THE BIBLE IN ITS LITERARY MILIEU

Contemporary Essays

THE BIBLE IN ITS LITERARY MILIEU

Contemporary Essays

Edited by
Vincent L. Tollers
and
John R. Maier

WILLIAM B. EERDMANS PUBLISHING COMPANY
GRAND RAPIDS, MICHIGAN

Library of Congress Cataloging in Publication Data

Main entry under title:

The Bible in its literary milieu.

    1. Bible—Criticism, interpretation, etc.—
Addresses, essays, lectures. I. Tollers,
Vincent L. II. Maier, John R.
BS511.2.B5 220.6 79-14253
ISBN 0-8028-1799-8

Contents

12.95

IV. LITERARY FORMS AND LITERARY INFLUENCE

V. APPROACHES TO A LITERARY CRITICISM OF
THE BIBLE

Acknowledgments

Luis Alonso Schökel, "The Psychology of Inspiration," in *The Inspired Word*, tr. Francis Martin, pp. 177–215. Copyright © Burns & Oates, London. Reprinted by permission of The Seabury Press.

Permission to reprint poems in the above essay has been granted as follows:

From: The Poems of St. John of the Cross, pp. 42–43. Copyright © Hughes Massie Ltd., London. Reprinted by permission.

From: Rainer Maria Rilke, *Selected Works II, Poetry*. Copyright © 1960 by The Hogarth Press Ltd. Reprinted by permission of New Directions Publishing Corporation.

From: "Ash Boughs," by Gerard Manley Hopkins, in *Poems of Gerard Manley Hopkins*. Copyright © 1959 by Oxford University Press, Inc. Reprinted by permission.

Northrup Frye, "Theory of Archetypal Meaning: Apocalyptic Imagery," and "Theory of Archetypal Meaning: Demonic Imagery," in *Anatomy of Criticism: Four Essays*. Copyright © 1957 by Princeton University Press; Princeton Paperback, 1971. Reprinted by permission of Princeton University Press.

Johannes Lindblom, "Symbolic Perceptions and Literary Visions," in *Prophecy in Ancient Israel*. Copyright © 1962 by Basil Blackwell and Mott Ltd., London. Reprinted by permission.

David Noel Freedman, "Pottery, Poetry, and Prophecy: An Essay on Biblical Poetry," *Journal of Biblical Literature* 91 (1972), 5–26. Reprinted by permission.

Walter C. Kaiser, Jr., "The Old Promise and the New Covenant: Jeremiah 31:31–34," *Journal of the Evangelical Theological Society* 15/1 (1972), 11–23. Reprinted by permission.

John R. Collins, "History and Tradition in the Prophet Amos," *Irish Theological Quarterly* 41 (1974), 120–133, St. Patrick's College, Maynooth, Ireland. Reprinted by permission.

Stanley Brice Frost, "Apocalyptic and History," in *The Bible in Modern Scholarship*, ed. J. P. Hyatt, pp. 98–113. Reprinted by permission of the Society of Biblical Literature.

William F. Albright, "The Antiquity of Mosaic Law," in *Yahweh and the Gods of Canaan*, pp. 172–182. Reprinted by permission.

William O. Walker, Jr., "The Origin of the Son of Man Concept as Applied to Jesus," *Journal of Biblical Literature* 91 (1972), 482–490. Reprinted by permission.

G. Ernest Wright, "What Archaeology Can and Cannot Do," *Biblical Archaeologist* 34 (1971), 70–76. Reprinted by permission.

Sigmund Mowinckel, "The Method of the Cultic Interpretation," in *The Psalms in Israel's Worship*, tr. D. P. Ap-Thomas, vol. 1, pp. 23–39. Reprinted by permission of Basil Blackwell and Mott Ltd.

Ralph W. Klein, "Aspects of Intertestamental Messianism," *Concordia Theological Monthly* 43 (1972), 507–517. Reprinted by permission of the author.

Bleddyn J. Roberts, "The Old Testament: Manuscripts, Text and Versions," in *The Cambridge History of the Bible: The West from the Fathers to the Reformation*, vol. 2, ed. G. W. H. Lampe. © Cambridge University Press 1969. Reprinted by permission.

Bruce M. Metzger, "The Practice of New Testament Textual Criticism," in *The Text of the New Testament: Its Transmission, Corruption, and Restoration* (2nd ed.), pp. 207–246. Copyright © 1968 by Oxford University Press. Reprinted by permission.

Roland Mushat Frye, "Introduction," in *The Reader's Bible, A Narrative: Selections from the King James Version*, pp. xxviii–xxxix. Copyright © 1965 by Roland Mushat Frye. Reprinted by permission of Princeton University Press.

Samuel Noah Kramer, "Sumerian Literature and the Bible," *Analecta Biblica* 12 (1959), 185–204. Reprinted by permission of the author.

W. G. Lambert, "A New Look at the Babylonian Background of Genesis," *Journal of Theological Studies* 16 (1965), 287–300. Reprinted by permission.

Roger L. Cox, "Tragedy and the Gospel Narratives," *The Yale Review* 57 (1968), 545–570. Copyright © Yale University. Reprinted by permission.

William Whallon, "Biblical Poetry and Homeric Epic," in *Formula, Character, and Context*, pp. 214–220. Copyright © 1969 by Harvard University Press. Reprinted by permission.

S. Van Tilborg, "A Form-Criticism of the Lord's Prayer," *Novum Testament* 14 (1972), 94–105. Reprinted by permission of the author and E. J. Brill, Leiden.

Norman Perrin, "Redaction Criticism at Work: A Sample," in *What is Redaction Criticism?*, pp. 40–63. Reprinted by permission of Fortress Press.

James Muilenburg, "Form Criticism and Beyond," *Journal of Biblical Literature* 88 (1969), 1–18. Reprinted by permission.

Kenneth Burke, "On the First Three Chapters of Genesis," in *The Rhetoric of Religion: Studies in Logology*, pp. 201–222. Copyright © 1961. Reprinted by permission of the University of California Press.

John Macquarrie, "Symbolism Case Study: Light as a Religious Symbol," in *God-Talk: An Examination of the Language and Logic of Theology*, pp. 192–211. Copyright © 1967. Reprinted by permission of SCM Press Ltd., London, and The Seabury Press.

Edmund R. Leach, "Genesis as Myth," in *Genesis as Myth and Other Essays*, pp. 7–23. Reprinted by permission of Jonathan Cape, Ltd., London.

Charts are reprinted from *The Interpreter's One-Volume Commentary on the Bible*. Copyright © 1971 by Abingdon Press. Used by permission.

List of Abbreviations

AB	Anchor Bible	JETS	*Journal of Evangelical Theological Society*
AJSL	*American Journal of Semitic Languages and Literature*	JNES	*Journal of Near Eastern Studies*
ANET	J. B. Pritchard, ed., *Ancient Near Eastern Texts*	JR	*Journal of Religion*
		JSS	*Journal of Semitic Studies*
Apoc. Bar.	Syriac, Greek Apocalypse of Baruch	LXX	Septuagint (ancient Greek translation of the OT)
BA	Biblical Archaeologist		
BASOR	Bulletin of the American School of Oriental Research	McCQ	*McCormick Quarterly*
		NT	*Novum Testamentum*
		NTS	*New Testament Studies*
BJRL	Bulletin of the John Rylands University Library of Manchester	PG	J. Migne, *Patrologia graeca*
		RB	*Revue biblique*
BR	Biblical Research	RGG	*Religion in Geschichte und Gegenwart*
BZAW	Beihefte zur ZAW		
CBQ	Catholic Biblical Quarterly	SBT	*Studies in Biblical Theology*
CR	Critical Review	SPCK	Society for Promoting Christian Knowledge
CTM	Concordia Theological Monthly		
ET	Eglise et theologie	Str-B	[H. Strack and] P. Billerbeck, *Kommentar zum Neuen Testament*
Eth. Enoch	Ethiopic Enoch		
EvT	*Evangelische Theologie* (EvTh)	TDNT	G. Kittel and G. Friedrich, eds., *Theological Dictionary of the New Testament*
ExpT	*Expository Times*		
HTR	*Harvard Theological Review*	ThRu	*Theologische Rundschau*
		USQR	*Union Seminary Quarterly Review*
HUCA	*Hebrew Union College Annual*		
IPQ	*International Philosophical Quarterly*	VT	*Vetus Testamentum*
		VTSup	*Vetus Testamentum, Supplements*
JAOS	*Journal of the American Oriental Society*	ZAW	*Zeitschrift für die alttestamentliche Wissenschaft*
JBL	*Journal of Biblical Literature*		
JCS	*Journal of Cuneiform Studies*	ZDMG	*Zeitschrift deutschen morgenländischen Gesellschaft*

General Introduction

H OW many of those to whom Shakespeare still speaks would not
remember the witches' chorus in *Macbeth* with its insidious refrain:

Double, double, toil and trouble,
Fire burn, and caldron bubble. (IV,1,10-11)

These lines are not as intense as, for example, Macbeth's soliloquy in
which he laments:

Tomorrow, and tomorrow, and tomorrow
Creeps in this petty pace from day to day,
To the last syllable of recorded time,
And all our yesterdays have lighted fools
The way to dusty death. (V,5,19-23)

Nor are those lines as wild as Macbeth's hallucination that he is being led
to the murder of the king by a dagger; or as moving as Lady Macbeth's
mad scene. But the witches' refrain lingers in the reader's mind. It may
well be the most easily recalled piece of poetry in the play.

Does it matter that Shakespeare probably did not write the witches'
song? Shakespearean scholars tell us the "Hecate scenes" (including the
witches' song in act IV, scene 1) are most likely not the Bard's. His
contemporary, Thomas Middleton, is the best candidate for authorship.
But does it matter? Tradition keeps the disputed scenes in performances
of the play. There is a kind of relevance to the witches' singing over their
pot, and few are disturbed by this intrusion of an outside author.

To the literary critic the question of authorship is not easily laid
aside. Interpolations—additions by a hand other than Shakespeare's—
can be distressing. How well does the witches' song square with Shakespeare's intention in the play? The practical critic today is concerned with
the unity of a literary work. Should the "eye of newt" and "wool of bat" be
considered in an analysis of the play's "natural" imagery; in the recurrent
patterns of "vision" images and images of clothes that give the "real"
Shakespearean sections their great intensity? What about two themes of
the play: "foreknowledge" and "freedom?" Do the Hecate scenes blur the
themes or, worse, alter them? Should a modern text keep the Hecate
scenes in or relegate them to an appendix? To be sure, they present

1

problems to the play as a unified, organic whole. How can we be sure of Shakespeare's final intention in *Macbeth*?

The Hecate scenes are worth remembering as interest in the Bible "as literature" grows. It has become customary to point out that the world of the biblical scholar and the world of the literary critic are still far apart. Indeed, the very term "literary criticism" means one thing to biblical scholars and quite another to literary critics.

There is certain validity in this differentiation. "Literary criticism" is still used by biblical scholars in the analysis of the biblical text to determine the different "strands" of narrative that constitute the text. Determining the history of combining "strands" and parallel accounts of stories is the task of the biblical scholar. For example, there are not one, but two accounts of Creation: Genesis 1:1–2:4a and 2:4b–2:25. God's appearance to Moses on Mount Sinai in Exodus 19 is reported in three ways by three writers (or editors or schools or traditions) who had a hand in composing what we usually think is one unified report. Scholars have come to label these as the Yahwist, the Elohist, and the Priestly writers (or traditions). These three writers (or five, if the "lay" source and the Deuteronomist are accepted) have contributed to the Pentateuch.

The "strandedness" of the Bible is of great importance for our understanding, as the Flood story makes clear. Is the tension between God's "promise" to his people and the "covenant" established with Noah a careful blend of two accounts, each having its characteristic habits of thought, imagery, and theological purpose? The nature of the blend very likely will affect any theology or moral principles drawn out of the text, not to mention the aesthetic appreciation of the Flood story as an artistic whole.

Such "literary criticism" is at the very heart of biblical scholarship— or at its root in nineteenth-century historicism. What this "literary criticism" examines is not the same as what the Dickens literary critic or the Gerard Manley Hopkins scholar examines.

A glance at what literary scholars were doing a century ago, however, will show how the gap between "literary criticism₁" and "literary criticism₂" has been exaggerated: Philologists worked with *Piers Plowman*. Editors struggled with apocryphal passages in Chaucer. Grammarians examined *Beowulf*. Scholars searched for the reconstructed original form, the *ur*-form, of *Sir Gawain and the Green Knight*. Their work was marked by precise, disciplined methods of historical research. They wanted to be scientific, objective, and dispassionate in their work. And a glance at a recent *Modern Language Association International Bibliography* will show that similar work is continuing today.

Yet problems do exist. The Bible not only provides examples of nearly every kind of problem literary scholarship has had to deal with, but also the problems of faith, inspiration, prophecy, and "inerrancy." These latter problems do not confront the student of *Oliver Twist*. The aim of this book is to bring together essays by biblical scholars and literary critics centered around questions of interest to both disciplines. How is the Bible a "literary" work? How does it contain literary works? How does "literariness" influence our reading? How do we enter the literary work?

"Literature" is basically "something written" (as the Bible is basically a "book"). For the most part, however, "literature" in this book will be restricted to the kind of writing taught in literature courses. This includes poetic forms, narratives, and songs.

Even so, the Bible is an awesome collection of *literary* work. If we ignore for a moment the long oral tradition behind much of what comes to be written and concentrate only on what *is* written, we will note that it took over a thousand years for the Bible to take form (from approximately 1100 B.C. to A.D. 150). During those centuries great empires came and went. Some periods are well known and documented, while others are known only after great efforts have been made to reconstruct them. In addition there are many biblical "authors," but even biblical "authorship" is problematic. Apart from the question of divine inspiration of biblical writings, the question of oral tradition is especially thorny. The different languages of the Scriptures—Hebrew, Aramaic, and Greek—present complex problems of translation that are implicit in nearly every essay presented here. Finally, the Bible is remote from us in time and distant from our "mind set." Compared with the complexities in, for example, the meaning of *ṣelem* (image) in Genesis, or in the diction of Job, or in the "unity" of Isaiah, the difficulties with *Macbeth*'s witches are small indeed.

The questions that occupy biblical scholars today have occupied and continue to occupy literary scholars. The question raised frequently by literary critics today is the question of unity. Is "The Song of Deborah and Barak" a literary unity? What about the Pentateuch? Or Genesis? How do we "enter" a work, as some "postmodern" critics ask us to do? What are the reader's expectations in a given form? What does the work tell us about authorship and audience? These are questions asked of both Hopkins and Hosea. This book will attempt to explore these questions.

The essays in this volume include three important concerns shared by literary critics and biblical scholars. Approaches to any text removed from the present are likely to include the following concerns: first, recovering the "original" meaning of the text—what it meant for the composer and audience when it was first written; and second, identifying the final intention of the author or editor—taking the text as it is (without losing the development of the text through earlier authors and editors). Both of these concerns are largely the province of literary history. The third concern deals with history itself. History is a problem because of the concern for language and codes that are both historical (diachronic) and *an*historical (synchronic); because of concern for the meaning of the text for us in our modern existential situation; and because of concern that human experience is at some level universal or "archetypal," with symbols, myths, and images that are not totally bound to specific time periods and cultures. These challenges to history are broadly the approaches of structuralism, phenomenology or hermeneutics, and various sorts of archetypal and myth criticism.

The present moment in literary studies is valuable because it is intensely self-reflective. Notions and basic assumptions about literature that previously have been taken for granted, are now being challenged. What is a text? What is a symbol? What is a story? Narrative theory is being discussed in a number of journals. Several new journals have devoted entire issues to the theory of metaphor.

At the center of the controversy is the "work itself." The majority of literary students (in the United States at least) have been trained in both conflicting schools of criticism: literary history and formalist criticism generally known as new criticism. New criticism, which has been around since the 1920s, is best known in the work of Cleanth Brooks, William K. Wimsatt, John Crowe Ransom, and William Empson. New criticism was at first a direct challenge to literary history. To approach a literary work properly was to understand its inner coherence. "Explicating the text" and uncovering its unity required attending to the "work itself." Biographical information about the author, these critics thought, was unnecessary and often a nuisance. Even an artist's own statements about his intention in writing a work were suspect. Once written, a work was no longer the property of the author; he had no privileged position from which to enter it. Historical background was largely irrelevant. A long, savoring pause over a striking image or a quotable phrase taken out of context was a cardinal sin. It was rather in the interplay of images, in the rich ambiguity, the ironic twisting, and the paradoxical and "concrete" character of language itself that the critics found their work. The new critics' intense concern for the "work itself" was dry, objective, and largely unrelated to existential questions. The delightful paradoxes in Archibald MacLeish's lines that claim, "A poem should not mean / But be," provide both a testament to and an example for the movement.

Although at first enemies, literary history and new criticism have made peace over the years. No one is surprised to find studies of the "theme and structure" of a work as remote as *Beowulf* or a study of paradox and ambiguity in, for example, Chaucer's "The Knight's Tale." Literary critics of the Bible are beginning to apply the new criticism. The rhetorical criticism advocated by James Muilenburg (pp. 362–380) is an example. Like much of the new criticism in practice, rhetorical criticism is potentially anhistorical, but has not lost its connection with textual, "literary," and form-critical concerns, all of which are interested in the original shape and meanings of the text.

Just when peace between new criticism and literary history seemed most secure, different tendencies emerged that challenged the peace. The archetypal criticism of Northrop Frye, various structuralist approaches, phenomenological or hermeneutical, and linguistic-symbolical analyses have in different ways attacked both literary history and the formalism of the new critics. There are rough parallels between trends in biblical scholarship and literary studies in the last century which seem to operate even today. The earlier parallels, going back as far as the mid-eighteenth century, are rooted in historicism. The newer trends, which have come to be known as the new literary history and postmodernism, share in the critique of historicism.

A convenient example is provided by Shakespearean criticism in the last two hundred years. Certain landmarks in Shakespearean criticism have a strange way of reflecting landmarks in biblical criticism, though there is almost no possibility of one influencing the other. In the 1780s, when Johann Gottfried Eichhorn was proposing that Genesis showed three or more fragmentary sources combined by an unknown redactor (the beginning of "literary criticism" on the basis of style and content analysis), scholars like the influential Samuel Johnson were examining Shakespearean plays for textual inconsistencies that indicated somebody other than the Bard had written a particular passage. A century later, when Julius Wellhausen proposed that the Hexateuch was composed in four historical stages with four sources J-E-D-P (Yahwist, Elohist, Deuteronomist, and Priestly), in that order, he was influenced strongly by the philosophies of history (Hegel's) that were important to nineteenth-century developmentalist thought. At the same time, Edward Dowden was mapping out Shakespeare's "spiritual" development in four evolutionary stages. The schema he pursued showed the Bard marching through periods "in the workshop," "in the world," "out of the depths," and "on the heights." Dowden's developmental schema still lingers in introductions to modern editions of Shakespeare.

As Hermann Gunkel was challenging the literary critics of the Bible and proposed form-critical analysis in this century, a landmark in Shakespearean criticism was established by E. E. Stoll. Stoll challenged previous assumptions about Shakespeare's plays. Like Gunkel, who wanted to establish the typical forms imbedded in the biblical text and place them in their original situation in the living community, E. E. Stoll directed scholars back to the highly conventional devices, forms, and characters of Shakespeare's plays. Stoll's underlying premise was that attention to the play in its sixteenth- or seventeenth-century context— before living Elizabethan and Jacobean audiences—would reveal the authentic and original Shakespeare.

There are further parallelisms in Shakespearean and biblical criticism. It would be interesting to compare Rudolf Bultmann's demythologizing phenomenological studies with studies by G. Wilson

Knight or C. L. Barber—two very influential twentieth-century Shake-speareans. The point is not, of course, to suggest influences between the scholars. On the contrary, the enormity of the tasks have kept the disciplines apart. An E. E. Stoll may or may not have learned anything from Gunkel which is applicable to Shakespearean studies. Still, large concerns, problems, and methods have a kind of family resemblance, perhaps since the *Zeitgeist* operates on scholars more pervasively than on other people. Not surprisingly, then, very recent Shakespearean scholarship, while still retaining textual and historical interests, has come to include a great many formalist as well as archetypal, structural, and phenomenological studies.

American literary criticism is increasingly using the term "postmodernism" to include these last three approaches. It may be rash to label as postmodern the interest biblical scholars have shown recently in narrative theory, structuralism, and phenomenology. In both disciplines the term postmodern perhaps would obscure the great diversity of approaches to the literary work. The large parallels are useful to note, however, if only to show that a community of interests has certainly formed. Courses such as "The Bible as Literature" are in large measure signs of the interdisciplinary interests. So are courses in Religion and Literature. It would not be wrong to see *The Bible in its Literary Milieu: Contemporary Essays* as a primer in "approaches to the study of literature" with a focus on one major work with a strongly historical character—the Bible.

The design of *The Bible in its Literary Milieu: Contemporary Essays* is not meant to exhaust the approaches to the Bible as literature. Nor is it meant to pursue one theoretical line. Rather, the anthology is designed to show the rich variety and promise of literary studies. It is hoped that this is a book of openings. Certainly it does not try to suggest that these are the only essays available or the only selections that should be made. We selected these essays, in part, because they are readable representations of various critical approaches to biblical problems which have recently interested scholars. Our hope is that they will stimulate more work in the areas highlighted.

The Bible in its Literary Milieu: Contemporary Essays is divided into five sections.

SECTION I: THE WORD

Friedrich Nietzsche, as we will see in greater detail in the introduction to this section, saw revelation and inspiration in the process by which he produced *Thus Spake Zarathustra*. He prefaced his description, however, with a caution: "Provided one has the slightest remnant of superstition left, one can hardly reject completely the idea that one is the mere incarnation, or mouthpiece, or medium of some almighty power." Rudolf Otto illustrated the "numinous" in the *Bhagavad-Gita* and the works of John Ruskin. The sense that one is being dominated and yet attracted to the Other has been claimed by many outside the Bible.

The problem of inspiration is raised immediately by Luis Alonso Schökel's "The Psychology of Inspiration." As the first barrier to understanding the literary character of Scripture, inspiration becomes a very positive force for understanding the process of composing biblical literature. Alonso Schökel sees a threefold process of inspiration: intuition, the impulse to write, and execution. He is guided in large part by the biblical texts themselves. He uses equally well, however, examples from modern authors.

The essays by Northrop Frye, Johannes Lindblom, and David Noel Freedman also look at biblical writings from the writer's point of view. Northrop Frye, architect of archetypal criticism, writes in "Archetypal Meaning: Apocalyptic and Demonic Imagery" that the central images of the Scriptures are gathered together brilliantly in Revelation. The images are a key to works outside the Bible. The dream of total freedom and fulfillment (apocalyptic imagery) is a universal dream; a static vision shared by all men. Variations appear in writings from all periods and cultures. Demonic imagery, the opposite of apocalyptic imagery, is the nightmare vision of powerlessness and total bondage, the Satanic world of torture and estrangement. In the larger scheme of archetypal criticism, Frye shows how the myths or basic narrative patterns—romance, tragedy, comedy, and irony—are "generated" from these static visions of freedom and bondage. The Bible—and Revelation in particular, which Frye sees as the grand climax of the Bible as a whole—illuminates the workings of other writers.

Johannes Lindblom's "Symbolic Perceptions and Literary Visions" concentrates on the prophets. Not all visions are of one sort, and Lindblom carefully distinguishes the "symbolic perception" and the "literary vision" from the ecstatic trance. Although the prophet's life may be recounted in the prophetic works, as is the case of Jeremiah and Isaiah, the focus is the sayings of the prophets—the poetry.

David Noel Freedman, in "Pottery, Poetry, and Prophecy," makes much of the connection between the poet and the prophet. (Ancient writers outside the biblical tradition—such as Homer and Plato—knew of the "inspired" poet. Our language of poetic composition—the Muses, "creativity," and the "imagination"—flows from this connection.) Again and again during moments of crisis in biblical history, the prophet resorted to the oldest form of exalted, oracular speech: poetry. The prophets before the period of Exile turned to it, and the apocalyptic writings of the time before Christ are filled with it. In this regard, Jesus Christ also is appreciated as a poet.

The essays by Frye, Lindblom, and Freedman may take different tacks from Alonso Schökel's, but all of them write about the visionary, "mythopoeic" imagination that is the chief medium of inspired speech.

SECTION II: THE CONTEXT

The great themes of biblical literature reveal much of the literary character of the Bible. "Promise" and "covenant," "Son of Man" and "Messiah," are but a few themes. Do the themes appear once or often in Scripture? in different periods? in different traditions? The "history of ideas" is a discipline that considers such ideas and develops methods for dealing with them. Nearly every preacher has wrestled with these and other themes which unify the Bible, and even the casual reader is likely to dwell on them. After all, they have profoundly shaped our beliefs and values. Systems of theology and ethics have been raised on them.

Nonetheless, recovering the context and studying the development of the great central themes in Scripture is neither simple nor obvious. In fact, the texture of a character or an event that is indivisible from the theme is often elusive, and subject to opinion even after the biblical historian has done all possible homework. The prophetic roles of Amos and Jeremiah are studied by John J. Collins, pp. 121–133, and Walter C. Kaiser, Jr., pp. 106–120, in their analyses of a major theme—salvation history—God's way of caring for his people. We learn from these critics that the prophets' messages differ because the historical upheavals of the Israelites called for a new type of prophetic utterance. In general, themes, characters, and events are in constant flux. To understand a passage as fully as possible, we must be prepared to examine all of them as they come together in a single context.

To pursue the nature of the problem further, we should see how it applies to characters and events. Even major personalities such as David or Jesus are difficult to sketch. Before he assumes the throne, David's character is strikingly inconsistent: in I Samuel he oscillates between a strapling boy and a seasoned warrior; between a good-hearted fellow and a crafty politician. Then there is the paradox of Jesus: his personality and message dominate the New Testament, yet only a minuscule portion of his speech—printed in red in some Bibles—has survived. And that portion obviously has been shaped by the gospel writers. Note how the writers of Matthew, Mark, and Luke organize their accounts so Jesus moves from obscurity to sudden prominence in the passion week prior to Crucifixion, while the writer of John has an altogether different organization of much the same material. But the problems of identifying the essence of Jesus begin well before Calvary. The essays by William O. Walker, Jr., "The Origin of the Son of Man Concept as Applied to Jesus," and Ralph W. Klein, "Aspects of Intertestamental Messianism," show the historical and religious context into which Jesus was born. A repeated theme of the New Testament is the way in which Jesus fulfilled God's promises in the Old Testament.

And finally, we can group the remaining essays in Section II under the rubric of "events." G. Ernest Wright's "What Archaeology Can and Cannot Do" reveals the interconnectedness of biblical studies disciplines. As he writes, "Archaeology, dealing with the wreckage of antiquity, proves nothing in itself. It must be analyzed in a variety of ways, and then with all other data available, its meaning in the overall picture of a cultural continuum is expressed by interpretation." To excavate a perfectly preserved biblical city might bring to light some specific event, but that event is only the means to understanding history—not an end. William F. Albright, in "The Antiquity of Mosaic Law," helps us understand why the Hebrew people drew up and preserved the case laws of Exodus. By extension, it should be apparent that the Bible survived because it once met and still may continue to meet the needs of its readers. What is interesting about this article is how Albright looks closely at the dietary laws, particularly about eating fish, in order to date this part of Exodus. The last article which attempts to illuminate the Bible by looking at an event is from Sigmund Mowinckel's *The Psalms in Israel's Worship*. Starting from the position that all ancient art has a social function, the noted Norwegian scholar examines the oriental cult rituals during the Period of the Monarchy (1020-930 B.C.). Each psalm, he concludes, filled a specific need in the community's religious life. Thus this section underscores the mutual dependence of those working in biblical studies. While a Shakespearean scholar can ignore with impunity most research that has been published on American writers, those who identify a problem connected with spiritual writing are likely to find a satisfactory solution only after they have applied an interdisciplinary approach.

SECTION III: TEXTUAL CRITICISM

For many people the Bible occupies a valued place in the home because it was given at an important point in one's religious life or handed down through the generations. Often this is the King James Version—seldom read because of its Elizabethan English, but culturally and aesthetically important to its owner because it is *the* Bible. The transmission of early manuscripts, the establishment of the canon of Scripture, and the translation activities in the ancient world indeed are removed from feelings associated with this family treasure which is thought of only when it is dusted.

Although these textual concerns are far removed from the ordinary reader of the Bible, the work of these critics—often called primary bibliographers in literary studies—is of the highest importance to the serious student. Only after the text has been established can others apply their diverse talents to its explication. In *The Art of Literary Research,* Richard D. Altick tells the anecdote of a critic who wrote a learned disquisition about Melville's use of *soiled fish* in *Whitejacket.* Unfortunately for the critic, the image was not a *discordia concors,* but merely a printer's error for *coiled fish* or an eel. "Today," Altick writes, "we realize that accurate texts are indispensable to the progress of literary study." The same holds true for biblical study. It may be, for example, that Mark 9:50 can never be understood because the text is corrupt—garbled in transmission. The King James Version reads: "Salt is good: but if the salt have lost his saltness, wherewith will ye season it?" The Jerusalem Bible reads: "Salt is a good thing, but if salt has become insipid, how can you season it again?" Neither of these versions, nor any others, makes sense of this and other passages in the Old and New Testaments.

The fact that nothing more can be learned about the original intention of biblical authors is no reason to despair. Textual critics who deal with such difficulties have had major breakthroughs in their sub-disciplines of content and methodology. As Bleddyn J. Roberts notes in his "The Old Testament: Manuscripts, Text and Versions," the post-World War II discoveries of Hebrew and Aramaic Scripture and writings near the Dead Sea prove that the Massoretic (Hebrew) texts of the ninth and tenth centuries A.D. are more accurate than the Greek codices which predate them by five hundred years—the Vaticanus, Sinaiticus, and the Alexandrinus being the most famous. The full impact of these discoveries is yet to be felt. Although the best Greek codices were the basis of the current flood of biblical translations, we should expect at some point a more reliable Old Testament translation from the Hebrew versions.

Likewise, there has been significant advancement in the methodology of the textual critic, as Bruce M. Metzger demonstrates in "The Practice of New Testament Textual Criticism." Knowledge of relevant languages; of the history and religion of the Jews, Christians, and their neighbors; of transmission patterns and composition practices—these skills are among the many required of a modern textual critic. Metzger's history of this methodology illustrates, however, that scholars in this area have profited immensely from the work of their predecessors. Since Roberts' and Metzger's essays assume more knowledge than most readers of this anthology have, we have included in the introduction to Section Three some essential background—a sketch of the major events surrounding the canonization of the Old and New Testaments by various religious bodies, and a brief table of the major Hebrew and Greek manuscripts to which the authors frequently refer.

Since the King James Version has retained such an important place in our language and literature, Section Three concludes with Roland

Mushat Frye's "The Bible in English," in which he considers the translation in its milieu. His essay is useful in several ways. It supplements
Roberts' history of textual transmission of the Old Testament and Metzger's approach to translation—a key concern of textual critics. But
perhaps it appeals most strongly to the undergraduate reader when Frye
examines why the King James Version gained immediate popularity not
only as a translation of Holy Scripture, but as a work of literature whose
cadence and imagery became an indelible part of the English language.

SECTION IV: LITERARY FORMS AND LITERARY INFLUENCE

Literary works throughout the ancient world, especially in the ancient
Near East, share motifs and forms. Proverbs, hymns, disputations, and
prophecies appear in the literature of cultures influenced by the Hebrews. But direct influence of one literary text upon another is often
difficult to prove. The Egyptian maxims of Amenemope, which found
their way into the Book of Proverbs, are a conspicuous exception. Other
influences certainly are possible, such as Persian and Babylonian influences on the Book of Esther, or the Greek forms of historiography on the
Acts of the Apostles. But the way specific forms and texts travel in
societies where literacy is restricted to the few is complicated. Certainly it
is not like an example in English literature familiar to many: the story of
Troilus and Criseyde. This story was drawn by Chaucer from Boccaccio
and others in a way that can be pinpointed precisely, and later, Shakespeare used Chaucer's version. In each instance the author took a fixed
text, and from it created his own. The critic's attention is focused on what
use the author made of his predecessor's works.

Perhaps the most controversial form of ancient story is myth. Many
find it objectionable that ancient myths which describe creation, the
Flood, dying gods, and accounts of descent into the netherworld may
have influenced the biblical narratives. The presence of these myths in
Mesopotamia before the appearance of biblical texts renders interrela-
tionships between the Hebrew world and their powerful Mesopotamian
neighbors especially problematic. Two essays, Samuel Noah Kramer's
"Sumerian Literature and the Bible" and W. G. Lambert's "A New Look
at the Babylonian Background of Genesis," examine possible contacts
between these two societies. Creation, paradise, and the Flood are a few
of the myths existing in different variations in Mesopotamia. Kramer is
more positive than Lambert in pressing for the influence of Mesopotamian ideas and forms on the Bible; however, both essays present reasonable methods for detecting cross-cultural influences even where long
literary traditions are involved.

Literary tragedy would seem to be a form peculiar to the West. From its roots in ritual (both Greek and medieval Christian) to its brilliant expression in the Greek classical period and in the Elizabethan period in England, tragedy has been a form with special prestige. Northrop Frye considers it one of the four basic narrative types in all of literature. Philosophers such as Hegel and Nietzsche plumbed its depths. In biblical narratives, however, only Job is usually considered a tragic work. Far more often than not, the fundamental optimism of the Judeo-Christian tradition has been considered antipathetic to tragedy. Roger Cox's "Tragedy and the Gospel Narratives" takes a different view. Not only is the Bible compatible with the deep problems of human existence explored in tragedy; the very center of the gospel narrative is tragic. The literary form of the Bible relates to problems of human existence, to difficulties with freedom and necessity, and with suffering, not just specifically to exchanges between societies.

William Whallon's "Biblical Poetry and Homeric Epic" also examines Greek literary forms and the Bible. What makes the Greek epic poetry and Hebrew poetry comparable is traditional processes of oral composition. The demands of preliterate composition lead to parallel phenomena such as formulaic expression and the treatment of character in a certain way. The narrative prose of Hebrew Scripture departs from the distinctive features of oral composition in favor of specific detail and naturalistic speech patterns. Thus Whallon draws very tightly the distinctions between prose and poetry in the early writings of Scripture.

Form critics who study ancient Near Eastern forms, such as Mowinckel, Van Tilborg, and Muilenburg, are usually anxious to show a specific cult setting for a given form. The Creation story in the Mesopotamian *Enuma Elish*, for example, was read annually on the occasion of the New Year's festival which had been celebrated in the cities for centuries. Taken together, however, the four essays in this section more immediately illustrate the problems of literary history. The anonymity of traditional poetry, the peculiarities of oral composition, and the possibilities of archetypal narrative forms are barriers (and prods) to a modern understanding of biblical literature.

SECTION V: APPROACHES TO A LITERARY CRITICISM OF THE BIBLE

The first essay in this section, S. Van Tilborg's "A Form-Criticism of the Lord's Prayer," illustrates an approach to biblical literature that continues to grow—form criticism. Initially form criticism is far removed from the *formalist* criticism the new critics of literature proposed. The aim of form criticism is to isolate text-types and literary forms, and to establish their connection with a tradition, a community, or cult. (In this regard also see the essays by Muilenburg and Mowinckel.) The forms can be large or quite small. The Psalms, for example, contain a variety of song-types: royal songs, hymns, pilgrimage songs, and the like. Psalm 130 is a "Song of Ascent," but it contains another form—a "watchman's song." Sermons, speeches, prayers, contracts, myths, fables, parables, accounts of dreams and visions, and forms of address in epistles are some of the forms that form criticism pursues.

Van Tilborg initially demonstrates that the Lord's Prayer is a prayer-type which already existed in the Jewish community. He then explores its function in the early Christian congregations.

The attempt to reverse the form critic's analysis by concentrating on the way forms are built up into wholes is redaction criticism. Norman Perrin's "Redaction Criticism at Work: A Sample" exemplifies the approach by a close analysis of the incident at Caesarea Philippi. Looking closely at the account in the Gospel of Mark, Perrin demonstrates how previously existing sayings are brought together and modified by the redactor to create a new saying. In other words, he shows how a new saying is created. The historical situation of the church addressed by Mark accounts for his emphasis on suffering. The authors of Matthew, Luke, and John show their distinct understandings of Christ's life and death by their emphases: Matthew saw Christ's views of the Jewish heritage and deliverance of the Jews as important; Luke emphasized God's sacrifice of his Son; and John emphasized the mystical community of those who followed Christ. After Mark, other redactors show subtle differences in their handling of the episode.

At stake in redaction criticism is the history of the development of a text. Forms and the purposes of the redactor are both related to the communities they serve. Redaction criticism attempts to synthesize the whole work, the completed text, in order to arrive at the author's "final intention." Form criticism, on the other hand, works analytically to underlying forms—often to oral tradition. James Muilenburg, as the title of his essay, "Form Criticism and Beyond," makes clear, suggests an approach that uses form criticism but goes beyond it. He calls for rhetorical criticism to deal with the literary wholes. The *literary* character of the ancient text must be recognized, and the rhetorical critic should use parallel accounts from other ancient Near Eastern literature. The "structure of a composition" and the "configuration of its component parts" are what rhetorical criticism should examine.

Muilenburg recalls T. S. Eliot's phrase from the *Four Quartets* about the poem as a "raid on the inarticulate." In a stirring rephrase Muilenburg provides a motto for these studies of the literary character of biblical texts:

In the Scriptures we have a literary deposit of those who were confronted by the ultimate questions of life and human destiny, of God and man, of the past out of which the historical people has come and of the future into which it is moving, a speech which seeks to be commensurate with man's ultimate concerns, a raid on the ultimate, if you will.

The "raid on the ultimate" is very evident in the early chapters of Genesis. Kenneth Burke, in "The First Three Chapters of Genesis," studies those early chapters from a stance he calls "logology," or studies of words about words. How are great principles, which theologians prefer to reduce to *a*temporal and *im*personal propositions, involved in narratives about creation, Adam and Eve, and death? At the center of Burke's logological study is the symbol. Man is a symbol-using animal. In a very complex way, the symbols derived from nature and the social order transform the principles into story, a narrative. A narrative, as Burke demonstrates, is essentially temporal and personal, involving narrative sequence and characters.

Burke's essay—and in large measure the two that follow his—John Macquarrie's "Symbolism Case Study: Light as a Religious Symbol," and Edmund Leach's "Genesis as Myth"—are part of a tendency to go beyond a historical understanding of biblical literature. Burke's rhetorical criticism is curiously anhistorical. If the original meaning of a text is the meaning for its first audience, Burke is all that much interested in recovering the "original" meaning. Macquarrie goes further by stating that symbols die. Over the years even the most profound expressions lose their life. His chief example is the magnificent symbol of light. Throughout the ancient world, light is an important symbol, as the sun is a vital part of man's environment. Our situation is different—the symbol has been drained of its power. Macquarrie's new hermeneutical task leads him to a way of revivifying this symbol that *en*lightens our existence. Just as twentieth-century man can relate to "estrangement" rather than the old language of "sin," the "light" symbol must be, as Macquarrie calls it, "desymbolized." "Openness" is Macquarrie's choice for a "light" in which the symbol speaks to us, *en*lightening us once the "desymbolizing" is done.

Macquarrie is deep in the phenomenological movement of this century. Another postmodern movement that·challenges earlier historically-based analysis is structuralism. Its many advocates employ many very different approaches. Anthropologist Edmund Leach is guided in his structuralist reading of four chapters of Genesis mainly by twentieth-century communication theory and the study of myth by Claude Lévi-Strauss. The *opposed pairs* images in Genesis, like life and death, are mediated by anomalous figures. The function of binary opposition and mediation in myth is to resolve intolerable problems that arise in contradictory principles under which a society operates. The highly repetitive nature of myth—the same story, the same pattern, is repeated time and again—is an essential feature of myth. The repetition also makes certain the audience is informed—that the message is not lost. Repetition in myths also validates the imaginative resolution of the society's problem.

John H. P. Reumann once noted that no one in antiquity would ever have dreamed of publishing a "Bible as Literature." The ancients, he reminded us, saw books as things of power and sacred books as vehicles for the deity. Books were not mere "literature." There is a large measure of truth in that, but only if the concentration is on stylistic features—formal devices that can easily be separated from and opposed to content. However, the modern schools of literary criticism represented in this anthology—from formalists through structuralists and phenomenologists—challenge the old habit of separating form and content, and seek rather to find literature in their unity. There is still time to pause quietly in delight at a well-turned phrase or a striking image—in T. S. Eliot or in Qoheleth—but most critics keep a wary eye out for such impressionism. The reader who seeks in a book about "The Bible as Literature" that simple delight in a beautiful phrase is apt to be disappointed with the selections in this volume. Probably the most hopeful sign that a meeting of minds is possible between literary critics and biblical scholars is the energy both camps take to overcome the form/content opposition. This is true even of the form criticism which at first glance might seem committed to the opposition. This is true as well of "desymbolizing," which initially would seem to demand the split.

T. S. Eliot was thinking of the poet when he proposed the phrase James Muilenburg recalled, a "raid on the inarticulate." But we might without too great a distortion take Eliot's somber and yet hopeful reflections as a comment on the critic's task.

> And what there is to conquer
> By strength and submission, has already been discovered
> Once or twice, or several times, by men whom one cannot hope
> To emulate—but there is no competition—
> There is only the fight to recover what has been lost
> And found and lost again and again: and now, under conditions
> That seem unpropitious.

"Each venture," Eliot says, is "a new beginning." The critical venture, as the essays in this volume hope to show, is complicated and yet open. The methods and approaches to the literary work are many, and some have only begun to be used in the study of the Bible. Much of the book will seem to be sophisticated ways of telling old truths. Pulsating in the heart of the venture, however, will be the living and awesome spirit of the Numinous.

I: THE WORD

Introduction

O FTEN the student of the Bible is understandably nervous about treating Scripture as if the Bible were a work of art. Apart from the problems of dating parts of the Bible, different text-traditions, translations, and historical backgrounds, the student is apprehensive about the notion that the Bible is inspired and sacred—a direct revelation of the Divine to man. How can the claim to truth—particularly the claim that the Bible cannot err—survive if the Bible is seen as cultural process and the work of individual humans?

The essays in this section offer partial answers to this difficult question. Without losing sight of the sacred, the essayists present four different but complementary ways of dealing with the human activity of receiving the inspired Word and transforming it into literature.

There are two related problems that prevent us from using our experience of literature to illuminate our readings of Scripture. We have developed certain expectations about what writers of poems and stories produce. Ordinarily we expect lyric poets to express their unique "vision" of things in their work. We tend to value lyric poetry and novels for their relationship to authors who are first of all individuals, a William Wordsworth or a Charles Dickens. On the other hand, we tend to expect writings to show a high degree of craftsmanship and conscious control.

It is at least arguable that the exaltation of the writer as an individual speaking mainly by himself and even for himself is a modern, "romantic" phenomenon. To a great extent, the romantic writer produced in reaction to modern, industrial, and alienated society in the West. It is dangerous to read this writer back into the early years of the Western literary tradition—for example, back to Shakespeare, Chaucer, or the *Beowulf* poet—let alone back to the years in which the Bible was slowly forming. Once the expectations of the modern reader are "deconstructed," as it were, the writer of traditional works, closely linked to the community and often to cultic and political institutions, can come forward to speak to us.

On the other hand, the high degree of conscious control over materials that we have come to expect from a T. S. Eliot or an Ernest Hemingway seems too tame and rational to deal with the explosive force and grand visionary quality one finds in the great prophets, for example, or in apocalyptic works such as Revelation. That explosive force seems far removed from the picture of an editor quietly and carefully composing the documents in the traditions to produce a synthetic text or "redaction." A glance at what writers have said of the process of finding, shaping, and bringing their intuitions into a coherent form, however, should quickly dispel this image. For example, Friedrich Nietzsche, who would not have wanted his name associated with any conventional religious piety, said the following about his experience of writing *Thus Spake Zarathustra:*

> The notion of revelation describes the condition quite simply; by which I mean that something profoundly convulsive and disturbing suddenly becomes visible and audible with indescribable definiteness and exactness. One hears—one does not seek; one takes—one does not ask who gives: a thought flashes out like lightning, inevitably without hesitation—I have never had any choice about it. There is an ecstasy whose terrific tension is sometimes released by a flood of tears, during which one's progress varies from involuntary impetuosity to involuntary slowness. There is the feeling that one is utterly out of hand, with the most distinct consciousness of an infinitude of shuddering thrills that pass through one from head to foot;— there is a profound happiness in which the most painful and gloomy feelings are not discordant in effect, but are required as necessary colors in this overflow of light. . . . Everything occurs quite without volition, as if in an eruption of freedom, independence, power and divinity. The spontaneity of the images and similes is most remarkable; one loses all perception of what is imagery and simile; everything offers itself as the most immediate, exact, and simple means of expression.[1]

We know that rational problem-solving is a complex process. How much more complex is the ecstasy of the artist's "inspiration"?

Poets have spoken for some time of their inspiration and Muses; of this non-rational element; of their being seized by a great intuition. Well over a thousand years before Homer, a Sumerian poetess, Enheduanna, wrote of her nocturnal inspiration to write a magnificent exaltation-poem to her goddess, Inanna:

> With "It is enough for me, it is too much for me!" I have given birth,
>   oh exalted Lady, to this song for you.
> That which I recited to you
>   at midnight
> May the singer repeat it to you
>   at noon![2]

But does this help us with biblical literature? Luis Alonso Schökel would answer yes. To the question of inerrancy and inspiration Alonso Schökel proposes a three-level schema. The poet's living experience provides the stuff of which literature is made. But according to Schökel, the experience only becomes relevant to the creative process when "in a flash, the formless mass of our experience takes shape." The intuition becomes the "life center," the "initial idea" of the process. Finally, the intuition expresses itself in language, transforming "his material and his experience into an organic significant system composed of words." This process is as much the case with biblical literature as it is for any other. And Alonso Schökel illustrates the process by the words and works of poets themselves.

Unlike Alonso Schökel's discussion, which concentrates on the individual author such as Jeremiah, Gerard Manley Hopkins, Hosea, Rilke, Northrop Frye's discussion of apocalyptic and demonic imagery is (at least initially) at the other extreme. The archetypes—images, symbols, myths—which fill up the universe of discourse are universally human. The Bible gives evidence of the archetypes—enough so that Frye can see the Bible as the "main source for undisplaced myth in our tradition." For Frye, the apocalyptic is the dream of total fulfillment, and the demonic is the nightmare of total bondage. Frye sees the vision of total fulfillment and total bondage in most direct terms in Revelation, which he believes is the symbolic climax of the Bible, and a grand literary unity in itself. Recurrent images such as the city, the garden, and the sheepfold are grounded in this vision which all men share. So, too, are the story lines, such as the patterns of ascent and descent.

Johannes Lindblom is not concerned with saving "poetic" inspiration, but his study of "symbolic perceptions" and "literary visions" sheds light on the nature of prophecy, vision, and poetry. Lindblom considers the Old Testament prophets closely. Besides ecstatic visions Lindblom finds other types of "vision" in the prophets. The other types of vision are subject to greater conscious control than ecstatic vision, but nonetheless, they are authentic responses to the Divine. They may take the form of Jeremiah's taking notice of the twig of an almond tree or his vision of the battle of Carchemish. The "night visions" of Zechariah can be separated, Lindblom thinks, into those that are genuine ecstatic visions—fanciful, unreal, irrational, and unreflective—and those which are literary visions—completed, controlled, and reflective—although the impulse from the Divine is present in both instances.

David Noel Freedman pursues the inspired poet-prophet from still another starting point. The earliest writings in Scripture are poetic, and behind them stretch the traditions of oral composition. The poetic sections are usually prophetic as well, as in the case of "The Song of Deborah and Barak" and the songs of Moses. In times of crisis, when the history of Yahweh's people (written in prose) is in need of renewal, the prophets utter their oracles in traditional poetic forms. The association between poetry and prophecy persists at least through the period of Exile. After the Exile, prophecy ceases, to be renewed later under different crisis situations. With its renewal, particularly in apocalyptic vision, comes the renewal of poetry. Jesus himself, in his parables and sayings, renews the poetic tradition. The "sequence-dating" method of dating poetic compositions advocated by Freedman, is more than a technical device to establish chronology. It would seem to fix the place of the poet-prophet in his vital role during periods of crisis. The poetry which is embedded in prose history is a useful indicator of the way literature transforms very old and traditional poetic ways.

(For a different view, see Collins, pp. 121–133. Wright, pp. 166–172, deals with archaeology and ancient documents as well. Klein, pp. 191–203, connects apocryphal writings and Dead Sea Scrolls with Messianism. On the sociological functions of poetry see Mowinckel, pp. 173–190.)

Later sections in this book will deal with the literature of the Bible from the point of view of traditions, influences on the poet, and the reader. The essays in this section are concerned mainly with the producers of the literature. The prophets and the writers of visionary pieces are the most likely subjects to give us insight into the psychology of inspiration.

Questions raised in this section about symbolism and imagery will also be discussed later. (In particular, see the essays by Macquarrie, pp. 396–410, and Burke, pp. 381–395.)

Many thinkers in this century have been intrigued by the poet and the Sacred. Some, like Rudolf Otto, Gerardus van der Leeuw, and Mircea Eliade, have been anxious to show that poetry outside the Judeo-Christian tradition and poetry that is not ostensibly religious (not connected with a cult or sect) can manifest the Sacred. The philosopher Martin Heidegger has even claimed that "the writing of poetry is the fundamental naming of the gods."[3] Commenting on a poem written by Hölderlin, Heidegger tells us that "the poetic word only acquires its power of naming when the gods themselves bring us to language." For Heidegger the gods speak through "signs from antiquity":

> The speech of the poet is the intercepting of these signs, in order to pass them on to his own people. This intercepting is an act of receiving and yet at the same time a fresh act of giving; for "in the first signs" the poet catches sight already of the completed message and in his word boldly presents what he has glimpsed, so as to tell in advance of the not-yet-fulfilled.

One need not illustrate the nature of poetry and even prophecy by biblical literature. To show the nature of inspired authorship through the Bible itself gives point and immediacy to the question. It is to that task that the essays in this section are written.

NOTES

1. "*Thus Spake Zarathustra:* A Book for All and None," *Ecce Homo,* tr. Clifton P. Fadiman, *The Philosophy of Nietzsche,* Modern Library (New York: Random House, 1954), pp. 896–97.

2. *The Exaltation of Inanna,* ed. and trans. William W. Hallo and J. J. A. Van Dijk (New Haven: Yake Univ. Press, 1968), p. 33.

3. "Hölderlin and the Essence of Poetry," trans. Douglas Scott, *Existence and Being* (Chicago: Henry Regnery, 1949), p. 287. The following two passages are also from this source.

The Psychology
of Inspiration

Luis Alonso Schökel, S.J., advocates what has been called "aesthetic criticism" (see Muilenburg, pp. 362–380). In this essay he confronts the problems of inerrancy and literary authorship. Examination of biblical authors and other writers sheds light on the psychology of inspiration—on the psychology of the "inspired literary process." A central intuition brings the poet into being. Examination of texts helps us recover something of the poetic intuition which produced it. The flash of insight, the charismatic inspiration, is followed by an impulse to write, and is completed by the writer's skill in using words. Both powerful hierophanies (in which the Sacred manifests itself) and the often humble task of choosing the right word for the right situation are parts of the creative process. Even a psalm that shows Canaanite influences is taken up in its new significant religious context—one poet is touched by the work of another.

The author's creative combination of "sources" is a particularly important element in the "inspired literary process," since source studies are classified as "literary criticism" (discussed in the General Introduction, pp. 1–15).

Inspiration, then, attends all stages of composition. The creative process is seen relative to the material of a literary work, the intuition, and the execution of the work.

T HE charism of inspiration, considered formally as an action of the Holy Spirit, cannot be scrutinized by psychological investigations. However, the human literary activity which is moved and directed by the Holy Spirit can be subjected to speculative study and its result called "a proposed psychology of inspiration." A title for this chapter which would

From Luis Alonso Schökel, S.J., *The Inspired Word* (1967), pp. 177–215.

be more exact though less manageable would be something like, "The Psychology of the Inspired Human Literary Process."

Someone might ask if an analysis such as we propose is legitimate or even useful; perhaps it would be better to leave inspiration wrapped in its mystery. While, again, someone might object that the study of the human process of literary creation in an effort to understand the charism of inspiration is no more helpful than an analysis of the mathematical reasoning of a professor (who teaches in the state of grace and with a supernatural intention) to an understanding of the workings of grace.

But this objection overlooks an important distinction. Grace has no specific reference to mathematics, but inspiration is directed specifically to the act of language, and it is this which differentiates it from the other charisms. In undertaking a study of this question, we are but following in the footsteps of those who have written treatises on the subject of prophecy and inspiration.

THE LEONINE DESCRIPTION

Modern manuals usually base their treatment of the question on the following description of inspiration given by Leo XIII in his encyclical, *Providentissimus Deus:*

> Hence, the fact that it was men whom the Holy Spirit took up as His instruments for writing does not mean that it was these inspired instruments—but not the primary author—who might have made an error. For by supernatural power He so moved and impelled them to write—He so assisted them when writing—that the things which He ordered, and those only, they, first, rightly understood, then willed faithfully to write down, and finally expressed in apt words and with infallible truth. Otherwise, it could not be said that He was the Author of the entire Scripture.[1]

We find this passage in that part of the encyclical in which Leo XIII is talking about inerrancy, and rejecting the false opinion of those who maintained that there were errors in the Bible but that these were due to the human authors, not to God. The Pope denies the validity of such a distinction and bases himself on the principle already defined: "God is the author of the entire Scripture," adding to this a speculative elaboration of what is meant by "author." The description of inspiration which is here given is thus not presented for its own sake, but is subordinated to and in the context of the question of inerrancy.

Any discussion of this Leonine description of inspiration should begin with an affirmation of its fundamental validity. A psychological schematization retains its validity so long as it is taken as such; it loses its validity the moment that it offers itself as the complete and adequate expression of the reality.

If we leave aside cases of completely mechanical writing or other instances of abnormal or pathological phenomena, we can schematically break any literary process down into the following stages: an intellectual stage in which there is knowledge of one kind or another, a volitional stage in which there is a free decision to objectify knowledge in writing, and a stage of execution in which the intention is realized. In reality, these three stages intermingle, and as each unfolds it may adopt different forms, yet this does not invalidate the fundamental correctness of the schematization.

In a study of the problems connected with the inspired literary process, it is quite helpful to adopt this schematization and then pursue the investigation by differentiating further within each stage of the schema. This is the method followed by most modern manuals; we wish first merely to reproduce and summarize their presentation.

THE DESCRIPTION GIVEN BY THE THEOLOGY MANUALS

(1) The Intellectual Stage: The human author can receive his knowledge directly from God through a previous revelation, and this can come about in diverse ways: a vision, the ordering of phantasms in the imagination, or an intellectual perception. It is also possible that the human author arrive at his knowledge by his own efforts: his experience, his study, the consultation of sources, etc. In this case, the inspired writer makes an interior judgment concerning his acquired knowledge and affirms, explicitly or implicitly, that "it is so." This judgment is made with the aid of divine light, "in the light of divine truth," and his illumination forms an integral part of the process of inspiration. Because the light is divine, the judgments made in virtue of this light are divine. Note that it is not only the statement as such which is the matter of the judgment that is inspired, but the affirmation of its truth—the formal element in the judgment. And since this formal element is of divine truth, it demands the assent of our faith to the reality revealed. It is not necessary or even usual that the hagiographer be conscious of the divine influence in his soul.

(2) The Volitional Stage: "No prophecy ever came about by the will of man." God moves the will of a man to write without destroying his freedom. This usually transpires without any conscious awareness of the movement on the part of the one inspired, though the divine action infallibly achieves its purpose. The movement must be interior and physical; it may at times also be moral, governing the circumstances which prompt the author to write. Under this motion of God, a man's decision is divine: God is the author of the process by which the book comes about, and thus He is the author of the book.

(3) The Stage of Execution: This is the act of writing which the author accomplishes by himself or through others; it is the act of expressing the message in apt terms, without error. The process by which the work is realized is not under a special supernatural influence, but is carried out with the aid of a certain divine assistance which guarantees that the terms are apt and that there is no error. This assistance does not consist in a physical motion acting directly on the executive faculties.

We are sure that, as the reader studied the above description, he felt a veritable surge of questions and objections welling up within him—more even than he could express to himself: "The outline has become much too schematic.... The description is oversimplified.... It concentrates on the one example of a writer.... Is the creative imagination of a poet an executive faculty?... What about all those things in the Bible which are not formal judgments or doctrine?... The whole question of literary expression is treated as secondary.... There is no appreciation of the psychology of language.... The restriction of a prophetic insight to a charism of knowledge seems awkward...."

We can remain calm, however, and proceed with our investigation. Others also have felt the inadequacy of the schematization, and have attempted in their theological speculations to render the description more realistic and more supple.

THE DESCRIPTION GIVEN BY BENOIT

We give Benoit's name to this description since he is responsible for its present and justifiable notoriety. Benoit himself tells us that the first person to propose the distinction was Nicolaus Serarius, an exegete of the sixteenth century. We find the following text in his *Prolegomena Biblica* (Mainz, 1612):

> ... Secondly, God illumines the mind of the writer with a certain light which is either entirely supernatural, or natural but supernaturally conferred or increased. This light is given in order to enable him to perceive what is dictated or to judge, or to do both. Thirdly, this judgment, which is made by the writer concerning what has been dictated, is either theoretical or practical. It is the former when the writer judges that what has been dictated, is true. It is the latter when he judges that he should write these things, in just these words, in this way, and at this time.[2]

The theoretical judgment has as its object, the true; the practical judgment has as its object, the good—an end to be achieved. The theoretical judgment is in the order of knowledge, the practical judgment has to do with activity. Both these judgments exist and are diversely operative in the inspired authors.

In the case of the prophet, for instance, his announcement of the certainty of coming doom—"You are going into exile"—is the statement of a true proposition made in the name of God. The predominant factor in the oracle was the speculative judgment. However, when the prophet preaches a sermon to the people, his aim is to persuade and convert them, his intention is centered on the good end to be achieved. Here the practical judgment predominated, initiating and directing the literary activity, willing a certain goal and selecting the means toward it.

When the speculative judgment predominates, it elicits a practical judgment concerning the advisability and the means of communicating itself. When the practical judgment predominates, it utilizes various aspects of speculative judgments, ordering them to its own end. An evaluation of any text must first take into account which type of judgment predominates; if it is the theoretical judgment, we seek the truth of the statement and affirm its inerrancy; if, however, the practical judgment is predominant, we seek the practical truth, or the correspondence between what is intended and how and whether it is achieved.

Both procedures are inspired, each realizing the charism analogically according to its own nature, and each judgment gives rise to a process of execution in which the faculties engaged are operative with the aid of a special divine assistance.

Benoit has lately summed up his thought in three propositions:

1. The writing of the sacred Scriptures calls for speculative judgments as well as practical judgments.

2. These speculative judgments need not precede the practical judgments; they may accompany these latter or come after them.

3. Again, these speculative judgments may be modified under the influence of the practical judgments.[3]

Further on in the same article, enlisting the aid of another distinction proposed by A. Desroches,[4] Benoit enumerates three types of judgments, not merely two:

> [1] An absolute speculative judgment, or one "purely speculative," which is made in regard to the truth considered in itself. . . . [2] A speculative judgment with regard to action, which considers the truth in relation to activity . . . the thing to be done is viewed as possible. . . . [3] A practical judgment which has as its proper object practical truth, that is, truth considered in its relation to a right desire . . . which tends unerringly to the goal of art—the work achieved.[5]

The distinction of Benoit is elaborated with an eye to the problem of inerrancy. It enables him to gradate the various degrees of commitment with which the authors make their affirmations, down to and including those cases in which, while in the process of achieving a practical goal, they utilize statements without being completely committed to their speculative validity.

This same article includes an historical survey of recent discussion concerning the nature of the two judgments. We find there the opinions of Franzelin, Levesque, Crets, Clames, Pesch, Merkelbach, Lagrange, and Bea.

This line of thought, which we have named Benoit's, has undoubtedly made a great contribution, and has refined and nuanced the Leonine description considerably, bringing it closer to the psychological reality of literary creation. However, we still believe that the needs of the problem have not been entirely met, first, because the whole outlook gravitates too closely around the question of judgment, and secondly, because the operative or executive powers—so eminently creative in a poet—are assigned a negligible function. While recognizing, then, the value of these investigations, it seems that the time is ripe to essay another direction in the study of the problem, one that is more positive and more open to modern acquisitions in contiguous areas of research. That is to say, we would like to relate this problem to the study of literary creativity.

A DESCRIPTION DRAWN FROM LITERARY CREATION

We will proceed in this analysis first by elaborating a description of literary creation in general, basing ourselves on what writers themselves have said. Then we will attempt an application of this description to the biblical authors, again basing ourselves on what these authors have said and also on what their works can tell us.

Both stages in this investigation are liable to objection. In relation to the first stage, it might be pointed out that there is no "common doctrine" in this matter: There are only disparate testimonies whose selection and classification cannot result in a representative description. The second objection is more serious in that it denies that there is any parallel between an author in our culture and the men who wrote the Bible: The whole concept of "author" is so different that if the term is not equivocal, the analogy is too remote to be useful in an intellectual inquiry.

It is certainly true that the biblical authors are not romantic or modern poets. Their approach to literature is quite different. Their composition often consists more in working with material already formed than in true creativity. The prophet is not concerned with his success as a literateur, but with announcing the message of God. And the biblical authors in general do not attempt to express their own personality or style in their work.

Let these differences be granted. Still, we do not think we have the right to exaggerate them; an analogy is still possible. Sometimes we wonder whether those who so vigorously deny any resemblance between literature in general and the Bible are not really trying to pacify their own consciences in order to leave themselves free to approach the biblical authors with an utterly unique set of criteria and methods; other investigators give the impression of possessing little appreciation of literary values. Whoever would maintain that the Old Testament contains no literature and no poetry has a rather unique concept of these realities.

Think for a moment of the Canticle of Canticles—or the smaller units which compose it; think of the Book of Job—minus its additions; or of the introduction to Ecclesiastes; or of some Psalm or page from the prophets. If, while reading these, our artistic sense is awakened, then the literary world in which they move cannot be so alien to our own. And as we study each work in turn, the spiritual affinity which we discover is quite sufficient justification for the analysis we are about to undertake. Then, too, we need only reflect on the distance between works which we include within the ambit of our own culture: The differences between the *Ars Poetica* of Horace and that of Verlaine are great indeed, yet no one thinks them insuperable.

AN ARTIST WITH LANGUAGE

Let us begin with a pen-sketch of an artist in our own culture. Usually, he is a man possessing a capacity to experience many things intensely. These experiences need not be specifically poetic; much of what he lives is shared by the lot of men: disappointment in love, for example. He is capable of deeply personal experiences and at the same time, by reason of some mysterious sympathy with men and things, he can enter into the experiences of others and relive them. Life itself breaks in to make its impact and set up these intense vibrations, but then, so does literature: An artist usually has a unique grasp of poetry. In art, a man gives himself up to his experiences, admitting all their vividness and their pain.

> O ancient curse of poets!
> Being sorry for themselves instead of saying,
> forever passing judgment on their feeling
> instead of shaping it; forever thinking
> that what is sad or joyful in themselves
> is what they know and what in poems may fitly
> be mourned or celebrated. Invalids
> using a language full of woefulness
> to tell us where it hurts, instead of sternly
> transmuting into words those selves of theirs,
> as imperturbable cathedral carvers
> transposed themselves into the constant stone.
>
> That would have been salvation. Had you once
> perceived how fate may pass into a verse
> and not come back, how, once in, it turns image,

nothing but image, but an ancestor,
who sometimes, when you watch him in his frame,
seems to be like you and again not like you:
you would have persevered.[6]

Recall, for instance, the complexity of Shakespeare, or Lope de Vega, the intensity of Antonio Machado or Donne, the self-surrender of which Rilke speaks, or the sublime experience of St. John of the Cross, occasioned by a love poem. Though such people may seem to have something of the romantic about them, they are not all of this school of literature (none of the authors just mentioned is a romantic). Much of what is being written today, and many of the greatest classics, can lay claim to like intensity, complexity, sympathy, and self-surrender—Petrarch or Fra Luis of Granada, for example—yet the same cannot be said of those exercises in imitation practiced by many notable writers, such as those responsible for the Petrarchism so prevalent in sixteenth-century Europe.

Curiously enough, the artist, even as he abandons himself to the flood tide of his experience, remains somehow aloof from it, as though he had to divide himself in order to contemplate his own experience. To the entirety of the self-surrender there is opposed this distant vantage point from which the surrender is surveyed. The artist gives himself up to the intensity of love or pain as few men can, and yet he preserves a clear reflective consciousness of himself, observing himself in love or pain, and drawing from this quarry the stones for his trade. Rilke has magnificently described these aspects of an artist, and Thomas Mann has taken them as the theme for some of his stories: "Tonio Kröger" or "Tristan," for example. In some writers, this reflective distance is very great; it is a characteristic of the classical writers, but it can also be the sign of a self-scrutiny which is wholly modern. Then, again, as an artist views the experiences of others, he can keep too great a distance, replacing sincere sympathy with cold curiosity, and defensively erecting his vantage point into an unpitying, egotistical security. However, a man must be somewhat detached from an experience, be it his own or another's, if he is to write of it.

A great artist begins with an intuition which forms the dominant life center and unifying principle of his work; such, for instance, was the experience of a playwright such as Shakespeare or Calderón or the great Russian novelists. Poets, too, of lesser breadth, also begin with a dominating and unifying intuition: Keats, Juan Ramón, Valéry, etc.

Finally, the literary artist has the gift of language. Easily or painstakingly, he makes language serve him, harnessing it, or forging it to his task. The facility of Lope de Vega is in marked contrast with the struggles of Schiller; Tolstoy wrote *War and Peace* six times.

If we wish now to convert these four characteristics of linguistic artistry into a process, we should maintain the same order: experience, reflective vision, intuition, and execution. For the moment, let this schema (one more schema) rest at that, and let us look now at the other extreme in literary creation; not now at the massive geniuses, but rather at the honest craftsman of language with his modest poetic grace and unspectacular insights, and even at the craftsman copier who has not received the gift of poetry at all. There are times when even the greatest artist finds himself alone with his craft as his only resource; and it is at such times that creativity can begin from craftsmanship. Valéry can be our witness:

> The poet is awakened in a man by some unexpected happening, some event outside himself or within him: a tree, a face, a "subject," an emotion, a word. Sometimes it is the desire for expression which sets the thing in motion, a need to translate experience; but sometimes it is just the opposite, there is some fragment of style, some hint of expression which is searching for a cause, which seeks a meaning somewhere in my soul. . . . Note this possible duality: sometimes a thing wishes to be expressed, at other times a means of expression is looking for something to serve.[7]

SOME BIBLICAL EXAMPLES

With this preliminary information, let us undertake to explore the Promised Land of the Old Testament. We do not know if we will return with grape clusters the size of a man, or whether the complex terrain will overwhelm us. At any rate, it is worth the try.

A Great Poet

One of the most intense lyric pieces of the Old Testament is, undoubtedly, the poem of Hosea about his unfaithful wife.[8] Aside from some questions of detail, there is general agreement concerning the basic meaning of the poem, its substantial unity, and the power of its language. Everyone can appreciate, either immediately or on reflection, the powerful way in which marriage, the Promised Land, and the divine mystery are fused in the forge of his intuition.

One may question the possibility of reconstructing the creative process by which this poem came into being, but it will be worth the effort to try, availing ourselves of the narrative material in other chapters. Hosea appears to have been someone deeply in love with his wife; his love was strong, exclusive, and irrevocable, but his wife was unfaithful. He feels within him a deep, persistent pain which sinks down and lodges in his heart. Total love has become grief, and grief gives rise to anger, which, in turn, strives to turn into hate in order to dull the pain, but it cannot—this love refuses to be destroyed, it lives on in memory and finally conquers. Now, up to this point in our reconstruction, Hosea is not yet a poet; he is only a husband who has been tragically deceived.

At some point, he succeeded in stepping back from himself and looking at his pain. Perhaps he started to ask himself the reason for his grief, or perhaps he began to complain of a choice which he considers to have been made by God. In this atmosphere of heavy storm clouds, there is a sudden flash of blinding light and his experience is illumined from above; it becomes transparent and reveals in an instant its own deepest meaning. There now appears, not Hosea and his beloved, but God and His people, or, better, this very real experience of Hosea is seen to be a reflection and imitation of God's love for Israel. The prophet's experience had to be deep and painful if it was to convey any notion of the depth of the divine passion.

The insight was poetic: The prophet now feels the urge to transform his intuition into poetry so that in this form it will continue to have existence and reveal to others the love of God which he has discovered. So he sets himself to work, bringing to bear all his mastery of language and his craftsman's patience: He listens to the sound of his words as he combines them; he measures the rhythm of his phrases; he elaborates his images with consistency; and he intensifies the dramatic movement of his piece, sustaining it up to the conclusion. As he works, he receives new insights which round out and support his original intuition, and as he manipulates words, his meaning becomes clearer, richer, and more delicately blended.

Hosea passes from the scene, but his poem remains. He knows that his poem is an oracle. He passes it on as the word of God, and it is as such that we receive it and read it.[9]

Accepting the above hypothesis as substantially correct, we can go on to ask the question: At what point did the motion of the Spirit begin to be operative? Pesch's remark that "Many times, poets are obliged to endure a cold sweat in their effort to clothe their thought fittingly,"[10] does not adequately describe the process. This picture of a poet as a tailor seeking to outfit his ideas is a bit rationalistic. Poetry is not that kind of a sweatshop, or even a designer's salon.

What makes Hosea the author of his poem? The experience of life as such does not pertain to the creative process, except as preparatory for it; it provides the material for the poem. Literary activity has its true beginning in an intuition which provides the force and directive energy to the whole process in which it itself achieves objective existence. Thus, in our case we have to consider that the intuition of Hosea pertains to the realm of the charismatic: At this point, at least, the action of the Spirit must begin. The process which follows, in which intuition is given literary existence and solidity, transforming the preëxisting material into a poem, will then be dominated by this intuition under the influence of the charism.

The process of execution is a creative function. It is here that the powers of the poet in respect to language are acting in creative harmony:

> ... this state in which we are intimately affected, and in which all the properties of our language are indistinctly but harmoniously evoked.[11]

The error of many authors who treat of inspiration is found in the fact that they envisage the poem or the work to be written as already existing before it is given verbal form. This latter factor is considered quite secondary, and all that is demanded of it is that it be "apt." In poetry, and in literature more generally, the work only exists in its verbal expression; the central intuition becomes objective and communicable only in its literary realization, and the activity by which this existence is conferred characterizes a literary author or poet. (Let us recall here the words of Mallarmé: "Poetry is made with words.")

Obviously, then, we cannot place the specifically literary activity of the author outside the realm of inspiration. Neither can we decompose the process into a series of practical or speculative-practical judgments concerning the aptitude of a given literary formulation. We do not deny the existence of such judgments: Sometimes they are explicit and extend to the very last effort at expression; sometimes they are implicit, contained in the joy of a single, dazzling discovery. But we maintain that literary realization is greater than, and prior to, any such judgments. We cannot equate an intuition which contemplates its object with a speculative judgment which affirms explicitly or implicitly the truth of a proposition. The intuition may be accompanied by some tacit affirmation, "it is so"; but we find it difficult to reduce a poetic intuition to some form of speculative judgment.

The poetry of the Old Testament, at least a large portion of it, cannot be explained by the psychological description and its enumeration of various judgments; consequently, the charism in virtue of which it is inspired does not correspond to the schema proposed.

The example taken from Hosea has its limits as an hypothesis. For some centuries past, commentators, on account of a certain moral scrupulosity, have considered the matrimonial incident related by Hosea to be pure fiction—a species of allegory. Many modern commentators, however, accept the historicity of the fact, since it provides a psychological basis for the oracle. Others insist on what is called "symbolic action," which can be a real historical episode or merely pantomime. Even if we are inclined to see the action as symbolic, we believe that it is a genuine historical occurrence. Those who minimize the psychological factor do not hesitate to recognize the intensity of feeling present in the poem. This means that, though they deny the historical basis of Hosea's experience, they must by that very fact accord to him an extraordinary poetic capacity to enter into the experiences of others, and use them as the raw material for his own poetic creation.

A Simple Craftsman

Let us pass now from the great poet and prophet of love to an anonymous craftsman of a later date who had not a pennyworth of poetic temperament. He is a lover of the law, that law which is beginning to be an intermediary reality while at the same time maintaining its immediate link with God. It has occurred to our author to express his love and the glories of his beloved, the law, in verse. It will be a series of phrases which will convey the sense of totality and perfection. He has decided to use a stylistic artifice, an alphabetical acrostic which consists in beginning each verse with a letter of the alphabet. This technique had been used before in Hebrew literature: in a few Psalms, in the description of an "ideal wife,"[12] and in the lamentations attributed to Jeremiah. In the lamentations, there are passages in which each strophe contains three verses, all beginning with the same letter. The author of our Psalm is going to surpass them all: In order to express the idea of plentitude, he will begin eight consecutive verses (seven plus one) with the same letter, which, multiplied by the twenty-two letters of the alphabet, gives to the "poem" a length of one hundred and seventy-six verses, each having six accents. Already the inspiration and proposal are not very poetic.

And so he sets to work: for the first strophe—the letter "aleph." This gives us two "happy's"; a conjunction, "but"; an adverb, "then"; a preposition, "to"; a pronoun, "you"; an interjection, "would that"; and a verb in the first person future, which in Hebrew begins with aleph. Naturally, the first word sets the tone for the rest of the verse or hemistich, with the result that from verse to verse there is no continuity—only succession.

The first strophe succeeded in avoiding a superabundance of "filler words." The second strophe, beginning with the letter "beth," repeats the preposition "*be*" (with, in) six times, and adds one "blessed": The author has not sweated unduly over this. The third strophe—the letter "gimel"—reads nicely: "ideal," "open," "stranger," "consumed," "rebuke," "take away," and then concludes with two "indeeds." The fourth strophe—the letter "daleth"—has to resort five times to the word "ways."

Our author arrives at the fifth strophe, which has to begin with the letter "he." (In our Hebrew dictionaries, the letter "h" takes up but a few pages.) He counts on using "*hinne*" (behold, lo), which he saves for the last verse. He searches painstakingly, and finally resorts to a colorless artifice. There is in Hebrew a conjugation which in the perfect tense has as preformative "*ha*." This conjugation is called "*hifil*," and it expresses the notion of causation. We will translate the initial word of each verse, using our English "make" as an auxiliary: "make me understand," "make me appreciate," "make me walk," "make my heart incline," "make my eyes turn away," "make your words firm," "make shame pass from me," and then "behold I desire your precepts." We ought to say in defense of the author that perhaps he did not have our outsider's awareness of verbal roots and conjugations; in any case, his literary activity consisted at this point in a hunt for "h's." Where, then, is the poetic inspiration? There is none. However, the charismatic inspiration must be present.

If someone were to read this last strophe with a theological preoccupation, he would be positively enthusiastic; the author has voiced a profound truth. With all his love for the Law, and with all his expressions of the desire to keep it, he has enunciated here the most important fact about the Law: that its observance is more the work of God than of man. These causative verbs are the proof of it: "make my heart incline," "make my eyes turn away," "make me walk," "make me appreciate that I might keep your law." God not only gives commandments, but also the power, the grace, to keep them. This is the great theological lesson contained in this rather prosaic prayer.

But if we turn our attention back to the literary efforts of the author, we see that his intention was not so much to teach theology as to find "h's." How should we interpret this craftsman's work in terms of inspiration? In general, we would say that the initial idea of the acrostic form multiplied by the number eight occurred under the influence of the Spirit; the patient pedestrian realization of the idea was also directed by the Spirit in such a way that, as the author strove to compose his work, he received new insights with which he could express and develop his love for the law. This love was the remote material for his verses, the point at which it took on the nature of inspiration is found in his craftsman's choice of a literary form.

Someone wishing to use the description of Benoit or Desroches, would say that the Psalm began with a practical judgment or a speculative judgment concerning action, and that this initial judgment gave rise to and modified subsequent speculative judgments. But he should not neglect to complete Benoit's description, acknowledging the decisive importance of verbal realization as a truly formative factor in the process by which the work is composed. This factor must also be accorded a place within the influence of the charismatic motion of the Spirit.

Joining now these examples of the two extremes, Hosea and Psalm 119, we can better appreciate the words of Valéry, which are worth repeating here:

> The poet is awakened in a man by some unexpected happening, some event outside himself or within him: a tree, a face, a "subject," an emotion, a word. Sometimes it is the desire for expression which sets the thing in motion, a need to translate experience; but sometimes it is just the opposite, there is some fragment of style, some hint of expression which is searching for a cause, which seeks a meaning somewhere in my soul. . . . Note this possible duality: sometimes a thing wishes to be expressed, at other times a means of expression is looking for something to serve.

This is the place to defend the Leonine description against the inhibiting strictures it has had to endure in some theological manuals. The Pope speaks of the sacred authors as "conceiving correctly in their mind," but this term "concept" is quite broad. It can refer to concepts which are clearly defined, or to a very general idea, or it can even refer to the "conceiving" of a literary work. Why must we interpret this term in the encyclical as referring exclusively to concepts and judgments? In our description of the creative process in Hosea, the first thing "conceived" was an intuition from which grew the general plan of the work. There then followed an intermediary stage characterized by a movement toward its realization, and finally the actual execution by which the intuition was given verbal existence. This same amplitude can be accorded the other Leonine phrase, "aptly express," which can refer to the authentic literary contours given to the initial conception (the phrase which follows, "with infallible truth," need not be identical with "apt"). If the Pontiff's words are thus understood, we can place emphasis on this third stage of composition, leaving for a later moment the question of "writing."

A Tree

Here is a very likely example of the same process of intuition. Valéry, in his list of things which can touch off poetry in a man, puts "a tree" at the head of the enumeration. One morning, just before Spring, a prophet was walking in the countryside and suddenly came upon a tree already in flower. The sight of it suggested its name, and the prophet said it aloud. As he pronounces the word, its obvious etymology comes into his mind: the almond tree has a name in Hebrew which is derived from the word "to watch," because it seems to be so anxiously on the watch for Spring and ready to flower early. As he hears himself say the name, there is a flash of association: "the watching tree"—"God on the watch" (*maqqel shaqed— Yahweh shoqed*). The name of the tree resounds with the echoes of a higher reality: God watching in history to make good His word. The spark of intuition contained a transcendent analogy.

Jeremiah recognized the insight as a message from God, and set to work to transform it into a communicable form. For this purpose, he enlisted the aid of a device already known since the time of Amos,[13] and perhaps even topical in prophetic utterances:

> The word of Yahweh came to me:
> What do you see, Jeremiah?
> I said:
> I am looking at a branch of the vigilant tree.
> And Yahweh said to me:
> Well seen!
> For I am keeping vigil over my word
> bringing it to completion.[14]

As we have constructed it, the inspired process begins with a flash of insight, is followed by a movement or impulse to write, and finally is completed by the exercise of the writer's craft. The last step could hardly be called creative in this instance, since it consisted in "re-filling" a used formula.

We like to compare this example from Jeremiah with a *poema Castellano* by Antonio Machado Ruiz. As the poet walked along, his eyes rested on an elm tree: A ray of light passed through its dormant branches and somehow caught the color of a few tiny leaves just appearing on the tip of one of its shoots. In this tree, just about to regain its verdure, the poet sees the mystery of life itself with its Spring and its hope: the gray melancholy of the branches intimates the secret. He decides to record this discovery before the tree be cut down and disappear.

. . . . .
Elm tree, let me record on this paper,
the favor of your vernal branches.

My heart is looking
also, toward the light and toward reliving,
another miracle of springtime.[15]

And though the medium is more complex, the same intuition resounds in these lines of Hopkins:

Not of áll my eyes see, wandering on the world,
Is anything a milk to the mind so, so sighs deep
Poetry tó it, as a tree whose boughs break in the sky.
Say it is ásh-boughs: whether on a December day and furled
Fast ór they in clammyish lashtender combs creep
Apart wide and new-nestle at heaven most high.
They touch heaven, tabour on it; how their talons sweep
The smouldering enormous winter welkin! May
Mells blue and snow white through them, a fringe and fray
Of greenery: it is old earth's groping towards the steep
Heaven whom she childs us by.[16]

The poet of Castile and his English counterpart recognized in elms and ash boughs a human meaning in their cosmic mystery; the prophet from Anatoth, magnetized by his calling, saw divine meaning in an almond tree. The prophet couched his message in an accepted literary formulation of incisive brevity; the Spanish poet used the form of a "confession," revealing the state of his soul as it faced the vision of the elm tree; and the nineteenth-century English Jesuit adopted a sonnet form.

The Area of Probability

Our description of a walk in the countryside is a reconstruction. Perhaps the thought occurred while the poet looked out of the window. Some say that the flowering branch was really a staff made of almond wood (we don't know if the grain is that easily recognizable); even so, the role of the name "watching tree" remains, though its poetic resonances be somewhat diminished. Those who consider that the branch was seen in a vision or was only imagined, must still allow for the poetic role of its name. However, there is no need to have recourse to extraordinary visions when we know, for instance, that Jeremiah received an oracle while watching a potter at work (18:1ff.); and when there is the example of something as homespun as a boiling pot about to tip over (1:13ff.), we need not imagine a preternatural occurrence.

The example taken from Jeremiah provides us with a good illustration of the way in which the actual craft of poetry writing was profoundly influenced by tradition, and this may serve as a sample characteristic of most of the poetry of the Old Testament in which traditional forms and formulas played such a large role.

Jeremiah also tells us in his "confessions" of the interior impulse he felt, which he could not restrain, driving him to give to the words he heard within himself an objective literary existence:

You led me on, O Yahweh,
and I let myself be led.
You forced me, and you won.
And I?—a laughingstock all day,
sport for every passer-by.

Whenever I speak, I shout Violence!
Plunder is my cry.

For Yahweh's word to me—
scorn and derision all the day long.
I said:
I will not remember it,
no more will I speak in his name.
Then in my heart it turned to fire
burning, imprisoned in my bones.
I am weary holding it in,
I can no longer.[17]

This reminds us of the "spiritual compulsion" which Stephen Spender avows in his article, "The Making of a Poem."[18]

In the poem of Jeremiah which we quoted above, he refers to his oracle as consisting of the word "Violence!" According to von Rad, this is the cry by which someone who is being oppressed demands protection or justice.[19] The role of the word in context can be variously explained: (1) It could be a summary of Jeremiah's message put here in this form for functional reasons. (2) It might be a germinal word, capable of being articulated in a full oracle, as for example in the oracle of the almond tree; a single cry becomes the seed of a whole poem, setting its tone and providing its theme. (3) It could be the oracle in its entirety; an elemental inspiration suggests but one word and causes it to be pronounced. In such a situation, intuitions and judgments in regard to literary realization count for nothing. The unadorned cry acquires its concrete meaning within the vital context of the people. We ought to note, of course, that such single-worded oracles were not left in their isolation in the collections of prophetic sayings as we have them, but this does not exclude the possibility of their existence in the prophetic preaching.

A Detail of Style

We are going to take a quick glance at the prophet Isaiah as he gives literary shape to a matrimonial litigation carried on between God and his people or his city. The exclamation "*ay*" could, in the instance we are studying, be said either as "*ayka*" or "*ayk*" (which became in later pronunciation "*eka*" and "*ek*" respectively); Isaiah chooses the bisyllabic form. There are two words for city, "*ir*" and "*qirya*": here he chooses the latter. In order to see the reason behind these choices, it will suffice to read out loud the following alternatives:

> 'ayk hayetá lezoná 'ír ne' maná
> 'ayká hayetá lezoná qiryá ne'maná.[20]

The reality of the verse, and consequently of the poem, is changed because of the emphatic fivefold rhyme scheme found in the second of the two lines. Here, if we wish to speak of a judgment, we must place it in the choice between stylistic alternatives (Marouzeau—style consists in choice). The verse is not a simple statement or a judgment of truth; it is a cry and a complaint uttered by God. The intelligible content is dissolved in the expressive utterance. If the poet chooses to give to the divine complaint a form in which there are two more rhymes than need have been, then this choice is inspired, because the total message is more impressive and more revealing in this heightened literary form. Intensity is a dimension of the spirit (Bruno Snell) which plays an important role in interpersonal communication and in literary language. We have to realize that the technique and the style of Isaiah were elaborated under the influence of the Holy Spirit, and that the resulting literary work in all its dimensions is an inspired message. We may note in passing how aptly this verse illustrates the manner in which literary language assumes and exploits the possibilities inherent in common language.

Imitation in a Psalm

We are going to prescind for a moment from the origin of Psalm 29. The activating force in the poem is the experience of a storm which, in itself, is but the material for the work. In an overpowering experience of the tempest, a man perceived the awesome yet fascinating presence of God. The storm is to his symbolic intuition a theophany—a manifestation of

God in power. This perception of transcendence is the igniting point of the poem. In order to give his intuition an objective existence, the poet chooses the form of a liturgical hymn, and this selection of form dominates the whole tenor of the piece, which appears as a communal song of praise. As he shapes the poem, the author stylizes the storm in a series of seven thunderclaps, nouns which can almost be felt, and which are dynamic subjects for his phrases. These factors came to light as he strove to execute his poem in an *élan* of genuine creativity.

So far, this example seems to be exactly the same as that of Hosea. But there is a new factor. This Psalm is in all probability of Canaanite origin, and has been adapted by an inspired biblical author. The probable provenience of the Psalm poses a new question: Who is inspired? At what point in the process did the action of the Spirit begin, and in what terms are we to describe this action? We will attempt an answer.

The Hebrew author experienced a storm in a way very similar to his Canaanite predecessor. There need be nothing unusual in this, considering the fact that a storm is a common enough occurrence, and taking into account the symbolic thought context in which both minds moved. Seeking to objectify his experience, the biblical author recalls or finds this Canaanite Psalm whose aptitude he easily recognizes and on which he works, retouching it and making additions and changes. It is almost the same process which we saw in the case of the question-and-answer formula employed by Jeremiah: more imitative than creative, but no less inspired.

Or there can be another explanation: An Israelite poet reads this Canaanite Psalm and is deeply and sympathetically affected. The power of the poetic word, re-creating the event and manifesting its content, causes in the reader the same experience as that first had by the author, except that this time the intuition vibrates within the context of a faith in Yahweh. There is continuity and communion between the two experiences insofar as the Israelite relived the previous emotion and intuition; and there is a real transposition insofar as the religious meaning of the poem has been specified in a new, significant context. As the Hebrew reader strives to give form to the experience touched off by the poem, he finds that the best medium is the poem itself, and in this phase of literary execution, he adapts it to a new context of faith making use of the name of God, and God's relation with His people. His adaptation was a creative process in that it substantially modified the meaning of the poem. This is not a thing which can be established statistically by counting the number of words he changed, but must be appreciated by observing the resonances set up by replacing the preëxisting word figure in a new context, most probably with a marked economy of artifices. In this second hypothesis, we can locate the action of the Spirit in the moment when there was a relived experience in a new key, and then in the fundamental choice to repeat the previous poem, as well as in the actual technique by which it was adapted to a new religious purpose. Observe, however, that we admit a religious plane common to both experiences.

This is, as a matter of fact, that which would distinguish our example from another, whose process of transposition we can control quite closely: We refer to the poem about the shepherd boy by St. John of the Cross. We now possess the original love poem which served as his model; it does not really excel other poems of its type and era. The mystic, whose whole life force was polarized by the Lord Jesus, read the poem and felt a living flame. Seeking to confer existence and a communicability to the fire he felt within him, he took the poem, retouched it here and there, and transposed it to a completely new image-context. The result is astounding:

A shepherd lad was mourning his distress,
Far from all comfort, friendless and forlorn.
He fixed his thought upon his shepherdess
Because his breast by love was sorely torn.

He did not weep that love had pierced him so.
Nor with self-pity that the shaft was shot,
Though deep into his heart had sunk the blow,
It grieved him more that he had been forgot.

Only to think that he had been forgotten
By his sweet shepherdess, with travail sore,
He let his foes (in foreign lands begotten)
Gash the poor breast that love had gashed before.

"Alas! Alas! for him," the shepherd cries,
"Who tries from me my dearest love to part
So that she does not gaze into my eyes
Or see that I am wounded to the heart."

Then, after a long time, a tree he scaled,
Opened his strong arms bravely wide apart,
And clung upon that tree till death prevailed,
So sorely was he wounded in his heart.[21]

A critic with a positivist turn of mind, before the original was discovered, suspected a similar process and sought to establish the lines of dependence for the verses of St. John of the Cross. Another critic, now that the model has been found, might see in it the complete explanation of the mystic's poem. He would go back to the "original," not bothering with the work of St. John since, for him, this is "a pure plagiarism with hardly an original detail." This critic, whom we have invented for the sake of illustration, has not entered into the poem: He has not understood it, and thus, of course, cannot explain it. He is forced to maintain that the work of St. John of the Cross has no interest for him. But genetic analysis and statistics are not the instruments by which poetry is detected. The example of St. John of the Cross illustrates a common literary procedure in Spain during "*el siglo del oro*" known as "*a lo divino*," by which profane works were taken as the inspiration for other works "with a divine intention." The originals were at times quite pedestrian as literature, though at other times they possessed a certain poetic charm.[22]

St. John of the Cross effected a transposition from a profane level to one intensely religious by the analogy of love. This process sheds light on similar transpositions made by the biblical authors: For example, the chant of field workers—a love song—made expressive of God's love for his people (the song of the vineyard—Is 5:1-7), or a sentinel's song (Is 21:11-12), and most probably the love poem which we call the Canticle of Canticles, are the result of this type of transposition.

We do not doubt that in the case of Psalm 29 it is possible to isolate speculative judgments directed toward activity—concerning the aptitude of a Canaanite Psalm for the Israelite liturgy; and practical judgments—concerned with the adaptation necessary to effect this transposition. If the first judgment is explicit, the others are concomitant with the exercise of the technique required to realize it, and are thus consequent on the effort and the choice. However, we are not sure that this type of analytic dissection is particularly useful here, whereas the moments of conception and execution mentioned in the Leonine description when they are broadly interpreted can provide real insight.

A Narration

The story of the ten plagues in the Book of Exodus[23] is not a lyrical composition, nor does it burst forth from an intensely lived experience; it is a narrative of epic proportion, manifesting a calculated process of composition. No one can reasonably doubt that the author of the story as we now have it utilized preëxisting narrative material, some of which was contained in the Yahwistic account, while other elements pertained to the Priestly tradition. Some of the plagues were duplicated in these two compositions, others varied in their telling, and still others were simply diverse. The role of the personages involved, the tenor of the refrains used, as well as some other fixed formulas, were also different in the "J" and "P" traditions. But this does not matter: Our author took the two versions as the basis and source for his own composition. He chooses the number ten, because it is a simple figure on which to structure a story, and because of its capacity to signify seven plus three. The first and second plagues finish ambiguously; the third is decisive—"The finger of God is here." The fourth plague begins a mounting wave of affliction which subsides at the sixth plague, in order to prepare for the solemn entrance of the seventh: a theophany, which is announced in sonorous tones and culminates in the confession, "I have sinned." The eighth plague is preceded by a new prologue, announcing God's intentions and initiating a fresh series of calamities and concessions which culminate in the slaying of the first-born. We will not stop here to point out other ways in which the differences in the two preëxisting accounts are smoothed out or covered over (not always successfully). The final result is an epic narration of dynamic composition which, as such, is the work of the last author. (We presume, of course, that no one will equate "epic" with "pure fiction.")

In this instance, the most creative activity of the author lay in his work of composition, since the material and the formulas were already given. The execution was subordinated to a predetermined structure, and the whole was permeated by an epic tone which was intended to reveal the grandeur of the divine activity. We must, then, situate the impulse of charismatic inspiration within the whole process of composition from the very first choice of a structure until the whole work was realized. It is not difficult to describe this case in terms of speculative and practical judgments, or, indeed, in terms of conception and execution.

SUCCESSIVE INSPIRATION

The last example which we have just considered is of special importance, because many parts of the Old Testament as it has come down to us were composed in much the same way. The explanation of these passages forces on us a question which could be phrased like this: Are the preëxisting formulas and materials inspired, or is only the last stage of composition, the canonical text, inspired?

This is the question of "successive inspiration." Back in the time when Pesch and others were writing their manuals, it was possible to envisage the process of composition as having taken place in a way similar to our modern experience. Moses wrote his Pentateuch, Isaiah wrote his book, etc. But such thinking is untenable today. Many books of the Bible were composed in successive stages of literary creation: There were the traditions of local cult shrines, the composition of the Yahwist, the Elohistic variant on the same theme, the Priestly account with its cultic and legal interest, the various redactions and combinations of the above and other traditions; there were "*chansons de geste*," both secular and religious, collected in larger groups, unified on the basis of a religious theme, and rounded out by some passages of theological reflection (the Book of Judges); there were additions made to bring a text "up to date" (the last lines of Psalm 51); the insertion of the name "Judah" in oracles first addressed only to Israel as a commonplace. We find such procedures as the collection in a new dynamic unity of three oracles which were at first separate and of slightly different intent (as in Is 8); and so forth.

Must we imagine the Holy Spirit standing by with arms folded watching the whole process and then, just at the very last minute, stepping in to "inspire" the final stage of composition? Are we obliged to consider only the collector, or editor, or corrector as inspired? Ought we then to think that "inspiration" was only operative in the later period of Jewish history, between the Exile and the time of Esdras?

Such questions, obviously, answer themselves. A theory of inspiration so meager that it shuts out the Holy Spirit during the most creative moments in the composition of a work and then opens the door when there is practically nothing left to do, seems to us quite unacceptable. We are obliged to allow for some form or other of "successive inspiration" in order to explain the facts and apply the principles correctly. Wherever there is a real literary and religious contribution, there the Spirit acted. At the level of profane composition of non-Israelite origin, it is not necessary to invoke the charism of inspiration, and the same is true of a level of simple collection with no literary contribution. The books of the Bible grew along with the life of the people, and the Holy Spirit, far from looking on indifferently, was active in this process of growth and concomitant literary activity, breathing into it mysteriously yet powerfully.

Grelot treats this question by distinguishing three types of charisms which are related: (1) the prophetic charism in the Old Testament and the apostolic charism in the New Testament for the proclamation of the word of God; (2) the functional charism of language, by which the proclaimed word is preserved, elaborated, and developed; (3) the literary charism of language, by which the results of the former are fixed in written form. These three charisms all have relation to the word, that is, to language, but in varying degrees; the last mentioned is the least intense, but nonetheless essential in the constituting of the "Sacred Book."

THE TONE OF A WORK

The example we gave above of the story of the plagues in Egypt suggests some other considerations. We spoke there of an "epic tone," which in the poet was an attitude of soul in the presence of his theme, and in the work was its unifying structure. We can attribute to this "tone," as a subjective attitude of the author, a creative function, because of its influence over the whole of the execution of the work in its structure and unity. If this attitude is not to be identified with the initial intuition, it certainly flows easily from it, and as such must be considered to be under the influence of the Spirit.

The author of the Book of Judith envisaged his protagonist in an "heroic tone," while the tone of gentle irony pervades the characterization of Jonah. Joel (1:17–18) hears the bellows of the starving cattle with a compassion that is almost lyric. The tone of drama is felt in Nahum's contemplation of Nineveh's fall (2), or in the Book of Daniel's description of the scene in Belshazzar's dining hall where an empire changed hands (5).

The attitude or "tone" of soul on the part of the author determines the way in which the work is concretized as it receives its objective existence; in turn, the work determines the "tone" which the sympathetic reader will derive from it. For this reason, the tone of a biblical work assumes an important function as revelation, one which is at times as important as the thing being told. We find it very difficult to reduce this attitude or tone to any kind of "judgment," yet we cannot imagine that such an important factor could lie outside the influence of the charism of inspiration.

THE NEW TESTAMENT

The New Testament presents us with less variety. The Gospels began to acquire their consistency in a stage of oral tradition which was nevertheless Gospel. It was at this stage that they received many of their literary forms: There were larger units of composition such as the Passion narrative, and smaller unities which can be discerned because of the similarity of their structure: miracle stories, conflict stories, parables, etc. All of this provided the preëxisting material for the evangelists in their original work of literary composition.[24]

The literary efforts of the evangelists were profoundly personal contributions, and that is why each of them offers us a picture of Christ which is different yet complementary. They retain many of the forms and phrases which were found in the material that lay before them, imposing on it a higher unity deriving from an overall narrative schema and theological interpretation. Without a doubt, the literary work of the evangelists was inspired from the moment of the original intuition or intention which grew out of a personal understanding of Christ, until the last patient touches of redaction. It is not as certain that the previous stages of composition were inspired, but considering the extent of the influence that this stage had on the later literary Gospels, it seems reasonable to suppose that the successive elaborations of the material which later became the Gospels were inspired also.

The letters are in large measure doctrinal, with parenetic material interspersed. Often, they give literary stability to formulas which were part of the apostolic preaching, thus posing for us the problem of where to place the emphasis in an analysis of their compositions: Is it in their writing or in their speaking? The First Epistle of St. Peter is presented as a collaborative undertaking: "I write you this brief appeal through Silvanus, our trusty brother" (5:12). It appears as though the work of Silvanus was more than secretarial, and that he played a real role in the framing of the inspired message, which means, of course, that he was also inspired. The Epistle to the Hebrews seems to be a homily approved and recommended by St. Paul; but we cannot imagine that inspiration began with his "subsequent approval." The letters, especially of St. Peter and St. Paul, incorporate material found in the ancient liturgy. They refer to "spiritual canticles" (Eph 5:19; Col 3:16), and even quote from early hymns (Phil 2:5-11), or professions of faith (1 Cor 15:3ff.).

The New Testament has effected an immense work of transposition in which the Old Testament is placed within the new context of the Christ-fact. There is more here than the simple application of a few explicit prophecies, or the attempt to elucidate others that are more obscure; nor is it merely a question of the homiletical, theological, or pastoral use of a few passages from the ancient writings. The whole of the Old Testament is seen in the light of the glory shining on the face of Christ Jesus that transforms and elevates it by conferring on it a fullness of meaning which crowns its insights and tendential aspirations with a perfect but unsuspected plentitude. The new context is charged with transforming power. The original sense of the text is not denied but is rather transposed by its new context, being caught up in a dynamic movement and sharing a higher life. Thus, the Old Testament, to use Origen's favorite theme, becomes Gospel.

> Once the Logos had touched them, they raised their eyes and saw only Jesus, no one else. Moses, the law, and Elijah, prophecy, had become one thing; they had become one with Jesus who is the Gospel. And so things are not as they were before; there are no longer three, for these three have become one Being.[25]

This transposition was effected by Christ, first of all by the very fact of His Incarnation, and then by His words which conveyed His own mystery and explained it. We see Him at Nazareth proclaiming: "Today in your hearing, this text has come true" (Lk 4:21); we hear Him explain, "but let the Scriptures be fulfilled" (Mk 14:49), and in a special way after the Resurrection, when "He began with Moses and all the prophets and explained to them the passages which referred to Himself in every part of the Scriptures" (Lk 24:27). It is not quite exact to say that the Church received the Bible directly from the Synagogue. The Bible was given to the Church by Christ, and all the apostles, fathers, doctors, and saints of the Church have understood and followed this example.

This transposition of meaning, this filling with meaning, is a true literary activity, one which Lohfink calls the "hagiographical act." It is an activity by which literary form is given to a new and mysterious reality that completes the meaning of the older texts by joining them in a transcendent unity toward which they tended, but which they could never attain or demand. If this view is correct, then the activity by which the fullness of meaning is conveyed was performed under the action of the

Holy Spirit, and the necessity for a "spiritual understanding" of the Old Testament follows ineluctably.

SYNTHESIS

Now that we have seen the variety existing in the ways and results of literary activity, we would like to propose another schema, intended as complementary to those which we have already seen. It has three levels: the material, the intuition, and the execution.

(1) *The Material of a Literary Work.* The stuff of which literature is made is living experience—one's own or another's—which has been appropriated. It may be a single vivid occurrence, or a series of events which accumulate in the consciousness with the rhythm: experience—reflection. The material that a novelist uses can be the experience of his own life, or it can be the life around him which he considers or discovers; it can come directly from life, or through the medium of something which is read. This material can be theoretical knowledge, or a series of facts, or some preëxisting literary elaboration.

Strictly speaking, the material does not pertain to the creative process, and has interest only because of its relation to the future literary work, insofar as it is transformed by the productive activity of the writer. It is in this light that we should view the biblical events, the court records, the preëxisting profane literature, etc. These things may exist as the result of a special action of God; they may be instances of a divine intervention in history, but they are not yet the object of the charism of inspiration.

(2) *The Intuition.* At times, the light of understanding comes only after a long and painful period of gestation, and then in a flash the formless mass of our experiences takes shape, and we see the results of our searching. At other times, the intuition comes suddenly, without any awareness of a period of preparation, and our soul is held, as it were, in suspense. We experience the insight as something unsuspected, imperative, or serene, which fills us with a sense of light and of the joy of discovery. It may be that we have caught the message of a symbol, or perhaps some analogy reveals a new dimension of reality.

This intuition becomes the life center, activating and illuminating the whole process to follow. It is what Stephen Spender calls the initial idea, it is masculine or germinal. Proust has pointed out how intuition precedes the work of the intellect, and Virginia Woolf has stressed its unifying power; it is itself simple. Pirandello, in a memorable passage, describes how, as he was at grips with some personalities which had presented themselves to his imagination, there came to him an intuition which shed light on the whole complex and was the seed of his *Six*

Characters in Search of an Author. Writers are all in accord in assigning intuition as the true starting point for a work, and as the catalytic energy which fuses preëxisting material.

If the biblical authors have this in common with their literary counterparts, then we must maintain that this intuition in them takes place under the influence of inspiration, and that it manifests a reality, though not in propositional form. There must, of course, be some latitude allowed for variation in the intensity and extent of these germinal intuitions. The Bible is not a collection of nothing but masterpieces.

(3) *Execution.* Consequent on the intuition, there may occur an impulse, felt as an inner necessity, to write or to compose. Goethe speaks of some poems which occurred to him all of a sudden, and demanded to be composed without delay with such insistence that he felt an instinctive or hypnotic force impelling him to write immediately.

This interior urge sets the whole process of execution in motion. It is directed toward an activity which the writer performs in regard to language; that is to say, the whole process by which the "poetic idea," or seed, or intuition is made objective, is ordered from the very moment of its inception toward language.

We ought not to consider language as some lifeless stone; it is a medium possessing a certain capacity to work along with the artist. By language we mean, not merely the dictionary and the grammatical dimension of words, but the whole complex of possibilities and resonances assembled in a given linguistic entity.

But language can also present to the writer an aspect of resistance. Anyone can appreciate this quality of language who has tried to translate poetry, while maintaining the force and shades of the original. But even when we compose in our own language, we can encounter this resistance which will give rise either to a sense of challenge or to a "lapidary style," in which language is treated like a stone. When certain poets complain that their poem does not correspond to their interior vision, it is possible that, apart from the exaggerations of the romantics, they are referring to this resistance of language which has not been overcome by their intuition and technique. This is true not only of poetry or literature, but even didactic treatises can experience the intractability of words, thwarting the attempt of a teacher to hit upon the right formulation. Pesch speaks of this common experience in his discussion on the psychology of inspiration:

> Someone can have the intention to write, and know what he wants to write, and still hesitate and labor in order to find the right expression of what he wants to say. This is true not only of poets who sweat and shiver in order to find apt clothing for their thought, but also of other writers who, after having removed all doubt as to what they want to say, still often cannot find the right way to say it, except after a long series of attempts, and then not infrequently in later editions they say the same thing in different words.[26]

Pesch does not sufficiently consider the act of expression as a creative element in composition. But to a large extent, the talent of a writer is found precisely in the art of expression. We do not readily accept the excuses of a bad writer who makes appeal to his profound and genial intuitions.

Actually what a writer does, is to transform his material, the world and his experience, into an organic, significant system composed of words. This takes place by an act of language in which all the possibilities and resonances of language collaborate.

In the process of giving expression, new intuitions occur and are subordinated, and other, lesser insights are gained; but sometimes a greater intuition arises, dethroning and enlisting the former, and the work takes a new direction.

This collaboration of language in the act of realizing a work stands out clearly in writers who have a great sensitivity for language. Such men—trained perhaps in philology—have a feeling for the roots of words, and are often able to pass from a verbal analogy to one that is ontological.

At the end of the process, which may have been easy or painful, direct or intricate, the finished work emerges. It contains the preëxisting material in a different mode of being. It confers on the intuition an objective existence, though not enunciating it by way of proposition, and the work of execution, either manifest or hidden, receives stability.

An attentive analysis of the biblical writings sometimes reveals to us the work of execution. We do not know if it came easily to the writers, or if it cost them something, but the fact is there. These men labored over a language they had received and allowed it to come to their aid. Sometimes they capitalized on the sound of its words; sometimes they employed the alternating rhythm of parallelism to convey a sense of balance; sometimes they quickened the rhythm in order to concentrate their message.[27] All of this labor must be seen as having taken place under the motion of the Holy Spirit, for it is mainly here that we find the charism. The role of the sacred writers consisted in transforming into a significant word-system the history of the people, their own personal experiences, the insights they received from God, the meaning of history, the works of salvation, the response of the people of God. Inspiration is a charism of language, and language is forged at this stage of literary production. There is no problem in imagining two expressions of the same thing, both inspired, and one better than the other; they can even be from the same author, and indeed often are.

Before this stage of activity, the word does not exist, there is no word of God. It is in this process of expression that the word is realized, and if the Bible is the word of God, it is because He has directed this process. The being of the words is their signification or meaning, and the being of the work is in the system of significant words. In the word of the Bible, revelation is present and available—it is the meaning of the words. We have avoided here using the expression "revelation is contained" in the words. Such terminology tends to make one think that there is some real distinction between the word as receptacle and the meaning as its content. But this is false; the meaning is realized in the word, and the being of the word is its meaning. Otherwise, it is nothing but fruitless sound.

The motion of the Spirit hovers over the language act of the sacred writer, and makes of it an act of revelation. The context of the Spirit and the context of the Logos—these two, which are united ontologically, meet here again at the term of our analysis.

POSTSCRIPT

There are some who would not wish to see this chapter conclude without a more detailed discussion of the operation of the faculties which collaborate in the process of execution. But such a discussion would be interminable. There would have to be some treatment of the sense of rhythm which plays such a large part in some passages, and which can register the most delicate shades of emotions; then there is the question of phonetics—the role of sound and tone in literary expression; we would have to enter into the question of imagination as creative and imitative, for this is essential in poetry. There should also be some consideration for the discernment of various shades and resonances of meaning, as well as an attempt to assess the various semi-conscious factors which find expression in a literary work.

It will be sufficient and briefer to invoke the principle of Benoit with regard to the analogous nature of inspiration: The charismatic influence extends to all the faculties according to their specific function in literary activity. To complete this statement, we will only add that this functioning is not parallel, but organically interrelated, and thus the charismatic influence should be conceived as central and all-pervasive.

BIBLIOGRAPHY

The Description Given by Benoit. It is probably best to begin with Benoit's most recent article, "Révélation et Inspiration," *RB* 70, 1963, pp. 321–370. (See *Aspects of Biblical Inspiration,* translated by J. Murphy-O'Connor and S. K. Ashe, Chicago, 1965.) His other works are referred to there and the positions they set forth modified and clarified. The first part of the article "Revelation and Inspiration According to St. Thomas" is dedicated to giving a more ample and flexible view of the Angelic Doctor's thought. The second part, "Revelation and Inspiration in the Bible," is also marked by a suppleness of treatment in regard to the sacred text. The third part, "Criticism and Suggestions in regard to the Modern Discussions," terminates the work and attempts to interpret the data in the light of the categories of speculative and practical judgment. The work of A. Desroches, *Jugement pratique et jugement spéculatif chez l'Ecrivain inspiré*, Ottawa, 1958, is a thesis of one hundred and forty pages. Its orientation is descriptive, its documentation meager. There is also the very competent thesis of Denis Farkasfalvy, *L'inspiration de l'Ecriture Sainte dans la théologie de Saint Bernard*, Studia Anselmiana, no. 53, Rome, 1964.

An Artist with Language. Since this aspect of the psychology of inspiration is seldom treated at length in manuals, the bibliography will be somewhat ample in order to familiarize readers with the names and opinions most current in this field. Monographs on inspiration have sometimes attempted to describe the psychology of inspiration: H. Lusseau in his *Essai sur l'inspiration scripturaire*, Paris, 1930 (a thesis defended in 1928), dedicates a chapter to this topic before discussing the description of *Providentissimus Deus;* it consists of thirteen pages. Among the authors cited, one finds Pesch, Billot, Schiffini, and St. Thomas; there is a citation from Boileau, and Pascal is also represented, along with some nineteenth-century French orators. A. Desroches in his work also dedicates a chapter to the psychology of the literary author (pp. 107–123). His authorities are Cajetan, St. Thomas, John of St. Thomas, and Aristotle. There is one quote from Chateaubriand, one from Maritain, and two from Longhaye. Such a method is simply insufficient. In order to discuss this question properly, we must begin from a wider experience of literature and techniques of composition. It would be impossible to cite all the authors who have exercised some influence on the ideas which we propose in the "Description Drawn from Literary Creation." The purpose of the enumeration which follows is, as we have said, to provide a point of departure for those who wish to study this aspect of the problem more fully.

From a philosophical point of view, the question of creativity has been studied only recently. The essays of Heidegger are an interesting beginning. There is a good article by Carl Hausman, "Spontaneity: Its Rationality and Its Reality," in *IPQ* 4, 1964, pp. 20–47, in which there is a review of the opinions of Whitehead, Husserl, Hartmann, etc.; the bibliographical material in the footnotes is also valuable. J. Maritain in *Creative Intuition in Art and Poetry*, New York, 1953, treats of this theme in Thomistic categories (on Thomism's effort to account for the fact of poetry, cf. Curtius, *European Literature and the Latin Middle Ages*, p. 227). Maritain writes from his own experience as an author, and with a real sympathy and familiarity with poetry. The most important chapter for the topic which interests us here is ch. 4, "Creative Intuition and Poetic Knowledge." In the same tradition, but harder to follow, is the little study by T. Gilby, *Poetic Experience* (Essays in Order, no. 13), New York, 1934; ch. 9, "Presence," is especially good.

It is very important in a study of artistic creation to consult the statements of artists themselves, and in this regard we are fortunate to have good material in English. Brewster Ghiselin in *The Creative Process*, New York, 1955, collects the testimony of mathematicians (Poincaré, Einstein), musicians (Mozart), painters (van Gogh, Picasso), sculptors (Moore), and various literary authors. Charles Norman in *Poets on Poetry*, New York, 1962, presents the views of sixteen different English-speaking poets on their art; not all of these speak of the creative process, but all make interesting reading; the same can be said of the collection of essays in *The Limits of Language*, compiled by W. Gibson, New York, 1962, which includes in part 2, "Consequences of the Problem, Testimony from Artists and Writers"—articles written by Sartre, Virginia Woolf, Wallace Stevens, etc. There are four other excellent studies of the same type: H. Block and H. Salinger, *The Creative Vision. Modern European Writers on their Art,* New York, 1960; W. Allen, *Writers on Writing,* New York, 1948 (the essays here are all good and they are organized with great perception. We have used this book a great deal); M. Cowley, *Writers at Work,* New York, 1959 (a series of interviews, treats of the techniques of composition); and John W. Aldridge, *Critiques and Essays on Modern Fiction. 1920–1951,* New York, 1952, which contains a wealth of valuable material, and a good bibliography: under part 2, ch. 2, "Writers on their Craft," there are fifty-six titles listed, and under part 3, ch. 3, "The Artist and the Creative Process," there are eighty-nine books and articles listed.

There are some good works that treat of creativity by an analysis of the works and the artists who produce them: A. Maurois, *The Art of Writing,* New York, 1960; Wallace Fowlie, *Jacob's Night,* New York, 1947. P. Valéry discusses both aspects in the series of essays which make up *The Art of Poetry,* New York, 1961; cf. especially "Problems of Poetry."

NOTES

1. "*Quare nihil admodum refert, Spiritum Sanctum assumpsisse homines tamquam instrumenta ad scribendum, quasi, non quidem primario auctori, sed scriptoribus inspiratis quidpiam falsi elabi potuerit. Nam supernaturali ipse virtute ita eos ad scribendum excitavit et movit, ita scribentibus adstitit, ut ea omnia eaque sola, quae ipse iuberet, et recte mente conciperent, et fideliter conscribere vellent, et apte infallibili veritate experimerent: secus, non ipse esset auctor Sacrae Scripturae universae.*" EB 125; RSS, p. 24.
2. "*Secundo. Intellectum scriptoris illuminat Deus luce quapiam vel omnino* SUPER-

NATURALI, *vel naturali quidem, sed* SUPERNATURALITER DATA *vel aucta. Et hoc vel ad* PERCIPIENDUM *tantum, quod dictatur; vel ad* IUDICANDUM *tantum, vel ad utrumque. Tertio. Hoc autem iudicium, quod a scriptoribus de dictatis fit, vel* THEORETICUM *est vel* PRACTICUM. *Illud est, quando scriptor iudicat ea quae dictantur, esse vera. Hoc autem practicum est, quando iudicat ea sibi scribenda, et his quidem verbis, isto modo, isto tempore.*" Both Desroches and Grelot cite Serarius. Most probably, the source for all these citations is the ample quotation from Serarius found in *Institutiones Biblicae*, put out by the Pontifical Biblical Institute, 6th ed., Rome, 1951 (the above text was taken from the 5th ed., Rome, 1937, vol. 1, p. 32—tr.).

3. "*1. La composition des livres saints exige des jugements spéculatifs surnaturels en plus des jugements pratiques. 2. Ces jugements spéculatifs ne sont pas forcément antérieurs aux jugements pratiques, mais peuvent leur être concomitants ou postérieurs. 3. Ces jugements spéculatifs peuvent être qualifiés par l'influence des jugements pratiques.*" *RB* 70, 1963, p. 358.

4. "*Jugement pratique et jugement spéculatif. . . .*"

5. "*1. Le* JUGEMENT SPÉCULATIF ABSOLU *ou 'purement spéculatif,' qui porte sur la vérité considéré en elle-même, sans aucun rapport, même possible, à l'opération; 2. le* JUGEMENT SPÉCULATIF D'ACTION, *qui a pour objet 'la vérité dans son rapport à l'oeuvre,' mais ne la considère encore 'que comme objet de connaissance, comme mesure et norme appréciative des moyens'; 'l'opérable y est considéré comme possible.' On peut songer à l'appeler 'spéculativo-pratique,' encore que A. Desroches y répugne; 3. le* JUGEMENT PRATIQUE, *qui a proprement pour objet la vérité pratique, c'est-à-dire la vérité 'prise par rapport à l'appétit droit . . . qui tend d'une façon impeccable à la fin de l'art, qui est l'oeuvre.'*"

6. "*O alter Fluch der Dichter,*
die sich beklagen, wo sie sagen sollten,
die immer urteiln über ihr Gefühl
statt es zu bilden; die noch immer meinen,
was traurig ist in ihnen oder froh,
das wüssten sie und dürftens im Gedicht
bedauern oder rühmen. Wie die Kranken
gebrauchen sie die Sprache voller Wehleid,
um zu beschreiben, wo es ihnen wehtut,
statt hart sich in die Worte zu verwandeln,
wie sich der Steinmetzeiner Kathedrale
verbissen umsetzt in des Steines Gleichmut.

"*Dies war die Rettung. Hättest du nur* EIN *Mal*
gesehn, wie Schicksal in die Verse eingeht
und nicht zurückkommt, wie es drinnen Bild wird
und nichts als Bild, nicht anders als ein Ahnherr,
der dir im Rahmen, wenn du manchmal aufsiehst,
zu gleichen scheint und wieder nicht zu gleichen:
du hättest ausgeharrt."

Rilke, from "Requiem for Wolf Graf von Kalckreuth." German text, *Sämtliche Werke*, Insel-Verlag, 1955, vol. 1, p. 663. English translation by J. B. Leishman, *Rainer Maria Rilke, Selected Works*, vol. 2, New York, 1960, p. 209.

7. "*Le poète s'eveille dans l'homme par un événement inattendu, un incident extérieur ou intérieur: un arbre, un visage, un 'sujet,' une émotion, un mot. Et tantôt, c'est une volonté d'expression qui commence la partie, un besoin de traduire ce que l'on sent; mais tantôt c'est, au contraire, un élément de forme, une esquisse d'expression qui cherche sa cause, qui se cherche un sens dans l'espace de mon âme. . . . Observez bien cette dualité possible d'entrée en jeu: parfois quelque chose veut s'exprimer, parfois quelque moyen d'expression veut quelque chose a servir.*" Paul Valéry, *Oeuvres*, ed. by J. Hytier, Bibl. de la Pleiade, 1962, vol. 1, p. 1338.

8. Hos 1:2–3:5.

9. Even though it is not introduced by "Thus says the Lord," or something similar.

10. "*. . . ut exemplo sunt non soli poetae, qui saepe sudant et algent ad inveniendum vestitum aptum cogitationum suarum.*" No. 414.

11. *"Mais cet état de modification intime, dans lequel toutes les propriétés de notre langage sont indistinctement mais harmoniquement appelées, ..."* Paul Valéry, *Oeuvres*, vol. 1, p. 1334.

12. Prv 31:10ff.

13. Am 7.

14. Jer 1:11-12.

15. *"olmo, quiero anotar en mi cartera
la gracia de tu rama verdecida.*

*"Mi corazón espera
también, hacia la luz y hacia la vida,
otro milagro de la primavera."*
Antonio Machado, "A Un Olmo Seco," *Poesías Completas*, Madrid, 1955, p. 169.

16. "Ash Boughs," *Poems of Gerard Manley Hopkins*, ed. W. H. Gardner, New York, 1959, p. 164.

17. Jer 20:7-9.

18. Cf. R. W. Stallman, *Critics and Essays in Criticism. 1920-1948*, New York, 1949.

19. G. von Rad, *Genesis*, Philadelphia, 1961; cf. pp. 123, 187.

20. Is 1:21.

21. *"Un pastorcico solo está penado,
Ajeno de placer y de contento,
Y en su pastora puesto el pensamiento,
Y el pecho del amor muy lastimado.*

*"No llora por haberle amor llagado,
Que no le pena verse así afligido,
Aunque en el corazón está herido;
Mas llora por pensar que está olvidado.*

*"Que sólo de pensar que está olvidado
De su bella pastora, con gran pena
Se deja, maltratar en tierra ajena,
El pecho del amor muy lastimado,*

*"Y dice el Pastorcico¡ Ay, desdichado
De aquel que de mi amor ha hecho ausencia,
Y no quiere gozar la mi presencia,
Y el pecho por su amor muy lastimado!*

*"Y a cabo de un gran rato se ha encumbrado
Sobre un árbol do abrió sus brazos bellos,
Y muerto se ha quedado, asido de ellos,
El pecho del amor muy lastimado."*
Text and translation taken from *The Poems of St. John of the Cross. The Spanish Text with a Translation by Roy Campbell*, New York, 1951, pp. 42-43.

22. Cf. Dámaso Alonso, *Poesía española. Ensayo de metodos y límites estilísticos*, Madrid, 1950, pp. 256-258.

23. Ex 7-12.

24. In regard to the formation of the Gospels, cf. X. Léon-Dufour, *Les Évangiles et l'Histoire de Jésus*, Paris, 1963; V. Taylor, *The Formation of the Gospel Tradition*, New York, 1957; C. Dodd, *The Apostolic Preaching and its Development*, 1st ed., London, 1936; J. R. Scheifler, *Así nacieron los Evangelios*, Bilbao, 1964. The bibliography and notes in this latter work are especially valuable.

25. Ἀλλὰ μετὰ ἀφὴν τοῦ λογοῦ, τοὺς ὀφθαλμοὺς ἐπαράντες εἶδον Ἰησοῦν μόνον, καὶ οὐδένα ἄλλον. Ἕν μόνον γέγονε Μωϋσῆς ὁ νόμος καὶ Ἡλίας ἡ προφητεία Ἰησοῦ τῷ Εὐαγγελίῳ. καὶ οὐχ ὥσπερ ἦσαν πρότερον τρεῖς οὕτω μεμενήκασιν, ἀλλὰ γεγόνασιν οἱ τρεῖς εἰς τὸ ἕν. "On Matthew, t. 12, 43," *PG* 13, 1084.
The same thought is expressed in a slightly different way in his sixth homily on Leviticus:
"Doceat te Evangelium, quia cum transformatus esset in gloriam Jesus, etiam Moyses et Elias simul cum ipso apparuerunt in gloria, ut scias quia lex et prophetae, et Evangelium

in unum semper conveniunt, et in una gloria permanent. Denique et Petrus cum vellet eis tria facere tabernacula, imperitiae notatur, tanquam qui nesciret quid diceret. Legi enim, et prophetis, et Evangelio non tria, sed unum est tabernaculum, quae est Ecclesia Dei. "Hom 6 in Lev," PG 12, 468.

26. *"Potest aliquis velle scribere et scire, quid scribere velit, et interim anxius haerere et laborare de elocutione rerum scribendarum, ut exemplo sunt non soli poetae, qui saepe sudant et algent ad inveniendum vestitum aptum cogitationum suarum, sed etiam alii scriptores, qui saepe omni dubitatione iam remota de rebus, quae dicendae sint, modum dicendi convenientem non inveniunt nisi post multa tentamina, et in posterioribus editionibus easdem res non raro aliis verbis exprimunt."* No. 414.

27. We have treated this aspect, with many illustrative analyses, in *Estudios de Poética Hebrea*, Barcelona, 1963.

Theory of Archetypal Meaning: Apocalyptic and Demonic Imagery

Northrop Frye's "Archetypal Criticism" of literature draws heavily on the Bible, which he claims is "the main source for undisplaced myth in our tradition." By examining genres, modes, and archetypes in Western literature, Frye opens a way for biblical criticism to deal with larger literary forms and typical patterns of imagery in Scripture.

Two "undisplaced" worlds are examined in this essay for their structure of imagery. Frye's is a study of literature that, unlike Alonso-Schökel's (pp. 24–56), initially de-emphasizes the individual literary artist and the historical situation of the artist. To Frye, the larger patterns of imagery and symbolism are archetypal and universally human. As such, archetypal criticism offers a powerful entry into mythopoeic design. Literature consists of the forms of human desire in various degrees of displacement from the apocalyptic and the demonic.

Frye's notion of the great "organizing metaphors" of the Bible is a striking and useful concept in biblical criticism.

(On symbolism, see also Burke, pp. 381–395, and Macquarrie, pp. 396–410).

I N looking at a picture, we may stand close to it and analyze the details of brush work and palette knife. This corresponds roughly to the rhetorical analysis of the new critics in literature. At a little distance back, the design comes into clearer view, and we study rather the content represented: this is the best distance for realistic Dutch pictures, for example, where we are in a sense reading the picture. The further back we go, the more conscious we are of the organizing design. At a great distance from, say, a Madonna, we can see nothing but the archetype of the Madonna, a large centripetal blue mass with a contrasting point of interest at its center. In the criticism of literature, too, we often have to

From Northrop Frye, *Anatomy of Criticism* (1957), pp. 137–59.

"stand back" from the poem to see its archetypal organization. If we "stand back" from Spenser's *Mutabilitie Cantoes,* we see a background of ordered circular light and a sinister black mass thrusting up into the lower foreground—much the same archetypal shape that we see in the opening of the Book of Job. If we "stand back" from the beginning of the fifth act of *Hamlet,* we see a grave opening on the stage, the hero, his enemy, and the heroine descending into it, followed by a fatal struggle in the upper world. If we "stand back" from a realistic novel such as Tolstoy's *Resurrection* or Zola's *Germinal,* we can see the mythopoeic designs indicated by those titles. Other examples will be given in what follows.

We proceed to give an account of the structure of imagery, or *dianoia,* of the two undisplaced worlds, the apocalyptic and the demonic, drawing heavily on the Bible, the main source for undisplaced myth in our tradition.

APOCALYPTIC IMAGERY

Let us proceed according to the general scheme of the game of Twenty Questions, or, if we prefer, of the Great Chain of Being, the traditional scheme for classifying sense data.

The apocalyptic world, the heaven of religion, presents, in the first place, the categories of reality in the forms of human desire, as indicated by the forms they assume under the work of human civilization. The form imposed by human work and desire on the *vegetable* world, for instance, is that of the garden, the farm, the grove, or the park. The human form of the *animal* world is a world of domesticated animals, of which the sheep has a traditional priority in both Classical and Christian metaphor. The human form of the *mineral* world, the form into which human work transforms stone, is the city. The city, the garden, and the sheepfold are the organizing metaphors of the Bible and of most Christian symbolism, and they are brought into complete metaphorical identification in the book explicitly called the Apocalypse or Revelation, which has been carefully designed to form an undisplaced mythical conclusion for the Bible as a whole. From our point of view this means that the Biblical Apocalypse is our grammar of apocalyptic imagery.

Each of these three categories, the city, the garden, and the sheepfold, is, by the principle of archetypal metaphor, the concrete universal, identical with the others and with each individual within it. Hence the *divine* and *human* worlds are, similarly, identical with the sheepfold, city and garden, and the social and individual aspects of each are identical. Thus the apocalyptic world of the Bible presents the following pattern:

divine world	=	society of gods	=	One God
human world	=	society of men	=	One Man
animal world	=	sheepfold	=	One Lamb
vegetable world	=	garden or park	=	One Tree (of Life)
mineral world	=	city	=	One Building, Temple, Stone

The conception "Christ" unites all these categories in identity: Christ *is* both the one God and the one Man, the Lamb of God, the tree of life, or vine of which we are the branches, the stone which the builders rejected, and the rebuilt temple which is identical with his risen body. The religious and poetic identifications differ in intention only, the former being existential and the latter metaphorical. In medieval criticism the difference was of little importance, and the word "figura," as applied to the identification of a symbol with Christ, usually implies both kinds.

Now let us expand this pattern a little. In Christianity the concrete universal is applied to the divine world in the form of the Trinity. Christianity insists that, whatever dislocations of customary mental processes may be involved, God *is* three persons and yet one God. The conceptions of person and substance represent a few of the difficulties in extending metaphor to logic. In pure metaphor, of course, the unity of God could apply to five or seventeen or a million divine persons as easily as three, and we may find the divine concrete universal in poetry outside the Trinitarian orbit. When Zeus remarks, at the beginning of the eighth book of the *Iliad*, that he can pull the whole chain of being up into himself whenever he likes, we can see that for Homer there was some conception of a double perspective in Olympus, where a group of squabbling deities may at any time suddenly compose into the form of a single divine will. In Virgil we first meet a malicious and spoiled Juno, but the comment of Aeneas to his men a few lines later on, "deus dabit his quoque finem" [God will also give an end to these], indicates that a similar double perspective existed for him. We may compare perhaps the Book of Job, where Job and his friends are much too devout for it ever to occur to them that Job could have suffered so as a result of a half-jocular bet between God and Satan. There is a sense in which they are right, and the information given to the reader about Satan in heaven wrong. Satan is dropped out of the end of the poem, and whatever rewritings may be responsible for this, it is still difficult to see how the final enlightenment of Job could ever have returned completely from the conception of a single divine will to the mood of the opening scene.

As for human society, the metaphor that we are all members of one body has organized most political theory from Plato to our own day. Milton's "A Commonwealth ought to be but as one huge Christian personage, one mighty growth, and stature of an honest man" belongs to a Christianized version of this metaphor, in which, as in the doctrine of the

Trinity, the full metaphorical statement "Christ *is* God and Man" is orthodox, and the Arian and Docetic statements in terms of simile or likeness condemned as heretical. Hobbes's *Leviathan,* with its original frontispiece depicting a number of mannikins inside the body of a single giant, has also some connection with the same type of identification. Plato's *Republic,* in which the reason, will, and desire of the individual appear as the philosopher-king, guards, and artisans of the state, is also founded on this metaphor, which in fact we still use whenever we speak of a group or aggregate of human beings as a "body."

In sexual symbolism, of course, it is still easier to employ the "one flesh" metaphor of two bodies made into the same body by love. Donne's "The Extasie" is one of the many poems organized on this image, and Shakespeare's "The Phoenix and the Turtle" makes great play with the outrage done to the "reason" by such identity. Themes of loyalty, hero-worship, faithful followers, and the like also employ the same metaphor.

The animal and vegetable worlds are identified with each other, and with the divine and human worlds as well, in the Christian doctrine of transubstantiation, in which the essential human forms of the vegetable world, food and drink, the harvest and the vintage, the bread and the wine, *are* the body and blood of the Lamb who is also Man and God, and in whose body we exist as in a city or temple. Here again the orthodox doctrine insists on metaphor as against simile, and here again the conception of substance illustrates the struggles of logic to digest the metaphor. It is clear from the opening of the *Laws* that the symposium had something of the same communion symbolism for Plato. It would be hard to find a simpler or more vivid image of human civilization, where man attempts to surround nature and put it inside his (social) body, than the sacramental meal.

The conventional honors accorded the sheep in the animal world provide us with the central archetype of pastoral imagery, as well as with such metaphors as "pastor" and "flock" in religion. The metaphor of the king as the shepherd of his people goes back to ancient Egypt. Perhaps the use of this particular convention is due to the fact that, being stupid, affectionate, gregarious, and easily stampeded, the societies formed by sheep are most like human ones. But of course in poetry any other animal would do as well if the poet's audience were prepared for it: at the opening of the Brihadaranyaka Upanishad, for instance, the sacrificial horse, whose body contains the whole universe, is treated in the same way that a Christian poet would treat the Lamb of God. Of birds, too, the dove has traditionally represented the universal concord or love both of Venus and of the Christian Holy Spirit. Identifications of gods with animals or plants and of those again with human society form the basis of totemic symbolism. Certain types of etiological folk tales, the stories of how supernatural beings were turned into the animals and plants that we know, represent an attentuated form of the same type of metaphor, and survive as the "metamorphosis" archetype familiar from Ovid.

Similar flexibility is possible with vegetable images. Elsewhere in the Bible the leaves or fruit of the tree of life are used as communion symbols in place of the bread and wine. Or the concrete universal may be applied not simply to a tree but to a single fruit or flower. In the West the rose has a traditional priority among apocalyptic flowers: the use of the rose as a communion symbol in the *Paradiso* comes readily to mind, and in the first book of *The Faerie Queene* the emblem of St. George, a red cross on a white ground, is connected not only with the risen body of Christ and the sacramental symbolism which accompanies it, but with the union of the red and white roses in the Tudor dynasty. In the East the lotus or the Chinese "golden flower" often occupied the place of the rose, and in German Romanticism the blue cornflower enjoyed a brief vogue.

The identity of the human body and the vegetable world gives us the archetype of Arcadian imagery, of Marvell's green world, of Shakespeare's forest comedies, of the world of Robin Hood and other green men who lurk in the forests of romance, these last the counterparts in romance of the metaphorical myth of the tree-god. In Marvell's "The Garden" we meet a further but still conventional extension in the identification of the human soul with a bird sitting in the branches of the tree of life. The olive tree and its oil has supplied another identification in the "anointed" ruler.

The city, whether called Jerusalem or not, is apocalyptically identical with a single building or temple, a "house of many mansions," of which individuals are "lively stones," to use another New Testament phrase. The human use of the inorganic world involves the highway or road as well as the city with its streets, and the metaphor of the "way" is inseparable from all quest-literature, whether explicitly Christian as in *The Pilgrim's Progress* or not. To this category also belong geometrical and architectural images: the tower and the winding stairway of Dante and Yeats, Jacob's ladder, the ladder of the Neo-platonic love poets, the ascending spiral or cornucopia, the "stately pleasure dome" that Kubla Khan decreed, the cross and quincunx patterns which Browne sought in every corner of art and nature, the circle as the emblem of eternity, Vaughan's "ring of pure and endless light," and so on.

On the archetypal level proper, where poetry is an artifact of human civilization, nature is the container of man. On the anagogic level, man is the container of nature, and his cities and gardens are no longer little hollowings on the surface of the earth, but the forms of a human universe. Hence in apocalyptic symbolism we cannot confine man only to his two natural elements of earth and air, and, in going from one level to the other, symbolism must, like Tamino in *The Magic Flute,* pass the ordeals of water and fire. Poetic symbolism usually puts fire just above man's life in this world, and water just below it. Dante had to pass through a ring of fire and the river of Eden to go from the mountain of purgatory, which is still on the surface of our own world, to Paradise or the apocalyptic world proper. The imagery of light and fire surrounding the angels in the Bible, the tongues of flame descending at Pentecost, and the coal of fire applied to the mouth of Isaiah by the seraph, associate fire with a spiritual or angelic world midway between the human and the divine. In Classical mythology the story of Prometheus indicates a similar provenance for fire, as does the association of Zeus with the thunderbolt or fire of lightning. In short, heaven in the sense of the sky, containing the fiery bodies of sun, moon, and stars, is usually identified with, or thought of as the passage to, the heaven of the apocalyptic world.

Hence all our other categories can be identified with fire or thought of as burning. The appearance of the Judaeo-Christian deity in fire, surrounded by angels of fire (seraphim) and light (cherubim), needs only to be mentioned. The burning animal of the ritual of sacrifice, the incorporating of an animal body in a communion between divine and human worlds, modulates into all the imagery connected with the fire and smoke of the altar, ascending incense, and the like. The burning man is represented in the saint's halo and the king's crown, both of which are analogues of the sun-god: one may compare also the "burning babe" of Southwell's Christmas poem. The image of the burning bird appears in the legendary phoenix. The tree of life may also be a burning tree, the unconsumed burning bush of Moses, the candlestick of Jewish ritual, or the "rosy cross" of later occultism. In alchemy the vegetable, mineral, and water worlds are identified in its rose, stone, and elixir; flower and jewel archetypes are identified in the "jewel in the lotus" of the Buddhist prayer. The links between fire, intoxicating wine, and the hot red blood of animals are also common.

The identification of the *city* with fire explains why the city of God in the Apocalypse is presented as a glowing mass of gold and precious stones, each stone presumably burning with a hard gemlike flame. For in apocalyptic symbolism the fiery bodies of heaven, sun, moon, and stars, are all inside the universal divine and human body. The symbolism of alchemy is apocalyptic symbolism of the same type: the center of nature, the gold and jewels hidden in the earth, is eventually to be united to its circumference in the sun, moon, and stars of the heavens; the center of the spiritual world, the soul of man, is united to its circumference in God. Hence there is a close association between the purifying of the human soul and the transmuting of earth to gold, not only literal gold but the fiery quintessential gold of which the heavenly bodies are made. The golden tree with its mechanical bird in "Sailing to Byzantium" identifies vegetable and mineral worlds in a form reminiscent of alchemy.

Water, on the other hand, traditionally belongs to a realm of existence below human life, the state of chaos or dissolution which follows ordinary death, or the reduction to the inorganic. Hence the soul frequently crosses water or sinks into it at death. In apocalyptic symbolism we have the "water of life," the fourfold river of Eden which reappears in the City of God, and is represented in ritual by baptism. According to Ezekiel the return of this river turns the sea fresh, which is apparently why the author of Revelation says that in the apocalypse there is no more sea. Apocalyptically, therefore, water circulates in the universal body like the blood in the individual body. Perhaps we should say "is held within" instead of "circulates," to avoid the anachronism of connecting a knowledge of the circulation of the blood with Biblical themes. For centuries, of course, the blood was one of four "humors," or bodily liquids, just as the river of life was traditionally fourfold.

DEMONIC IMAGERY

Opposed to apocalyptic symbolism is the presentation of the world that desire totally rejects: the world of the nightmare and the scapegoat, of bondage and pain and confusion; the world as it is before the human imagination begins to work on it and before any image of human desire, such as the city or the garden, has been solidly established; the world also of perverted or wasted work, ruins and catacombs, instruments of torture and monuments of folly. And just as apocalyptic imagery in poetry is closely associated with a religious heaven, so its dialectic opposite is closely linked with an existential hell, like Dante's *Inferno,* or with the hell that man creates on earth, as in *1984, No Exit,* and *Darkness at Noon,* where the titles of the last two speak for themselves. Hence one of the central themes of demonic imagery is parody, the mocking of the exuberant play of art by suggesting its imitation in terms of "real life."

The demonic divine world largely personifies the vast, menacing, stupid powers of nature as they appear to a technologically undeveloped society. Symbols of heaven in such a world tend to become associated with the inaccessible sky, and the central idea that crystallizes from it is the idea of inscrutable fate or external necessity. The machinery of fate is administered by a set of remote, invisible gods, whose freedom and pleasure are ironic because they exclude man, and who intervene in human affairs chiefly to safeguard their own prerogatives. They demand sacrifices, punish presumption, and enforce obedience to natural and moral law as an end in itself. Here we are not trying to describe, for instance, the gods in Greek tragedy: we are trying to isolate the sense of human remoteness and futility in relation to the divine order which is only one element among others in most tragic visions of life, though an essential one in all. In later ages poets become much more outspoken about this view of divinity: Blake's Nobodaddy, Shelley's Jupiter, Swinburne's "supreme evil, God," Hardy's befuddled Will, and Housman's "brute and blackguard" are examples.

The demonic human world is a society held together by a kind of molecular tension of egos, a loyalty to the group or the leader which diminishes the individual, or, at best, contrasts his pleasure with his duty or honor. Such a society is an endless source of tragic dilemmas like those of Hamlet and Antigone. In the apocalyptic conception of human life we found three kinds of fulfilment: individual, sexual, and social. In the sinister human world one individual pole is the tyrant-leader, inscrutable, ruthless, melancholy, and with an insatiable will, who commands loyalty only if he is egocentric enough to represent the collective ego of his followers. The other pole is represented by the *pharmakos* or sacrificed victim, who has to be killed to strengthen the others. In the most concentrated form of the demonic parody, the two become the same. The ritual of the killing of the divine king in Frazer, whatever it may be in anthropology, is in literary criticism the demonic or undisplaced radical form of tragic and ironic structures.

In religion the spiritual world is a reality distinct from the physical world. In poetry the physical or actual is opposed, not to the spiritually existential, but to the hypothetical. The transmutation of act into mime, the advance from acting out a rite to playing at the rite, is one of the central features of the development from savagery into culture. It is easy to see a mimesis of conflict in tennis and football, but, precisely for that very reason, tennis and football players represent a culture superior to the culture of student duelists and gladiators. The turning of literal act into play is a fundamental form of the liberalizing of life which appears in more intellectual levels as liberal education, the release of fact into imagination. It is consistent with this that the Eucharist symbolism of the apocalyptic world, the metaphorical identification of vegetable, animal, human, and divine bodies, should have the imagery of cannibalism for its demonic parody. Dante's last vision of human hell is of Ugolino gnawing his tormentor's skull; Spenser's last major allegorical vision is of Serena stripped and prepared for a cannibal feast. The imagery of cannibalism usually includes, not only images of torture and mutilation, but of what is technically known as *sparagmos* or the tearing apart of the sacrificial body, an image found in the myths of Osiris, Orpheus, and Pentheus. The cannibal giant or ogre of folk tales, who enters literature as Polyphemus, belongs here, as does a long series of sinister dealings with flesh and blood from the story of Thyestes to Shylock's bond. Here again the form described by Frazer as the historically original form is in literary criticism the radical demonic form. Flaubert's *Salammbo* is a study of demonic imagery which was thought in its day to be archaeological but turned out to be prophetic.

The demonic erotic relation becomes a fierce destructive passion that works against loyalty or frustrates the one who possesses it. It is generally symbolized by a harlot, witch, siren, or other tantalizing female, a physical object of desire which is sought as a possession and therefore can never be possessed. The demonic parody of marriage, or the union of two souls in one flesh, may take the form of hermaphroditism, incest (the most common form), or homosexuality. The social relation is that of the mob, which is essentially human society looking for a *pharmakos,* and the mob is often identified with some sinister animal image such as the hydra, Virgil's Fama, or its development in Spenser's Blatant Beast.

The other worlds can be briefly summarized. The animal world is portrayed in terms of monsters or beasts of prey. The wolf, the traditional enemy of the sheep, the tiger, the vulture, the cold and earth-bound serpent, and the dragon are all common. In the Bible, where the demonic society is represented by Egypt and Babylon, the rulers of each are identified with monstrous beasts: Nebuchadnezzar turns into a beast in Daniel, and Pharaoh is called a river-dragon by Ezekiel. The dragon is especially appropriate because it is not only monstrous and sinister but fabulous, and so represents the paradoxical nature of evil as a moral fact and an eternal negation. In the Apocalypse the dragon is called "the beast that was, and is not, and yet is."

The vegetable world is a sinister forest like the ones we meet in *Comus* or the opening of the *Inferno,* or a heath, which from Shakespeare to Hardy has been associated with tragic destiny, or a wilderness like that of Browning's "Childe Roland" or Eliot's *Waste Land.* Or it may be a sinister enchanted garden like that of Circe and its Renaissance descendants in Tasso and Spenser. In the Bible the waste land appears in its concrete universal form in the tree of death, the tree of forbidden knowledge in Genesis, the barren figtree of the Gospels, and the cross. The stake, with the hooded heretic, the black man, or the witch attached to it, is the burning tree and body of the infernal world. Scaffolds, gallows, stocks, pillories, whips, and birch rods are or could be modulations. The contrast of the tree of life and the tree of death is beautifully expressed in Yeats's poem "The Two Trees."

The inorganic world may remain in its unworked form of deserts, rocks, and waste land. Cities of destruction and dreadful night belong here, as do the great ruins of pride, from the tower of Babel to the mighty works of Ozymandias. Images of perverted work belong here too: engines of torture, weapons of war, armor, and images of a dead mechanism which, because it does not humanize nature, is unnatural as well as inhuman. Corresponding to the temple or One Building of the apocalypse, we have the prison or dungeon, the sealed furnace of heat without light, like the City of Dis in Dante. Here too are the sinister counterparts of geometrical images: the sinister spiral (the maelstrom, whirlpool, or Charybdis), the sinister cross, and the sinister circle, the wheel of fate or fortune. The identification of the circle with the serpent, conventionally a demonic animal, gives us the ouroboros, or serpent with its tail in its mouth. Corresponding to the apocalyptic way or straight road, the highway in the desert for God prophesied by Isaiah, we have in this world the labyrinth or maze, the image of lost direction, often with a monster at its heart like the Minotaur. The labyrinthine wanderings of Israel in the desert, repeated by Jesus when in the company of the devil (or "wild beasts," according to Mark), fit the same pattern. The labyrinth can also be a sinister forest, as in *Comus*. The catacombs are effectively used in the same context in *The Marble Faun*, and of course in a further concentration of metaphor, the maze would become the winding entrails inside the sinister monster himself.

The world of fire is a world of malignant demons like the will-o'-the-wisps, or spirits broken from hell, and it appears in this world in the form of the *auto da fe*, as mentioned, or such burning cities as Sodom. It is in contrast to the purgatorial or cleansing fire, like the fiery furnace in Daniel. The world of water is the water of death, often identified with spilled blood, as in the Passion and in Dante's symbolic figure of history, and above all the "unplumbed, salt, estranging sea," which absorbs all rivers in this world, but disappears in the apocalypse in favor of a circulation of fresh water. In the Bible the sea and the animal monster are identified in the figure of the leviathan, a sea-monster also identified with the social tyrannies of Babylon and Egypt.

Symbolic Perceptions
and Literary Visions

_The degree of conscious reflection and control over vision is
a way of distinguishing types of prophetic "visions." The
psychological study of "symbolic perceptions" and "literary
visions" sheds more light on the process of inspiration (see
Alonso Schökel, pp. 24–56)._

_Ecstatic visions (fanciful, unreal, irrational, and unre-
flective) are not the only kinds the biblical prophets experience. There are also symbolic perceptions, which have a
real, objective foundation in the material world. Furthermore, there are literary visions—inspiration in the
form of a visual creation of the imagination. It is not that
one kind of vision is more or less true than the others. What
is seen in the vision is taken to be particularly significant
and symbolic of a higher reality._

_Since the prophets provide the best cases in Scripture
for a psychological study of inspiration and authorship (see
Alonso Schökel, pp. 24–56 and Frye, pp. 57–66), Lindblom's
careful study of the differences among types of visionary
experience enables us to see the connections that may exist
between religious and poetic inspiration, and problems of
authorship in the Bible._

I T is characteristic of a symbolic perception that it has a real, objective
foundation in the material world; that which is seen is, however, conceived of as something particularly significant and interpreted as a symbol of another, higher reality.

The genuine vision and the symbolic perception have this in common, that they are both regarded as given by God to provide insight into
the spiritual world, thus playing an essential role in the life of him who
has the favour of receiving them. Further, both are connected with inspiration, the supernormal mental state which makes it possible for men to
assign a supernatural significance to what they see. Because they have

From Johannes Lindblom, _Prophecy in Ancient Israel_ (1962), pp. 137–48.

the form of visions, the symbolic perceptions have often been confused with, and interpreted as, ecstatic visions.

The differences are, however, equally manifest. The vision proper has no basis in outward reality; the symbolic perception is an observation of a real object in the material world. The former is an insight into the invisible world by 'the inward eye', the latter is an apprehension of a material object by the bodily eye; only through divine illumination does the object perceived become a revelation of invisible realities. The content of a vision is, finally, something supermundane, something beyond space and time; the primary content of a symbolic perception is temporal, material, everyday.

All over the world men are in the habit of using exterior things as revelations of secrets. Everywhere omens and portents have played a great role in human life. Auguring from the flight of birds, from the movements and cries of birds and beasts, from the behaviour of sacrificial animals and the appearance of their entrails is well known in all quarters of the world. The conditions which it presupposes are technical skill and traditional methods.

Students of life and customs among modern Arabs have observed various methods of drawing omens and important indications from purely occasional phenomena. The appearance of a water-seller with water confined in his skin can under certain circumstances indicate that someone is in prison. A raven croaking three times in succession indicates that someone will die after three days. A person carrying a burden indicates that a child is unborn but waited for. A male sparrow noticed in this connection shows that the child is a male child.

Such prognostications from everyday phenomena have a certain resemblance to what we have called symbolic perceptions. There is, however, a great difference. In the last mentioned cases the divination is throughout trivial, secular, and fortuitous. The symbolic perceptions among the Old Testament prophets are connected with revelations from the divine world. Yahweh stands behind them, Yahweh arranges them; and what they reveal has a deeply religious significance.

. . . .

An example of symbolic perception is the 'vision' of the basket of summer-fruit (perhaps ripe figs) upon which Amos's eye fell one day (viii. 1. f.). What the prophet saw in this moment became to him an indication of the end which was impending over Israel. The connection between the summer-fruit and the end is based on a pun: 'summer-fruit' is in Hebrew *qayiṣ,* 'end' is *qēṣ,* two words which sounded much alike in a Hebrew ear. The idea of the end of Israel was regarded by Amos as a revelation from God coming to him through the medium of the basket of summer-fruit. Therefore he said, 'Thus Yahweh, the Lord, showed me.' So the seeing of the basket took the form of a vision. But in the strict sense this seeing was not a vision. The object seen was throughout trivial and had nothing in it of the characteristics of an ecstatic vision. The question, 'What do you see, Amos?' and the following answer belong to the reproduction of 'the vision', not to 'the vision' itself. This is a stylistic form probably taken from the didactic methods used in the Wisdom schools.

One day when Jeremiah was walking in the field he noticed a twig of an almond tree which captured his attention. We may imagine that he walked in prophetic reverie. He pondered over the problem whether his preaching of doom really would be fulfilled, or whether he would one day be put to shame before his people. We know that the prophet was later frequently concerned with this problem. While gazing upon the twig, the Hebrew name of an almond tree, *šāqēd*, became actualized to him. The name *šāqēd* led him to the idea of something that watched—'watch' is in Hebrew *šāqad*. This association of ideas came to him as an answer to the question he was just pondering. Had not Yahweh let him see this almond tree in order to show him that He at all events would watch over the accomplishment of His words spoken by His prophets? This occurrence, too, has the form of a vision and is introduced by the common revelatory formula, 'Yahweh's word came to me, saying.' The whole had for the prophet the character of a revelation. The trivial impression was by inspiration from God lifted up to a higher level. The everyday observation was sublimated, carried over into the divine and supernatural sphere. In short, we have here a typical 'symbolic perception'. Also in this 'vision' the didactic Wisdom formula is used (Jer. i. 11 f.).[1]

Another example of the same group of visions is the 'vision' of the cauldron in Jer. i. 13 f. Jeremiah was absorbed by thoughts concerning the judgement to come. How would the punishment come to pass, and through whom? Palestine also was affected by the rumour of the upheavals in the northern countries where various peoples strove for power. Would the catastrophe come upon Judah from those quarters? As Jeremiah pondered such questions, his attention was drawn to a cauldron placed upon a flaming fire blown upon by the wind, a cauldron of which it is said in the narrative that its face was turned to the north. This expression is somewhat obscure. But everything becomes clear if we realize that the cauldron was sunk down in an open air hearth of stones or bricks forming a circle round it, but open towards the north, from where the wind blew on the fuel consisting of wood or dry thorns. The face of the cauldron is thus a somewhat inexact expression for the face of the hearth in which the cauldron was placed. The cauldron on the fire blown upon from the north gave the prophet an answer to his questions. From the northern countries the judgement was to come upon Judah, the apostate nation. Here the common sight of the wind blowing from the north upon a cauldron standing on its hearth was a fact from which the prophet drew the significant omen. As arranged by Yahweh this phenomenon together with its interpretation became to the prophet a revelation from God. It was reproduced by him as a vision and cast in the usual didactic form.

The present writer is of the opinion that the two baskets of figs which, according to ch. xxiv, Jeremiah saw in front of the temple likewise were real baskets upon which the eyes of the prophet chanced to fall. Several scholars think of a vision seen in ecstasy; but in the light of what has been said above I think it most likely that the baskets of figs belong to the same category as the almond twig and the cauldron in Jeremiah and the baskets with summer-fruit in Amos. One basket contained fresh and good figs, delicious as early figs, the other rotten and uneatable figs. The two baskets with their contents became to the prophet a revelation from Yahweh. He saw in them symbols of the two parts of his people, on one hand the exiled Jews, on the other those who were left behind in the homeland. With the former Yahweh was well pleased; upon the latter His wrath rested. The former were destined to be bearers of the new age, the latter would be struck with destructive judgement. It was significant to the prophet that he saw the baskets against the background of the temple. There is no hint that they were destined for offering (that is in fact out of the question). He says only that the baskets were placed just there. The objects seen were things of everyday occurrence, but standing side by side against the background of the temple building they became to the inspired prophet the basis of a highly important revelation. Here again the didactic formula is used.

Finally we must consider the passage about the potter in Jer. xviii. One day Jeremiah went down to the potter's house and found him engaged in work on the wheels. Whenever the vessel at which he was working became spoiled, he changed it into another vessel, such as seemed suitable in the potter's own eyes. The observation of this procedure in the potter's shop suggested to the prophet the idea of the sovereignty of Yahweh in His dealing with His people. Here, too, the providential character of the occurrence is strongly emphasized. It is said that the prophet was ordered by Yahweh to arise and go down to the potter's house, to obtain there a message from Yahweh. The whole is regarded as a revelation, as appears from the introductory words: 'The word that came to Jeremiah from Yahweh.'

The symbolic perceptions resemble in some measure what the psychologists call illusions, but must not be confused with them. In illusions something real is seen, but what is seen is transformed by error, either by a hypersensitive imagination or by a hallucinatory procedure in the brain. In the symbolic perception again the object seen is not changed in the apprehension of the observer, but is interpreted by a more or less spontaneous act of reflection. That which is seen is not perverted into something else, but becomes a symbol of ideas of a higher character. For this reason we may speak of sublimated or symbolic perceptions. I have not found any illusions proper in the Old Testament prophets.

LITERARY VISIONS

The symbolic perceptions could be described as in some sense pseudo-visions. There is also another group of visual pictures which could be called pseudo-visions, although of another nature. Without being in ecstasy, although in an exalted state of mind, a prophet receives an inspiration in the form of a visual creation of the imagination. What the prophet produces in such a psychic state resembles the products of visual poetry; but the prophetic imagery differs from the products of the poets in so far as it appears in the form of revelations given by God. I have called such creations of the prophetic imagination 'revelatory fancies'. Another suitable term for them is 'literary visions'.

When the medieval visionaries speak of *figurata locutio,* in which their writings are so abundant, they mean approximately the same as we here call 'revelatory fancies' or 'literary visions'.

The descriptions in Jeremiah of the enemy from the north are not ecstatic visions, but typical revelatory fancies.

Behold, he comes up like clouds,
his chariots like a whirlwind;
his horses are swifter than eagles—
woe to us, for we are ruined (iv. 13).

(Thus says Yahweh:)
Behold, a people is coming from the north land;
a mighty nation is stirring from the ends of the earth.
They lay hold on bow and javelin;
they are cruel and pitiless.
The sound of them is like the roaring sea;
and they ride upon horses—
arrayed every man for the battle,[2]
against you, O daughter of Zion!

We have heard the report of it,
and our hands fall helpless;
anguish lays hold on us,
pain like that of a woman in travail.
Go not out to the fields,
nor walk on the way!
For there is the sword of the enemy,
terror all around.
O daughter of my people, gird on sackcloth,
and wallow in ashes;
take up mourning, as for an only son,
wailing most bitter!
For suddenly will come
the despoiler upon us (vi. 22–26).

While these examples take the form of visual revelations, the little poem of Rachel's lamentation is in the form of an audition:

(Thus says Yahweh:)
Hark! in Ramah is heard lamentation,

bitter weeping!
It is Rachel weeping for her children,
refusing to be comforted
for her children,
because they are not (xxxi. 15).

A splendid specimen of this genre is the poem of Jeremiah about the battle of Carchemish (ch. xlvi). Here the picture is in the form of a dramatic vision.

Other examples of literary visions are the poems of the advancing Assyrians in Isaiah, the *maśśâ'* on Moab in Isa. xv, the picture of the capture of Nineveh in the book of Nahum, etc. Such passages (there are several examples of this genre in the prophetic literature) are poetical compositions, but with the character of revelations. Accordingly, we may apply to them the term 'revelatory fancies'.

Why do we not regard such poems as ecstatic visions? First of all they are not presented to us as visions in the strict sense but as oracles. They are introduced by the usual oracle formulas and sometimes expressly called *maśśâ'* or even *māśāl*. Further, the visionary style is not accurately adhered to; the pictures often glide into other types of prophetic preaching: exhortation, lamentation, announcement of doom, hymn. Finally, the descriptions of this kind are as a rule more realistic and less fanciful than ecstatic visions usually are. The conscious reflection of the author is more evident.

The so-called night visions of Zechariah offer a special problem. There are eight of them: four riders reporting that the earth is at peace, Yahweh having not yet begun His planned Messianic work; four horns representing the world-powers and four blacksmiths who are coming to break them down; the man with a measuring-line in his hand going to measure Jerusalem but being informed that Jerusalem of the future can have no walls on account of the multitude of men and cattle; the high priest Joshua dressed in dirty garments and accused by Satan but vindicated by Yahweh and clothed in festal and clean garments; the golden candlestick with seven lamps and two olive trees at the side thereof symbolizing Yahweh, the all-seeing God, and Joshua and Zerubbabel as His servants; the flying roll, a symbol of the curse which strikes the evil-doers in the land; the woman within the ephah-measure representing the wickedness which is to be taken forth from the land; the four chariots going out to the four quarters of the earth, probably indicating the return of the dispersed Jews to the homeland.

What the prophet here describes is given the form of ecstatic visions. The first vision is introduced by these words: 'Last night I saw.' Most of the following visions are introduced by one or other of the phrases, 'I lifted my eyes and saw', or 'he showed me'. In one case a very interesting phrase is used, namely in the introduction to the vision of the candlestick:

'The angel who was talking with me waked me again like a man who is waked from his sleep.' This expression does not mean that the prophet had been sleeping and now awoke; he *compares* his transition from one state of mind to another with the awakening from sleep. As a man, when awakening, sees the light and the shapes of the day, Zechariah, when passing into the ecstatic state of mind, saw figures and shapes appearing from the invisible, spiritual world. Similar descriptions of revelatory experiences are common among the medieval visionaries. St. Birgitta says that God frequently rouses her soul as from sleep to see and hear in a spiritual way. The mystic says that, while the soul is making its orison, it sometimes feels its spiritual sense suddenly awakening; it becomes conscious of the presence of God in a way quite new.

Now the question arises whether these 'visions' really are ecstatic visions or have only been given the form of visions. The latter is of course conceivable. As we have seen above, the prophets often give their inspired utterances the form of visions. The introductory phrases mentioned above, particularly some of them, seem, however, to tell in favour of the other explanation. But there are several facts which tell against it, at least so far as certain of the visions are concerned. A number of the visions entirely lack the characteristics of genuine visions. In the descriptions of the 'visions' the visionary features are often very scanty and fragmentary. The visionary pictures are not completed. We miss the conclusion which should have accomplished and rounded off the scene. Irrespective of the fact that the descriptions of the visions in most cases are confused by extended explanations of an allegorical nature, oracles by the prophet from different times, and secondary additions, the visions have given the interpreters much trouble, precisely because of their fragmentary character.

Four of the visions are noteworthy exceptions: the flying roll, the woman within the ephah-measure, the clothing of the high priest in clean clothes, and, above all, the candlestick with the two olive trees at its side.

These four visions (including the Joshua vision) have this in common that they are all pictorial, completed, and do not need any additions to be fully intelligible. They have all the characteristics of genuine ecstatic visions. Their contents are highly fanciful, unreal, irrational, and unreflective. The introductory phrase with which the vision of the candlestick begins points decidedly to the fact that we have here an ecstatic vision. Saying that he was roused *again,* the prophet possibly indicates that the preceding vision also was an ecstatic one.

The present writer suggests the following solution of the problem of the night visions in the Book of Zechariah. Four of the eight visions are visions in a strict sense, namely those mentioned above.[3] The others are products of the imagination of the prophet, although he was in a state of inspiration. He wanted to complete the genuine series with a number of 'visions' in order to give a more comprehensive picture of the Messianic age which in his opinion was about to dawn. One cannot say that what came into his mind was particularly excellent. The fundamental idea of the genuine visions is the new Messianic community in its cultic and national organization, and the moral and ritual cleansing necessary for its realization. In the four literary visions, as we consequently may call them, the prophet, in addition, intended to depict the waiting for the wonderful events, the crushing of the hostile nations, the future immensity of the Messianic capital, and the return of the dispersed Jews.[4]

In the visionary literature we find many examples of such a combination of genuine visions and literary visions, in which the reflection of the visionary played a more marked part. The Apocalypse of John is a fine specimen of this sort in our Bible. The revelations of Birgitta and many other medieval visionaries consist to a great extent of literary visions combined with genuine ones. The visionary in the Book of Zechariah was stimulated by his ecstatic visionary experiences to create new fanciful visions expressing his ideas concerning the heavenly secrets of the age to come. The very order of the visions in the present book may of course be owing to the man who has given the Book of Zechariah its present form.

In the second part of the Book of Zechariah, the so-called Deutero-Zechariah, we meet with a passage which in all probability should be assigned to the same category, namely the description of the shepherd and the sheep, xi. 4–16+xiii. 7–9.[5] A prophet received the divine command to be a shepherd of a flock which was to be slaughtered and to be badly treated by sellers and buyers. He took over the charge and took for himself two rods, called 'Grace' and 'Union'. The shepherd got weary of his task, abandoned the flock to destruction, and broke the rods. Wages were weighed out to him, a ridiculous sum: thirty shekels of silver, which he threw to the metal founder. Then the prophet was ordered to be a bad shepherd of the flock. As such he had to be killed, whereupon the flock would be scattered. Only a small part would be rescued.

That these happenings occurred in reality is out of the question. Of an ecstatic vision one would expect more pictorial detail and less reflection. The picture has all the characteristics of a literary vision of a pronounced allegorical nature. Thus it may be classed among the category which we have called 'revelatory allegories'. The interpretation is rendered a little difficult because of the fact that later hands have applied the original text to specific historical events (e.g., the three shepherds in xi. 8) and because of the blend at different points of allegory and interpretation, which is common in descriptions of this kind.

What the allegory means is the following. The Jews are in a miserable situation. They are ill-treated by evil rulers. The nation is itself stubborn and not even worthy of a good leader. Yahweh's covenant with it is broken. So is the bond between the Jews and their northern neighbours in Samaria. Severe judgement is imminent. A cruel tyrant will rise in the land. He will be killed and the nation itself will be destroyed. Only a small remnant will be saved.

I think it most probable that the great vision of Ezekiel in ch. xl–xlviii concerning the new temple, the new city, and the new land is to be judged in a similar way. The visionary frame of the whole is manifest. Not all the details, however, can have been seen in ecstasy. But the introduction to the whole section points so palpably to a basic ecstatic experience as to make it very unlikely that this is only a literary form. It is stated that on a certain day 'Yahweh's hand' came upon the prophet; in divine visions he was transferred to the land of Israel and found himself set on a high mountain, where something like the structure of a city was raised. The expression 'divine visions' is also used in the undoubtedly ecstatic vision in Ezek. viii–xi (viii. 3; cf. xi. 24). Thus my thesis concerning the great temple vision of Ezekiel is that the prophet, after having been transferred in ecstasy to Mount Zion, saw the future city and the future temple in their general contours in an ecstatic vision. The vision of the glory of Yahweh in xliii. 2 f. seems also to be an ecstatic experience. After the passing of the ecstatic rapture the prophet worked out all the details contained in the nine chapters, giving to all that emerged in his imagination and reflection the form of a long series of visionary experiences linked to the basic ecstatic visions. Most of the 'visions' in Ezek. xl–xlviii are consequently to be classified as literary visions.

A very interesting parallel to the great temple vision of Ezekiel is the immense 'vision' of St. Birgitta in her *Regula Salvatoris*. The Swedish visionary 'saw' in all details the Nunnery in Vadstena, the church with its altars, ornaments, etc., the garments of the nuns, the lodgings and garments of the various functionaries, the holy ceremonies, and so on. Obviously most of what she 'saw' must be regarded as 'literary visions', but the exceptionally concrete and lively description of the ecstatic experience in the introduction to the revelation of the Nunnery rule makes it difficult to deny that an ecstatic rapture gave the first impulse.

Visions of various kinds (ecstatic visions, symbolic perceptions, or literary visions) played a central role in the religious life of the prophets. It seems that the prophets themselves as well as their contemporaries regarded their visionary endowment as the essential element in their prophetic equipment. Like the early prophets, the later prophets are frequently called 'seers'. 'Prophet' and 'seer' stand as synonyms (Isa. xxix. 10; xxx. 10; Am. vii. 12). To be a prophet and to have visions are almost the same (Ezek. xxi. 34; Joel iii. 1). In the book of Hosea it is said that Yahweh speaks to the prophets and gives many visions (xii. 11). Deutero-Zechariah in his experience of the decay of prophecy in his time says that in the future age it shall come to pass that the prophets will each be ashamed of his visions when he prophesies (xiii. 4). In the Book of Lamentations a poet complains of the fact that the prophets do not receive any visions from Yahweh (ii. 9).

The prophetic oracles and messages can in general be called visions irrespective of whether they really are, or have simply been given the literary form of, visions. The words of the prophets are called 'vision words' (Ezek. xii. 23). The collections of the revelations of Amos, Isaiah, Micah, Nahum, and Obadiah are described as visions. Individual oracles, too, can be called 'visions' irrespective of their general character: Isa. xiii. 1; xxix. 11; Jer. xxxviii. 21; Hab. ii. 2 f.

NOTES

1. Williams (in *A Stubborn Faith,* pp. 91 ff.) refers the almond twig in an original fashion to Aaron's rod in Num. xvii.

2. I read *'ārûk 'iš*.

3. That they were seen in one single night (i. 7 f.) is curious, but not impossible. These are analogies in the visionary literature. Julian of Norwich had fifteen 'shewings' from four o'clock till after nine in the same morning (*Rev.*, xix, p. 164).

4. The prophetic words linked to the visions surely belong to different times; but I see no cogent reason for going against the assertion of the prophet that he saw the visions at the beginning of the reign of Darius.

5. While xiii. 7–9 seems to be a continuation of xi. 4–16, the passage xi. 17 gives the impression of being an interpolation by a later hand to serve as a substitute for the original passage, after it had been removed from there and placed after xiii. 6.

Pottery, Poetry, and Prophecy:
An Essay on Biblical Poetry

*Statistical analysis has shown that prose and poetry in He-
brew Scripture can be clearly distinguished from one
another. The distinction between prose and poetry in turn
brings out the originality of the prose history of Yahweh
and his people—a new literary form in ancient Near Eastern literature. Hebrew poetry, on the other hand, has its
roots in traditional, oral composition (see also Whallon, pp.
318–325).*

*More striking is the persistent linkage of poetry and
prophecy in the Bible. In Moses, Miriam, and Deborah; in
the oracles of the "writing prophets"; and again in the revival of prophecy in Greek and Roman times, the expectation persists that poetry is the main vehicle for prophecy.
The prophet's role involves Yahweh's spirit upon the poet,
from before the Monarchy through Jesus' time and particularly in the late apocalyptic writings.*

*As the footnotes of the article demonstrate, many
scholars have written about the basic forms of Hebrew
poetry (see also Muilenburg, pp. 362–380). Freedman distinguishes two basic structural types—regular metrical
patterns and symmetrical stanzas. Statistical analysis offers the possibility of "sequence-dating" poetry to establish
the time of composition, a technique similar to sequence-
dating of pottery.*

P OETRY is not only central in the title, but for the study of the Hebrew
Bible. There is no intention here of disvaluing the prose of the Bible,
which constitues the first major literary composition in that medium ever
produced, so far as I am aware, whether we speak of the so-called Court
History and the J source of the Pentateuch of the 10th century B.C., or the
composite whole which we may call the Primary History (Genesis
through Kings) of the 6th century.[1] The preponderance of prose is even

From David Noel Freedman, *Journal of Biblical Literature*, 96/1 (1977), 5–26.

greater in the NT, where we speak of the narratives of the Gospels and Acts, or the essays on religion and ethics contained in the Epistles.[2] There is little danger that the prose of the Bible will be lost or forgotten, neglected or abandoned by scholars, much less by the vast constituency which holds this literature sacred. On the contrary, the Bible will be read and studied, admired and absorbed, primarily as a prose work in the future as in the past.

The case with the great poetic tradition of the Bible is far otherwise. While particular compositions and certain books of the Bible have always been identified and acknowledged as poetic in form and content, much of the poetry of the Bible has been incorporated into the prose tradition. The rediscovery of the poetry of the prophets is a major contribution of modern scholarship, as is the recognition of the poetic tradition behind the earliest prose narratives.[3] Since some large fraction, perhaps a quarter to a third of the Hebrew Bible, must be reckoned as poetry or poetic in character, just its bulk would demand serious attention, but its quality and difficulty make it even more important. In many respects it is older and more basic than the prose materials; at the same time it is more obscure and challenging. The form and style, the selection and order of words, all play a vital role in conveying content, meaning, and feeling. In poetry, the medium and message are inseparably intertwined to produce multiple effects at different levels of discourse and evoke a whole range of responses: intellectual, emotional, and spiritual.

In the present paper, I intend to discuss two aspects of Hebrew poetry in the light of recent research and discussion: (1) its character, including (a) definition; (b) sequence-dating; (c) forms and structures; (2) its function as the vehicle of revelation, including (a) pagan patterns: myth, epic, ritual, oracle; (b) Israelite adaptation: echoes and remnants of epic traditions, surviving poems; (c) continuation: worship (Psalms), wisdom (Proverbs, Job), oracles (Prophets).

I. THE CHARACTER OF HEBREW POETRY

(a) *Definition.* Poetry is well delimited by its differences from prose. While there is an area of overlap, generally it is not difficult to distinguish the two without precisely defining the difference. Since the distinction is often quantitative rather than qualitative, and in terms of degree rather than kind, it may be asked why it is important to draw the line at all and try to separate one corpus from the other. The answer is that in spite of some blending of types and blurring of the lines of demarcation, prose and poetry are basically two different ways of using language. Each has its own rules of operation, and it is obligatory to understand each category according to its own pattern, even if the dividing line is not always certain.

We have devised recently a mechanical test to separate poetry from prose in the Bible, and preliminary tests show that it will work efficiently in most cases. The particles *'ēt* (the sign of the definite direct object), *'ăšer* (the relative pronoun), and *ha-* (the definite article) all have been identified as prosaic elements, not common in or suitable to poetry.[4] But with one partial exception, no systematic study of the distribution of these elements in biblical literature has been made.[5] In a comprehensive investigation, the results of which are now being prepared for publication, a graduate student of mine, working with statisticians at the University of Michigan, has collected extensive samples of prose and poetry in the Bible, has determined the frequency with which these particles occur, their distribution, and the ratios between prose and poetry. Then on the basis of standard formulas and tables, she has been able to fix the value of these particles as a discriminant and calculate the probability that their distribution in the Bible is the result of chance or convention. The conclusion is that the criterion works, *grosso modo,* very effectively and serves to separate prose from poetry without difficulty. Prose passages cluster at the high end of the frequency spectrum while poetry is found at the other extreme. There are exceptions and some overlapping; and we must reckon with a modest amount of contamination: i.e., the addition of one or more of these particles where they did not originally occur, and more rarely their omission where they were present. There is no evidence, however, for the normalization of prose practice through the text or the wholesale revision of "poetry" into "prose," even though no distinction was made in the manner of copying the material, or most of it, in the manuscripts. Otherwise the distinction could not have been preserved, as in fact it has been. In general, these particulars occur six to eight times more frequently in prose passages than in poetic ones. Statistically the results are even more important, since they establish beyond cavil that the occurrence of these particles is a valid discriminant, and the difference in distribution reflects an intrinsic distinction between prose and poetry.[6] What it means is that, when a writer composed a prose work, he naturally and inescapably used these particles in the normal fashion described in the grammars; but when he or anyone composed poetry, he naturally did not use them, or if he did, very sparingly. Some of these exceptions can be explained as the result of transmissional errors, since the tendency of scribes would be in the direction of normal prose practice. But the residue would require further investigation and explanation.

Refinements in the use of this criterion may show some fluctuation in the occurrence of these particles in poetry and offer clues to a more discriminating classification of the poems in the Bible. Hypothetically, we might expect this difference between prose and poetry to break down gradually during the long period of biblical composition and compilation. Thus a higher incidence of these particles in poetry might point to a later date of composition, but other potential influences must be reckoned with, screened out, or otherwise accommodated.

We must issue a *caveat* at this point concerning the possible use of this statistically important criterion in textual restoration and in the care and cure of ailing passages in poetry. It would be irresponsible to conclude that these particles were never used in poetry and that all such occurrences in the present text are the result of editorial revision or scribal error. At the same time, some contamination has occurred, and the elimination of intrusive particles will be justified in specific cases, especially where supporting data are available.[7] There must have been a slight tendency to add particles in poetry, chiefly because most of the poetry was copied as prose, which would blur this distinction. Furthermore, the Masoretes seem not to have recognized the difference between prose and poetry except where tradition had preserved it in stichometric writing, or in some other fashion.[8] While it is clear that they did not tamper with the existing text (the *kětîb*), when it came to vocalization they followed a uniform pattern, marking the presence of the article indiscriminately in prose and poetry wherever it seemed grammatically appropriate.[9]

(b) *Sequence-Dating.* This leads directly to a discussion of sequence-dating in poetry, and the reference to pottery in the title of the paper. Before proceeding on this fragile topic, however, I had best make a more emphatic disclaimer than usual with regard to lack of expertise, especially in the presence of qualified archaeologists. No one—friend or foe—has ever accused me of knowing more than the rudiments of pottery identification or dating. My acquaintance with this intricate science is so passive as to be inert. Nevertheless, the principles of sequence-dating of pottery are simple enough, and the application over the years has proved remarkably successful and perduring. Pottery chronology remains the best and most exact standard of measurement for all periods of the Bronze and Iron Ages (roughly from before 3000 to about 600 B.C.). What makes the lowly potsherd so valuable is that it has extraordinary durability (a quality that also attaches to clay tablets with cuneiform writing on them, as we are reminded repeatedly in these latter days), and occurs in enormous quantities everywhere human beings lived for the last 6000 years and more, and in great varieties of types, sizes, and shapes, and with all kinds of decorations. In addition to these statistically significant characteristics, they also underwent continuous and measurable change and thus constitute an ideal instrument for determining chronological sequence. When combined with accurate stratigraphic analysis, pottery dating is entirely reliable within necessary limits. Except in the most unusual circumstances, dates deriving from the study of pottery cannot be fixed more precisely than within a range of 50 to 100 years. Pottery analysis and sequence dating has been a critical factor in establishing archaeology as a reasonably exact science and in permitting the material findings to be integrated into the historical framework of the ancient Near East.

In principle, it should be possible to establish criteria for the sequence-dating of Hebrew poetry. As the late W. F. Albright was fond of saying, everything human beings set their minds to and their hands on is susceptible of typological classification and chronological ordering. Everything humans touch evolves in one way or another, and it only requires some experience with the material and the application of good sense to isolate those factors which are diagnostic for the process of change in the phenomena under investigation. By using these criteria adroitly, it should then be possible for us to measure both the direction and the degree of change from one period to the next. What may be relatively simple in principle, however, can turn out to be deucedly difficult in practice.

Albright himself attempted to establish a viable sequence-dating of Hebrew poetry, using as criteria certain widespread stylistic phenomena: repetitive parallelism and paronomasia.[10] As a pioneering effort, it was a brilliant *tour de force* and another example of his extraordinary ability to create new areas of research. The net results, however, can only be regarded as mixed, and he continued to refine the method and reorder the poems during the remaining years of his life. Using the same corpus of early Hebrew poetry, essentially, but applying an entirely different set of criteria, I also have worked out a sequence-dating of these poems, partly as a check on Albright's findings, and to develop a mechanism for dealing with other poems. My study, embodied in a major article, "Divine Names and Titles in Early Hebrew Poetry," has just appeared in the G. E. Wright Memorial Volume (edited by Frank M. Cross and others). I will refrain from repeating myself *in extenso*, except to say that the value for biblical studies of recovering a securely dated corpus of pre-monarchic poetry would be very great and should have an important impact on previous and current reconstructions of early Israelite history.

I can also report a subsidiary gain from the application of the techniques developed in that study to poems outside the corpus mentioned. In a recent examination of the Song of Hannah (1 Sam 2:1-10), another graduate student of mine and I had occasion to compare it with Psalm 113 in view of the close literary connections between them.[11] Converging tests show that the relationship is sequential, though not necessarily direct, and all the relevant indicia point to the Psalm as the older of the two poems. Since the Song, independently of this comparison, has been dated to the period of the United Monarchy (10th century),[12] we are required to date the Psalm earlier, in the 11th or even the 12th century, a conclusion which was quite unexpected. In the Song of Hannah, there is an explicit reference to the "king . . . anointed one," along with the use of divine names characteristic of the monarchic period; in the Psalm, on the other hand, along with other archaic features, the divine name Yahweh is used repeatedly and exclusively, which is characteristic of the earliest phase of Israelite poetry.

Other scholars have developed different criteria for determining the relative and absolute dates for the ten poems embedded in the narratives of the Pentateuch and Former Prophets (through 2 Samuel). Gradually a consensus is emerging that these poems are to be dated in the Iron I period (from about 1200 to about 900 B.C.), though there are differences about the placement of individual poems.[13] Sequence-dating of poems in the Bible is still in its infancy, but all the ingredients for a successful resolution of one of the most persistent and troubling problems in literary criticism are in hand: an adequate sample of materials, a sufficiently long period of time for the measurement of change, some dated and more datable poems to provide fixed points of reference, and a tested group of criteria which can be used independently or together to fix dates and check results.

(c) *Forms and Structures.* The quest for the key to Hebrew metrics may have reached a turning point. Hitherto the search and the struggle among scholars have been to uncover that governing principle or universal truth that not only would encompass all cases, but would also recover the fundamental patterns adopted by the biblical poets. Needless to say, the quest has proved futile, like some other scholarly quests of the past century; no such magic key has ever been found, or is likely to be. The actual situation is somewhat different. No regular, fairly rigid system will work with any large sample without extensive reshaping of individual poems and verses. The pages of scholarly journals and commentaries are strewn with the wreckage left by the advocates of this approach, and there is a general feeling that while the investment of time, effort, and ingenuity was great, the returns have proved to be small. Not many poetic reconstructions have survived critical scrutiny very long. While newer approaches and methods have been more respectful and conservative regarding the established text, and successes have been registered in the case of individual poems, overall the gains have not been impressive. Some poems exhibit formal metrical features, and even regular stanza structure, but it is rare indeed when two or more poems share the same structure. Many poems do not seem to have clear-cut metrical or strophic patterns and may never yield to this sort of analysis. Since an essentially descriptive and inductive method requires painstaking treatment of a large number of units, it will be a long time before syntheses and worthwhile generalizations are possible. In the meantime, we should restrict ourselves to modest statements and small claims.

Since we cannot resolve the problem at least on the terms which have been used in the past, we may try to redefine it in ways more appropriate to the tools at our disposal. Our objective is not to find or devise a key to Hebrew metrics, but rather to achieve an adequate description of the phenomena. This is much less ambitious, but by scaling down our expectations we may be surprised by the achievable results. There are three points to be made, and in the process we hope to focus attention on the attainable and dispel some illusions along the way:

(1) There is no single solution to the problem of Hebrew meter and poetic structure, but there are many possible descriptions, some more adequate than others, some more pertinent for different sets of questions than others. In comparing systems, we should give up the notion that the poets of Israel used any of them deliberately, or that our task is to find out which one it was. Lacking any useful literature from antiquity on the subject or clear-cut internal data, the best we can hope for is an evaluation of different systems in terms of economy (or parsimony), efficiency, utility, precision, and comprehensiveness. In general, the system which satisfies these criteria best should be adopted, but different systems may be used for different purposes, and it is always wise to check the results derived from one system by another. It is interesting and may be instructive that practically all the systems which have been devised in the past century have produced positive results in measuring and describing aspects of Hebrew poetry. At the same time none has been generally satisfactory, and all have demonstrable weaknesses. The conclusion is that there is no single best system, but that acceptable results will depend to a great extent on the purpose of the measurement and the kind of description desired. Since all systems reflect a certain rhythmic regularity in much of Hebrew poetry, the principal object is to devise a measuring system that is symmetry-sensitive and will describe the metrical pattern as clearly and as simply as the data permit. That is why I have opted for a syllable-counting system in preference to the more traditional stress-system used by most scholars.[14] Basically, the two methods describe the same phenomena in much the same way, but there are more arguments about the number of stresses than about the number of syllables, or I should say that syllable-counters tend to be more accommodating and less dedicated because one syllable more or less does not make as much difference as one stress more or less. In addition, the picture provided by syllable-counting is more precise. An equally simple system that also works with large samples is word-counting. We can define a word as any sequence of Hebrew letters between white spaces on a printed page, leaving open the question of the effect of a *maqqēp* (which is roughly

equivalent to a hyphen). I have tried more complex methods of counting, distinguishing between long and short vowels, and even adding in consonants in order to secure an exact calculation of the time-span of a poetic unit. For the most part, I think it has been wasted effort, as poets notoriously bend the rules, written and unwritten, and the point of diminishing returns is reached very rapidly in view of the extraordinary arithmetical effort required.[15]

(2) It is difficult if not impossible to draw the line between the conscious intention of the poet and what the attentive reader finds in a poem. On the whole, I think we have given insufficient credit to the poet for subtleties and intricacies in his artistic creation, and it is better to err on that side for a while. If we find some clever device or elaborate internal structure, why not assume that the poet's ingenuity, rather than our own, is responsible? It is a different matter if it is our ingenuity in restoring or reconstructing the text. In many cases, however, I believe that the process by which the poet achieves an effect is different from the process by which the scholar recognizes and describes it. What is the result of conscious effort on our part, may be spontaneous in the poet, or second nature. For one who is steeped in the tradition and draws on long experience in creating poems, it is not necessary to start from scratch, and the associations and intricate arrangements, which we discover only after painstaking investigation, may be byproducts of which he is not fully aware, while he centers attention on other aspects of composition. Since there is no way finally to resolve such questions about the intention of the poet, it is a safer and better procedure to restrict or extend ourselves to the visible data and describe what we see there, rather than try to probe the recesses of the poet's mind.

(3) Questions concerning oral or written composition and transmission cannot easily be resolved one way or another, and the common discussion does not shed much light on the nature of the process or the end result. These are very important matters, but with respect to Hebrew poetry at least it is difficult if not impossible to disentangle oral and written elements. Both processes are at work in the history of composition and presentation of any biblical poem; all of them finally were written down, no matter how they were composed or how they were transmitted. So there is a written factor at the end of the line, if not earlier, for biblical poems, and undoubtedly an oral factor at some point in the process as well. Needless to say, these factors affect each other: oral composition and transmission are very different in a community in which there is a strong writing-tradition from what they are in a community without any writing at all. In the case of the oracles which Jeremiah dictated to the scribe Baruch, there is a mutually interdependent process at work. The original oracles presumably were composed orally. Then they were dic-

tated by the prophet and written down by the scribe; in principle this was only a change in procedure not in substance. Once written, they begin a new career in manuscript form, with a history to come of editorial revision and scribal alteration. When the autograph is destroyed by the king, another copy has to be compiled, again at Jeremiah's dictation. Is the second version another instance of oral composition, or something else, viz., an effort to reconstitute a previously existing written work, itself a compilation of earlier composed oral pieces. Even without the special complications of the Jeremiah-Baruch composition, the process of composing, reciting, recording, and transmitting is endlessly involved. Rarely if ever can oral and written categories be kept separate, especially in the Near East where writing was a compulsive habit long before the time of the patriarchs.

Thus far I have been able to identify two basic structural types in Hebrew poetry: (1) In the first group are poems of a more traditional type, at least in comparison with the poetry of other cultures. These poems have fairly regular metrical patterns and symmetrical stanza structures, ranging from simple to complex and ornate. To illustrate this type we may consider Psalm 113 in relation to the Song of Hannah.[16] Psalm 113 has a very simple metrical and strophic structure: it consists of three stanzas of three bicola each. The standard line-length is 14 syllables, divided in the middle, 7:7; there is a slight variation in some bicola, which divide 8:6. No alterations or emendations in the text are needed, and except for the question whether the poem is complete or only a fragment, we can consider it a prime example of classic metrical Hebrew poetry. It apparently belongs to the earliest phase of Israelite verse, when presumably poems of this type were prevalent. There are slight deviations from the norm, but these can be regarded as reluctant concessions to the ultimate intractability of language when pressed into metrical patterns or the resistance of the poet to metrical requirements. We can also include transmissional errors as an element in the occurrence of such irregularities, but unless there is other compelling testimony, we need not appeal to such a contingency in order to achieve metrical conformity. Artistic freedom is a more persuasive alternative, or in fact artistic necessity as a guard against mechanical composition and the constant threat of monotony in the creation of metrically repetitive poetry.

Turning to the Song of Hannah, we find a much more complex strophic structure; even after the most painstaking efforts to recover the original, or a more original, form of the poem, it may have eluded us. Still it is possible to identify the basic three-line stanza of 42 syllables in vv. 4–5, and 8a-f. There are elaborations and embellishments, including a formal introduction (vv. 1–2) and complementary closing (vv. 9–10). Similar, though in no case identical, strophic patterns have been identified in other short Psalms (23, 29, 137), all of which have a striking chiasm at the midpoint of the poem. The net effect of these features is to produce an X-like structure within a frame.[17]

(2) Another type of poem exhibits much greater variation in line length and stanza construction, while at the same time there is an overall consistency and regularity which ensure that the poem generally is intact and that the pattern is deliberate. The problem is how to account for the great internal freedom and variety, on the one hand, and the predictable and repeated patterning of the poems as a whole, on the other. The best examples of such poems are the alphabetic acrostics of Lamentations 1–3.[18] Without repeating the extensive analysis of G. B. Gray or my own observations already published, it can be said that within an established framework of 22 stanzas per poem there is considerable freedom in the matter of line length (measured in syllables) and in stanza structure and length. In view of the mechanical structure of the poem, however, such free variations may have been regarded as welcome or obligatory relief from monotony. The great surprise, at least initially, was to discover that in spite of the wide variations from line to line and from stanza to stanza the three poems as a whole were virtually identical in length, again measured by the number of syllables (I:865; II:863; III:868).[19] However we try to explain the matter, the facts are beyond dispute; nor is the situation unique with respect to these three poems. The same results are obtained when eight other acrostic poems are compared: the internal range of variation in line and stanza length is great but the total length of the poems or the averages are again practically identical.[20]

When the distribution of line and stanza lengths (but not the position of the lines) is plotted on a graph, the results overall and for specific poems are the same: an almost perfect bell-shaped curve, which, as we all know, is the pattern for random distribution of practically everything. In this pattern, the bulk of instances will be concentrated around the mean or average figure; the remainder will be spread out above and below the center point, with short lines balancing long ones, thus producing the familiar curve. How do we account for this peculiar phenomenon and correlate a carefully wrought poem with a random-distribution curve for its metrical model? What factors produce uniformity in the overall configuration but a wide range of variation in the component parts?

Parts of the answer lie in the nature and structure of the Hebrew language, and other parts in the complex process of poetry composition. It is difficult to imagine that there was a set of rules governing such a poetic structure. After all, the bell-curve is a description after the fact, not a prescription for would-be poets to follow. In the case of the poet responsible for Lamentations 1–3, it might be argued that the special metrical pattern reflects the way in which he conceived and executed his work. The whole is a product of his genius, and many of the details are distinctive of this poet. But the distributional pattern we have described seems to be independent of the particular poet. It is observable in practically all the acrostic poems, which cover a wide range of subjects and which were composed by a number of poets, and is clearly the established pattern for poems of this type. For the present, the evidence links the pattern with acrostics, but I am sure that many other poems of different types conform to the same model. Since it is inconceivable that poets counted words or syllables into the hundreds (or thousands) to determine the shape of their poems, especially when they allowed themselves such wide variation in the matter of line and stanza length, we must reckon with a fundamental control deeply ingrained in the consciousness of poets generally. The result was a format at once regular and flexible, within whose fixed but not consciously recognized limits the poet was free to practice his art and express his individuality.

We may summarize the findings in these terms: There is a predictable and repeated total configuration (measured by syllable or word counts), fixed by tradition, experience, and practice. Poets in different places and times conform to this pattern, consciously or not, but inevitably. Within the large structure, however, there is a wide area of free choice, and variation is not only permitted but encouraged. The poet exercises his personal prerogatives in the internal arrangements and expresses his originality not only in the choice and arrangement of words and phrases and clauses, but also in the organization of lines and stanzas. This combination of rigid external control and of internal variety and freedom is distinctive; its roots lie deep in the nature of language, music, and poetry, and it belongs in its history to the sphere of oral composition. Whatever its origin and rationale, the "random-distribution" phenomenon must be reckoned with in the discussion of the nature of Hebrew poetry.

II. THE FUNCTION OF HEBREW POETRY AS A VEHICLE OF REVELATION

(a) *Pagan Patterns.* From time immemorial the language of heaven and of heroes has been poetic in form. In the ancient Near East and the Mediterranean basin, poetry has served as the vehicle of myth and epic alike; reflecting the same awareness, ritual and liturgy share this quality: oracles, incantations, prayers and hymns customarily appear in poetic guise. The basic and persistent medium of classic religion and revelation is poetry. But this intrinsic association has been obscured somewhat in the Bible, for several reasons: (1) The basic narrative, which is the story of Yahweh and his people Israel, is the first and great prose classic of antiquity. The genre itself is the creation of the biblical writers. There was never anything like it earlier, and there have only been imitators since. The fact that the Primary History—the first Bible—is a prose work has dominated the approach to and evaluation of all the biblical literature. (2) Much of the remainder of the Bible, though actually poetic in character, was copied as prose. (3) The treatment of the Bible as sacred, canonical literature has tended to erase all distinctions among the various types of literature, including the basic one between prose and poetry. Whether the concern was legislative or theological, the objective was to fix the exact wording of the text and establish an authoritative interpretation to settle questions and cases. In the process of making the Bible a constitutional authority, poetry was levelled out as prose. Reverence for the text nearly killed off its spirit and effectively suppressed the special features of its poetry.

(b) *Israelite Adaptation.* Without debating the question of prose versus poetry or denying the predominance of the prose tradition in the Bible, it is legitimate to call attention to the poetic element, which not only lies behind the prose end-product but always persisted alongside of it. With regard to the primary prose narrative, critical scholars have always recognized an important poetic component in it or aspect of it. Various attempts have been made to identify and classify that element: (1) E. Sievers (followed in general respects by E. Brønno) just read the narrative as poetry, in accordance with a very complicated set of rules, to which there was an equally complicated set of exceptions or modifications. The results were very mixed and few contemporary scholars, if any, accept either the premises or the conclusions, much less the rules. But we are all impressed by the incredible energy and ingenuity demonstrated by Sievers. In spite of the shortcomings of the system and of our misgivings about the procedure, we must acknowledge that the exercise has not been in vain; and if he erred, he erred on the right side by emphasizing the presence of poetry in the prose tradition.[21] (2) A second and more successful effort is represented by names like R. Kittel, U. Cassuto, and W. F. Albright, who believed that behind the present prose agglomerate there was a poetic substratum.[22] Moreover, bits and pieces of the original epic have survived, especially in the set speeches or sayings preserved in the present prose framework. Examples may be found by leafing through the pages of the Kittel Bible in which poetic passages have been set off from the prose. Succeeding editions of the Bible have identified more poetic passages but the net effect is about the same: poetry embedded in prose, most often in passages containing dialogue. While the work of the scholars mentioned, and of many others since, has had a massive impact on current scholarship—and a *prima facie* case must be acknowledged—there are difficulties with the position in whatever form it has been advocated. The theory of a poetic substratum or an underlying epic poem remains attractive, but so far it is not only unproved but unprovable. I doubt that this epic ever existed, although I am sure that there were many poems, perhaps some of considerable length, which arose out of and described the early experiences of Israel and its forebears, which did not survive, but which influenced the formation of the prose accounts. In addition there are numerous short passages, mainly in dialogue form, which are clearly poetic, and which form part of the prose narrative. This is simply a fact, but how is the prose-poetry combination to be explained? It is possible that these passages are remnants of an earlier stage of transmission and that the prose writers incorporated these dramatic and lyrical elements from the oral tradition into the larger works. The premise and the argument, however, are open to question: Do the theory and the data really match up? Is not the notion of such carpentering of a narrative rather artificial and out-of-date? (3) These inquiries lead to a third possibility, which combines features of the views just mentioned but presents the case for a poetic component in the prose narrative in a more appealing and less artificial manner. It also reflects the reality of the end-product, which is a genuine work of literature. The essential argument is that the same author is responsible for both prose and poetry in composing his work and has combined them deliberately to enhance the literary quality and dramatic impact. E. F. Campbell, Jr. has proposed just such a solution to the literary problem of the Book of Ruth, which in small compass has many of the same features as the Primary History: a prose framework and narrative with poetic elements (some of extraordinary beauty) embedded in it.[23] It is not necessary or desirable to think in terms of an original poem or poetic narrative, subsequently cast in prose form, while some elements of the older poem have been retained. It is better to regard the work as an independent prose composition in which the convention of putting some of the speeches, especially those of the central characters, in poetic form has been observed. It may be mentioned that in Elizabethan drama, for example, the nobles and other leading characters typically speak in poetry, whereas commoners and comedians are relegated to prose. The same person who composed the prose of Ruth is also responsible for the poetry; no doubt the whole story is based on older oral poetic traditions from the region of Bethlehem and the family of Boaz and his successors. The story itself was not invented, but it was handed down from the time when "the judges judged" in Israel.

Happily, we can leave the question of the poetic elements embedded in the larger prose narratives of the Bible and pursue the great poetic tradition of early Israel in a more fruitful way, by examining several major poems which have been preserved in the Pentateuch and Former Prophets. These poems are independent of their prose contexts, although in each case a title or framework has been provided, indicating that the poem was incorporated into the larger work when the prose narrative had already been composed. In these poems, we have authentic reminiscences of a time earlier than the prose narrative and examples of hymnic and lyric composition from the formative period of Israel's existence. The poems, which form a coherent group highlighting the great events and experiences of the early period, are as follows: the Testament of Jacob (Genesis 49); the Song of the Sea (Moses and Miriam, Exodus 15); the Oracles of Balaam (Numbers 23–24); the Song of Moses (Deuteronomy 32); the Blessing of Moses (Deuteronomy 33); the Song of Deborah (Judges 5). The survival and preservation of these poems are quite understandable, even though the prose accounts cover much the same ground (explicitly in the case of Exodus 15 and Judges 5, and in the story of Balaam in which the poems are interspersed among the prose paragraphs, Numbers 22–24). The poems were central and basic to Israel's life and could not be lost or forgotten. They mirrored Israel's self-consciousness as the people of Yahweh, who had led them out of bondage in Egypt, to freedom at Sinai and to nationhood in Canaan. For later generations they remained the fundamental expression of Israel's faith and commitment and served as a constant reminder of its origins and reasons for existence. They share in and convey the enthusiasm and exuberance of the early days of Israel and also portray the conflicts and crises of that era. Taken together, the poems form a corpus of tradition about the beginnings of Israel, which is free of later interpretation and adaptation to other situations and circumstances, a unique source from and for the premonarchic period in Israel.

Two aspects of the poetry may be distinguished: (1) The date of composition: on the basis of different analyses and by the use of a variety of criteria, it is possible to arrange these poems in a relative order of composition and then fit the whole group into a framework of fixed dates between the 12th and 10th centuries B.C. Since the subject has been treated in some detail elsewhere, I shall only summarize the conclusions. I distinguish three phases of composition, which may be assigned to the 12th, 11th, and 10th centuries respectively: (i) the period of militant Mosaic Yahwism: the Song of the Sea (Exodus 15), during the first half of the 12th century, and the Song of Deborah (Judges 5), during the second half of the same century; (ii) the archaic period, with the revival of patriarchal names and titles for God: the Testament of Jacob (Genesis 49), during the first half of the 11th century, and the Testament of Moses (Deuteronomy 33), during the latter part of the same century; the Oracles of Balaam (Numbers 23–24), perhaps in the middle of the century; (iii) the period of the monarchy: the Song of Moses (Deuteronomy 32), difficult to date, but there are tell-tale signs of later composition in the selection of divine names, which indicate that it belongs to phase iii, not earlier than the 10th–9th centuries, perhaps around 900 B.C.[24] (2) The contents: the poems describe the critical events in the early history of the sacred community, from its origins until its settlement in the land of Canaan.[25] These do not constitute a connected narrative, even in the sense of the prose accounts, but are rather the raw materials of history, selected, collected, reflected, and refracted in poetic form. The poems are only slightly later than the period which they describe and are themselves active elements in the material they transmit. The era they cover runs from perhaps the first half of the 13th century B.C. with the formation of the 12 tribe league in Canaan (reflected in the reference to Israel's presence there in the Marniptaḥ stele) to the latter part of the 12th century, when Canaanite resistance to Israelite settlement was crushed at the battle of Taanach by the waters of Megiddo. The Testament of Jacob reflects the establishment of a pre-Mosaic, pre-Yahwistic tribal federation in Canaan, apparently the creation of the patriarchal hero, Jacob. The Song of the Sea recounts the climactic episode in the flight from Egypt, the miraculous deliverance at the crossing of the Red Sea and its aftermath, the journey to the holy mountain of Yahweh, and the initial settlement there. The Oracles of Balaam recall a later phase of this settlement, presumably in trans-Jordan, though details are lacking. The Song of Moses is a long historical and theological survey of Israel's experience in the wilderness, with special concern for the generation that failed, the group that was delivered from bondage, but that was guilty of apostasy and rebellion against its redeemer and suffered the consequences. The Testament of Moses describes a tribal assembly at the time when the two groups and their traditions (patriarchal and Israelite from Canaan, on the one hand; Mosaic and Yahwistic from Egypt by way of the wilderness, on the other) were merged to form Israel, the people of Yahweh.[26] The Song of Deborah records the decisive victory of Yahweh and his people over the kings of Canaan, whereby possession of the land was finally secured, and title was transferred from one people to the other.

These poems were part of a larger corpus, the scope and contents of which are indicated by quotations and references found in the prose narrative, and which were gathered in collections like the Book of Jashar and the Book of the Wars of Yahweh.[27] The emergence of Israel as a small nation-state in the 13th–12th centuries may be one of the minor effects of the great upheaval all along the littoral of the eastern Mediterranean and the surrounding areas, but it must be linked with the saga of the exodus from Egypt and the religious pilgrimage to Sinai, the holy mountain of Yahweh. It is this combination of a new faith embodied in a reconstituted community which gives the story its unique importance and establishes the tradition of exodus, wanderings, and settlement, however difficult it may be to reconstruct it as history, as the major formative factor in the development of Western civilization. The point which we have been approaching with all deliberate speed is that this handful of biblical poems (along with a few bits and pieces of others now lost) constitute the Israelite version of the mythic-epic tradition of the ancient Near East; this episodic account in poetry was itself superseded by the great prose narrative. Nevertheless, some wise editor preserved the poems alongside the prose, as artifacts and mementos of that creative age when Israel came to be.[28]

The great battle hymns, the Song of the Sea and the Song of Deborah, describe events in Israel's history, victories that were crucial to Israel's survival and success and attributable to the direct intervention of Yahweh. This miracle or wonder, which is at the center of the story in both cases, consists in a sudden rainstorm with a following flood which disables and destroys the chariot force of the enemy, which otherwise would overwhelm the militia of Israel. But it is much more than a natural cataclysm: the violence, the split-minute timing, the complete reversal of fortunes, all point to the hand of God. When a miracle occurs, the causal connection between heaven and earth becomes visible and immediate, as explosive contact is made. As in any mythic or epic situation, involving the divine and the human and communication or action between heaven and earth, the appropriate language is that of poetry. Prose may be adequate to describe setting and circumstances and to sketch historical effects and residues; only poetry can convey the mystery of the miraculous and its meaning for those present. Just as the miraculous participates in history with the mundane and also transcends it, so poetry participates in language with prose but also transcends it. The miraculous action and the poetic utterance have a common source in the powerful spirit of God.

We may summarize this excursus into the realm of esthetics and apologetics by affirming that poetry is the traditional means of expressing and transmitting religious experience: in myth and epic, in ritual and liturgy. In the biblical tradition, the vehicle of communication of the action and word of God is predominantly the prose narrative of the Primary History, but the original medium was poetry (and this pattern persisted through the period of the First Temple), which, like the extraordinary events it embodied and depicted, is also a product of the divine spirit. The chosen leader can only produce signs and wonders through the power of the Spirit, and the poet can only produce his works through the power of the same Spirit. The poetry of religious saga is as much the work of God as the miraculous events it describes. Potentate and poet tend to merge into the same person, so far as tradition is concerned, because the same inspiration is present in the mighty deed as in the mighty word.

(c) *Continuations.* This brings us to the next and last proposition: that poetry and prophecy in the biblical tradition share so many of the same features and overlap to such an extent that one cannot be understood except in terms of the other; in short, they are different aspects or categories of the same basic phenomenon, viz., the personal contact between God and man, and the verbal expression of it through the action of the Holy Spirit. The argument is essentially that the prophets were the inheritors of the great poetic tradition of Israel's adventure in faith and maintained, enhanced, renewed, and recreated it in the face of increasingly bitter opposition of those who preferred their religion in more manageable prose forms and who conceded (grudgingly) only the realms of liturgy (hymnody) and wisdom (gnomic and speculative verse) to the poets. There are two points, though not of equal value or importance; nevertheless they complement each other: The first is that the old poems were captured for the prophetic tradition. With few exceptions, the authors were identified as prophets or presented as having prophetic powers, the poem itself being evidence of divine inspiration. Among the poems we have been considering, three are attributed to Moses (Exodus 15, Deuteronomy 32 and 33), who is the prophet par excellence and nonpareil of the Hebrew Bible. Miriam, who is assigned a collaborative role in the presentation and presumably the composition of the Song of the Sea, is explicitly called "prophetess" in that connection (Exod 15:20). Deborah, the composer of the song which bears her name, is also called "prophetess" (Judg 4:4). As for her collaborator, Barak, we are not informed about any prophetic tendencies on his part, only about his military status and prowess. Balaam was a well-known diviner from Aram, whose role in the biblical tradition, however reluctant, was that of an authentic messenger of God. While the term "prophet" or "prophecy" is not used, we may claim his oracles (Numbers 23–24) for that category. A similar argument can be made in the case of Jacob and the Testament attributed to him (Genesis 49). While the term is not used of him directly, the poem is introduced as a prophetic oracle concerning the last times (Gen 49:1).

The correlation between poetry and prophecy is maintained elsewhere in the tradition. David is credited with the composition of several poems which are preserved in 2 Samuel (the Lament over Saul and Jonathan, the Lament over Abner, the Psalm of Salvation, 2 Samuel 22 = Psalm 18, and the Testament of David, 2 Samuel 23:1–7), as well as almost half of the Psalms. The question is whether he also was considered to be a prophet. Generally speaking, the latter role is a late assignment, finding explicit notice in the NT (e.g., Acts 2:30 in connection with the citation of Psalm 110 which was regarded as a messianic, i.e., prophetic, utterance). But there is much earlier evidence supporting David's prophetic status. The Testament of David begins with the same words as two of the oracles of Balaam (Num 24:3, 15): *ně'um dāwīd,* "oracle of David." The term *ně'um* is used almost exclusively of divine oracles in the prophetic literature; and the more archaic usage here, as in the case of Balaam, reflects the conscious recognition that the person named was the bearer of an authentic word from God, precisely the role of the prophet. The conclusion is confirmed by the passage, 2 Sam 23:2, which reads:

rûaḥ yahweh dibber-bî	Yahweh's spirit has spoken by me,
ûmillātô 'al-lĕšônî	and his word is upon my tongue.

The first colon is both difficult and ambiguous: *rûaḥ* is regularly feminine and therefore can hardly be the subject of the verb *dibber;* but even if we took Yahweh as the subject, the meaning would not be affected seriously. Just how to interpret the prepositional phase *bî* is difficult to decide, but in this case the parallel passage makes it clear that the poet considers himself the messenger by whom God delivers his word. In other words he has a prophetic role. The same expression is used in Hos 1:2, where we read:

tĕḥillat dibber-yahweh bĕhôšēaʻ	At the beginning (i.e., the first time)
	when Yahweh spoke by Hosea

The roles of the poet (David) and the prophet (Hosea) are hardly distinguishable.

Among others credited as authors of Psalms, we find the names of Asaph (Psalms 50, 73-83), Heman (Psalm 88), and Ethan (Psalm 89). The first two were called seers, while the third is grouped with them at other places, and no doubt was thought of as having the same status and powers.[29] To sum up, many of the poets of the Bible were considered to be prophets or to have prophetic powers, and in some cases at least, the only tangible evidence for this identification is the poetry itself. On the other hand, most of the prophets for whom we have evidence in the form of speeches or oracles, were in fact poets. While the prose narratives about the prophets in the later historical books (Samuel and Kings) contain very little information about the formal utterances or oracles, there are hints here and there that the prophets composed poems, and were expected to do so in certain circumstances: e.g., Samuel (1 Sam 15:23, which may be authentic); Nathan (the parable of the lamb may be described as poetic prose or prose-poetry, 2 Sam 12:1-4); Micaiah (1 Kgs 22:17); Elisha (2 Kgs 13:17).

The main evidence for prophets as poets comes from the great corpus of the major and minor prophets. While a good deal of prose has been mixed in with the poetry, especially in the Books of Jeremiah and Ezekiel and of postexilic prophets like Zechariah and Haggai, most of these prophets were poets, and their oracles were delivered and have been preserved in poetic form. Most of the prose materials are narratives about the prophets (e.g., the Book of Jonah, which however contains a poem, probably not by the prophet) or paraphrases of their messages written down by others. The fact that a person was a prophet and a poet does not in itself rule out the possibility or even the likelihood that he spoke occasionally in prose, both formally and informally, and might have dictated or written in the same mode. The question is whether the primary equation of prophecy and poetry holds, and I think it is safe to say that from the beginnings of prophecy in Israel at least until the exile, poetry was the central medium of prophecy. The pattern persisted after the exile, but the data are less clear; in any case by the 5th century prophecy itself had declined so much that the question becomes academic and irrelevant. The great spiritual leaders of the postexilic period, Ezra and Nehemiah, regarded themselves as conservers and restorers of the old traditions, but by no stretch of the imagination could either have been considered a prophet or a poet. An age had ended.

It may be noted that in subsequent centuries the revival of prophecy brought with it a revival of poetry. The presence of the Holy Spirit of God was considered the necessary sign of the inauguration of a new age of revelation, and in turn prophecy and poetry were products of the Spirit's power. The new form of prophecy in the Greco-Roman age was apocalyptic, and it is in these mostly pseudonymous writings that the genre of prophetic poetry is renewed: the Enoch literature, *The Testaments of the Twelve Patriarchs, The Psalms of Solomon,* etc. The Qumran community also provides an instructive example. The Teacher of Righteousness is not called a prophet (that role is reserved for an eschatological figure of the future) but he is described as an inspired interpreter of the words of the canonical prophets, especially in forecasting future events; in other words he was regarded as having prophetic powers. At the same time, he is apparently the author of the *Hodayot,* or Thanksgiving Psalms, a poet like David.[30]

We may add a cautious note about the NT. With the appearance of John the Baptist and Jesus of Nazareth, it was believed that the age of prophecy had returned in the context of eschatological fulfillment. Luke especially emphasizes this theme in the nativity stories, and true to tradition the speeches of angels and other inspired persons are in the form of poetry, even though the Gospel itself is a prose narrative. Thus the angel makes the first announcement to Zechariah about John in Luke 1:14–17, and to Mary about Jesus in 1:28–34 (several small pieces). Mary herself makes a prophetic announcement in 1:46–55, while Zechariah prophesies under the power of the Holy Spirit in 1:68–79. Simeon, empowered by the same spirit, utters an oracle in 2:29–32, and another in 2:34–35. Anna is not quoted directly, but since she is called a prophetess, we may suppose that in her case too there was poetry in the picture.

More difficult and more important is the question concerning the utterances of John the Baptist and Jesus. Here we must be very cautious indeed, but there is some evidence to consider. Probably there is too little left of John's prophetic utterances to make a judgment, but in the case of Jesus a substantial corpus of authentic sayings has survived. How much of what he said belongs to the category of prophecy or apocalyptic, and how much to other categories like wisdom teaching, are serious questions which, however, need not detain us at this point. The classical prophets were not too careful about their categories and wandered from genre to genre in the delivery of their oracles. If Jesus was regarded as a prophet, and he seems to have been, then the question with which we are concerned is: Was he also a poet? While the efforts of competent scholars like C. F. Burney and J. Jeremias to recover an original Aramaic substratum in poetic form from the present Greek of the gospels have not achieved universal acceptance, and many details have been rejected or questioned, on the whole the results seem to me plausible and often persuasive.[31] Without pressing the point, it can be argued that there is a poetic quality and perhaps something more rhythmic and regular in many of his utterances. The parables strike me as a kind of prose poetry, while the sayings belong to the category of free verse. While neither his poetry nor his prophecy is in the classic mold, there are haunting reminiscences of both in his recorded utterances. Nor is poetry lacking in other parts of the NT: hymns of one sort or another are embedded in different epistles (e.g., Phil 2:6–10); more specifically the Book of Revelation is a mosaic of poetic compositions within a prose framework. At the same time it is a prophetic work, attributed to John the servant of Jesus.[32]

Our last example may be the most appropriate because while it belongs to the biblical tradition, it lies outside the Bible entirely. In Islam there is one final authentic prophet, Mohammed. The sacred scripture, the Quran, is a transcript of his utterances, and while they vary greatly in length and shape, they are all considered poetic. In this case, prophet and poet are one, and the two categories are coterminous. In the Quran, poetry and prophecy are the same.

What after all was the purpose of this exercise in demonstrating the obvious, that there is a close correlation between classical prophecy and poetry? The answer lies in the effort to come to grips with the larger underlying problem of inspiration, which in turn is related to questions of authority and canonicity. During the period of classical prophecy in Israel, there was a pressing existential question: Did God indeed communicate his will to men as tradition maintained? And how could one choose among the many self-styled messengers of the deity? The test of the prophet was the presence of the Spirit: by the power of the Spirit authentic miracles were performed and authentic oracles were uttered. The miracle or wonder validated the message, and the message interpreted the miracle. It is no accident that miracles and oracles are the province of the prophets. So the prophet could authenticate his mission by wonder as well as by word; but in these latter days miracles were part of the problem rather than the solution. Those in the past were safely embedded in tradition, but in the present, mastery of miracles seemed to have passed into unscrupulous hands, and the subject itself was suspect in the eyes of many. So we find frequent warnings in the Old and New Testaments against false prophets and false messiahs who in spite of being false have access to sources of supernatural power and can produce signs and wonders; but they are not to be believed or followed. The Book of Deuteronomy offers two pragmatic tests for dealing with prophets and their claims: (1) They must speak in the name of Yahweh, and not of other gods; (2) their predictions must come true. Although these tests are simple and clear, they are not workable in all situations. While the first test will screen out interlopers who represent foreign deities, the real problem is with the prophets who speak in the name of Yahweh, but say different and conflicting things. The case of Hananiah and Jeremiah, both of whom claimed to be prophets of Yahweh and who nevertheless offered contradictory diagnoses of the current situation and predictions about the future, exposes the weakness of this test (cf. Jeremiah 28). The second test will work when circumstances allow the community the leisure of delaying a decision about the challenge or the warning of the prophet until his predictions can be checked by events. Most prophecies mix a summons to decide with warnings or predictions about the future, so that people must respond immediately and settle the question as to whether the prophet is true or false long before the test can be applied. There are other ways in which the test might fail: It is entirely possible for a false prophet to make a true prediction; in fact, if two false prophets make opposite predictions, one is certain to be false, but the other may be true. It can also happen that a true prophet makes a false prediction. This may be a little more difficult to explain, but mistakes happen, and a prophet's career and standing could hardly be nullified by one stray prediction. While the situation is complicated, Ezekiel seems to have missed on a prediction about Nebuchadnezzar and the siege of Tyre (cf. Ezek 26:7–14 with 29:17–20); the prophet does not seem to have been unduly disturbed by the outcome and modified his prediction accordingly. There is no clear evidence that the latter forecast, that Nebuchadnezzar would conquer Egypt, was fulfilled either.

This quest too seems to have ended in failure. There are no certain tests, and no infallible guarantees by which to distinguish between true and false prophets. If we revise the question, however, we may find an answer. Instead of trying to decide the ultimate issues of truth and falsehood, which are best left to the *eschaton* and to the Almighty, we may examine the more immediate question facing Israel: the test of a prophet was the presence and power of the Spirit in his message, what he said, and how he said it. Since the Spirit was the direct source of both prophecy and poetry, they were the basic indicators and primary evidence of its presence and activity. In the case of the great prophets, there is a remarkable congruence between content and form, a welding of prophecy and poetry which authenticated both messenger and message. For Israel, the high points of its historical experience were represented, on the one hand, by the great poems of its formative period; and on the other hand, by the prophetic oracles of its later years, in both cases by a happy union of message and medium which directly confirmed the presence and action of the Spirit of God. These compositions, doubly validated as poetry and prophecy, constitute a basic Scripture within the Scriptures, the direct word of God, like one of his thunderbolts hurled from on high.

Pottery, poetry, prophecy. There is an old word-building game called "Anagrams," which can be played in a variety of ways. Here is one: If you add a "t" to "poetry," you can make "pottery." Then if you add a "c" (and make a few other emendations), you can produce "prophecy." As we have suggested, there is more to the connection than mere alliteration and assonance.

NOTES

1. D. N. Freedman, "The Law and the Prophets," *Congress Volume, Bonn 1962* (VT Sup 9; Leiden: Brill, 1963) 250–65; also "Pentateuch," *IDB* 3 (1962) 711–27.

2. Nevertheless, there is an important poetic component in the NT, which will be discussed later in the paper.

3. Bishop Lowth, while not the first to make this observation, nevertheless marked a turning point in the study of the prophetic literature and the poetry of the Bible generally. See G. B. Gray, *The Forms of Hebrew Poetry* (New York: Ktav, 1972; reprint of original edition 1915) 6–7; also my comments, "Prolegomenon," to Gray's volume (p. viii).

4. W. F. Albright routinely eliminated these particles in his reconstructions of Hebrew poetry, and scholars associated with the Baltimore School have followed the same practice.

5. The study by Y. T. Radday of the Technion in Haifa was limited to the occurrences of the definite article. In counting, the author made no distinction between the instances of the article indicated by the letter *he,* and those implied by the Masoretic vocalization of the preposition with following nouns. In spite of this qualification, Radday's results are very impressive: poetic books are grouped at the low end of the chart (with minimal use of the article), and prose books at the high end. Books that are mixtures of prose and poetry (as, e.g., Jeremiah and Ezekiel) fall between the extremes.

6. The key figure for each particle taken separately is less than .001 (and for all three taken together, which is the strongest criterion, even less than for the others), which means that the probability that this is a deliberate difference in the treatment of prose and poetry is so great as to be certain.

7. Compare Num 24:4b with 24:16c, which are identical except that the particle '$šr$ occurs before *mḥzh* in v. 4b, whereas it is omitted in v. 16. In view of the metrical balance of the bicolon v. 16cd, we must omit '$šr$ in v. 4b as a secondary addition. There may be some connection between the insertion of '$šr$ in v. 4b and the fact that the colon v. 16b (*wyd' d't 'lywn*), which is parallel to v. 16a = v. 4a, is missing in v. 4.

8. Some MSS with stichometric writing have been found at Qumran, e.g., Deuteronomy 32. Cf. P. W. Skehan, "A Fragment of the 'Song of Moses' (Deut. 32) from Qumran," *BASOR* 136 (1954) 12–15.

9. The statistics show a startling reversal from the pattern established for the use of the three particles, where the proportion is overwhelming, when prose is compared with poetry. When it comes to Masoretic vocalization, however, the difference between prose and poetry is practically erased. If one counts those cases in which, according to the Masoretes, the *he*

has been elided and its presence indicated by the appropriate vowels and dagesh forte, the frequency is practically the same (for the entire sample there were 229 occurrences in prose, and 219 in poetry). Even when the greater overall incidence of prepositions in poetry as distinguished from prose is taken into account, the ratio is about 3:2 which is a far cry from the ratio of almost 7:1, which we find when we count only those instances in which the *he* of the article actually appears. It is clear that the Masoretes seriously affected the results where they were able to do so.

10. W. F. Albright, *Yahweh and the Gods of Canaan* (Garden City: Doubleday, 1968), chap. 1.

11. I wish to acknowledge the extensive assistance of Mr. Clayton Libolt, a graduate student at the University of Michigan, in the preparation of this article, "Psalm 113 and the Song of Hannah," which is to appear in the H. L. Ginsberg *Festschrift*, to be published as one of the volumes in the Eretz Israel series.

12. Cf. "Divine Names and Titles in Early Hebrew Poetry," *Magnalia Dei: The Mighty Acts of God* (eds. F. M. Cross, W. E. Lemke, P. D. Miller; Garden City: Doubleday, 1976) 55–107; esp. 71–72, 96.

13. See discussion and bibliography in the following articles: "Divine Names and Titles in Early Hebrew Poetry"; "Early Israelite History in the Light of Early Israelite Poetry," *Unity and Diversity: Essays in the History, Literature, and Religion of the Ancient Near East* (eds. H. Goedicke and J. J. M. Roberts; Baltimore: The Johns Hopkins University, 1975) 3–35; "Early Israelite Poetry and Historical Reconstructions," which is to appear in the Jerusalem Symposium volume to be published by the American Schools of Oriental Research.

14. I have described the system in a number of articles: e.g., "Strophe and Meter in Exodus 15," *A Light unto My Path: Old Testament Studies in Honor of Jacob M. Myers* (eds. H. N. Bream, R. D. Heim, C. A. Moore; Philadelphia: Temple University, 1974) 163–203, esp. pp. 168–75; "Acrostics and Metrics in Hebrew Poetry," *HTR* 65 (1972) 367–92, esp. pp. 368–69; with C. F. Hyland, "Psalm 29: A Structural Analysis," *HTR* 66 (1973) 237–56, esp. pp. 238–39; "The Structure of Psalm 137," *Near Eastern Studies in Honor of William Foxwell Albright* (ed. H. Goedicke; Baltimore: The Johns Hopkins University, 1971) 187–205, esp. pp. 188–90.

15. See the discussion of these matters throughout the article, "Strophe and Meter in Exodus 15," and especially the tables at the end, pp. 193–201.

16. See the forthcoming study, "Psalm 113 and the Song of Hannah."

17. See the following articles: "The Twenty-Third Psalm," *Michigan Oriental Studies in Honor of George G. Cameron* (eds. L. L. Orlin et al.; Ann Arbor: University of Michigan, 1976) 129–66; "Psalm 29: A Structural Analysis"; "The Structure of Psalm 137."

18. See Gray's discussion in chap. 3 of *The Forms of Hebrew Poetry*, and elsewhere in his book; cf. my comments in the "Prolegomenon," pp. xi–xxiv.

19. The variation among the poems is less than 1%. Essentially the same results are achieved if we count words, i.e., the combinations of letters between spaces: I:376; II:381; III:381. We have ignored the presence of the *maqqēp*, but if we take this Masoretic flourish seriously and regard it as binding words together into single units, then the totals are somewhat different: I:329; II:332; III:350. The effect of the Masoretic intrusion is to obscure the equivalence of the poems, but the basic pattern is still visible.

20. D. N. Freedman, "Acrostics and Metrics in Hebrew Poetry," pp. 367–92.

21. E. Sievers, *Metrische Studien* (Leipzig: Teubner, I[1901], II[1904–5], III[1907]). E. Brønno, *Die Bücher Genesis-Exodus: Ein rhythmische Untersuchung* (Stockholm: 1954). There are many other volumes, which include Joshua, Judges, Ruth, Samuel, Kings, Isaiah, Jeremiah, and Psalms.

22. Albright's views are scattered among his many writings on the subject; Kittel's observations are embodied in his edition of the text of the book of Genesis in the Bible which bears his name. For Cassuto the basic works are: *A Commentary on the Book of Genesis: Part I: From Adam to Noah* (English translation; Jerusalem: Magnes, 1961); Part II: *From Noah to Abraham* (English translation; Jerusalem: Magnes, 1964); *Biblical and Oriental Studies. Vol. 1: Bible* (Jerusalem: Magnes, 1973). The translator in all cases was Israel Abrahams.

23. E. F. Campbell, Jr., *Ruth* (AB 7; Garden City: Doubleday, 1975) 5–23.

24. "Divine Names and Titles in Early Hebrew Poetry," pp. 77–80, 96.

25. "Early Israelite Poetry and Historical Reconstructions."

26. The setting of the poem is the plains of Moab shortly before the death of Moses, but it already reflects the transition to his successors and is doubtless of later composition, presumably the 11th century.

27. If Albright was correct in identifying Psalm 68 as a catalogue of *incipits* or opening lines of many different poems, then we have an indication of the extent and variety of ancient Israelite poetry; the Psalm itself may be dated in the 10th century, but that would mean that many of the poems mentioned in it were of premonarchic date. The Book of the Wars of Yahweh is mentioned in Num 21:14, in connection with some poetic pieces including the Song of the Well (21:17–18) and the victory song of Sihon (21:27–30); the unnamed book mentioned in connection with the diatribe against Amalek (Exod 17:14) may have been the same, and poems like the Song of the Sea (Exodus 15) and the Song of Deborah (Judges 5) may have been included in such a collection. The Book of Jashar is mentioned in Josh 10:13, in connection with the spectacular miracle of the sun and the moon, and again in 2 Sam 1:18, in connection with the Lament of David over Saul and Jonathan.

28. Comparison with the great Greek epic poems, the *Iliad* and the *Odyssey*, which constitute a literary cornerstone for Western culture, is inevitable and necessary. These works are the finest literary achievements of the ancient world (we draw the line in the 6th century B.C. between ancient and modern), with the exception of the Bible, but in terms of poetic art and esthetic quality they are unsurpassed. But they were products of their age and were suited to it; when that world perished, they became relics of a bygone era.

29. On Asaph as prophet and seer, see 1 Chr 25:2 and 2 Chr 29:30; on Heman as seer, see 1 Chr 25:5.

30. The relevant passage in the Habakkuk *pesher* is 7:1–5; " . . . its meaning concerns the Teacher of Righteousness to whom God has made known all the mysteries of the words of his servants the prophets." The translation is from W. H. Brownlee, "The Jerusalem Habakkuk Scroll," BASOR 112 (1958) 10.

31. C. F. Burney, *The Poetry of Our Lord* (Oxford: Clarendon, 1925); *The Aramaic Origin of the Fourth Gospel* (Oxford: Clarendon, 1922); J. Jeremias, *The Parables of Jesus* (rev. ed.; London: SCM, 1963). For a discussion and evaluation see M. Black, *An Aramaic Approach to the Gospels and Acts* (Oxford: Clarendon, 1954), esp. part III, "Semitic Poetic Form."

32. Cf. R. H. Charles, *A Critical and Exegetical Commentary on the Revelation of St. John* (*ICC*: 2 vols.; New York: Scribner, 1920); J. M. Ford, *Revelation* (AB 38; Garden City: Doubleday, 1975).

II: THE CONTEXT

Introduction

T HE Bible cannot be meaningfully studied, according to historical critics, when it has been separated from its historical environment. To them, the biblical writer is analogous to T. S. Eliot's author in "Tradition and the Individual Talent" who moves along in the perpetual stream of the tradition, but who changes it by his own contributions and, significantly for the biblical writer, by his reinterpretation of the past. For example, Christ is not a static figure to the writers of Matthew, Mark, Luke, and John. Although they wrote within approximately fifty years of each other, each has a radically different view of Christ. As indicated by the historical symbols associated with each gospel—lion, man, oxen, and eagle—Matthew's Christ is a king like David; Mark's is a common man; Luke's is a sacrifice for us; and John's is an eternal loftiness. Each gospel writer interpreted Christ out of an experience shaped by tradition; yet at the same time each writer reinterpreted that tradition of a coming Messiah in the light of how he personally saw Christ.

The objective of the modern scholar represented in this section is to resurrect the *Sitz im Leben* (the German term for "setting in life") so the right questions can be asked about the biblical text. David H. Kelsey's *The Use of Scriptures in Recent Theology* includes questions of twentieth-century theologians that the writers in this section implicitly asked of early Jewish and Christian thinkers: What view of God and Christ had they inherited? How had they reinterpreted them to express God's covenant in a world wrought by constant and sometimes violent upheaval? To illustrate some ways in which scholars frame their approaches, we have selected essays from a variety of disciplines associated with biblical studies: archaeology, linguistics, history, and comparative religion.

These essays focus on two important interdisciplinary inquiries: social and political concerns of the Hebrews and early Christians, and their individual and collective relationships with God and Christ. The complexity of these problems can be shown through the order of composition of the Old and the New Testaments, for each major social and political change can be directly related to an altered religious view. The earliest major narratives of the Old Testament—court chronicles written at the time of Saul, David, and Solomon (c. 1020–930 B.C.)—show Israel in her glory. As typically happens in societies, the nation soon began to search for or to create her past. Since the court writers believed that God had made several unique covenants with his people, the books from Genesis through Joshua use these as the unifying motif of the Creation and the nation's subsequent flowering. The third major phase of composition followed as Israel collapsed into political subjugation in the four hundred years following Solomon's death. In this phase the authors sought a new individual and corporate relationship with God in the present and future, as shown in the Writings (Psalms, Proverbs, Ruth, etc.), in the Later Prophets of the Old Testament, and in the entire New Testament. Like any work which was composed and subsequently altered numerous times over approximately fourteen centuries, generalizations about a prophet or a patriarch, for example, have to take into account the wide fluctations of history.

In "What Archaeology Can and Cannot Do," G. Ernest Wright raises the question of how much factual information can be obtained about the people of the Bible. Meanwhile, at the present time Near Eastern archaeologists continue to seek for a biblical city which is as exquisitely preserved as Pompeii or Herculaneum. Using highly developed digging techniques, they are rapidly expanding our knowledge of the Israelites and their neighbors. For example, ongoing excavations at Tell Mardikh (the site of ancient Ebla), reported by Paolo Mattiae and Giovanni Pettinato at the 1976 Society of Biblical Literature convention may well alter our views about Abraham and the other patriarchs. Or as the published findings by William F. Albright in "The Antiquity of the Mosaic Law" and Sigmund Mowinckel in "The Method of Cultic Interpretation" illustrate, archaeologists can tell us a great deal about the Israelites during their years of nomadic wandering. Despite these advances, however, much archaeological evidence has to be united with findings in other fields before it takes on significance to others in biblical studies. Note, for instance, that David Noel Freedman, in his essay in section one, figuratively pieces together the broken pottery found by the archaeologists on various sites with some thoughts about the Hebrew prophet. By using this eclectic approach he is able to formulate some major insights into the nature of biblical poetry.

Besides sifting through the physical ruins of the biblical world, scholars study the *Sitz im Leben* of Hebrew and Christian religion, often searching for differences between them and the religion of their neighbors. The theme of salvation history, that is, God's eternal covenant with the faithful, is the thread that ties together the remaining essays in this section. The view that the good are rewarded and the evil are punished is easy to accept for an Israel prospering under the rule of Solomon; but why did God punish the faithful who had the misfortune to be born when their broken nation suffered under a foreign yoke? Could a good person expect God's protection when leaders were corrupt? Why were the prophets of doom seen as God's oracles when they welcomed the end of the world? These are representative questions to which the essayists of this section write. In "Apocalyptic and History," Stanley Brice Frost discusses how the writers of chronicles and myths, and later the apocalyptic writers, interpreted historical events to prove that God would save his chosen. John J. Collins in "History and Tradition in the Prophet Amos" and Walter C. Kaiser, Jr. in "The Old Promise and the New Covenant: Jeremiah 31:31–34" complement Frost in that they show how Amos and Jeremiah had divergent views about God's covenant—views that arose from different crises. The assumption of power by Rome over the Near East and the coming of Christ forced Jews and Christians to reconsider the theme of salvation history. Ralph W. Klein's "Aspects of Intertestamental Messianism" and William O. Walker's "The Origin of the Son of Man Concept as Applied to Jesus" bring out the milieu into which Jesus was born and what various groups of organized religion expected of him. Thus, it should be apparent that some see the coming of Christ as the natural outgrowth of the Old Testament perception of salvation history.

These essays are, of course, almost indivisible in approaches and theses from those in the literary and textual sections. For example, Albright's discussion about the relationship of the Ten Commandments to other Near Eastern legal codes could be placed in any of the three. Or again, the essays by Frost and Collins have much to do with literary forms. But after some reflection, we placed the essays here because of the writers' frequent use of the milieu to substantiate their arguments. Relatively more than the scholars whose essays appear elsewhere in the anthology, these writers came to conclusions after exploring a host of contextual questions. Differing only in their fields of inquiry, the biblical and literary historian often find answers to what initially appeared to be textual problems in caches far removed from the Bible or literary work.

The Old Promise and the New Covenant: Jeremiah 31:31-34

This is the first of two essays which have conflicting views about the dominant theme of the Bible—salvation history or God's relationship with his people. The other essay, by John J. Collins, immediately follows. Walter C. Kaiser, Jr. advocates the view of dispensational theologians—those who believe that God will save those whom he has chosen simply because he so wills. Collins, on the other hand, advocates the view of covenant theologians—those who believe that people must prove their faithfulness, a condition of God's salvation. Kaiser writes that God's promise of salvation was initially thought to be only for the Jews, but Jeremiah and the New Testament writers make it apparent that through Abraham, the father of Jews and Gentiles, all people are eligible for God's dispensation. Collins, however, writes: "Salvation is by conduct: not by tradition"—Amos and the other prophets, as well as Jesus and the New Testament writers, are constantly lifting their voices against the false security of tradition.

It is not our place here to champion either view. Yet it should be noted that these essays illustrate once more the old adage that the search for truth is difficult—muffled by layers of quotes may be the sound of a grinding axe. Both of these essays demonstrate the breadth of knowledge that is required for intelligent writing on this complex topic. Kaiser not only studies the original language of the covenant theme to reveal that many key words have been misinterpreted, but also the structure of Jeremiah's passage to demonstrate the Old Testament writer's revolutionary insight into personal salvation, as well as the context in which Jeremiah concluded that salvation was available to both Jews and Gentiles. Collins, with his interest in modern theology, summarizes the main lines of reasoning of the

From Walter C. Kaiser, Jr., *Journal of the Evangelical Theological Society,* 15 (1972), 11–23.

*dispensational and covenant theologians written over the
past twenty years.*

*See Stanley Brice Frost's essay, "Apocalyptic and His-
tory," in this section for a view of history which totally
rejects those of Jeremiah, Amos, and the other prophets.*

O NE of the most important, yet most sensitive of all theological texts,
is the new covenant theme of Jeremiah 31:31–34. Hardly has the
exegesis of this passage begun when the interpreter discovers to his great
delight and consternation that he is involved in some of the greatest
theological questions of our day. No matter what he says, some evangelicals are bound to be scandalized because of their commitments either to a
covenantal or dispensational understanding of theology. Nevertheless,
the issues are too exciting and the passage is too important for a simple
retreat to past theological battlelines. For one thing, God's action in historical events has made the contemporary evangelical too responsible and
blameworthy for him to simply repeat the previous generation's theology.
For another, too many excellent points have been made by both of the
current evangelical schools of interpretation to abandon the attempt for a
rapprochement.

THE ISSUES AT STAKE

The time is now ripe for evangelical scholarship to restate for our age our
credos on the following relationships: (1) the amount of continuity and
discontinuity between the two testaments, (2) the separate and/or identical parts played by Israel and the Church in the composition of the people
and purpose of God in the past and the future, and (3) the crucial importance of authorial will, i.e., the truth as intended by the writers of Scripture as a basis for resolving the present stalemate on a hermeneutical
stance and a Biblical philosophy of history.

This latter question is handled so brilliantly in its basic theoretical
argumentation by E. D. Hirsch that no attempt will be made to repeat his
invincible arguments here.[1] Evangelicals would be well advised to study
this volume carefully and then apply its insights to such debatable areas
as eschatological hermeneutics.[2] The other two questions, however, will
be features in the ensuing discussion.

THE OLD PROMISE

The promise of God is one of the greatest unifying themes running
throughout the various books of the Bible and binding them into one

organic whole.[3] Interestingly enough, the Old Testament itself possesses no single, special word to designate the idea of "promise"; rather it has a series of rather ordinary words: *dibber,* "to speak";[4] *'amar,* "to say";[5] *sabac,* "to swear"; *sebucah,* "oath";[6] *berakah,* "blessing";[7] and *menuhah,* "rest."[8] When these words have God as their subject and his chosen people as the recipients of the divine word, action, or person, they are properly translated as "promise" or connected with the promise theme. In addition to these terms, there are repeated formulas which epitomize the content of the promise, e.g., the gospel itself is the heart of the promise: "In your seed, all the nations of the earth shall be blessed."[9] Another is the tripartite formula, "I will be your God, you shall be my special possession and I will dwell (*sakan*) in the midst of you."[10]

Contrary to most current exposition and thinking, the promise is actually God's single, *all*-encompassing declaration which is repeated, unfolded and ultimately completed "in that day" of our Lord. Highlights of this single promise can be located in the *proto-evangelium* of Genesis 3:15, the Abrahamic covenant of Genesis 12:1–3, the Davidic covenant of II Samuel 7[11] and the new covenant of Jeremiah 31; but under no condition must these predictions and actualizations of the promise be scattered into many separate disconnected Messianic prophecies. Willis J. Beecher's work, still the best commentary on this general theme, is at pains to make just this point.[12]

The New Testament has more than forty references to the promise and uses the technical term *epaggelia,* and its cognates *epaggelma* and *epaggelomai.* In Luke-Acts, the promise is still the same one made with Abraham and his seed (Acts 7:5, 17; 26:6–7). In his ten references to the "promise," Luke centers on the work of the risen Lord (Luke 24:49; Acts 1:4; 2:33) and the Holy Spirit (Acts 1:5; 2:33).

Paul's letters also refer the promise back to Abraham (Gal. 3:16, 19), but Paul also carries it way beyond Abraham's day to include not only the present offer of the gospel in our age (Gal. 3:8; Rom. 4:20–21), but even to the "inheritance of the world" at the conclusion of this age (Rom. 4:13)—the Holy Spirit being God's down payment and guarantee of this inheritance "until we acquire possession of it" (Eph. 1:14). Amazingly, Paul repeats the same tripartite formula so frequently cited by the Old Testament in II Corinthians 6:16, i.e., "I will dwell among them, . . . and I will be their God and they shall be my people." This formula he contends is part of the "promise" and he claims that these realities are now being fulfilled among believers in II Corinthians 7:1.

Hebrews also makes the promise the center of its message of grace and hope in some 18 references (Heb. 6:17–18). More importantly this book "notes the difference between receiving *the promise* and receiving *what is promised.* In receiving the promise, recipients are declared heirs; in receiving what is promised, they obtain their inheritance"[13] (Heb.

9:15). Therefore the promise is one continuous, unfolding declaration, consummated not only in the arrival, death and resurrection of Christ, or even in the spiritual seed now receiving the gospel which previously evangelized Abraham (Gal. 3:8); but as the general epistles declare, this single promise will only reach its most glorious realization when we "abide in the Son and in the Father" (I John 2:24) and "eternal life" is fully realized. It reaches to the second coming of Christ (II Peter 3:4, 9–10), to our receiving "the crown of Life" (I John 2:5), and even on into the enjoyment of "the new heavens and the new earth" (II Peter 3:13). Finally, as John concludes the book of Revelation by describing the new heavens and the new earth, he hears the tripartite formula once more: "God shall dwell with them, they shall be his people and he shall be their God who is always with them" (Rev. 21:3). This single promise is so unified, yet so all encompassing in its numerous specifications and span of time, that it must be reexamined as the Bible's own key category for theological organization.

Covenant theologians have stressed the covenant form rather than the total promise content of those covenants; therefore the emphasis has fallen on the church's present reception of *the promise* as God's new Israel. Dispensationalists, on the other hand, have stressed the ultimate reception of *what is promised;* therefore the emphasis has fallen on Israel's inheritance of the land and the kingdom of God. Obviously, both are pointing to valid Biblical teaching found in the single promise spanning both testaments. If rapprochement is that close, let us investigate the possible connections the Scripture makes between this old promise and Jeremiah's new covenant.

THE NEW COVENANT

The only place in the Old Testament where the expression "new covenant" occurs is Jeremiah 31:31. However, it would appear that the idea is much more widespread. Based on similar content and contexts, the following expressions can be equated with the new covenant: the "everlasting covenant" in seven passages,[14] a "new heart" or a "new spirit" in three or four passages,[15] the "covenant of peace" in three passages,[16] and "a covenant" or "my covenant" which is placed "in that day" in three passages[17]—making a grand total of sixteen or seventeen major passages on the new covenant.

Still, Jeremiah 31:34 is the *locus classicus* on the subject. This may be validated from several lines of evidence. Firstly, the unique appearance of the word "new" in this passage stimulated Origen to be the first to name the last 27 books of the Bible "The New Testament."[18] Secondly, it was the largest piece of text to be quoted *in extenso* in the New

Testament—Hebrews 8:8–12. The writer of Hebrews even partially repeats the same long quotation a few chapters later in 10:16–17. Thirdly, it was the subject of nine other New Testament texts: four dealing with the Lord's Supper,[19] three additional references in Hebrews[20] and two passages in Paul dealing with "ministers of the new covenant" and the future forgiveness of Israel's sins.[21] Again, we are presented with another important Biblical theme which promises to unify the two testaments. This is the theme we now wish to explore.

THE BOOK OF COMFORT: JEREMIAH 30-33

Probably the best analysis of the first half of Jeremiah's little book of comfort is the work by Charles Briggs. Observing the introductory formula of "thus says the Lord" and its expansion, he divided chapters 30–31 into six strophes. The resulting topics and sections are: (1) the time of Jacob's trouble, 30:1–11; (2) the healing of the incurable wound, 30:12–31:6; (3) Ephraim, God's firstborn, 31:7–14; (4) Rachel weeping for her children, 31:15–22; (5) the restoration of Israel in Judah and the new covenant, 31:23–34; and (6) God's inviolable covenant with the nation Israel, 31:35–40.[22] The whole context meticulously connects the new covenant strophe with a literal restoration of the Jewish nation. This includes not only the larger context of these six strophes and the second half of the "Book of Comfort" (Jer. 32–33), but also the immediate context of Jeremiah 31:27–28 and 31:35–36. On this point almost all commentators are agreed; at least initially so.

THE PERSONS ADDRESSED IN THE NEW COVENANT

Just as the Abrahamic and Davidic covenants were made directly with each of these men, so the new covenant was made with all the house of Israel and the whole house of Judah. Putting it in this form may open up some new paths for discussion, for while there seems to be no argument over who was originally addressed, there is everything but a consensus when it comes to identifying who participates in the benefits of all three covenants.

But haven't the dispensationalists conceded a point when they agree that the Christian's gospel and the Christian's spiritual seed were both announced in the Abrahamic covenant (e.g., Gal. 2:8, 29)?[23]

So also should the covenant theologians concede the point that it is too late in history to be arguing over whether God will restore a national Israel or not. There are just too many historical events and too many explicit texts (some well beyond the Babylonian Exile, e.g., Zech. 10:8–

12; Rom. 9–11) to shut the door on a revived Israelite nation thesis. Indeed, there are some real signs of encouragement that this subject is also open for renegotiation by many covenant theologians.[24]

With just this much concession on either side, the way would be opened for the synthesis provided us in two great works: the aforementioned work by Willis J. Beecher[25] on the promise doctrine and George N. H. Peters' *Theocratic Kingdom*.[26] Peters demonstrates that:

> We have decided references to... [a] renewed Abrahamic covenant, conjoined with the Davidic [as] being a distinguishing characteristic of, and fundamental to, the Messianic period, e.g., Micah 7:19–20; Ezekiel 16:60–63; Isaiah 55:3; etc.[27]

Further he argues that:

> The decided and impressive testimony of [the]... early fathers... [was] that they were living under this *renewed* Abrahamic covenant as the seed of Abraham [by adoption and engrafting into the covenanted elect nation], which the death and exaltation of Jesus ensured to them of finally realizing in the inheriting of the land with Abraham.[28]

Here is a new footing for an old stalemate. The new covenant is indeed addressed to a revived national Israel of the future, but nonetheless by virtue of its specific linkage with the Abrahamic and Davidic covenants and promises contained in all of them, it is therefore proper to speak of gentile participation. Under the promise doctrine, they were to be the seed of Abraham. They would be adopted and grafted into God's covenant nation Israel.[29] The hope of their final inheritance stood or fell with Israel's reception of the land and the kingdom. But what of the new covenant? Did it change all of this? The text itself must now be investigated.

THE RENEWED COVENANT

The most frequent title given to the new covenant in the Old Testament is the "everlasting covenant."[30] It was a ratification of the "sure mercies of David" (Isa. 55:3) and of God's covenant made with Israel "in the day of Israel's youth," i.e., with the patriarchs (Ezek. 16:60). Perhaps the key texts connecting the "everlasting covenant" with the future "covenant of peace" made with nature and with such contents of the Jeremiah covenant as "I will be their God and they shall be my people" are Ezekiel 37:26–27 and Jeremiah 32:38–42. These old promises are stated anew for a nation on the brink of national disaster and extinction. Notice then its continuity with the past.

Calvin did not miss this point when he commented on Ezekiel 16:61, for he called the "everlasting covenant" a "renewed covenant" and concluded by saying "that the new covenant so flowed from the old, that it was almost the same in substance while distinguished in form."[31]

Still some are apt to be misled by Jeremiah's use of the word "new." They will, therefore, deny that this is the same promise doctrine announced to Abraham, reiterated and enlarged for David. But Biblical usage must supply our definition here also. Both Hebrew *hadas* and Greek *kainos* frequently mean "to renew" or "to restore," as in the "new commandment" (which is actually an old one),[32] the "new moon," the "new creature in Christ," the "new heart," and the "new heavens and new earth."[33]

While the exact distinction between *kainos* and *neos* is often contested, the discussion in Kittel's *TDNT* appears convincing. *Neos* refers to something brand new or distinctive in time or origin, often lacking maturity. *Kainos,* on the other hand, refers to what is new in nature, better than the old or superior in value or attraction.[34] The Hebrew word, however, must serve both ideas: new in time and renewed in nature. Thus for Jeremiah 31, the context, content and New Testament vocabulary distinction decide in favor of a "renewed covenant."[35]

THE CONTRAST WITH THE MOSAIC COVENANT

Jeremiah 31:32 explicitly contrasts the new covenant with an old covenant made during the era of the Exodus. However, both Jeremiah and the writer of Hebrews are emphatic in their assessment of the trouble with the old covenant made in Moses' day: it was with the people, not with the covenant-making God, nor with the moral law or promises reaffirmed from the patriarchs and included in that old covenant. Jeremiah 31:32 specifically says "which covenant of mine they broke." And so is Hebrews explicit on the matter: ". . . finding fault with them . . . because they continued not in [his] covenant" (Heb. 8:8–9).

Was the Mosaic covenant conditioned on the people's obedience for fulfillment and all the other covenants unconditional as dispensationalists claim? Or were all the covenants conditioned on obedience and consequently, as covenant theologians claim, the Jewish aspect of the covenants is obviously to be deleted since Israel failed to obey?[36] But this may all be just a semantical battle. The word *heperu*, "they brake," also occurs in the Abrahamic covenant (Gen. 17:14: "the uncircumcised man . . . shall be cut off; he hath broken [*heper*] my covenant."[37] Even the eternal, irrevocable covenant with David contained some qualifications which allowed for *individual* invalidation, frustration, or destruction of the benefits of that covenant, e.g., I Chronicles 22:13; 28:7; Psalm 132:12. Obedience was no more an optional feature for a genuine trust in the promise or gospel in that day than it is in ours.

But neither was individual rejection or breaking of the covenant a sign that God's purpose had been frustrated and stopped.[38] Jeremiah 31:35–37 argued that the stars would fall out of the sky and the planets would spin out of their orbits before God would abandon his pledge to the nation of Israel!

Covenant theologians have properly emphasized the Biblical role of the "obedience of faith" which follows all genuine saving faith, but they have erred when they pressed the case for the conditionality of all of God's covenants as the condition for divine fulfillment of them especially in the sensitive area of national Israel's future.[39] They have confused the determined, sovereign will and on-going purpose of the promising God with the individual participation in that will in any given time or age.

On the other hand, dispensationalists stressed the unconditionality of the Abrahamic, Davidic, and New Covenants, which emphasis from the standpoint of the sovereign purpose was more than justified; but they failed to account for that Biblical human responsibility which was attached to these covenants. Since the "if" of individual participation was so clear in the case of the Mosaic covenant, dispensationalists wrongly isolated and lowered it below the other covenants. That covenant is lower, but only because of its planned obsolescence; not because it asked for obedience as an evidence of real faith and love towards God.[40]

THE CONTENTS OF THE NEW COVENANT

Now all of this discussion is what makes the new covenant so important; for one of its most perplexing features is that almost all of the items mentioned in Jeremiah's new covenant are but a repetition of some aspect of the promise doctrine already known in the Old Testament.

The section begins with the eschatological formula so frequently seen in the Old Testament—"Behold, the days are coming." It concludes with a motive-clause which has divine forgiveness as the foundation of the covenant. According to Bernhard W. Anderson's excellent structural analysis of the passage, the expression *ne'um yhwh*, "says the Lord," appears four times to set forth the main structure of the unit; twice in the first section: at its beginning (v. 31a), at its end (v. 32b) and twice in the second section: at the beginning (v. 33a) and at the end (v. 34b). The latter occurrence sets.off the climactic *ki* statement of v. 34c.[41]

The items of continuity contained in the new covenant are: (1) the same covenant-making God (*beriti*), (2) the same law (*torati*), (3) the same divine fellowship ("I will be your God"), (4) the same seed ("You shall be my people"), and (5) the same forgiveness. Each of these items merits some further discussion and documentation.

The same nation that had previously broken a divinely ordained covenant is now offered a renewal of that covenant with many of the same features and more. There is a diversity of covenants in the Old Testament but one God and one promise doctrine throughout all of them.

The kernel and essence of both the old and the new covenant was the law of the Lord.[42] Even the Mosaic exposition of the law urged its placement in the heart of the believer (Deut. 6:6, 7; 10:12; 30:6). Indeed some Old Testament righteous men did claim that it was in their heart: "Thy law is within my heart," Psalm 40:8 and Psalm 37:31; the difference seems to be a relative one only.

There was no greater or more frequent formula for the promise doctrine than the declaration, "I will be your God and you shall be my people." As observed above, this theme of divine fellowship and special ownership is one of Israel's most treasured concepts. But Gentiles also now claim the same promise *verbatim* in II Corinthians 6:16. Again, the difference can only be in extent and degree, but not in kind.

Even God's gracious forgiveness was experienced by the O.T. man. Not only did God announce himself at least eight times as "The Lord, a God merciful and gracious, slow to anger and abounding in steadfast love and faithfulness . . . forgiving iniquity and transgressions and sins,"[43] but he forgave and forgot Israel's sin as on the Day of Atonement[44] and in such great Psalms as 103, 32 and 51. Such is the scope of the continuity between the covenants.[45]

But there are also items of discontinuity. Some of these are: (1) a universal knowledge of God (Jer. 31:34), (2) a universal peace in nature and in military hardware (Isa. 2:4; Ezek. 34:25; 37:26; Hos. 2:18), (3) a universal material prosperity (Isa. 61:8; Jer. 32:41; Ezek. 34:26–27; Hos. 2:22), (4) an age of the spirit and (5) a sanctuary to exist forever in the midst of Israel (Ezek. 37:26, 28).

These passages sound like the "all Israel" of Romans 11:26 and "every knee bowing" and "every tongue confessing" of Philippians 2:10–11. Jeremiah emphasizes the words "all of them" by placing them first in the Hebrew clause and by the expression "from the most insignificant of them unto the greatest of them—they all shall know me."[46]

Then too the full realization of the tripartite promise formula is only totally realized in the *eschaton,* for a great voice out of heaven cries in Revelation 21:3, "Behold, the tabernacle [remember O.T. *sakan?*] is with men, and he will dwell with them, and they shall be his people, and God himself shall be with them and be their God."

We conclude that the new covenant is a continuation of the Abrahamic and Davidic covenants with the same single promise doctrine sustained in them all. No features have been deleted except the ceremonies and ordinances of the "old" Mosaic covenant whose phasing out was planned for long ago. The better covenant remained.

THE BETTER COVENANT:
THE ABRAHAMIC-DAVIDIC-NEW COVENANT

The key to understanding the "better covenant" of Hebrews 8:6 is to observe the equation made between the Abrahamic promise (Heb. 6:13; 7:19, 22) and the new covenant (Heb. 8:6-13). The Abrahamic is not the first covenant according to that writer's numbering, but a second, better covenant since the Mosaic covenant was the first to be actualized and experienced by the nation. The Mosaic covenant did have its faults (Heb. 8:7), not because of a fault in the covenant-making God, but because many of its provisions were deliberately built with a planned obsolescence. Its ceremonies and civil institutions were mere copies of the heavenly reality (Ex. 25:9; Heb. 9:23) and temporary teaching devices until the "surety" of the "better covenant" arrived (Heb. 7:22).

Indeed the Sinaitic covenant was an outgrowth of the Abrahamic; yet since many of its provisions were merely preparatory, its place had to be yielded to the more enduring one now that Jesus had died. In fact, "God, willing more abundantly to show unto the heirs of promise the immutability of his counsel, confirmed it by an oath." Thus "by two immutable things [i.e., the promise and the oath] in which it was impossible for God to lie, we . . . have a strong consolation" (Heb. 6:17, 18). "These two immutable things are God's original promise (Gen. 12:1-3) and his solemn oath on Mount Moriah."[47] Sinai could not eradicate these two things.

Some equate the person and work of Christ in this first advent with the sum and substance of the new covenant, using verses like Isaiah 42:6 and 49:8. Christ himself is a "covenant of the people" in the same sense as he is "a light to the gentiles," *viz.* the source, mediator, or dispenser of light and so the mediator of the new covenant. By his death (the cup of the last supper), Jesus renews the covenant, but it is not an entirely new covenant.

Neither is it a fulfilling of just the spiritual promises made to Abraham's seed. The middle wall of partition has been broken down between believing Jews and believing Gentiles, but this says nothing about national destinies (Eph. 2:13-18). Paul says that gentile believers have become part of the "household of God" (Eph. 2:19) and of "Abraham's seed" (Gal. 3:16-19). But they also are to be "heirs" according to the promise (Gal. 3:19) with an "inheritance" to come which is "the hope of their calling" (Eph. 1:18)—even the "eternal inheritance" promised to Abraham (Heb. 9:15).[48] With Christ's resurrection power shared with all of Abraham's seed, it is now possible to eventually realize all the promises made to Abraham: geographical, political and spiritual. The first advent will climax in the second advent and all the promises made to Abraham will then be realized.[49]

CONCLUSION

It would appear that Hebrews does not warrant a radical break between the "old" and the "new"... . The Old Testament saints already participate in the New Age in anticipation even though in time they still belong to the old order... . The "new" is only different from the old in the sense of completion.[50]

The "new" began with the "old" promise made to Abraham and David. Its renewal perpetuated all of those promises previously offered by the Lord and now more. Therefore Christians presently participate in the new covenant[51] now validated by the death of Christ. They participate by a grafting process into the Jewish olive tree and thus continue God's single plan.[52] However, in the midst of this unity of the "people of God" and "household of faith" there is an expectation of a future inheritance. The "hope of our calling" and the "inheritance" of the promise (in contradistinction to our present reception of the promise itself) awaits God's climactic work in history with a revived national Israel, Christ's second advent, his kingdom, and the heavens and the new earth. In that sense, the new covenant is still future and everlasting; but in the former sense, we are already enjoying some of the benefits of the age to come.[53] With the death and resurrection of Christ the last days have already begun (Heb. 1:1), and God's grand plan as announced in the Abrahamic-Davidic-New Covenant continues to shape history, culture and theology.

NOTES

1. E. D. Hirsch, Jr., *Validity in Interpretation*. New Haven: Yale University Press, 1967.

2. See the writer's paper "The Eschatological Hermeneutics of 'Epangelicalism': Promise Theology," *JETS*, XIII (1970), 91–99.

3. See Foster R. McCurley, Jr., "The Christian and the O.T. Promise," *Lutheran Quarterly*, XXII (1970), pp. 401–10 for the most recent exploration of this theme. Also F. C. Fensham, "Covenant, Promise and Expectation in the Bible," *Theologische Zeitschrift*, XXIII (1967), pp. 305–22. And Cleon L. Rogers, Jr., "The Covenant with Abraham and Its Historical Setting," *Bibliotheca Sacra*, CXXVII (1970), pp. 241–56.

4. McCurley, *ibid.*, p. 402, n. 2. He counts over 30 cases of *dibber* as "promise." The promised (*dibber*) items include: (1) the land: Ex. 12:25; Deut. 9:28; 12:20; 19:8; 27:3; Jos. 23:5, 10; (2) blessing: Deut. 1:11; 15:6; (3) multiplication of his possessions: Deut. 6:3; 26:18; (4) rest: Jos. 22:4; I Kings 8:56; (5) all good things promised: Jos. 23:15; and (6) a dynasty of David's throne: II Sam. 7:28; I Kings 2:24; 8:20, 24, 25, 56; 9:5; I Chron. 17:26; II Chron. 6:15, 16; Jer. 33:14. As a "promise" (*daber*) it appears in I Kings 8:56; Psa. 105:42.

5. *Ibid.* (about 7 cases); e.g. Num. 14:40; II Kings 8:19; Psa. 77:8; Neh. 9:15, 23; II Chron. 21:7.

6. Gen. 26:3; Deut. 8:7; I Chron. 16:15–18; Psa. 105:9; Jer. 11:5. See Gene M. Tucker, "Covenant Forms and Contract Forms," *Vetus Testamentum*, XV (1965), pp. 487–503 for use of "oath" with the promise.

7. Gen. 12:1–3 *et passim*.

8. Gen. 49:15; Deut. 12:9; I Kings 8:56; I Chron. 22:9; 28:2; Psa. 95:11; 132:8, 14; Isa. 11:10; 28:12; 66:1; Jer. 45:3; Mic. 2:10; Zech. 9:1.

9. Gen. 12:3; 18:18; 22:18; 26:4; 28:14. Cf. Paul's estimate of this in Gal. 3:8 and Norman C. Habel, "The Gospel Promise to Abraham," *Concordia Theological Monthly* (1969), pp. 346-55.

10. Gen. 17:7, 8; 28:21; Ex. 6:7; 29:45; Lev. 11:45; 22:33; 25:38; 26:12, 44, 45; Num. 15:41; Deut. 4:20; 29:12-13; Jer. 7:23; 11:4; 24:7; 30:22; 31:1; 31:33; 32:38; Ezek. 11:20; 14:11; 36:28; 37:27; Zech. 8:8; 13:9.

11. Otto Eissfeldt, "The Promises of Grace to David in Isaiah 55:1-5," in *Israel's Prophetic Heritage* (ed. Bernhard W. Anderson), pp. 196-207.

12. Willis J. Beecher, *The Prophets and the Promise*. Grand Rapids: Baker Book House, 1963 (rpt. of 1905 Thomas Crowell publication), pp. 175-85. He fails to make the previous point, i.e., the connection of the promise of the land and nation with the events of the second advent of Christ. See also the fine article by Paul S. Minear, "Promise," *Interpreter's Dictionary of the Bible*, III. Nashville: Abingdon Press, 1962, pp. 893-96.

13. Minear, *ibid.*, p. 895 (italics ours).

14. Jer. 32:40; 50:5; Ezek. 16:60; 37:26; Isa. 24:5; 55:3; 61:8.

15. Ezek. 11:19; 18:31; 36:26; Jer. 32:39 (LXX).

16. Isa. 54:10; Ezek. 34:25; 37:26.

17. Isa. 42:6; 49:8; Hos. 2:18-20; Isa. 59:21. For additional passages on the new covenant see Stefan Porubcan, *Sin in the Old Testament: A Soteriological Study*. Rome: Slovak Institute, 1963, pp. 481-512.

18. T. H. Horne, *Introduction to the Critical Study and Knowledge of the Holy Scriptures*, I, p. 37. Also Geerhardus Vos, *Biblical Theology*. Grand Rapids: Eerdmans, 1954, p. 321 for a similar assessment. Also Albertus Pieters, *The Seed of Abraham*. Grand Rapids: Eerdmans, 1950, p. 61.

19. Luke 22:20; I Cor. 11:25; Matt. 26:28; Mark 14:24.

20. Heb. 9:15; 10:13; 12:24.

21. II Cor. 3:6; Rom. 11:27.

22. Charles A. Briggs, *Messianic Prophecy*. New York: Scribners, 1889, pp. 246-57. The same outline was essentially repeated in George H. Cramer, "Messianic Hope in Jeremiah," *Bibliotheca Sacra*, CXV (1958), pp. 237-46.

23. When Charles Ryrie comments on the new covenant, he says, "The occurrences of the term *New Covenant* in the New Testament show that there is a wider meaning than to Israel alone. Some of the blessings of the new covenant with Israel are blessings which we enjoy now as members of the body of Christ." *The Basis of Premillennial Faith*. New York: Loizeaux Bros., 1953, p. 124. Again Ryrie says in *Dispensationalism Today*. Chicago: Moody Press, 1965, pp. 145-46: "If our concept of the kingdom were as broad as it appears to be in Scripture and our definitions of the Church as strict as they are in the Scriptures, perhaps nondispensationalists would cease trying to equate the Church with the Kingdom and dispensationalists would speak more of the relationship between the two." We agree wholeheartedly and urge this state of affairs to begin immediately.

24. Hendrikus Berkhof, *Christ the Meaning of History*. Richmond: John Knox Press, 1966, pp. 136-53. "At any rate, with the surprising geographical and political fact of the establishment of the state of Israel, the moment has come to begin to watch for political and geographical elements in God's activities, which we have not wanted to do in our Western dualism, docetism and spiritualism" (p. 153). Cf. also John Murray, *The Epistle to the Romans* (NIC NT), II. Grand Rapids: Eerdmans, 1965, pp. 65-100. Commenting on Romans 11:27 he concludes, "Thus the effect is that the future restoration of Israel is certified by nothing less than the certainty belonging to covenantal institution" (p. 100). In a footnote on that page he observes, "It is worthy to note that although Paul distinguishes between Israel and Israel, seed and seed, Children and children, (cf. 9:6-13) he does not make this discrimination in terms of 'covenant' so as to distinguish between those who are in the covenant in the broader sense and those who are actual partakers of its grace." The older view may be found in Albertus Pieters, *The Prophetic Prospects of the Jews, or Fairbairn vs. Fairbairn:* 1930. For the older literature on the subject consult David Brown, *The Restoration of the Jews: The History, Principles and Bearings of the Question*. Edinburgh, 1861.

25. Beecher, *op. cit.* See this writer's *JETS* paper cited in n. 2 for an enthusiastic endorsement of his main thesis.

26. George N. H. Peters, *The Theocratic Kingdom I.* Grand Rapids: Kregel, 1957.

27. *Ibid.,* p. 322.

28. *Ibid.,* p. 324 (italics his). The fathers he has in mind are chiefly Barnabas, Papias, Justin Martyr, Irenaeus, etc.

29. Refer to the above discussion on the old promise and the conclusion of this paper.

30. See above, n. 14.

31. See Marten H. Woudstra's fine recent article. Obviously this very question troubles Woudstra greatly as he tries to decide between Calvin and G. Charles Aalders in "The Everlasting Covenant in Ezekiel 16:59–63," *Calvin Theological Journal,* VI (1971), pp. 22–48.

32. Cf. John 13:34; I John 2:7; II John 5.

33. Cf. those verses where the perpetuity of the heaven and earth is taught: Psa. 104:5; 148:3–6; 89:34–36; Jer. 31:35–36. See Wilbur M. Smith's thoughtful comments in the *Biblical Doctrine of Heaven.* Chicago: Moody Press, 1968, esp. chap. XIII, "A New Heaven and a New Earth," pp. 223–38.

34. Johannes Behm, "Kainos," in *TDNT* (ed. by Gerhard Kittel and tr. by Geoffrey W. Bromiley), III. Grand Rapids: Eerdmans, 1965, p. 447. The suggested etymology for *neos* is an Indo-European word from the adverb *nu,* "now, of the moment." *Kainos* is probably from a root *ken,* "freshly come, or begun." Notice while the aspect of *kind* of newness is stressed in our word *kainos,* the aspect of time is also present. Brevard S. Childs in *Myth and Reality in the O.T.* (2nd ed.). Naperville: SCM, 1962, p. 77, stresses that *hadas* is cognate to Semitic roots like Akkadian *edēšu,* meaning "to restore" ruined altars or cities.

35. Only in Heb. 12:24 is *neos* used of the covenant to stress the recent mediation of Christ's death as a surety for the new covenant. Hence it was recent in time.

36. Notice the crucial importance of this feature in dispensationalism in Charles Ryrie, *op. cit.,* pp. 52–61 and the strong disavowal in O. T. Allis, *Prophecy and the Church.* Philadelphia: Presbyterian and Reformed Publ. Co., 1945, pp. 31–48. See George N. H. Peters, *op. cit.,* I, p. 176. See the distinction between obligatory types (Sinai covenant) and promissory types (Abrahamic and Davidic covenants) by M. Weinfeld, "The Covenant Grant in the O.T. and in the Ancient Near East," *Journal of the American Oriental Society,* XC (1970), pp. 184–203. The "royal grant" treaties of the Ancient Near East with their gifts of land and dynasty are the models for the promissory form. If sustained, this will open new avenues of conversation with covenantal theologians.

37. As pointed out by Woudstra, *op. cit.,* p. 28 (cf. Lev. 26:15 and Jer. 11:10 to Ezek. 16:59).

38. See the writer's discussion, "Leviticus 18:5 and Paul: Do This and You Shall Live (Eternally?)," *JETS,* XIV (1971), pp. 21–24, esp. n. 27.

39. See Archibald Hughes, *A New Heaven and A New Earth.* Philadelphia: Presbyterian and Reformed Publ. Co., 1958, pp. 115 ff. Also Martin J. Wyngaarden, *The Future of the Kingdom in Prophecy and Fulfillment.* Grand Rapids: Baker Book House, 1955, p. 133. He knows that Hebrews 6:17, 18 makes the Abrahamic covenant "immutable," but he quickly restricts it to the promise of children, passing the promise of the holy land over to the Christians' heavenly hope! Roderick Campbell, *Israel and the New Covenant.* Philadelphia: Presbyterian and Reformed Publ. Co., 1954, pp. 199–205, uses I Samuel 2:30, 35 (rejection of Eli's family from the priesthood) and I Samuel 13:13–14 (rejection of Saul from everlasting kingdom) as texts which put limits on the *colam* of what would otherwise appear to be unconditional prophecies. Cf. Patrick Fairbairn, *Prophecy . . .* (2nd ed., 1856), chap. IV and part I. But did God obliterate the priesthood or kingship in Israel? Wasn't it only a question of who participated in it, not whether or not it was fulfilled?

40. For a fuller discussion of this point, see the writer's paper, "Leviticus 18:5 and Paul," *op. cit.* Subsequent to writing this article I discovered J. O. Buswell, Jr., *A Systematic Theology of the Christian Religion.* Grand Rapids: Zondervan, 1962, pp. 314–20.

41. "The New Covenant and the Old," in *The O.T. and Christian Faith* (ed. by Bernhard W. Anderson). New York: Harper and Row, 1963, p. 230, n. 11. He also notes on p. 229 that "the particle *ki* is employed effectively to introduce the decisive moments in the movement of thought." The first in v. 33 is adversative, and the other two in v. 34 are

climactic *ki* usages. For this climactic use he cites James Muilenburg, "The Linguistic and Rhetorical Usage of the Particle *Ki* in the O.T.," *HUCA*, XXXII (1961), pp. 135 ff.

42. C. F. Keil, *The Prophecies of Jeremiah*, II. Grand Rapids: Eerdmans, 1956, pp. 38–39.

43. Ex. 34:6, 7; Num. 14:18; Deut. 5:9, 10; Psa. 86:15; Joel 2:13; Jonah 4:1; Jer. 34:18; Neh. 9:17.

44. Henry Melvill, *The Golden Lectures: Forty-Six Sermons Delivered at St. Margaret's Church, Lothbury on Tuesday Mornings from January 1 to December 23, 1856.* London: James Paul. The sermon delivered on March 18, 1856 entitled "The Jewish and Christian Sacrifices" is an excellent exposition of Leviticus 16. One of the most stimulating discussions on this general subject to appear recently from an evangelical pen is that by Geoffrey W. Grogan, "The Experience of Salvation in the Old and New Testaments," *Vox Evangelica* (ed. Donald Guthrie), 1967, pp. 4–26.

45. So great is the continuity factor that Wilbur B. Wallis believes Jeremiah is using an ironical figure of speech when he calls it a new covenant. "Irony in Jeremiah's Prophecy of the New Covenant," *JETS*, XII (1969), pp. 107–10.

46. Jeremiah does not mean possessing intellectual data only, but in accordance with his usage in Jeremiah 22:15, 16 it is a knowledge which results in appropriate action and living. No doubt this is the explanation of the apparent contradiction of not needing teachers in Jeremiah 31:34 and the need for the Lord to teach in that day in Isaiah 2:3. No one will need to say, "Get with it; don't you know Yahweh is King." All will "know" that and act accordingly!

47. John J. Mitchell, "Abram's Understanding of the Lord's Covenant," *Westminster Theological Journal*, XXXII (1969–70), p. 39. Cf. Gen. 22:16–18.

48. ". . . He is the Mediator of the New Covenant, that by means of death . . . they which are called might receive the promise of eternal inheritance" (Heb. 9:15). George N. H. Peters comments, "This promise, let the reader notice, of inheriting the land forever is found in the Abrahamic covenant." *Op. cit.*, p. 322. Again on pp. 397–98 he comments: "We cannot too strongly insist upon *this necessary engrafting* of Gentile believers, so that by virtue of a *real relationship* they . . . may inherit. For, it has become a great and radical *defect* in many, if not nearly all, of our systems of theology to overlook the reason *why* a seed must be raised up *unto* Abraham, and to proceed in their elucidations of the subject, as if Abraham and the Jews had very *little* to do with the matter. This is a very *serious fundamental* blunder, violating unity." For support he cites Ephesians 2:12 about Gentiles being "aliens from the commonwealth of Israel" and "strangers from the covenants of promise" and Ephesians 2:19 about our being "strangers and foreigners, but now fellow-citizens with the saints, and of the household of God." In Ephesians 3:6 the believing Gentiles become "fellow-heirs of the same body and partakers of his promise in Christ by the gospel." Engrafting into the Jewish olive tree (Rom. 11:17–25) is necessary because "salvation is of the Jews" (John 4:22); and since there is only one fold and one shepherd, Jesus wishes to bring the "other sheep . . . which are not of this fold" (John 10:16). To see a stimulating, but ambivalent attempt to handle this question of the "New Inheritance," consult Roderick Campbell's chapter in *Israel and the New Covenant*. Philadelphia: Presbyterian and Reformed Publ. Co., 1954, pp. 157–64. The best word study on the O.T. and N.T. words is by J. Herrmann in *TDNT*, III, pp. 769–76 and in the same vol. L. H. Foerster, pp. 781–85.

49. See John Bright, "An Exercise in Hermeneutics: Jeremiah 31:31–34," *Interpretation*, XX (1966), pp. 188–210, esp. pp. 144, 195, 198.

50. Jakob Jocz, *The Covenant: A Theology of Human Destiny*. Grand Rapids: Eerdmans, 1968, p. 244. Also E. W. Hengstenberg, *Christology of the O.T.*, II. Edinburgh: T.&T. Clark, 1872, pp. 424–45. On p. 433 he calls the difference between the old and the new "a relative one only, not an absolute one." On p. 432 he says, "The new covenant . . . is in substance the realization of the old." John Calvin in his commentary on Jeremiah 31:31 ff. agrees: "The substance remains the same."

51. Most recent dispensationalists see two (!) new covenants in the N.T. This only avoids half of the truth to which the covenantal theologians are pointing. For exceptionally clear, but similarly worded statements cf. John Walvoord, "The New Covenant with Israel," *Bibliotheca Sacra*, CIX (1953), pp. 193–205; John Walvoord, "The New Covenant with Israel." *Bib. Sac.*, CIII (1946), pp. 16–27; Charles Ryrie, *Basis of Premillennial Faith*. New

York: Loizeaux Press, 1953, pp. 105–25; Dwight Pentecost, *Things to Come: A Study in Biblical Eschatology*. Grand Rapids: Zondervan, 1964, pp. 116–28.

52. This is only to respect the authorial will in Romans 11. While we are in general agreement with the dispensationalist hermeneutic, we cannot go as far as Charles Ryrie goes in *Dispensationalism Today,* p. 154: "If the dispensational emphasis on the distinctiveness of the church seems to result in a dichotomy, let it stand as long as it is a result of a literal interpretation." This is to play Pentecost off against the promise and the engrafting process at the expense of the latter.

53. See the delightful study of George Ladd, *The Gospel of the Kingdom*. Grand Rapids: Eerdmans, 1959.

John J. Collins

History and Tradition
in the Prophet Amos

*This is the second of two essays on the important biblical
topic of salvation history. See the headnote to Walter C.
Kaiser, Jr.'s essay, pp. 106–107, for background information.*

T HE historical nature of revelation has very often been emphasized in
biblical theology in this century. All shades of scholarly opinion,
from German existentialists to American archaeologists, have agreed that
the biblical material is marked by a 'historical' character. This unanimity
has, however, been bought at the price of considerable ambiguity, as
various scholars have understood the term 'history' in widely different
ways.[1]

The ambiguities have been most clearly exposed in New Testament
scholarship in the contrast between Rudolph Bultmann and Oscar
Cullmann.[2] For Bultmann the important thing is 'historicity'—existence
in time within the limitations of humanity. For Cullmann, by contrast,
the important aspect of history is the recollection of the mighty deeds of
Yahweh as a history of salvation.

In Old Testament scholarship the role of the 'history of salvation' has
been seldom questioned. Some scholars, such as G. E. Wright, might
emphasize the objective occurrence of the events in question.[3] Others,
such as Gerhard von Rad, might stress the faith of the community.[4]
However, the great majority of biblical scholars have agreed that all the
main branches of the Old Testament literature (except perhaps the wisdom literature) are based on the traditions of Yahweh's saving acts in
history.[5] In particular the dependence of the prophets on tradition has
been emphasized.[6] Only recently has this consensus been challenged,
particularly in the work of George Fohrer and his student Jochen Vollmer.[7]

In this essay I will attempt to clarify the issues which divide von Rad
and Cullmann, on the one hand, and Fohrer and Vollmer on the other.[8]
Then I will discuss these issues with reference to the book of Amos, since

From John J. Collins, *Irish Theological Quarterly*, 41 (1974), 120–33.

this book offers least indication of dependence on tradition and so poses most problems for the widely accepted concept of 'salvation history'.

We may begin, then, with some remarks on what is meant by 'salvation history'. As expounded by Oscar Cullmann[9] it involves three stages:

First, there is the 'naked event', the brute historical occurrence. This can be seen by anyone present, but may be interpreted in various ways. It does not necessarily involve a revelation for everyone who witnesses it.

Second, there is the revelation to one or more witnesses that the event is an act of God. This means that the act is meaningful in view of a divine purpose.

Third, the event and the particular interpretation which construes it as a revelation are associated with other events which have been interpreted as revelations. Then these events are seen to be coherent and to form together a divine plan.[10]

We find such events grouped together in a number of places in the Old Testament in the form of historical credos. Von Rad has drawn attention to these credos in Deut 26:5-10; Deut 6:20-24 and Josh. 24:1-13.[11] Each of these, in the words of von Rad, is 'out and out a confession of faith'.[12] The confessional character survived even in the final form of the Hexateuch. The credos remained of relevance for each successive generation 'because of a latent contemporaneousness'.[13]

These credos, however, did not exhaust the history of salvation. That history was being constantly supplemented by new acts of God. Cullmann writes: 'Each time a new event is added, the whole perspective is simultaneously changed in the light of it, and so also is the relationship to the eschatological events yet to come. It must not, of course, be forgotten that the new events give the cause for the reinterpretations, and that the kerygma therefore develops further because it is bound to a sequence of events. . . . The notion of development is in fact quite basic to the Bible'.[14] The history of salvation then is not something which has been completed once for all. It is a series of ongoing events which can be described as a development in the sense that each new event provides new insights.

The association of these events is not arbitrary. There is a unifying principle which warrants their association. This principle is the election of Israel, and it is illustrated in some way in each event of the history of salvation. Again we quote Cullmann: 'The prophet is not just a solitary man; he still stands in the salvation-historical tradition. When because of new events and revelations he places this tradition in a new perspective, for instance in prophesying judgment, nevertheless the *constant* of the tradition, the *election of Israel* for the salvation of mankind, is not done away with, but is more closely defined on the basis of new events, and thus the idea of election is corrected.'[15] This is also affirmed by von Rad.[16]

The belief in the election of Israel is essentially what roots the prophets in the tradition of salvation history. Apart from that, von Rad admits that they are often at variance with tradition: 'The comfortable words of the tradition are, however, both called in question by the prophet's message of judgment and reconverted by him into an antitypical new form of prediction.'[17] Even more, 'This conviction of theirs, that what has existed till now is broken off, placed them basically outside the saving tradition as it had been understood up to then by Israel.'[18]

There is an apparent contradiction here in von Rad's thought. How can he 'regard their whole preaching as a unique discussion of these ancient inherited traditions, a discussion which submitted them to criticism, and made them relevant for the prophet's own day and generation'[19], and yet say that they were 'basically outside the salvation history'? It is important that they were 'outside the salvation history *as it had been understood up to then by Israel*'. They break, not with salvation history as such, but with the particular understanding of it prevalent in Israel. They still, according to von Rad, retain a belief in the essential element of salvation history, the election of Israel.[20]

The foregoing are the essential aspects of salvation history as described by von Rad and Cullmann. The understanding of the prophets which they have put forward in this context has been directly attacked by Fohrer, and in great detail, by Vollmer.

Fohrer agrees that the prophets knew and used old traditions and are not to be understood as great religious personalities who pioneered ethical monotheism.[21] However, he insists that the question '*how* the prophets used tradition' is more important than '*whether* they used tradition'. He finds that they typically inverted the meaning of traditions—especially using traditions which promise salvation, to threaten doom.

The prophets refer to certain past events, but these events do not constitute a continuous chain. Accordingly, Fohrer thinks it inappropriate to speak of 'salvation history' in any sense that might be given to the term.[22] He finds no trace of a belief in a divine plan comprehending all history in the prophets,[23] and in fact finds that the actions of Yahweh most often referred to by the prophets are actions of destruction. The operative factors in history are Israel's sins and Yahweh's acts of destruction.[24] Instead of a 'history of salvation' Fohrer would speak of a 'history of decision'.[25] What recurs are not saving acts by Yahweh, but situations in which Israel has to choose whether to continue sinning or return to Yahweh.

The idea of a 'history of decision' is not necessarily at variance with 'salvation history'. The fact, emphasized by Fohrer, that the prophets call for a *decision* to be made in the present is also fundamental to salvation history as conceived by Cullmann and von Rad. However, in the context of salvation history, the recurring *situations of decision* are unified by the constant element—the belief in the election of Israel. Fohrer denies that this concept of an election of Israel has any place, at least in the pre-exilic prophets. In fact he alleges that it originated with the book of Deuteronomy.[26]

Fohrer asserts that Israel's history was not essentially different, in the view of the prophets, from the history of the rest of the world. It was a 'particular case' of God's universal work, distinguished only by a 'close relationship' between Yahweh and Israel, by which Israel was 'my people'.[27] At this point it is difficult to regard Fohrer's argument as more than a quibble. If Israel stood in a 'close relationship' to Yahweh, so that it was 'his people', is not this an election, even if no technical term is used? However, Fohrer is trying to minimize the distinction between Israel and the other peoples, and to give this distinction a far less prominent role than it has in the salvation history approach. He also eliminates the distinction between 'salvation history' and 'history' which is stressed by Cullmann.

Again in his treatment of the historical flashbacks in the prophets, Fohrer's difference from the salvation history approach is not as great as it may seem. Referring to the references to the Exodus in Hosea and Jeremiah, and to David and Solomon in Isaiah, he admits that there was an ideal period in the past and that it would have persisted if Israel had been obedient.[28] So he speaks of an 'initial possibility' which Israel failed to realize. This conception is essentially compatible with the salvation history approach. By creating the initial possibility Yahweh began the history of salvation. This history did not then develop in a straight line: Israel deviated. However, while the possibility remained open to Israel, it was still possible to speak of Israel as 'elected' by God and of God's will for Israel's salvation—and so at least of the possibility of a salvation history.

The real point at issue in Fohrer's criticism of the salvation history approach is whether it is conceivable that Yahweh might actually remove the possibility of decision and so doom Israel to definitive destruction.

We now turn to the evidence of the prophetic texts. I choose the prophet Amos, because in his oracles the problem of the relation to tradition is most acute. Unlike most of the other prophets, Amos does not speak of a new beginning which might make possible a renewal of salvation history,[29] but preaches unqualified doom.

INDICATIONS OF AN ELECTION-TRADITION IN AMOS

There are a few passages in the book of Amos which indicate that he was aware of a tradition of election and of Yahweh's acts of salvation. The clearest of these passages can be found in Amos 3:1-2: 'Hear this word, O men of Israel, that the Lord pronounces over you, over the whole family that I brought up from the land of Egypt. You alone have I known, from all the families of the earth. Therefore will I punish you for all your crimes.'[30]

Two things are apparent from this. First, Amos knows and accepts the tradition that Yahweh chose Israel exclusively from among the nations of the earth. This in itself should refute Fohrer's argument that the election of Israel was a later, Deuteronomic idea. Second, Vollmer is probably right that the statement of election was taken over by Amos from his adversaries. The unexpected consequence which Amos derives from it—that Yahweh will punish Israel—is clearly intended to shock by the contrast with the popular expectation that Yahweh would bless Israel. Amos is prepared to accept the fact of the election provided the consequences are properly understood.

The reasoning of Amos in this passage is probably identical with what we find in 5:18, where he speaks of the day of Yahweh: 'Woe to you who desire the day of Yahweh . . . it is darkness, not light'. Here again he evidently accepts the datum of popular tradition but inverts its consequences. There would indeed be a day of Yahweh, but it would not have the result expected by Israel.

The question arises whether Amos really accepts the fact of the election of Israel, or whether he merely takes it over from his adversaries for the sake of argument. The latter view has been strongly argued by Vollmer. The statement that Yahweh knew only Israel from all the nations of the earth is contradicted by Yahweh's interest in the nations in 1:3–2:3. Most of all it is contradicted by a striking passage in Amos 9:7: 'Are you not like the Cushites to me, sons of Israel, says Yahweh. Did I not bring Israel up from the land of Egypt and the Philistines from Caphtor and Aram from Kir?'

Here Amos seems to obliterate any distinction between the history of Israel and that of other nations. Are we to conclude that there had never been any distinction, or simply that the distinction is no longer valid? I believe the latter is the easier conclusion. Yahweh acted in the history of several nations but Amos could scarcely have claimed that he 'knew' them in the sense of revealing himself to them. Certainly this passage poses problems for any theory of salvation history, and we will return to those problems. It does not, however, prove that Amos was ignorant of, or rejected, the tradition that Yahweh elected Israel. He does at least admit that Yahweh brought Israel out of Egypt.

What then is the meaning of those two passages? They are primarily denunciations of the way in which Israel had abused the election-tradition by making it a basis of false hopes and security. The election had not given Israel any unconditional status. Rather it gave responsibility. That is why it can be the cause of punishment for Israel. If the conditions inherent in the election are not met, then the acts of Yahweh, such as the Exodus, cannot guarantee salvation. Salvation may be a gift of Yahweh, but it is given on condition of Israel's obedience. Without that obedience Israel's 'history of salvation' is no different from the history of the Cushites.

The conditional nature of Yahweh's activity for Israel is emphasized in Amos 2:9–12:

> It was I who destroyed the Amorites before them, who were as tall as the cedars, and as strong as the oak trees. I destroyed their fruit above and their roots beneath. It was I who brought you up from the land of Egypt, and who led you through the desert for forty years, to occupy the land of the Amorites; I who raised up prophets among your sons and Nazirites among your young men.

This is Amos' closest approximation to a recitation of salvation history, but his story lacks the happy ending of the credos in the Hexateuch. Israel failed to respond: 'You gave the Nazirites wine to drink, and commanded the prophets not to prophesy'. Therefore the salvation history becomes null and void: 'I will crush you into the ground as a wagon crushes when laden with sheaves'.

Vollmer (p. 27) denies that this passage shows any recognition of an election-tradition on Amos' part. It is true that Amos cannot be said to proclaim the *actualization* of the tradition or its continued validity, but he surely recognizes that this tradition is the basis on which the present situation must be understood. If Israel is about to be destroyed, this is not the result of an arbitrary decision of Yahweh, but of its own failure to respond to Yahweh. If Israel had never been chosen, its crime would be less grave. This is apparent to the prophet because he stands at the end of the tradition and he owes his insight not to the tradition but to revelation.[31] However, in the actual course of events as the prophet expounds them, the end is a consequence of the tradition.

Vollmer and Fohrer underestimate the role of tradition. Vollmer hints at a better understanding on p. 28 when he asserts that Amos bases his proclamation of the end of the tradition on the tradition itself.[32] The tradition is important for Amos because it determines the horizons of his understanding. This is true not only of the obvious fact that both he and his audience recognize the same God Yahweh and acknowledge that he has acted in the past. Even the new action of Yahweh which Amos sees is patterned on his traditional mode of action. In the 'day of Yahweh' Yahweh will destroy Israel, rather than her enemies, but he will indeed be manifest as a warrior. The way in which the tradition determines the new event is more obvious when the prophets look ahead to a new beginning—such as the 'new exodus' in Hosea or Second Isaiah.

The tradition is important in that it supplies the prophet's basic ideas about God. Is this, however, what we normally mean by salvation history? When Amos threatens the destruction of the chosen people does he not negate what Cullmann alleged was the 'constant' of the tradition—the election of Israel?

THE CONDITIONAL NATURE OF THE ELECTION

The answer to this question depends on whether we conceive the original election to have been absolute or conditional. If the tradition asserted that God had chosen Israel as the instrument for his divine plan for the world, then it appears that he abandoned his original plan in the eighth and seventh centuries B.C. If on the other hand the tradition had merely asserted that God had set an option before Israel, and would punish or bless her according to her choice, then we can indeed affirm that the tradition was not disrupted.

The question whether the original election was a conditional one is essentially the question whether the covenant, as we find it in the book of Deuteronomy, can be dated back to the time of Moses or was original with Deuteronomy and a product of the preaching of the prophets. The majority of scholars in recent years have favoured an early date, especially since the work of G. E. Mendenhall.[33] A number of scholars have sharply disputed this, however, notably Fohrer and his disciples.[34]

The question of the origin of the covenant is too wide to be discussed here. However, no one can deny that the application of the idea of the covenant has cast much light on the use of history in the prophets. In the covenant form, as described by Mendenhall, the recitation of history is not an end in itself but provides the motivation for the observance of the covenant law. In the prophets the recall of history gives the reason why Israel will be punished for breaking the covenant law. The prophetic oracles can often be understood as lawsuits impeaching Israel for breach of covenant.[35]

Whether the prophetic oracles were composed with reference to covenant-form then in existence, or rather shaped that form by their own new vision, that form provides a very illuminating model for their use of history. In this context the election was essentially conditional and could be completely revoked. There is no pre-determined plan of history. God acted in history in the past to make possible an option for Israel. The future of history depended on Israel's response.

If this view of history which the prophets preached corresponded to an original covenant in the time of Moses, then we can say that the prophets are pitting one tradition against another or recalling Israel to the original form of the tradition. However, it is quite certain that they opposed the election-tradition in the unconditional form current at their time. This is quite clear from the way in which Amos inverts the expectations of the people and foretells darkness where they expected light.

TRADITION AS A STYLE OF THEOLOGY

The prophetic attack on tradition is even more fundamental in another respect. It involves not only the rejection of specific traditions but also the rejection of the whole style of theology which relies on the recitation of the past as a source of security in the present.

In general, the preaching of the prophets was directed against all forms of false security. In particular, they often attacked the sacrificial cult for this reason.[36] It is important to realize that the recitation of salvation history was just as big an occasion for complacency as the sacrificial cult.

There are a number of instances where this is made explicit in the prophetic writings. Yahweh had chosen the temple as his dwelling place according to the traditions of Jerusalem. Yet Jeremiah scoffs at the people: 'Put not your trust in the deceitful words: "This is the temple of the Lord! the temple of the Lord! the temple of the Lord!"' (Jer 7:4). Yahweh would only abide in the land if the people reformed their ways, but 'here you are, putting your trust in deceitful words to your own loss' (Jer 7:8).

The 'words' in which Israel trusted were nothing other than the tradition of her own election, a tradition which had been perverted: 'How can you say, "We are wise, we have the law of the Lord?" Why, that has been changed into falsehood by the lying pen of the scribes' (Jer 8:8).

The use of tradition as a false source of security is also evident in Hosea (8:1): 'They have violated my covenant while to me they cried out, "God, we Israel know you".'

This abuse of salvation history is what led Amos to set the Exodus on a par with the history of the Cushites, and to say that the only fruit of Israel's election would be her utter destruction. Amos was not saying that Yahweh had never chosen Israel or brought her out of Egypt. He was saying that the recitation of past events is not a substitute for an ethical response to God.

The point Amos was making and its significance in cultural history may be illustrated by a comparison with Plato's criticism of Homer and the use of epic poetry in Greek education. E. A. Havelock has analysed that criticism rather well:

> There was a state of mind which we shall conveniently label the 'poetic' or 'Homeric' or 'oral' state of mind which constituted the chief obstacle to scientific rationalism, to the use of analysis, to the classification of experience, to its rearrangement in sequence of cause and effect. That is why the poetic mind is for Plato the arch-enemy and it is easy to see why he considered this enemy so formidable. He is entering the lists against centuries of habituation in rhythmic, memorized experience. He asks of men that they should think about what they say, instead of just saying it. And they should separate themselves from it instead of identifying with it; they themselves should become the 'subject' who stands apart from the 'object' and reconsiders it and analyses it, and evaluates it, instead of just 'imitating' it.[37]

The analogy is particularly apt in several respects—primarily for the similarities between the use of Homer in the Greek tradition and of the cultic credo in Israel. Recent research has made clear that the basic Exodus tradition was originally passed on in the form of an epic poem.[38] It used all the poetic devices of rhythm and structure to facilitate assimilation by its audience. It was originally passed on orally, so that a great emphasis was placed on retention by memory. Because of this technique of transmission, constant recitation in the cult (or elsewhere) was necessary. Accordingly the energies of the faithful were concentrated on the preservation and repetition of the past.

The prophets reacted against this style of theology, even as Plato reacted against the 'poetic state of mind'. Unlike Plato, their protest was not made in the name of rational science. There was, however, considerable similarity. Like Plato, their objective was to break down complacency and routine, and stimulate consciousness in the activities of men. Both desired that people deal critically with the situation at hand and not automatically glide along in the status quo.

Plato sought to replace the repetition of the past by the contemplation of timeless ideas. Amos, bound by the traditional conception of a God who acts in history, sought to replace the repetition of the past with the expectation of a new event in the future. This future expectation became the hallmark of prophetic religion. It marks a decisive point of transition in Israelite religion. Hitherto the religion had been focused on the past as a source of security. Henceforward it was focused on the future. Since the future was not yet decided, it was less likely to be a source of complacency.[39]

I suggest, then, that the understanding of history which we find in the prophet Amos is distinct both from the salvation history of Cullmann and von Rad and from the viewpoint of Fohrer. It attaches more importance to tradition than Fohrer would allow, in the sense that the horizons of the prophet's vision and his conception of God are determined by tradition. On the other hand, it rejects, first, the recitation of history as a style of theology. Second, it refuses to regard the election of Israel as an absolutely fixed datum. Because nothing is determined, and there is no plan for the world's history which is not absolutely dependent on conditions, Fohrer's 'history of decision' appears more appropriate for Amos' view of history than the term 'history of salvation'.

THE DEFICIENCIES OF THE 'SALVATION HISTORY' APPROACH

The validity of the latter two points as criticism of the salvation history approach may be questioned, and requires further elaboration. Neither von Rad nor Cullmann would deny that there was a conditional element in the election of Israel or that the recitation of history must lead to decision. However, there are important details in which 'salvation history' is not applicable to the preaching of the prophet.

First, we may consider the prophetic criticism of theology as the recitation of history. Undoubtedly, the recitation of history is quite compatible with good ethical conduct. Within the prophetic literature we often find recitations of history as a basis for judgment. The implication is that the recall of God's saving deeds should have evoked an ethical response from Israel. This is the logic of the so-called 'prophetic lawsuit', as we find it, for example, in Amos 4:4–13.[40] Within the framework of the covenant the recitation of history had a place as the motivation for action.

However, the fact remains that the recitation of history had failed to produce the intended response in Israel, and had on the contrary become a further source of complacency. The salvation history approach of Cullmann and von Rad seems to lack awareness of this danger. This lack of awareness is related to a failure to appreciate the full significance of the prophet's openness to the future. Nothing is finally decided by the past. Not even the election of Israel.

This brings us to the second and major criticism. The salvation history approach underestimates the absolutely conditional nature of divine election. Cullmann describes the conditional element in history as follows:

> From the human point of view, quite apart from man's sin contingency belongs to the manner in which God's plan develops. In the Bible, the movement and purpose of the plan are revealed at the start, but not the particular stages in it. They are disclosed for the first time in the events as they occur. The continuing execution of the divine plan, and its association with contingency, lapses and detours, is expressed in a Portuguese proverb. . . . 'God writes straight, but with crooked lines'.[41]

Cullmann is here taking over a viewpoint from later Jewish apocalyptic and the New Testament, that God had planned out the course of history from creation to the last judgment. Neither he nor von Rad would claim that a prophet such as Amos was aware of this, but both would feel justified, as Christian theologians, in applying this viewpoint in their interpretation of the prophets. The destruction by Assyria and Babylon may have seemed to the prophets to mark the end of salvation history, but time proved that this was not so. In fact the election of Israel was maintained after the exile, irrespective of the prophecies of Amos. Amos then did not share the viewpoint of salvation history, but nevertheless was himself a particular instant of that history, though without perspective on the whole.

This viewpoint is essentially derived from the Christian conviction that the New Testament is the culmination of the Old, and provides categories by which the Old can be understood.[42] Even within this Christian perspective, objections can be raised. The element which was allegedly constant in salvation history—the election of Israel—is either broken off or only preserved in a very weakened analogical sense in the New Testament. St Paul tries valiantly in Romans 3 to establish that there was some advantage to being a Jew, but his final conclusion was that 'God has no favourites' (Rom 2:11). In the New Testament, as in Amos, ethical decision was of greater importance than adherence to a tradition. Also, the recognition of God in the present situation was of greater importance than recognizing him in the past.

There remains some place for salvation history. Past revelation is one source of the knowledge of God. But this place is entirely subordinate. Most of all, it determines nothing finally. While the revelation of God in the history of Israel is a useful pointer to his character, it is not an exclusive or even necessary revelation. Salvation is by conduct, not by tradition. Even the tradition itself affirms this.

HISTORICAL CONTINUITY IN THE BIBLE

There remains the fact of a certain undisputed degree of continuity in biblical history. The prophets show links with the earlier religion of Israel. Apocalyptic was largely a development of prophecy. This continuity cannot establish a special category of 'salvation history'. It is no more than the continuity to be found in the history of any nation.

The idea of the election by Yahweh played a prominent part in the developing continuity of Israelite religion. However, the greatest impulses in that religion—the teaching of the prophets, and again of Jesus—appear as correctives of that idea, and ultimately deny it. It should be noted that even the idea of a remnant, found in the pre-exilic Isaiah, represents a departure from the idea of a chosen people. Election was no longer determined purely by race. In this way the door was opened for universalism and the belief that all races are equal before God.

The idea of election played its part in the formation of the nation with its distinct consciousness. Later, when it became a source of false security, it constituted an obstacle in the way of true religion. The final message of the Israelite (and Christian) tradition is that no people can claim to be the exclusive elect of God or depend on a past tradition for salvation.[43]

NOTES

1. On the role of the category 'history' in biblical theology and the problems to which it has given rise see especially B. S. Childs, *Biblical Theology in Crisis* (Philadelphia:

Westminster Press, 1970) 39–44; 62–66; J. Barr, *Old and New in Interpretation* (London: SCM, 1966) 65–102.

2. Bultmann, *History and Eschatology* (New York: Harper and Row, 1957) and 'History of Salvation and History' in *Existence and Faith. Shorter Writings of Rudolf Bultmann*, ed. Schubert M. Ogden (London: Fontana, 1964) 226–40; Cullmann, *Christ and Time* (London: SCM, 1962) and *Salvation in History* (London: SCM, 1967).

3. G. E. Wright, *God Who Acts* (London: SCM, 1952).

4. G. von Rad, *Old Testament Theology*, Vol. I (Edinburgh and London: Oliver and Boyd, 1962) 105–28. For the contrast between Wright and von Rad, see Wright, 'History and the Patriarchs', *Expository Times* 71 (1960) 292–96 and von Rad's reply, 'History and the Patriarchs', *Expository Times* 72 (1961) 213–16.

5. Von Rad writes in *Old Testament Theology*, I, 106: 'In principle Israel's faith is grounded in a theology of history. It regards itself as based upon historical acts, and as shaped and re-shaped by factors in which it saw the hand of Yahweh at work. The oracles of the prophets also speak of events though there is the definite difference, that in general they stand in point of time not after, but prior to, the events to which they bear witness. Even where this reference to divine facts in history is not immediately apparent, as for example in some of the Psalms, it is, however, present by implication, and where it is actually absent, as for example in the Book of Job and Ecclesiastes, this very lack is closely connected with the grave affliction which is the theme of both these works.'

6. This emphasis has been largely a reaction against the view of Wellhausen and Duhm that the prophets were great creative personalities who developed a spiritual religion which owed little to tradition.

7. Fohrer, 'Prophetie und Geschichte' in *Studien zur Alttestamentlichen Prophetie* (Berlin: Töpelmann, 1967) 265–93; Vollmer, *Geschichtliche Rüchblicke und Motiv in der Prophetie des Amos, Hosea und Jesaja* (Berlin: de Gruyter, 1971).

8. These differences are far from obvious. So, for example, Cullmann believes he can dismiss Fohrer's objections by attributing to him 'a narrow concept of salvation history' (*Salvation in History* 86 n. 1).

9. *Salvation in History* 90.

10. I am not concerned here with the relationship between the event and the interpretation (or 'kerygma') which has been the subject of much debate. The prophets were not troubled by such epistemological and hermeneutical problems but believed, however naively, that their interpretation simply coincided with the facts. My concern here is simply with the views of the prophets, however naively held.

11. *Old Testament Theology*, I, 121–28.

12. *Idem* 122.

13. *Idem* 125.

14. *Salvation in History* 122.

15. *Idem* 92.

16. *Old Testament Theology*, II, 130. Cf. also Wright, *God Who Acts* 50.

17. *Idem* 130.

18. *Idem*, I, 128.

19. *Idem*, II, 138.

20. *Idem*, II, 130; von Rad says that 'tensions created by three factors bring the prophet's *kerygma* into being. These are the new eschatological word with which Yahweh addresses Israel, the old election-tradition, and the personal situation'.

21. Fohrer, 'Prophetie und Geschichte' 285.

22. *Idem* 288: 'Gewiss wird dieser Begriff in der Theologie in verschiedener Bedeutung gebraucht; doch keine Bedeutung trifft für die prophetische Bedeutung zu.'

23. The idea of a divine plan in history in the Old Testament is also disputed by Bertil Albrektson, *History and the Gods* (Lund: Gleerup, 1967) 68–97.

24. Fohrer, 'Prophetie und Geschichte' 279: '*Israels Sünde einerseits und Jahwes mahnende und warnende Plagen* sowie seine sonstigen Bemühungen *andererseits* sind für Propheten *die beiden hauptsächlichen Faktoren* zum Verstehen der palästinischen Geschichte Israels'.

25. *Idem* 289: 'immer war die Geschichte eine *Entscheidungsgeschichte*, war die jeweilige Gegenwart nach der prophetischen Gesamtbeurteilung der Widerfahrnisse Israels

eine *Entscheidungssituation* für Volk und Mensch—Entscheidung zwischen dem weiteren oder erneuten Abfall von Jahwe und der Rückkehr zu ihm'.

26. *Idem* 274-75.

27. *Idem* 274: 'Grundsätzlich erblicken sie im Wirken Jahweh in und an Israel eine Ausschnit aus seinem Handeln in bezug auf das Geschick der Völker und Menschen überhaupt. Es ist ein Sonderfall seines weltumfassenden Wirkens, bedingt durch seiendes Verhältnis zu Israel das "mein Volk" ist.'

28. *Idem* 276.

29. Von Rad, *Old Testament Theology*, II, 138, argues for the authenticity of the prophecy about the 'booth of David' in Amos 9, but admits that 'grave doubts' have been raised about it. I agree with Vollmer (p. 53) and most commentators, who regard this passage as a later addition. Even though Amos was a Judean, there is no other trace in the book of Amos of any interest in the Davidic monarchy. The passage could very naturally be explained as an addition when the oracles were being passed on in Judah.

30. Vollmer brackets the reference to the Exodus as a gloss because of the abrupt transition from the third to the first person (p. 29).

31. So Vollmer, rightly, p. 19. See also M.-L. Henry, *Prophet und Tradition* (Berlin: de Gruyter, 1969).

32. Cf. also R. Knierim, 'The Vocation of Isaiah', *Vetus Testamentum* 18 (1968) 63: 'Isaiah uses the theological tradition exclusively in order to justify his vision and the new message which proclaims the end of traditions.'

33. G. E. Mendenhall, 'Law and Covenant in Israel and the Ancient Near East', *Biblical Archaeologist* 17 (1954) 26-46 and 49-76. See also Klaus Baltzer, *The Covenant Formulary* (Oxford: Blackwell, 1971); Delbert Hillers, *Covenant, The History of a Biblical Idea* (Baltimore: Johns Hopkins Press, 1969); D. J. McCarthy, *Old Testament Covenant: A Survey of Current Opinions* (Oxford: Blackwell, 1972).

34. G. Fohrer, 'Altes Testament—"Amphiktyonie" und "Bund"?', *Theologische Literaturzeitung* 91 (1966) 801-16; 893-904; *Geschichte der Israelitischen Religion* (Berlin: de Gruyter, 1969) 78-83. Most recently E. Kutsch, *Verheissung und Gesetz* (Berlin: de Gruyter, 1973) has denied that there was any idea of a covenant between Yahweh and Israel before the book of Deuteronomy. For a typically comprehensive discussion of the election of Israel see H. H. Rowley, *The Biblical Doctrine of Election* (London: Lutterworth, 1950).

35. On the 'covenant lawsuit' see H. B. Huffmon, 'The Covenant Lawsuit in the Prophets', *Journal of Biblical Literature* 78 (1959) 285-95; J. Harvey, 'Le Rib-Pattern', *Biblica* 43 (1962) 172-96; G. E. Wright, 'The Law-suit of God' in *Israel's Prophetic Heritage*, eds. Anderson and Harrelson (New York, 1962) 41-67; W. Brueggemann, *Tradition for Crisis* (Richmond, Virginia: John Knox Press, 1968).

36. E.g. in the famous passage in Hosea 6:6, 'It is love that I desire, not sacrifice, and knowledge of God rather than holocausts.'

37. E. A. Havelock, *Preface to Plato* (Oxford: Blackwell, 1963) 47.

38. See W. F. Albright, *Yahweh and the Gods of Canaan* (New York: Doubleday, 1962) 1-52.

39. This is at least true of prophecy and the apocalyptic strands of later Judaism.

40. Cf. W. Brueggemann, 'Amos IV 4-13 and Israel's Covenant Worship'. *Vetus Testamentum* 15 (1965) 1-15.

41. *Salvation in History* 124-25.

42. For criticism of the application of the idea of a divine plan in history to the prophetic literature see Albrektson, *History and the Gods* 68-97.

43. Cf. H. J. Muller, *The Uses of the Past* (Oxford: University Press, 1952) 110-11: 'Ultimately both the glory and the tragedy of Israel sprang from the exalted inhuman conviction that they, and they alone, were God's chosen people. Chosen peoples are not apt to make good neighbours . . . In general the people were incapable of the humble, charitable attitude implicit in the teaching of their greatest prophets. The history of Israel, like the history of Christian Europe, suggests that no nation and no sect can afford to regard itself as the elect of God.'

_____Stanley Brice Frost_____

Apocalyptic and History

This is the revelation given by God to Jesus Christ so that he could tell his servants about the things which are now to take place very soon. (Rev. 1:1)

In Greek, "apocalyptic" means "to reveal." Between 200 B.C. and A.D. 100, a period of intense, intermittent persecution of the Jews and later the Christians, a literary form flourished which symbolically revealed to the faithful the eschatology or teachings of the end of time. The most extensive examples of this form are Daniel in the Old Testament, II Esdras in the Apocrypha, and Revelation in the New Testament. This is also the form of parts of Joel, Isaiah 24–27, Ezekiel 38–39, Zechariah 9–14, and the "little apocalypse" in the New Testament: Mark 13, Matthew 24, and Luke 21.

As Kaiser and Collins have demonstrated in the two previous essays, the court writers and prophets based their belief that God cared for the Israelites on the historical premise that he made them a great nation. However, the apocalyptic writers "did not, indeed could not," as Frost writes, "take mundane history seriously." Their faith in God's covenant with his people was founded instead on a revolutionary view of history: at a time known only to himself, God will end time. Meanwhile, the faithful must remain firm: their persecutions somehow offer proof that the end is drawing near.

Frost's essay reinforces our emphasis on milieu. In this case, the persecution of the Jews and later the Christians resulted in the birth of a new literary form and an alternate view of history.

MY TITLE, if spelt out in fuller detail, is the apocalyptic contribution to the biblical consideration of history.

From Stanley Brice Frost, *The Bible in Modern Scholarship* (1965), ed. J. P. Hyatt, pp. 98–113.

Much has indeed been claimed for the apocalyptic school of writers with regard to their view of history. Thus, for example, R. H. Charles wrote in the Introduction to his *Commentary on Daniel:* "Apocalyptic was a Semitic philosophy of religion and concerned itself with the questions of whence? wherefore? whither? It sketched in outline the history of the universe, and of the angelic and human worlds, the origin of evil, its course and ultimate overthrow. It was thus apocalyptic and not prophecy that was the first to grasp the great idea that all history, human, cosmological and spiritual, is a unity—a unity that follows inevitably as a corollary to the unity of God as enforced by the O.T. Prophets."[1] Similarly I myself wrote of the apocalyptists: "If their task was a theodicy, then their answer must be made good in the one sure medium of revelation— and that for the Hebrew was *history,* the story of what God had done in creation and providence . . . in their own strange way they were trying to view all history *sub specie aeternitatis,* and if they did not always get their facts clear, they were at least the first men to essay a philosophy of history."[2] D. S. Russell has recently expressed a more moderate view. He writes: "Such a claim, however, does less than justice to the Old Testament prophets and enhances the reputation of the apocalyptists in a way they hardly deserve. It is more accurate to regard the apocalyptists as middle men than as pioneers in this regard. What they did was to carry still further the sense of divine purpose, which was already to be found in the prophets, as the unifying principle of all human history."[3] The purpose of the present paper is to suggest that apocalyptic is best described neither as pioneering a philosophy of history nor as acting as interpreter of the view of history which had been expressed by the prophets, but rather as departing from that view as untenable, and turning to an expression of religious reality which, indeed, draws upon historical thinking but also upon prehistorical thinking, and offers a new and distinctive synthesis. We are well accustomed to calling the latter kind of thought myth, and the element derived from historical thinking we often call eschatology.[4] Thus, from the time of Gunkel, apocalyptic has been freely described as eschatologized myth. The tag ran *Urzeit wird Endzeit.* That apocalyptic thus identified represents within the complex of biblical thought a rejection of history as the medium in which religious truth is to be sought and expressed, has not, I believe, been so widely recognized.[5]

I

To give substance to this view we must see the apocalyptists in the perspective of the Bible as a whole and particularly in relation to some aspects of the biblical treatment of history, and so we begin by commenting on the nature of historiography in the OT. E. H. Carr has recently reminded us that: "It used to be said that the facts speak for themselves.

This is of course untrue. The facts speak only when the historian calls on them: it is he who decides to which facts to give the floor, and in what order and in what context," and reminds us that as long ago as 1894 James Anthony Froude remarked that history is "a child's box of letters with which we can spell any word we please."[6] The word which the Hebrews chose to spell was, they believed, the Word of God, but it is important to recognize that this was, from the human point of view, consciously or unconsciously, a matter of choice.[7] Further, we have to break down that "Word of God" into its constituent ideas, and in this way to inquire what were the ideas which the Hebrew history writers chose that their history should express.

It can be shown, I suggest, that Israel took over (as one would expect) the ideas of religion as they were familiar to her in the myths of the ancient Near East and reclothed those same fundamental notions in the dress of her own history. As a result of the work of Gunkel, Hooke, Frankfort, Engnell, Mowinckel, and others, we have been able to recognize that the dominant themes of ancient mythology were six-fold: the divine conflict with and victory over the forces of chaotic evil, the divine creation of the existing order, the kingly relation of the divine to the creation, the worship which is the creation's proper response to that sovereignty, the vitality of the divine as expressed in the death and resurrection motif, and the divine fertility expressed in the sacred marriage. It is fundamentally these same ideas which Israel's history is made to express by the early biblical historiographical tradition, though, of course, there is much modification, redistribution of emphasis, and an all-important selectivity.[8] The result is a fresh, highly characteristic Hebrew version of the basic complex of religious ideas which evolved in the ancient Near East. Thus the conflict of Marduk and Tiamat (to use the terminology of the Babylonian variant) becomes the conflicts of Yahweh and the successive enemies of Israel.[9] The creation of the world is paralleled by the creation of Israel,[10] and the kingly relationship is expressed very appropriately in terms of covenant.[11] The motif of worship appears in the mythology as the need for Marduk to have built for him *esagila,* the ziggurat of Babylon; or again as the need for Baal, fresh from the conquest of Prince Yamm, to have a house built for him by 'El's command. This is expressed in Hebrew historiography as the need to provide a tabernacle or house for Yahweh after his victory—especially the success of Israel under David over the Canaanites, the last and greatest in the series of victories that were recorded no doubt in the "Book of the Wars of Yahweh."[12] Israel was, however, hesitant as to how to express the vitality of God as testified by the dying and rising myth. Her teachers shifted the relationship of the motif from Yahweh to a number of surrogates closely allied to him and yet separate from him. Thus the story of the defeat of Israel and the capture of the ark, its descent into the House of Dagon and its triumphant return from thence, has been recognized as one of the Hebrew expressions of this theme; and A. R. Johnson has found reason to think that the theme also expressed itself in the role of the king in the Jerusalem cultus. Again, the dying and rising role is transferred from the divinity not only to his ark, or to his Messiah, but also later to his people, Israel, who undergo death at the exile and are resurrected to life in the return.[13] Perhaps the most striking feature of Hebrew religion is its almost total rejection of the fertility motif. True, it provided the metaphor of the marriage relationship of Yahweh and Israel and its converse, the adultery metaphor which referred to the worship of other gods, but otherwise the divine sexuality was the one major theme of ancient Near Eastern mythology which Israel refused.[14] In the early days, this resulted in a divorce between Yahweh and the natural order, but it was later corrected by a vigorous doctrine of world creation and world providence, as distinct from Israel creation and Israel providence.[15]

The history was made to convey these ideas by means of a teleological interpretation. The patriarchal traditions, the descent into Egypt, the exodus, the wanderings in the desert, the conquest, were built into a saga wherein Israel was the chosen people of Yahweh and wherein his activity could be plainly discerned as bringing the tribes through many crises to the splendid goal of being a people, with a god, an identity, a law, a land of their own. No doubt the *telos* to which the history led was not a wholly static concept, and by the time *Heilsgeschichte* first achieved something like literary form at the hands of the Yahwist, it had become the Davidic Kingdom, with the reigning Judean king as Yahweh's Messiah. A little later, when the division of the kingdom and the resultant political weakness made the present seem less than wholly desirable, the goal was no longer thought of as attained, but was put off into the future as something yet to come. The *Yom Yahweh*, the *telos* in which *Heilsgeschichte* must finally fulfill itself, became in the teaching of the prophets the sustaining hope of Israel. It was an end which had indeed once been achieved, in the time of David and Solomon,[16] and would assuredly be given to a loyal Israel once again. But it is important to notice that this Golden Age was to come within history, and as a result of Yahweh's control of history.

II

History, then, and not myth, was the medium in which Israel's religious understanding found expression. A change of medium, however, inevitably affected profoundly the character of the ideas themselves. Notably, the covenant relationship became more prominent and with it the Torah, in which the Hebrew's obligations to his god were set forth. In the hands of the prophets, however, this appeal to history was given a natural but dangerous turn. If Israel was asked to read her past history in terms of a revelation of her God, his nature, his power, his will, it was only to be expected that this same divine activity should also be looked for in current events. This task the prophets undertook; but whereas it had been comparatively easy to impose a standard interpretation upon past history, it was by no means so easy to do so with regard to contemporary history. First, there was the problem that the interpreters disagreed among themselves. The disagreement came to a head at the time of the great crisis of Israel's existence, the Babylonian attack upon the Judean state at the beginning of the sixth century B.C. How deep was the cleavage and how bitter the quarrel between the adherents of the two interpretations, the book of Jeremiah reveals in numerous passages.[17] This inability of her experts to agree upon the interpretation of those all-important events dealt a severe blow to the belief that history could convey a revelation of the divine mind, a blow from which that belief never fully recovered. Secondly, while it was possible in the early post-exilic period to make a massive effort to interpret the disaster which had befallen Israel as the punitive will of Yahweh, the long Persian domination and its immediate sequel, the prolonged Greek domination, made a similar explanation of contemporary history more and more unconvincing. The burden laid upon credulity is well expressed by the seer in II Esdras, a comparatively late work in which this dissatisfaction is given overt expression: "Then I answered and said, 'I beseech you, my lord, why have I been empowered with the power of understanding? For I did not wish to enquire about the ways above but about those things which we experience daily: why Israel has been given over to the Gentiles as a reproach; why the people whom you loved have been given over to godless tribes, and the law of our fathers has been made of no effect and the written covenants no longer exist; and why we pass from the world like locusts and our life is like a mist.' "[18] Another aspect of the increasing difficulty of belief in a revelation of God in history was that if the purpose of God thus revealed was the salvation of Israel, why then was the scale of history so unnecessarily large? What was to become of all the Gentiles? And indeed, what was to become of all the Jews who were not "wise," i.e. members of the apocalyptic movement? It is again the seer of II Esdras who puts these thoughts into words. He can at a pinch, though with obvious reluctance, summon up sufficient orthodoxy to dismiss the Gentiles as of no moment: "As for the other nations which have descended from Adam, thou hast said that they are nothing, and that they are like spittle; and thou hast compared their abundance to a drop from a bucket."[19] He can also make his angelic interlocutor say: "The Most High made this world for the sake of many, but the world to come for the sake of few . . . many have been created, but few shall be saved,"[20] but the problem remains in his heart unanswered. The frame of history was, in fact, too large for the *Heilsge-*

schichte it was supposed to contain, and earnest minds were increasingly aware of the incongruity.

History thus lost favor as the great medium for the expression of religious ideas. The only motive Israel had had in writing her history had been thereby to demonstrate her faith and to use that history as a medium for its expression. Once that motive was pre-empted, Israel lost interest in the writing of history and (apart from a tendentious reworking of earlier writing by the Chronicler) history writing ceased in Israel. When it recommenced in the Maccabean period, it was a very difficult thing, no longer *Heilsgeschichte* but rather history as the Greeks understood it.[21]

The apocalyptists came therefore at a critical period in the development of Israel. At the turn of the first millennium B.C., myth had been outgrown and abandoned, and faith-expressive historiography had taken its place. But in the fourth and third centuries B.C. the limitations of history as the medium in which religious ideas might be expressed, had become woefully apparent. How were believing men to meet this challenge?

III

Gerhard von Rad recognizes that history had already been effectively abandoned by the Priestly school, in their case for law. He writes: "In understanding the law in this way, Israel parted company with history, that is, with the history which she had hitherto experienced with Jahweh. She did not part company with her relationship to Jahweh. But once she began to look upon the will of Jahweh in such a timeless and absolute way, the saving history necessarily ceased moving on. This Israel no longer had a history, at least a history with Jahweh. From now on she lived and served her God, in, as it were, an enigmatic 'beyond history.' "[22] This was the response of what might be called normative Judaism to the question "What to do with history?" but it is clearly not so much an answer to the question as an evasion of it. The apocalyptic movement at least did not ignore history, but earnestly tried to come to terms with it. Their response was to revert to mythological ways of thought, but just as when Israel left myth for history she could not make a clean break with her past, and her history in fact includes much myth and considerable legend, so when the apocalyptists reverted to myth they could not wholly leave behind the habits of thought engendered by almost a millennium of thinking in terms of history. They tended therefore on the one hand to historicize myth and on the other to mythologize history, and in fact very effectively blurred the distinction between the two. But a review of their work in the light of our greatly increased understanding of the role of myth in the ancient Near East (an advantage which has accrued to us almost wholly since Charles's death in 1931) will enable us I believe to see that basically their thought is neither "historiological" nor mythological but a new blend of the two for which the term "eschatological" should be strictly reserved.

At this point we have to attempt to isolate the major characteristics of mythological thought and, following the guidance of Henri and H. A. Frankfort,[23] I suggest that it was characterized by three major elements. First it was aetiological, in that it attempted to make comprehensible the human situation. Man had to come to terms with his environment and, even more importantly, he had to come to terms with the strange contradictions of his own nature.[24] The second characteristic is that the events which myth described are located in a world related to but not identical with this present order. It is as it were a mirror-image world, but like Alice's world *Through the Looking-Glass* it has its own reality, its own flow of events, its own patterns of behavior, which impinge very effectively, at times even determinately, upon this world. The third characteristic is that the world of myth is in another order of time—what Frankfort calls "absolute time." The mythical past never recedes any further into the distance, and the Annus Magnus in its revolution never brings the future Golden Age any nearer.[25]

In turning again to mythological ways of thinking, the apocalyptists did not, however, simply put the clock back a whole millennium. The historiological period left its mark, and we find the new style of apocalyptical thinking repeating these three characteristics of mythological thought with subtle but unmistakable differences. Thus the burden of the aetiological task of myth had been transferred by Israel to the broad back of historiography, but with this difference, that the task was no longer to accommodate man to his environment and to himself; this could be taken fairly unreflectively from the earlier period. The contemporary task was to explain what Israel was, and how Israel was to relate herself to her situation and to her God. Similarly, the apocalyptic movement did not go back to the concerns of the Israelite period. The new aetiological task was two-fold. Consequent upon the work of Jeremiah and Ezekiel in particular, and the atomizing effect upon Israel of its *diaspora* experience, the first need was to meet the concern of the individual believer for personal reassurance. As early as the book of Daniel, the "wise," that is, the members of the apocalyptic movement, are in fact being thus reassured: "And those among the people who are wise shall make many understand, though they shall fall by sword and flame, by captivity and plunder, for some days . . . and some of those who are wise shall fall, to refine and cleanse them, to make them white . . . and many of those who sleep in the dust of the earth shall awake, some to everlasting life, and some to shame and contempt. And those who are wise shall shine like the brightness of the firmament; and those who turn many to righteousness, like the stars for ever and ever."[26] Thus the role played by aetiology in the pre-Israelite mythology is played by soteriology in the post-Israelite mythology.

But not by soteriology alone. As the long centuries of Persian and Greek rule creep past, so the historiological idea that God's nature may be discerned in current events gives rise to the unwelcome thought that the only God an honest mind can discern in these unhappy years is an ineffectual deity, a deity indifferent to the experience of his people.[27] To defend God against such impious thoughts, the apocalyptists drew on the ancient myths to say that this world was governed, or rather misgoverned, by the angels into whose hands God had consigned it for a stated term. The disorders of man's terrestrial experiences are due to the celestial disobedience of the angels. In Ethiopic Enoch God says: "Observe and mark everything that the shepherds [i.e., angels] will do to those sheep [i.e., Israel]; for they will destroy more of them than I have commanded them."[28] Because God can never go back on his word, he cannot intervene to rescue the "wise" and to punish the angels, until the predetermined time has come. This is not a very effective theodicy, but it does fill out the role previously played by aetiology.

Turning to the second of the three features of myth, we are reminded that the most familiar characteristic of apocalyptic is its doctrine of the two ages, the time of this present age and the time of the age to come. This is indeed the mirror-world of myth brought back into Jewish thought, after it had been largely banished for the historiological Israelite period. It is true that during that period there is a lingering tradition from the mythological period, whereby the Hebrew seer could conceive of Yahweh "in heaven," surrounded by his sôd, conducting the affairs of heaven and earth, but the characteristic concept of the Israelite period is of Yahweh resident on Zion and conducting the business of his people from his holy hill. He is thought of as active and operative in this world, not as removed and distant in some other, parallel existence. The apocalyptists, however, picked up the older tradition, and for them the realm of God was a transcendent order, perfect, ideal, removed, having its communication with this world only by means of its ambassadors and plenipotentiaries, that is, the angelic interlocutors who play such a large role in all the apocalyptic works.

The third feature which we remarked of myth was that it located the other world in absolute time, while in this world it conceived of time in a cyclic fashion. The Hebrews, on the other hand, in inventing history had at the same time invented teleology; that is, they conceived the historical process as moving to a climax, in time, on earth, called the Day of Yahweh. The apocalyptists took over this teleological or progressive thrust of the historiological period and applied it to the transcendent order of the kingdom of God. Thus, they reversed their previous practice, and instead of mythologizing history, they historicized myth. They took the timeless myth of the other world and, identifying it with the Golden Age of historiological thought, they brought it down on to the stage of human affairs. That is, they conceived of the other, mirror-image world as breaking into this world, at a particular moment in time. In so doing, they created the idea of the Fifth Kingdom, the future Rule of the Saints, the coming kingdom of God.[29]

There was, however, almost as it were inevitably, a corresponding development whereby myth was made part not only of future history but also of past history. As the two worlds were to become one in the future, so it was reasonable to think they might have been originally one, and had been divorced only by great wickedness. This moment of divorce was, in the apocalyptic tradition, the flood.[30] Those who lived prior to the flood, then, obviously had greater access to that other world and to its secrets, so that men like Enoch, Lamech, Noah, or even Adam himself, could be expected to have left traditions of arcana behind them for the guidance and information of later generations. This meant that the flood became very definitely an historical event, and as an historical event, the critical event of all this-worldly time. Thus for the apocalyptists, neither the exodus nor the return is the climactic of time; for them it is the flood. As the judgment day, the day of Yahweh, lies in the future, so the judgment day, the day of the flood, lies in the past. In both directions, as it were, past and future, myth is historicized and made part of the chronological process. But the effect of blending the teleological approach to time and the mythological absolute character of time produces a new concept. It is the idea of that other order of time, often called eternity, as that from which this present order is divorced and to which this present order nevertheless properly belongs, and to which it is one day to be re-related. It is this concept which we rightly call eschatology.

In this process of historicizing myth and mythologizing history, the apocalyptists have thus reached eschatological concepts. At the same time, however, they have effectively robbed mundane history of its significance. For these writers it is the other world which is the real world. It is there that events on earth are initiated and there that their outcome is determined. In the book of Daniel, for example, we hear of the mysterious "prince of the Kingdom of Persia" and of "the prince of Greece" and of "Michael the great prince who has charge of your people." It is these powers who are deciding Israel's fortunes. In Ethiopic Enoch it is the angelic Watchers and "Shepherds" whose activities decide the destinies of earth. Moreover the time schedule is fixed by divine decree and nothing can interfere with its fulfillment. This indeed gives the seers an opportunity to display their knowledge of the foreordained chronology. Thus Daniel produces seventy weeks of years as his schedule of predetermined time. The "Dream-Visions" of Enoch have similarly seventy shepherds, and the Apocalypse of Weeks has ten "weeks" into which the history, past and future, of the whole world is schematized. Almost every work has its own variant scheme.[31] The classic comment is that of II Esdras: "For he has weighed the age in the balance, and measured the times by measure, and numbered the times by number; and he will not move or arouse them until that measure is fulfilled."[32] But a world in which what happens on earth is predetermined by a heavenly timetable, and where the outcome of events is not dependent upon the balance and interrelationship of forces and personalities on earth, but rather on the outcome of struggles on another plane of existence, is a world in which mundane history has been deprived of any meaning. Such a world is far removed from the world of Amos, for example, who was confident that in history Yahweh did nothing without informing his prophets; or of Jeremiah, who conceived his role to be that of a prophet to the nations, and by his divinely inspired word to build them up or to tear them down; or again of Deutero-Isaiah, who confidently predicted the rise of Cyrus, because it was Yahweh's purpose through him to release Israel. For the prophets history was the sphere in which Yahweh worked out his purposes, but for the apocalyptists it was a mere succession of events with which God would not, indeed could not, interfere until the ordained moment arrived. History, so far from being the medium in which religious ideas could be expressed, had become literally a marking time until the *eschaton* should come.[33] The apocalyptists in this way released men from the overburdening task of trying to find any meaning or significance in the succession of mundane events. For them only the final event is significant.

IV

There are four comments to be made. First, while mundane history has become insignificant in the eyes of the apocalyptists, time has not. All man's existence is proceeding according to a predetermined plan. Mundane events are thus, paradoxically, both determined and insignificant. But human existence is not insignificant. It is full of hope. He that endures to the end shall be saved! The time of the kingdom is at hand! When Daniel calculated that from the setting up of the "abomination of desolation" to the end was a mere period of three and a half years, he was speaking for all his fellow apocalyptists. For all of them, the time of the end is very soon, it is *now*. It is only those who do not share in the positive convictions of the apocalyptists that time is predetermined and that the end is now, who find their outlook negative.

Secondly, it is their attitude to history which explains the notorious historical inaccuracies of the apocalyptic writers. Actually, they are more notorious than numerous. Nevertheless they are significant. History has in fact become so unimportant that the apocalyptists do not hesitate to make it fit into their numerical and other schemes, even at the cost of somewhat rearranging the past. Thus in Daniel, Belshazzar the Chaldean becomes the son of Nebuchadrezzar, and Darius the Mede and his empire interpose between the Babylonian and the Persian kingdoms in a most unhistorical manner.

Thirdly, just as in the myths gods and goddesses blend and merge, borrowing each other's traits and exchanging personalities, so too in the Enoch literature the central figure is more than a little confused with Lamech and with Noah in the earlier strata, and in the Similitudes he is enigmatically identified with the Son of Man himself. In the hands of the apocalyptists, history itself takes on an unhistorical character.[34]

The fourth observation is that the reason for the apocalyptists acquiring such a high but undeserved reputation as historians and philosophers of history was their frequent use of historical surveys and retrospects. Their purpose, however, was to gain credence for their prognostications of the future by putting them into the mouth of some long dead seer, whose "prophecies" were thus seen to have been proved so far amazingly correct, and therefore might confidently be trusted with regard to what was yet to come. The really important point is that whether the history of the four empires is being sketched in Dan. 2 or 7, or the wearisome marching to and fro of the kings of the north and of the kings of the south is being mapped in ch. 11, the *eschaton* interrupts the history; it is not something which the history prepares for, or in any way causes to occur. Similarly, in II Esdras, after much confused coverage of many events, the eagle finally achieves unitary rule of the earth; then the lion of the Most High announces its doom, not because of this achievement, but because "the Most High has looked upon his times and behold they are ended and his ages are completed."[35] Thus apocalyptic, while using history surveys freely, nevertheless did not, indeed could not, take mundane history seriously.

We may conclude, then, that, so far from being the first philosophers of history, the apocalyptists are in fact a school of biblical writers who recognized that the burden which Hebrew religion had laid upon history was greater than it could bear. They therefore returned from history to myth, myth in a new amalgam with history, which we have learned to call eschatology. In so doing, however, they abandoned the teleological view of history and with it the attempt to justify in mundane events the ways of God to man.

It is worthy of remark that none of the NT writers resumed the task. St. Augustine indeed sought to undertake it in the fifth century A.D. with his *Civitas Dei,* and since his day theologians have struggled to preserve for the Christian account of mundane history that element of purposiveness of which a thoroughgoing apocalyptic would deprive it.[36] The difficulties they have encountered, and the modesty of their success, lead us to recognize that the apocalyptists were not imagining or creating difficulties. Rather they were men who found the thought-forms of their religious tradition inadequate for the age in which they lived, and while in looking for a new medium of expression they may not have found a full answer, they at least arrived at a sufficient one, whereby faith could still be cogently affirmed. It may be that a sense of fellow feeling will lead us to be not unappreciative both of their sincerity and of their achievement.

NOTES

1. *Commentary on Daniel*, Oxford, 1929, p. xxv.

2. S. B. Frost, *Old Testament Apocalyptic*, London, 1952, p. 8.

3. *The Method and Message of Jewish Apocalyptic*, Philadelphia, 1964, p. 218.

4. Eschatology is in fact a misnomer as applied to pre-apocalyptic writers; teleology is the more correct term, seeing that an end was envisaged *in* history rather than *of* history.

5. The matter is not, I venture to suggest, one of small importance. The so-called "biblical theology" movement would not perhaps have trusted the idea of revelation through biblical history so unquestioningly if it had been realized that not only eminent secular historians but also some biblical writers themselves were clearly warning us: "Put not your trust in history." For an extreme example of such overconfidence, cf. *Offenbarung als Geschichte*, ed. W. Pannenberg, Goettingen, 2nd ed., 1963.

6. *What Is History?* London, 1961, p. 5. He cites on p. 21 J. A. Froude, *Short Studies in Great Subjects*, I, 1894, p. 21.

7. This does not of course rule out a doctrine of inspiration, except in the extreme form that the writers were wholly dominated by the Holy Spirit. [Ed. note: See also Alonso Schökel, pp. 24–56.]

8. The attempt to express the age-old religious ideas of mankind in terms of Israel's history can first be traced in the sagas which we know as the Pentateuchal sources J and E, though it probably antedates them. It appears more characteristically in the works of the Deuteronomic tradition.

9. This is particularly well illustrated in the case of Yahweh's conflict with Egypt by the cycle called "The Ten Plagues." [Ed. note: See also W. G. Lambert, pp. 285–297.]

10. Later, however, the history-period is extrapolated back into the past, so that the creation of the world itself can become an event in time, and thus become an event in Israel's history. This has the result that it becomes unclear whether the memorial of creation, the weekly sabbath, is to celebrate the creation of Israel or the creation of the world. Cf. the Deuteronomic and Priestly recensions of the Fourth Commandment, Deut. 5:15; Exod. 20:11.

11. The relationship of Hebrew covenant forms to second millennium treaty-structures setting out kingly relationships has been discussed by G. E. Mendenhall, "Law and Covenant in Israel and the Ancient Near East," *BA*, XVII, No. 2, May, 1954, 26–46, and No. 3, September, 1954, 49–76.

12. Num. 21:14.

13. Cf. J. R. Porter, "The Interpretation of II Sam. 4–6 and Ps. 132," *JTS*, N.S. V, 1954, 161–73; A. R. Johnson, "The Rôle of the King in the Jerusalem Cultus," in *The Labyrinth*, ed. S. H. Hooke, London, 1935, pp. 73–111; Ezek. 37:1–14.

14. The divinity of the reigning king was another idea which Israel by and large refused, but while it has been the subject of much modern study, it was a relatively minor theme of ancient religion.

15. Hos. 2:8–9; cf. also Ps. 65 and the evidence for rain-making ceremonies at the

Feast of Tabernacles in N. H. Snaith, *The Jewish New Year Festival,* London, 1947, pp. 62 f. Also Ps. 104, itself modeled upon the nature-hymn attributed to Ikhn-aten (Pritchard, *Ancient Near Eastern Texts,* 2nd ed., 1955, pp. 369 f.).

16. Cf. I Kings 4:20–34.

17. Cf. I Kings 22:1–28; Isa. 9:15–16, 29:10; Deut. 18:15–22; Jer. 4:9–10, 14:11–15, 23:16–17, 18–22, 23–32, and especially Jer. 27—29.

18. II Esdras 4:22–24. Wilfred Cantwell Smith draws attention to the fact that this same dilemma, arising out of a reading of history which is controverted by hard facts, is the major problem of modern Islam. Cf. *Islam in Modern History,* Princeton, 1957, p. 41: "The fundamental *malaise* of modern Islam is a sense that something has gone wrong with Islamic history."

19. II Esdras 6:56.

20. II Esdras 8:1–2.

21. The difference is so marked that R. G. Collingwood, taking the Greek style of historiography as the norm, will not concede that the Hebrews wrote any history before the Maccabean period: "These two forms of quasi-history, theocratic history and myth, dominated the whole of the Near East until the rise of Greece." *The Idea of History,* Oxford, 1946, p. 16.

22. *O. T. Theology,* New York, 1962, I, 91–92. The notion of *Heilsgeschichte* was not, of course, wholly rejected; it was rather relegated to a sacred, unassailable past. To continue the comment made in n. 5 above, we may observe that the question now raises itself (and on none does it press more hardly than on von Rad himself): if the idea of *Heilsgeschichte* proved inadequate for the men of the post-exilic period, are we right in making it the all-important interpretative principle of the whole of the Old Testament? (Cf. the introduction to von Rad's deservedly acclaimed book.) Even more pertinent is the question whether such a "biblical theology" should then be made the basis for a systematic theology in which a "theology of history" is assumed to be intrinsically superior to a "theology of nature."

23. Cf. H. and H. A. Frankfort, "Myth and Reality" in *The Intellectual Adventure of Ancient Man,* Chicago, 1946, pp. 23 f. [Also appears as *Before Philosophy.*]

24. While a word based on so philosophical a concept as the Greek *aitia* is perhaps too intellectual a term for the process of mental accommodation we are describing, nevertheless it serves to indicate that the myths of the ancient world enabled man to relate to his own environment and to his own self-awareness. This as we have seen was achieved by the use of the six dominant themes of mythology described above.

25. It is because the cycle of the Annus Magnus is associated with the "absolute time" of the mirror-image world that the ancient Near East could believe in a future Golden Age without achieving teleology or eschatology.

26. Dan. 11:33, 35; 12:2–3. The same concern shows itself in the Ethiopic book of Enoch, in all its major components, and, as we have seen, while the seer of II Esdras accepted the divine justice as impeccable, he was greatly concerned that of all created humankind only a favored few were to be saved. The salvation of the individual looms large in the *Apocalypse of Baruch* and in the *Secrets of Enoch,* while in the great Christian apocalypse, *The Revelation to John,* the concern becomes central: "To him who conquers I will grant to eat of the tree of life. . . . He who conquers shall not be hurt by the second death. . . . He who conquers shall be clad thus in white garments and I will not blot his name out of the book of life" (Rev. 2:7, 11; 3:5. Cf. 20:11–12; 21:7, 27; 22:14).

27. Just such charges lie barely concealed beneath the surface of Ps. 44. Similarly the problem of the book of Job is basically the question: "Is God good?" a question which could not have arisen before the disillusionment with the idea of salvation-history. Job, it should be remarked, is both an individual and also the righteous sufferer, Israel.

28. Eth. Enoch 89:61.

29. The relation of this-worldly teleology to other-worldly absolutism was not, however, easy to achieve, and the device of "the Days of the Messiah," or "the Millennial Reign of Christ," had to be invented before the new eschatology and the old teleology could be rightly accommodated each to the other.

30. It was only in later apocalyptic, e.g. II Esdras and Apoc. Bar., that the divorce was attached to the Adam and Eve myth. Cf. N. P. Williams, *The Ideas of the Fall and of Original Sin:* "The Ezra-Apocalypse [II Esdras] which dates from the last quarter of the first

century A.D. seems to mark the complete disappearance of the Watcher-story and the triumph of the Adam-narrative as the generally accepted Fall-story" (p. 30; cf. also pp. 75 f.).

31. D. S. Russell (see n. 3 above) gives many instances of these schemes, pp. 224 f.

32. II Esdras 4:36–37.

33. Cf. J. A. T. Robinson's comment: "It is a transition from an understanding of time as *kairos* to an understanding of it as *chronos* that perhaps more than anything else distinguishes the prophetic from the apocalyptic outlook." *In the End God*, London, 1950, p. 47. Given the general validity of the distinction between *kairos* and *chronos* (despite James Barr, *The Biblical Words for Time*, London, 1962), the comment is perceptive.

34. D. S. Russell (see n. 3 above) comments that two incidents having similar "psychological" content or two persons partaking of a similar "psychological" character were readily given a "psychological identity" or "contemporaneity" and so the givenness of history is overruled (p. 211). He also argues that history remains meaningful for the apocalyptists because they allowed for the exercise of free will by individuals. Cf. pp. 230 f. But so long as the major movements of mundane time are predetermined, individual free will cannot restore significance to world history.

35. II Esdras 11:44.

36. Not, however, all Christian theologians. Karl Löwith, for example, appears to embrace a negative view of history with considerable enthusiasm. His summary of the matter runs: "Historical processes as such do not bear the least evidence of a comprehensive and ultimate meaning. History as such has no outcome. There never has been and never will be an immanent solution of the problem of history, for man's historical experience is one of steady failure. Christianity, too, as a historical *world* religion, is a complete failure. The world is still as it was in the time of Alaric; only our means of oppression and destruction (as well as of reconstruction) are considerably improved and are adorned with hypocrisy" (*Meaning in History*, Chicago, 1949, p. 191). But can we be content with such a heartless view of human endeavor? Does it not, to adapt the memorable phrase of Dionysius of Alexandria, "slander our most merciful God as merciless"? As the Israelites abandoned myth, and the apocalyptists abandoned history, in order to embrace new concepts, may not we, too, be called, not only to establish how our fathers thought, but also how, in a new age, we ourselves should think? A more preceptive approach is that of R. L. Shinn (*Christianity and the Meaning of History*, New York, 1953). He finds the Christian view of history to be compounded of the ideas of the church, purposiveness and eschatology. This may still leave many questions to be answered, but it has the virtue of recognizing that no view of history which does not give a man a reason for entering into it can ever be satisfactory.

The Antiquity
of Mosaic Law

You may eat any animal that has a divided and cloven hoof and that is a ruminant. Of those, however, that are ruminant and those that have a divided and cloven hoof you may not eat the following: the camel, the hare and the hyrax, which are ruminant but have no cloven hoof; you must hold them unclean. (Deut. 14:6–7)

The Pentateuch, the first five books of the Old Testament, which tradition attributes to Moses, is studied for clues about the Hebrew people prior to their forming a nation under Saul in 1020 B.C. Modern scholars support the Graf-Wellhausen theory that the "J" (Yahwist), "E" (Elohist), "D" (Deuteronomist), and "P" (Priestly) editors extensively altered the original Pentateuch between the tenth and fifth centuries to meet their evolving religious philosophies. The Old Testament scholar, William F. Albright, looking carefully at this hypothesis, concludes that much of the original—the dietary, moral, and civil laws which appear in Leviticus and Deuteronomy—survived the various editings. After comparing the language and structure of the Hebrew laws with contemporary ones by the Egyptians and Babylonians, Albright asserts that the Hebrews were far superior to their contemporaries in their ability to analyze their world and then to establish general laws about it.

See also Bleddyn J. Roberts' "The Old Testament: Manuscripts, Text and Versions," pp. 212–234, for a textual approach to the Pentateuch and another perspective on the Graf-Wellhausen theory.

THE case-laws of Exodus are much more ancient than their present context suggests; and they must have been—at least in large part—brought from Mesopotamia by the ancestors of the Hebrews and kept alive in Egypt as well as Palestine. Among them is, however, some mate-

From William F. Albright, *Yahweh and the Gods of Canaan* (1968), pp. 172–82.

rial of apodictic and generalizing character which points to Mosaic or post-Mosaic reworking or editing.

This apodictic material appears as insertions scattered in blocks through Ex. 21–23, especially at 21:12–17, 22:17 (Heb.)–23:3, and 23:6 ff. It is scarcely ever stated in the conditional form of case-laws but always as declarations, either in the form of prohibitions or more rarely as positive commands. Their content is religious, moral and humane; the brilliant analysis by Albrecht Alt[1] clarified the difference between the originally non-Hebrew customary law in case form and the apodictic law found in the Book of the Covenant and elsewhere in the Books of Moses. Their general character reminds one of the Egyptian Negative Confession (Book of the Dead, Ch. 125),[2] which goes back at least to the sixteenth century B.C. and was very popular during the centuries immediately preceding and following the time of Moses. The Egyptian statements are couched as protestations of innocence, e.g.: 'I have not committed murder, I have not ordered murder to be committed, I have not treated anyone unjustly, I have not reduced the food offerings in the temples, I have not debased the bread of the gods, . . . I have not had homosexual relations, I have not defiled myself, I have neither increased nor diminished measures (of capacity), I have not tampered with the balance', etc. The Negative Confession shows a remarkable lack of systematic order or selectivity with regard to different types of sin which will cause a man to be rejected by the judges of the Nether World. A striking difference is the relative lack of specific cultic regulations among the apodictic rules in the Book of the Covenant. At the same time the Hebrew texts lay much greater stress than the Egyptian on humane treatment of men and animals. The Decalogue consists of a similar intermixture of prohibitions and positive commands, but its content was remarkably well selected from a much larger body of similar material in the apodictic law. We have no way of telling whether the Decalogue is younger than the apodictic law as such, or not; the differing recensions found in Ex. 20 and Deut. 5 show that different forms of it had diverged early, while, on the other hand, use of words like *melā'kāh* in the sense of 'labour' or 'business' shows that the text was put into Classical Hebrew form at a date subsequent to the time of Moses.[3] But the use of relatively late words does not mean that the Decalogue as such is necessarily later than Moses, since the wording of such a popular list of moral norms for behaviour might easily be changed quite often in the course of its history, and there has obviously been some expansion of items. Elsewhere I shall present extrinsic arguments for an original date of the Decalogue no later than the thirteenth century B.C.[4] The generalized pattern of the norms of the Decalogue is very striking and places it in a different category from the Negative Confession or corresponding Babylonian lists of sins and taboos, also from the latter part of the second millennium B.C. Most remarkable is the generalized statement of the *lex talionis* in Ex. 21:23-25. Alt pointed out in 1934 that the formula in question appears in very similar terms in Punic inscriptions of about the third century A.D. from North Africa. In the Latin text we have *anima pro anima, sanguine pro sanguine, vita pro vita,* which is so like the Hebrew formula in Exodus (together with its variants in Lev. 24:20 and Deut. 19:21) as to be unmistakably derived from the same ultimate source.[5] On the other hand, the two formulas are not sufficiently alike to make direct borrowing likely, even if it were not excluded by the totally different context in each case: the Punic formula involves substitution of animal for human sacrifice, whereas the Hebrew adumbrates the principle of equal justice for all. We may, therefore, be reasonably sure that this formulation of the *lex talionis* goes back to not later than the seventh century B.C., after which there was little fresh influence from Phoenicia on Carthage.

In the Hebrew formula, we have what may be the earliest enunciation of a generalized legal principle known anywhere in the world. Though it has not yet attained the level of a generalized abstract proposition, it reaches its purpose by listing several related concrete propositions to illustrate the scope of the generalized principle. Since the Old Testament shows little trace of protological thinking after the thirteenth-twelfth centuries B.C. but is throughout a monument of empirical logic, we need not have any hesitation about tracing this legal generalization back to the beginnings of the Mosaic revolution—either to Moses himself or to a 'school' of interpreters who endeavoured to harmonize the ancient case-law with the body of apodictic law which had been developing since the time of Moses. The latest probable date for the collection of their material is the tenth century B.C., as will be argued below.

Since it is not our purpose here to discuss the entire Mosaic *corpus* of apodictic law, we shall limit ourselves to a necessarily brief discussion of certain features of the dietary and sanitary codes attributed to Moses.

A detailed analysis of the dietary and hygienic rules of the Pentateuch is still premature. We have much material for the laws of purity in the ancient Near East in the collections of ritual taboos which were prepared in Egypt and especially in Babylonia during the second millennium B.C. It is noteworthy that the Hebrew rules are much more highly developed than the corresponding ancient Near Eastern lists of taboos. For this we may adduce a number of reasons. In the first place, there is a strong flavour of sympathetic magic—sometimes even of professional magic—about the taboos in such cuneiform collections as Shurpu and Maqlû. If we knew more about corresponding Egyptian forms of ritual, we should doubtless find much the same situation in Egypt where some aspects of Egyptian culture tended to resemble newly hatched chicks which carry bits of eggshell about on their backs for days after they emerge from the shell. It must also be recognized that there had probably been much more revision and interpretation of the content of the Hebrew laws of purity, with addition of later interpretation and commentary, than would be true of case-law or simple apodictic declarations. This is probably because the case-law as preserved in the Pentateuch is at best extremely fragmentary, containing essentially only laws about homicide, slavery, and torts, and because the early apodictic law is even more fragmentary and less systematic. The relatively systematic presentation of the rules of purity strongly suggests a later date for them than for the less complete tradition of civil and moral law. The codification of the laws of purity may well come down to the seventh century B.C. in their present form (chiefly in 'P' and 'D'). On the other hand, we shall see that no part of the Hebrew Bible is more clearly empirico-logical in its background than the rules of purity; the body of rules in question carries us directly back to the lessons learned from common experience.

After a long period in which anthropologists were accustomed to explain all such regulations as going back to totemism or animism, there is now a striking reaction. It is being increasingly recognized that men have always learned from experience and observation, especially in the ancient Near East, where sedentary culture began long before its origin in most other parts of the world. Everywhere man has a natural capacity, not only for observing closely, but also for remembering what he has observed. Such memories are carried down by collective activity. In other words, the elders teach what they have heard from the elders of their generation, supplemented by their own experience, to younger people who, in turn, transmit it to the next generation, in such a way that the experience of one person is checked by that of others and that of one chronological group by the experience of the following. I have repeatedly pointed out that the Hebrew Bible is the greatest existing monument of empirical logic and that this logic is more exact than formal logic in some important respects. After all, it is based on the cumulative experience of men, and not on postulates or presuppositions which may or may not be correct, as is inevitably true of most postulational reasoning outside of mathematics and the exact sciences.

Just as the Chinese had long known the curative properties of *mahuang* before it was exported to the West and finally replaced by its active alkaloid, ephedrine, so the ancient Egyptians discovered the curative function of many medicinal plants and preparations, which they duly transmitted to the Greeks, who in turn passed on their pharmacopoeia to mediaeval Europe.

It is equally natural that men should have learned through the experience of many centuries to distinguish between poisonous and non-poisonous serpents, mushrooms, etc. For example, they early learned the danger involved in eating pork. Since trichinosis has been endemic in all Near Eastern lands from antiquity, and since there are several other dangerous maladies which come from eating insufficiently cooked pork, some connexion must have been recognized at an early date, at least in areas where the habits of domesticated pigs had become unusually filthy. Since they knew nothing specific about the causes of illness contracted by eating pork, they did not realize that adequate cooking would dispose of the dangers. The common explanation for the biblical legislation concerning pork—that it was not eaten because it was sacred among pagan people—is sheer nonsense. The pig was sacred in certain places and periods, but large and small cattle were even more generally sacred, so that it is quite irrational to single out the economically and religiously much less important pig, and to explain its prohibition in Israel by its alleged religious significance. If there were any doubt about the empirical explanation, it should be removed by the fact that both the hare and the hyrax (šāfān) were also prohibited. This can be explained only by the fact that both animals are carriers of tularemia, which comes from infected cuts received in the process of skinning and dismembering the animals. While it is true that the hyrax belongs to an entirely different mammalian family from the hare, it is also true that their habits of life have converged almost completely, and it is now well known that the hyrax, like the hare, carries this disease.

The most remarkable distinction of this kind in the regulations distinguishing clean from unclean animals in Lev. 11 and Deut. 14 is that made between fish with fins and scales and fish without fins and scales. It is only in the water of extremely muddy and slow-flowing rivers such as the Nile that the distinction is important for health. Fish with scales and fins are normally free-swimming, whereas fish without scales and fins, such as eels, are usually mud-burrowers and therefore hosts to a great many more parasites than free-swimming fish. (Of course there are periods in the life cycles of some aquatic animals when they are free-swimming, and periods when they are not, but in general this distinction holds true.) Animal parasites and native inhabitants often establish a symbiosis, but foreign visitors to the Nile valley have not established immunity, so that parasites can be quite lethal, for the number of diseases carried by aquatic animals in the Nile valley is prodigious. For foreigners, then, the distinction is extremely significant. The most reasonable explanation of its origin seems to be that this distinction was discovered by early Semitic settlers in Egypt, and passed on by them to the Hebrews during the centuries in which they lived in the Nile valley. It is thus a vivid example of the antiquity of some of this legislation which is often thought to be very late. In salt water the distinction is not generally valid, and it could not have been noticed in the clean salt waters of the Mediterranean, or in the Dead Sea, where there are no fish at all. It might conceivably have arisen in the Jordan Valley and the Sea of Galilee, but there is nothing to show that fisheries played a significant economic rôle there in Israelite times. An ultimate Babylonian origin is possible but not very likely, since we have no trace of it in our extensive Babylonian rituals of purity such as the Shurpu and Maqlû codes.

Another case is that of the camel. The camel, as far as we know at present, was not generally domesticated even in Arabia until the end of the Bronze Age. By the late twelfth century it was being used to mount large-scale raids, as well as presumably for trade. The camel was certainly known through this entire period and had been since Pleistocene times, at least. Since camels are notoriously stupid, it is highly probable that herds of them were kept in a half-wild state in order to provide milk, flesh, hair and skins for the nomads. Camel flesh, as far as known to medical science, is harmless though extremely tough. But the Egyptians were much less hospitable to the camel than the Semites. In fact there is no evidence for domesticated camels in Egypt until the Persian period—and this evidence comes from texts copied in Roman times. The Arabian camel was not introduced into North Africa west of Egypt until still later. It is therefore probable that the prohibition against camel flesh was also Egyptian in origin.

The most striking feature of the dietary laws in the Pentateuch is that for the first known time in history we have a generalized classification of complex zoological phenomena according to observed criteria. In this connexion it is scarcely relevant to point out that the classification of clean and unclean animals according to parting the hoof and 'chewing the cud' is not quite accurate, since hares, for example, do not actually chew their cud but merely move their lips. Nor is it significant that these rules can scarcely have been drawn up on the basis of any knowledge of the aetiology underlying the prohibition of certain mammals, fish and other animals. It is rather a kind of mnemonic device to make abstention from certain kinds of flesh easier for the young or unsophisticated person. And yet we find no classification as logical as this in any of the elaborate cuneiform lists of fauna or of ritual taboos.

In the case of hygienic regulations, it is perfectly obvious that their ultimate basis rests on the observed facts of contagion and infection. It could not possibly escape the sharp eyes and active mind of the proto-physician that certain diseases were communicated from person to person or from contaminated locations or areas to persons. In this case the background is reasonably clear. Both in ancient Near Eastern medicine and post-biblical Jewish folklore the rôle played by demons in transmitting disease was well known. (In practice there is little difference between belief in demons and in pathogenic organisms as a basis for transmitting infection!) In the Mosaic tradition the rôle of demons had been almost always cancelled by the process of demythologizing which set in with Moses. But the facts of experience remained and were presupposed in the hygienic laws. Thanks to the dietary and hygienic regulations of

Mosaic law, held firmly together and developed along empirico-logical lines by post-Mosaic commentators down to the seventh century B.C., subsequent history has been marked by a tremendous advantage in this respect held by Jews over all other comparable ethnic and religious groups. It is only in our own times that advances in medicine have made it possible to replace rule-of-thumb regulations of former times by medical and hygienic practices which obtain similar results by scientific methods.

One of the most remarkable features of Mosaic legislation—always using the term in its widest sense, of laws approved or introduced by Moses and developed in later Israel—is its humanity to man. It is the most humanitarian of all known bodies of laws before recent times. The laws about slavery, which envisage the liberation of Hebrew slaves after seven years, are a good example. But there are also laws protecting the poor: interest (always high in the ancient East) was prohibited, and again there was a moratorium on payments after a term of years. Furthermore, it was not permitted to take a man's clothing in payment for a debt. Even strangers, who normally had very little protection in antiquity, except when they were citizens of a strong neighbouring state which might step in and protect them by force of arms, are exceptionally well cared for by Mosaic law. Not only do we find numerous special provisions for the humane treatment of human beings, but even the well-being of animals receives attention; as for example in the command, 'Thou shalt not muzzle the ox that treads out the grain' (Deut. 25:4). The original practice may well have been connected with pagan cult, as so often was the case, but the apodictic law has been depaganized.

In 1950 I pointed out that the laws of Exodus could scarcely be later than the ninth century B.C., because they contain no hint of the royal appointment of judges which was introduced under King Jehoshaphat, according to II Chron. 19.[6] We can be reasonably sure that the tradition has an historical basis for three reasons: (1) The compiler of Chronicles was very much interested in legal matters and should therefore be particularly reliable in treating them. This reason would be even stronger if I am correct in maintaining that the first edition, at least, of this work is due to Ezra, who was himself a jurist.[7] (2) The reform is said to have involved setting up a mixed tribunal of royally appointed judges of both priestly and non-priestly origin, which can be closely paralleled in fourteenth- and thirteenth-century Egypt. (3) Our respect for the accuracy of both the written and the oral tradition recorded by the Chronicler has been notably enhanced in recent years.[8]

The legislative material of Exodus was not intended to be a digest of current or proposed legislation, but just what it purports to be—an account of the legislation of Moses, drawn up and edited in its present form in the seventh and sixth centuries B.C., but not including anything then known to date after the Mosaic Age. It is no longer rational to deny the antiquity of the Pentateuchal laws in general. There is no reason why we should date the case-laws later than the Patriarchal Age. The older legislation was presumably accepted by Moses and adapted where necessary to the situation of Israel in his day. The apodictic law also reflects pre-Mosaic sources, but has been so thoroughly reworked in the spirit of the Mosaic movement that its originality cannot be denied.

NOTES

1. *Die Ursprünge des israelitischen Rechts,* originally published in the *Verhandlungen* of the Leipzig Academy, LXXXVI:1 (1934) and now reprinted in KSGVI I, 278–332.

2. See J. A. Wilson in ANET, 34 ff., and for the latest treatment see T. G. Allen, *The Egyptian Book of the Dead* (Chicago, 1960), pp. 196 ff.

3. On the meaning of Ugar. *ml'akt* at that time (a meaning which it still has occasionally in Hebrew verse), see BASOR 150 (1958), 38, n. 14.

4. See my *History of the Religion of Israel.*

5. ZATW, N.F. XI (1934), pp. 303 ff., KSGVI I, 341 ff.

6. See my study, 'The Judicial Reform of Jehoshaphat' in the *Alexander Marx Jubilee Volume* (New York, 1950), pp. 61–82.

7. See H. H. Schaeder, *Esra der Schreiber* (Tübingen, 1930).

8. On the historical value of the Chronicler's work see Jacob M. Myers, *Chronicles,* Anchor Bible (Garden City, 1965), especially the introduction to Vol. I.

_____William O. Walker, Jr._____

The Origin of the
Son of Man Concept
as Applied to Jesus

I gazed into the visions of the night.
And I saw, coming on the clouds of heaven,
one like a son of man. (Dan. 7:13)

*In this essay, Walker explores how and why the writers of
Mark, Matthew, and Luke shaped from the prophecies in
Psalms and Daniel their views of Christ as the Son of Man.
Employing form-critical and historical analysis, Walker
studies selected texts as well as the historical forces which
motivated the New Testament writers to claim after
Christ's death a characteristic he did not claim in his life.
The reader is directed to Norman Perrin's The New Testa-
ment: An Introduction (1974), pp. 39–61, for a detailed
consideration of the four periods of the primitive church:
Jewish Christianity (centered in Jerusalem); Palestinian
Jewish Christianity; Hellenistic Jewish Mission Christianity; and Gentile Christianity. In this essay, Walker
concerns himself with the first two periods.*

T HE "Son of Man problem in the Gospels," as Matthew Black so aptly
put it, "is one of the most perplexing and challenging in the whole
field of Biblical theology."[1] More than a decade ago, A. J. B. Higgins spoke
of the "bewildering mass of material" which had been produced on the
subject during the previous quarter of a century,[2] and this "mass" has
continued to grow since he wrote.[3] Most of the recent discussion has
revolved around two interrelated questions: (1) the derivation and consequent meaning of the term and concept "Son of Man," and (2) the
authenticity and interpretation of the various Son of Man sayings in the
NT gospels.[4] As regards the first question, despite some continuing dis-
sent and disagreement concerning details, there has emerged a significant consensus among NT scholars that "Son of Man" is intended in the
gospels as a kind of "messianic" title[5] from the world of Jewish apocalyp-

From William O. Walker, Jr., *Journal of Biblical Literature*, 91 (1972), 482–90.

ticism,[6] which, it is widely assumed, held "the conception of a transcendent, pre-existent heavenly being, the Son of Man, whose coming to earth as judge would be a major feature of the drama of the End time."[7] As regards the second question, some scholars still hold that all or most of the Son of Man sayings are genuine self-references of the historical Jesus,[8] and others find an authentic element primarily in those sayings which allude to the present situation, activity, and authority of the Son of Man,[9] but increasingly the tendency is either, on the one hand, to reject all but certain of the apocalyptic Son of Man sayings and to deny that these are *self*-references of Jesus[10] or, on the other hand, to attribute all of the Son of Man sayings without exception to the early church.[11]

Recently, Norman Perrin re-opened the Son of Man question in a fresh and exciting way by (1) vigorously challenging the widespread assumption of a Son of Man concept in Jewish apocalypticism; (2) denying the authenticity of all of the Son of Man sayings in the NT gospels and attributing the Son of Man christology to an exegetical process at work in the early church similar to that which has been detected in the Qumran community; and (3) ascribing to the author of Mark the major role in the creative use of Son of Man traditions in the NT period.[12]

On the basis of a critical examination of the use of "Son of Man imagery" in Jewish apocalyptic and midrashic literature, Perrin concludes:

> There is no sufficient relationship between the use of Son of Man in I Enoch and IV Ezra for us to suppose that they are both reflections of a common conception. What we have is the imagery of Dan. 7.13 being used freely and creatively by subsequent seers and scribes. These uses are independent of one another; the common dependence is upon Dan. 7.13 on the one hand and upon the general world of apocalyptic concepts on the other. Similarly, the scribes of the midrashic traditions in their turn use the imagery of Dan. 7.13 in connection with the Messiah. Although they abandon the general world of apocalyptic concepts, nonetheless they find Dan. 7.13 every bit as useful in their presentation of the Messiah as did the seer of IV Ezra in his.[13]

If this is true, and, in my opinion, Perrin's argument is convincing, then Jewish literature and thought provided no unified and consistent Son of Man concept in the first century. What was at hand, rather, was simply the precedent of "the varied use of 'Son of Man imagery,'"[14] and the apocalyptic Son of Man concept which appears in the NT gospels must, therefore, have originated either with Jesus himself or with the early Christian community.

Perrin then maintains that the apocalyptic Son of Man concept originated not with the historical Jesus, but with the primitive church. A careful form-critical and tradition-historical analysis of the Son of Man sayings in the synoptic gospels indicates "that Jesus could not have spoken of the coming of the Son of Man, either in reference to himself or in reference to an eschatological figure other than himself," since all of the apocalyptic Son of Man sayings, under close scrutiny, turn out to be products of an exegetical tradition in the early church.[15] Following Barnabas Lindars in particular,[16] Perrin points out that

> the earliest Christians made most significant use of the OT in their theologizing. They developed major aspects of their belief and expectation from OT texts, interpreting the texts in the light of their experience and their experience in the light of the texts. The Christian practice here paralleled that of the Qumran scribes and, like those scribes, the Christians read the OT texts as strictly relating to themselves and their experiences, and they exercised very considerable freedom in regard to the wording of the texts.[17]

Specifically, Perrin claims that the expectation of the coming of Jesus as apocalyptic Son of Man is a "product" of such an "exegetical process" which was at work in the early church.[18]

Apparently, according to Perrin, "the first christological step taken by the early church was that of interpreting the resurrection in the light of" the first verse of Psalm 110:

> The Lord says to my lord: "Sit at my right hand,
> till I make your enemies your footstool."[19]

The Christian exegesis of this verse produced the *mār* [sic] christology, as well as the particular eschatological expectation expressed in *maranatha*. The beginning of the Son of Man christology, however, can be traced to a secondary "Christian exegetical tradition in which the original interpretation of the resurrection in terms of Ps 110.1 was expanded by the use of Dan 7:13: the resurrection of Jesus is now interpreted as his ascension to God *as Son of Man*."[20] "Just as Enoch became Son of Man on the basis of an interpretation of his translation, so Jesus became Son of Man on the basis of an interpretation of his resurrection."[21]

II

I am strongly inclined to accept Perrin's basic reconstruction of the origin of the Son of Man christology, so far as it goes. What he fails to explain, however, is precisely why Ps 110:1 first came to be interpreted by the further use of Dan 7:13. What caused the two texts to be combined in the early Christian exegetical tradition? In general terms, of course, it could be pointed out that the two passages have a natural affinity in that they both speak of exaltation to a position of pre-eminence by God and, indeed, in the presence of God, and this might explain their association. Moreover, some scholars believe that Jewish exegetes had already, as early as the first century, given a "messianic"[22] interpretation of both Psalm 110[23] and Dan 7:13–14,[24] although this is debatable.[25] Apparently, however, it was characteristic of early Christian exegesis, at least in many instances, to combine OT texts not on the basis of mere general affinity, but rather on the basis of specific verbal similarities.[26] Perrin himself suggests a possible precedent in Jewish exegetical practice when he points out that the Similitudes of Enoch 37–71 interpret the translation of Enoch on the basis of Ezekiel 1 and Daniel 7, and thus identify him as "Son of Man." The term "Son of Man" is applied to Ezekiel[27] and also occurs in Daniel 7, and thus forms a natural link between the two passages.[28] In the light of this precedent, the apparent absence of such a link between Ps 110:1 and Dan 7:13 in the early Christian exegetical tradition is all the more remarkable.

I suggest, however, that the combination of Ps 110:1 and Dan 7:13 occurred in two stages, that a link between the two texts can be found in Psalm 8, and that the key passage in demonstrating this link is Mark 12:36b.

Ps 110:1, which Perrin regards as the starting point for the exegetical tradition which eventually produced the Son of Man christology, reads as follows in the LXX version (LXX 109:1): εἶπεν ὁ κύριος τῷ κυρίῳ μου κάθου ἐκ δεξιῶν μου ἕως ἂν θῶ τοὺς ἐχθρούς σου ὑποπόδιον τῶν ποδῶν σου (The Lord said to my lord, 'Sit at my right hand, until I make your enemies your footstool'"). This is quoted almost *verbatim* in Acts 2:34b–35, the only difference being the absence of the article before κύριος, and its application to Jesus. It is also quoted in Mark 12:36b, but this time an apparently insignificant difference appears:[29] in place of ὑποπόδιον ("footstool"), the text reads ὑποκάτω ("under"), resulting in the phrase ὑποκάτω τῶν ποδῶν σου ("under your feet") rather than the ὑποπόδιον τῶν ποδῶν σου ("footstool of your feet") of Ps 110:1.[30] Now, the interesting fact is that the phrase ὑποκάτω τῶν ποδῶν appears also in the LXX version of Ps 8:6 (LXX 8:7), which reads: καὶ κατέστησας αὐτὸν ἐπὶ τὰ ἔργα τῶν χειρῶν σου πάντα ὑπέταξας ὑποκάτω τῶν ποδῶν αὐτοῦ ("And you placed him over the works of your hands, you subjected all things under his feet"). It is quite possible, then, that the ὑποπόδιον τῶν ποδῶν σου of Ps 110:1 suggested to the early Christian mind the ὑποκάτω τῶν ποδῶν σου of Ps 8:6 and that Mark 12:36b reflects a conflation of the two verses, either intentional or unintentional, in the Christian exegetical tradition.[31] This possibility becomes virtually a certainty when it is noted, as Lindars points out, that the two texts are quite regularly combined or associated elsewhere in the NT.[32]

Apparently, then, the early Christians initially used Ps 110:1, particularly the first half of the verse (εἶπεν ὁ κύριος τῷ κυρίῳ μου κάθου ἐκ δεξιῶν μου), to interpret the resurrection of Jesus as an exaltation to the right hand of God as "Lord," but the second half of the verse (ἕως ἂν θῶ τοὺς ἐχθρούς σου ὑποπόδιον τῶν ποδῶν σου), which served the purpose of explaining the delay of the *parousia,* subsequently led them to Ps 8:6 with its strikingly similar ending (πάντα ὑπέταξας ὑποκάτω τῶν ποδῶν αὐτοῦ), with the result that Psalm 8 was then also applied to Jesus. Thus far, the exegetical development seems clear and logical, but how does Ps 8:6 then serve as the link between Ps 110:1 and Dan 7:13? The answer is equally clear and logical: Psalm 8 also refers in verse 4 (LXX 5) to a "son of man" (υἱὸς ἀνθρώπου), here used, of course, simply as a synonym for "man" (ἄνθρωπος). To the early Christian mind, however, which had already come to regard Psalm 8 as referring to Jesus on the basis of its association with Ps 110:1,[33] this would undoubtedly be understood as an identification of Jesus as "Son of Man," and it would almost inevitably suggest a connection with another reference to the term "Son of Man," viz., Dan 7:13. I suggest, therefore, that Psalm 8 forms the most probable link between the primitive Christian use of Ps 110:1 to interpret the resurrection of Jesus as his exaltation to the right hand of God as "Lord" and the subsequent use of Dan 7:13 to interpret further that exaltation as the exaltation of Jesus as *"Son of Man."*

Once Ps 110:1 and Dan 7:13 were combined in this way,[34] further exegetical developments followed, as Perrin has shown.[35] Originating, then, in a particular Christian exegetical tradition having to do with the exaltation of Jesus, the apocalyptic Son of Man concept was taken up and used in a variety of early Christian forms[36] and, ultimately, was employed more or less systematically by the author of Mark in his attempt to correct what he regarded as a "false christology" in the early church.[37]

III

One problem remains. This use of Ps 8:6 to serve as a link between Ps 110:1 and Dan 7:13 and thereby to create a Son of Man christology for Jesus is possible only on the basis of the Greek texts of the passages in question; it cannot be worked out in Hebrew.[38] Thus, if my reconstruction of the origin of the Son of Man christology is valid, we must conclude that it was the Greek-speaking, not the Aramaic-speaking, church which first understood Jesus in apocalyptic terms as Son of Man. This, however, constitutes no real weakness in or objection to the reconstruction. Ferdinand Hahn has argued, primarily on linguistic grounds, that even the chronologically earlier use of Ps 110:1 to speak of Jesus' exaltation cannot have originated in the Aramaic-speaking Palestinian church,[39] Howard M. Teeple, among others, has maintained that the Son of Man christology originated in hellenistic Jewish Christianity—perhaps with Stephen and the hellenistic Jewish Christians in Jerusalem or, more likely, among hellenistic Jewish Christians in Syria.[40] The former possibility is particularly intriguing.

It has frequently been noted that one of the very few occurrences of "Son of Man" outside the gospels is Acts 7:56, where it is applied to Jesus by "the radical hellenistic Jewish convert, Stephen."[41] It may be that this is simply an indication "that the author of Acts associated the Son of Man christology with hellenistic Jewish-Christianity, not with the primitive Jerusalem church,"[42] or it may be that it reflects a correct memory that Stephen and his group actually held a Son of Man christology.[43] Clearly, the conflict between the "Hellenists" and the "Hebrews" in the early Jerusalem church was over more than just the daily distribution of food (Acts 6:1).[44] Teeple points out that "the hellenistic Jewish-Christians were unorthodox enough in Jewish sight to be persecuted, while the original church was traditional enough to be allowed to remain," and he poses the question: "Did the hellenists' unorthodoxy include the belief that Jesus is the Son of Man?"[45] If the Son of Man christology did begin with Stephen and the hellenistic Jewish Christians in Jerusalem, then "the split between the original Jerusalem church of the disciples and the hellenistic converts from the diaspora is quite understandable."

> The earlier belief, that Jesus was the Messiah who had been raised from the dead and exalted to heaven, was not theological heresy. Judaism contained traditions that certain human beings (Enoch, Moses, Elijah, Isaiah, and Jeremiah) had been exalted to heaven and that all righteous Jews would be raised from the dead. But the claim that the human Jesus who had lived on earth is the divine, pre-existent Son of Man, was a belief that bordered on blasphemy because it was a threat to monotheism. . . . The fears of the orthodox were justified, for the Son of Man christology helped to prepare the way for the fuller deification of Jesus later in gentile Christianity.[46]

The apparent absence of a full-blown Son of Man concept in pre-Christian Judaism which has been noted by Perrin calls into question certain details of Teeple's reconstruction; but it may well be, as he suggests, that the Son of Man christology originated with the "Hellenists" in Jerusalem and that the differences between "Hellenists" and "Hebrews" included, among other things, a conflict between a Son of Man christology and a Son of David christology. In any case, I suggest that it was among Greek-speaking, not Aramaic-speaking, Christians that the exegetical tradition produced the Son of Man christology.

NOTES

1. Matthew Black, "The Son of Man Problem in Recent Research and Debate," *BJRL* 45 (1963) 305.

2. A. J. B. Higgins, "Son of Man-*Forschung* since 'The Teaching of Jesus,'" *New Testament Essays: Studies in Memory of Thomas Walter Manson* (ed. A. J. B. Higgins; Manchester: Manchester University, 1959) 119.

3. The more important recent books on the Son of Man problem include: E. Sjöberg, *Der verborgene Menschensohn in den Evangelien* (Lund: Gleerup, 1955); H. E. Tödt, *The*

Son of Man in the Synoptic Tradition (Philadelphia: Westminster, 1965); A. J. B. Higgins, *Jesus and the Son of Man* (Philadelphia: Fortress, 1964); F. H. Borsch, *The Son of Man in Myth and History* (Philadelphia: Westminster, 1967); M. D. Hooker, *The Son of Man in Mark* (London: SPCK, 1967); and F. H. Borsch, *The Christian and Gnostic Son of Man* (SBT 2/14; London: SCM, 1970). Other books which contain significant treatments of the subject include: S. Mowinckel, *He That Cometh* (New York/Nashville: Abingdon, 1956) 346–450; O. Cullmann, *The Christology of the New Testament* (Philadelphia: Westminster, 1959, rev. ed., 1963) 137–92; M. S. Enslin, *The Prophet from Nazareth* (New York/Toronto/London: McGraw-Hill, 1961) 137–48; F. Hahn, *The Titles of Jesus in Christology: Their History in Early Christianity* (London: Lutterworth, 1969) 15–67; E. Jüngel, *Paulus und Jesus: Eine Untersuchung zur Präzisierung der Frage nach dem Ursprung der Christologie* (2d ed.; Tübingen: Mohr, 1964) 215–62; R. H. Fuller, *The Foundations of New Testament Christology* (New York: Scribner, 1965) 34–43, 65, 119–25, 143–54, 229–30, 233–34. Recent articles dealing with the Son of Man are much too numerous to list, but mention should be made of the extremely thorough and important treatment by Carsten Colpe, "ὁ υἱὸς τοῦ ἀνθρώπου," *TDNT* 8 (1972) 400–77.

4. For surveys of the discussion, see, e.g., F. J. Foakes Jackson and Kirsopp Lake, *The Beginnings of Christianity, I: The Acts of the Apostles* (London: Macmillan, 1920) 345–408; N. Schmidt, "Recent Study of the Term 'Son of Man,'" *JBL* 45 (1926) 326–49; A. S. Peake, "The Messiah and the Son of Man," *The Servant of Yahweh: Three Lectures Delivered at King's College, London, during 1926 Together with The Rylands Lectures on Old Testament and New Testament Subjects* (Manchester: Manchester University, 1931) 220–37; H. Riesenfeld, *Jésus transfiguré: l'arrière-plan du récit évangélique de la transfiguration de Notre-Seigneur* (Copenhagen: Munksgaard, 1947) 307–13; C. C. McCown, "Jesus, Son of Man: A Survey of Recent Discussion," *JR* 28 (1948) 1–12; W. Bauer, *A Greek-English Lexicon of the New Testament and Other Early Christian Literature* (tr. W. F. Arndt and F. W. Gingrich; Chicago: University of Chicago, 1957) 842–43; P. C. Hodgson, "The Son of Man and the Problem of Historical Knowledge," *JR* 41 (1961) 91–108; R. H. Fuller, *The New Testament in Current Study* (New York: Scribner, 1962) 37–43; N. Perrin, *The Kingdom of God in the Teaching of Jesus* (Philadelphia: Westminster, 1963) 90–129; R. Marlow, "The *Son of Man* in Recent Journal Literature," *CBQ* 28 (1966) 20–30; I. H. Marshall, "The Synoptic Son of Man Sayings in Recent Discussion," *NTS* 12 (1966) 327–51; G. Haufe, "Das Menschensohn-Problem in der gegenwärtigen wissenschaftlichen Diskussion," *EvT* 26 (1966) 130–41; A. J. B. Higgins, "Is the Son of Man Problem Insoluble?" *Neotestamentica et Semitica: Studies in Honour of Matthew Black* (eds. E. E. Ellis and M. Wilcox; Edinburgh: Clark, 1969) 70–87.

5. H. M. Teeple ("The Origin of the Son of Man Christology," *JBL* 84 [1955] 213–50) interprets the terms "Messiah" and "messianic" in a very broad sense, insisting that the proper distinction to be drawn is not between "Son of Man" and "Messiah," but rather between "Son of Man type Messiah" and other types of "Messiah" (e.g., "Son of David type Messiah"). Norman Perrin ("The Son of Man in Ancient Judaism and Primitive Christianity: A Suggestion," *BR* 11 [1966] 24; *Rediscovering the Teaching of Jesus* [New York/Evanston: Harper and Row, 1967] 170–71), on the other hand, prefers "apocalyptic redeemer figures" as the broad category and makes a distinction between "Son of Man" and "Messiah."

6. See, e.g., H. E. Tödt, *The Son of Man in the Synoptic Tradition*, 22. Numerous suggestions have been offered as to the possible origin of the Son of Man image in Jewish apocalypticism, but the present evidence points increasingly to a Canaanite origin; see, e.g., C. Colpe, "ὁ υἱὸς τοῦ ἀνθρώπου," 406–20.

7. The quotation is from N. Perrin (*Rediscovering the Teaching*, 164) who, however, does not accept this view (see below). It should be noted that the weaknesses in this assumption have often been recognized even by scholars who accept it; see, e.g., H. E. Tödt, *The Son of Man in the Synoptic Tradition*, C. Colpe, "ὁ υἱὸς τοῦ ἀνθρώπου," 420–30; and the comments by N. Perrin, "The Son of Man in Ancient Judaism and Primitive Christianity," 19.

8. E.g., T. W. Manson, *The Teaching of Jesus: Studies of Its Form and Content* (2d ed.; Cambridge: Cambridge University, 1935) 211–34; V. Taylor, *The Names of Jesus* (New

York: St. Martin's, 1953) 33–34; E. Stauffer, *New Testament Theology* (New York: Macmillan, 1955) 109–11; O. Cullmann, *The Christology of the New Testament*, 152–64.

9. Particularly E. Schweizer, *Erniedrigung und Erhöhung bei Jesus und seinen Nachfolgern* (Zurich: Zwingli, 1955) 88–93; "Der Menschensohn (Zur eschatologischen Erwartung Jesu)," *Neotestamentica: Deutsche und Englische Aufsätze 1951–1963; German and English Essays 1951–1963* (Zurich/Stuttgart: Zwingli, 1963) 56–84; *Lordship and Discipleship* (SBT 28; London: SCM, 1960) 39–41; "The Son of Man," *JBL* 79 (1960) 119–29; *Erniedrigung und Erhöhung* (2d ed., 1962) 33–52, 65–71; "The Son of Man Again," *Neotestamentica* (1962–63), 85–92. Cf. also J. A. T. Robinson, *Jesus and His Coming: The Emergence of a Doctrine* (New York/Nashville: Abingdon, 1957) 37–82.

10. E.g., J. Knox, *The Death of Christ: The Cross in New Testament History and Faith* (New York: Abingdon, 1958) esp. 86–102; R. Bultmann, *Theology of the New Testament* (2 vols.; New York: Scribner, 1951–55) I, 26–32; and, for individual texts, *History of the Synoptic Tradition* (New York/Evanston: Harper and Row, 1963; rev. ed., 1969); cf. also his "Reich Gottes und Menschensohn," *ThRu* n.s. 9 (1937) 1–35; G. Bornkamm, *Jesus of Nazareth* (New York: Harper, 1960) 175–78, 228–31; F. Hahn, *The Titles of Jesus*, esp. 21–28; E. Jüngel, *Paulus und Jesus*, 215–62; R. H. Fuller, *Foundations*, 119–25; and especially H. E. Tödt, *The Son of Man in the Synoptic Tradition*. A. J. B. Higgins (*Jesus and the Son of Man*) agrees on the question of authenticity, but maintains that Jesus did identify himself with the coming Son of Man.

11. Especially P. Vielhauer, "Gottesreich und Menschensohn in der Verkündigung Jesu," *Aufsätze zum Neuen Testament* (Munich: Kaiser, 1965) 55–91; "Jesus und der Menschensohn: Zur Diskussion mit Heinz Eduard Tödt und Eduard Schweizer," ibid., 92–140; "Ein Weg der neutestamentlichen Theologie? Prüfung der Thesen Ferdinand Hahns," ibid., 141–98. See also, e.g., E. Käsemann, "Sentences of Holy Law in the New Testament," *New Testament Questions of Today* (Philadelphia: Fortress, 1969) 66–81; "The Beginnings of Christian Theology," ibid., 82–107; "On the Subject of Primitive Christian Apocalyptic," ibid., 108–37; H. Conzelmann, "Present and Future in the Synoptic Tradition," *God and Christ: Existence and Province* (New York: Harper and Row, 1968) 26–44; "Jesus Christus," *RGG* 3 (1959) 630–31. Cf. also H. M. Teeple, "The Origin of the Son of Man Christology."

12. N. Perrin, "Mark XIV.62: The End Product of a Christian Pesher Tradition?" *NTS* 12 (1966) 150–55; "The Son of Man in Ancient Judaism and Primitive Christianity," 17–28; *Rediscovering the Teaching*, 164–99; "The Creative Use of the Son of Man Traditions by Mark, *USQR* 23 (1968) 357–65; "The Son of Man in the Synoptic Tradition," *BR* 13 (1968) 3–25; "The Literary *Gattung* 'Gospel'—Some Observations," *ExpT* 82 (1970) 4–7.

13. N. Perrin, *Rediscovering the Teaching*, 172, and cf. 164–73; "The Son of Man in Ancient Judaism," 25–26. See also R. Leivestad, "Exit the Apocalyptic Son of Man," *NTS* 18 (1971–72) 243–67.

14. N. Perrin, *Rediscovering the Teaching*, 166; "The Son of Man in Ancient Judaism," 20.

15. N. Perrin, *Rediscovering the Teaching*, 198 (for the analysis of the sayings, see 173–99) and "The Son of Man in the Synoptic Tradition," 6–20. Perrin does accept the authenticity of certain of the "present" Son of Man sayings (e.g., Luke 7:34 = Matt 11:19), but he insists that "Son of Man" here is not a title, but "simply an idiomatic self-designation of the speaker in contrast to another person, the idiom known to us from the rabbis" ("The Son of Man in the Synoptic Tradition," 14; cf. Geza Vermes, "Appendix E: The Use of *br nš / br nš'* in Jewish Aramaic," in M. Black, *An Aramaic Approach to the Gospels and Acts* [3d ed.; Oxford: Clarendon, 1967] 310–28).

16. B. Lindars, *New Testament Apologetic: The Doctrinal Significance of the Old Testament Quotations* (London: SCM, 1961).

17. N. Perrin, *Rediscovering the Teaching*, 23.

18. N. Perrin, "The Son of Man in the Synoptic Tradition," 4.

19. N. Perrin, "The Son of Man in the Synoptic Tradition," 4; see *Rediscovering the Teaching*, 175–76. More recently, Perrin ("Recent Trends in Research in the Christology of the New Testament," *Transitions in Biblical Scholarship* [ed. J. Coert Rylaarsdam; Chicago: University of Chicago, 1968] 222) has apparently accepted the view of R. H. Fuller

and others that behind the exaltation christology based upon Ps 110:1 can be found traces of a still more primitive christology which held that "Jesus is the one who at his resurrection/ascension was predestined to appear as the Christ at the parousia." This does not necessarily affect, however, his conclusions regarding the origin of the Son of Man christology.

20. N. Perrin, *Rediscovering the Teaching*, 179; see the full discussion, 175–84.

21. N. Perrin, "The Son of Man in Ancient Judaism," 26; *Rediscovering the Teaching*, 173; cf. "The Son of Man in the Synoptic Tradition," 5, n. 7: "The parallels between the Son of Man in I Enoch and the New Testament are to be explained . . . by the fact that two roughly contemporary groups in the same Jewish apocalyptic milieu have done the same kind of thing in the same kind of way. The Enoch saga interprets the translations of Enoch by means of Ezekiel and Dan 7; the Christian traditions understood the fate of Jesus as a translation/assumption and interpreted it by means of Ps 110:1; Zech 12:10ff. and Dan 7:13."

22. See note 5 above.

23. This was frequent in late and rabbinic Judaism; see, e.g., Str-B, 4. 452–65.

24. See, e.g., Sigmund Mowinckel, *He That Cometh*, 335–36; G. F. Moore, *Judaism in the First Centuries of the Christian Era: The Age of the Tannaim* (Cambridge: Harvard, 1927) II, 334–37.

25. Regarding Psalm 110, F. H. Borsch (*The Son of Man in Myth and History*, 396, n. 2) says: "There is little evidence that Ps 110:1 was employed messianically by Jews in Jesus' lifetime, but its use here [in Mark 12:35ff.] shows that someone could make the connection. If the Church could have done this, there is no reason why someone before it could not have done so also."

26. For example, the phrase "right hand" is apparently the verbal link between Ps 16:8–11 and Ps 110:1 (see, e.g., Acts 2:25–36). See also my argument below for the verbal link between Ps 110:1 and Ps 8:6; cf. B. Lindars, *New Testament Apologetic*, 50–51. For a parallel to this in the Qumran material, see 4QFlor 10–13, where the verbal link between 2 Sam 7:11–14 and Amos 9:11 is "I will raise up."

27. Ezek 2:1 and frequently thereafter.

28. N. Perrin, "The Son of Man in Ancient Judaism," 21–22; *Rediscovering the Teaching*, 167–68.

29. See B. Lindars (*New Testament Apologetic*, 46–47), who argues, on other grounds, that the quotation of Ps 110:1 in Mark 12:36b reflects a later exegetical development than that in Acts 2:34b–35.

30. Matt 22:44 follows Mark's ὑποκάτω, but Luke 20:43 returns to the ὑποπόδιον of Ps 110:1.

31. The presence of ὑποκάτω in Mark 12:36 and Matt 24:44, rather than ὑποπόδιον, has, of course, been noted before, as has the probability of its derivation from Ps 8:6; see, e.g., K. Stendahl, *The School of St. Matthew and Its Use of the Old Testament* (Philadelphia: Fortress, 1968) 78.

32. B. Lindars, *New Testament Apologetic*, 50–51.

33. N. Perrin (*Rediscovering the Teaching*, 181) observes that, once the use of a particular text is established, "it would be natural to go on to use other aspects of the passage." C. H. Dodd (*According to the Scriptures: The Sub-Structure of New Testament Theology* [New York: Scribner, 1953]; *The Old Testament in the New* [Philadelphia: Fortress, 1963]) has argued that the early Christians tended to draw material from whole blocks of OT texts (e.g., entire chapters), rather than from individual sentences or phrases, and that the context in which a particular word, phrase, or statement originally stood was very much in the mind of the Christian exegete. This may be overstated, but the context would obviously have been in the mind of the exegete and would quite easily have suggested to him further possibilities of interpretation and application.

34. The two are used together in Mark 14:62 and parallels, and in Acts 7:56. N. Perrin (*Rediscovering the Teaching*, 179) argues that the two usages "cannot be dependent upon one another" and that they, therefore, constitute double testimony for the combination of Ps 110:1 and Dan 7:13 in the Christian exegetical tradition. Cf. also the Ascension story in Acts 1:9, which Perrin regards as dependent ultimately upon the Ps 110:1 tradition but containing "an echo" of Dan 7:13 in the reference to the "cloud."

35. N. Perrin, *Rediscovering the Teaching*, 184.

36. N. Perrin, "The Son of Man in the Synoptic Tradition," 7–10.

37. N. Perrin, "The Creative Use of the Son of Man Traditions by Mark"; "The Literary *Gattung* 'Gospel'—Some Observations."

38. Ps 110:1 in the Hebrew ends *âd-'āšît 'ōyᵉbe̞(y)kā hᵃdōm lᵉragle̞(y)kā*. Ps 8:6 (8:7) in the Hebrew ends: *kōl šattāh taḥat-raglā(y)w*. Thus, the similarities are much less striking than in the Greek. Moreover, Ps 8:4 (8:5) uses *be̞n-'ādām* for "son of man," while Dan 7:13 has the Aramaic *bar-'ᵉnāš*."

39. F. Hahn, *The Titles of Jesus*, 104–7.

40. H. M. Teeple, "The Origin of the Son of Man Christology," 237–50. Teeple (238) also acknowledges that the Son of Man sayings "may have originated in Greek."

41. H. M. Teeple, "The Origin of the Son of Man Christology," 241; cf., e.g., H. E. Tödt, "Excursus II: Discussion of the Concept of the Heavenly Son of Man in Acts 7:56," *The Son of Man in the Synoptic Tradition*, 303–5; C. K. Barrett, "Stephen and the Son of Man," *Apophoreta: Festschrift für Ernst Haenchen* (ed. W. Eltester; Berlin: Töpelmann, 1964) 32–38.

42. H. M. Teeple, "The Origin of the Son of Man Christology," 248.

43. E. Schweizer ("The Son of Man," 123) says: "This scene of the Son of Man standing upright, as well as the use of this term outside the words of Jesus, is so unusual that the report seems to go back to the very event of the execution of Stephen." Similarly, O. Cullmann (*The Christology of the New Testament*, 181–88) argues that "the little known but very important early Christian group of the Hellenists" was "the circle which fostered the Son of Man Christology" (183); Cullmann also believes, however, that the history of the Son of Man concept can be traced from what he terms "esoteric Judaism" through the teaching of Jesus and the Christology of the Hellenists to the Fourth Gospel. On the importance of Stephen and the Hellenists, see M. Simon, *St. Stephen and the Hellenists in the Primitive Church* (New York: Longmans, Green, 1958).

44. See, e.g., O. Cullmann, "Dissensions within the Early Church," *USQR* 22 (1967) 85–87.

45. H. M. Teeple, "The Origin of the Son of Man Christology," 248.

46. Ibid., 249–50.

What Archaeology Can and Cannot Do

Following a brief look at the contributions of those who shaped biblical archaeology before 1960 and at the methodological advancements which were made up to 1970, G. Ernest Wright illustrates the ways in which archaeology can be used in biblical studies. His premise is timeless: when archaeological evidence is considered from fresh angles and when new findings become known in the Near East, our view of the Bible alters. For instance, David Noel Freedman makes a major statement, pp. 77–100, about Hebrew poetry based on a study of relevant archaeology, literature, and history. Also, Paolo Mattiae's continuing dig at Tell Mardikh is motivating scholars to reconsider the prevailing opinion that Genesis contains little fact—that it is chiefly a mythic fabrication of later editors. Mattiae's discovery of the names of Abraham and other patriarchs among thousands of ancient non-biblical writings gives considerable credence to that book's historical accuracy. And as Giovanni Pettinato and others publish translations of texts discovered at Tell Mardikh, biblical historians may be able to fill in some of the innumerable blank pages about the patriarchal period.

F OR a majority in the Biblical world Albright's work has established the basic chronology for the events related in Joshua (a 13th century date of the conquest) and the historical support for the background of the narrative. Yet a carefully defined statement of what archaeology is and is not, does and does not, has been hard to articulate. Such a statement must follow the experiments of reconstruction, and first attempts may need future modification when the polemical period which is always created when general assumptions are badly shaken, is past.[1]

While the term "archaeology" was first used by classical authors simply to mean "ancient history", its revival in modern times has meant a

From G. Ernest Wright, *Biblical Archaeologist*, **34** (1971), 70–76.

narrowing of its meaning to the ruins of past civilizations and cultures, especially their excavation. For Albright and his students archaeology has included both epigraphic and non-epigraphic discoveries, even though the investigation of the two must develop each its own set of disciplines. Yet in the antiquarian field generally, philologists and archaeologists are usually separate, the former studying documents and the latter the methodologies of conducting an excavation and the study and presentation of what is found. The field has suffered from too much compartmentalization at this point.

Furthermore, archaeologists themselves have suffered from too great a separation from one another in their various fields, and usually too great a separation from humanistic disciplines on the one hand and from the natural sciences on the other. Anthropological archaeology, for example, starting from its primary point of reference, primitive man, has developed methodology and cooperation with natural sciences more quickly than other fields, because the very nature of most of the deposits dealt with required them to do so in order to extract a maximum of information from a minimum of deposit. On the other hand, the humanistic aspects of the subject have often been short-changed and the results impoverished by over-zealous attempts to remain non-historical and "scientific" when actually they are simply trying to reconstruct all they can about human beings for whom "science" has only a partial application.

Classical and most of early Near Eastern archaeology has been dominated by a museum mentality which requires objects for display to a contributing public primarily interested in art and art history. Archaeologists from this background have been slowest of all to develop an interest in ever more precision and control in methodology. They have to their glory maintained their full humanistic interest, but separation from the natural sciences with exceptions has been most notable in the information derived from the queries put to their material.

Excavation of the great Near Eastern tells has brought such wealth of architecture and objects that there seemed no need to ask further questions than those of the historian regarding chronology, interconnections and typological history.

The conceptual framework and methodology of excavation has been most highly developed and refined in the historical period by a few exceptional persons whose primary training has been in other countries, but who for one reason or another began excavations in Palestine, Petrie and Kenyon from England, Reisner and Albright from the United States. That small corridor between continents has few natural resources, and thus was and is very poor as compared with the centers of world power in antiquity. To gain any positive result from work in the country requires one's turning his attention from an expectation of rich stores of anything, and certainly not great palaces and a wealth of inscriptions, the latter forming the primary guide to where in time one is located while digging. Pottery chronology and the stratigraphy of the deposits of earth have to be the primary concentration. It was Petrie who in 1890 left Egypt for a short period of work at Tell el-Ḥesī in the southern coastal plain. There he proved that ceramics could be a primary chronological tool by demonstrating the differences in pottery between levels cut into the steep cliff of the tell eroded by a winter stream. It was Reisner who left Egypt in 1909 and 1910 for two seasons of work at Samaria and encountered an intricate jumble on the tell which required entirely different strategy from anything he had used in Egypt.

It was Albright, beginning in 1920, who developed the pottery tool into an instrument of some precision by taking it out of the mists of oral tradition, articulated its use in writing, and provided a critical assessment of the whole discipline in the light of his knowledge of the entire Near East. Following his work one could begin to write archaeological histories of the country—something impossible before the discipline had been subjected to his critical work and his ceramic sequences.

Reisner's methodological principles were generally not followed, except for the new care with which recording and find spots were handled and the ideal evolved of being able to reproduce on paper a tell's stratigraphy in which the exact location of all artifacts could be spotted. It was with Kenyon's re-introduction of Reisner's principles independently, as they had been developed in the archaeology of England, that the new revolution in precision and field control was now put in practice for all to see in East Mediterranean archaeology. The key to this control lay in digging and distinguishing the soil layers as a geologist would do, rather than focusing primarily on building or wall sequences, following the lead of the chief interests of the expedition's architect.

Palestine west of the Jordan is the most intensively dug and explored area of its size in the world. Its very poverty has been a major factor in the development of precision in archaeological field work to a level seldom reached in the historical periods anywhere else in the classical and Near Eastern worlds. Consequently, it cannot be overstressed that the proper use of archaeology as a "scientific" tool in Biblical study was impossible before the work of Albright, while the period of the 1960's is the time of a revolution in controlled archaeology, following the period 1952–1958 of the Kenyon expedition to Jericho.[2]

Even these new methodologies fail to extract a maximum of information from the occupational debris of antiquity. Beginning in Palestine in 1970, certain American explorations were able to staff their expeditions with a more or less full complement of natural scientists. Such cross-disciplinary approaches were a "first" in the Near East's historical period. They were modeled after the great pioneering prehistoric enterprises of Robert J. Braidwood in the 1950's, which have refocused our knowledge of human prehistory with regard to what happened before, during, and after *the Neolithic revolution* when the first villages were established in the Near East. Hence it can be predicted that the 1970's will see far more controlled information made available to the Biblical student than the archaeologist has hitherto been able to provide.

With regard to Biblical events, however, it cannot be overstressed that archaeological data are mute. Fragmentary ruins, preserving only a tiny fraction of the full picture of ancient life, cannot speak without someone asking questions of them. And the kind of questions asked are part and parcel of the answers "heard" because of predispositions on the part of the questioner. Archaeology can *prove* very little about anything without minds stored with a wide-ranging variety of information which carefully begin to ask questions of the mute remains in order to discover what they mean. It is all too easy for lack of information and imagination to gain less than the remains can supply, or for fertile imaginations to suppose that the ancient trash heaps tell them more than a more controlled mind can believe they do. It is small wonder, then, that disagreement and debate arise. A destruction layer in the ruins does not tell us the identity of the people involved. Indeed, we know that certain black soot and charcoal layers do not necessarily mean destruction. An accidental fire in one part of the town or city, certain industrial pursuits, or even an earthquake may be the answer.

Yet the mute nature of the remains does not mean that archaeology is useless. It simply means that ancient cultural and political horizons and sequences can only be reconstructed by hypothesis from every kind of critically sifted evidence available. At some points more data are available than at others. Hence the historical reconstructions have only varying degrees of probability. Yet in antiquity it is most important to recall that models and hypotheses are the primary means by which reconstruction is possible after the basic critical work is done. And, furthermore, it takes a great deal of humility to say frankly what the physical sciences have had also to say; predisposition of minds at any one period frame the type of questions asked of the material and become a part of the "answers" we suppose we have obtained from our investigations. Final *proof* of anything ancient must be confined to such questions as how pottery was made, what rock was used, and what food and fauna were present. Certainly that proof does not extend to the validity of the religious claims the Bible would place upon us, and we must remember that the Bible is not a mine for scientifically grounded certainties about anything. It is instead a literature that places before us one of history's major religious options.

What archaeology can do for Biblical study is to provide a physical context in time and place which was the environment of the people who produced the Bible or are mentioned in it. Inscriptional evidence is of exceptional importance for Biblical backgrounds and even for occasional mention of Biblical people and places. For the rest, archaeology provides evidence to be critically sifted. It then is used along with other critically assessed data, where it exists, in order to form *hypotheses* about the how, why, what and when of cultural, socio-political and economic affairs in 13th century Palestine, for example. These hypotheses will stand or be altered as new information makes change necessary. Final and absolutely proven answers are impossible to provide. One generation's questions may not be another's, and in every case the questions asked are integral to the answers. Thus one generation's research differs from another's.

Furthermore, Martin Noth's predisposition, for example, has led him to a negative view of the historical background of the confessional events surveyed in the Books of Exodus and Joshua, along with many of his predecessors and contemporaries. To this writer, such a negative assessment, deriving from the last century's criticism, is not only a defensible, but an indispensable tool in historical *methodology*. But when the tool becomes the dominant item of the conclusion, it then is most often a bias or predisposition of the author. There is no reason whatever that the opposite predisposition should not be held, namely one toward a positive view of the evidence, even though the actual course of events may have been far more complex than tradition has remembered. Whether optimism or pessimism is the predisposition, the fact is that in Exodus and Joshua we have dominant and central confessional and literary themes presented both in the book and in confessional liturgical statements. This requires explanation. A necessity is upon us to explain their presence in the earliest literature (e.g., Exod. 15) as well as in the latest. Something formative to Israel's worldview happened in her earliest historical experience. Can a hypothesis be suggested which explains without claiming too much or too little? By definition such a hypothesis is devised to explain most completely what we *now* know, *not* what it may be necessary or possible for another generation to say.

The situation with regard to Joshua, ranging from extreme negative assessment to positive, has numerous parallels in other fields where scholars try to assess literary tradition, philological analysis, tradition-history, form, language, text, archaeology and historical background— and then try to come up with a story of what *really* happened! Faulty analysis or overemphasis at the wrong place can throw the resulting hypothesis "out of gear" entirely. Yet one must forge ahead, under the critical light of his peers, in the knowledge that the work has to be as carefully done as early as possible, and then restudied a generation later, if not sooner!

Father Roland de Vaux has reviewed the evidence for the Trojan War and that for the Phoenician colonization of the Mediterranean, and finds precisely the same problems being struggled with in the same way, with the same radically different conclusions.[3]

With regard to the Phoenicians, ancient authors assert that Cadiz and Utica, for example, were founded as early as 1100 B.C., while Carthage was founded in 814 B.C. and became the Phoenician power of the west *par excellence* for centuries. Yet Rhys Carpenter in 1958, basing his results on purely archaeological evidence, disregards the literary tradition completely and says the cities in question were not founded much before *ca.* 700 B.C., and only gradually during the next two centuries spread to Sicily, Sardinia, Cadiz, Spain and the Balearic Islands. Now with 10th and 9th century inscriptions existing on Cyprus and Spain, which Carpenter had no training to handle critically, 8th century specimens in Sicily, Sardinia, and Malta, the skeptics can only defend themselves by challenging the archaeologist's methods, especially the discipline of paleography. Nevertheless, the basic point has been made by the archaeologists in general agreement with the ancient authors: Phoenician colonization preceded the arrival of the Greeks.

What can be said about the tradition made immortal by Homer in the *Iliad* and the *Odyssey*? Schliemann evidently found the ruined tell of Troy, but then came the debate as to which stratum was destroyed and by what agency at the site. Carl Blegen, the last excavator, accepts the city's identification, and claims the city destroyed in Homer's traditions must be identified with Stratum VIIa, in which Mycenean pottery still occurs in abundance. Thus Homer's story of the expedition against Troy must have a historical basis. Archaeology for Blegen thus "proves" that there must have been some kind of coalition of Achaeans or Myceneans who fought Troy and its allies and defeated them.

Yet a more "judicial" answer has been that Troy VIIa was destroyed by human violence, but the excavations have provided not one scrap of evidence of a Greek coalition or any identification whatever to answer the question of "Who did it?" Perhaps it was destroyed by the Sea Peoples. The best procedure of all, in this viewpoint, is to dissociate the whole archaeological discovery from myth and poetry, and even from the legend of Troy itself.

Yet in both instances still other scholars raise basic questions with regard to both viewpoints as to whether the two extremes are really in methodological tune with the use of archaeology as "proof" or as evidence. The skeptic always has the advantage because archaeology speaks only in response to our questions and one can call any tradition not provable. Thus since no proof can be attained anywhere, one extreme simply asks that archaeological data be presented and the attempt to prove anything in literary tradition cease forthwith.

Both sides of the controversy use the term "proof" in ways inadmissible, even absurd, with regard to any past cultural, political, socioeconomic history.

Whether it is Trojan history, Phoenician history, or what history remains in the book of Joshua, we must begin with the fact that we have *actual* texts. These must be interpreted by all the means of literary analysis available to us. Then we must reconstruct the archaeological and ecological context as best we can both in the given area and in the widest possible context. Only then can we examine the question as to whether the one illumines the other, or whether a reasonable hypothesis can be reconstructed which best explains what we know at this time. The dictum of de Vaux is axiomatic: "Archaeology does not confirm the text, which is what it is, it can only confirm the interpretation which we give it."[4] Conversely, archaeology, dealing with the wreckage of antiquity, proves nothing in itself. It must be analyzed in a variety of ways, and then with all other data available, its meaning in the overall picture of a cultural continuum is expressed by interpretation. Here again it is the interpretation that is at all usable, and that is the product of a human brain with the use of tools available, not in a pure vacuum mistakenly called by some "science." Instead the brain belongs to a limited person, living and working in a given time and space. A person is not more infallible than his sources and predecessors. Ambiguity and relativity enter every sphere of human activity. Some minds rise above others as masters of their peers, but the solid *proofs*, which so many assume possible at the end of either scientific or historical work, cannot be attained by finite beings. We are historical organisms by intrinsic nature, and ambiguity is always a central component of history, whether of the humanities, of social science, or of natural science.

NOTES

1. For outstanding attempts at such statement, see especially Roland de Vaux, O.P., "On Right and Wrong Uses of Archaeology," *Near Eastern Archaeology in the Twentieth Century*, pp. 64–80. For a treatment of the same subject from the standpoint of a classicist, see M. I. Finley, "Archaeology and History," *Daedalus* (Winter, 1971), pp. 168–186.

2. Cf. Kenyon, *Beginning in Archaeology* (1952); *Digging up Jericho* (1957); and G. Ernest Wright, "Archaeological Method in Palestine—An American Interpretation," *Eretz Israel*, IX (1969), pp. 120–133.

3. See R. de Vaux, *loc. cit.* (n. 1).

4. R. de Vaux, *op. cit.*, p. 78.

The Method of the
Cultic Interpretation

The Psalms, written over several centuries to meet a wide
range of personal and national religious needs, remain the
most frequently read yet imperfectly understood books of
the Old Testament. In a review of the research, Sigmund
Mowinckel focuses on the leading Psalms scholar, Hermann
Gunkel. For further reading of Gunkel's seminal work, see
Thomas M. Horner's translation, The Psalms: A Form-
Critical Introduction *(1967). After giving some illuminat-*
ing insights into conditions under which the Psalms were
written, Mowinckel discusses why they have a perennial
literary appeal. For additional views about their literary
appeal, see the essays in Section IV: "Literary Forms and
Literary Influence," as well as the essays by David Noel
Freedman, pp. 77–100, and Roland Mushat Frye, pp.
253–264.

A CULTIC interpretation—and a real understanding—of the psalms means setting each one of them in relation to the definite cultic act—or the cultic acts—to which it belonged.

All scientific research demands a proper arrangement of material, a classifying and a grouping, so that the things which belong together may be seen in their mutual connexions and illuminate one another. But the principles and criteria of classification must be derived from the material itself, not from disparate fields or modern interests and points of view. Not seldom the 'catchwords' for classification have been taken from the loci of Christian dogmatics, e.g. from the different divine attributes. But the ancient Israelites did not shape their thoughts to the pattern of Christian dogmas and morals. Nor can a classification according to the religious ideas represented in the different psalms be considered satisfactory: we cannot be sure that the idea which to us seems most prominent was so for the poet. It is quite unsystematic to group together 'nature psalms', 'creation psalms', 'psalms on the majesty of God', with 'prayer

From Sigmund Mowinckel, *The Psalms in Israel's Worship*, I (1967), 23–39.

psalms', 'thanksgiving psalms', and 'penitential psalms'. The creation and the majesty of God, etc., may well be mentioned both in a 'prayer psalm' and a 'thanksgiving psalm'; the question is: why, and with what aim? There is no psalm which does not accept God's majesty and his power to intervene everywhere and all the time, or which does not acknowledge him as creator; the question is: why does, e.g., *this* special psalm speak at greater length and in more detail about creation than is usual in the psalms? It is misleading to speak of a 'nature psalm', because 'Nature'— this modern conception—plays no independent part in the psalms at all, but only occurs as an example of God's creative work. But why do certain psalms call 'heaven and earth, mountains and oceans, trees and fields, beasts and birds', etc., to praise the Lord, while the regular call to praise in the psalms is directed to the congregation of Israel, or the like?

All this modern grouping only leads us to ask the poets about things which interest *us*, but to which *they* often have no answer, instead of trying to see things from *their* point of view, and asking what is in *their* mind, e.g. when they appeal to God's omniscience, or call upon nature to praise Yahweh. The usual interpretations of Pss. 90 and 139 are examples of such a mistaken way of putting the question. We read them as contemplations of the eternity or the omnipresence of God—but that is not what the poems seek to convey. They speak out of a definite situation, and it is in order to make God intervene in this situation that they speak of his eternity and omniscience. We must first listen to the emotion in the psalmist's own heart, and to be able to do that we must try to find the actual situation in which he is placed. Only then can we ask what he—and God through him—has to say to *us* in *our* situation.

A proper classification must try to find the different fundamental types or species of psalms according to their own rules. How can these rules be recognized and described?

This is where Gunkel's 'form-critical' ('form-historical', *formgeschichtliche*) or 'type-critical' (*gattungsgeschichtliche*) method comes in.

Even a superficial consideration shows that, in form and in details of content and structure, the psalms largely fall into a certain number of markedly different groups, which usually show a close conformation in form and matter within each individual group.

A number of psalms, for instance, are immediately recognizable as praises of Yahweh and of his great works and attributes. We soon discover that certain fundamental elements recur in such psalms with great regularity, and that in regard to their structure also, the psalms of this group have certain traits in common. Another group consists of prayers and lamentations, in which a 'we' or 'I' voices his distress and begs Yahweh's help. Here too we meet with a number of characteristic details and common formulas both of prayer and lamentation, and with particular motivations for granting the prayer (*Gebetserhörungsmotive*), which in many variations constantly recur. Thus we are here confronted with special 'kinds' or 'types' of psalms whose peculiarities of content and form are amenable to description and explanation, and in which the agreement between form and content can be studied. These conformities cannot be accidental.

The first task is to classify the different forms and styles, thoughts and moods, of the psalms which are more or less distinctly alike in all these respects, and which thus form a special group or 'type' (species), for the moment leaving the dubious cases aside. Thus we become able to give a more or less complete description of the characteristics and peculiarities of every single group or species, each one containing those psalms which show a fund of common forms, thoughts and moods. The work may be compared with that of the botanist, who decides the species of the individual plant and its place within the system on the basis of such objective criteria as the form and number of stamens, petals and sepals, and the place of these organs above or below the ovary.

We have to do with fixed style forms, where the similarities between the individual pieces within the group cannot be due to one poet having imitated the other, but to the fixity of a traditional and conventional style.

In a closed cultural orbit, both in a primitive culture and in the ancient high civilizations, the power of tradition and custom over form was much stronger than in modern times, when both an open exchange of cultural values and a much higher appreciation of the individual and his peculiar qualities have broken up the formerly closed and uniform circles of culture. The durability of form, and the power of convention over what is to be thought and said and done in the different constantly recurrent, typical situations of life, we Norwegians, for example, until quite recently have had the opportunity of studying in our own remote valleys and communities. The conditions in ancient Israel were very much the same. Thus the hold of style over the poet was very great; from one point of view poetic composition was a thing which might be learned by anyone who cared to familiarize himself with the ideas and forms which custom demanded on typical occasions. Poetry, then, exists in definite traditional types or kinds, each with its own special rules as to content and form.

Content and form belong together. There exists no form without a content, and no content without a form. The psalms are poetry, and poetry is an art, and in art both content and form are determinants. Good art means a work in which there is unity of content and aim on the one hand, and of form and style on the other—where the form serves and adequately expresses the content, makes it living, and allows it to appear with its full weight and to exhibit its real character. But especially in a remote culture, the forms are easier to detect, and they are often more fixed and more durable than the content. A form may live, even if the content has become more or less incomprehensible, and the ideas connected with it have changed, or have gotten a different emphasis. It goes without saying that in the classification of the psalms due attention must be paid to the motifs or themes included in the different form elements and thus recurring in several psalms as characteristic of the group. Essential parts of the content lie concealed in the form elements. Each motif or theme must be followed up in the different psalms and its quality be determined by comparison.

But even so, the fixed forms provide the easiest point of departure, and that is just what Gunkel has seen. So he came to call his method the *formgeschichtliche*, the form-historical, or form-critical method. The term is not quite adequate, and has given rise to misunderstanding. We might better call it the 'type-critical' or 'type-historical' method. The fixed form elements will usually begin to appear in the opening words of the psalm. Anyone could at once classify a piece of writing that began: 'Once upon a time', or 'Dear Friend', or 'We are in receipt of your favour'. In the same way we find that a certain group of psalms, a 'psalm-type', quite regularly starts with 'Praise Yahweh', or 'Let us praise', and so on. Another starts with a mention of Yahweh's name (the 'invocation') and a supplication, 'LORD (i.e. Yahweh), I cry unto thee'.

Just as important as the opening words are the closing ones. Compare 'and they lived happily ever after', or 'Yours faithfully'. In the psalms we very often find that the closing words, in some form or other, reiterate or correspond to the opening ones.

But even the central portion or main part has its typical elements of form and content. Religious experience and custom had long ago decided what details of content, what thoughts and formulas in the cult were 'right' and 'appropriate' in each type of psalm and situation in the cult. And these forms persist, even where the individual poet does not think consciously of a purpose any longer, or of gaining anything by his prayer. Thus we see that with the exhortation to praise God in the opening words, there usually goes an enumeration of Yahweh's great and glorious works, his *tĕhillôth*. Very often a description of the sorry state and need of the suppliant corresponds to the opening invocation and prayer, and an appeal to the attributes of Yahweh or his deeds which make it likely that help may be given.

The realization of which elements of form normally belong to a certain type not only makes it possible to define the individual psalm and the cultic situation from which it originates, but is also of considerable importance for the exegesis, and for the interpretation of any obscure passage. The problem is frequently solved when we find out to what fundamental type the psalm in question belongs. It is also important when solving the question of how to divide a psalm into stanzas. The form may decide whether a verse belongs to the preceding or to the succeeding part. The determination of type can also answer the question we often meet with in the commentaries as to whether a psalm is a unit or should be divided into two; in the light of form criticism we can tell which subject matter and elements of form regularly belong to, or may belong to, a certain type.

Gunkel also realized that there is a close connexion between the fixed forms and contents on the one hand, and certain typical, more or less regularly recurring situations in the life of the community in question. Each 'literary' type has its special *place in life,* from which it has sprung.

As hinted above, there are in the life of every society, and especially in a closed cultural orbit, like that of the Hebrews, certain ever recurrent situations where certain things have to be done and certain words to be said. That applies both to what we call secular life, and to the sacred, cultic life. That means that even what we call secular, but important, situations in life tend to become hedged by fixed 'rituals'. In his book *Rites de passage,* A. van Gennep has demonstrated this as a very important side of man's culture and cult. In the decisive situations of life, in life's supreme moments, it is necessary that something vital be created and obtained; and the means by which it was to be attained were the efficacious rites and words. As an element in these acts and words, art has always found its place, from the cave paintings of the Mousterians to the cultic poetry, song and music of the higher religions.

Poetry, like all other sorts of art, may have come into existence by the eruptive expression of what filled man's soul, without any other aim and purpose than just to express, to give birth to what demands expression, just because it 'presses on' the soul. But even this is an 'aim', although perhaps an unconscious one; man at once experiences that he has gained something by the expression, and that what he has created is useful to obtain certain results. What he expresses makes an impression on the others. It can and shall be used.

To primitive man, art and poetry have their aim and purpose, their 'tendency' in the good sense of the word. The ancient civilizations do not know of poetry which is not 'tendentious'. Even the fairy-tale has its purpose: to entertain, to move, to excite and to release. No ancient oriental could have conceived of 'Art for art's sake'. Art and poetry are individual and personal, but also social. Primitive poetry has its place in definite situations in life, and aims at expressing what then happens and should happen, what is felt and should be felt, what should then be said, because the situation demands a lofty form of expression. Poetry itself was an expression of a sociological function. Certain emotions, thoughts and words were to be expressed so as to bring about a certain result, important for the life of the community, and the form had to be the 'impressive', creating, efficacious form of poetry. At the marriage ceremony the rhythmic blessing was meant to induce fertility in the bride and numerous offspring for the husband and his clan, as in the narrative of the betrothal of Rebekah. Before the battle a curse was flung against the enemy to break his 'luck', put 'bane' and evil 'charms' into his soul, to enable Israel to stand up to him and drive him away, as in the Balaam story (Num. 22–24). At the holy places, when the council sat and cases were brought forward, the priests gave their directions from Yahweh in traditional forms. Before the battle they and the prophets gave oracular answers. When the army came home, the women sang paeans. At a burial the 'mourning-women' sang their dirge, the *qînâ*. Each of these 'literary categories' has its traditional form and its traditional subject. No chance words were then spoken, but words of a defined content, worked by a poet or poetess into a poem according to set rules governed by a long tradition. The content was determined by the aim, and the aim, again, was dictated by the situation.

In the same way the situations also determined the form. The form is the one which, in each case, was felt to be the most natural and most suitable means of expressing the word to be said and of reaching the goal to be attained. This consideration consciously or unconsciously decides the choice of the details to be included, the expressions and imagery employed, the fundamental mood, and the composition as a whole into which the details have been fitted.

This general principle must also be applied to the psalms. The classification into different groups, each with its specific peculiarities as to style, form and content, is no subjective arrangement of the material, based on aesthetic considerations and feelings. By taking the fixed forms as a starting point, the form-critical method shows that it is founded on something objective and amenable to control, dependent on external observations, which it classifies, systematizes and explains. In the forms— here taken in the widest sense of the word—some essential information is found. The study of the formal criteria of the different stylistic 'types' shows the way to the different situations in life from which they have sprung. To each of the main psalm types corresponds a definite situation; they all have their definite setting or place in life. It then becomes quite clear that all these situations are cultic situations.

The content and the style of the 'public psalm of lament', such as, e.g., Pss. 44; 74; 79; 80, are just those which can be singled out from the description in I Sam. 7 of what was done and said as the Philistines oppressed the Israelites and the latter 'gathered together to Mizpah, and drew water, and poured it out before the LORD, and fasted on that day, and said there, We have sinned against the LORD . . . and the children of Israel said to Samuel, Cease not to cry unto the LORD our God for us, that he will save us out of the hand of the Philistines. And Samuel took a sucking lamb, and offered it for a whole burnt offering unto the LORD: and Samuel cried unto the LORD for Israel'. What, at a similar celebration 'in the time of dearth' (according to Jer. 14), used to be said to Yahweh is, as to content and form and style, in the closest correspondence with the same psalm type. What, according to Isa. 38 or Jonah 2, a man used to say to Yahweh when bringing his thanksgiving gift after being saved from great danger—sickness or the like—has also its close parallels in a definite type of psalm represented by Pss. 32, 116, and others. When the Chronicler describes a cultic celebration of some sort, he often lets the singers sing a hymn of praise which, in all essentials, often even in the wording, has its formal and material parallels in the Psalter.

So Gunkel could confidently draw the conclusion that psalm poetry as such, all the main psalm types with their formal and material characteristics, have sprung from definite cultic situations. Every psalm type as such has been created to serve cultic performances in a definite cultic situation with its own specific aim—hence its typical content, its structure and its formal expression.

With an objective inner logic the cultic situations demand a particular content in a particular form. Within the framework of a divine service of worship nothing is accidental. Everything has its significance and its purpose, which we must try to fathom. All the formal and material peculiarities of a type are explained by that origin and that purpose. To find these definite cultic situations was to Gunkel an integrating part of his form-historical research. So far, he was, in principle, absolutely right; and all further investigations of the psalms must be based on the foundations thus laid by him.

2

But, as already mentioned, Gunkel has not drawn the full consequences from his own fundamental discovery. His commentary on the psalms (*Die Psalmen*) and the Gunkel-Begrich 'Introduction to the Psalms' (*Einleitung in die Psalmen*) have gone only half-way. His method led him to see that psalm poetry as such was old in Israel, and that many psalms must be dated to pre-exilic times; but in the main he kept to the opinion ruling at the beginning of this century, that the greater number of extant psalms were post-exilic and came from small, more or less private 'conventicles' of pious laymen—for the existence of which he has given just as little proof as did his predecessors. The majority of extant psalms were in Gunkel's opinion no real cult psalms; they were 'spiritualized' imitations of the old, now mostly lost, cultic psalm poetry. In the many allusions to cultic rites and performances he would see only metaphors, and in this supposed emancipation from the cult, in the psalmists' 'freedom from the cult religion', he saw just that religious 'progress' which gave the psalms their religious value. The psalms had, so to say, to apologize for their cultic origin. He clung, like most of the older psalm interpreters, to the curious prejudice that direct cultic destination—'cult' formulas', as they said—was more or less incompatible with deep personal feeling and experience—and the presence of these latter traits in many psalms they of course could not deny.

From this position, however, arose a serious problem which neither Gunkel himself nor his nearest followers perceived, or which, at least, they left unsolved. Both the titles of the psalms and express notes in the Jewish tradition in the Mishna and Talmud show that several psalms have definitely been used in the temple service. But since we know that Judaism, like all other ancient cult religions, always demanded that everything concerning the cult should rest on old and sacred heritage and tradition, and that the cult should be a kind of closed world which no 'profane' influence might enter, it is inconceivable how any younger, private, lay poetry could possibly have made its way into the cult, and even supplanted most of the genuine old ritual poetry.

If the many psalms in which 'the suffering ones' or 'the hapless ones' ('ŏnîyîm, 'anāwîm) complain about their oppressors originate from the 'suppressed' lower classes in the congregation, how can it then be explained that they later on found their way into the official cult, which was in the hands of the supposed oppressors of the authors, the mighty and wealthy priesthood and the rulers of the congregation? In fact those 'oppressed ones' are the nation of Israel itself, suffering under the oppression of its heathen neighbours or the oriental world empires. Or, to take another instance, if the Korah psalms, Pss. 42–44, as Snaith has tried to demonstrate, originated in the circles which Nehemiah drove out from Jerusalem, and Pss. 50; 73–83 from the Jewish rigorists at that time, can it be conceived that this private polemical poetry has been taken up into the official cult, at a time when its true nature must still have been known to everyone?

To this problem there is only one satisfying answer: the psalms are—with very few exceptions—real cult psalms, made for cultic use.

Another consideration points in the same direction.

We do have a Jewish psalm poetry which came into existence as 'private religious lyrics' without any connexion with the temple cult, and without cultic destination. This psalmody emanated from certain 'pious circles', which really existed in later Judaism, after the days of the predominance of the written law on the one hand, and the Hellenizing influences among the upper classes before and after the Maccabean revolt on the other. It is to be found in the so-called Psalms of Solomon, and the newly found Essenian Hodayoth from the Qumran caves. Owing to the emancipation from the temple cult and the individualistic spirit of the poets concerned, they demonstrate a far-reaching disintegration of the old fixed forms and a mixture of elements from different styles and types not found in the biblical psalms, where in all essentials the old fixed formal and stylistic rules predominate.

What strikes us in the biblical psalms is the uniformity and formality which characterize most of them. One is often so like another that they are difficult to differentiate. The personal, individual element is pushed into the background. Imagery and phraseology are often the stereotyped traditional ones. Rarely is there a clear allusion to the poet's personal situation, rarely anything definite and concrete, almost invariably only what is typical of a whole circle, in the most general terms. This cannot be explained as only the usual lyric dependence on a particular style with its partiality for that in which everybody can join; for even then there can be room for personal variations, as may be seen from the dirge over Saul and Jonathan in 2 Sam. 1.19ff., compared with the usual stereotyped dirge. The set formality of the psalms can only be explained on the basis that they are not primarily meant to be personal effusions, but are, in accordance with their type and origin, ritual lyrics. It is of the nature of the cultic psalm that it cannot express the individual's definite, once-for-all experiences and emotions. It voices those moods and experiences which have common currency within the cult community. Hence everything which is too concrete and individual is pushed into the background. In its original form the cultic psalm springs from set formulas, suiting all occasions. We meet the same formality to a much higher degree in Babylonian-Assyrian cultic psalms.

This does not imply that the personal element has been cut out, or that type analysis pays no heed to it.

But also in another respect Gunkel—and after him many of his followers—went only half-way. He often stuck too much to the mere formal registration and labelling of the single elements of a psalm and did not see clearly enough that his own form-historical method demanded that it be developed into a real *cult-functional method.*

The form may be overrated so as to arrest one's vision and understanding through purely formal limitations, and make one overlook important inner correspondences between psalms which outwardly appear to belong to different groups, but which are governed by the same ideas, and thus prove to belong together, perhaps as psalms for some specific festival.

In course of time an old form may have become the bearer of new contents in a new situation.[1] That also must be taken into consideration.

On the other hand, an alien form may have been used as an effective means of expressing the content. Thus although the prophets often used the psalm-style to underline and emphasize their message, nevertheless their utterances are prophecies and neither hymns nor lamentations. And the psalm-writer may use the form of the 'wisdom-poetry' for his personal expression of the praise of God, or thanksgiving for a blessing received—without his psalm becoming a wisdom or problem poem.

Occasionally we meet with 'compound' psalms, whose different parts use two completely different form types, e.g. hymn of praise plus lamentation, or thanksgiving plus lamentation. In such cases the older critical psalm interpreter often solved the problem by declaring that here two different psalms had been joined together 'by chance'. This was possible when the psalms were still viewed from a purely literary and aesthetic point of view, and one did not raise the question about their background in an actual cultic situation. Even Gunkel's interpretation, which on principle took its point of departure from the latter point, sometimes failed here and was content to classify and establish the facts instead of explaining them. An instance of such a failure is his treatment of Pss. 9–10, which form *one* psalm bound together by 'the alphabetical scheme', that is, each new stanza starts with another letter, in alphabetical order. The first part of this, the letters *aleph* to *kaph* (*a–k*), make a hymn; while the second part, the letters *lamedh* to *taw* (*l–t*), is a lament. Gunkel's explanation is that when the poet reached *lamedh* he could not, on the spur of the moment, find any other word starting with an 'l' than *lamma*, 'why', and hence he plunged into the lament style, where the lamenting phrase 'Why hast thou forsaken me?' and the like, frequently recur, and continued in this lamentation style! This is a curiously superficial explanation, poorly corresponding with the firm and conscious style of the poem, and is only possible because Gunkel, with regard to the individual psalms, usually betrays his own cultic principle, maintaining that they are not real cult psalms, but only 'literary' imitations.

Sometimes Gunkel stressed the formal identity between the psalms of a definite species at the risk of drawing too narrow limits for the species in question, thus failing to see an important idea that at least has some inner connexion with that species. There can be no doubt that Gunkel is wrong in excluding Ps. 95 from the category of the 'enthronement' psalms: 93; 96–99. Ps. 95 has all the characteristics of the others, *plus* something more: and this plus in fact opens the way to a deeper understanding of the enthronement psalms, and widens the number of psalms belonging in the same ideological connexion. We then see that the narrow group of enthronement psalms, in the strictest sense of the word, tells us very little about religious experience, life and thought in ancient Israel, compared with the great complex of experiences and ideas that we grasp when we put the real cult-functional question: to which cultic occasion must this psalm group have belonged, and what has the congregation experienced and felt on that occasion? The definition 'enthronement psalms' must be made not only from the formal literary, but also from the cult-functional point of view, and the latter is the more important.

That the psalms belong to the cult will in many cases mean that they belong to some definite festival cult, which to the ancient Israelite meant primarily 'festival'.

But the experience, thought and mood involved in a particular cultic festival are generally many-sided, and complex enough to cover the whole range of religious content and experience. The ritual of a festival service is in fact a very complex affair with many subdivisions, each intended to express a certain aspect of the experience and of the 'cultic drama', and the corresponding religious need and mood. Corresponding to these different aspects are different kinds of style, evolved to express each of them. So to the same festival there may have belonged both plaintive prayers for help in distress and need, and joyous hymns to the living God, thanking him for salvation promised or 'seen' and grasped by the believer in the symbols of the cult. The festival cult involved a number of very different acts and ceremonies. This point Gunkel of course had seen, when he recognized a 'sacramental' element, an oracle of Yahweh, in some psalms, and defined a group of psalms as '(compound) liturgies'. But each festival also has its main idea, with many varying notions and conceptions. This main idea and the conceptions which accompany it will of course characterize most of the appertaining 'words' and psalms. With us, for instance, the main idea of Easter or Whitsun, and the reality of salvation which these festivals express and revive, will in many ways stamp all true Easter or Pentecost hymns, and appear in prayer and confession as well as in hymns of thanks and praise. There is no Christian Easter hymn—of whatever style—that does not in some manner refer to Christ's victorious resurrection and its power and hope. It is not sufficient, then, to define a psalm as a lamentation or prayer-psalm, if its main idea suggests in addition a connexion with the idea and experience of a particular festival. This must become perfectly clear, and we shall have understood neither the psalm nor its place in actual life, its cultic situation and its aim, until we have connected it with the festival in question, and with its idea and cultic forms.

In other words, the purely form-historical classification and interpretation of Gunkel, the pure 'examination of types', and grouping of the psalms according to the form categories found by the form critic, have to be enlarged and replaced by proper cult-historical ones. The formal point of view is only a provisional help.

This point of view, then, will lead us to a modified division of the psalms and to another principle of interpretation than that of Gunkel, viz. to the form- *and* cult-historical one. If we take this seriously, at the same time remembering the old Israelite 'collective' (corporate) view of people and community, as it appears in the cult, we shall see that a purely formal classification often has only a relative value. We shall not have reached our goal by, e.g., dividing the 'lamentation-psalms' into 'we-psalms' and 'I-psalms', and imagining that we have in that way reached two really different categories and cultic situations. The I-form in reality includes psalms of two very different cultic types, each with its own cultic and historic background and causation. One of these groups—the so-called public (congregational) lamentations—is objectively and cult-historically much more closely related to the 'we-psalms' than it is to the proper 'I-psalms'. There is a series of 'I-psalms' where the 'I' is not the single, private member of the congregation, but the social, political and cultic representative of the people—that is to say, the king. In this case the occasion and the corresponding cultic situation is a public matter, not the experience and situation of a single, private individual. This leads both to somewhat of a return to older positions in the interpretation of the 'I' in the psalms,[2] and to a view of the so-called 'royal psalms' diverging from Gunkel's.

In practice the form-critical and the cult-functional method cannot be separated from each other, but must work hand-in-hand when we arrange the psalms in groups or species, according to such common forms, thoughts and moods as are in accordance with that cultic situa-tion, or that special festival, which is supposed to be the background of the species in question. True enough, the common elements must be the essential ones in the psalms in question; but if a whole coherent complex of ideas is included in the supposed cultic festival, it may well happen that one of the components of this complex is predominant in one psalm, another component in another. Here it will be necessary to bear in mind the old Israelite way of 'thinking in totalities': if one note of a chord is struck, all the others sound in his mind; one important component of a complex of ideas being mentioned, the others are recalled in his con-sciousness.

The present author has for a good many years in his studies on the psalms endeavoured to apply a really cult-functional interpretation, and to bring out all these features in the psalms and in what we know about the Israelite and Jewish cult which help to prove that the psalms of the Psalter, on the whole, are real cult-psalms and an expression of that experience of God which the cult seeks to further.

The cult-functional method includes the attempt to understand every surviving psalm as a real cult psalm, made for a definite cultic situation. The foundation has been laid by Gunkel's explanation of the cultic origin of the different types. But in trying to trace the consequences for the surviving psalms, we shall find ourselves concerned with more of such situations than he thought, and realize that the connexion between psalm and cult is much closer than he imagined.

To understand a psalm means to see it in the right cultic connexion. This is, in fact, a quite elementary truth. Everybody will agree that a Christian baptismal hymn or a communion hymn acquires full significance only when seen in connexion with the holy act to which it belongs.

From the cult new light falls on the psalms, and from the psalms light falls on new sides of the cult. There is no first and last here. In the actual process of research these two points of view must be kept in a constant reciprocity.

Our method will afford a possibility of distinguishing between real cult psalms and a 'private' psalmody which partly uses the old styles and forms, but in many ways points to another 'place in life'. There *are*, even in the Psalter, some non-cultic psalms, but they are few.

A true interpretation of the psalms must try to form as complete and vivid a picture as possible of the old Israelite and Jewish cult and its many situations and acts.

3

Apparently we are quite well informed about the cult in Israel. The whole central part of the Pentateuch consists of cultic and ritual laws. But these are mostly to be found in a relatively late form and system, such as the 'Priestly Document' (P), the latest of the Pentateuchal sources, collected in post-exilic, Jewish times. As is shown by a comparison with the allusions in older sources and in the historical books, the view taken of important ritual acts (e.g. of the importance of the sacrifice) has changed and developed; so that it would be a mistake to base our conception of the psalms on the later stages of Israelitic-Jewish cultic development. The psalms are to a very great extent much older, and date from the time of the monarchy (before the exile). Further, the picture which the priestly source gives us of the cult is both one-sided and fragmentary. It presents ritual and other features of the service from the priests' own technical point of view. The laws (priests' agenda) speak of the kind and number of beasts to be sacrificed, and how the priest is to conduct himself in the course of the sacrificial act. We are also told what sacrifices and contributions the lay people are to offer, and the rituals at certain purifications and sacrifices are described from the point of view of the officiating priest. But they never give a living picture of a ritual festival as a whole. We hear practically nothing about the part played by the congregation, e.g. in the great festal processions which, from other sources, we know belonged to it. Nor do they say anything about the words which belonged to the cult, the prayers which were prayed, and the psalms which were sung. But from other sources, e.g. the book of Chronicles, we know that they formed part of the service. Only very rarely do the laws record a cultic

prayer (Deut. 21.7–9; 26.1ff.), and we hear very little about hymn singing, even though other sources contain allusions to ritual acts where
hymns were sung.[3]

In addition to what is given in the laws, we find, in historical and
legendary accounts and in the prophets, more incidental remarks and
allusions which may serve to amplify the picture.

But, to a certain extent, the situations can and must be pictured from
hints in the psalms themselves. When once we have grasped that each
situation creates its own formal language around a definite subject-
content, then we are able, from the characteristics of the content and
form in a certain group of psalms, to reconstruct the precise cultic occasion which has produced them, and which also supplies their natural
explanation. In this way Gunkel and others after him re-discovered important parts of the ancient Israelite cult which were not mentioned in
the laws. We shall look more closely at this when treating of the particular
types of psalms and their origin.

This process of induction from the types of psalms to the underlying
cultic situation of course becomes increasingly convincing as it can be
confirmed by analogies from neighbouring oriental civilizations. We must
realize that in matters of the framework of the cult, and incidentally, of
many of the ideas expressed through it, the partially Canaanized Israelites took as models the temple cults of neighbouring peoples. The
Yahweh religion in the period immediately following the immigration
(and especially after the blending with the indigenous population had
been achieved with the rise of the monarchy) had been deeply influenced
by Canaanite religion, that is to say, by oriental religion generally. The
religious history of Israel in the following period largely consists of a
dramatic struggle to expel the obviously syncretistic, and to work out the
peculiar historical significances of the Yahweh religion. Israel's cult
places were to a great extent the same as those of the ancient Canaanites,
and there followed, as a matter of course, the adoption of many Canaanite
cultic traditions. The three great annual festivals are characteristic agricultural festivals, which Israel adopted from the natives and adjusted to
the religion of Yahweh, giving them a new, historically orientated interpretation. The first of them, the festival of the barley harvest, the
Maṣṣôth festival, corresponded in time to the old Israelite cattle-breeding
festival of Easter (_Pesaḥ_), and could be combined with it. The very Temple in Jerusalem was built according to Canaanite patterns. To worship
Yahweh in temples was a novel custom. In Jerusalem, Yahweh was 'identified' with the ancient deities, and inherited their names and titles of
honour. There can, for instance, be no doubt that the name El Elyon,
'The Highest God', which in the Old Testament means Yahweh, originally signified the chief god of Jebusite Jerusalem. There are even signs
that point to a connexion between the new priestly family to whom David

entrusted the Yahweh cult in the Temple—the Zadokites—and the ancient dynasty of priest-kings in Jerusalem. Israel had no tradition as to the framing of a temple cult which went back to the period of desert wandering. That was adopted from outside.

Hence it goes without saying that the knowledge of other oriental cult rituals—as Gunkel has already shown[4]—will throw light on much in the cult of Jerusalem, and thereby yield important contributions for a correct location of the psalms in the cult—not least because they so often support the conclusions one can draw from the psalms themselves.

In several respects—e.g. in the way we look at the collective element in many of the 'I-psalms'—our presentation will mean a return to older positions in psalm-interpretation,[5] but in new connections and in a new light. Such is often the way of science.

In spite of a definite and fundamental cult-historical view we shall, in what follows, resist the one-sided exaggeration of this view which has cropped up in certain quarters lately, where it has even been suggested that all psalms and all details in them allude to cult-mythical happenings and experiences, leaving no room for an historical background or for allusions in any of the psalms to historical events. This can be understood as a reaction against older interpretations which paid no heed to the cultic side, and of each psalm asked first of all, 'what historical occasion is here alluded to, and who can the author of this psalm be?' That is an untenable position; but the reaction goes too far. Even though the lamentation-psalms belong to a cultic situation, there can be no doubt that they have for their background and cause historical events in the life of Israel, such as a definite national catastrophe or defeat in the fight against known enemies. Sometimes this is expressly stated. The duty to take this into account in the interpretation cannot be put aside by speaking slightingly of 'historicism', and the like.

4

A classification of the psalms must—like every understanding of them—be in accord with the 'divisions' in the cult itself, its different occasions, situations and acts.

At the present stage there is only the question of a rough classification according to the main features.

What main types of divine service were there in ancient Israel and in Judaism? From what points of view can we classify them?

As we have already mentioned, the service is always essentially a communion, a matter that concerns both God and the congregation. To ancient Israel this was a matter of course, in accordance with the 'collective' or 'corporate' view of the relation between the society and the individual. From the human point of view, the protagonist in the cult, the one in whose name the action and speaking takes place, is the congregation.

But the congregation is also positively interested in the individual members, regardless of the degree to which they represent the whole. There are cultic actions on behalf of the individual, in which he or she is the centre. From our own divine service we may mention baptisms, churchings, weddings and funerals. But here too it is the congregation which is the real actor. The individual is regarded as a member of the congregation. To us, therefore, the natural form of the cultic psalm is the first person plural, 'we'. But the I-form, too, may be the right one, either when the cultic act in question is performed for the sake of the individual, or when he is so representative a person that he appears on behalf of the people, and in such a way that what is done to him is also done to the whole. The last train of ideas is characteristic of ancient religions, including that of ancient Israel.

In the psalms we meet with both the we-form and the I-form. How is this to be explained?

The simplest solution would be to say—like Gunkel and others—that the I-form means there is an individual who is speaking, a Mr. So-and-so who is in need of that special cultic act, or a certain person who has composed the psalm or has had it composed to express his personal situation and experience. Only the psalms in the we-form are then congregational psalms proper.

There can be no doubt that this view contains a substantial truth. The psalms may be divided into those which concern the congregation or the people, that is *national* psalms or *congregational* psalms, and such as are connected with the individual's, possibly a private person's, religious and ritual need, that is, *personal or individual* psalms.

But the problem is not solved yet. The matter cannot be decided simply on the basis of I- or we-forms. There are also psalms where there is no doubt that the 'I' in question speaks on behalf of a plurality (as in Ps. 118), or where a 'we' appears together with and in the same sense as an 'I' (e.g., Ps. 44). There are also 'I-psalms' where the matter that caused the supplication to Yahweh obviously is a public one, concerning the whole people, and not only a single person (e.g., Ps. 66).

To this may be added that it is only to us moderns that it seems a matter of course that the natural form of plurality should be 'we'. In reality this 'we' presupposes a mental attitude and outlook which is individualizing compared to the old corporate one—a mental attitude proper to each individual person who has begun to be conscious of his own individuality, the congregation being a sum of 'I's (a 'we'). In the religion and common prayer of ancient peoples and civilizations the I-form is the usual and natural one, because there it is the whole and not the individual that is given reality, a 'corporate personality' which may act through a representative personality who 'incorporates' the whole. According to such an attitude it will be natural for the representative of the collective prayer to use the I-form. We see this for instance in Babylonian hymns, and it has persisted through the ages.

An apparent I-psalm therefore may be really a congregational psalm, because the 'I' is the national and cultic representative of the congregation.

But there are also real I-psalms where the suppliant is the single member of the congregation. They belonged to cultic acts performed on behalf of the individual as a 'private' person—no matter who he was, a king, or a nobody. That Israel had such cultic acts is seen from many of the ritual laws of the Pentateuch.

There is, then, after all, a reality in the distinction between congregational or national psalms, and individual or private psalms. This distinction must be the point of departure in psalm interpretation, even though it is only of relative value and cannot be carried through in all its details.

Another division is that between joy and thanksgiving festivals, and days of penitence. They demand each their own type of prayer and psalm. From these two principles of division spring the *four main types* of psalms in the Psalter, the praises and thanksgivings of the congregation, private (that is, individual) thanksgivings, and besides them both congregational and individual lamentation and prayer psalms.

The praise and thanksgiving psalms of the congregation divide into two kinds: the common praises or hymns, about God's excellence and benefactions in general, and the special thanksgiving psalms, giving thanks for a particular, just experienced salvation. This may be a special historical act of salvation, or one renewed at regular intervals.

In the same way we can distinguish between the common prayer psalms of the congregation and lamentation and prayer psalms on a special occasion such as a catastrophe or a threatening danger. Within the latter group we can distinguish between real lamentations, when a catastrophe has already taken place, and 'protective psalms', where the event is as yet only a threat. The last-mentioned distinction of course also obtains for the 'I-psalms', which are really royal or congregational psalms.

Besides these six or seven important types there are a certain number of less frequent kinds and types of psalms.

I want to underline again that the foundations for such an investigation were laid by Gunkel, even if I, on many points already hinted at, disagree with his results.

NOTES

1. Gunkel is of course fully aware of this, for instance, when he maintains that a new sense has been 'spiritually' assigned to the cultic psalms of illness, so as to change them into individual cult-free prayers. But this theory of a new reading is itself untenable.

2. This applies for instance to the view of the so-called 'collective ego', which has more of truth in it than the purely form-historical school has been willing to admit. It also applies to the view of the political background and the events occasioning the I-laments, which are actually 'national' (royal) psalms.

3. Cf. Am. 5.23; Job 33.27; 2 Sam. 6.5; I Kgs. 8.12; I Chron. 16.8ff.; 2 Chron. 6.1f.; 6.41f.

4. This applies to the whole 'religio-historical school' and was an important point in the scientific programme of the latter.

5. See note 2 above.

_____ _Ralph W. Klein_ _____

Aspects of Intertesta-
mental Messianism

_The discovery in 1947 of the Dead Sea Scrolls—several
hundred manuscripts stored in caves by the Essene community at Qumran on the northern shore of the Dead
Sea—has recently provoked scholars to study the "silent
centuries" for clues about the Jewish expectations for a
Messiah. They are called the "silent centuries" because
theologians excluded from the Old Testament a spate of
religious books written after Nehemiah (445 _B.C._) and Ezra
(397 _B.C._). Ultimately, fourteen of them appeared as the
Apocrypha (which in Greek means "obscure" or "hidden"
author). Today, however, the Roman Catholic Bible includes only eleven of them. Along with a number of non-
canonical books, Klein mentions several books from the
Apocrypha: 1 and 2 Maccabees and the Wisdom of Solomon.
Together, these scriptural stories of questionable authorship record an important period in Old Testament history,
which included a Jewish uprising against their oppressors,
intrigue among Jewish leaders which led to the Essene
withdrawal to Qumran, and a wide variety of definitions of
a coming Messiah. In short, they describe the type of deli-
verer they sought in Jesus._

_For another view of these "silent centuries" and the
writing that went on during them, see Bleddyn J. Roberts'
"The Old Testament: Manuscripts, Text and Versions," pp.
212–234._

W HEN we confess Jesus as Messiah we do so through the prism of
His cross and resurrection. These events reveal the fulfillment as
well as the transformation of Israel's messianic hope, a hope grounded in
God's promise through Nathan to David and eschatologized through
Isaiah and his successors in a series of well-known passages (2 Sam. 7;

From Ralph W. Klein, _Concordia Theological Monthly_, 43 (1972), 507–17.

Is. 9 and 11; Micah 5:2 ff.; Jer. 23:5 f.; Hag. 2:23; Zech. 3:8; 6:12; 9:9; and others).

In confessing Jesus as Messiah the early Christians, however, were not living in Isaiah's Assyrian crisis, in the disaster of the Exile, or in the heady days of Zechariah and Haggai. Part of their context was shaped by their brother Jews who had faithfully remembered and preserved God's promises and had freely adapted them for their own tumultuous times. It is this latter context of Jewish messianic expectations[1] that we shall explore in order to appreciate better the radical claim: Jesus of Nazareth is the Messiah.

MESSIANIC PRETENDERS

In many ways the Maccabees ushered in one of the greatest moments in Israel's religious history. Mattathias and his five sons were able to stymie the military forces of Antiochus Epiphanes (175–163 B.C.) and his successors and to rally the people around the Law and the rededicated sanctuary. For some this movement seemed to be the fulfillment of God's greatest promises; to others it became only an arrogant, presumptuous and oppressive establishment. The books of 1 and 2 Maccabees respectively give us both sides of the story.[2]

For our inquiry two events are of special importance. The first is Jonathan's usurpation of the high priestly office in 152 even though he was not a Zadokite; the other was the decision of the Jews and their priests in 140 to make Jonathan's successor Simon leader and high priest forever. This dynastic understanding of the high priestly office and the approval by the people of the non-Zadokite Hasmoneans for this office were the central provocations leading to the establishment of the Essene community at Qumran.[3] Together with these ecclesiastical power plays came the assumption of the political title "leader" which was to culminate in the claim by Aristobulus I (104–103) to be king. Thus people who could claim only Levitic ancestry assumed the functions of priest and king. The writer of the poem in 1 Macc. 14:4–15 was a political propagandist for the Hasmoneans. He suggested that the reign of Simon marked the dawn of the messianic age and the fulfillment of a number of Old Testament prophecies:[4]

> They farmed their land in peace,
> the land gave its produce,
> the trees of the plain their fruit.
> The elders sat at ease in the streets,
> all their talk was of their prosperity;
> the young men wore finery and armour.
> (vv. 8–9)

Each man sat under his own vine and his own fig tree,
and there was no one to make them afraid.
No enemy was left in the land to fight them,
and the kings in those days were crushed.
He gave strength to all the humble folk among his people
and cleared away every renegade and wicked man. (vv. 12–14)

It is interesting to see how the blessings of the messianic age are understood in material terms. This reveals not only a wholesome attitude toward creation, but also the theological expectations of kingship. Psalm 72 records a prayer appropriate for every king, but especially for the ideal king of the future:

May he [the king] be like rain that falls on the mown grass,
like showers that water the earth!
In his days may righteousness flourish,
and peace abound, till the moon be no more!
May there be abundance of grain in the land;
on the tops of the mountains may it wave;
may its fruit be like Lebanon;
and may men blossom forth from the cities
like the grass of the field! (vv. 6–7, 16)[5]

NO! THE MESSIAH IS DAVIDIC

The pretensions of the Hasmonean house were not allowed to go unreproved, especially as its internal corruption became more manifest. The Psalms of Solomon, for example, written in the second half of the first century B.C., express strong, Pharisaic (?)[6] opposition:

You, O Lord, chose David as king over Israel,
And swore to him . . . that his kingdom should never fail before you.
But, for our sins, sinners rose up against us; they assailed us and thrust us out; what you had not promised to them, they took away with violence.
They in no wise glorified your honorable name;
they set a [worldly] monarchy in place of [that which was] their excellency;
They laid waste the throne of David in tumultuous arrogance. (17:4–6)

The sinners listed here are the Hasmoneans who had pushed aside the (Pharisaic) author(s) of this psalm. Although the Hasmoneans were Levitic in ancestry, they appropriated the throne of David. With almost undisguised glee the psalm hails Pompey and the Romans for attacking Palestine and taking Aristobulus II and his children as hostages to Rome. But just as Isaiah changed his mind about the Assyrians—once he thought they were the tool of Yahweh, but then he threatened them with destruction for their arrogance—so now this psalmist prays for the coming of David's Son to destroy the Romans, using a collage of Old Testament citations:[7]

> Behold, O Lord, and raise up unto them, their king, the Son of David,
> At the time in which you see, O God, that he may reign over Israel your
> servant.
> Gird him with strength, that he may shatter unrighteous rulers,
> And that he may purge Jerusalem from nations that trample her down
> to destruction.
> Wisely, righteously he shall thrust out sinners from the inheritance,
> He shall destroy the pride of the sinner as a potter's vessel.
> With a rod of iron he shall break in pieces all their substance,
> He shall destroy the godless nations with the word of his mouth;
> At his rebuke nations shall flee before him, and he shall reprove sinners
> for the thoughts of their heart. (17:21–25)

What is the function of this Messiah? In a sense he is only a sign of and a pointer to God's reign since the psalm begins and ends with a prayer for God the king to come! For this reason little attention is given to the person of the king. Nor is mention made of his death or of a successor. God's kingship is renewed through this earthly king. Yet the human king will have responsibilities both toward the nations and toward Israel. He will overthrow the oppressing nations by his rod of iron, but trust in God, and not armaments, is the real source of his power:

> For he shall not put his trust in horse and rider and bow,
> Nor shall he multiply for himself gold and silver for war.
> The Lord Himself is his king. . . . (17:33–34)

One of his major weapons is his "word" by which he destroys nations and smites the earth,[8] although it is not completely clear from the context whether by this is meant a war cry or his authoritative word as judge. In any case, all nations will eventually be made subservient to him and will come from the ends of the earth to see his glory in Jerusalem.[9]

Toward Israel, on the other hand, he is a judge endowed with the Spirit just like the leaders in the Book of Judges. He is also a shepherd and a wise teacher of the Law who will allow none of his people to stumble. In fact, he can almost be called a scribe-king and the spiritual aspects of his reign receive considerable emphasis.[10] So he will be free from sin, without pride, the righteous king who saves his people, governs justly, and punishes the wicked. He is the leader and example who directs "man in the works of righteousness by the fear of God" (18:8). He will banish unrighteousness, purify Jerusalem, and gather a holy people.

Small wonder, then, that the psalmist pronounces a benediction on anyone who lives to see his day ("Blessed be they that shall be in those days" [17:44]) and prays for God to carry out his deliverance through his anointed one speedily: "May the Lord hasten his mercy upon Israel!" (17:45).

This psalm documents the belief in a vindictive, nationalistic Messiah, to whom all nations will come thronging in pilgrimage; it shows how the coming of the Messiah is usually seen in tandem with and subservient to the kingship of Yahweh; it highlights the spiritual qualifications of the king; and finally, it provides some of the earliest attestation for the technical use of titles like "Son of David" and "Messiah."[11]

MESSIAH OR MESSIAHS?

The Essene community at Qumran apparently shared in the antipathy toward the Hasmonean leadership; its founders may even have been among the first to disassociate themselves from it. Although the picture that emerges from the Qumran documents is vastly different from the Psalms of Solomon, it is equally instructive for students of late Judaism and of Christian origins.

Before turning to these texts several Old Testament passages must be briefly canvassed. In Jer. 33 a secondary hand has reworked an earlier text about the righteous Branch (Jer. 23:5). Instead of a single figure *yahweh sidqenu*,[12] the prophet speaks of a whole new line of Davidites beside whom will function an unending line of Levitical priests. These promises are part of an irrevocable covenant. This promised structure for the future of Israel seems to be fulfilled in the fifth vision of Zechariah (6:1–14). There the prophet sees in symbolic fashion two olive trees, representing two sons of oil (anointed ones) or, more concretely, Zerubbabel and Joshua, the royal and priestly leaders of the postexilic community.[13]

This "dyarchic" leadership reappears—in somewhat altered fashion—at Qumran.[14] The clearest text comes from the Community Rule (= the Manual of Discipline). We are told that the members of the community are not to depart from the counsels of the Law until the "eschaton," that is, "until there shall come the Prophet and the Messiahs of Aaron and Israel." One could debate whether the words Prophet and Messiahs should be capitalized and whether the latter might not be better rendered as "anointed ones." But the most important thing to notice is that three eschatological figures are to come and that the two anointed figures correspond to the priesthood and to lay Israel.

A similar picture is presented by the Damascus Document, discovered over half a century ago in the Cairo Genizah but now conclusively linked to the Qumran community.[15] In a series of four texts the Messiahs' advent again marks the inauguration of the new age: "Those who follow these statutes in the age of wickedness [= this world] until the coming of the Messiah of Aaron and Israel shall form groups of at least ten men . . ." (XII, 23 f.). Or again, commenting on the words "star" and "scepter" in

Num. 24:17, the document reads: "The star is the Interpreter of the Law who shall come to Damascus;[16] as it is written, 'A star shall come forth out of Jacob, and a scepter shall rise out of Israel.' The scepter is the Prince of the whole congregation, and when he comes he shall smite all the children of Seth." The star or interpreter of the Law corresponds to the anointed one of Aaron while the scepter or prince corresponds to the anointed one of Israel. A third document refers to these figures as the priest and the Messiah of Israel. This text, known popularly as the Messianic Rule, describes a messianic banquet at the end time. Here, after the priest blesses the bread and wine, the Messiah of Israel blesses the bread.

The dyarchic eschatological structure is perhaps also reflected on coins from the second Jewish revolt of 132–135 which record the name of Simon bar Kokheba on one side and Eleazar the priest on the other. Even in the second century A.D., therefore, it was felt that God would effect his new age through two messianic figures.

The Qumran documents accord clear superiority to the priestly figure which no doubt shows their own strong priestly predilections. In the War Scroll, for example, the priest offers the prayer and says the blessing, arranges the battle lines, urges the troops to have courage, and praises God after the victory in the eschatological battle. The "king" is only a shadow figure in this text without an essential function. This priestly superiority is a reversal of Old Testament roles and is not continued in the Bar Kokheba incident.

The superiority of the eschatological priest is affirmed in other texts as well. Not only is he listed before the Messiah of Israel in both the Community Rule and the Damascus Document, but great stress is given to his priority in giving the blessings at the messianic banquet in the Messianic Rule. In fact, here he and all the other priests take precedence over the lay leader. The priests are to serve as the instructors of the "Branch of David" according to a commentary (*pesher*) on Isaiah and according to a collection of messianic passages known as 4Q Florilegium.

As for the Messiah of Israel, he is often presented in military dress, partly corresponding to his role in the Psalms of Solomon, and heavily drawing on the words of Is. 11. In the manuscript known as 1QSb, an appendix to the Community Rule, the following blessing is given to the "prince of the congregation":

[May you smite the peoples] with the might of your hand and ravage the earth with your scepter; may you bring death to the ungodly with the breath of your lips.

[May he shed upon you the spirit of counsel] and everlasting might, the spirit of knowledge and of the fear of God; may righteousness be the girdle [of your loins] and may your reins be girdled [with faithfulness]! [Cf. Is. 11:1–5.]

May he make your horns of iron and your hooves of bronze; may you toss like a young bull [and trample the peoples] like the mire of the streets! [Cf. Num. 24:17.]

For God has established you as the scepter. The rulers . . . [and all the kings of the] nations shall serve you. [Cf. Gen. 49:8–10.]

According to the commentary on Isaiah from Cave IV, the Branch will rule and judge all nations.

In addition to these martial images, the Messiah(s) will usher in the new age and will celebrate a banquet of victory with the people. A broken line in the Damascus Document even links the coming of this new messianic age with the bestowal of forgiveness: "This is the exact statement of the statutes in which [they shall walk until the coming of the Messiah] of Aaron and Israel who will pardon their iniquity."

We cannot quit our discussion of Qumran, however, without mentioning 4Q Testimonia.[17] The work consists of four Biblical citations: (1) Deut. 5:28–29 and 18:18–19; (2) Num. 24:15–17; (3) Deut. 33:8–11; (4) Joshua 6:6 plus a commentary from the Psalms of Joshua. The order of texts was unclear until P. Skehan demonstrated that the first set is really a proto-Samaritan text tradition of Ex. 20:21. Thus the ordering of texts follows their order in one recension of the Bible. In any case the first set of texts refers to the prophet like Moses who is to come, a figure whom some identified with John the Baptist in the New Testament (Mark 1:2), while at other places, especially in Luke-Acts, Jesus is declared to be that prophet (Luke 4:24–26 and Acts 3:22). With the cessation of prophecy in Israel (1 Macc. 4:46 and 14:41), Deut. 18 came to be understood eschatologically.

The second text is from the oracles of Balaam and refers to the star of Jacob and the scepter of Israel, which are interpreted in other Qumran texts as the priestly and royal Messiahs. In the third text we read of one who "taught your judgments to Jacob, your teaching to Israel," presumably indicating the Righteous Teacher who had founded the eschatological Qumran community. The final text is a curse on anyone who would rebuild Jericho, a curse also involving that man's two sons. Since the Essenes believed that all Scripture was written for the end time and that they themselves lived in that end time, they would take this text as referring to their own days.[18] The most likely candidate for this cursed one is Simon the high priest who was painted in messianic colors in 1 Macc. 14. He and his two sons were killed by men of Ptolemy in the city of Jericho!

Thus this series of texts refers to a number of figures of the eschatological age in which the Qumran community believed it was living. The Righteous Teacher and Simon (the wicked priest?) were figures of the very recent past. The others—prophet, priestly Messiah, and royal

Messiah—were figures whose advent would mark the beginning of the new age.

THE MESSIAH AND HIS TEMPORARY KINGDOM

A final type of messianic expectation occurs in the apocalyptic writings of Enoch, 4 Ezra, and 2 Baruch. Almost all these texts expect the messianic age to be a time of peace, prosperity, and joy, but an added feature that distinguishes them is that they are set in the context of the final apocalyptic judgment. The Messiah functions in a kind of *"Zwischenreich"* or millennial period before the final judgment. Many scholars believe that this structure of an intermediate messianic period followed by the final judgment is a conflation of two sets of ideas: (1) the Old Testament expectation of the prosperity to be brought by the coming Davidic prince and (2) the apocalyptic picture of the world according to which the present age is locked in a hopeless struggle between good and evil that will only be resolved with God's coming in judgment.[19]

Enoch 85—90 portrays the history of the world from Adam to the judgment with transparent symbolism: all people are represented as animals. Enoch (the pseudonymous name used by the author) rehearses the history of the Jews and announces a final onslaught of the Gentiles. Then judgment will be rendered on the stars or angels who intermarried with women (cf. Gen. 6) and on the 70 wicked shepherds or kings from the fall of Jerusalem to the end. All apostates are cast into Gehenna before a new temple is provided and the Gentiles are converted. After all this— that is, after the judgment—the Messiah is born as a white bull and all generations likewise become white bulls in imitation of him. He is later further transformed into a white lamb.

Note that the usual "messianic works" are here done by God himself and the Messiah has no specific function. He is merely the king who is self-evidently needed in the new age. According to the symbolism of this apocalypse, his depiction as an animal is a way of emphasizing that he is human. All beasts of the field and all birds of the air (= the Gentiles) will make petition to him all the time. Although various items could be correlated with the New Testament, the primary interest of this passage in our discussion is to demonstrate one way in which the Messiah is included in an apocalyptic program. The idea of an intermediate age has not yet developed.

Another series of such attempted correlations occurs in 4 Ezra and 2 Baruch, two Jewish works written later than the destruction of Jerusalem but which are not anti-Christian and consequently can be used for understanding the type of Jewish thinking on the Messiah current about the time of our Lord.

In 4 Ezra 7 the Messiah is revealed after the messianic woes, that is, the period of final persecution. Accompanied by immortal companions (perhaps Elijah, Enoch, Ezra, Baruch, and Jeremiah) he makes the survivors rejoice for 400 years.[20] At the end of this *Zwischenreich* he dies, together with all human beings. Significantly, this is the only certain place in all of Jewish literature where the Messiah dies. Here, however, it is without any kind of atoning significance. After 7 days of primeval silence, there follows the general resurrection and judgment by the Most High (= God). We are not told what is to happen to the Messiah in the new age, but we can see how His former royal function of providing good things for the people has now been transferred to the intermediate age.[21]

The eagle vision (4 Ezra 10:60—12:35) provides another glimpse of Jewish messianic thought. In this case the Messiah is represented as a lion who upbraids, rebukes, and finally destroys an eagle, a symbol for the Roman empire. The eagle vision differs from the animal apocalypse and 4 Ezra in that the Messiah himself brings an end to the present world order. His function, however, is only quasi-military, for the eschatological battle has merely been "legalized" or turned into a judicial situation. His activity for Israel in the intermediate age is described as follows:

> But my people who survive he shall deliver with mercy, even those who have been saved throughout my borders, and he shall make them joyful until the End come, even the day of Judgment, of which I have spoken unto you from the beginning. (12:34)

Thus he delivers the people and makes them rejoice, just as Israel hoped every king would do. Only now this is fitted into an apocalyptic understanding of history. Several other features are worthy of note. It is explicitly stated that the Messiah is pre-existent (12:32) and that he is of Davidic descent. He makes his appearance in Palestine when the wickedness of the last kingdom is at its peak. His function resembles in part that of an Old Testament prophet, although the power of his word also has precedents in such messianic texts as Isaiah 11. His kingdom is temporary—"until the End come, even the Day of Judgment"—and no assignment is listed for him in the new age.

A strikingly similar understanding is reflected in the vision of the vine in 2 Baruch 36—40. The vine represents the messiah and from beneath it issues a stream symbolizing his dominion. After the stream overwhelms a forest and destroys it except for one last cedar, the vine scolds the cedar for its wicked rule and pronounces a curse on it: "Recline in anguish and rest in torment till your last time come, in which you will come again, and be tormented still more" (36:11). After this the cedar bursts into flames, while the vine continues growing in a field full of unfading flowers. This vision is then given an interpretation. The forest represents the Babylonians, Persians, Diadochi, and the Romans who will be rooted out by the principate of the Messiah.[22] After this victory the last pagan leader will be bound and taken to Mt. Zion. "My Messiah will convict him of all his impieties, and will gather and set before him all the works of his hosts" (40:1). Then the Messiah will kill this ruler and protect the rest of the people as he rules them during the intermediate age. This age lasts only until "the world of corruption is at an end and until the times aforesaid are fulfilled" (40:3). The picture of the messianic age as a temporary time of bliss between the final outbreak of evil and the great day of judgment differs only slightly from 4 Ezra.

2 Baruch 27—30 also asserts that a time of terrible tribulation, divided into twelve parts, will ensue, threatening even the elect. Only Palestine (this land) will be spared. After the Messiah has been revealed he will provide food for all the survivors by serving them Behemoth and Leviathan. This idea has roots as deep as ancient Canaan. After defeating the Sea or Leviathan, Baal presented a victory banquet for all his retainers. Now at the messianic banquet, the main course will be the chaotic monsters themselves, although here their subservience to God is indicated by the assertion that God made them on the fifth day of creation. In this messianic age the vine will produce a thousandfold and more—each grape in fact will yield 120 gallons![23] Winds from God will bring the fragrance of aromatic fruit and the fertile dew of evening. The end time will bring back the good old wilderness days: "The treasury of manna shall again descend from on high, and they will eat of it in those years, because these are they who have come to the consummation of time" (29:8). After the Messiah's departure in glory, the general resurrection will occur. From then on the righteous will rejoice while the wicked waste away more and more. It is not specifically stated that the Messiah will bring all the good things of the intermediate kingdom; his presence, however, is the sign of the time of salvation. With the end of the intermediate kingdom, his importance ceases. A final reference comes from the Cloud Vision of 2 Baruch 53—76. Through an alternating sequence of black and white waters the author traces the 12 bad and good periods of world history from Adam to the rebuilding of Jerusalem and the erection of the second temple. There follows a period of terrible tribulations, the so-called messianic woes. Men will hate one another, the impious will exalt themselves over the heroic; the wise will be silent and only the foolish will speak. War, earthquake, fire, and famine will utterly decimate the ranks of men. Then the Messiah will appear as bright lightning.[24] He will spare the nations that have not known Israel or oppressed the seed of Jacob. All others will be given over to the sword. When all this has taken place, it shall come to pass "that joy shall then be revealed and rest shall appear. And then healing shall descend in dew . . . and anxiety and anguish and lamentation pass from among men, and gladness proceed through the whole earth. . . . And wild beasts shall come from the forest and minister unto men [cf. Is. 11:6–9!], and asps and dragons shall come forth from their holes to submit themselves to a little child." Even the curse of Eden will be reversed: "And women shall no longer then have

pain when they bear, nor shall they suffer torment when they yield the fruit of the womb."

Those who wrote this literature longed for this great messianic day. They were sure that the course of history was determined (12 periods, followed by a period of intense tribulation), that the length of this aeon was fixed, and that they were living immediately before the end.

CONCLUSION

Our survey of intertestamental messianism outlines the matrix within which the early Christians confessed: Jesus is the Messiah! To correlate this data with the New Testament evidence would be a major article in itself, but the following four observations can be made:

1. There is a great deal of continuity between certain aspects or details in late Jewish messianic thought and the New Testament. The expectation of a priestly and royal Messiah is fulfilled by Jesus the Christ, the high priest after the order of Melchizedek, according to Hebrews. The belief in the Messiah within an apocalyptic context unlocks the code of Rev. 20. The feeding of the 5,000, the eucharistic banquet, Jesus' care for the physical needs of people are all signs of continuity.

2. Almost every messianic expectation of the Old Testament and the intertestamental period is shattered and refracted in Jesus of Nazareth. His renunciation of power and vindication and especially His death and resurrection confounded those who expected the Messiah to reinforce nationalistic hopes or to annihilate the wicked.

3. His death, His embodiment of the Suffering Servant, shows another change within continuity. Instead of a series of figures—Priest, Prophet, King, Son of Man, Son of God, Servant—God sent one Man who combined in His person and work all of Israel's eschatological expectations.

4. Finally, we must say a positive word about the way in which the Messiah was confessed in Jewish circles. They believed that God was faithful to His old promises and relationships, but they also confessed that God was free to adapt these promises to fit their new situation and their new and unique needs. In bearing witness to this faithful and free God, they saw from afar the same God whom we believe was manifested in Jesus the Messiah.[25]

NOTES

1. No future Messiah is mentioned in the following major writings: 1 and 2 Maccabees, Tobit, Wisdom of Solomon, Judith, Ben Sirach, Jubilees, Enoch 1–36 and 91–104,

the Assumption of Moses, 1 Baruch, and 2 Enoch. A useful survey of intertestamental messianic ideas is that of Ulrich Kellermann, "Die politische Messias-Hoffnung Zwischen den Testamenten," *Pastoral Theologie* LVI (1967), 362–377 and 436–449.

2. See George W. E. Nickelsburg, Jr., "1 and 2 Maccabees—Same Story, Different Meaning," *CTM* XLIII (September 1971), 515–526.

3. Frank M. Cross, Jr., "The Early History of the Qumran Community," *McCormick Quarterly* XXI (March 1968), 249–264.

4. See especially 1 Kings 4:25, Micah 4:4, Zech. 3:10 and 8:4–23.

5. As time went on, others pretended to be the Messiah as well, often with fanatical revolutionary intent: Theudas (Acts 5:36); Judas the Galilean (Acts 5:37); a false prophet from Egypt who wanted to storm Jerusalem; Menahem; Simon bar Giora; and Simon bar Kokheba.

6. These psalms are customarily ascribed to the Pharisees, but Jerry O'Dell has demonstrated in them several departures from Pharisaic thought. He ascribes their authorship to a wider eschatological movement. See his "The Religious Background of the Psalms of Solomon," *Revue de Qumran* III (1961–62), 241–257.

7. 2 Sam. 7, Ps. 2, and especially Is. 11 are very prominent. The latter passage in fact is one of the key texts for intertestamental messianism. A complete list of allusions can be found in Ulrich Kellermann, *Messias und Gesetz* (Neukirchen: Neukirchener Verlag, 1971), pp. 98–99.

8. Cf. Is. 11:4: "His word is a rod that strikes the ruthless" and Rev. 19:15: "From his mouth issues a sharp sword."

9. This worldwide rule of Israel's King is common in the royal psalms and is part of the messianic promise of Is. 11:10: "The root of Jesse shall stand as an ensign to the peoples. It will be sought out by the nations. . . ."

10. M. de Jonge, "The Use of the Word 'Anointed' in the Time of Jesus," *Novum Testamentum* VIII (1966), 136.

11. Mark 12:35 and Luke 1:32 f. Although the Davidic origin of the Messiah is quite ancient, this title is unattested before the first century B.C.

12. Jeremiah is implicitly rejecting the messianic pretension of Zedekiah's admirers and making a pun on his name at the same time.

13. If space permitted, this pattern of royal *and* priestly leadership could be documented from Ezek. 40—48 as well.

14. The Testaments of the Twelve Patriarchs also speak of two anointed or messianic figures. T. Levi 18:2–3 refers to God's raising up of a new priest whose "star shall arise in heaven as a king." In T. Judah 24:5–6 we read of a stem from the root of Judah from which will come "a rod of righteousness to the Gentiles, to judge and save all who call upon the Lord." Some assert that both figures are original while R. H. Charles dismissed the passages about the Messiah from Judah as Christian interpolations. M. de Jonge believes that the Testaments are Christian compositions. Because of this lack of consensus, we have decided to limit ourselves in this article to Qumran.

15. Several copies of this document were discovered in Cave IV. Reinhard Deichgräber has ably defended the presence of two Messiahs in this document. See "Zur Messiaserwartung der Damaskusschrift," *ZAW* LXXVIII (1966), 333–343.

16. Damascus has been plausibly explained as the "prophetic name" applied to the desert of Qumran. See Frank M. Cross, Jr., *The Ancient Library of Qumran* (Garden City, N.Y.: Doubleday, 1961), pp. 81–83.

17. My interpretation here is basically that of Cross, "The Early History of the Qumran Community," pp. 259–264.

18. This hermeneutical principle, by the way, is similar to that employed in Matthew's citation of texts like Hos. 11:1 and Jer. 31:15.

19. In some apocalypses the Messiah disappears from consideration while in others the Messiah becomes a figure in the age following the judgment. For a helpful synthesis see Josef Schreiner, *Alttestamentlich jüdische Apokalyptik* (München, Kösel Verlag, 1969), pp. 141–147.

20. Neither Elijah nor Enoch died, according to the Bible. A similar blessing is ascribed to Ezra in 4 Ezra 14:9; to Baruch in 2 Baruch 76:2 and to Jeremiah in 2 Macc. 2:1. The number 400 seems to derive from a combination of Gen. 15:13 and Ps. 90:15. Rev. 20:3

expects a 1,000-year reign. In the apocalypse of Elijah, from the third century A.D., the number is set at 40.

21. A perceptive analysis of the messianic passages in 4 Ezra has been provided by Michael Stone, "The Concept of the Messiah in IV Ezra," in *Religions in Antiquity*, edited by Jacob Neusner (Leiden: E. J. Brill, 1968), pp. 295–312.

22. This is an updating of the four kingdom expectations. In Dan. 2 and 7 the kingdoms are the Neo-Babylonians, Medes, Persians, and Greeks.

23. This belief in the fecundity of the vine became current also in Christian tradition. The following quotation from Irenaeus is interesting, not only because the statistics have been considerably inflated, but also because it is stated to be a saying of Jesus Himself! "As the elders who saw John, the disciple of the Lord, related that they had heard from him how the Lord used to teach in regard to these times and say: The days will come, in which vines shall grow, each having ten thousand branches, and in each branch ten thousand twigs, and in each true twig ten thousand shoots, and in every one of the clusters ten thousand grapes, and every grape when pressed will give five and twenty metretes of wine" (Irenaeus *Against Heresies*, Book V, Ch. XXXIII).

24. While this sequence fits perfectly with our other patterns, there is some evidence that 72-74 are secondary from a literary point of view. See Wolfgang Harnish, *Verhängnis und Verheissung der Geschichte* (Göttingen: Vandenhoeck & Ruprecht, 1969), p. 261.

25. I have demonstrated this essential confessional and hermeneutical principle elsewhere. See my article, "Yahweh Faithful and Free—A Study in Ezekiel," *CTM* XLII (September 1971), 493–501.

III: TEXTUAL CRITICISM

Introduction

T HE starting place of biblical study is the Word—the most reliable text available. But just what *is* the Word? Who determines what is the most reliable text, and how? What can be learned from tracing the versions of the Bible, which seem to supersede each other like the latest model cars? These questions are elemental to a textual critic.

Section One, including both the introduction and the essays, deals in part with what the Word is—the creative process by which God's intention is transmitted through writers. But after a work appeared, others, generally those who were religious leaders far removed from the writer, had to establish if it would be accepted in the canon (the authoritative list of works which received official sanction). Unlike the Magna Carta or the Declaration of Independence, which can be consulted in the original manuscript if there is ever a question about a specific wording, not a single original word of the Bible has survived. And the thousands of ancient texts which preserve the various parts of the Bible seldom, if ever, can be arranged in neat order. If one can believe in salvation history, that a writer is the vehicle through whom God's will is expressed, then it is easy to believe that God's will survives the vicissitudes of textual transmission through the centuries.

Since Bleddyn J. Roberts and Bruce M. Metzger begin their studies of textual transmission at an advanced level, some readers may think it necessary to read the next several paragraphs about canonization history which fill in the background.

The history of the Old Testament, the Apocrypha (the eleven books between the Old Testament and the New Testament in the Roman Catholic canon or the fourteen books of the Septuagint included in the Vulgate Bible), and the New Testament is so diverse that each must be discussed separately. Perhaps the two greatest pressures to establish the Hebrew canon were (1) the emergence of Christianity from the Jewish world, and (2) the weakening of a central religious authority following the Diaspora (dispersion of the Jews from Palestine) in A.D. 70. As we read in Acts, Jerusalem Christianity began in the synagogue and, after an internal struggle between factions, moved to the church. When the temple in Jerusalem was destroyed by the Romans in A.D. 70, the schisms among the dispersed Jews grew. The manuscripts considered by Roberts were written before and during these years of upheaval. The agreement reached by the Pharisees gathered in Jamnia in A.D. 90—that only those books now included in the Old Testament were canonical—overcame for all times any threat of further fragmentation due to the Christian schism or the Jewish dispersion.

Much of the confusion about why the Torah (the combined Jewish literature and oral tradition) and the several Christian versions of the Bible include different books, stems from who establishes what is normative. The Hebrew canon is divided into three parts: Laws, Prophets, and Writings. The first to be accepted as authoritative was the Law. In 621 B.C., a scroll which is now part of Deuteronomy was recognized as the Law by King Josiah and his people. After Genesis, Exodus, Leviticus, and Numbers were added to an expanded Deuteronomy in approximately 400 B.C., the collection called the Pentateuch or Torah was canonized by general acclaim. Similarly, the twenty books of the Prophets were canonized in 180 B.C.—several hundred years after they were written. The remaining fourteen books of history, poetry, prophecy, and special occasions (Ruth, Ecclesiastes, and others), called the Writings, were canonized at Jamnia because they too met a significant criterion—they were written in Hebrew.

Greek-speaking Jews, however, who lived during the decades surrounding Jesus, also accepted the books of the Apocrypha which were originally written in languages other than Hebrew. Jerome included them in the Vulgate Old Testament in A.D. 405, and there they remained unchallenged until Martin Luther refused to include them in his 1534 translation. At the Council of Trent in 1546, the Roman Catholic Church accepted most of the Apocrypha as canonical. Thus we can see, even without going into what motivated most of the decisions behind the process, that the decisions were often based as much on theology as they were on textual accuracy.

The New Testament canonization process can be discussed more easily. Paul's letters, written between A.D. 50 and 62, are accepted by most to be the oldest writings in the New Testament. By A.D. 367, Athanasius, the Bishop of Alexandria, accepted them and the other books which constituted the twenty-seven books. Thus in a mere three hundred years, the New Testament as we now know it became canonized. Metzger, however, shows that even within these years heretics such as Marcion and the Gnostics had their impact on even those books which were included. To more fully understand the history of New Testament transmission, Metzger implies, we must also read the writings of the Apostolic Fathers—another name for the New Testament Apocrypha. These writings include 1 and 2 Clement, the Epistle of Barnabas, and the letters of Ignatius.

With canon history in mind, we can now pass to the second question raised at the beginning of this section: What can be learned from tracing a text's transmission history? Roberts, Metzger, and, to a lesser degree, Frye are all concerned about textual transmission, for it informs us about the authors and the environment in which they wrote. Theological differences between Roman Catholics and Protestants can be traced back to Jerome's and Luther's attitudes about the Old Testament Apocrypha. This section of the Scriptures also broadens our appreciation of the imaginative literature not found elsewhere—such as the book of Susanna and additions to the book of Esther. It is unfortunate for a variety of reasons that this Apocrypha is not more widely read. As a final example, Frye demonstrates how the King James Version was an ideal match of a type of literature, of translators, of ancillary knowledge about the biblical world, and of a particular Renaissance mind which was controlled, yet lively. Thus we see that textual and historical studies are like love and marriage. Each needs the other. Just as the textual critic needs substantial historical knowledge, the historical critic must have a firm grasp of biblical and related texts.

Since Roberts and Metzger assume more knowledge than most undergraduates bring to their essays, we suggest they first skim the table on pp. 210–211, which summarizes the main points of the most important Hebrew and Greek manuscripts. This comes from John Reumann's article, "The Transmission of the Biblical Text" in the *Interpreter's One-Volume Commentary on the Bible*: it is an excellent supplementary essay.

Finally, while Metzger and Roberts look at ancient texts, Frye, in "The Bible in English," studies the milieu of the King James Version (1611). After discussing the translators and their works that precede it, Frye turns to the effect of the King James Version on its readers. As Peter Levi writes in *The English Bible: 1534 to 1859* (1974):

> The most modern English versions are none of them convincing on the level of language; I find this morally and intellectually confusing, since I find it means I am incapable of taking seriously anything that they say. Since I cannot think that I am unique in this experience, I am forced to regard the new versions as ill-judged, and their imposition as an act of folly. I am clear that the principles of English style are a moral matter, not just a question of taste. Reticence, clarity and sobriety, strength and simplicity, logical coherence and a decent habit of speech have their foundations in moral sensibility. The modern English Bibles are written in the language, or the non-language, of a class, and of a class that has no authority in spoken English.

We glimpse why its cadences have survived in our hearts long after the King James Version has been superseded on other grounds.

TRANSMISSION OF THE BIBLICAL TEXT

by John Reumann

TABLE I. OLDEST MSS OF THE MASORETIC TEXT

Designation	Date	Contents	Location	Other Information
Or. 4445	820-50?	Gen. 39:20–Deut. 1:33	British Museum	Text of Aaron ben Asher
Cairo Codex (C)	895	Former and Latter Prophets	Karaite Synagogue, Cairo	Copied by Moses ben Asher
Petersburg Codex (P)	916	Former and Latter Prophets	Public Library, Leningrad	Ben Asher text, but with earlier "Babylonian" vowel pointing
Aleppo Codex	900-950	Complete	Hebrew Univ., Jerusalem	Vocalization and masorah by Aaron ben Asher; used by Israeli scholars as basis for new ed.
Leningrad Codex B 19a (Leningradensis, L)	1008	Complete	Public Library, Leningrad	Copied from MSS written by Aaron ben Asher; used in 1937 as basis for Kittel-Kahle *Biblia Hebraica*, third ed.

TABLE II. CHIEF UNCIAL GREEK PARCHMENT MSS

Number	Letter	Name	Cent.	Contents	Location	NT Text Type	Discovery
01	ℵ (aleph)	Sinaiticus	4th	Last half of OT; all of NT	British Museum; 43 OT leaves in Univ. Library, Leipzig	Alexandrian with Western touches	By Tischendorf at Mt. Sinai 1844, 1859
02	A	Alexandrinus	5th	Almost complete	British Museum	Alexandrian but gospels Byzantine	Gift to king of England from patriarch of Constantinople in 1627
03	B	Vaticanus	4th	Most except Gen. 1:1–46:28; Heb. 9:14–13:25, Pastorals, Philem., Rev.	Vatican Library	Alexandrian	In Vatican Library since before its first catalog in 1475 but opened to scholars only in latter half of 19th cent.
04	C	Ephraemi Rescriptus	5th	Palimpsest of scattered parts of OT & NT	National Library, Paris	Mixed, mostly Byzantine	Noted ca. 1700; deciphered by Tischendorf, 1840–45
05	D	Bezae	5th/6th	Greek & Latin of Gospels, Acts	Cambridge Univ. Library	Western	At Lyons in 1562
06	Dᴾ	Claromontanus	6th	Greek & Latin of Pauline letters, Heb.	National Library, Paris	Western	At Clermont, France
032	W	Washingtoniensis	5th	Gospels	Smithsonian Inst., Washington, D.C.	Mixed	Egypt, 1906
038	Θ (theta)	Koridethi	9th	Gospels	Georgian Museum, Tiflis, U.S.S.R.	Caesarean in Mark, elsewhere Byzantine	In a monastery at Koridethi, Georgia (Russia) 1853, but later lost and rediscovered in 1901

The Old Testament:
Manuscripts, Text
and Versions

The Old Testament was written in Hebrew c. 900–125 B.C.
*Yet until the Dead Sea Scrolls were discovered after World
War II, the oldest extant Hebrew transcription of the Old
Testament was the Cairo codex of the Prophets, dated* A.D.
*895—a thousand years after the last parts of the Old Tes-
tament appeared. Until recently, translations of it were
based on fourth and fifth century Greek versions, the oldest
in any language. Careful reading of the Dead Sea Scrolls,
however, makes clear that these texts, which were written
in Massoretic (Hebrew) between 100* B.C. *and* A.D. *125, are
less "corrupt" (have fewer errors of transmission) than even
the Greek uncial manuscripts (so named because of the
large size of the script). The Dead Sea Scrolls, as Roberts
implies, have caused a revolution in Old Testament textual
criticism. The quantum jump in our knowledge about the
intentions of the original authors and about its transmission
process will, undoubtedly, have a major impact on future
translations.*

*The reader should find the table on pp. 210–211 a useful
supplement to this complex and difficult subject of the establishment of the Old Testament canon and the history of
its transmission. The table lists the Massoretic and Greek
manuscripts in chronological order and briefly notes which
books of the Bible they include.*

T HE Old Testament textualist is today more concerned with the story
of the textual transmission up to the middle ages than ever before. It
is from its manuscripts that he derives both the text itself and the variants
for his *apparatus criticus,* and his interpretation of the medieval transmission controls, to a large extent, his choice of readings. Consequently,
the relevance of the present survey of the medieval transmission lies not

From Bleddyn J. Roberts, *The Cambridge History of the Bible,* II (1971), ed. G. W. H.
Lampe, pp. 1–26.

so much in providing information about textual activities but in an appraisal of their use in the contemporary textual situation. The topic as a whole falls into two fairly exclusive sections, namely the Hebrew (Massoretic) text and the Versions.

THE HEBREW (MASSORETIC) TEXT

The traditional view of the Hebrew transmission was that the textual minutiae of the Law as the most significant part of the Scriptures were fixed for all time under the influence of Rabbi Aqiba (c. A.D. 55–137), and the standardization of the remainder followed soon afterwards, to produce the official Massoretic text. From that time onward all manuscripts were scrupulously transcribed according to the archetype, and scrutinized by official scribes, so that a correct transmission was assured. Rabbinic evidence, it was said, supported this reconstruction.

On four occasions in rabbinic writings we are told, with a few variations, that three scrolls of the Law, with minor textual divergences, were deposited in the Temple court, and in each case of divergence it was ruled that the majority reading was authoritative. The fact that the legend is set in the Temple area shows that discussion about text standardization goes back at least to the time before A.D. 70, the date of the sack of Jerusalem. Again, it is stated that Rabbi Aqiba studied each instance of the use of the grammatical particles and based his exegesis on their usage, and this, it is argued, must surely represent a definitive phase in the standardization. The fact that the comment is derived from the Babylonian Talmud (*Shebu'oth 26 a*), a standard rabbinic work redacted in the sixth century, shows that the rabbinic tradition was soundly based.

During the past hundred years, however, and especially because of the work of Paul Kahle in the present century, the tradition has been challenged, and counter-challenged. At present, experts who can rightly claim outstanding authority are not only contradictory but often mutually exclusive in their testimony. The present survey cannot pretend to offer a verdict on either side, but rather, by means of introducing an independent perspective, seeks to tell the story as a whole with a reasonable sense of proportion.

The discovery of the Dead Sea scrolls provides a suitable starting-point, because they provide actual specimen texts from the time before Aqiba's 'standardized' text-form. But the fact that there are two distinct groups of 'Dead Sea' biblical texts is highly important. On the one hand we have the texts from Qumran, which are sectarian and probably from the pre-Christian and early Christian era, and, on the other, we have the texts from Murabba'at and Masada, which represent the orthodox rabbinic transmission from the second century A.D.

The latter are less well known to the average reader, but for the present survey they demand pride of place. It is beyond dispute that they form part of the literary remains of the Jewish army in the bar Cochba revolt in A.D. 132–35, the last vain attempt to oppose Roman domination. Not all the texts are available for general scrutiny, but it is reported that they contain fragments from the three sections of rabbinic scriptures, the Law, the Prophets and the Writings, and are identical with the text which became recognized as standard. Rabbi Aqiba, whose name figures so prominently in the so-called standardization, was directly involved in the revolt, and consequently it is reasonable to assume that the standardized text was available before his time. The relevance of the conclusion, however, will be discussed when the question of standardization must once again be raised.

The Qumran biblical manuscripts do not represent the orthodox transmission, and consequently it is only by implication that they relate to the Massoretic text. They belong to a dissident sect, whose independence of orthodoxy was fundamental and is to be observed in such important issues as the religious calendar, the priestly hierarchy, apocalyptic teaching and the interpretation of Scripture—all matters on which orthodox Judaism of those times held rigid views. It lies to hand to suggest that in its transmission of Scripture the sect of the scrolls was no less nonconformist, and consequently it is at least precarious to use the Qumran scrolls indiscriminately to demonstrate the early history of rabbinic textual transmission.

In actual fact, the Qumran biblical scrolls, mainly from caves one, four and eleven, range from near-identity with the Massoretic text to a text-form which closely approximates to the parent text of the oldest of the Versions, the Greek Septuagint, with instances, too, of variations between the two. That is, there is a considerable variety of text-forms, with far-reaching divergences; it does not appear that the sect subscribed to any one traditional or established text-form of the Hebrew Old Testament.

But among the variety the one text-form which is predominant has strong affinities and probable identity with the rabbinic text. One of the Isaiah manuscripts from cave one is particularly relevant, namely *1 QIsb*. It belongs to the first century A.D. and, though it is badly worn and consequently has lost a substantial amount of text, it is generally regarded as practically identical in both text and orthography with the current text. Indeed, so similar are they and so insignificant are the divergences that the scroll has hardly been given the notice it deserves from scholars. But from the text-historian's point of view it is just these features that make it one of the most significant of the Qumran scrolls. Its comparatively late date places it in a period when any tendency by the sect to accept an orthodox text-form can be discounted. By the same token, it is very unlikely that orthodox Judaism at that time would have chosen as archetype for its own text-form a text out of those transmitted by the Qumran sect. The obvious conclusion is that its existence among the scrolls points to its existence also in orthodox circles long before the time of Aqiba, and it could be as early as the beginnings of the Qumran sect itself.

Another Isaiah text from cave one indirectly supports this view, namely *1 QIsa*. Compared with the accepted text, the divergent readings in this scroll are numerous and more far-reaching than in *1 QIsb*. In the main, however, they fall into clearly defined categories of grammar, orthography and normal textual corruption, scribal errors and the replacement of difficult readings by simple ones; only rarely do they point to recensional divergences in the sense presupposed, for instance, by some of the Samuel texts from cave four. That is, *1 QIsa* again postulates the existence, at a time earlier than its own date, of a text which agrees essentially with the Massoretic text. Thus the cumulative evidence of Qumran, albeit by implication, points to the existence in the period before Christ of a text which approximates as nearly as is possible to the Massoretic text.

Finally, it may be noted that other fragments of biblical texts from caves one and four, and the lengthy scroll of Psalms from cave eleven, agree to such an extent with the Massoretic text that what was said above about *1 QIsb* may well apply to the whole of the Old Testament.

We cannot discover how orthodox Judaism functioned in the period before Christ, but it is unlikely that the authorities countenanced such a wide freedom of textual transmission as that which obtained in Qumran. Josephus, in *Contra Apionem* i. 8, from the second century A.D., says that one mark of the sacred writings of the Jews is their textual inviolability, and it is consistent with what we know of Judaism, with its particularism and its strict hierarchical control, that it transmitted one text-form, whereas the sects were accustomed to the transmission of popular variant versions.

Historical data from rabbinic writings suggest how the rabbis proceeded with the task of transmitting the text. After the fall of Jerusalem in A.D. 70 the Pharisees, relieved of preoccupation with the Temple-bound Sadducees, turned their wrath on the apocalyptic sectarians such as the Zealots, the Essenes and the Christians, persecuted them and expelled them from the Synagogue. Constructively, they established under Johanan ben Zakkai of the first generation of Tannaite teachers (c. A.D. 10–80) a centre of study and piety at Jamnia (Jabne-el of biblical times) on the coastal plain, and this became the prototype of similar academies throughout Palestine. It is often assumed that final questions connected with the canonicity of some of the books of Scripture were settled at the Synod of Jamnia, but it is still an open question whether the interpretation is correct. It is still more difficult to decide whether or not steps were taken to establish the definitive text of the Old Testament. What Jamnia does show is that henceforth orthodox Judaism was to be rigidly controlled by the rabbis, who, in turn, were themselves bound to the Massorah, i.e. the tradition. There was freedom within the Massorah to debate and to decide, as is abundantly shown by references within the complex of rabbinic writings down to the middle ages, and controversy waxed strong, but it was always ordered and controlled and never again was orthodoxy to be torn asunder by schism or secession.

The existence of the Massorah can be traced back as far as any rabbinic activity; its usage in the Mishna, the earliest codification of rabbinic teaching, produced in the second century A.D., shows that it had always functioned in the disputations. 'The Massorah is a fence to the Law', said Rabbi Aqiba, who, though he belonged to the third generation of teachers, was primarily concerned with the maintaining of the Massorah, the tradition which he had received. The academy to which he belonged was at Bne Baraq (to the east of Joppa), although he had also attended those of Lydda and Jamnia. Obviously, Massoretic studies in this period were pursued at a number of centres and under the guidance of a variety of families of rabbis in Palestine, and their *dicta* were treasured and transmitted, to a large extent orally, until the final redaction of the Mishna in the second century, and later in the Talmuds of Palestine and Babylonia, and in other rabbinic works down to the middle ages. And it is in this sense that biblical scholars always refer to the Hebrew Old Testament as the Massoretic text.

Rabbinic studies flourished also in Babylonia, for from the second century and later there is evidence of centres at Nehardea and at Sura. The former was destroyed in 259 and was replaced by the academy at Pum Bedita. Verdicts of the rabbis in these centres, too, were included in the collections referred to. It is from these sources that data are recoverable for the historical reconstruction of the textual transmission, and it is significant that they contain no hint of any divergent recension of the text, but rather assume that every care and attention was devoted to the transmission of the accepted, 'correct' form. The Babylonian Talmud, *Kethuboth 106a,* from the sixth century included among the officers who had been paid by the Temple authorities the 'book readers', men who corrected biblical manuscripts, and it is apparent that the office persisted into later Talmudic times.

This account, however, is oversimplified, as we have been forcibly reminded in a recent survey (1966) by H. M. Orlinsky. Most of the material he uses as evidence was previously known, but his conclusions are new and quite sensational. He summarily denies that the Massoretic text as such ever actually existed, or can ever be constructed; divergences within the transmitted texts, as witnessed by rabbinic discussions and also by collations in subsequent biblical editions, demonstrate traditional and legitimate divergences. For Orlinsky, then, all that can be claimed for any given edition is that it represents *a* Massoretic text, and not *the* Massoretic text. This is hardly the right occasion to enter into the controversy: what may be stressed, however, is that the key-word is still Massoretic—whether it be *a* or *the* Massoretic text.

In a general sense, then, it is correct to think of the transmission as the work of the scribes, including, possibly from the time of Ezra, an expertise in matters of interpretation. At the same time, the title *sopher,* 'scribe', is both traditionally and etymologically attached to the official copyists. A ninth-century rabbinic work, *Massekheth Sopherim,* contains the traditions of scribal instructions and data; and numerous Talmudic references connect with the word *sopher* the work of counting. Thus, the scribes reckoned every letter of the Torah, established that the middle consonant in the Torah was in Lev. xi. 42, the middle word in Lev. x. 16, the middle verse Lev. xiii. 33. The middle of the Psalter was Ps. lxxviii. 38.

These and other products of scribal activity came to be inserted in the margins of manuscripts, at the top and bottom of columns, and at the end of individual books. Much later they were assembled in separate collections, of which a few have survived. Particular interest attaches to three or four which, in part at least, are still extant. They include the above-mentioned *Massekheth Sopherim, Diqduqe Ha-te'amim,* attributed to Aaron ben Asher in the tenth century, and *Ochla we-Ochla,* which was edited from manuscripts and published by Frensdorff in 1864; but the most convenient for current usage, despite some serious basic misconceptions, is the collection made by C. D. Ginsburg, and published in four volumes, *The Massorah, 1880-1905.* Appropriately, the scribal notes contained in these collections are collectively called *Massorah* or *Massoreth*—'the body of tradition'—and the persons responsible for its transmission *ba'ale ha-massoreth,* 'the masters of the tradition'. The notes include such items as irregularly shaped letters and unusual features of grammar, and draw attention to textual interference by the scribes in matters of exegesis, especially where the traditional, consonantal text was still retained. But it must be stressed that they are not uniform, nor do they always agree with the texts they accompany.

An outline of such Massoretic annotations obviously needs to be illustrated from actual texts, but the following will serve to indicate the kind of material included in them: *Tiqqune Sopherim*—scribal emendations—which often avoid anthropomorphism in the original text; *'Itture Sopherim*—scribal omissions; *Qre* and *Kethib*—divergences between what was recited and the written consonantal text (although most of these first became obvious only after the introduction of vocalization). There are also scribal marks which denote that the text was corrupt or wrong, and such passages were designated (in the Babylonian Massorah)

Demish. Lists of such marks—actually dots, *puncta extraordinaria*—have been transmitted and their existence is postulated even as early as the Mishna.

Other scribal peculiarities, such as the suspended consonants *nun* in Judges xviii. 30, and *ayin* in Ps. lxxx. 14, and a number of enlarged and diminished consonants, have only incidental significance and denote the initial or the middle consonant of a book. Some interest may attach to the presence in some manuscripts of an enlarged initial consonant for Isa. xl. 1.

The survival of the two main traditions of Massoretic activity in Babylon and Palestine is seen in the two divergent Massoroth, those of *Madinhae* (eastern) and *Ma'arbae* (western) respectively. Failure to recognize the distinction between them resulted in the erroneous view, prevalent until the work of Paul Kahle in the present century, that the Massorah of the text was uniform because it reflected a basic uniformity in the text transmission. Nowhere is the divergence more obvious or more relevant than in the systems of vocalization which were superimposed on the consonantal text and which were developed both in Palestine and Babylon between the late fifth century and the ninth century A.D. In Babylon sporadic use of vocalic consonants and dots was made to assist and to formalize the correct recitation of the hitherto unvocalized, consonantal text in synagogue worship. In the eighth century, probably under the influence of the Qaraites, a non-rabbinic Jewish sect, refinements were introduced into the vocalization which ultimately produced the complicated scheme of supralineal pointing which still survives in the so-called Babylonian vocalization. During the same period, and under the same impetus, a parallel process was applied to the texts transmitted in Palestine. A primitive Palestinian supralineal vocalization was in due course replaced by the Tiberian pointing, which is the one normally used today for the Hebrew Bible. The supremacy of the Tiberian system over the Babylonian is to be explained mainly by the disappearance of Babylon from Jewish history as a result of the Islamic conquest of Mesopotamia, though it is to be noted in passing that Babylonian influences, inspired by the Qaraite movement and perpetuated by outstanding personalities such as Saadya Gaon and the academies at Pum Bedita and Sura, played an important part in the subsequent history of European Judaism.

The earlier, primitive phases of the vocalization in both transmissions are almost wholly unknown, except for incidental and until recently incomprehensible references in late rabbinic works, but actual examples were discovered in fragments of biblical texts from the Cairo Genizah, an ante-chamber in the synagogue in which discarded manuscripts were deposited. The account of their significance forms an important part of Kahle's Schweich Lectures (published as *The Cairo Geniza*, 1947, and its second edition, 1959). Subsequent scrutiny of important fragments of these texts has been published in the Annual of the Hebrew University, *Textus*.

The Genizah fragments—over 200,000 in all—were removed from the Cairo synagogue, where they had been assembled in the ninth and tenth centuries A.D., and deposited in the main in libraries in Leningrad, in England, notably at the Cambridge University Library, the Bodleian at Oxford, the British Museum and the John Rylands Library, Manchester (which acquired what previously formed the Gaster Collection), and in the U.S.A. They range from about the sixth century to the tenth and relate to all aspects of synagogue worship and pedagogy, and include biblical texts (many of them vocalized), Mishna, Talmuds, Targums, liturgies, hymns and prayers, and even private papers. Recent discoveries among the Genizah fragments contain texts with both Babylonian and Tiberian vocalizations, and form a valuable addition to other fragments by which it is now possible, albeit tentatively, to reconstruct the framework for the whole history of vocalization. They also include fragments where the words are only partly written and vocalized, the so-called 'abbreviated system'; and whereas specimens of Palestinian and Tiberian pointings had been available since early in this century, a recent fragment with Babylonian abbreviated texts has thrown further light on this interesting phase. Moreover both this and another fragment from the Rylands collection contain both Babylonian and Tiberian vocalizations. From the standpoint of textual transmission, it might be argued that the main body of the fragments generally supports the traditional view that the text had long been fixed. But the exception of one very significant feature, namely the transmission of the divine name, indicates that such a generalization is misleading. It is remarkable how frequently the manuscripts show divergences not only in the change from Yahweh to Adonai and conversely, but also of interchange between Elohim and Yahweh. That there were ancient divergent transmissions of the divine name is shown by the Elohistic and Yahwistic redactions in collections of Psalms, but it is remarkable that a similar divergence was allowed to persist long after the text was apparently established in other respects, and this underlines the need to scrutinize other, less obvious, inconsistencies.

The adoption of one scheme of vocalization from the rather chaotic multiplicity of Simple and Complex Babylonian, and the Palestinian and Tiberian, and various modified forms within each group—for they were not in any way homogeneous—was not the end of a phase in the struggle for supremacy, for controversy still persisted. There were disputes between two contemporary families of Tiberian Massoretes, ben Asher and ben Naphtali. The former flourished in the ninth and tenth centuries, presumably also the latter, though so apparently complete was the ultimate supremacy of ben Asher that most of the traces of the history of the ben Naphtali tradition have been expunged, and the main evidence of its existence lies in Massoretic lists of variations between the two transmissions. In their present form, the lists indicate that the conflict dealt mainly with minutiae of vocalization and especially accentuation, but underlying these apparently innocuous variants are issues of more far-reaching significance. What might appear to be the concern of the Massoretes simply for the 'correct' rendering of Scripture in synagogue worship was actually their desire to retain divergent traditions. For the general purposes of the Old Testament textualist, however, its main importance lies in its providing the means of identifying biblical manuscripts from the middle ages. The oldest and best list of differences between ben Asher and ben Naphtali is that by Mishael ben Uzziel, *Kitab al Khilaf*, probably composed in the tenth century but now reconstructed from later works and Genizah fragments. This work is now completely edited by L. Lipschütz; the first part, *ben Ascher—ben Naftali*, appeared in 1937, and the remainder was published as an appendix to *Textus*, vol. II, in 1962, with an introduction in vol. IV, 1964.

With the introduction of the name ben Asher we move into the period when lengthy and complete manuscripts of the text are available, for there are codices extant which carry ben Asher colophons. They are the oldest copies of the Old Testament Scriptures apart from the Dead Sea scrolls and the Genizah fragments, and consequently need to be listed separately; they also form the basis of most modern editions of the text, or at least provide important sources for the *apparatus criticus*. They are:

1. The British Museum manuscript *Or. 4445*, which consists of the Pentateuch, written probably in the early tenth century, on the authority and during the lifetime of Aaron, the chief though not the first of the ben Asher family.

2. The so-called Babylonian codex of the Prophets, actually dated A.D. 916. At one time it was known as the St Petersburg Codex, but it is now catalogued in the Leningrad Library, *MS Heb. B. 3*. It was edited and published under the title *The Petersburg Codex of the Prophets* by H. L. Strack, 1876.

3. The Cairo codex of the Prophets, preserved in the Qaraite synagogue in Cairo from 895, is the oldest dated Hebrew manuscript extant, and was produced by Moshe ben Asher, the father of Aaron.

4. The Aleppo codex comes from the first half of the tenth century, and once contained the whole Old Testament; consequently it is the most significant of all the ben Asher manuscripts. Furthermore it is argued that this text was acclaimed by Maimonides in the twelfth century as the model codex. At least from the fifteenth century it was preserved in the Sephardic synagogue in Aleppo, and so carefully was it guarded that it was almost impossible to consult. Even so, one page was photographed, and in 1887 formed the frontispiece of a book on Hebrew accents

(Wickes, *A Treatise on the Accentuation of the Twenty-One So-Called Prose Books of the Old Testament*). The codex was reported destroyed in the upheavals in Lebanon in the 1940s, but in 1960 the President of the State of Israel proclaimed that it had been recovered, and it has now become the basis of a new edition of the Massoretic text edited by M. H. Goshen-Gottstein in the Hebrew University, and in 1965, *A Sample Edition of the Book of Isaiah* appeared.

5. Finally, the *Leningrad Codex, B 19a,* written in 1008 and vouched for by the copyist in a colophon as based on the text of Aaron ben Asher. Since 1937 it has been used as the basis of the only current critical edition of the Massoretic text, namely Kittel's *Biblia Hebraica*, third and subsequent editions.

It has been assumed that the ben Asher text marks the end of the formal history of the Massoretic text, but not all manuscripts from the middle ages belong to this tradition. Three Erfurt codices from the eleventh to the fourteenth centuries, and the *Reuchlin Codex*, the oldest biblical manuscript in Germany, contain elements which are recognizably ben Naphtali. In the past, they have not been rated as significant for the history of the classical text, but, as scholars become better informed about Massoretic activities in general, it is more than likely that renewed attention will be paid to these divergent transmissions. One is again conscious of Orlinsky's assertion, already referred to, that there never was really a text which could be designated as *the* Massoretic text.

The establishment of the ben Asher text, however, produced an interesting side-effect on the transmission of the accompanying Massoretic notes. The Massorah became conventional because it had no longer any real purpose to serve; and gradually its minutely written script became rendered in geometric and artistic designs as embellishments around the margins of the manuscript, sometimes in grotesque shapes of dragons and occasionally in intricate and fanciful lines, to give an outlet to the artistic urges of the scribe.

An exquisite example of the ornamental Massorah is to be found in a fifteenth-century Spanish manuscript in Aberdeen University, and in a discussion of it (*The Aberdeen Codex of the Hebrew Bible,* 1958) Dr Cecil Roth gives the history of this feature of Hebrew scribal activity, with three excellent photographs from the manuscript itself. The codex also contains eight folios of ben Asher and ben Naphtali variants, which were included in the manuscript. Dr Roth urges that they are to be regarded simply as a convenient vehicle for introducing scribal art and letter illumination into the initial pages (in this instance eight) of the scroll. Another instance of ornamental Massorah is *B.M. Or. 2626–28,* again of Spanish provenance, late fifteenth century.

In the late fifteenth and early sixteenth centuries, printed Hebrew bibles begin to appear, and outstanding among them are rabbinic bibles, because they contain along with the Massoretic text important Targumic renderings to which reference will be made later, and the polyglot texts, because they include many of the Versions. For the history of the Massoretic text, however, special interest attaches to the *Second Rabbinic Bible* of 1524/25 edited by Jacob ben Chayim. The edition is a critical one, based on the collation of a considerable number of manuscripts, and supplied with a Massorah created by the editor himself. It became the main basis of practically every subsequent edition of the text until Kittel's *Biblia Hebraica*[3]. But it had two serious faults. First, the manuscripts available to ben Chayim were, by his own plaintive admission, recent and of unknown provenance. Secondly, he seems not to have been able to deal with the vicissitudes which had beset the transmission even during the four or five centuries since the emergence of the ben Asher text. The Erfurt Codices provide an instance of what had happened, and there is hardly a manuscript—and there are a goodly number from this period—which had retained a pure ben Asher text. The very fact that ben Chayim composed his own Massorah shows that he was not ignorant of the divergent elements which were present in his manuscript sources, but was unable to accommodate them.

Subsequent printed bibles perpetuated the hybrid text of ben Chayim and occasionally introduced additional, equally mixed, text-forms, but they served well. They include the Hebrew text of the *Complutensian Polyglot* (1514-17), and the editions of Michaelis (1720), Kennicott (1776-80), and J. B. de Rossi (1784-98). Lists of variants from nearly 700 and 1,500 manuscripts and printed bibles accompanied the last two respectively, and during the heyday of biblical criticism the editions of Baer-Delitzsch and C. D. Ginsburg were published with their Massoroth, and Kittel's first two editions were supplied with an *apparatus criticus* to include manuscript evidence, Version variants and conjectural emendations to the text.

There appears to be no doubt that *Biblia Hebraica*[3] with its return to an authentic ben Asher text from the early eleventh century marks an important step in the scientific study of the textual transmission. It renders possible, too, an appreciation of the relevant Massorah, rather than assuming a Massoretic composition which has no textual value at all. The edition is a lasting tribute to Paul Kahle and his assessment of the Cairo Genizah fragments and of subsequent manuscripts. But the extent to which this departure really involves a drastic modification of earlier theories is still a controversy, and the edition might well be displaced as a definitive text either by the Hebrew University Bible, or by Orlinsky's conclusion that it can be no better than *a* Massoretic text, one among many.

To some degree the reaction is illuminated by the latest Hebrew Old

Testament to be published in Britain, namely N. H. Snaith's edition for the British and the Foreign Bible Society (*Sepher Torah u-Nebi'im u-Kethubim*), which will replace the Letteris and Ginsburg editions. A detailed introduction to the edition is still awaited, but Snaith has briefly outlined the background ('New Edition of the Hebrew Bible', *Vetus Testamentum*, VII, 1957, pp. 207/8, and again in *Textus,* vol. II, 1962). The text is based on the original readings of some fifteenth-century Spanish manuscripts (*B. M. Or. 2626–28*, the Yemenite *B.M. Or. 2375*), and the *Shem Tob MS* from the Sassoon Library, and the editor claims that the resultant text is practically identical with the Kahle (*Biblia Hebraica*[3]) edition of the ben Asher standard text.

That Principal Snaith decided that only the ben Asher type of text can henceforth really satisfy the Hebraist is a tribute to the epoch-making work of Kahle and the publication of *Biblia Hebraica*[3], but if his claim that the ben Asher text is not limited to strictly ben Asher manuscripts is substantiated, further scrutiny of Spanish manuscripts might well be worthwhile. In any case it is a challenge to the view, popularly accepted, that, soon after the ben Asher text appeared, scribal interference with it was universal and brought all later manuscripts into disrepute. Thus, recent textual studies emphasize that for the Hebrew Old Testament actual medieval manuscripts are basic. At present, and unless some discovery is made of more fundamental significance than the Dead Sea scrolls, critical editions must be based on medieval codices, whether they be regarded as *the* Massoretic or merely *a* Massoretic text.

THE VERSIONS

The relevance of the middle ages for the Versions of the Old Testament is quite different from that for the Hebrew text, for it is in this period that we see much of their origin and early history. In a sense this is true even of the oldest of the Versions, and the most important, namely the Greek rendering commonly known as the Septuagint; it is obviously true of the Latin renderings—both the early Old Latin and the later Vulgate—as well as the Aramaic renderings of the Targums and the others. Nevertheless, the prehistory of the Versions must be included, for without it we fail to see the whole significance of many prominent features in the medieval transmission. At the same time, it is necessary to note that much of this prehistory actually results from recent discussion as well as discovery; consequently the present survey must often be concerned with items undreamed of by the medievalists themselves.

The actual Versions consist, of course, of the Septuagint and its daughter versions on the one hand, and renderings more closely related to the Massoretic text such as the Targums, the Samaritan recension and the Arabic version on the other. The Syriac Peshitta, as we shall see, has its own category.

The Septuagint

Throughout the history of the Christian Church the most important of the Versions has been the Septuagint. It assumed priority as early as the first century: apparently it was used by Paul when he wrote to the churches, and on the whole it was the rendering used for the Gospels in their present form. On the other hand, orthodox Judaism either refused to recognize it from an early period or quickly expunged it from among its Scriptures, for there are but few and indirect indications of its existence in any of the rabbinic works. Consequently, the history of its transmission must be regarded as largely independent of the Massoretic text except that, from time to time, significant attempts were made by Christian Fathers to achieve its alignment with the more fixed and, in a sense, more authentic Hebrew text.

Recently discovered manuscripts from the pre-Christian and early Christian periods provide pointers for the early history. They include the *John Rylands Papyrus 458* from the second century B.C., and *Papyrus Fouad 266* in Cairo from the late second or early first century B.C., both of which contain fragments of Deuteronomy. Qumran cave four has produced a papyrus fragment of Leviticus, and two leather fragments of Leviticus and of Numbers. The last mentioned still await publication. Their major importance is that on the whole they confirm the implications of the Letter of Aristeas, and the testimony of Philo and Josephus that by the second century B.C. the Greek rendering of the Torah was not only complete and uniform but was also well distributed throughout the Hellenistic Diaspora and in Palestine itself. The only caveat that should be entered is that the scholars who have collated the Rylands papyrus are not wholly agreed on its affinities (e.g. Kahle argues that it is related to one of the recensions, namely the Lucianic).

From Qumran caves one, four, five and six come biblical texts in Hebrew which, according to reports, are related to the parent text of the Septuagint historical books. Particular interest attaches to Samuel fragments from cave four, because the text-form shows more obvious affinities with the Septuagint than do the others. Of course, it has long been agreed that the parent text of the Septuagint Samuel contained recensional divergences from the Massoretic text, but the extent of the recension has been debated. Those who minimized it argued that many of the textual differences merely reflect Hellenistic tendencies, others explained them as deriving from actual Hebrew variants. The present discovery obviously supports the second alternative, and it may be assumed that since the rendering of Samuel is demonstrably a fairly literal translation of its Hebrew parent text, the presence of interpretation elsewhere, at least in the historical books, should be admitted only where no other explanation is possible.

But the problem of Greek–Hebrew relationships is not thereby disposed of, for though the presence of interpretation in the Septuagint generally is undoubted, its nature and its extent are debated. It is probable that during the third century B.C. a rendering of the Torah in *koiné* Greek was produced by a duly commissioned body of Jerusalem (orthodox) Jews for apologetic purposes and for liturgical use in the synagogues of the Hellenistic Diaspora. This agrees with the historical core of the Letter of Aristeas. In the rendering, interpretative elements bear typically Jewish characteristics, in which such items as antianthropomorphisms and antianthropopathisms loom large, as they also do in the Aramaic Targums. Likewise the Septuagint rendering of the historical books may well be a true rendering of a Hebrew parent text, albeit in a different recension from the Massoretic. It used to be claimed for it that some legendary features in the Massoretic Samuel–Kings had been rationalized and the persons of the kings idealized, all under the influence of Greek interpretation. But discrepancies of this kind are not necessarily Hellenistic, or confined to the Greek–Hebrew texts; one need only think of the similar discrepancies between Samuel–Kings and Chronicles in the Hebrew Bible. The question is further complicated by traces of multiple translators as well as divergent parent texts. At the same time we cannot deny Hellenistic influence; for instance, it is difficult to explain away such obvious interpretative elements as the polemic against Hellenistic heathenism in the Greek Isaiah—a text whose parent Hebrew is almost identical with the Massoretic. There are other hints of what has been appropriately called 'Galuth-psychology', that is, the introduction of Hellenistic philosophical overtones. Thus, Proverbs and Job can be regarded as a fruitful source of Hellenistic hermeneutics, and even the comparatively literal rendering of Ecclesiastes betrays occasional Hellenisms. The theory has inevitably evoked opposition, which is mainly based on the view that the only satisfactory key to the Version is Jewish (orthodox) hermeneutics. If, however, the history of the Old Testament text and interpretation in the pre-Christian era must be regarded from one basic standpoint, with one uniform parent text and one uniform exegesis, more questions seem to be raised than answered. The debate continues, vigorously conducted with scholars such as G. Gerleman and J. W. Wevers on opposite sides, and promises to be one of the most fruitful examinations of the Septuagint of recent times.

A parallel controversy is centred on the nature of the Greek text and the early textual transmission of the Version. On the one hand Kahle has a considerable following for his view that during the pre-Christian era there were numerous Greek renderings of the Old Testament and that what the Letter of Aristeas describes is the standardization rather than the rendering of the Torah text in Greek. The other books were subsequently standardized by the Christian Church and the name Septuagint, having lost favour among the Jews, was given to it for convenience. In other words, despite the evidence of Philo and Josephus and the statement in the Prologue to Ecclesiasticus, it is assumed that there was no authorized Septuagint text before the second century A.D. On the other hand, the traditional view is still strongly defended by many scholars and has the implicit approval of the editors of modern critical texts of the Septuagint. Obviously this does not deny the existence of variant Greek texts in the pre-Christian era, for in the New Testament itself, although the quotations are predominantly Septuagintal, use is made of other renderings—some of them identifiable, such as the pre-Theodotionic readings in the Book of Revelation and elsewhere. It would appear, however, that Kahle and his school are overstating the case when they make it depend on the assumption that the existence of other Greek versions necessarily precludes the existence of the Septuagint as a recognized version in the time immediately before the New Testament.

The Chester Beatty and related papyri from the early Christian era, whose discovery was a sensation in the 1930s, seem now to be assuming their proper place in the textual history of the Version; and, especially in their contribution to post-Pentateuchal books, their importance is even greater than the Dead Sea scrolls or the pre-Christian Septuagint fragments. For Ezekiel, *Pap 967/68* provides a substantial amount of text from the secondary century A.D. which, it has been argued, either helps to establish the case for an early alignment of the Septuagint with the Hebrew text, or for the view that already doublets occur in the text which betoken a conflation of two divergent traditions, one of which had a strong affinity with the Massoretic text. For Daniel, the same papyrus manuscript gives a text which is true Septuagint and not Theodotionic, which is the source of all other extant manuscripts of this book, with one late exception. Yet another collection of early Greek manuscripts, housed in Berlin until their destruction in the last war, but fortunately discussed by O. Stegmuller in 1939, can be briefly mentioned. They are on papyrus and parchment from the early third to the seventh centuries A.D. and contain texts which range from straightforward Septuagint to a fifth- or sixth-century lectionary which clearly stands outside the normal Septuagint transmission and which represents either a far-reaching recension or a completely new Greek translation.

The rival Greek translations from the second century A.D.—Aquila, Symmachus and Theodotion—have again become the centre of attention because of yet another of the Dead Sea scrolls. It is a leather fragment from an unidentified cave, probably in the Murabba'at area, and contains fragments of the Minor Prophets in Greek. There are two conflicting views about their significance. Father Barthélemy, writing in *Revue Biblique*, 1953, asserts that the text, from the late first century A.D., consists of a revision of the old Septuagint from the pre-Christian era, similar in pattern to the later renderings of Aquila, Symmachus and Theodotion, and is also the text used by Justin Martyr in the second century in his *Dialogue with Trypho*, in which he refutes Jewish charges of Christian interference with the Septuagint. That is, Barthélemy continues, the text of the Greek Minor Prophets shows that there was current among both Jews and Christians in the second century A.D. a common Greek Bible acceptable to both parties, and which was itself a revision of the earlier Septuagint. The opposite view is taken by Kahle, and published in *Theologische Literaturzeitung*, 1954, and his *Cairo Geniza* (2nd edition), 1959. Accepting a verdict by C. H. Roberts that the fragment belongs to the period 50 B.C. to A.D. 50, and asserting that agreement with the three translations of Aquila, Symmachus and Theodotion is only sporadic, he concludes that the manuscript is yet another of the *Vulgärtexte* which were abundant in Judaism before the Bible texts, both Hebrew and Greek, were standardized. The similarity with the text of Justin Martyr, Kahle continues, is to be explained by his having made use of Lucian's recension which, in turn, can be showed to have existed in pre-Christian times, as witness Kahle's interpretation of the above-mentioned *Rylands Papyrus* of the Pentateuch. According to this hypothesis, texts used by the Fathers postulate a variety of text-forms current during the early stages of the history of the Greek Bible. The present manuscript of the Minor Prophets belongs to the same group, and, together with Aquila, Symmachus, Theodotion and Lucian, reflects attempts made at that time to establish agreement between the Greek and Hebrew texts.

It is difficult to see how a compromise solution satisfactory to both sides can be offered. The Chester Beatty and other papyri show textual divergences, as indeed do all the manuscripts of the Septuagint; throughout its history, free transmission was always one of its characteristic features, and, despite attempts to fix a standard form, there appears to have been no recension for which the claim was made that it was an authoritative text. In other words, if there was at any time a recognized Septuagint text-form it was at the beginning, and the divergences were introduced during the transmission over the centuries.

It is against this background that we look at Origen's *Hexapla*. At some time between 230 and 240 Origen, the first scholar in our sense in the history of the Church, produced what was to become yet another recension of the Septuagint on the basis of the Hebrew text. That the latter was supremely important to him is suggested by the order of columns in the *Hexapla*—first the Hebrew text and the same in transcription, columns three and four Aquila and Symmachus, and only in column

five does his reconstructed Septuagint appear, with the use of Aristar-
chean signs to mark additions and omissions in relation to the Hebrew.
Why Theodotion's version is placed in column six, after the Septuagint, is
not clear, nor why parts of the poetical books were placed in additional
columns, though from a note by Eusebius that they were found in a jar in
a cave near the Dead Sea we might venture a guess that these were early
precursors of the Dead Sea scrolls, and that the relevance of the Greek
Minor Prophets, from the caves, is thereby still further increased.

Of the colossal *Hexapla*, and of its abbreviated *Tetrapla*, there are no
extant remains, but mention should be made of the *Milan Palimpsest*
from the tenth century, discovered in 1894 by Cardinal Mercati, which
contains some Psalms in all columns except the Hebrew. Unfortunately,
the manuscript is still unpublished, but the transcription column has
been examined from the point of view of Hebrew orthography and
grammar. Field's collection of Hexaplaric material in 1895 (reissued in
1965) is now being superseded by a section in the *apparatus criticus*
of the latest critical edition of the Septuagint text, the *Göttingen
Septuagint.*

The controversy about the early history of the Version is bound to
affect modern views about the recensions of its text. It is at first sight
difficult to dismiss a tradition, which goes back to Jerome in the late
fourth century, that there were three recensions current at this time: the
Hesychian in Alexandria, the Lucianic in Constantinople and Antioch,
and the Hexaplaric in Palestine; but reference has already been made to
Kahle's view that at least the Lucianic was based on a pre-Christian
divergent text. There is, moreover, abundant evidence from before and
after Jerome's time that the transmission of the text itself was by no
means controlled by local or recensional principles. The sources for the
evidence, of course, are the Great Codices and the uncials and minuscules from the fourth century onwards. They are all admittedly 'mixed'
texts. For instance, whereas it is generally agreed that *Codex Mar-
chalianus* (Q) belongs, with others, to a fairly well-defined family of texts
with Hesychian characteristics, and that Hexaplaric readings are to be
recovered largely from another group of manuscripts, it is nevertheless
from the margins of Q that many of the best Hexaplaric readings are
actually obtained. Again, the well-known *Codex Vaticanus* (B) is regarded as the best of the so-called non-recensional texts, but the presence
of Hexaplaric infiltration in this text is admitted. So little is known about
the early history of the recensions and their purpose that any assessment
of their relevance for the general transmission is inconclusive, and also
carries with it a possible danger in that it might suggest a completely
wrong standpoint for their use in textual reconstruction.

Nowhere is this more obvious than in current attempts to produce
critical editions of the Septuagint. There have been two major projects,

each with its independent approach to the task. The one is the Cambridge edition, *The Old Testament in Greek,* begun in 1906 under the editorship of Brooke and McLean, later joined by St John Thackeray and subsequently taken over by T. W. Manson, and abandoned at his death. It largely adopts the principles applied by H. B. Swete for the three-volume *The Old Testament in Greek* (1887–91, with several later editions), and uses as basic the text of *Vaticanus,* whose lacunae are supplied from the text of *Codices Alexandrinus and Sinaiticus.* The *apparatus criticus* provides variants from uncials, selected minuscules, daughter translations, Philo and Josephus, and some early Christian writings. Obviously there is no pretence that the result represents a standard critical text; by using the British Museum *Codex Alexandrinus,* which is largely a Hesychian witness, to augment *Vaticanus,* the editors implied that their text was to be little more than a conventional rendering which, together with the *apparatus criticus,* could be used by each individual student to reconstruct or to explain the Version as he wished. It is significant that Professor Manson more than once explained that in his view to reconstruct an 'original' Septuagint is not only hypothetical but also impossible on *a priori* grounds. The edition covers Genesis (1906) to Tobit (1940), and the regrettable and untimely death of the editor in 1958 caused its cessation. A re-issue of Swete, however, with a revised *apparatus criticus,* might go far towards redeeming the situation.

In some ways Rahlfs' *Septuaginta* (1935) follows the same principle, for the text is based on the three Great Codices, *Vaticanus, Sinaiticus* and *Alexandrinus,* with a much shorter *apparatus criticus* of variant readings than the Cambridge edition.

The other edition is the *Göttingen Septuagint,* which, since 1922 and more ambitiously since 1931, has appeared with regularity and colossal industry. The origins of the edition are to be found in the principles formulated by de Lagarde late in the nineteenth century. Essentially it means that in the first instance all available sources for Septuagint readings, which include manuscripts of all kinds, daughter translations and quotations from the Fathers, should be classified according to the recensions—Hexaplaric, Lucianic and Hesychian—to provide 'Text-Families' on lines similar to those of the New Testament. The next step was to reconstruct the pre-recension text, which should, in theory, correspond to the original text. The work obtained its main inspiration and impetus through Rahlfs and later Ziegler, who, however, has established the case for the addition of one further recension, called *The Catena Group* and based originally on early commentaries of the Fathers from which readings were included in later manuscripts. But it has been pointed out that the texts in this group contain readings which overlap with the older recensions—a conclusion which reduces the validity of their witness to the existence of a self-contained 'family' or recension.

A still more ambitious edition along the lines of de Lagarde and the *Göttingen Septuagint* is the *Text of Joshua in Greek,* produced by Max L. Margolis and published in four fascicles in 1931-38.

The comparative merits of the two principles of editing as exemplified in the Cambridge and Göttingen texts are difficult to assess. The former, it may be complained, is inconclusive and does little more than provide material for further analysis and speculation; but it has the advantage of being realistic. Its text is produced from actual historical text-forms, particularly *Codex Vaticanus,* which, since the appearance of the Sixtine edition in 1587, has provided the basis for the major Septuagint studies of Holmes and Parsons, Swete, and, to a large extent, the *Concordance* of Hatch and Redpath. Indeed it is the only manuscript from among the Great Codices which can safely be used; for *Alexandrinus* is, as we have seen, representative of the Hesychian recension, and comparatively large portions of the Old Testament have been lost from *Sinaiticus,* which, in any case, is so closely related to *Vaticanus* as to make its choice arbitrary. Moreover, it is only such an edition as the Cambridge that can possibly accommodate the view that there never actually existed an *Ur-Septuagint* in the sense postulated by the Göttingen edition.

On the other hand the Göttingen text has the merit of being the logical product of a recognized historical method and analysis, and has to a considerable extent justified itself by demonstrating the existence of some well-defined text-families. Furthermore, the practical benefits of the classification are clearly indicated in the *apparatus criticus,* and the fact that a very large number of readings are adduced from a great variety of sources adds to the immediate practical uses of the edition. Obviously the main criticism, and a fundamental one which is almost universally recognized, is that the resultant text is hypothetical, eclectic and unreal, and one which probably never existed except in the mind of the editor; a corollary is that even the system by which the text is achieved is not without possible criticism along the same lines. Nevertheless, the practical benefits of the edition far outweigh its academic shortcomings, and its use is not limited to the scholars who subscribe to its postulates.

Other Versions

The other Versions may briefly be divided into two groups according to their Jewish and Christian origins. Jewish renderings come under the general title of Targums and consist mainly of translations and expansions into Aramaic. How ancient these renderings may have been is difficult to say, but the Babylonian Talmud, *Megillah 3a,* attributes their origin to Ezra, and Kahle has argued that unofficial Aramaic translations were current from the fourth century B.C., when, under the Persian regime, Aramaic became an official language in Asia Minor.

Hypotheses about the history and transmission of the Targums reflect the same two basically different standpoints as in the case of the Septuagint. Kahle's interpretation assumes that the standardized translation was a later emergence from a number of unofficial, free and popular renderings. The other view which, in the absence of contemporary outstanding Targum exponents, must be called traditional, assumes that free renderings are developments from an earlier fixed translation.

Extant Targumic texts are generally to be found in printed editions of the rabbinic printed bibles and the polyglots from the fifteenth and sixteenth centuries, but many later and critical editions have been produced in the nineteenth and twentieth centuries. Substantial manuscript additions have become available from the Cairo Genizah, and augmented in 1956 by the identification of a complete Targum manuscript of the Pentateuch, the *Neofiti Codex I* of the Vatican which belongs to the fifteenth century, but whose significance is far greater than its date would suggest.

Targums are divided into two groups: those which, by their adherence to the Massoretic text and the prestige they claim in the tradition, were official translations, and others, free and paraphrastic, which were unofficial. Of the former, the Pentateuch Targum of Onqelos is usually explained as having been officially redacted in the second century A.D. as a literal rendering of the newly produced Massoretic text, and parallel to Aquila's Greek translation—indeed, the two names have frequently been identified. An important edition was produced by A. Berliner in 1884, but substantial additions of manuscripts from the middle ages in the Genizah fragments have changed some of the readings as well as modified the general picture of the transmission. The standard Targum to the Prophets is called by the name of Jonathan ben Uzziel, but again the version is sometimes identified with Theodotion, and a possible pointer in favour of this view is that the Mishna itself is confused in its references both to the identity of Jonathan and of the Targum. As a rendering it is not so faithful to the Massoretic text as is Onqelos, and it bears obvious traces of having been redacted from earlier renderings; the fact that it quotes Onqelos, especially in passages relating to the Torah, bears out both the fact that it had mixed origins and also had official status as a translation. As with Onqelos, the most common sources of the Targum Jonathan are the rabbinic and polyglot bibles. But mention should be made of de Lagarde's *Prophetae Chaldaice* (1872) and of critically edited texts of Joshua and Judges by Prätorius (1899–1900) and Isaiah by Stenning (1949, reprinted 1953) and a concordance to the whole Targum Jonathan by Kosowski (1940). More important is the recent publication, in four volumes, of A. Sperber, *The Bible in Aramaic*, 1959–62. Volume I has Targum Onqelos; vol. II, the Former Prophets (Targum Jonathan); vol. III, the Latter Prophets (Targum Jonathan). Volume IV is to contain treatments of textual problems raised by the edition.

Unofficial Targums are numerous and vary considerably, both intrinsically and in interest for the textualist. Indeed, even Targums to the Pentateuch from this class need careful scrutiny because freedom of paraphrase has permitted, for example, not only the final compilation of the Mishna to be presupposed (second century A.D.) but also one of the wives of Mohammed and a daughter to be mentioned as wives of Ishmael in Gen. xxi. 21! Nor is this an isolated historical pointer to the middle ages.

The most interesting of the Targums are those of the Pentateuch, and, because of the recently discovered Neofiti I, pride of place goes to what was previously called the Fragment-Targum, or Jerusalem II. There is now a complete copy of 450 folios of this Targum excellently preserved, and it also provides evidence for a degree of 'infiltration' of the Onqelos text into the text of the unofficial Targums. Portions of the text of this Targum were printed in the first rabbinic Bible, 1516–17, and later reprinted; other texts were published in 1899 by Ginsberger (*Das Fragmententhargum*); still other material was discovered in the Genizah manuscripts and discussed by Kahle (*Cairo Genizah*[2], 1959), and undoubtedly Neofiti I, under the direction of its editor, Diez Macho, will necessitate a fresh examination of the whole Targum.

Another Pentateuch Targum, wrongly called Jonathan, hence Pseudo-Jonathan, is based on Targum Onqelos with numerous elaborations of rabbinic provenance. The question of their relationships and period is still unsettled, but additions to the text from the Cairo Genizah manuscripts help to clarify the picture.

Targums to the Writings obviously come into the list of unofficial Targums for, because of the omission of these books from the synagogue lectionaries, there was no need of an official Targum. The texts vary from literal renderings as in the Targum to Esther (which may be official, as witness the important role played by this book in the history of the synagogue) to very free paraphrases, as in some Psalms.

The text of the Samaritan Pentateuch has recently become a subject of concern. It is well known that the Abisha scroll at Nablus was always regarded as a standard text, and because of its antiquity it ranked as a major source of textual variants. And especially under the influence of Paul Kahle it has become one of the most important witnesses to the early, pre-Massoretic text of the Pentateuch. But the Abisha scroll has now been twice photographed, and in 1959 its text was edited and published by Pérez Castro, accompanied by photographs and a lengthy introduction. The scroll, far from being a pre-Christian text, is merely a collection of medieval texts, written by Abisha ben Pinhas in 1085. Consequently the actual text of the Samaritan Pentateuch cannot claim antiquity except by implication. The fact that in some cases Samaritan readings are paralleled by some Qumran texts does not mean that the former text-form receives complete vindication. The full implications of Castro's publication have not yet been assessed, but it appears unlikely that in future an appeal to the Samaritan text will carry the same authority as previously. In this context, too, mention should be made of the Arabic rendering of the Pentateuch by Saadya Gaon in the tenth century, which became part of the Samaritan transmission.

The second group of early Versions relates to the history of the Septuagint, and as part of the Christian transmission of Scripture they reflect the vicissitudes of the Church in the same way as its dogma and politics. For western Christendom the main interest lies in the Latin Versions. As early as the late second century A.D. there appear to have been free renderings of the Septuagint to produce daughter translations in Latin, and fragments from Europe and North Africa were later assembled and became known as Old Latin texts (or *Itala*). The standard list of these texts, made by Sabatier in 1743-49, has received continuous though sporadic additions; the most recent and ambitious collection made by the abbots of Beuron, 1949-54, goes to the end of Genesis.

The Vulgate marks a departure from the Septuagint, at least theoretically, for its original text cannot any longer be constructed. It is well known that Jerome, commissioned by Pope Damasus in 383 to produce a Latin Bible, first of all revised Old Latin texts on the basis of the Hexaplaric Septuagint, and extant remains include the Psalter and, possibly, parts of Job and Song of Songs. After 390, however, Jerome produced the Vulgate based on the Hebrew text, and explained his principle and methods in the *Prologus Galeatus,* which accompanied the first section of his translation, Samuel-Kings. Opposition to the rendering was violent from the outset, and it was not until the eighth century that the Vulgate was popularly received. Meanwhile the rendering had been interspersed with readings from the Old Latin, and the uncertain nature of its transmission is well illustrated by two editions of the Vulgate which appeared in the late sixteenth century. After the Council of Trent a revision—the Sixtine—was produced under the auspices of Pope Sixtus V in 1590, but four years later, under Clement VIII, it was replaced by the Clementine, which is still recognized as the official version, except that since 1945 the Pontifical Biblical Institute's new translation of the Psalms from the Hebrew has been included in the breviary. In 1907 the Benedictines began a critical edition of the Vulgate, and books have appeared regularly since 1926. The work, *Biblia Sacra iuxta latinam Vulgatam,* is based on the modern principle of the establishment of manuscript families, but it is generally admitted that, despite some very important clarifications in the history of the Version, the resultant text cannot confidently be claimed to represent the original Vulgate.

Finally, the Syriac Peshitta. This is yet another Version transmitted by the Church, though possibly having Jewish provenance and consequently a somewhat greater relevance for the Hebrew Old Testament. Its origins are unknown, but there are traces in quotations by Syriac Fathers of a pre-Peshitta rendering, possibly for propaganda among proselyte Syrians such as the royal family in Adiabene, eastwards of the Tigris, who became converts around the beginning of the Christian era. But there was also a pre-Peshitta New Testament, whose existence strengthens the opposite view, that the Syriac Version always was Christian; and the fact that the Peshitta—like the Vulgate—represents a Hebrew parent text and contains sporadic traces of rabbinic exegesis does not necessarily preclude a Christian origin. Some of the numerous Christian Peshitta manuscripts, such as the Codex *Ambrosianus* (sixth to seventh century A.D.), stress that the Psalms were translated from Hebrew.

At the same time, the characteristically free transmission of the Bible text characterizes the Peshitta as much as any other Version, and it is demonstrable that the influence of the Septuagint is frequently present; consequently the textual evidence of the Version, especially where it departs from the Massoretic text and confirms the Septuagint, loses force.

As a whole, two distinct standpoints may be seen emerging from a mid-twentieth-century survey of the Old Testament Text and Versions. On the one hand, the authenticity of the Massoretic text stands higher than at any time in the history of modern textual criticism, a standpoint which is based on a better assessment of the history of the Jewish transmission. Coupled with it is an increased knowledge of Hebrew lexicography and of the cognate languages which shows that difficulties in the *textus receptus* do not always justify textual emendation. On the other hand, interest in the Versions has become increasingly centred on their own intrinsic relevance and their intricate history. Appeal to the Versions for purposes of textual emendation, though obviously still valid, is made with the greatest caution; but the scrutiny of the Versions, especially of the Septuagint and Targums, for exegesis and interpretation has produced important results, and is likely to prove interesting and profitable.

The Practice of New Testament Textual Criticism

This essay is telescoped to include Metzger's criteria and methodology of textual criticism and four of the fourteen examples he cites in his definitive Text of the New Testament *(2nd ed., 1968). His principles, however, broadly apply to textual criticism in any discipline. Critics in search of the best possible redaction (editing) of a selected passage, he asserts, combine the best of art and science—intuition and methodology. It should be evident that such critics require an extraordinary range of skills. Translating words from a single Hebrew or Greek manuscript into English is only one step in a complex process.*

Those unfamiliar with the numbers, letters, and names of the Greek texts which Metzger discusses should consult the table on pp. 210–211.

I. BASIC CRITERIA FOR THE EVALUATION OF VARIANT READINGS

PERHAPS the most basic criterion for the evaluation of variant readings is the simple maxim 'choose the reading which best explains the origin of the others'. We all follow this common-sense criterion when confronted with errors and 'variant readings' in modern printed books. For example, two editions of John Bunyan's classic, *Pilgrim's Progress*, diverge in the story of Christian's finding and using a key by which he was able to make his escape from Doubting Castle. One edition reads 'The lock went desperately hard', while another reads 'The lock went damnable hard.' Which is the original reading and which has been

From Bruce M. Metzger, *The Text of the New Testament* (2nd ed., 1970), pp. 207–29, 246.

altered? Did Bunyan write 'desperately' and a modern editor change it to 'damnable' for some inexplicable reason? Or did Bunyan write 'damnable' (using the word in its non-profane sense) and someone subsequently alter it in order to remove what was deemed to be an offensive expression? There can surely be no doubt what the answer is.[1]

Another criterion which we instinctively recognize to be basic is that the reconstruction of the history of a variant reading is prerequisite to forming a judgement about it. For example, in the earlier printings of the second edition of the unabridged *Webster's New International Dictionary of the English Language* (Springfield, 1934) there stands the entry:

> **dord** (dôrd), *n.* *Physics & Chem.* Density.

Now, it is a fact that there is no English word 'dord'; its presence in this venerable dictionary is the result of what may be called an accidental 'scribal error'. As was acknowledged later by the publishers, the entry originated in the confusion of the abbreviation, given both as a lower-case letter and an upper-case letter, of the word 'density', and was intended to stand thus:

> **d** or **D**, *Physics & Chem.* Density.

Not noticing the periods, someone took the collocation of letters as a word and called it a noun. The remarkable thing is that the error escaped detection for more than a decade, during which the volume was reprinted several times.

Another example of a clerical mistake, this one occurring in the highly esteemed *Who's Who in America*, arose because of incompetent judgement. The first time that the biography of Thomas Mann appeared in this distinguished cyclopedia of famous persons, he was given, quite gratuitously, a middle name. In the volume for 1939 the entry reads, in bold-face type, 'Mann, Thomas Schriftst'; in subsequent volumes, however, 'Schriftst' is lacking. Which form of the name is correct? An examination of the volume *Wer Ist's*, which is the German counterpart of *Who's Who*, discloses that 'Schriftst.' is the customary abbreviation of the German word for 'author' (*Schriftsteller*). Obviously, someone who prepared the biographical sketch for the American volume mistakenly took the abbreviation of Mann's occupation to be his middle name.

The two criteria mentioned earlier are capable of very wide application, and include by implication a great many other subsidiary criteria. It will be useful, however, to specify in more precise detail the various considerations which scholars take into account in evaluating variant readings of New Testament witnesses. It is usual to classify these criteria in terms of (1) External Evidence and (2) Internal Evidence; the latter involves what Hort termed Transcriptional Probabilities and Intrinsic Probabilities.

An outline of basic criteria and considerations to be taken into account in evaluating variant readings

I. EXTERNAL EVIDENCE, involving considerations bearing upon:

(1) The date of the witness. (Of even greater importance than the age of the document itself is the date of the type of text which it embodies. The evidence of some minuscule manuscripts [e.g. 33, 81, and 1739] is of greater value than that of some of the later or secondary uncials.)

(2) The geographical distribution of the witnesses that agree in supporting a variant. (One must be certain, however, that geographically remote witnesses are really independent of one another. Agreements, for example, between Old Latin and Old Syriac witnesses may be due to influence from Tatian's Diatessaron.)

(3) The genealogical relationship of texts and families of witnesses. (Witnesses are to be weighed rather than counted. Furthermore, since the relative weight of the several kinds of evidence differs for different kinds of variants, there can be no merely mechanical evaluation of the evidence.)

II. INTERNAL EVIDENCE, involving two kinds of probabilities:

A. Transcriptional Probabilities depend upon considerations of palaeographical details and the habits of scribes. Thus:

(1) In general the more difficult reading is to be preferred, particularly when the sense appears on the surface to be erroneous, but on more mature consideration proves itself to be correct. (Here 'more difficult' means 'more difficult to the scribe', who would be tempted to make an emendation. The characteristic of most scribal emendations is their superficiality, often combining 'the appearance of improvement with the absence of its reality'. Obviously the category 'more difficult reading' is relative, and a point is sometimes reached when a reading must be judged to be so difficult that it can have arisen only by accident in transcription.)

(2) In general the shorter reading is to be preferred, except where (*a*) parablepsis arising from homoeoteleuton may have occurred; or where (*b*) the scribe may have omitted material which he deemed to be (i) superfluous, (ii) harsh, or (iii) contrary to pious belief, liturgical usage, or ascetical practice.

(3) Since scribes would frequently bring divergent passages into harmony with one another, in parallel passages (whether involving quotations from the Old Testament or different accounts of the same event or narrative) that reading is to be preferred which stands in verbal dissidence with the other.

(4) Scribes would sometimes (*a*) replace an unfamiliar word with a more familiar synonym, (*b*) alter a less refined grammatical form or less elegant lexical expression in accord with Atticizing preferences, or (*c*) add pronouns, conjunctions, and expletives to make a smooth text.

B. *Intrinsic Probabilities depend upon considerations of what the author was more likely to have written*, taking into account:

(1) the style and vocabulary of the author throughout the book,

(2) the immediate context,

(3) harmony with the usage of the author elsewhere, and, in the Gospels,

(4) the Aramaic background of the teaching of Jesus,

(5) the priority of the Gospel according to Mark, and

(6) the influence of the Christian community upon the formulation and transmission of the passage in question.

Not all of these criteria are applicable in every case. The critic must know when it is appropriate to give primary consideration to one type of evidence and not to another. Since textual criticism is an art as well as a science, it is understandable that in some cases different scholars will come to different evaluations of the significance of the evidence. This divergence is almost inevitable when, as sometimes happens, the evidence is so divided that, for example, the more difficult reading is found only in the later witnesses, or the longer reading is found only in the earlier witnesses.

One of the perennial dangers which confront scholars in every discipline is the tendency to become one-sided and to oversimplify their analysis and resolution of quite disparate questions. In textual criticism this tendency can be observed when a scholar, becoming enamoured of a single method or criterion of textual analysis, applies it more or less indiscriminately to a wide variety of problems.

II. THE PROCESS OF EVALUATING VARIANT READINGS

To teach another how to become a textual critic is like teaching another how to become a poet. The fundamental principles and criteria can be set forth and certain processes can be described, but the appropriate application of these in individual cases rests upon the student's own sagacity and insight. With this caveat in mind, the beginner will know how to estimate the following simplified description of text-critical methodology.

As a preliminary step in analysing and evaluating the evidence found in a critical apparatus, the several variant readings should be set down in a list, each with its supporting witnesses. This will help one to see clearly the point at issue, and whether the documents have two principal readings or more.

In the evaluation of the evidence the student should begin with external considerations, asking himself which reading is supported by the earliest manuscripts and by the earliest type of text. Readings which are early and are supported by witnesses from a wide geographical area have a certain initial presumption in their favour. On the other hand, readings which are supported by only Koine or Byzantine witnesses may be set aside as almost certainly secondary.[2] The reason that justifies one in discarding the Koine type of text is that it is based on the recension prepared near the close of the third century by Lucian of Antioch, or some of his associates, who deliberately combined elements from earlier types of text. Despite the fact that it appears in a large majority of Greek manuscripts (for it was adopted, with subsequent modifications, as the received text of the Greek Orthodox Church), the abundance of witnesses numerically counts for nothing in view of the secondary origin of the text-type as a whole.

To facilitate the process of ascertaining which types of text support the several variant readings, the student should become thoroughly familiar with the following tables of witnesses. One must beware, however, of supposing that these text-types are static and exactly defined entities; on the contrary, each text-type involves a process[3] of textual development which, though distinctive and characteristic as a whole, cannot be isolated within precisely determined boundaries.

KOINE OR BYZANTINE WITNESSES

Gospels: A E F G H K P S V W (in Matt. and Luke viii. 13–xiv. 53) ΠΨ (in Luke and John) Ω and most minuscules.
Acts: Hᵃ Lᵃᵖ Pᵃ 049 and most minuscules.
Epistles: Lᵃᵖ 049 and most minuscules.
Revelation: 046 051 052 and many minuscules.

PRE-KOINE TYPES OF TEXT

The forms of text which antedate the Koine or Byzantine text include the Western group of texts, the so-called Caesarean text, and the Alexandrian (Hort's 'Neutral') text.[5]

The Western Group of Texts

Though some have held that the Western text was the deliberate creation of an individual or several individuals who revised an earlier text, most scholars do not find this type of text homogeneous enough to be called a textual recension; it is usually considered to be the result of an undisciplined and 'wild' growth of manuscript tradition and translational activity.

The Western type of text can be traced back to a very early date, for it was used by Marcion (and probably Tatian), Irenaeus, Tertullian, and Cyprian. Its most important witnesses are codex Bezae and the Old Latin manuscripts, all of which are characterized by longer or shorter additions and by certain striking omissions. So-called 'Western' texts of the Gospels, Acts, and Pauline Epistles circulated widely,[6] not only in North Africa, Italy, and Gaul (which are geographically 'Western'), but also in Egypt and (in somewhat different text-forms) in the East. These latter text-forms are represented by the Sinaitic and Curetonian manuscripts of the Old Syriac, by many of the marginal notes in the Harclean Syriac, and perhaps by the Palestinian Syriac.

Westcott and Hort regarded the Western text as almost totally corrupt and accepted as original in it only what they called 'Western noninterpolations'. Subsequent scholars (e.g. Adelbert Merx and A. C. Clark) reacted against this one-sided view with an equally one-sided preference for the Western text. Today such extreme positions for and against Western forms of text find little favour, for most textual scholars recognize that all of the pre-Koine forms of text deserve a hearing, and that any one of them may preserve original readings which have been lost to the other text-types.

WESTERN WITNESSES

Gospels: D W (in Mark i. i–v. 30) 0171, the Old Latin; Syr^s and Syr^c (in part), early Latin Fathers, Tatian's Diatessaron.

Acts: $\mathfrak{p}^{29}$ $\mathfrak{p}^{38}$ $\mathfrak{p}^{48}$ D 383 614 Syr$^{h\ mg}$, early Latin Fathers, the Commentary of Ephraem (preserved in Armenian).

Pauline Epistles: the Greek–Latin bilinguals D^p E^p F^p G^p; Greek Fathers to the end of the third century; the Old Latin and early Latin Fathers; Syrian Fathers to about A.D. 450.

The Caesarean Text and Its Witnesses

B. H. Streeter identified the text that Origen used at Caesarea and associated it with the text in Θ, fam. 1, fam. 13, and other witnesses. Subsequent investigations by Lake, Blake, and New showed that the Caesarean text probably originated in Egypt and was brought by Origen to Caesarea, from where it was carried to Jerusalem (a number of Caesarean witnesses contain the so-called 'Jerusalem colophon' to the Armenians (who had a colony in Jerusalem at a very early date), and thence to the Georgians (codex Koridethi belongs to Georgia).

The special character of the Caesarean text is its distinctive mixture of Western readings and Alexandrian readings. According to Lagrange, evidently its maker knew both and made a kind of compromise; in substance he followed the Alexandrian text while retaining any Western readings which did not seem too improbable, for the latter text was widely current, although the former was the better. One may also observe a certain striving after elegance, and thus consideration for the needs of the Church.[7]

According to more recent investigations made by Ayuso and others, it is necessary to distinguish two stages in the development of the Caesarean text (at least for Mark). The Old Egyptian text which Origen brought with him to Caesarea may be called the pre-Caesarean text. This is preserved in $\mathfrak{p}^{45}$, W (in Mark v. 31–xvi. 20), fam. 1, fam. 13, 28, and many Greek lectionaries. At Caesarea and in its subsequent development, the pre-Caesarean text took on the form to which we are led back by the common evidence of Θ, 565, and 700, many of the citations of Origen and Eusebius, and the Old Armenian and Old Georgian versions (this form is the Caesarean text proper). There also seems to be some degree of affinity between the Old Syriac (Syr[s, c]) and the Caesarean text. In short, the Caesarean text appears to be the most mixed and the least homogeneous of any of the groups which can be classified as distinct text-types.

The Alexandrian Text

It is widely agreed that the Alexandrian text was prepared by skillful editors, trained in the scholarly traditions of Alexandria.[8] The text on which they relied must have already been an ancient text in all-important points. Until recently the two chief witnesses to this form of text were B and ℵ, dating from about the middle of the fourth century. With the discovery, however, of $\mathfrak{p}^{66}$ and $\mathfrak{p}^{75}$, both dating from about the end of the second or the beginning of the third century, proof is now available that Hort's 'Neutral' text goes back to an archetype which must be put early in the second century. This earlier form of the Alexandrian text, which may be called the proto-Alexandrian text, is generally shorter than the text presented in any of the other forms, the Western being the longest. Furthermore, the proto-Alexandrian text appears not to have undergone the systematic grammatical and stylistic polishing that was given to other texts, including the later form of the Alexandrian text itself.

Though most scholars have abandoned Hort's optimistic view that codex Vaticanus (B) contains the original text almost unchanged except for slips of the pen, they are still inclined to regard the Alexandrian text as on the whole the best ancient recension and the one most nearly approximating the original.

ALEXANDRIAN WITNESSES

(1) Proto-Alexandrian:

$\mathfrak{p}^{45}$ (in Acts) $\mathfrak{p}^{46}$ $\mathfrak{p}^{66}$ $\mathfrak{p}^{75}$ ℵ B Sahidic (in part), Clement of Alexandria, Origen (in part), and most of the papyrus fragments with Pauline text.

(2) Later Alexandrian:

(C) L T W (in Luke i. 1–viii. 12 and John) (X) Z Δ (in Mark) Ξ Ψ (in Mark; partially in Luke and John) 33 579 892 1241 Bohairic.

Acts: $\mathfrak{p}^{50}$ A (C) Ψ 33 81 104 326.

Pauline Epistles: A (C) H^{p} I Ψ 33 81 104 326 1739.

Catholic Epistles: $\mathfrak{p}^{20}$ $\mathfrak{p}^{23}$ A (C) Ψ 33 81 104 326 1739.

Revelation: A (C) 1006 1611 1854 2053 2344; less good $\mathfrak{p}^{47}$ ℵ

After having ascertained the text-types represented by the evidence supporting each of the variant readings under examination, the student should draw a tentative conclusion as to the preferred reading on the basis of considerations bearing on the age of the manuscripts, the geographical spread of the witnesses which join in support of a given reading, and the textual types to which they belong. Due appreciation of the implications of genealogical relationship among manuscripts prevents one from favouring a reading merely because a large number of witnesses may support it.

The next step in the process of evaluating variant readings is to appeal to internal evidence, beginning with transcriptional probabilities. Which reading is the more difficult—that is, more difficult to the scribe? Other things being equal, the reading which puzzled the scribe is most likely to be correct. On the other hand, there is a point at which what is relatively difficult becomes absolutely difficult, and therefore impossible to be regarded as original.

Some readings were favoured by scribes because they supported current beliefs and practices in their part of the Christian world. Hence the textual critic will need to have the fullest knowledge of the development of Christian doctrine and cultus, as well as all the heretical aberrations in the early Church. It goes without saying that acquaintance with palaeographical features of uncial and minuscule hands, along with a knowledge of dialectical variations in Greek orthography and syntax, will often suggest the correct evaluation of a variant reading. When dealing with a passage in the Synoptic Gospels it is necessary to examine the evidence of parallel passages. The harmonization of the Evangelists is by definition a secondary procedure; therefore the supreme rule for editors of the text is to give each Gospel its own proper character. This means that ordinarily the reading which differs from a parallel passage (particularly when the evidence for the reading of the parallel is firm) should be preferred. Likewise, in instances of quotations from the Old Testament, the text and apparatus of the Septuagint must be consulted. Since scribes tended to make New Testament quotations conform to the text of the Septuagint, readings which diverge from the Old Testament should not be rejected without the most careful consideration.

Finally, the student may appeal to intrinsic probability. The reading deemed original should be in harmony with the author's style and usage elsewhere. Since, however, it is conceivable that several variant readings may fulfil this requirement, the textual critic should be guided more by negative judgements delivered by intrinsic evidence than by positive judgements. The appropriate question to ask is whether intrinsic evidence *opposes* the conclusion commended by genealogical considerations, the geographical distribution of witnesses, and transcriptional probabilities.

Sometimes it happens that the only reading which seems to be in harmony with the author's usage elsewhere is supported by the poorest external evidence. In such cases the decision of the textual critic will be made in accord with his general philosophy of textual methodology. It is probably safest for the beginner to rely upon the weight of external evidence rather than upon what may be an imperfect knowledge of the author's usage.

In the course of time the student will observe that generally the reading which is supported by a combination of Alexandrian and Western witnesses is superior to any other reading. There is, however, an exception to this observation; in the Pauline Epistles the combination of B D G is ordinarily not of great weight. The reason for this is that though B is purely Alexandrian in the Gospels, in the Pauline Epistles it has a certain Western element. Hence the combination of B plus one or more Western witnesses in Paul may mean only the addition of one Western witness to others of the same class.

The combination of Western and Caesarean witnesses does not usually possess exceptional weight, for the Caesarean text was probably formed from a base which had Western affiliations.

In the evaluation of readings which are supported by only one class of witnesses, the student will probably find that true readings survive frequently in the Alexandrian text alone, less frequently in the Western group alone, and very rarely only in Caesarean witnesses. As a rule of thumb, the beginner may ordinarily follow the Alexandrian text except in the case of readings contrary to the criteria which are responsible for its being given preference in general. Such a procedure, however, must not be allowed to degenerate into merely looking for the reading which is supported by B and ℵ (or even by B alone, as Hort was accused of doing); in every instance a full and careful evaluation is to be made of all the variant readings in the light of both transcriptional and intrinsic probabilities. The possibility must always be kept open that the original reading has been preserved alone in any one group of manuscripts, even, in extremely rare instances, in the Koine or Byzantine text.

It remains now to put into practice these principles. Lest, however, the student imagine that the procedures of criticism are stereotyped and doctrinaire, this section may be concluded on a lighter vein with a quotation from a scintillating essay on textual criticism by A. E. Housman:

> Textual criticism is not a branch of mathematics, nor indeed an exact science at all. It deals with a matter not rigid and constant, like lines and numbers, but fluid and variable; namely the frailties and aberrations of the human mind, and of its insubordinate servants, the human fingers. It is therefore not susceptible of hard-and-fast rules. It would be much easier if it were; and that is why people try to pretend that it is, or at least behave as if they thought so. Of course you can have hard-and-fast rules if you like, but then you will have false rules, and they will lead you wrong; because their simplicity will render them inapplicable to problems which are not simple, but complicated by the play of personality. A textual critic engaged upon his business is not at all like Newton investigating the motions of the planets: he is much more like a dog hunting for fleas. If a dog hunted for fleas on mathematical principles, basing his researches on statistics of area and population, he would never catch a flea except by accident. They require to be treated as individuals; and every problem which presents itself to the textual critic must be regarded as possibly unique.[9]

III. THE TEXTUAL ANALYSIS OF SELECTED PASSAGES

The following passages have been chosen in order to provide illustrative examples of various kinds of text-critical problems. To prevent monotony in the exposition and to emphasize that no one stereotyped method of textual analysis is suited to all problems, the presentation of the kinds and nature of the evidence will be varied in sequence and in development of argument. The discussion begins with relatively simple problems, for which one can usually find clear and unambiguous solutions, and concludes with more complex problems, where the probabilities are much more evenly divided and where the critic must sometimes be content with choosing the least unsatisfactory reading, or even with admitting that he has no clear basis for choice at all.

It is customary in a critical apparatus to use abbreviations of certain Latin words as a concise and 'international' working language. The following are in general use:

pc (*pauci*)	=	a few other manuscripts
al (*alii*)	=	other manuscripts
pm (*permulti*)	=	very many other manuscripts
pl (*plerique*)	=	most other manuscripts
rell (*reliqui*)	=	the remaining witnesses
vid (*videtur*)	=	as it seems, apparently
omn (*omnes*)	=	all manuscripts
codd (*codices*)	=	manuscripts of a version or Church Father as distinguished from the edition
ap (*apud*)	=	in the writings of, on the authority of (e.g. Papias ap Eusebius)

ᵖᵗ (*partim*) = divided evidence (e.g. Orig^ᵖᵗ signifies that Origen is inconsistent in his quotations of the same passage)

2/4 = divided evidence (e.g. Orig 2/4 signifies that in two cases out of four quotations of the same passage Origen supports a given reading)

An asterisk (*) placed after the siglum of a manuscript indicates that the manuscript at the passage referred to has been corrected and that the original reading is being cited; a superior letter (ᶜ) placed after the siglum indicates that the corrected reading is being cited. Sometimes the work of more than one corrector can be differentiated. When the siglum of a manuscript is enclosed within parentheses, this signifies that the manuscript supports the chief point of the variant reading but differs in minor respects.

In this connexion a warning may not be out of place: in some *apparatus critici* of the New Testament the sigla of uncial manuscripts are often cited without the superior letter (or the inferior numeral) that serves to distinguish certain manuscripts from others designated by the same siglum. Thus D *simpliciter* often stands for codex Claromontanus (instead of Dᵖ [or D₂]) as well as for codex Bezae. In such instances one must be alert to distinguish between the two manuscripts by observing whether the variant reading occurs in the Gospels or Acts (in this case D = codex Bezae), or whether the variant occurs in the Pauline Epistles (in this case D = codex Claromontanus). In the following textual analyses the witness' siglum with the superior letter (when this is appropriate) will be used: the superior letter ᵃ after a siglum indicates a manuscript that contains the Acts and the Catholic Epistles, ᵖ indicates the Pauline Epistles, and ʳ the Book of Revelation.

In the King James version of Acts vi. 8 Stephen is described as 'full of faith and power' (πλήρης πίστεως καὶ δυνάμεως), whereas in the Revised Standard Version and the New English Bible he is said to be 'full of grace and power' (πλήρης χάριτος καὶ δυνάμεως). The difference in the English versions represents not variant renderings of the same Greek word but variant readings in the basic Greek text. The textual evidence, which involves four variant readings, is as follows:

(1) 'grace' (χάριτος) is read by 𝔭⁷⁴ ℵ A B D, more than twenty minuscule manuscripts, the Vulgate, Sahidic, Bohairic, Syriacᵖ, Armenian, and Ethiopic (the last reads χάριτος θεοῦ).

(2) 'faith' (πίστεως) is read by Hᵃ Pᵃ, many minuscule manuscripts, Syriacʰ, and Chrysostom.

(3) 'grace and faith' (χάριτος καὶ πίστεως) is read by Eᵃ.

(4) 'faith and grace of the Spirit' (πίστεως καὶ χάριτος πνεύματας) is read by Ψ.

Of these four variant readings it is obvious that either the first two are independent abridgements of the longer readings, or the third and fourth readings have arisen from combining the elements of the first two. Consideration of both external evidence and internal probability unite to demonstrate that readings (3) and (4) are secondary, being alternative conflations of the other two. Reading (3) is supported by the uncial manuscript E[a], which dates from the sixth century and is one of the earliest representatives of the Koine or Byzantine type of text in Acts. Reading (4) is supported by the uncial manuscript Ψ, which dates from the eighth or ninth century and has a mixed type of text in Acts. Transcriptional considerations lead one to conclude that both (3) and (4) presuppose the priority of the other two readings, for it is easier to believe that a scribe, knowing the existence of readings (1) and (2), decided to join them, lest the copy which he was writing lose one or the other, than to believe that two scribes independently took offence at the longer reading and that each chose to perpetuate half of it in his copy. Thus external evidence, which is meagre in extent and relatively late in date, and transcriptional probabilities unite against the originality of readings (3) and (4).

Variant reading (2) is supported by two uncial manuscripts, H[a] of the ninth century and P[a] of the tenth century, both representative of the Koine or Byzantine types of text. The majority of the minuscule manuscripts join these two uncial witnesses. The earliest witness to reading (2) is Chrysostom, who died A.D. 407.

Variant reading (1) is supported by a wide variety of witnesses, including representatives of the major pre-Koine types of text. Codices Sinaiticus and Vaticanus, both of the fourth century, are the earliest and best uncial representatives in Acts of the Alexandrian type of text. Codex Bezae, of the fifth or sixth century, is the chief Greek representative of the Western group of witnesses. Codex Alexandrinus, of the fifth century, and p[74], dating from about the seventh century, have a mixed type of text. The evidence of the early versions, including the Latin, Syriac, Coptic, and Armenian, reflect the wide geographical area over which the reading was accepted. The external evidence in support of reading (1) is, therefore, far superior in point of age and diversity of text-type to that supporting reading (2).

Internal probabilities likewise favour reading (1). If the account originally stated that Stephen was 'full of faith', there is no discernible reason why a scribe should alter it to 'full of grace'. On the other hand, in view of the statement made three verses earlier that Stephen was a man 'full of faith and the Holy Spirit' (vs. 5), it is easy to understand that in transcribing the later statement in verse 8 copyists would be likely, either consciously or unconsciously, to substitute πίστεως, which they recalled from the earlier passage, for the correct reading χάριτος. The presence of πνεύματος in reading (4) is to be explained in the same way.

Thus the converging of several strands of evidence, both external and internal, leads one to the firm conclusion that the author of Acts vi. 8 wrote πλήρης χάριτος καὶ δυνάμεως.

Not a few New Testament manuscripts incorporate here and there interesting details, some of which may be historically correct. The story of the woman taken in adultery, for example, has all the earmarks of historical veracity; no ascetically-minded monk would have invented a narrative which closes with what seems to be only a mild rebuke on Jesus' part: 'Neither do I condemn you; go, and do not sin again.' At the same time the pericope, which is usually printed as John vii. 53–viii. 11, must be judged to be an intrusion into the Fourth Gospel.

The account is lacking in the best Greek manuscripts: it is absent from 𝔓66 𝔓75 ℵ B L N T W X Δ Θ Ψ 33 157 565 892 1241 fam. 1424, etc. Codices A and C are defective at this point, but it is highly probable that neither contained the section, for there would not have been space enough on the missing leaves to include it along with the rest of the text. The Old Syriac (Syrs, c) and the Arabic form of Tatian's Diatessaron betray no knowledge of the passage, nor is it contained in the best manuscripts of the Peshitta. Likewise the old Coptic Churches did not include it in their Bible, for the Sahidic, the sub-Achmimic, and the older Bohairic manuscripts lack it. Some Armenian manuscripts as well as the Old Georgian version omit it. In the West the passage is absent from the Gothic version and from several Old Latin manuscripts (a f l* q).

Even more significant is the fact that no Greek Church Father for a thousand years after Christ refers to the pericope, including even those who, like Origen, Chrysostom, and Nonnus (in his metrical paraphrase), dealt with the entire Gospel verse by verse. Euthymius Zigabenus, who lived in the first part of the twelfth century, is the first Greek writer to comment on the passage, and even he declares that the accurate copies of the Gospel do not contain it.

When one adds to this impressive and diversified list of external evidence the consideration that the style and vocabulary of the pericope differ markedly from the rest of the Fourth Gospel, and that it interrupts the sequence of vii. 52 and viii. 12 f., the case against its being of Johannine authorship appears to be conclusive.

The earliest Greek manuscript known to contain the passage is codex Bezae, of the fifth or sixth century, which is joined by several Old Latin manuscripts (b c e ff²j). The pericope is obviously a piece of floating tradition which circulated in certain parts of the Western Church. It was subsequently inserted into various manuscripts at various places. Most scribes thought that it would interrupt John's narrative least if it were inserted after vii. 52 (D E F G H K M S U Γ Λ Π 28 579 700 1579, etc.). Others placed it after vii. 36 (MS. 225) or after xxi. 24 (fam. 1 1076 1570

1582). The revision of the Old Georgian version, made in the eleventh century by George the Athonite, contains the passage after vii. 44. The scribe of an ancestor of fam. 13 inserted it in another Gospel altogether, after Luke xxi. 38. Significantly enough, in many of the manuscripts which contain the passage it is marked with an obelus (as, for example, in S) or an asterisk (as, for example, in E M Λ), indicating that, though the scribes of these manuscripts included the account, they were aware that it lacked satisfactory credentials.

A few of the manuscripts which report the incident also include an interesting expansion at the close of viii. 8. More than one reader of the statement that Jesus 'bent down and wrote with his finger on the ground' must have wondered what it was that the Lord wrote. An unknown copyist satisfied this natural curiosity by adding the words, 'the sins of each of them'.[10]

The best disposition to make of the pericope as a whole is doubtless to print it at the close of the Fourth Gospel, with a footnote advising the reader that the text of the pericope has no fixed place in the ancient witnesses.

An interesting example of several different attempts to clarify a comment made by the Fourth Evangelist, which was felt to be open to misinterpretation, is found in John vii. 37–39:

> On the last day of the feast, the great day, Jesus stood up and pro-claimed, 'If any one thirst, let him come to me and drink. He who believes in me, as the scripture has said, "Out of his heart shall flow rivers of living water".' Now this he said about the Spirit, which those who believed in him were to receive; for as yet the Spirit had not been given, because Jesus was not yet glorified.

In the final sentence the clause 'for as yet the Spirit had not been given' (οὔπω γὰρ ἦν πνεῦμα δεδομένον) appears in seven different forms:

(1) πνεῦμα p[66c] p[75] ℵ K T Θ Π Ψ 1079 1546 Cop[bo] Arm.

(2) πνεῦμα ἅγιον p[66*] L W X Γ Δ Λ 28 33 565 700.

(3) πνεῦμα ἅγιον ἐπ᾽ αὐτοῖς D f Goth.

(4) πνεῦμα δεδομένον a b c e ff[2] g l Vulg Syr[s, c, p] Eusebius.

(5) πνεῦμα ἅγιον δεδομένον B 053 1230 e q Syr[pal, h].

(6) 'for they had not yet received [the] Spirit' Cop[sah, sub-ach.]

(7) 'for the Holy Spirit had not yet come' Eth.

A little reflection will make it obvious that the reading which ex-plains the rise of all the others is (1) πνεῦμα. Many scribes were doubtless perplexed by the bare and ambiguous statement 'for as yet the Spirit was not, because Jesus was not yet glorified'. Lest this be taken to affirm that the Spirit was not yet in existence prior to Jesus' glorification, modifications were introduced to relieve the difficulty. Several Western witnesses (D ƒ Goth) read (3), 'for the Holy Spirit was not yet in them'. Other witnesses add the verb 'given' (as in readings 4 and 5), or 'received' (reading 6), or 'come' (reading 7).

The introduction of the adjective ἅγιον (readings 2, 3, and 5) is a most natural kind of addition that many scribes would make independently of one another. (The correction found in 𝔭⁶⁶, deleting ἅγιον, is in keeping with the observed vigilance of this scribe in correcting his own inadvertent errors.) It is noteworthy that in this case codex Vaticanus is doubly in error (5), having added both ἅγιον and a predicate verb.

The evidence for (2) can be joined to that of (1) in respect of resisting the temptation to add a predicate verb. There is thus a very widespread and diversified constellation of witnesses in support of the more difficult and shorter reading. It can scarcely be doubted, therefore, that the original text had simply οὔπω γὰρ ἦν πνεῦμα.[11]

How did Mark end his Gospel? Unfortunately, we do not know; the most that can be said is that four different endings are current among the manuscripts, but that probably none of them represents what Mark originally intended to stand as the close of his Gospel. These four endings may be called the short ending, the intermediate ending, the long ending, and the long ending expanded. The evidence for each of them is as follows:

(1) The last twelve verses of Mark (xvi. 9–20) are lacking in the two earliest parchment codices, B and ℵ, in the Old Latin manuscript k, the Sinaitic Syriac, many manuscripts of the Old Armenian version, the Adysh and Opiza manuscripts of the Old Georgian version, and a number of manuscripts of the Ethiopic version. Clement of Alexandria, Origen, and Ammonius show no knowledge of the existence of these verses; other Church Fathers state that the section is absent from Greek copies of Mark known to them (e.g. Jerome, *Epist.* cxx. 3, *ad Hedibiam*, 'Almost all the Greek copies do not have this concluding portion'). The original form of the Eusebian sections makes no provision for numbering sections after xvi. 8. Not a few manuscripts which contain the passage have scholia stating that older Greek copies lack it (so, for example, MSS. 1, 20, 22, etc.), and in other witnesses the passage is marked with asterisks or obeli, the conventional sigla used by scribes to indicate a spurious addition to a literary document.

(2) The intermediate ending ('But they reported briefly to Peter and those with him all that they had been told. And after this Jesus himself sent out by means of them, from east to west, the sacred and imperishable proclamation of eternal salvation') is present in several uncial manuscripts of the seventh, eighth, and ninth centuries (L Ψ 099 0112), as well as in a few minuscule manuscripts (274[mg] 579), and several ancient versions (k Syr[h mg] Coptic[pt] Eth[codd]).[12]

(3) The long ending, so familiar through the King James version

and other translations of the Textus Receptus, is present in the vast number of witnesses (including several which also contain the intermediate ending), namely A C D L W Θ, most of the later uncials, the great majority of the minuscules, most of the Old Latin witnesses, the Vulgate, Syr[c, p], and the Coptic[pt]. It is probable that Justin Martyr at the middle of the second century knew this ending; in any case Tatian, his disciple, included it in his Diatessaron.

(4) The long ending in an expanded form existed, so Jerome tells us, in Greek copies current in his day, and since the discovery of W earlier this century we now have the Greek text of this expansion.

None of these four endings commends itself as original. The obvious and pervasive apocryphal flavour of the expansion in (4), as well as the extremely limited basis of evidence supporting it, condemns it as a totally secondary accretion.

The long ending (3), though present in a variety of witnesses, some of them ancient, must also be judged by internal evidence to be secondary. For example, the presence of seventeen non-Marcan words or words used in a non-Marcan sense; the lack of a smooth juncture between verses 8 and 9 (the subject in vs. 8 is the women, whereas Jesus is the presumed subject in vs. 9); and the way in which Mary is identified in verse 9 even though she has been mentioned previously (vs. 1)—all these features indicate that the section was added by someone who knew a form of Mark which ended abruptly with verse 8 and who wished to provide a more appropriate conclusion. An Armenian manuscript of the Gospels, copied A.D. 989, contains a brief rubric of two words in the space at the end of the last line of verse 8 and before the last twelve verses, namely *Ariston eritsou* ('of the Presbyter Ariston'). Many have interpreted this as a reference to Aristion, a contemporary of Papias in the early second century and traditionally a disciple of John the Apostle. But the probability that an Armenian rubricator would have access to historically valuable tradition on this point is almost nil, especially if, as has been argued, the rubric was added in the thirteenth or fourteenth century.

The internal evidence of the so-called intermediate ending (2) is decidedly against its being genuine. Besides containing a high percentage of non-Marcan words, its rhetorical tone differs totally from the simple style of Mark's Gospel. The mouth-filling phrase at the close ('the sacred and imperishable message of eternal salvation') betrays the hand of a later Greek theologian.

Thus we are left with the short ending, witnessed by the earliest Greek, versional, and patristic evidence. Both external and internal considerations lead one to conclude that the original text of the Second Gospel, as known today, closes at xvi. 8. But did Mark intend to conclude his Gospel with the melancholy statement that the women were afraid (ἐφοβοῦντο γάρ)? Despite the arguments which several modern scholars have urged in support of such a view,[13] the present writer cannot believe that the note of fear would have been regarded as an appropriate conclusion to an account of the Evangel, or Good News. Furthermore, from a stylistic point of view, to terminate a Greek sentence with the word γάρ is most unusual and exceedingly rare—only a relatively few examples have been found throughout all the vast range of Greek literary works, and no instance has been found where γάρ stands at the end of a book. Moreover, it is possible that in verse 8 Mark uses the verb ἐφοβοῦντο to mean 'they were afraid of' (as he does in four of the other occurrences of this verb in his Gospel). In that case obviously something is needed to finish the sentence.

It appears, therefore, that γάρ of Mark xvi. 8 does not represent what Mark intended to stand at the end of his Gospel. Whether he was interrupted while writing and subsequently prevented (perhaps by death) from finishing his literary work, or whether the last leaf of the original copy was accidentally lost before other copies had been made, we do not know. All that is known is that more than one person in the early Church sensed that the Gospel is a torso and tried in various ways to provide a more or less appropriate conclusion.[14]

It should not be overlooked that the text-critical analysis of the endings of Mark's Gospel has an important bearing on the historical and literary source criticism of the Gospels. Since Mark was not responsible for the composition of the last twelve verses of the generally current form of his Gospel, and since they undoubtedly had been attached to the Gospel before the Church recognized the fourfold Gospels as canonical, it follows that the New Testament contains not four but five evangelic accounts of events subsequent to the Resurrection of Christ.

. . . .

By way of conclusion, let it be emphasized again that no single manuscript and no one group of manuscripts exists which the textual critic may follow mechanically. All known witnesses of the New Testament are to a greater or lesser extent mixed texts, and even the earliest manuscripts are not free from egregious errors. Although in very many cases the textual critic is able to ascertain without residual doubt which reading must have stood in the original, there are not a few other cases where he can come only to a tentative decision based on an equivocal balancing of probabilities. Occasionally none of the variant readings will commend itself as original, and he will be compelled either to choose the reading which he judges to be the least unsatisfactory or to indulge in conjectural emendation. In textual criticism, as in other areas of historical research, one must seek not only to learn what can be known, but also to become aware of what, because of conflicting witnesses, cannot be known.

NOTES

1. James B. Wharey collates the first eleven editions of *Pilgrim's Progress* (Oxford, 1928), all of which read 'damnable hard'.

2. Theoretically it is possible that the Koine text may preserve an early reading which was lost from the other types of text, but such instances are extremely rare. For a survey of previous evaluations of such readings, see the chapter on the Lucianic Recension in B. M. Metzger, *Chapters in the History of New Testament Textual Criticism* (Leiden and Grand Rapids, 1963), pp. 1–31.

3. Cf. E. C. Colwell's discussion of 'The Origin of Text-types of New Testament Manuscripts', *Early Christian Origins: Studies in Honor of Harold R. Willoughby*, ed. by Allen Wikgren (Chicago, 1961), pp. 128–38.

4. The Byzantine text of the Book of Revelation is less homogeneous than it is in other books of the New Testament, for the Greek Orthodox Church has never included readings from the Apocalypse in its lectionary system—a system which exerted a stabilizing influence on the Byzantine text of other books of the New Testament.

5. For fuller descriptions of each of these three pre-Koine types of text, as well as lists of witnesses that support each type in the several natural divisions of the New Testament (Gospels, Acts, Pauline Epistles, Catholic Epistles, and Revelation), see M.-J. Lagrange, *Critique textuelle;* ii., *La Critique rationnelle* (Paris, 1935). Somewhat different lists are given in the preface of August Merk's *Novum Testamentum graece et latine*, 8th ed. (Rome, 1957).

6. The Catholic Epistles and the Book of Revelation seem not to have existed in a characteristically Western form of text.

7. Lagrange, *La Critique textuelle*, pp. 163 ff.

8. See G. Zuntz, *The Text of the Epistles: A Disquisition upon the* Corpus Paulinum (London, 1953), pp. 272–76.

9. A. E. Housman, 'The Application of Thought to Textual Criticism', *Proceedings of the Classical Association, August, 1921*, XVIII (London, 1922), pp. 68–69; or John Carter, ed., *Selected Prose* (Cambridge, 1961), pp. 131–50.

10. See David C. Voss, 'The Sins of Each One of Them', *Anglican Theological Review*, XV (1933), pp. 321–23.

11. This is the text lying behind the King James Version, the Revised Version of 1881, and the American Standard Version of 1901, all of which use italics to show what the translators added for the sake of English readers: '... was not yet *given*'. Since neither the Revised Standard Version nor the New English Bible employs italics in this way, the inclusion of the verb 'given' in these two versions is to be accounted for either as the result of licence in translation or the choice of what appears to be a secondary variant reading as the basic text.

12. For detailed evidence of the Coptic versions, see P. E. Kahle, *Journal of Theological Studies*, N.S., ii (1951), pp. 49–57.

13. E.g. J. M. Creed, *Journal of Theological Studies*, xxxi (1932), pp. 175–80; Ernst Lohmeyer, *Das Evangelium des Markus* (Göttingen, 1937), pp. 356–60; N. B. Stonehouse, *The Witness of Matthew and Mark to Christ* (Philadelphia, 1944), pp. 86–118; A. M. Farrer, *The Glass of Vision* (London, 1948), pp. 136–46; R. H. Lightfoot, *The Gospel Message of St. Mark* (Oxford, 1950), pp. 80–97, 106–16.

14. Almost all textual studies and critical commentaries on the Gospel according to Mark agree that the last twelve verses cannot be regarded as Marcan; typical is the monograph by Clarence R. Williams, *The Appendices to the Gospel according to Mark: A Study in Textual Transmission*, vol. xviii (New Haven, 1915).

The Bible in English

The Bible continues to be the most frequently printed book in English, yet no translation has captured the minds of its readers or has entered into the written language like the King James Version of 1611. It is appropriate, therefore, that the textual section close with an essay which traces the compositional history of this version and suggests some reasons why it retains such a hold on the modern reader. It is interesting to read Frye's comments on poetry alongside those of Freedman on pp. 77–100, particularly regarding the Hebrew technique of versification.

A CCORDING to Hugh Blair, the great eighteenth-century literary critic, "the style of the poetical books of the Old Testament is, beyond the style of all other poetical works, fervid, bold, and animated." That sentence superbly characterizes the literary quality of that period in England which produced Shakespeare, Spenser, Donne, and the King James Version of the Bible. No other age in the history of English or American literature has been so admirably suited to reproducing the tone of the Biblical literature in appropriate English. The Augustan period, for example, lacked the spontaneity, the aggressiveness of spirit: its conception of regular and correct expression could scarcely have done justice to the verve and direct involvement of the Jewish writers. The Romantics could, and did, appreciate the Bible both in the original and in the Authorized Version, but Romanticism lacked the sense of the austere, the controlled majesty which was so important in the Biblical materials. The literature of our own time moves usually on a different plane, and though it can sound many of the depths of human existence, it rarely manages to reach the heights of the human spirit and has been singularly lacking in its ability to convey awe, reverence, and mystery. Of all the periods in our literary history, only the English Renaissance contained within itself so full an appreciation of literary style and expression as to allow its trans-

From Roland Mushat Frye, *The Bible. Selections from the King James Version* (1965), pp. xxviii–xxxix.

lators and editors to do full justice to the tone as well as the meaning of the Bible.

The structural character of Hebrew poetry is particularly suited to translation. For poetry such as our own which relies heavily on meter and rhyme, the problems of reproducing the poetic structure in a different language are immense and perhaps even insuperable. Translators of such poetry find it impossible to reproduce meaning, rhyme, and meter: almost always, one or more important elements must be sacrificed. Of course, something must be sacrificed in all translation, for as there are no perfect and complete synonyms within a single language, so there are even less adequate synonyms between languages. But the basic formal principle of Hebrew literature is far better suited to translation than that of almost any other literature, for Hebrew poetry is structured on parallel thoughts in successive lines or half lines, so that thought and form itself are in fact one. This poetic method is known as parallelism of members.

Psalm 24 is a fine example of this poetic system, in which a succession of carefully constructed parallels beautifully conveys the development of the psalmist's sense. In the opening verses of the psalm, we see the exaltation of God set forth in parallel phrases and followed by parallel questions which involve man's relationship with God:

> The earth is the Lord's, and the fulness thereof;
> The world, and they that dwell therein.
> For he hath founded it upon the seas,
> And established it upon the floods.
> Who shall ascend into the hill of the Lord?
> Or who shall stand in his holy place?

Here we begin with the exaltation of God in the earth and among his creatures, and move to a question involving man's place before God. The central use of the question as a device is significant and representative, for no literature with which I am familiar employs questions so frequently and so pivotally as does the literature of the Bible. The answer to the question moves us into the central portion of the psalm:

> He that hath clean hands, and a pure heart;
> Who hath not lifted up his soul unto vanity,
> Nor sworn deceitfully.
> He shall receive the blessing from the Lord,
> And righteousness from the God of his salvation.

Advancing still by the movement of corresponding ideas, the psalmist clarifies the character of the just individual, and then moves into the character of the righteous community, the ideal Israel or Jacob:

> This is the generation of them that seek him,
> That seek thy face, O Jacob.

Seeking God and seeking a righteous community (here personified as

Jacob, after the name of the founding patriarch) are not equated but are inseparably related by the parallel structure. It is on the basis of this relationship that the Lord God may be expected to come to the community which seeks the divine and which also pursues human righteousness. God is thus expected to enter into Jerusalem, and even the gates are commanded to prepare for him, as the righteousness of the people becomes the gate for God's entrance:

> Lift up your heads, O ye gates;
> And be ye lifted up, ye everlasting doors;
> And the King of glory shall come in.

What follows now employs not merely parallelism, but the interlocking of parallels and the repetition of former phrases:

> Who is this King of glory?
> The Lord strong and mighty,
> The Lord mighty in battle.
> Lift up your heads, O ye gates;
> Even lift them up, ye everlasting doors,
> And the King of glory shall come in.
> Who is this King of glory?
> The Lord of hosts,
> He is the King of glory.

As the basis of Biblical poetic form, parallelism of members is capable of an almost infinite variation in use, complexity, and effect. It also makes possible translations of Hebrew poetry which are characterized at once by beauty of English form and essential faithfulness to the original. "The effect of Hebrew poetry can be preserved and transferred in a foreign language as the effect of other great poetry cannot," Matthew Arnold wrote, for it "is a poetry, as is well known, of parallelism; it depends not on meter and rhyme but on a balance of thought, conveyed by a corresponding balance of sentence; and the effect of this can be transferred to another language."[1]

Another striking characteristic of Biblical literature which facilitates translation is the concreteness of its imagery and allusion. We are rarely dealing with abstractions and abstract nouns, which are so nearly impossible to translate from one language to another, for the Biblical writers persistently define, illustrate, and present their message through the most concrete symbols. The Biblical themes, even when unique in meaning, are expressed through universally relevant and understandable means. For a Greek, God might be a vast, noble, and impersonal abstraction, but for the Jew, he was intimately personal—a father caring for his children, or a husband for his wife, or a shepherd for his sheep. Faithful men are not described as well-adjusted or mature, but are said to feast at a table prepared for them by God in the presence of their enemies, and are pictured as drinking from a cup which runs over. The symbols of the

Bible are simple and universal symbols, such as men and women everywhere can understand: food and drink, hunger and thirst, love and hatred, pilgrimage towards a goal or aimless wandering, light and darkness, laughter and tears, birth and death, and myriads of others in fascinating and meaningful combinations.

These symbols are as intelligible in English as they were in Hebrew and Greek. Coleridge, who was among the finest poets and was the finest literary critic produced in England, declared that "after reading Isaiah, or St. Paul's Epistle to the Hebrews, Homer and Virgil are disgustingly tame to me, and Milton himself barely tolerable."[2] It is the great good fortune of English-speaking people to have an English version of the Bible which stands with the original in literary power and excellence. Sir Arthur Quiller-Couch, editor of Shakespeare and of the Oxford Books of Verse, judged that the Authorized or King James Version of the Bible was the greatest literary achievement in the English language, with the possible exception of Shakespeare, and that it had influenced our literature "far more deeply" even than Shakespeare.[3] Discussing qualities of style, Matthew Arnold wrote that there is "one English book, and one only where, as in the *Iliad* itself, perfect plainness of speech is allied with perfect nobleness, and that book is the Bible."[4]

The history of the English Bible, honored as it is for style as well as for content, is both interesting and significant. The King James Version bears the name of the English sovereign who in 1604 authorized work to begin on an improved and "perfected" English Bible. Under the King's authorization, the work was divided among forty-seven of the leading Biblical scholars of the time, who were formed into panels or committees, three for the Old Testament, two for the New, and one for the Apocrypha. The work of these separate committees was then submitted to a twelve-man committee of the whole, made up of two men drawn from each of the panels. These men reviewed the entire work before its appearance in print in 1611. They did not, however, attempt to achieve an absolute uniformity of translation, as we can see in the treatment of Old Testament proper names in the New Testament, for example. Thus the Hebrew prophet who appears in the Old Testament under the name "Elijah" is referred to in the New Testament as "Elias," and even greater confusion occurs when Moses' successor Joshua is referred to as "Jesus" in the translation of Stephen's sermon at Acts 7:45. While the original names could justifiably be Anglicized in either of these ways, the confusion arises from the failure to hold consistently to one form. There are remarkably few instances of confusion of this kind, however, when we consider the scope of the work and the number of men engaged upon it.

King James' committee of "learned men" did not regard their task as the creation of a new translation, nor did they claim to have introduced a new translation. The tradition of English Bibles upon which they drew extended back to William Tyndale, whose English New Testament appeared in its first version in 1526. In the succeeding three-quarters of a century a considerable number of Bibles appeared in English. Tyndale himself carefully revised his New Testament before his final version appeared in 1535, and produced as well a translation of the Pentateuch and of Jonah. After his death there appeared a translation of the Old Testament historical books from Joshua to Second Chronicles which most scholars attribute to him. His work as the greatest English translator of the Bible came to an end in 1535 when he was betrayed into the hands of the Inquisition by a friend, and he was executed in 1536.

After Tyndale's arrest, the translation of the Old Testament was completed by Miles Coverdale. Relying heavily on the version of those Biblical books which Tyndale had been able to complete, Coverdale in 1535 brought forth on the Continent the first English rendering of the complete Bible. Coverdale was not of the same stature as Tyndale in learning, but he ranks directly after him in influencing the development of the English Bible. Whereas Tyndale had worked from the original Hebrew and Greek, though also consulting the Latin of Erasmus and the Vulgate along with the German of Luther, Miles Coverdale translated from the Vulgate and the recent Latin translation of the Dominican Father Pagninus, as well as from the German versions of Luther and of Zwingli. Coverdale's work has distinctive stylistic qualities of its own, of course, but he did follow the general tone of elegant simplicity established by Tyndale. Between these two pioneers, the noble style of the English Bible was firmly established.

Neither Tyndale's translation nor Coverdale's had been properly licensed for printing in England either by church authority or by the royal approval of King Henry VIII. The first English Bible to appear under royal permission was the so-called Matthew Bible, printed in 1537. The "Thomas Matthew" whose name appeared on the title page of this Bible appears actually to have been Tyndale's former associate, John Rogers, who for this volume merged the translations of Tyndale and of Coverdale. The use of the pseudonym seems to have made it possible for King Henry now to permit the appearance of those Biblical translations which had formerly appeared without his authorization and even in defiance of his government's prohibition.

The Matthew Bible was published with notes, explanations, and certain phrases in the text itself which some conservative readers found offensive, and so the authorities decided to have it revised. The revision began in the spring of 1538 and was entrusted to Miles Coverdale himself, now granted both royal and ecclesiastical favor. Coverdale revised the text with some thoroughness, but still in basic reliance upon his own translations and those of Tyndale. The result was called the Great Bible because of its size. It appeared first in 1539, and went through a number of editions. From 1540 onwards it carried a preface by Archbishop Thomas Cranmer, and is therefore sometimes known as Cranmer's Bible.

The next major version of the English Bible was undertaken by a group of scholarly English refugees who had fled from Queen Mary's England to Geneva. The Geneva Version was to become the most popular version in Elizabethan England, and was the version which Shakespeare principally knew. It went through over a hundred editions in its various forms from the appearance of the New Testament in 1557 and of the whole Bible in 1560 to the end of Elizabeth's reign in 1603. Its scholarly excellence was acknowledged even among those who disagreed with the Calvinist theology of its marginal notes and explanations.

The marginal comments of the Geneva Version made it too partisan for official use in the Church of England services, though its high quality at the same time rendered the Great Bible obsolete. Hence in 1561 Elizabeth's Archbishop of Canterbury, Matthew Parker, led a number of his bishops in revising the Great Bible. The resulting Bible, known as the Bishops' Bible, appeared in 1568, and was further revised in an edition of 1572. Though never officially recognized by the Queen, this Bible was appointed for official use by the Convocation of Canterbury in 1571 and continued in such use until the appearance of the King James Version of 1611. It was not able, however, to displace the Geneva Version in popular favor and as time passed there was increasing demand for a new version which could attain more nearly universal use.

This need was not met until the appearance in 1611 of the King James Version, but meanwhile another significant development was taking place among English Roman Catholic refugees on the Continent. As the Geneva Version had been produced by Protestants living in exile from the Roman Catholic Queen Mary, so a Roman Catholic translation was prepared by Father Gregory Martin, who was living in exile from the Protestant Queen Elizabeth. Martin had completed his English translation of both Testaments by 1582, but though his New Testament appeared in that year, his complete English Bible was not published until 1609–10. The work was carried out at the English College founded on the Continent by Cardinal William Allen for the preservation of English Roman Catholicism. As the College was located in Rheims when the New Testament appeared and at Douai when the Old Testament was issued, the translation is generally known as the Rheims-Douai. It was based on the Latin Vulgate as the officially accepted text of the Bible for Roman Catholics, and represented an original translation which stands apart from all the versions thus far discussed. Martin's translation did, however, occasionally contribute important readings to the King James Version, and so has a place in this account. After Martin's completion of his translation, there was no significant development in English Biblical translation until after the death of Elizabeth I and the accession of James I in 1603.

Early in 1604 a group of churchmen representing various shades of theological opinion within the Church of England met with King James at Hampton Court, and in the course of the conference considered Dr. John Reynolds' proposal that a new version of the English Bible be prepared. The proposal met with James' hearty approval, for he found the explanatory notes of the popular Geneva Version "seditious and savoring too much of dangerous and traitorous conceits," and yet was aware of the drawbacks of the Bishops' Bible. It was thus determined that a new version should be prepared "of the whole Bible, as consonant as can be to the original Hebrew and Greek, and this to be set out and printed without any marginal notes."[5]

It was to this task that the forty-seven leading scholars, to whom we have already referred, devoted themselves. Their basic method was to work both with the Biblical texts in the original languages and with the existing English versions, principally traceable to Tyndale and Coverdale; to select the best readings; and, where necessary, to introduce new readings which seemed preferable to those already existing. To think of them as original translators of the Hebrew and Greek is quite false, and to expect that as a large committee working through various subcommittees they could produce a great work of art belies not only the facts of the case but also common sense. No committee has ever by itself *created* a great work of art. What they did was to *perfect* a great work of art.

To say this is to clarify, not diminish, their achievement. They were not only men of learning, but also men of rare taste and discernment. As such they were able to bring out of the basic work of Tyndale and Coverdale—along with the improvements which had already been made upon that work by later versions, and also in honest consultation with the independent Roman Catholic translation—a version which was superior to anything that had yet appeared in English. Of their own work the King James translators declared that "we never thought from the beginning that we should need to make a new translation, nor yet to make of a bad one a good one; . . . but to make a good one better, or out of many good ones one principal good one, not justly to be excepted against; that hath been our endeavor, that our mark."[6]

We may get a clearer impression of the development of the English Bible if we turn now from this brief and generalized account and examine certain specific passages as they appeared in the principal versions which we have been considering. There were, of course, other English translations both prior to and after Tyndale and Coverdale, but we are concerned here only with the major work leading up to the King James Version. The following tables will allow a comparison of well-known verses in these different renditions. To the left of each verse there is an identifying mark, "T" standing for Tyndale, "C" for Coverdale, "M" for Matthew, "Gr" for Great Bible, "Ge" for Geneva Bible, "B¹" for Bishops' Bible of 1568, "B²" for Bishops' Bible of 1572, "B³" for the Bishops' Bible of 1602, "R-D" for Rheims-Douai, and "KJV" for King James Version.

PSALMS 23:1-2a

C. The Lord is my shepherd, I can want nothing. He feedeth me in a green pasture,

M. The Lord is my shepherd, I can want nothing. He feedeth me in a green pasture,

Gr. The Lord is my shepherd, therefore can I lack nothing. He shall feed me in a green pasture,

Ge. The Lord is my shepherd, I shall not want. He maketh me to rest in green pasture,

B¹. God is my shepherd, therefore I can lack nothing: He will cause me to repose myself in pasture full of grass,

R-D. Our Lord ruleth me, and nothing shall be wanting to me: in place of pasture there he hath placed me,

KJV. The Lord is my shepherd, I shall not want. He maketh me to lie down in green pastures:

The base in the King James Version lies in Coverdale and Geneva, but a very great improvement is made by substituting "to lie down" for "to rest" and by introducing the plural "green pastures." The treatments of the next verse and a half of the same Psalm are also instructive.

PSALMS 23:2b-3a

C. and leadeth me to a fresh water. He quickeneth my soul,

M. and leadeth me to a fresh water. He quickeneth my soul,

Gr. and lead me forth beside the waters of comfort. He shall convert my soul,

Ge. and leadeth me by the still waters. He restoreth my soul.

B¹. and he will lead me unto calm waters. He will convert my soul.

R-D. Upon the water of reflection he hath brought me up, he hath converted my soul.

KJV. He leadeth me beside the still waters. He restoreth my soul:

Here the Authorized Version has adopted the reading of Geneva, but with one very telling change: the connective "and" is dropped, and "He" is substituted, thus providing a considerably more forceful expression.

Let us now take a descriptive passage and note its development through the principal versions. The passage is from Luke's account of the nativity.

LUKE 2:8

T. And there were in the same region shepherds abiding in the field and watching their flock by night.

Gr. And there were in the same region shepherds, watching and keeping their flock by night.

Ge. And there were in the same country shepherds, abiding in the field, and keeping watch by night because of the flock.

B³. There were in the same country shepherds abiding in the field, keeping watch over their flock by night.

R-D. And there were in the same country shepherds watching, and keeping the night watches over their flock.

KJV. And there were in the same country shepherds abiding in the field, keeping watch over their flock by night.

Here the 1611 editors simply took over the Bishops' wording. A few verses later comes the song of the angels.

LUKE 2:14

T. Glory to God on high, and peace on earth: and unto men rejoicing.

C. Glory be unto God on high, and peace upon earth, and unto men a good will.

M. Glory to God on high, and peace on earth, and unto men rejoicing.

Gr. Glory to God on high, and peace on earth, and unto men a good will.

Ge. Glory be to God in the high heavens, and peace in earth, and towards men good will.

B¹. Glory be to God on high, and peace on the earth, and unto men a good will.

B². Glory to God in the highest, and peace on earth, and among men a good will.

R-D. Glory in the highest to God, and in earth peace to men of good will.

KJV. Glory to God in the highest, and on earth peace, good will towards men.

There is some difference of meaning between several of the translations of the final phrase here, and none of these versions quite captures what modern scholars regard as the meaning of the Greek text—that peace is granted among men with whom God is well pleased. But this advance in understanding is due to the advances which have taken place in the knowledge of New Testament Greek in the course of several centuries of study. Having taken this fact into account, we can still see the consummate literary taste which led to the final wording and (no less important) order of words in the King James rendering. Here the editors took the initial phrase from the second editions of Bishops', followed the second phrase of Rheims-Douai with very slight variation, and inverted Geneva's rendering of the final phrase. At other times our editors would simply take the best single rendering of a passage, and follow it with little or no change, as we have seen with the description of the shepherds and as with the opening words of the Lord's Prayer shown below.

MATTHEW 6:9b–10a

T.   O, our father which art in heaven, hallowed be thy name. Let thy kingdom come.

Gr. Our father, which art in heaven, hallowed be thy name. Let thy kingdom come.

Ge. Our father which art in heaven, hallowed be thy name. Thy kingdom come.

B³. Our father which art in heaven, hallowed be thy name. Let thy kingdom come.

R-D. Our father which art in heaven, sanctified be thy name. Let thy kingdom come.

KJV. Our father which art in heaven, hallowed be thy name. Thy kingdom come.

Here the Authorized Version has merely incorporated Geneva, while Geneva had in turn but slightly modified Tyndale.

Let us turn next to one of the most famous passages from the Epistles, and examine the treatment of Paul's definition of charity.

FIRST CORINTHIANS 13:4–5a

T. Love suffereth long, and is courteous. . . . Love doth not frowardly, swelleth not.

C. Love is patient and courteous. . . . Love doth not frowardly, is not puffed up.

M. Love suffereth long, and is courteous. . . . Love doth not frowardly, swelleth not.

Gr. Love suffereth long, and is courteous. . . . Love doth not frowardly, swelleth not.

Ge. Love suffereth long, and is bountiful. . . . Love doth not boast itself; it is not puffed up.

B¹. Love suffereth long, and is courteous. . . . Love doth not frowardly, swelleth not.

B². Charity suffereth long, and is courteous. . . . Charity doth not frowardly, swelleth not.

R-D. Charity is patient, is benign; . . . dealeth not perversely, is not puffed up.

KJV. Charity suffereth long and is kind . . . charity vaunteth not itself, is not puffed up.

A number of comments are in order here. In the first place, the substitution of "charity" for "love" resulted from a growing recognition that the English word "love," with its vast ambiguities, was not a suitable vehicle for conveying the sense of the Greek *agape*, and so the translators returned to using an Anglicized form of the Vulgate's word *caritas*. In this, the King James Version followed its two immediate predecessors. Beyond this point, however, we see two quite original translations—"is kind" and "vaunteth not itself"—which are less stilted, more simple, and more graphic than the previously used words.

The selections which we have been studying here were chosen to illustrate the process by which the Authorized Version was developed. That process, as the forty-seven editors themselves affirmed, was more a matter of choosing from available riches than of creating something absolutely original. At every point, of course, they acknowledged their responsibility, whether for introducing new translations or relying on the translations of others, and we must also acknowledge not only the good taste but the good scholarship which lay behind their work. That a precise accuracy must be denied to the Authorized Version at certain points does not reflect unfavorably upon the editors and their predecessors so much as it reflects favorably upon the development of the knowledge of the original languages and advances in discovery and reconstruction of earlier texts which have come since their time. The work of King James' editors has certainly been surpassed in accuracy by a number of modern translations, though not to such an extent as to impugn the essential and overall validity of their work. Nor can any more recent translation be said to equal or even approach the literary stature of their achievement. Their achievement, and that of their predecessors, was to impart to the English Bible what Longinus had found in Genesis: the highest quality of sublimity. Indeed, whatever flaws we may find in it, the King James Version is pervasively marked by what Aristotle called "the perfection of style," which is "to be clear without being mean."[7]

NOTES

1. *Isaiah of Jerusalem* (London: Macmillan and Company, 1883), p. 4.

2. Quoted in *In Praise of the Bible*, ed. Geoffrey Murray (London: Frederick Muller, 1955), p. 38.

3. "On Reading the Bible," in *The English Bible: Essays by Various Writers* (London: Methuen and Company, 1938), p. 101.

4. *On the Study of Celtic Literature and On Translating Homer* (London: Macmillan and Company, 1903), pp. 239–40.

5. F. F. Bruce, *The English Bible: A History of Translations* (New York: Oxford University Press, 1961), pp. 96–97.

6. *Ibid.*, p. 101.

7. *The Art of Poetry*, trans. Lane Cooper (Ithaca: Cornell University Press, 1947), p. 71 (22.1).

IV: LITERARY FORMS AND LITERARY INFLUENCE

Introduction

M ANY great civilizations rose and collapsed in the ancient world in which the Bible appeared. The Bible took shape over a millennium in which boundaries, alliances, and governments altered, and trade bound together people who were widely separated from one another geographically. Most people today have heard of the Assyrians, Babylonians, Persians, Greeks, and Romans. The modern reader is only now coming to know many other great peoples, including Sumerians, Amorites, Hittites, the inhabitants of Ebla and Ugarit. But all these civilizations of the ancient world influenced biblical songs, prayers, and stories of gods and heroes. Biblical literature is varied, diverse, and often difficult for the modern reader to fathom. What typical forms did the songs and stories take? One expects that a period so remote in time and place from our own would not necessarily produce the forms we know well—the novels, plays, lyric poems, and short stories of the modern Western world.

The movement known as form criticism (actually form-historical criticism; see Muilenburg, pp. 362–380) developed out of an awareness of forms that scholars were beginning to recognize. ("Form" in this instance is typical form, or genre.) Speeches, such as the farewells given by political leaders; sermons; myths, fairy tales, and fables; folktales, sagas, and legends, varieties of reports and songs—all were found in the ancient world. But form criticism (e.g., Van Tilborg's essay on the Lord's Prayer, pp. 333–343) was not content merely to describe a given form. It sought the place of that form in a given community, particularly in ceremonial and cultic settings. To establish the forms and their *Sitz im Leben,* scholars used not only biblical literature but also the literary records that accumulated during the latter half of the nineteenth century and early twentieth century. Of late the most rewarding literature for biblical scholars has been the Canaanite literature discovered at Ugarit. But Egyptian proverbs, Hittite treaties, and the very old records of written cuneiform have proved extremely valuable as well. Sumerian literature is the oldest of the literary material in cuneiform, and it deeply influenced Babylonian and Assyrian literature (both written in Akkadian, the language common to the Babylonians and Assyrians).

It would be premature to think that a one-volume literary history of the ancient Near East and the early Western civilizations (which would include the Bible) will soon appear. But such a literary history is at least thinkable now, and the discovery of over twenty thousand clay tablets at the site of ancient Ebla (perhaps ten percent of which are likely to be relevant to literary studies) will offer even more materials toward such a project.

It is true that even today, with thousands of books, newspapers, and magazines flooding the market annually, only a tiny fraction of our language finds its way into writing. Ordinarily, a person in our culture will not write down in his entire lifetime the equivalent of a week's worth of speech. Still, there are many kinds of things we have come to expect in written form: long stories, for example, and a surprising variety of poetic forms. But while nearly all literary *forms* with which we are familiar were in fact already in evidence by the sixth century B.C.—the major exception being the novel, which is a mere three hundred years old—the situation in the ancient world was quite different. Songs and stories were handed down primarily through oral tradition. As often as not the "author" is anonymous in a very profound sense. The tale is told through him, continued in his performance, but it is not his tale in the same way "A Rose for Emily" is William Faulkner's. There is little cause to attribute to the traditional poet the "originality" (let alone "absolute uniqueness") we value so highly today.

What has been written down (only a small part of which has survived), then, does not capture much of the original situation, composition, performance, instruments used, or the mode of singing or chanting. Often the occasion of the singing has to be recovered by very exacting scholarship; often it cannot be recovered at all. Nor does the written text of an ancient composition tell us how long a song or story existed in oral tradition or, with rare exceptions, where it came from. Whole areas of composition are in all likelihood irretrievably lost, because the vagaries of ancient writing or the demands of court and cult gave no reason for writing down a work in the first place.

The act of writing itself transforms a work. Plato complained that writing meant the loss of memory. The written word can take on a magical aura. Composites, stylistic changes, reworkings of material—such as one sees in the masterpiece of Akkadian literature, *The Epic of Gilgamesh*—are possible with writing in a much freer way than in oral composition.

Literary criticism for biblical scholars had come to mean primarily the analysis of the biblical texts to find the history of their composition. Different strands, representing different writers, schools, or traditions, could be detected in the composition of the Pentateuch, for example. Early Elohist (E) and Yahwist (J) strands differ from one another and from those of a later "author" or editor designated as Priestly (P). Stylistic analysis allowed scholars to make decisions about which tradition stood behind a given passage in the text. Differences were found in the use of divine names (Elohim/Yahweh) and in words for persons and places (e.g., Canaanite/Amorite; Sinai/Horeb). And different motifs appeared in parallel and combined accounts, for example, the battle of Jericho (Joshua 6) or the theophany at Sinai (Exodus 19). Vestiges of oral tradition such as one finds in Moses' "Song of the Sea" (Exodus 15), in Psalms, and in Job further add to the complexity of the written text.

Nevertheless, in spite of the complexities, considerable work has been done in what might be regarded as a literary history of the ancient world. The four essays in this section illustrate that we can gain new insights into the Bible by studying those literary works written earlier which may have influenced the Bible. We may not be able to trace as clear a line of development as we can see in, for example, the story of Troilus and Criseyde as it moves through three distinct and individual writers—Giovanni Boccaccio, Geoffrey Chaucer, and William Shakespeare. But influences, through written or oral forms, remain.

The area of greatest dispute over influence on biblical literature is with Mesopotamian literature. Writing was invented in the area that is now Iraq at a very early period—as early as two thousand years before it appeared in the oldest biblical writings. (If a date of approximately 1100 B.C. is accepted for a very early work, "The Song of Deborah and Barak" in Judges 5, Hebrew literature is clearly centuries earlier than the emergence of literature in the West with the Homeric poems and Hesiod.) The earliest corpus of songs, proverbs, and narratives that may through one channel or another have influenced the Bible is in Sumerian. Samuel Noah Kramer describes the kinds of literary works found in Sumerian, mainly in late third millennium works. Kramer then assesses the possible carry-over of beliefs, ideas, themes, motifs, and values from one culture to the other.

W. G. Lambert is much more cautious than Kramer when he examines Assyrian and Babylonian influences on the Bible. For over a hundred years now the Flood narrative in the Akkadian *The Epic of Gilgamesh* has been known to scholars of the ancient world. Parallels between that narrative and the Flood in Genesis have been examined many times. In a similar vein, the poem known to the ancients as *Enuma Elish* and sometimes referred to as "The Creation Epic" has been studied for its cosmological ideas and for its possible influence on the Creation stories in Genesis. Both the Flood narrative and *Enuma Elish* are "myths" and provide a useful way to measure the mythic mode in biblical writing as well as the probability of direct influence on biblical writers.

While parallels between the biblical Flood story and those in Sumerian and Akkadian demonstrate a close link between biblical narrators and neighboring peoples (a fragment of a Flood narrative has also been discovered recently at Ebla), the connection between *Enuma Elish* and Genesis is not all that close. Lambert's careful sifting of the literary evidence is a model for comparative literary-historical study. (For another comparative study of ancient Near Eastern myth and the Bible, see Frost, pp. 134–147).

In the sense that Kramer's and Lambert's essays are about literary influence, Roger Cox's essay is not about influence at all. Although he cites Greek tragic playwrights, Cox nowhere suggests their influence on the writing of the gospels, which he contends are "tragedies." In a larger sense, however, the essay is about literary history. Tragedy is a literary form which shows certain constant features. It is best known through Greek and Elizabethan examples such as *Oedipus Rex* and *Hamlet*. Cox argues that an understanding of the complexity of tragedy leads one to reverse a judgment that has long held sway: that tragedy is incompatible with Christianity. Far from it, the gospels—with the Crucifixion as the central event in the narratives—are tragedies. Christ should be seen as a tragic hero who necessarily suffers, an agent of destiny—reluctant and yet partly responsible for his suffering. That is not to say the New Testament borrowed a classical Greek form. "Tragedy" is a genre which appears when the demands for it (e.g., in the double nature of the God-man, or the problem of destiny and human freedom) arise.

William Whallon uses the same technique as the other essayists in this section, but with yet another objective. He again asks the question raised by Erich Auerbach in his book *Mimesis*. What are the significant contrasts in the narratives of the Old Testament and the Greek epic of approximately the same era? Whallon challenges Auerbach's stylistic comparison, which is keyed to his idea of *mimesis* or the representation of reality in literature. Whallon sees Old Testament poetry sharing many features of the Greek epic. Here again there is no argument for direct borrowing, one way or another. Both Hebrew and Greek poetry show familiar signs of oral composition. Old Testament poetry is used for speeches—speeches which are often only loosely related to context and the character delivering them. Old Testament poetry is generalized and lofty in style. It is in the realm of prose that the contrasts Auerbach saw between Greek and Old Testament writings are important. High and low styles emerge, since the prose narratives are highly specific, highly economical in using detail, and naturalistic in presentation. This would seem to agree with David Noel Freedman's discussion (pp. 77–100) that prose history is the single original literary form invented by the Hebrews.

Of the four essays, Kramer's and Lambert's come close to familiar approaches of literary history. Sumerian and Akkadian culture was spread by scribal schools, and literary influences may be quite direct. What Scripture shares with Greek literary culture of the classical period, on the other hand, may be important, but is not a case of borrowing. The essays by Cox and Whallon explore resemblances that emerge not through direct influence, but through similar traditions (oral composition) on the one hand, and similar problematical issues (heroic suffering) on the other.

Sumerian Literature
and the Bible

*The Sumerians developed a literary tradition well over a
thousand years before Hebrew literature of the Bible.
Sumerian influences on both oral and written traditions
would, if they can be demonstrated, be basic to a literary
history of the ancient Near East. Samuel Noah Kramer first
discusses the nature of Sumerian literature that has been
discovered and translated thus far, and then turns to the
possible influences of Sumerian ideas, beliefs, tenets,
themes, motifs, and values on the Bible.*

*Sumerian literature includes myths, epic tales, hymns,
lamentations, "historiography," and "wisdom" literature.
While the search for ancient "forms" is often a search for
oral traditions, the Sumerian materials show a breadth of
literary forms that were already developed in the third millennium* B.C.

*Literary forms and themes offer many parallels be-
tween the Bible and ancient Sumerian thought.*

See also Lambert, pp. 285–297.

O NE of the major contributions of our century to the humanities in
general and world literature in particular consists of the restoration
and translation of the Sumerian literary documents, a rather remarkable
achievement in view of the fact that less than a century ago nothing was
known, or even suspected, of the existence of a Sumerian people and
language, let alone a Sumerian literature. Today, as a result of the
cumulative and devoted efforts of quite a number of scholars, living and
dead, there are available copies and transliterations of hundreds of Sumerian literary tablets and fragments scattered far and wide in the various
museum collections, as well as reasonably trustworthy translations of
many of the texts inscribed on them. The present paper will summarize
briefly the nature and content of the available Sumerian literary docu-

From Samuel Noah Kramer, *Analecta Biblica*, 12 (1959), 185–204.

ments, and then proceed to isolate numerous ideas, beliefs, tenets, themes, motifs, and values, which they have, or at least seem to have, in common with the Bible.

The Sumerians probably first began to write down their literary works some time about 2500 B.C., although the earliest literary documents as yet available date from about a century later. Their literary output increased with the centuries, and became quite prolific towards the end of the third millennium, when the Sumerian academy known as the *e-dubba*, "house of tablets"—note the parallel Hebrew word *beth-sepher*—came to be an important center of education and learning. Sumerian literary activity continued unabated throughout the first half of the second millennium, in spite of the fact that during this time the Semites were infiltrating the land so thoroughly that the Sumerian language was gradually being replaced by the Semitic Akkadian as the spoken language of Sumer. In the *e-dubba*'s which functioned throughout this, the first *post*-Sumerian period, the earlier literary works were studied, copied, and redacted with zest and zeal, with loving care and sympathetic understanding. In fact, almost all the Sumerian literary works which have come down to us are known only from copies and redactions prepared in these post-Sumerian *e-dubba*'s. The presumably Akkadian-speaking teachers, poets, writers, and scribes who comprised the *e-dubba* personnel—the *soferim,* as it were—even created new Sumerian literary works, following closely the form and content, the style and pattern of earlier documents.

Sumerian literature, in the restricted sense of belles-lettres, consists of myths and epic tales, hymns and lamentations, "historiography" and "wisdom". The large majority of the Sumerian literary works are written in poetic form. The use of meter and rhyme was entirely unknown, but practically all other poetic devices and techniques were utilized with skill, imagination, and effect: repetition and parallelism, metaphor and simile, chorus and refrain. Sumerian narrative poetry—the myths and epic tales, for example—abounds in static epithets, lengthy repetitions, recurrent formulae, leisurely detailed descriptions, and long speeches.

To be sure, these compositions are not without some rather serious defects, at least from our point of view. They show little feeling for closely-knit plot structure; the narratives tend to ramble on rather disconnectedly and monotonously, with but little variation in emphasis and tone. Above all, the Sumerian poets and writers seem to lack a sense of climax; they do not seem to appreciate the effectiveness of bringing their stories to a climactic head. There is little intensification of emotion and suspense as the story progresses, and the last episode is often no more moving or stirring than the first. Nor is there any attempt at characterization and psychological delineation; the gods and heroes of the Sumerian narratives tend to be broad types rather than recognizable flesh-and-blood individuals. All of which differs rather markedly and significantly from the Semitic literary effects, and especially the Bible.

As of today, there have been recovered wholly, or in large part, twenty myths, that is, twenty narrative poems in which the gods are the major protagonists, although in case of several, mortals play a not insignificant role. These are (1) "Enlil and Ninlil; The Birth of the Moon-god"; (2) "Enlil and the Creation of the Pickax"; (3) "Enki and the World Order: The Organization of the Earth and its Cultural Processes"; (4) "Enki and Ninhursag: A Sumerian 'Paradise' Myth"; (5) "Enki and Ninmah: The Creation of Man"; (6) "Enki and Eridu"; (7) "The Journey of Nanna-Sin to Nippur"; (8) "The Deeds and Exploits of Ninurta"; (9) "The Return of Ninurta to Nippur"; (10) "Inanna and Enki: The Transfer of the Arts of Civilization from Eridu to Erech"; (11) "Inanna and the Subjugation of Mt. Ebih"; (12) "Inanna and Shukallituda: The Gardener's Mortal Sin"; (13) "Inanna's Descent to the Nether World"; (14) "Inanna and Bilulu"; (15) "Dumuzi and Enkimdu: the Wooing of Inanna"; (16) "The Marriage of Dumuzi and Inanna"; (17) "Dumuzi and His Sister Geshtinanna"; (18) "Dumuzi and the Gallē" (19) "The Marriage of Martu"; (20) "The Flood".

There are now restorable, wholly or in large part, nine Sumerian epic tales, that is, nine narrative poems in which mortal heroic figures play the major roles, although deities may also participate in the action in one way or another. The poems vary in length from a little over one hundred to more than six hundred lines, and revolve about the Sumerian heroes Enmerkar, Lugalbanda, and Gilgamesh.

One of the most carefully cultivated literary arts in Sumer was hymnography. Scores of hymns varying in length from less than fifty to close to four hundred lines have been recovered to date, and there is every reason to believe that this is only a fraction of the hymns composed in Sumer throughout the centuries. There were hymns extolling gods and kings; hymnal prayers in which paeans of praise to the gods are interspersed with blessings and prayers for the kings; as well as a number of hymns glorifying the temples of Sumer. Hymnography had become so sophisticated a literary art that it was subdivided into various categories by the ancients themselves, and many of the extant hymns are ascribed to their appropriate category by a special ·subscription at the end of the work. Thus, to name only some of the categories, there were "harmony hymns", "hymns of heroship", "musical hymns", "hymns of shepherdship", "lyre (?) hymns", and "drum (?) hymns". Some of the hymns are broken up by their ancient composers into sections or stanzas separated by various types of notation, and a number of them make use of antiphons and choral refrains.

The Sumerian lamentations are primarily of two kinds: those bewailing the destruction of the Sumerian cities and city-states, and those lamenting the death of the god Dumuzi or one of his counterparts. Of the former, two of the best preserved concern the destruction of Ur. A third concerns the destruction of Nippur, but ends on a note of joy with the restoration of the city by Ishme-Dagan, the fourth ruler of the Dynasty of Isin. A fourth lamentation as yet restorable in part only, bewails the destruction of Sumer and Akkad as a whole. As for the Dumuzi laments, they range in size from less than fifty to over two hundred lines. Quite a number have been published to date, but for one reason or another their meaning and interpretation still remain obscure in large part.

The "historiographic" genre is not too well represented in the extant Sumerian literary documents. The longest "historiographic" text available is "The Curse of Agade," an excellently preserved composition which attempts to explain the catastrophic destruction of the city of Agade by the barbaric Guti. Another well-preserved document revolves about the defeat of the Guti by Utuhegal, a ruler of Erech. A third and rather unusual "historiographic" text concerns the successive restorations of the Tummal, the shrine of the goddess Ninlil in the city of Nippur. There are also indications that there had existed a series of legendary tales clustering about Sargon the Great and his contemporaries, Lugalzaggesi of Erech, and Ur-Zababa of Kish.

Finally, to turn to the Sumerian "wisdom" documents, these include "disputation" poems, essays large and small, and collections of precepts and proverbs. The extant "disputation" texts are seven in number and consist largely of verbal battles between deified or personified protagonists: "Summer and Winter", "Cattle and Grain", "Bird and Fish", "Tree and Reed", "Silver and Copper", "Pickax and Plow", "The Mill and the Gulgul-stone"; interestingly enough, they generally begin with a mythological passage which is quite revealing for the Sumerian notions about the creation of the universe and its organization. As for the longer essays, except for the poem with the "Job" motif, "Man and His God", they are all written in prose, and deal in one way or another with the Sumerian academy, the e-dubba, and its faculty, student body, and graduates. At present, five of these are restorable wholly or in large part: "Schooldays", "A Scribe and His Perverse Son", "The 'Supervisor' and the Scribe", "Enki-mansi and Girni-ishag", "Enki-hegal and Enki-ta".

Three Sumerian collections of precepts and instructions are now known: "The Farmer's Almanac", which contains the instructions of a farmer to his son; "The Instructions of Shuruppak to His Son Ziusudra", which consists of a series of admonitions for wise and effective behaviour; and a third which also consists of admonitions, but is too fragmentary for closer identification. As for Sumerian proverbs, they run into the hundreds and include all types of maxims, sayings, apothegms, and even short Aesop-like fables. About a dozen well-preserved proverb collections have now been identified by Edmund Gordon. He has now translated a large part of them and his resulting publications are opening up new vistas in the comparative study of ancient "wisdom" literature.

Now it goes without saying that a written literature so varied, comprehensive, and time-honored as the Sumerian, left a deep impress on the literary products of the entire ancient Near East. Particularly so, since at one time or another practically all the peoples of Western Asia—Akkadians, Assyrians, Babylonians, Hittites, Hurrians, Canaanites, and Elamites, to name only those for which positive and direct evidence is available at the moment—had found it to their interest to borrow the cuneiform script in order to inscribe their own records and writings. For the adoption and adaptation of this syllabic and logographic system of writing, which had been developed by the Sumerians to write their own agglutinative and largely monosyllabic tongue, demanded a thorough training in the Sumerian language and literature. To this end, no doubt, learned teachers and scribes were imported from Sumer to the schools of the neighboring lands, while the native scribes travelled to Sumer for special instruction in its more famous academies. All of which resulted in the wide spread of Sumerian culture and literature. The ideas and ideals of the Sumerians—their cosmology, theology, ethics, and system of education—permeated, to a greater or lesser extent, the thoughts and writings of all the peoples of the ancient Near East. So too, did the Sumerian literary forms and themes—their plots, motifs, stylistic devices, and aesthetic techniques. To all of which, Palestine, the land where the books of the Bible were composed, redacted, and edited by the Hebrew men of letters, was no exception.

To be sure, even the earliest parts of the Bible, it is generally agreed, were not written down in their present form much earlier than 1000 B.C., or not long thereafter. There is therefore, no question of any contemporary borrowing from the Sumerian literary sources. Sumerian influence penetrated the Bible through the Canaanite, Hurrian, Hittite, and Akkadian literature. Particularly through the last, since, as is well known, the Akkadian language was used all over Palestine and its environs in the second millennium B.C. as the *lingua franca* of practically the entire literate world. Akkadian literary works must therefore have been well known to Palestinian men of letters, including the Hebrews. But not a few of these Akkadian literary works went back to Sumerian prototypes, remodelled and transformed over the centuries.

However, there is one possible source of Sumerian influence on the Bible which is far more direct and immediate than that just described. In fact, it may well go back to Father Abraham himself. Most scholars agree that, while the Abraham saga as told in the Bible contains much that is legendary and fanciful, it does have an important kernel of truth, including the fact that Abraham was born in Ur of the Chaldees, perhaps some time about 1700 B.C., and lived there with his family during the early part of his life. Now Ur was one of the most important cities of ancient Sumer; in fact, it was the capital of Sumer at three different periods in its history. It had an impressive *e-dubba,* and in the joint British-American excavations conducted there between the years 1922–34, quite a number of Sumerian literary documents have been found. Abraham and his forefathers may well have had some acquaintance with the Sumerian literary products copied or created in his home town academy. And it is by no means impossible that he and the members of his family brought some of this Sumerian lore and learning with them to Palestine, where they gradually became part and parcel of the traditions and sources utilized by the Hebrew men of letters in composing and redacting the books of the Bible.

Be that as it may, here are a number of Biblical parallels from Sumerian literature which unquestionably point to traces of Sumerian influence.

1. *Creation of the Universe.* The Sumerians, like the ancient Hebrews, thought that a primeval sea had existed prior to creation. The universe, according to the Sumerians, consisted of a united heaven and earth engendered in some way in this primeval sea, and it was the air-god Enlil—perhaps not unlike the *ruach elohim* of Genesis—who separated heaven from earth.[1]

2. *Creation of Man.* Man, according to both the Hebrews and the Sumerians, was conceived as fashioned of clay and imbued with the "breath of life". The purpose for which he was created was to serve the gods—or Yahweh alone in case of the Hebrews—with prayer, supplication, and sacrifices.[2]

3. *Creation Techniques.* Creation, according to both the Biblical and Sumerian writers, was accomplished primarily in two ways: by divine command, and by actual "making" or "fashioning". In either case, the actual creation was preceded by divine planning, though this need not be explicitly stated.[3]

4. *Paradise.* No Sumerian parallel to the story of the Garden of Eden and the Fall of Man has yet been found. There are, however, several "paradise" motifs significant for comparative purposes, including one which may help to clarify the "rib" episode in Genesis 2:21–23. Moreover, there is some reason to believe that the very idea of a divine paradise, a garden of the gods, is of Sumerian origin.

5. *The Flood.* As has long been recognized, the Biblical and Sumerian versions of the Flood story show numerous obvious and close parallels. Noteworthy, too, is the fact that according to at least one Mesopotamian tradition there were ten antediluvian rulers, each with a life span of

extraordinary length. All of which is reminiscent to some extent of the Biblical antediluvian patriarchs.[4]

6. *The "Cain-Abel" Motif.* The rivalry motif depicted in the undoubtedly much abbreviated Cain-Abel episode of the Bible was a high favorite with the Sumerian writers and poets.

7. *The Tower of Babel and the Dispersion of Mankind.* The story of the building of the Tower of Babel originated no doubt in an effort to explain the existence of the Mesopotamian *ziggurats*. To the Hebrews these towering structures, which could often be seen in a state of ruin and decay, became symbols of man's feeling of insecurity and the not unrelated lust for power which brings upon him humiliation and suffering. It is most unlikely, therefore, that a parallel to this story will be found among the Sumerians, to whom the ziggurat represented a bond between heaven and earth, between god and man. On the other hand, the idea that there was a time when all peoples of the earth "had one language and the same words", and that this happy state was brought to an end by an irate deity, may have a parallel in a "Golden Age" passage which is part of the Sumerian epic tale "Enmerkar and the Lord of Aratta".

8. *The Earth and Its Organization.* The Sumerian myth "Enki and the World Order: The Organization of the Earth and Its Cultural Process" provides a detailed account of the activities of Enki, the Sumerian god of wisdom, in organizing the earth and in establishing what might be termed law and order on it. First he blesses Sumer in a passage which indicates that the Sumerians, not unlike the ancient Hebrews, thought of themselves as a rather special and hallowed community more intimately related to the gods than mankind in general, a community noteworthy not only for its material wealth and possessions, but also for its honored spiritual leaders—one which all the fate-decreeing heaven gods, the Anunnaki, have selected as their special abode.

From Sumer, Enki turns to Sumer's capital Ur, and blesses it as well. He then proceeds to bless Meluḫḫa, that is, ancient Ethiopia, and Dilmun, which may turn out to be northwest India. He proceeds to fill the Tigris and Euphrates with fresh and sparkling water and with fish galore. He turns to the sea and sets up its rules; calls the winds and harnesses their violence; gives instructions to the yoke and plow, and sees to it that the fields become fertile and productive. He gives orders to the pickax and brickmold, lays foundations, and builds houses. Finally he fills the plain with plant and animal life, builds stables and sheepfolds, fills them with milk and fat. To see to it that the world order remains stable and enduring, he appoints a host of minor deities in charge of each of these natural and cultural entities. All of which finds its echoes in such Biblical songs as Deuteronomy 38—especially verse 8—and Psalm 107.

9. *Personal God.* To judge from the covenant between God and Abraham—note, too, the reference to a "god of Nahor" in Genesis 31:53—the ancient Hebrews were familiar with the idea of a "personal" god. Now the belief in the existence of a "personal" god was evolved by the Sumerians at least as early as the middle of the third millennium B.C.[5] According to Sumerian teachers and sages, every adult male and family head had his "personal god", a kind of "good angel" whom he looked upon as his divine father. This "personal god" was in all probability "adopted" by the Sumerian *pater familias* as the result of an oracle, or a dream, or a vision, involving a mutual understanding or agreement not unlike the "covenant" between the Hebrew patriarchs and Yahweh.

To be sure, there could have been nothing exclusive about the "covenant" between the Sumerian and his tutelary deity, and in this respect, therefore, it differed very significantly from that between Abraham and his god. All that the Sumerian expected of his "personal god" was to talk up in his behalf and intercede for him in the assembly of the gods, whenever the occasion demanded, and thus insure for him a long life and good health. In return, he glorified his god with special prayers, supplications, and sacrifices, although at the same time he continued to worship the other deities of the Sumerian pantheon. Nevertheless, as the Sumerian literary document "Man and His God" indicates, there existed a close, intimate, trusting and even tender relationship between the Sumerian and his "personal god", one which bears no little resemblance to that between Yahweh and the Hebrew patriarchs, and in later days, between Yahweh and the Hebrew people as a whole.

10. *Law.* That the Biblical laws and the long-known Hammurabi Law Code show numerous similarities in content, terminology, and even arrangement, is recognized by practically all students of the Bible. But the Hammurabi Code itself, as has been shown in recent years, is an Akkadian compilation of laws based largely on Sumerian prototypes. In fact there is good reason to infer that the extraordinary growth and development of legal concepts, practices, precedents, and compilations in the ancient Near East goes back largely to the Sumerians and their rather one-sided emphasis on rivalry and superiority. Sumerian behaviour was characterized by an ambitious, competitive, and aggressive drive for preeminence and prestige, for victory and success. Particularly revealing in this respect are the Sumerian literary compositions categorized by the ancient scribes themselves as "contests" or "disputations", which consist largely of bitter and abusive arguments, full of sneers, jibes, and humiliating insults. One of these is particularly noteworthy, for its implications in regard to the psychological origin of the strong Sumerian penchant for law and legality, for legal documents and law-codes. The essay treats of a bitter dispute between the two school worthies, Enki-mansi and Girni-

ishag, and ends in the following revealing words: "In the dispute between Enki-mansi and Girni-ishag, the headmaster gives the *verdict*". The Sumerian word here used for "verdict" is the same which designates the "verdict" at court trials, and one cannot refrain from concluding that the extraordinary importance which the Sumerians attached to law and legal control, stemmed not altogether from lofty moral and ethical convictions, but at least in part from the contentious and aggressive behavioural pattern which characterized their culture.[6]

11. *Ethics and Morals.* The Sumerians, like the Hebrews, cherished goodness and truth, law and order, justice and freedom, wisdom and learning, courage and loyalty, honesty and forthrightness, mercy and compassion, in short all of man's most desirable virtues and qualities. Like the Bible, Sumerian literature contains numerous passages revealing a touching solicitude for the poor, the weak, and the oppressed, and especially the orphan, the widow, and the refugee. The step by step development of these ethical values is as difficult to trace for the ancient Sumerian culture as it is for our own, but it stands to reason that they were evolved gradually and painfully over the centuries from the social and cultural experiences of the Sumerian people. To be sure, the Sumerians attributed all the credit for man's high moral qualities and ethical virtues to the gods they worshipped while the Hebrews attributed it to Yahweh. But faith and revelation aside, this hardly makes their ethics less sublime, or their ideals less lofty.

Now while the Sumerians had developed ethical concepts and moral ideals which were essentially identical with those of the Hebrews, they lacked their almost palpable ethical sensitivity and moral fervor, especially as these are exemplified in the Biblical prophetic literature. Psychologically, the Sumerian was more distant and aloof than the Hebrew—more emotionally restrained, more formal and methodical. He tended to eye his fellow men with some suspicion, misgiving, and even apprehension. All of which inhibited to no small extent the human warmth, sympathy, and affection so vital to spiritual growth and well being. In spite of their high ethical attainments, the Sumerians never reached the lofty conviction that "a pure heart" and "clean hands" are more worthy in the eyes of the gods than lengthy prayers, profuse sacrifices, and elaborate ritual.

12. *Divine Retribution and National Catastrophe.* Yahweh's wrath, and the humiliation and destruction of the people which incur it, constitute an oft-repeated theme in the Biblical books. Usually the national catastrophe comes about through a violent attack by some neighboring people, especially selected as Yahweh's scourge and whip. To all of which an historiographic document which may be entitled "The Curse of Agade" offers a rather interesting parallel: Enlil, the leading

deity of the Sumerian pantheon, having been deeply angered by the blasphemous act of a ruler of Agade (Biblical Akkad), lifted his eyes to the mountains and brought down the barbarous and cruel Guti, who proceeded not only to destroy Agade, but almost all Sumer as well.

13. *The "Plague" Motif.* The Sumerian myth "Inanna and Shukallituda: The Gardener's Mortal Sin" contains a "plague" motif which parallels to some extent the Biblical "plague" motif in the Exodus story: in both cases, a deity, angered by the misdeeds and obduracy of an individual, sends a series of plagues against an entire land and its people.

14. *Suffering and Submission: The "Job" Motif.* Quite recently there was made available a Sumerian poetic essay, which is of rather unusual significance for Biblical comparative studies. Its central theme, human suffering and submission, is identical with that treated so sensitively and poignantly in the Biblical Book of Job. Even the introductory "plot" is the same: A man—unnamed in the Sumerian poem—who had been wealthy, wise, righteous, and blessed with friends and kin, is overwhelmed one day, for no apparent reason, by sickness, suffering, poverty, betrayal, and hatred. Admittedly, however, the Sumerian essay, which consists of less than one hundred and fifty lines, compares in no way with the Biblical book in breadth, depth, and beauty; it is much closer in mood, temper, and content to the more tearful and plaintive psalms of the Book of Psalms.[7]

15. *Death and the Nether World.* The Biblical *Sheol* and, for that matter, the Hades of the Greeks, has its counterpart in the Sumerian *Kur*. Like the Hebrew *Sheol*, the *Kur* is the dark, dread abode of the dead. It is a land of no return, whence only exceptionally the shade of a once-prominent figure might be called up for questioning. In the Sumerian literary documents there are found several interesting Hebrew-Sumerian parallels relating to the Nether World: its depiction as the pitiful home of former kings and princes; the raising of the shades of the dead from it; the imprisonment in it of the god Dumuzi,[8] the Biblical Tammuz, for whom the women of Jerusalem were lamenting as late as the days of the prophet Ezekiel.

So much for some of the more obvious and significant Biblical parallels from Sumerian literature. Needless to say this list only "skims the milk", and "scratches the surface". In the coming years, as more and more of the Sumerian literary documents become available, the number of Sumerian parallels will grow and multiply—particularly for such books as Psalms,[9] Proverbs,[10] Lamentations,[11] and Song of Songs.[12] All of which brings up a question which may already have occurred to the reader: If the Sumerians were a people of such outstanding literary and cultural importance for the ancient Near Eastern world as a whole that they even left their indelible impress on the literary works of the Hebrew men of letters, why is it that there seems to be little trace of them in the Bible? In Genesis, chapters 10 and 11, for example, we find lists of quite a number of eponyms, lands, and cities. But except for the rather obscure word Shinar which scholars usually identify with Sumer, but which actually stands for the Sumerian equivalent of the compound word Sumer-Akkad, there seems to be no mention of the Sumerians in the entire Bible, a fact which is hardly reconcilable with their purported preeminence and influence.

Interestingly enough a solution to this rather puzzling enigma was suggested over a quarter of a century ago, by my teacher and colleague, Arno Poebel.[13] To be sure, Poebel's suggestion has found no responsive echo among Orientalists and it seems to have been relegated to scholarly oblivion. It is my conviction, however, that it will stand the test of time, and will in due course be recognized as a significant contribution to Hebrew-Sumerian interconnections.[14]

Before evaluating Poebel's explanation, however, the reader who is not a cuneiformist will have to bear in mind a rather curious, but well-founded and generally accepted, Sumerian phonetic law, which is essential to an intelligent approach to the problems involved. This law, the formulation of which marked a milestone in the study of the Sumerian language, may be stated as follows: Sumerian final consonants were amissible, and were not pronounced in speech unless followed by a grammatical particle beginning with, or consisting of, a vowel. Thus, for example, the Sumerian word for field, *ashag,* was actually pronounced *asha* (without the final *g*). But when this same word appeared in the Sumerian complex *ashag-a,* "in the field", where the *-a* is a grammatical element equated with the English "in", it was pronounced *ashag,* not *asha.* Similarly the Sumerian word for "god", *dingir,* was actually pronounced *dingi,* with the final *r* silent. But in the complex *dingir-e,* "by god", where the *-e* stands for the English "by", the word was pronounced *dingir,* not *dingi.*

Now to return to our problem and the quest for the word Sumer, or rather Shumer, to use the form found in the cuneiform documents— Poebel was struck by its resemblance to the name Shem, Noah's eldest son, and the distant ancestor of such eponyms as Ashur, Elam, Aram, and above all, Eber, the eponym of the Hebrews.

The equation Shem–Shumer presented, however, two difficulties: the interchange of the vowels *e* and *u,* and the omission of the final *-er.* Now the first of these presents no difficulty at all, the Akkadian *u* often becomes *e* in Hebrew—a particularly pertinent example is the Akkadian *shumu* "name", and the Hebrew *shem.* As for the second difficulty, the omission of the final *er* of Shumer in its Hebrew counterpart Shem, this can now be explained by applying the Sumerian law of amissibility of final consonants. For the word Shumer was pronounced *Shume* or even more probably *Shum* (the final *e* is a very short, schwa-like vowel), and the Hebrews thus took it over from Sumerian as Shem.

Nor is Shem the only example of a Hebrew name borrowed for a Sumerian word without its final consonant. The name of the city where Abraham was born, is written as Ur in the Bible. But the Sumerian name, as has long been known, is not Ur but Urim; "in Ur", for example is *urim-a*, not *ur-a* or *uri-a*. In this case, too, therefore, the Biblical authors had borrowed the name as actually pronounced in Sumerian, when not followed by a grammatical element beginning with a vowel.

If Poebel's hypothesis turns out to be correct, and Shem is identical with Shumer-Sumer, we must assume that the Hebrew authors of the Bible, or at least some of them, considered the Sumerians to have been the original ancestors of the Hebrew people. Linguistically speaking, they could not have been more mistaken since Sumerian is an agglutinative tongue poles apart from the inflected Semitic family of languages of which Hebrew forms a part. But there may well have been considerable Sumerian blood flowing in the veins of Abraham's forefathers who lived for generations in Ur or some other Sumerian cities. As for Sumerian culture and civilization, there is no reason to doubt that these proto-Hebrews had absorbed and assimilated much of the Sumerian way of life. In brief, Sumerian-Hebrew interconnections, echoed in such talmudic and midrashic expressions as "the house of study of Shem and Eber" or "the court of justice of Shem and Eber", may well have been closer than suspected hitherto.

NOTES

1. For details, see my *Sumerian Mythology*, rev. ed. (New York: Harper, 1961), pp. 38ff.

2. For details, see my *Sumerian Mythology*, pp. 68ff. Note, too, that according to the 18th line of the "Creation of the Pickax" poem (see *SM*, p. 52) which reads literally "The head of man he (i.e., Enlil) placed in the mould", there seemed to be a mythological version of the creation of man, in which Enlil, rather than Enki or Ninmah, played the dominant role. Furthermore in the "Deluge" myth man was fashioned by all four creating deities: An, Enlil, Enki, and Ninhursag (the phrase there used is "black headed people" which is usually, but not always, the epithet given to the Sumerians, rather than mankind as a whole). In *JNES* 5:134 ff. Thorkild Jacobsen, after translating and analyzing the initial lines of the "Creation of the Pickax" poem, concludes that man, after "developing" below the surface of the earth, "shot forth" from the earth through a hole made by Enlil in the top crust of the earth. But his translation of the pertinent lines is by no means certain.

3. The principal planner of creation was no doubt the god Enlil (or the composite deity An-Enlil, that is, the Enlil who, at least by about 2500 B.C., had taken over the "kingship" of the gods from An as well as his power. It was probably Enlil, too, who had planned all the human institutions, activities, and attitudes which went to make up culture and civilization for the Sumerian thinkers; it was probably he who devised the *me*'s, the rules and regulations by which the universe operated effectively and without interruption. Just how Enlil

did his actual creating is not stated explictly, but to judge from the available material, the likelihood is that he merely gave the command and uttered the "word", or "name", while other deities, particularly Enki, the god of wisdom, attended to details. But even in the case of Enki, it was primarily the "word" by which he operated; note, however, that he waters the dikes and reeds by means of his phallus (cf. *ANET*, p. 38, lines 67–68) and "fashions" the KURGARRU and KALATURRU from the dirt of his fingernails (cf. *ANET*, p. 56, lines 219–220). In general, to judge from the available material, the Sumerian men of letters speak only in the vaguest terms when it comes to describing the diverse creative acts by which fertility, abundance, and prosperity were brought to earth. Only in case of the creation of man is some attempt made to furnish at least a few important details.

4. See Alexander Heidel, *The Gilgamesh Epic and Old Testament Parallels* (Chicago: University of Chicago Press, 1946), pp. 224ff. and André Parrot, *The Flood and Noah's Ark* (New York: Philosophical Library, 1955).

5. Some of the known personal gods are Šulutulua for Eannatum, Entemena, and Entemena II; Ninšubur for Urakagina; Nidaba for Lugalzaggesi; Ningišzida for Gudea; Ninsun for the rulers of the Third Dynasty of Ur.

6. Cf. now B. Gemser's interesting study: "The Rîb or Controversy Pattern in Hebrew Mentality" (*Supplement to Vetus Testamentum* 3:120–137), which points to a rather close similarity between Hebrew and Sumerian character.

7. Cf. *Supplements to Vetus Testamentum* 3:170–191.

8. As far as the present evidence goes, Dumuzi's death is not, as is commonly assumed, due to physical violence at the hands of either god, man, or beast. Dumuzi "dies" when he is carried off bound hands and arms to the Nether World by the seven *gallê*, as a substitute for his wife, the goddess Inanna, who according to the divine rules governing "the land of no return" could not be permitted to reascend from the Nether World to the world above, unless someone took her place.

9. This will be especially true in case of the "royal" psalms and the "cultic" hymns; but even the "individual lament" type of psalm now has its Sumerian parallel to a certain extent in "Man and His God", a poem which no doubt represents a special literary type of which additional examples will be recovered sooner or later.

10. As yet there have been identified relatively few Sumerian parallels to individual Biblical proverbs. But this number will undoubtedly grow in time, although it may never be too large, since the Biblical proverbs are largely prescriptive and moralistic, while the Sumerian proverbs tend to be descriptive, ironic, and caustic. It is probably in the Sumerian precept collections, rather than the proverb collections, that a considerable number of parallels to the Biblical Book of Proverbs will be uncovered. The precept collection known as "The Instructions of Šuruppak to his Son Ziusudra" may turn out to be particularly fruitful in this respect. Indeed even its more obvious stylistic features show a number of parallels with those of the Book of Proverbs. Thus the fact that these precepts were attributed to King Šuruppak, shows that as early as 2000 B.C. or thereabout, the "wisdom" writers and redactors of Sumer had come upon the idea of ascribing whole "wisdom" collections to a presumably very wise ruler of "long ago", just as the Biblical authors of a much later day ascribed some of their precept collections to the "wise" King Solomon.

11. There is little doubt that it was the Sumerian poets who originated and developed the "lamentation" genre—there are Sumerian examples dating possibly from as early as the Third Dynasty of Ur and as late as the Parthian period—and that the Biblical Book of Lamentations, as well as the "burden" laments of the prophets, represent a profoundly moving transformation of the more formal and conventional Mesopotamian prototypes.

12. See my *The Sacred Marriage Rite* (Bloomington: Indiana University Press, 1969), pp. 85–106.

13. *AJSL* 58:20–26.

14. [Ed. note. See the *BA* issues 39:2 and 3 (1976), devoted to recent studies of Ebla, esp. p. 84, and Giovanni Pettinato's "The Royal Archives of Tell-Mardikh–Ebla," pp. 44–54.]

A New Look
at the Babylonian
Background of Genesis

*The interest in Akkadian literature of Mesopotamia dates
to the period when biblical scholars such as Hermann Gunkel were advancing form criticism (see Muilenburg, pp.
362–380). Since then the background to Genesis has been
studied with special intensity. The review of that study
presented by W. G. Lambert adopts a cautious view on the
question of Akkadian influences in the Bible. (Compare
Kramer's views on the even earlier Mesopotamian influences on the Bible, pp. 272–284.)*

 *Close attention to the diversity in Babylonian and As-
syrian ideas, and the differences as well as the similarities
between accounts of Creation and the Flood make the study
of possible influences very complicated. Many parallels and
many differences exist between biblical accounts and
Mesopotamian accounts. Lambert shows the dangers in
"pan-babylonism"—of concluding that parallels in the literature automatically show literary influences.*

 *The Flood story in the Bible has been borrowed from
Mesopotamian materials. Creation stories, however, show
a marked diversity. After carefully examining the Hebrew,
Babylonian, and Assyrian accounts of the days of Creation,
Lambert concludes that the latter had less obvious influence
on Hebrew poetry.*

M Y subject arose in the first place from study of the cuneiform tablets
from Ashurbanipal's library in Nineveh, which had been dug up for
the British Museum in the 1850's. The most important discoveries were
published in the 1870's by George Smith: first, in 1872, a Babylonian
version of the flood story was made known,[1] and three years later a
Babylonian account of creation was announced, translation of the pieces
being given in Smith's book, *The Chaldean Account of Genesis*, which
appeared in the following year, 1876.

From W. G. Lambert, *Journal of Theological Studies*, 16 (1965), 287–300.

The attention of Old Testament scholars was now assured.[2] Even the most sceptical had to yield when confronted with the passage in the Babylonian text which described how three birds were sent out of the ark as the waters were subsiding. With the creation account the similarities were not so great. Although the Babylonian cosmology began with a primaeval Tiāmat, which is the etymological equivalent of $t^e h\hat{o}m$, 'the deep', in Gen. i, the major item of the Babylonian text, the battle between Marduk and Tiāmat, does not appear in the Hebrew accounts of creation. The German scholar Gunkel supplied the missing link in his book *Schöpfung und Chaos in Urzeit und Endzeit* (1895). He drew attention to a series of passages in the poetic books of the Old Testament in which a battle between Yahweh and the sea, or sea monsters, is alluded to. On this basis it could be affirmed that a conflict had existed in Hebrew traditions of creation, but had been washed out of the monotheistic formulation of Genesis i. Gunkel was not in fact the first to propound this idea. Our own Cheyne, in the year in which this book appeared, took the author to task in the *Critical Review* for not acknowledging that as far back as 1877 he himself had been advancing such views.[3] Cheyne had in fact mentioned the battle with Tiāmat as a possible parallel to the poetic allusions, whereas Gunkel was asserting that all the references to Rahab, Leviathan, etc., were but borrowed versions of Marduk's fight. However, another scholar had much greater claim to have been plagiarized. George A. Barton, a young American, had read a paper in 1890 in which he cited the main passages about Rahab, Leviathan, and the dragon of the Book of Revelation, and drew the conclusion that these were direct reflections of the Babylonian myth. This paper was published in 1893[4] and was known to Gunkel in the preparation of his book, since he quoted it on various minor points.

Whoever first propounded the idea (Barton seems to have the better claim), he provided the justification for assuming a direct connexion of some kind between the Babylonian and Hebrew accounts of creation. By the turn of the century the idea of dependence on a Babylonian original in the two cases of creation and flood was an accepted opinion in critical circles, so much so that strong assertions usually covered up the differences in the case of the former. Few thought it necessary even to admit of any problem, as did S. R. Driver in his commentary on Genesis, where he says about the creation narrative:

> In estimating these similarities, it must further be remembered that they do not stand alone: in the narrative of the Deluge we find traits borrowed unmistakably from a Babylonian source; so that the antecedent difficulty which might otherwise have been felt in supposing elements in the Creation-narrative to be traceable ultimately to the same quarter is considerably lessened.[5]

This amounts to saying that even though the case for the creation narrative is dubious, the better case of the flood can be used to prove it, a very debatable procedure. It should be added that another factor involved in the acceptance of this opinion by the turn of the century was the date assigned to the Babylonian texts. While the copies then available were not earlier than 750 B.C., the texts were believed to go back to at least 2000 B.C., well before the earliest possible date for Genesis.

The last sixty years have witnessed vast increases in knowledge of the various factors involved in this problem. It is no longer possible to talk glibly about Babylonian civilization. We now know that it was composed of three main strands. First, it inherited much from the Sumerians, who built up the first great civilization in Southern Mesopotamia. A second element was derived from a group of Semites who probably came down the Euphrates valley in the middle of the third millennium B.C. Thirdly, it owed something to the Amorites, who likewise came down the Euphrates valley, but at the end of the third millennium, and took over the country. The Sumerians were the most original and dynamic in cultural matters, and the other two groups owed something to them even before they had settled down. Consequently it is often difficult to know if a particular item of Babylonian civilization originated with one of these three groups or was a new creation. More is known of the Amorites than of the earlier Semitic migrants, and their influence can be found in words of Babylonian literature. In my opinion the *lex talionis* in the Code of Hammurabi depends on an Amorite legal tradition, since it was an innovation in Mesopotamian law. Also the location of the Sumero-Babylonian pantheon on Mount Hermon in the Babylonian *Epic of Gilgamesh* is certainly Amorite in conception.[6] Thus Babylonian civilization was a highly composite thing, and it is no longer scientifically sound to assume that all ideas originated in Mesopotamia and moved westwards. This is pan-babylonism. Parallels to Genesis can indeed be sought and found there, but they can also be sought and found among the Canaanites, the ancient Egyptians, the Hurrians, the Hittites, and the early Greeks. When the parallels have been found, the question of dependence, if any, has to be approached with an open mind.

Another qualification which is often overlooked in comparative studies of this kind is the inner diversity of so large and so long-lasting a civilization as the Babylonian. Our remoteness often causes the inquirer to attach an exaggerated importance to whatever fragment from this vast complex he happens to be working on. The doctrine of one text may be carelessly styled 'the Babylonian view', as though it were proved to have been held by all Babylonians of all periods and areas. More systematic study reveals what could very well have been conjectured, that a great variety of ideas circulated in ancient Mesopotamia. Sumerian religion crystallized in city-states, each with its particular gods and cults. Mutual tolerance was manifested in a generally accepted hierarchical order of the chief gods from the different cities. While Hammurabi welded the same cities into a single Babylonian state, religion continued its city-bound organization, though quite substantial changes gradually took place in the official hierarchy. And in all matters the 1,100 years between Hammurabi and Nebuchadnezzar II witnessed tremendous development. Yet, to the end, despite the political unity based on the city of Babylon, matters of thought still reflected local attachments. In the first millennium B.C. creativity in myth was no longer expressed in literary compositions of epic style. Instead, expository texts and scholarly commentaries of a highly esoteric character were compiled. The distinction between those expounding the myths of Nippur and those the myths of Babylon, for example, is easily discerned.

One matter can be disposed of very quickly. The recovery of the Ugaritic texts has shown that the allusions to Yahweh's battle with Leviathan and the *tannîn*, but not Rahab, are derived from Canaanite Baal myths, and these show no signs of dependence on Mesopotamian sources. Accordingly, one of the main supports for assuming the dependence of Genesis on Babylonian myths has gone, and the whole question needs reconsideration. Yet not all Old Testament scholars have really faced the facts. The following random quotations of recent opinion illustrate the position. Kaufmann in his *Religion of Israel* (1961) does indeed assert the Canaanite rather than Babylonian origin of the poetic allusions to battles with monsters. Similarly Hans-Joachim Kraus in his commentary on the Psalms refers to the Babylonian epic only as a parallel, and insists on the prior relevance of the Ugaritic material.[7] Contrast this with Eissfeldt's article on Genesis in the *Interpreter's Dictionary of the Bible*, which repeats essentially what Gunkel said, only modernizing the terminology: instead of Babylonian origin he speaks of 'Sumerian-Akkadian prototypes' (II, 375). Von Rad, in his commentary on Genesis, asserts the 'unbestreitbare Zusammenhang' of the Babylonian Tiāmat and *tᵉhôm* in Gen. i, meaning a mythological and not only a philological connexion.[8] Similarly, Orlinsky asserts: 'Scholars have long recognized that the biblical version of creation has great affinity with what we know of the Mesopotamian versions, that the former—whether directly or indirectly—derives ultimately and in significant measure from the latter.'[9]

On the Sumero-Babylonian side, matters are hardly more satisfactory. New editions of *Enūma Eliš*, or the *Babylonian Epic of Creation* as it is commonly called, have been made by merely adding new material to the old edition, with all their inevitable and, in their cases, excusable faults. L. W. King's excellent edition of 1902[10] was the truly critical edition based on first-hand study of all the textual evidence. In addition to this major and several minor texts, there is a mass of allusions and other secondary material comparable with the allusions in Hebrew poetry, which no one has hitherto collected, much less studied. The greatest failure, however, has been in the general interpretation of the major epic.

Views put out as plausible conjectures at the end of the last century have, by frequent repetition, become endowed with canonical status, and are now asserted in such terms as 'it is generally admitted' (which means that no one has ever proved) and 'there is no convincing reason against' (which patently confesses the lack of conclusive reasons for). Under these circumstances I have tried to get to the bottom of the various questions and to assemble neglected material. Some of my results, for what they are worth, must be used in the following notes.

The first major conclusion is that the *Epic of Creation* is not a norm of Babylonian or Sumerian cosmology. It is a sectarian and aberrant combination of mythological threads woven into an unparalleled compositum. In my opinion it is not earlier than 1100 B.C. It happens to be the best preserved Babylonian document of its genre simply because it was at its height of popularity when the libraries were formed from which our knowledge of Babylonian mythology is mostly derived. The various traditions it draws upon are often perverted to such an extent that conclusions based on this text alone are suspect. It can only be used safely in the whole context of ancient Mesopotamian mythology. With this introduction let us turn to the matter in hand.

The flood remains the clearest case of dependence of Genesis on Mesopotamian legend. While flood stories as such do not have to be connected, the episode of the birds in Genesis viii. 6–12 is so close to the parallel passage in the XIth tablet of the Babylonian *Gilgamesh Epic*[11] that no doubt exists. The only other Babylonian testimony to these birds is that of the priest Berossus, about 300 B.C. That edition of the *Gilgamesh Epic* which contains the flood story is the latest; no copies earlier than 750 B.C. are known, though it was a traditional text, and the late form may well have been put in shape between 1200 and 1000 B.C. Parts of earlier editions survive, for its origins go back, at least in Sumerian, to the third millennium, but none of them is known to have contained any flood narrative. In the late edition it is a digression, and was inserted from another Sumero-Babylonian epic, known in its later forms from the hero of the flood, Atra-ḫasīs. The Sumerian prototype, of which one incomplete copy of about 1800 B.C. alone survives, is very concise and its account of the flood has no mention of birds.[12] The first Babylonian edition known, from copies of about 1600 B.C., is incomplete, but so far there is nothing about birds. The late Babylonian editions are similarly incomplete.[13] Thus the only surviving testimony to the most telling parallel happens to be later than the Biblical account, but nevertheless I hold that there is a certain dependence of the Hebrew writers on a Mesopotamian tradition. First, there is no dispute that the late Mesopotamian forms of the flood story are local developments of the earlier Sumerian accounts, and these we know from copies of about 1800 B.C. This virtually excludes any possible Amorite influence in the initial formation of the Mesopotamian tradition. Thus priority rests on the Mesopotamian side, where floods are an annual phenomenon. Secondly, it is inconceivable that the Hebrews as such influenced the development of Babylonian epics. There seem, then, to be only two ways of escape from acknowledging Hebrew borrowing. The one is to assert that both Sumerians and Amorites held independent flood traditions, and from the latter the episode of the birds passed to both Hebrews and Babylonians. I can think of no refutation of such a view, though it seems most improbable to me. Alternatively it could be argued that the Hebrew and Babylonian accounts go back to the event rather than to a common source of tradition. This is unacceptable to me for reasons to be explained later.

Neither in Mesopotamia nor in Palestine did the flood story stand alone. In Berossus ten long-reigning kings precede it. A similar tradition, but of nine kings, occurs on a bilingual fragment from Ashurbanipal's library. Several Sumerian tablets from about 1800 B.C. attest this line of kings, but either eight or ten in number, extending from the beginning of civilization to the flood.[14] The Sumerian prototype of the *Atra-ḫasīs Epic* lacks the kings, but describes the founding of the five cities in which they are said to have reigned. In Genesis, the ten long-lived patriarchs from Adam to Noah lead up to the flood. It appears certain to me that this is no coincidence, and since the Sumerian character of this traditional history assures priority on the Mesopotamian side, borrowing on the part of the Hebrews seems certain.

The creation narratives are altogether more difficult. We shall start from the beginning of the first biblical account. Much has been made of the similarity of the Hebrew *tᵉhôm* and the Babylonian Tiāmat in *Enūma Eliš*. Both are primaeval and watery. The etymological equivalence is of no consequence, since poetic allusions to cosmic battles in the Old Testament use *yām* and *tᵉhôm* indiscriminately. So far as the concept is concerned, the idea of a watery beginning was by no means the only Mesopotamian notion. There were three basic doctrines. According to the most commonly attested, earth came first and all else emerged in some way from this. Less commonly attested is the conception of primaeval water; and thirdly, time was considered the source and origin of all things. Earth in this cosmological sense is first attested about 2600 B.C. Water is not known before 2000, and time makes its first appearance about 1700 B.C. Since the evidence for all three is scanty, these dates have no absolute value. In contrast with these different Mesopotamian ideas, the ancient Egyptians quite generally acknowledged the god of the primaeval waters Nu (Nun) as the source of all things.[15] In early Greece there were different opinions, as in Mesopotamia, but Ocean is described as the father (γένεσις) of the gods in Homer,[16] and water is the prime element in the cosmologies of Thales and Anaximander. Thus the watery beginning of Genesis in itself is no evidence of Mesopotamian influence.

The activity of the second day is more explicit. God divided the cosmic waters into two parts on the vertical plane. Similarly in *Enūma Eliš* Marduk splits the body of Tiāmat. These seem to be the only two examples of the splitting of a body of water from the area and periods under discussion (apart from Berossus), so a parallel must be acknowledged. However, Gunkel and his followers have wanted to push the matter further. In *Enūma Eliš* a battle precedes the splitting, and since there are poetic allusions to a battle of Yahweh with the sea, it is urged that there is dependence on *Enūma Eliš,* and that a battle did precede the separation of the waters in earlier forms of the tradition recorded in Genesis i. This involves most intricate problems. This splitting, whether in *Enūma Eliš* or Genesis, is, of course, only a variant of the common mythological theme of the dividing of heaven and earth,[17] the only difference being that these two accounts involve water, not a solid mass. This separation of heaven and earth does not necessarily presume a conflict. There are three Sumerian versions,[18] and in none is the matter being cut asunder the body of a monster slain in battle. The whole process is peaceful: a job of work. In a version in the Hittite language a saw is used to do the cutting, not a weapon of war.[19] In Egypt, Shu pushes apart Nut, the heaven, and Geb, the earth, without any antecedent battle.[20] The doctrine of the world egg, as found in some forms of Phoenician[21] and Orphic[22] cosmogony, similarly involves a peaceful sundering.

Is there, then, good reason to presume a battle behind the second day of creation in Genesis? The poetic allusions nowhere speak of Yahweh splitting the sea, except for Ps. lxxiv. 13 in the traditional English rendering: 'Thou didst divide the sea by thy strength.' However, the meaning of פוֹרַרְתָּ has been disputed on purely lexicographical evidence, and an Arabic cognate favours rather: 'Thou didst set the sea in commotion.'[23] Thus the case for a battle as a prelude to God's dividing of the cosmic waters is unproven.

On the Mesopotamian side the matter is very confused. Tiāmat is not uniform in the *Epic of Creation*. At times she is presented as a solid-bodied monster, at other times as a mass of water. The author is conflating two traditions. Berossus combined the two traditions more systematically: he presents Tiāmat advancing against Marduk as a woman yet at the same moment as a body of water so that monsters are swimming inside her! To me this is obviously a combination of two ideas. The question is whether the separating of the body of water really belongs to the dragon-slaying episode, or is just hitched on, to the greater glory of Marduk. To answer this question we must survey briefly the Mesopotamian traditions of cosmic water. The only one known from the Sumerians pictured a watery goddess Nammu as the mother of heaven and earth and of all the gods. She, however, was not split and no battle with her is known of. Another view, associated especially with Marduk, makes the primaeval waters merely a substratum on which the earth was placed. In some cases the water was an impersonal, passive element, in other cases this sea had to be subjugated before the work of creation could be done on top of it. In either case there is no splitting: all the water stays below. Thus *Enūma Eliš* and Berossus have something unique so far in Mesopotamia. No other tradition of a watery beginning involves the separation.

One other aspect remains, the cultic. Although much that has been written on this subject is altogether wrong, there is good circumstantial evidence that Marduk defeated Tiāmat each New Year in the Akītu house of Babylon.[24] But this only applies to Babylon in the time of the Late Babylonian empire, not to any other Akītu house of any other city. There are only very scrappy hints about the precise conception of Tiāmat involved in this annual rite, but they all savour of underworld connexions, which means that concept of a sea beneath the earth, not of a sea both above and beneath. Too much has been made of the recitation of *Enūma Eliš* in the New Year rites. The epilogue contradicts the suggestion that it was written expressly for use in the month Nisan, and nothing in the formulation of the epic implies a specific cultic use.

We are left, then, with the fact that the sequence of the battle and the splitting of the cosmic waters may be only the result of conflation of no particular antiquity, and it is only one of two traditions associated with a single Mesopotamian god. *Enūma Eliš* is the first testimony to it. Thus neither on the Hebrew side nor on the Mesopotamian is there any clear proof that a battle is necessarily tied to the dividing of the waters. More generally, there is no proof that the conflict of a deity with the sea is of Mesopotamian origin. So far it is only known in the cult and literature of Babylon. It was an Amorite dynasty that made Babylon from an unimportant settlement into the capital of an empire, and it is always possible that they introduced the ideas into Mesopotamia. If so, the Babylonians were as much borrowers as the Hebrews.

To sum up discussion of the second day, there is one close parallel between Genesis and *Enūma Eliš*, but no evidence of Hebrew borrowing from Babylon.

The third day can be dealt with more briefly. God separates the sea from the dry land. My opinion is that the second and third days contain originally unrelated traditions, put in this sequence by the Hebrew author. Three clear poetic allusions refer to Yahweh's pushing back the cosmic waters from the land and defining their limits: Ps. civ. 6–9, Prov. viii. 29, and Job xxxviii. 8–11. A conflict is definitely involved. The last passage is the most explicit: the section occurs in a cosmological setting, and involves not simply the separation of sea and dry land, but tells of the waters breaking forth 'from the womb' and being forced back by God within fixed limits. There is a Mesopotamian parallel for this, connected with Ninurta, the Sumero-Babylonian god of war, who was, incidentally, the dragon-slayer of ancient Mesopotamia. The story goes that 'the mighty waters' began to rise and threatened to overwhelm the land, so Ninurta built a stone wall to hold them back until eventually they receded. Thereby Ninurta saved the land. This is part of a composite Sumerian myth first known from copies of about 1800 B.C., though later bilingual copies also survive. There seems to be an allusion to this one episode in Cylinder A of Gudea of Lagash (c. 2100 B.C.), who describes how he went into the house of Ninurta and prayed to him, beginning, 'Lord, who held back the savage waters. . . .'[25] This Mesopotamian story reads very much like an account of the annual flood projected on to the mythological plane. The parallel with the Hebrew material is striking, since these seem to be the only two narratives of a god holding back savage waters from the ancient Orient. It is true that the water is conceived somewhat differently in the Old Testament: there it is sea, a term not used of Ninurta's exploit. But if the account were of Mesopotamian origin and had been borrowed in Syria and Palestine, where there is no annual flood, it would be very natural for such a change to take place. Since it is a traditional Sumerian myth, it is quite possible that this is the correct explanation of the facts.

For me the seventh day of creation offers a still more convincing case. The sabbath has, of course, been the subject of much study, both the institution and the name. My own position, briefly, is that the Hebrew term *šabbāth*, meaning the completion of the week, and the Babylonian term *šapattu*, meaning the completion of the moon's waxing, that is, the fifteenth day of a lunar month, are the same word. But since there is no genuine Sumerian equivalent of, nor Babylonian etymology for, *šapattu*, and it first appears only about 1700 B.C., I believe that Hebrews and Babylonians depend on a similar Amorite source.[26] The attempt to find days of rest in the Mesopotamian calendars has hardly succeeded. There is, however, another approach to the question. The Hebrews left two explanations of the sabbath. The first is that of Gen. i–ii and Exod. xx, that it repeats cyclically what God did in the original week of creation. The second, in Deut. v, regards it as a repeated memorial of the Hebrews' deliverance from Egypt. This divergence suggests that historically the institution is older than the explanations. On this assumption the use of the week as the framework of a creation account is understandable as providing divine sanction for the institution, but unexpected in that God's resting hardly expresses the unlimited might and power that are His usual attributes: 'See, Israel's guardian neither slumbers nor sleeps.' It is generally assumed that the use of the week as the framework of the account simply required that God rest on the seventh day. But there is no compulsion to have a week of creation at all. Furthermore, this implies that the development of the doctrine of God's rest came from pure, deductive reasoning, which I doubt very much. The authors of ancient cosmologies were essentially compilers. Their originality was expressed in new combinations of old themes, and in new twists to old ideas. Sheer invention was not part of their craft. Thus when the author tells us that God rested, I believe he drew on a tradition to this effect. Therefore in seeking parallels to the seventh day, one must look not only for comparable institutions, but also for the idea of deities resting.

Here Mesopotamia does not fail us. The standard Babylonian account of man's creation is not found in *Enūma Eliš*, but in the *Atra-ḫasīs* epic. An earlier form of this myth occurs in the Sumerian *Enki and Ninmaḫ*. The essentials of the story are that the gods had to toil for their daily bread, and in response to urgent complaints man was created to serve the gods by providing them with food and drink. On the last point all the Mesopotamian accounts agree: man existed solely to serve the gods, and this was expressed practically in that all major deities at least had two meals set up before their statues each day. Accordingly, man's creation resulted in the gods' resting, and the myths reach a climax at this point. Even in *Enūma Eliš* this is clear, despite much conflation. At the beginning of Tablet VI Ea and Marduk confer on what is called 'the resting of the gods', and thereupon man is created and the gods are declared free from toil. This common Mesopotamian tradition thus provides a close parallel to the sixth and seventh days of creation. Since the particular concept of the destiny of man goes back to the Sumerians, but is unparalleled in other parts of the ancient Near East, ultimate borrowing by the Hebrews seems very probable.

These, in my opinion, are the significant points of similarity between Mesopotamian and Hebrew accounts of origins. Other scholars, from the time of George Smith and onwards, have attached importance to other points, though to me they are inconclusive.[27] No sure Babylonian parallels have yet been found even for the Tower of Babel or the kingdom of Nimrod.[28] We are left, then, with the succession of long-lived worthies culminating in the flood, perhaps God's holding back of the primaeval waters, and, more probably, God's rest. So far the similarities have been stressed, but the differences must not be overlooked. The Sumero-Babylonian tradition is of a line of kings from the founding of civilization to the flood, not of a line of patriarchs, the ancestors of the Hebrew nation, from creation onwards. In the one case the names are mostly Sumerian, but in the other Semitic, nor do they bear any kind of relationship to the corresponding name in the other series. The differences are indeed so great that direct borrowing of a literary form of Mesopotamian tradition is out of the question. But if the case for borrowing is to be established, at least a suggestion of the manner and time of transference must be made. The exile and the later part of the monarchy are out of the question, since this was the time when the Hebrew traditions of creation and the early history of mankind were being put in the form in which they were canonized. That the matters spoken of were included in Genesis is proof that they were long established among the Hebrews. Kaufmann has rightly argued that prophetic use of the traditions of Yahweh's battle with the sea implies that these traditions were therefore long established on Hebrew soil. Thus one is forced back at least to the time of the Judges, and even this may be too late. Also, knowledge of this time does not suggest that Babylonian myths and legends would have gained currency then if they were not established earlier. The present writer's opinion is that only the Amarna period has any real claim to be the period when this material moved westwards. This is the period when the Babylonian language and cuneiform script were the normal means of international communication between countries from Egypt to the Persian Gulf. From within this period the Hittite capital in Asia Minor has yielded a large quantity of fragments of Mesopotamian literature, both Sumerian and Babylonian, including the *Gilgamesh Epic*. A smaller quantity of similar material has been yielded by Ras Shamra, including a piece of the *Atra-ḫasīs Epic*. Megiddo has given up a piece of the *Gilgamesh Epic*,[29] and Amarna itself several pieces of Babylonian literary texts. This spread of Babylonian writings at this period of history is not only the result of the use of cuneiform writing for international communication, but also is owed to the cultural activities of the Hurrians, for they were great borrowers from all the peoples in which they moved and settled, so much so that they were rapidly absorbed and lost their identity. Thus in the Amarna age the Hittites had not only Babylonian and Sumerian literature in addition to native texts, but also works translated from West Semitic.[30] Cultural barriers were indeed broken down in Syria and adjacent lands at this time. Nor was knowledge of borrowed Mesopotamian works restricted to the small number of scribes competent in cuneiform. Among the Hittites the *Gilgamesh Epic* was available in both Hittite and Hurrian translations. Also that version of *Nergal and Ereshkigal* from Amarna is so completely different from the traditional Mesopotamian one in its wording as to give the impression that oral tradition alone will explain it.[31]

Earlier borrowing of the material is ruled out, in the present writer's opinion, because Genesis shows no knowledge of Mesopotamian matters prior to 1500 B.C., a point of considerable importance. The description of Nimrod's kingdom and the account of the Tower of Babel both presume a period when legends were clustering around the city of Babylon. Up to the sudden and unexpected rise of Babylon under Hammurabi (c. 1750 B.C.) it was an utterly unimportant and obscure place. One must surely allow a century or two before it could become the centre of legends about early times, as indeed it did in Mesopotamia by about 1200 B.C. Negatively the case is equally strong: Genesis shows no knowledge of Mesopotamian matters prior to about 1500. The very existence of the

Sumerians is nowhere hinted at. While the borrowing may have been something altogether more involved and complex than we have suggested, all the known facts favour the idea that the traditions moved westwards during the Amarna period and reached the Hebrews in oral form.

NOTES

1. In a paper read to the Society of Biblical Archaeology on 3 December 1872, which was printed in the *Transactions* of the Society the following year.
2. In a letter to the *Daily Telegraph*, 4 March 1875.
3. *CR*, V (1895), 256–66.
4. *JAOS*, XV (1893), 1ff.
5. *The Book of Genesis*, (1907), p. 30.
6. See W. G. Lambert, *Babylonian Wisdom Literature* (1960), pp. 12–13.
7. *Biblischer Kommentar, Altes Testament*, XV/1 (1960), 518.
8. *Das Alte Testament Deutsch*, Teilband 2, p. 38.
9. *JBL*, LXXXII (1963), 256.
10. L. W. King, *The Seven Tablets of Creation*. One of the best English translations, and the most convenient, is that of A. Heidel, *The Babylonian Genesis* (1963).
11. The most recent translations are: A. Schott and W. von Soden, *Das Gilgamesch-Epos* (1958); E. A. Speiser, *ANET* (1955), pp. 72–99; A. Heidel, *The Gilgamesh Epic and Old Testament Parallels* (1949).
12. The only translations of this are by A. Poebel, *Historical Texts* (1914), pp. 17–20; and by S. N. Kramer, *ANET* (1955), pp. 42–44.
13. See W. G. Lambert, 'New Light on the Babylonian Flood', *JSS*, V (1960), 113–23.
14. See T. Jacobsen, *The Sumerian King List* (1939), and J. J. Finkelstein and W. W. Hallo, both in *JCS*, XVII (1963), 39ff. and 52ff.
15. See H. Bonnet, *Reallexikon der ägyptischen Religionsgeschichte* (1952), pp. 535–36.
16. *Iliad*, XIV, 201.
17. See W. Staudacher, *Die Trennung von Himmel und Erde* (1942).
18. S. N. Kramer, *Sumerian Mythology* (1944), p. 37; T. Jacobsen, *JNES*, V (1946), 134; E. Ebeling, *ZDMG*, LXX (1916), 532; and A. Heidel, *The Babylonian Genesis*, p. 68.
19. H. G. Güterbock, *JCS*, VI (1952), 29, 52–54.
20. H. Bonnet, *Reallexikon*, pp. 685–89; R. T. Rundle Clark, *Myth and Symbol in Ancient Egypt* (1959), pp. 48–50, 250.
21. See H. W. Haussig, ed., *Wörterbuch der Mythologie*, I. Abteilung, Teil 1, pp. 309–10.
22. W. K. C. Guthrie, *Orpheus and Greek Religion* (1952), ch. 4.
23. So L. Koehler, *Lexicon in Veteris Testamenti Libros* (1953), p. 782.
24. W. G. Lambert, *Iraq*, XXV (1963), pp. 189–90.
25. A. Falkenstein and W. von Soden, *Sumerische und akkadische Hymnen und Gebete* (1953), p. 146.
26. The best discussion of this word is still that of B. Landsberger, *Der kultische Kalender der Babylonier und Assyrer* (1915), pp. 131–35.
27. A collection of such material is given by J. Plessis in *Dictionnaire de la Bible, Supplément*, ed. L. Pirot, (1928), pp. 714ff., and detailed comparisons of *Enūma Eliš* and Genesis have been made by A. Deimel, '*Enuma Eliš*' *und Hexaemeron* (1934), and by A. Heidel, *The Babylonian Genesis* (1963), ch. 3. Among the more recent and reputable suggestions of particular scholars the following may be noted. W. F. Albright in *JBL*, LXII (1943), 369, on the basis of the translation of Gen. i. 1, 'When God began to create . . .', proposed a definite borrowing from a Sumero-Babylonian 'When . . . then . . .' period. S. N.

Kramer, *Enki and Ninḫursag, A Sumerian 'Paradise' Myth* (*BASOR*, Supplementary Studies, no. 1, 1945), p. 9. Kramer suggests a connexion between the word play on the Sumerian homophones *ti*, 'life', and *ti*, 'rib' and the fashioning of Eve ('Life') from the rib of Adam. The relevance of this Sumerian myth for the location of Eden has been maintained by E. A. Speiser, 'The Rivers of Paradise', *Festschrift J. Friedrich* (1959), pp. 473–85. The name Eden itself has often been derived from the Sumerian *'edin*, 'open country, desert', though the *'ayin* is inexplicable, and the meaning unsuitable. Also the *'ēd* (of unknown meaning) in Gen. ii. 6 has been given at least two Mesopotamian etymologies, on which see most recently E. A. Speiser, *BASOR*, cxl (1955), 9–11. J. J. A. Van Dijk in *Acta Orientalia*, XXVIII (1964), 40–44, has pointed out a Sumerian parallel to the content of this part of Genesis.

28. E. A. Speiser in 'Word Plays on the Creation Epic's Version of the Founding of Babylon', *Orientalia*, XXV (1956), 317–23, put forward an ingenious theory of a literary derivation of the biblical episode of the Tower of Babel from the Babylonian *Enūma Eliš*. Also, in *Eretz-Israel*, V (1958), 22–36, he proposed that the biblical Nimrod is a dim reflection of the Assyrian king Tukulti-Ninurta I (*c.* 1240–1200 B.C.). The present writer prefers the more usual opinion that the Sumero-Babylonian war god Ninurta is meant.

29. A. Goetz and S. Levy, *'atiqot*, II (1959), 121–28.

30. H. G. Güterbock in S. N. Kramer, ed., *Mythologies of the Ancient World* (1961), pp. 143 and 155.

31. See O. R. Gurney, *Anatolian Studies*, X (1960), 107.

Roger L. Cox

Tragedy and the
Gospel Narratives

Among narrative forms in Western tradition, "tragedy" has consistently held the greatest prestige. Despite this, not only has it been denied that the Bible contains tragic narratives; it is the only literary form that has been considered opposed to Christianity itself. Roger L. Cox challenges that point of view.

The situation of the tragic hero is as true of Christ as of Oedipus. Tragedy is a "literary work, predominantly somber in tone, in which the main character encounters some significant misfortune for which he himself is partly, though not wholly, responsible." The key is "responsible." Antigone, Oedipus Rex, Hamlet, and the gospel accounts of Jesus portray the hero's suffering as necessary and the hero in some significant way responsible for it. The Crucifixion is the central event of the gospels. Christ is presented as an agent of destiny who is yet free to embrace that destiny.

Cox sees the literary form relative to the writer and his purpose in writing. Literary influence between Greek plays and the gospels is not at stake. The analysis of tragedy has implications for the larger literary forms in Scripture.

P HILOSOPHERS, literary critics, and theologians often contradict each other's conclusions, but upon one matter they have reached almost universal agreement—that there can be no such thing as "Christian tragedy." In _Tragedy Is Not Enough_, Karl Jaspers asserts that "no genuinely Christian tragedy can exist," and he further claims that "what is essential to the Christian cannot even emerge in tragedy." Walter Kaufmann's _Critique of Religion and Philosophy_ denies that the book of Job is tragic and insists that there can never be "any Jewish or Christian tragedy." Richard Sewall, in _The Vision of Tragedy_, relegates to footnotes (presumably because they are almost self-evident) such statements as this: "Christian tragedy, to put it briefly, is not Christian; if it were, it

From Roger L. Cox, _Yale Review_, 57 (1968), 545–70.

would not be tragedy." And Edmond Cherbonnier contends in an article called "Biblical Faith and the Idea of Tragedy" that "at nearly every point [biblical philosophy] stands in flat contradiction to tragedy." Many thoughtful people share such a view, including Reinhold Niebuhr, who sums it up clearly and finally in his statement, "Christianity stands beyond tragedy." These assertions admit of no qualification; they totally exclude Christian literature from the category of tragedy.

When we contemplate a play which nearly everyone regards as belonging to the most select company of tragic dramas and we strongly suspect that the world view which it embodies is genuinely and specifically Christian, we wonder whether the claims of Jaspers and others are actually true. Do their statements have the status of fact, supported by a staggering amount of empirical evidence? Are they generalizations which, though they cannot be absolutely proven, seem to be justified by what evidence we have? Or, are they statements of private belief by men better acquainted with Christian doctrine than with tragic literature, or the reverse? If these statements are true, we should be able to verify them; and if we cannot verify them, we should hesitate to accept them unqualifiedly. They are not, after all, articles of faith—they are merely conclusions as to the relationship between Christianity and literature.

A persistent doubt about the assertion that no literary work can be both Christian and tragic leads to the more basic question, are not the gospel narratives themselves fundamentally tragic stories? They certainly seem so to the disinterested observer—the main character, who possesses both courage and integrity, conducts his life as he believes he must, even in the face of overwhelming opposition; and as a direct result of this behavior, he is put to death. Indeed, the similarity of the gospel narratives to the pattern of tragedy is so obvious that we wonder why no one has ever seriously advanced such an interpretation. We also wonder, since no one has done so at all systematically, why Jaspers and Niebuhr take such pains to deny that the gospel stories are tragic in any significant sense. In discussing "failure" as an aspect of tragedy, Jaspers remarks that "Christ is the deepest symbol of failure in this world, yet he is in no sense tragic." And Niebuhr observes that "Jesus is, superficially considered, a tragic figure; yet not really so." Against whom and to what purpose are they arguing? They are apparently asserting that appearances are deceptive and that their conception of tragedy is incompatible with their interpretation of the New Testament. But they fail to convince anyone (except persons who already agree with them) that *any* valid conception of tragedy inevitably conflicts with *any* serious view of the New Testament.

As we read their arguments, we soon notice the strongly partisan tone of those who most energetically deny the possibility of any Christian tragedy; each one is doing his best to show either that tragedy is "superficial" when compared to the Christian gospel, or else that Christianity, because it offers the believer a "way out" of any desperate situation, never really comes to grips with tragic conflict. Edmond Cherbonnier creates the impression that only a dilettante, who relishes emotions which are "to be savored by the connoisseur for their psychological effect," can respond sympathetically to literary tragedy. And Walter Kaufmann, with equal sarcasm, takes the opposite position: "By what is today called religion one cannot live, nor could one die for it. How much more profound is the outlook of the great tragic poets! What is there to prevent a man from living and dying like Antigone?" Cherbonnier seems serenely confident that no Christian will merely "savor" Christ's suffering and death from a comfortable distance, secure in the knowledge that his sacrifice was all-sufficient; and Kaufmann fails to indicate how it happens that Antigone can show us the way to live and die when Christ cannot. Obviously, both men are passionate believers, and each scoffs at what the other believes in. Since both are concerned to assert the superiority of their own positions, both feel compelled to demonstrate the supposed differences between Christianity and tragedy; and, as one might expect, both conclude that there can be no such thing as Christian tragedy.

The belief that Christianity and tragedy are mutually exclusive has a highly unfortunate double effect: the Christian, consciously or unconsciously, avoids the tragic implications of the gospel narratives; and the skeptic who admires tragedy is confirmed in thinking that the Christian takes a facile and unrealistic view of the world. The believer who sees nothing really tragic in Christ's suffering is not disquieted by the words, "Whoever does not bear his own cross and come after me, cannot be my disciple" (Luke 14:27, RSV; cf. Matt. 10:38 and 16:24, Mark 8:34, Luke 9:23). The command "Render therefore to Caesar the things that are Caesar's, and to God the things that are God's" (Matt. 22:21, Mark 12:17, Luke 20:25) holds no terror for him, because he somehow assumes that Caesar and God will never make contradictory demands upon him as Creon and the Greek gods did upon Antigone—or as political authority and religious imperative did upon Jesus himself. And Christ's words upon the cross, "My God, my God, why hast thou forsaken me?" (Matt. 27:46, Mark 15:34) seem to reflect only momentary discouragement, since we all know that the resurrection soon makes everything right again.

Since the confusion about Christianity and tragedy thrives upon partisanship—acceptance of Christianity and rejection of tragedy, or vice versa—it should not be surprising that a key to understanding the problem should come from a man whose primary interest was neither religious nor literary. I refer to Sigmund Freud's brief discussion of tragedy in *Totem and Taboo*. His remarks about "the oldest Greek tragedy" are highly significant and should be quoted verbatim rather than paraphrased (A. A. Brill translation):

A group of persons, all of the same name and dressed in the same way, surround a single figure upon whose words and actions they are dependent, to represent the chorus and the original single impersonator of the hero. Later developments created a second and a third actor in order to represent opponents in playing, and off-shoots of the hero, but the character of the hero as well as his relation to the chorus remains unchanged. The hero of the tragedy had to suffer; this is today still the essential content of a tragedy. He had taken upon himself the so-called "tragic guilt," which is not always easy to explain; it is often not a guilt in the ordinary sense. Almost always it consisted of a rebellion against a divine or human authority and the chorus accompanied the hero with their sympathies, trying to restrain and warn him, and lamented his fate after he had met with what was considered fitting punishment for his daring attempt.

But why did the hero of the tragedy have to suffer, and what was the meaning of his "tragic" guilt? We will cut short the discussion by a prompt answer. He had to suffer because he was the primal father, the hero of that primordial tragedy the repetition of which here serves a certain tendency, and the tragic guilt is the guilt which he had to take upon himself in order to free the chorus of theirs. The scene upon the stage came into being through purposive distortion of the historical scene or, one is tempted to say, it was the result of refined hypocrisy. Actually, in the old situation, it was the members of the chorus themselves who had caused the suffering of the hero; here, on the other hand, they exhaust themselves in sympathy and regret, and the hero himself is to blame for his suffering. The crime foisted upon him, namely, presumption and rebellion against a great authority, is the same as that which in the past oppressed the colleagues of the chorus, namely, the band of brothers. Thus the tragic hero, though still against his will, is made the redeemer of the chorus.

When one bears in mind the suffering of the divine goat Dionysos in the performance of the Greek tragedy and the lament of the retinue of goats who identified themselves with him, one can easily understand how the almost extinct drama was reviewed [*sic*] in the Middle Ages in the Passion of Christ.

Though his discussion is helpful, there are at least two ambiguities in the tragic situation which Freud apparently misses. One of these is reflected in his statement that "the tragic hero, *though still against his will*, is made the redeemer of the chorus." In Greek tragedy the hero frequently becomes the instrument for "punishing" himself—Antigone hangs herself, and Oedipus puts out his own eyes. This being the case, it does not quite make sense to say that the hero acts "against his will" in doing so. It would be far more accurate to say that the hero *voluntarily though reluctantly* becomes the redeemer of the chorus. Unless we make this qualification, we get into an absurd discussion like the one in Act V of *Hamlet,* where the gravediggers argue about whether or not Ophelia "drowned herself wittingly." Affecting an academic tone, the clown argues in this manner:

Give me leave. Here lies the water—good. Here stands the man—good. If the man go to this water and drown himself, it is, will he nill he, he goes, mark you that. But if the water come to him and drown him, he drowns not himself. Argal, he that is not guilty of his own death shortens not his own life.

Because Ophelia was mad, it is true that she did not have her wits about her when she drowned herself. But we certainly cannot argue about whether or not Oedipus "put out his eyes wittingly." There is no question of insanity, and there is no question of the brooches' coming to him and putting out his eyes "against his will." Even Walter Kaufmann, who has no interest in revising such a statement as this one of Freud's to make it fit the passion narrative, says that "the downfall and death of the tragic hero was originally, if we remember the genesis of tragedy, a self-sacrifice. The guilt which the hero takes upon himself transcends his own person: by accepting the guilt as his own and paying for it with his own destruction he sacrifices himself for others." The other ambiguity, which involves the hero's being "to blame for his suffering," we shall consider fully in a moment. With these two qualifications, Freud's discussion is both illuminating and accurate.

When those who deny the possibility of Christian tragedy attempt to describe the main features of tragic drama, their generalizations apply at least as well to the gospel narratives as they do to any literary tragedy. Ironically, this happens just as surely when the skeptic (Kaufmann) tries to analyze tragedy to show why it is more meaningful than Christianity as it does when the Christian (Niebuhr, Cherbonnier) tries to differentiate tragedy from Christianity to show the latter's superiority. Only by juxtaposing representative tragedies and the gospel narratives without any attempt to demonstrate that one is superior to the other, whether in kind or merely in degree, can we gain real insight into the intimate connections between the two. By this procedure we can begin to evaluate the claim, which we hear on every side, that there can be no such thing as Christian tragedy.

A "tragedy" is a literary work, predominantly somber in tone, in which the main character encounters some significant misfortune for which he himself is partly, though not wholly, responsible. If misfortune is treated comically throughout, then the somber tone is lost, and the work is not tragic no matter what the degree of the main character's responsibility. Unless the protagonist encounters significant misfortune, the plot of the work would be indistinguishable from that of pure comedy; and unless the main character is partly though not entirely responsible, his misfortune would be indistinguishable from sheer accident on the one hand and from quite reasonable punishment on the other. That is to say, tragedy deals basically with the timeless problem of necessary injustice; and since it involves the *mis*fortune of a person who is at least partly good rather than anyone's *unmerited good* fortune, it deals with necessary suffering. The human condition is such that when human suffering is seen in a literary work to be the product of absolute necessity, it affords some insight, some liberation—if not to the hero, at least to the audience. This insight or liberation is apparently what Aristotle means by "catharsis" and what Jaspers means by "transcendence."

Most misunderstandings about tragedy arise from a failure to comprehend the fundamentally double meaning of two terms in the preceding paragraph, the first of which is "responsible." When we say that an individual is "responsible" for something, we are designating his action as a cause, but we are not indicating whether that cause is *sufficient* or merely *necessary*. The difference here leads to whether or not we attach blame to the person in question. For example, Antigone's determination to bury her brother Polyneices leads directly to her suffering, but it does so only because Creon has declared that anyone who buries Polyneices must die. Her action is therefore a necessary but not a sufficient cause of her suffering, since under other circumstances her insistence upon the rite of burial for her brother could only be regarded as the proper fulfillment of a religious duty. As she says in one of her final speeches, "I stand convicted of impiety, / the evidence my pious duty done" (lines 924–25, translated by Elizabeth Wyckoff). Similarly, Oedipus suffers because of his determination to discover the identity of Laius' murderer and thereby free his people from the plague. It is only proper that he as head of government should do this, but the fact (unknown to him at the time) that he himself is the murderer functions in this play, just as Creon's edict does in *Antigone,* to create a situation in which his admirable determination to do right leads to his own suffering.

Let us analyze these two illustrations of "responsibility" more closely. *Antigone* and *Oedipus the King* both involve three significant elements, and the differences of construction result from the manner in which these elements are combined or separated within each of the two plays. Both works contain (1) a virtuous act by the protagonist, (2) an act which is an offense against the state, and (3) an edict which is designed to punish that offense. There are, moreover, three chief differences between the plays. First, in *Antigone* elements 1 and 2 are combined—Antigone's virtuous act (burying her brother) *is* an act which is an offense against the state—whereas in *Oedipus the King* elements 1 and 3 are combined—Oedipus' virtuous act as chief of state *is* the proclamation of an edict which is designed to punish an offense against the state. Second, as a consequence of the first difference, in *Antigone* a separate character (Creon) must be introduced into the play to proclaim the edict, whereas in *Oedipus* the protagonist performs this function himself. Hence, some people have mistakenly concluded that Creon is the main character in *Antigone;* Creon may be potentially a tragic hero, but he is *not* the hero of Sophocles' *Antigone.* Third, also as a consequence of the first difference, in *Antigone* element 3 (the edict) is beyond the control of the protagonist, whereas in *Oedipus* element 2 (the offense against the state) is beyond the protagonist's conscious control—he simply does not know that he is guilty of the offense. This third difference makes *Antigone* a battle of wills (Antigone versus Creon), while *Oedipus* represents a struggle for self-knowledge. In both cases, however, the protagonist performs at the beginning of the play an act which leads directly to his own suffering, and in both cases that act springs from a virtue, not a "fault." The character is therefore "responsible" for his suffering—he causes it, but he is not "to blame" for it. (Hence the ambiguity which Freud fails to recognize.)

The other term which involves double meaning is "necessary." This word points specifically to the tension which exists between the poles of fate on the one hand and personal choice on the other, between external and internal causes, between destiny and freedom. "Necessary" suffering results when the protagonist makes a decision (often a forced decision), and one of the alternatives leads directly to suffering while the other, which would normally be open to him, is eliminated because it would require him to deny his own identity. Using the same illustrations as before, we see that Antigone might easily have avoided suffering simply by denying her obligation to Polyneices—that is, by denying her identity as his sister. This, of course, is what Ismene does; and consequently she does not suffer in the same manner as Antigone, nor does she attain Antigone's heroic stature.

In *Oedipus the King* the situation is more complex, but the relationship between fate and freedom is fundamentally the same. The events which are regarded as inevitable or fated (the hero's killing his father and marrying his mother) are represented as having taken place in the remote past. Thus, they are utterly beyond the power of human beings to do anything about them. But the hero lives happily and prosperously for a long time afterward. His downfall and the tragedy itself result not merely from these events, but from the attitude which he takes toward them. When he carries through his determination to know all about the events over which he now has no control, Jocasta begs him, "O be persuaded by me, I entreat you; / do not do this." But Oedipus replies, "I will not be persuaded to let be / the chance of finding out the whole thing clearly" (lines 1064–65, David Grene's translation). Everyone urges him to leave well enough alone, not to bring down upon himself and Thebes the consequences of such a discovery; but he forces the truth out of all concerned: Jocasta, Tiresias, and the herdsman who disposed of the baby. In short, though the events which are the background for the action of the play are "inevitable," the hero's fall and the tragedy itself come about because Oedipus finds it "necessary" to pursue the knowledge which is his undoing. He cannot do otherwise without denying his identity—such is the case by definition, since the knowledge which he feels compelled to pursue *is* the knowledge of his own identity.

When we turn to Shakespearean tragedy, we find that though the structure of one tragedy is always different from that of any other, the content remains essentially the same. Hamlet, like Oedipus and Antigone, could easily avoid the whole tragic situation. He might simply ignore the ghost's commands and return to Wittenberg, but such an alternative would require him to deny his identity as the elder Hamlet's son. Also, it is precisely the meaning of Hamlet's apology to Laertes that Hamlet is "responsible" for what has happened in the limited sense which we have been describing—he has *caused* the suffering which the play represents, but he is not completely "to blame" for it: "If Hamlet from himself be ta'en away, / And when he's not himself does wrong Laertes, / Then Hamlet does it not, Hamlet denies it. / Who does it then? His madness" (V, ii, 223–26). Yet this apology has been so widely misunderstood that one nineteenth-century critic (E. H. Seymour, 1805) concluded that the passage was an interpolation because "the falsehood contained in it is too ignoble."

In *King Lear*, the protagonist (without fully realizing that he does so) denies his identity at the very beginning of the play by resigning his position as king and father because of his desire "To shake the cares and business from our age, / Conferring them on younger strengths while we / Unburdened crawl toward death" (I, i, 39–41). He soon discovers that he cannot abdicate in this manner and still retain "The name, and all th' addition to a king" (I, i, 136); and the rest of the play is devoted to the suffering he encounters in trying to reclaim his former identity. Because he is not compelled to abdicate, he might easily have avoided the whole situation; but because he does abdicate, he may be said to cause the suffering he encounters. It is also true, however, that his willful abdication is not a sufficient cause of his suffering, since that suffering is created in part by his daughters' reaction, which is completely beyond his conscious control and his ability to predict. In this respect, Cordelia's rigid truthfulness and innocence contribute no less directly to the suffering than do Goneril and Regan's hypocrisy and greed, even though it is finally Cordelia who "redeems nature from the general curse / Which twain have brought her to" (IV, vi, 202–03).

Some critics have argued that modern plays, such as Arthur Miller's *Death of a Salesman,* are bound to fall short of genuine tragedy because contemporary audiences reject the idea of human greatness, certainly, at least, in connection with a man like Willy Loman. But tragedy appeals to something far deeper in man than the conscious attitude which he holds at any given moment toward his fellow human beings and their potential for greatness. Such attitudes change from year to year and from generation to generation. If we judge *Death of a Salesman* to be less than tragic, it is because we are not convinced that Willy Loman's suffering is in fact necessary. That is, when Willy dies, we are not willing to say of him, as

Horatio does of Hamlet, "Now cracks a noble heart." In that statement, the word "noble" has little or nothing to do with Hamlet's being the son of a king—its meaning is generated in the course of the play, not imposed at the beginning by giving Hamlet the title of prince. We acquiesce in Horatio's judgment because we have witnessed the whole play and have found the protagonist's dilemma to be realistic and genuine, one that he could not have avoided except by turning his back on the situation he encounters and thereby denying his own (perfectly believable and apparently creditable) identity. If no literary work is now being produced that we can accept as tragedy, it is purely and simply because there is, at the moment, no writer who is capable of convincing us that the suffering of a particular character in a particular play or novel is really necessary in the sense we have been describing. Such writers have always been few and far between; but if we decide in advance that there can no longer be such a writer, we will be incapable of recognizing him when and if he does appear.

From this analysis it begins to be clear that several of the widely received generalizations about tragedy are meaningless or misleading. Karl Jaspers asserts, for instance, that "Absolute and radical tragedy means that there is no way out whatsoever." Because the world operates in terms of cause and effect, there is some truth to this statement; but it really tells us nothing about the essential nature of tragedy. Jocasta and Tiresias repeatedly offer Oedipus a "way out," and each time he refuses to take it. What is the function of Ismene's role in *Antigone* if not to show that there is a very simple "way out" for the protagonist? Why is Hamlet so distressed at his failure "to be" if indeed "not to be" is an avenue which is completely closed to him? And why is Lear's abdication represented as being so arbitrary if in fact he cannot do otherwise? If Jaspers means that once the causes are established, then the effects must follow, what he is saying is true though perfectly obvious. If, however, he means that not only the effects but also the causes are completely beyond the control of the characters in tragedy, then what he is saying is simply false. Misfortunes that befall someone when the causes are completely beyond his control are not tragic but pathetic. Unless the main character is in some significant sense "responsible" for the suffering which according to Freud is the "essential content of a tragedy," the pain (like that of a toothache) is simply meaningless, not tragic from a literary viewpoint. Jaspers' statement that "absolute and radical tragedy means that there is no way out whatsoever" is true only when we add the words "unless the protagonist irrevocably denies or abandons his identity."

Moreover, the Aristotelian doctrine of *hamartia* is completely misleading. Classicists are beginning to reexamine it after centuries of trying to discover the "flaw" in Greek tragic characters. In his book *Story Patterns in Greek Tragedy,* Richmond Lattimore says, "I find, of the thirty-two extant plays, fifteen in which the Tragic Fault has little or nothing to do with the main action, and ten more where one could establish it as a major theme only by straining the dramatic facts." Interestingly, Sophocles' *Antigone* and Euripides' *Hippolytus* are two of the plays to which, according to Lattimore, the *hamartia* doctrine may be said to apply. Of *Antigone* he says, "The Chorus charges the heroine with the fault of stubbornness. She is stubborn. It destroys her, of course, but it is not in the whole view seen as weakness, fault, or flaw. Few, certainly, will argue that this is meant to be Antigone's inner weakness which destroys her." Of *Hippolytus* he writes, "Euripides shows the flaw of self-satisfaction and pedantry in the young hero, but I am not sure he means to. He could equally well be trying—as Sophocles may be in *Ajax*—to show a man too good for the world he lives in; and what the world does to such a man." Lattimore indicates that the word *hamartia* as used by Aristotle in the *Poetics* "cannot signify a permanent characteristic in a person, pride, quickness to anger, etc., but must refer to a mistaken or wrong act or to a mistake that has been made." He concurs with Else in thinking that "Aristotle, in his context, must be talking about something much more narrow and specific, namely, the misidentification of a person."

This reinterpretation of *hamartia* is not very helpful though—what "misidentification of a person" is there in *Antigone* or *Hippolytus*? And how, if at all, does such a view illuminate those works as tragedies? The problem cannot be solved merely by redefining a word in Aristotle's *Poetics*, because the difficulty is much deeper than that. The doctrine of *hamartia* is simply an attempt to take into account the obvious fact that the protagonist is partly though not entirely responsible for the suffering which is essential to tragedy. This particular attempt is bound to be unsuccessful because it seeks to reconcile the meaningfulness of tragedy with the assumption that we live in a non-tragic world. Aristotle apparently takes it for granted that in the real world virtue always produces happiness, and evil conduct or error inevitably leads to suffering. If, in a literary tragedy, an apparently good man suffers, then it must be because of some *hamartia*, peculiar to him as an individual. Whether we take *hamartia* to mean "tragic fault" or simply "misidentification of a person," the conception still rests on the idea that the hero somehow blunders in a way that a really virtuous man ought to be able to avoid, and he is therefore "to blame" for the suffering which his action partly causes. The moralistic nature of Aristotle's thought emerges very clearly in a sentence which appears in the same section of the *Poetics* as the *hamartia* statement: "Good and just men are not to be represented as falling from happiness into misery; for such a spectacle does not arouse fear or pity in us—it is simply revolting" (Lane Cooper's translation). It follows from this that unless we can find some kind of *hamartia* in such characters as Antigone and Hippolytus, the plays in which they appear are not tragedies at all—just revolting spectacles. But Antigone speaks the un-varnished truth when she says, "I stand convicted of impiety, / the evidence my pious duty done." And Artemis is correct when she tells Hippolytus, "The nobility of your soul has proved your ruin" (line 1390, David Grene's translation). Aristotle derives the *hamartia* doctrine not from the tragedies but from his own moral views, and the fact remains that no moralizing can ever touch the real meaning of tragedy. As Walter Kaufmann rightly observes, "Tragedy occurs where men have come to see that even an exemplary devotion to love, truth, justice, and integrity cannot safeguard a man against guilt."

In attempting to describe the nature of tragedy, we are forced back to our own statement, that characterizes any given tragedy as "a literary work, predominantly somber in tone, in which the main character encounters some significant misfortune for which he himself is partly, though not wholly, responsible." Tragedy centers upon the idea of "necessary suffering," and we must bear in mind the essentially double meaning of the two words, "responsible" and "necessary." The suffering which tragedy represents is neither accidental nor inevitable; the hero's action is, to be sure, one cause of that suffering, but the effect goes far beyond what we can explain by means of that one cause. Nevertheless, the hero accepts the suffering voluntarily though reluctantly. He takes the guilt upon himself, and in so doing he "frees the chorus of theirs."

Let us turn now to the gospel narratives and analyze them in a way which will allow us to compare their content with the content of literary tragedies. The central event recorded in the gospels is the crucifixion, and it is here that the obvious similarity to the tragic pattern lies. When St. Paul reduces his message to its simplest form, it is this event which he emphasizes: "When I came to you, brethren, I did not come proclaiming to you the testimony of God in lofty words or wisdom. For I decided to know nothing among you except Jesus Christ and him crucified" (I Cor. 2:1–2). Whatever else it may also have been, the crucifixion was for Christ a "significant misfortune," which he accepted "voluntarily though reluctantly." This fact is clearly revealed in his Gethsemane prayer: "My Father, if it be possible, let this cup pass from me; nevertheless, not as I will, but as thou wilt" (Matt. 26:39; cf. Mark 14:36, Luke 22:42). Peter, upon whom the church is built (Matt. 16:18), thought the events leading up to the crucifixion so disastrous that he three times denied having any connection with Jesus (recorded in all four gospels). The crucifixion involves a self-sacrifice which, from the Christian viewpoint, redeems all who believe in Christ. In this sense, the words of John the Baptist, "Behold, the Lamb of God, who takes away the sin of the world!" (John 1:29) seem closely related to Freud's statement that the protagonist in tragedy takes the guilt upon himself "in order to free the chorus of theirs." All this seems relatively obvious. Our task will be to establish whether, according to the gospel writers, Jesus himself was "partly though not wholly responsible" for the crucifixion, whether the suffering he underwent was "necessary" in the sense we have described, and (as a separate matter) whether the resurrection destroys or even significantly diminishes the tragic meaning of that event.

According to all four gospel writers, Jesus repeatedly predicted his own suffering and death, but all four of them treat the effect of these predictions in a way that seems strange at first. Both Mark and Luke record the predictions in completely unambiguous terms and then add the words: "But they [the disciples] did not understand the saying, and they were afraid to ask him" (Mark 9:30–32, Luke 9:44–45, 18:31–34). Matthew makes the same point dramatically rather than narratively— after Christ makes his prediction, Peter exclaims, "God forbid, Lord! This shall never happen to you"; and Jesus responds, "Get behind me, Satan! You are a hindrance to me; for you are not on the side of God, but of men" (Matt. 16:21–23). John treats the matter least directly of all, and, as narrator, he gets ahead of his story in doing so. He offers Christ's statement about the rebuilding of the temple in three days as a prediction of his death and resurrection, and then says, "When therefore he was raised from the dead, his disciples remembered that he had said this; and they believed the scripture and the word which Jesus had spoken" (John 2:18–22). Furthermore, according to Luke, it is only *after* the crucifixion and resurrection that Jesus flatly declares that his suffering and death were in fact "necessary": "And he said to them, 'O foolish men, and slow of heart to believe all that the prophets have spoken! Was it not necessary that the Christ should suffer these things and enter into his glory?' And beginning with Moses and all the prophets, he interpreted to them in all the scriptures the things concerning himself" (Luke 24:25–27). Likewise, it is after the fact that Peter is represented as saying that Jesus was "delivered up according to the definite plan and foreknowledge of God" (Acts 2:23).

This manner of proceeding raises the question, why did the gospel writers insist first of all upon the fact that Christ made these predictions and at the same time upon the disciples' refusal to believe them until much later? The answer is perfectly clear. The gospel narrators were striving to present Christ as the agent of destiny and yet to preserve his freedom in embracing that destiny. They sought to convince their readers that his self-sacrifice was of cosmic significance and that it was at the same time freely offered. In order to do this, they had to show that the disciples arrived at such an understanding of Christ's role only retrospectively, whereas Christ himself was fully conscious of this destiny at a much earlier point.

This attitude of the gospel writers has very interesting implications. It means, for instance, that from their point of view Christ conducted his life with full consciousness of his destiny, and that when he took decisive action, knowing what the consequences would be, he acted in a way to *fulfill* that destiny, not to avoid it. (Compare Oedipus' flight from Corinth in an effort to escape his fate.) The extent to which one acts with consciousness of the probable results is precisely the measure of one's freedom. And the greater one's freedom in acting, the greater the responsibility for what happens. Thus, paradoxically, Christ is in a highly significant way represented as being "responsible" for his own crucifixion, though he dreaded that event, though "his sweat became like great drops of blood falling down upon the ground" in Gethsemane (Luke 22:44), and though he prayed that "this cup might pass from him." At the same time, of course, one cannot say that he was "fully responsible," for the obvious reason that it was people's reaction to Christ which finally determined the catastrophic conclusion—in different circumstances, his behavior would not have led to his crucifixion. That is to say, Christ's action as a whole was a necessary but not a sufficient cause of his suffering and death; or, in other words, Christ is represented in the gospels as being partly though not fully responsible for the significant misfortune which he encounters.

This conclusion is no trick of argument or rhetoric; it is an undeniable corollary of the gospel writers' attitude. Indeed, it is the ordinary, traditional mode of thinking which contains the trick of argument. That line of thought runs this way: the tragic hero's responsibility for what happens to him is to be explained in *moral* terms, by his *hamartia*—and this *hamartia* is of course some kind of "fault" or "error"; Christ has no "fault" and he commits no "error"; therefore, he is not a tragic figure. Strangely, no one who endorses this kind of thinking seems bothered by the obvious implication that if this is so, then Christ has no responsibility whatever for what happens to him, in which case he is the protagonist in the most naturalistic story ever written, crushed by forces he finds it utterly impossible to control or to avoid. Such a view makes Christ "non-tragic" not by placing him *above* the tragic level, but by reducing him far below it. It takes him out of the tragic realm and makes him merely pathetic. No believer, I think, would be willing to accept this view, and yet it follows necessarily from the denial of Christ's partial responsibility for his own crucifixion. And any believer who insists, on the contrary, that Christ was totally *free* (and therefore, of course, totally responsible for his own crucifixion) misses the whole point. The people crucified Jesus not because he was the son of God, but because from their point of view his claiming to be the son of God was blasphemy, pure and simple (Matt. 26:65–66; Luke 22:70–71).

At least two other points need to be stressed—first, the question which Freud articulates when he asks, "But why did the hero of the tragedy have to suffer?" and second, the more technical meaning of the word "necessary," as opposed to "accidental" on the one hand and "inevitable" on the other. For our purposes it will not be sufficient merely to quote the words of Jesus in which he *says* that it was "necessary that the Christ should suffer these things." Our task is rather to show the basis for that assertion and why the gospel writers considered it an essential part of the story.

Freud's answer to his own question about the necessity for the tragic hero's suffering is very simple: "He had to suffer because he was the primal father." It might be objected that this answer is not very helpful because it leads to the further question, "But why did the primal father have to suffer?" Nevertheless, as far as it goes, Freud's statement applies beautifully to the gospel narratives. It calls to mind the words of Jesus, "I and the Father are one" (John 10:30); and it drives home the point that it was this claim, which Jesus refused to withdraw even before the high priest, that led to his conviction in the eyes of the Jews. Thus, from the believer's viewpoint, Christ has to suffer as the result of a chain of facts: he was put to death because he would not renounce his claim to being the son of God; and he could not renounce that claim because he actually was God's son.

Such a chain of facts does not imply, however, that Christ's suffering was either accidental or inevitable. Because Jesus was at least partly responsible for what happened, his suffering cannot be described as accidental. The emphasis which the gospel writers place upon Christ's being an agent of destiny precludes this possibility. They make it perfectly clear that Christ knew his course of action would lead directly to a collision with the authorities—hence the predictions of his suffering and death. But on the other hand, the collision was not inevitable, because Jesus was at all times free to abandon his mission—that is, to deny his identity as the son of God. This indeed is the meaning of his being tempted in the wilderness (Matt. 4; Luke 4). Such a denial was the only "way out" for him; but unless we allow him that one, we assert that his self-sacrifice was not freely given. In other words, we deny the meaning of the gospel itself. There was in fact no way whatsoever that he could have avoided the crucifixion and retained his identity as the Christ.

Furthermore, we cannot argue that though there may have been no other way out for him as he faced suffering and death, by his doing so he provided one for us, since his sacrifice was all-sufficient. If that were the case, it would hardly be necessary, as Jesus said it was, for anyone to "take up his cross daily" in order to follow Christ (Luke 9:23). Nor can we argue that he transcends the crucifixion by means of the resurrection, and that therefore the whole series of events is no longer tragic. One of the categorical statements which Jaspers makes is this one: "*There is no tragedy without transcendence*" (italicized in Jaspers' text). If so, it would appear that the resurrection, far from diminishing the tragic character of those events, is one of the features which mark them as genuinely tragic, since without the resurrection the crucifixion would be meaningless—we would probably never have heard of it. (As St. Paul says, "If Christ has not been raised, then our preaching is in vain and your faith is in vain," I Cor. 15:14.) Such a line of argument defines tragedy right out of existence, because it asserts that *without* transcendence these events remain below the level of tragedy, and *with* transcendence they stand above the tragic level. At this rate there is no such thing as tragedy—a position which neither Jaspers nor anyone else attempts to defend.

The content of the gospel narratives thus lends itself to precisely the same kind of analysis as does the content of literary tragedy because both Christianity and tragedy spring from the problem of unmerited but necessary suffering. *For the moralist,* suffering which goes far beyond anything the sufferer may be said to deserve is ultimately meaningless; and its narrative or dramatic representation is, in Aristotle's words, a "revolting spectacle." Unless he can somehow convince himself that the punishment fits the crime, the moralist will be uncomfortable. But tragedy has as its center figures like Antigone and Hippolytus, Hamlet and Lear, who suffer and who cause others to suffer in a way which cannot be explained simply in terms of what any of them deserve; and Christianity has at its center a suffering God. That is, both tragedy and Christianity perceive a meaning in unmerited but necessary suffering which is bound to escape the moralist. Since the Christian clings to belief and hope no matter what happens, he, instead of being immune to tragic experience, is peculiarly susceptible to it, because the number of things which he can dismiss as meaningless is greatly reduced. To him, any disaster which brings suffering and death to his fellow human beings takes on the character of tragedy, though no tragic poet could ever use such a catastrophe for the end of his play.

In "Christianity and Tragedy" Reinhold Niebuhr differentiates Christ from the tragic hero by means of a simple comparison—he recalls Christ's words, "Weep not for me. Weep for yourselves and for your children"; he then asserts that "one weakness of the tragic hero is that he is always crying 'Weep for me.'" According to Niebuhr, "There is in other words an inevitable element of self-pity in classic tragedy." But one quotation is enough to cast doubt upon this generalization. In the first episode of *Antigone*, which consists entirely of dialogue between the heroine and her sister, Ismene exclaims: "Oh my poor sister. How I fear for you!" Antigone replies, "For me, don't borrow trouble. Clear your fate" (lines 82–83). Such a response suggests the opposite of self-pity. It may be true that "romantic tragedy" often involves an element of self-pity, but to insist that there is an "inevitable" element of self-pity in *classic* tragedy is to distort the truth.

Occasionally, someone embarks upon a more systematic comparison of the Bible and tragedy in an effort to prove that no Christian tragedy can exist. Edmond Cherbonnier makes such an attempt in "Biblical Faith and the Idea of Tragedy." His most interesting and complex argument is based upon the "double perspective," which he identifies as "the basis of the tragic view of life, from Aeschylus to Sartre." According to Cherbonnier, "The philosophical stage setting for tragic drama . . . consists of two shifting backdrops: the *ultimate perspective* of the detached observer, of the aesthete, in which all differences cancel each other out and in which no discord is possible; and the *finite perspective* of the man of action, in which strife and contradiction are the rule." He describes the implications of this double perspective at some length:

> The spectator thus becomes part of the act, deliberately maintaining a conscious ambivalence. The moment he relaxes the tension between the two perspectives, the tragic effect dissolves. If he adopts the finite perspective to the exclusion of the ultimate, tragedy becomes either a morality play or a picture of unrelieved frustration. If he relinquishes the finite in favor of the ultimate perspective, and allows himself to view the hero's world *sub specie aeternitatis*, he realizes that the whole play is really "much ado about nothing."

Cherbonnier's own attitude toward all of this soon becomes clear. He repeatedly makes such statements as the following: "What this really constitutes is an invitation to maintain a schizophrenic oscillation between the two perspectives, and thereby to become a party to one's own hypnosis."

But taken as a whole, his analysis of this aspect of tragedy is fairly accurate. The astonishing part of the argument comes in his interpretation of the Bible. He contends that in opposition to the double perspective of tragedy,

> biblical philosophy acknowledges no such convenient pretext for equivocation. Throughout the Bible there runs a single criterion of both truth and goodness, equally applicable "on earth as it is in heaven." This is the philosophical significance of the concept of God as Creator. . . . Whereas tragedy regards this present world as the negation of the "divine," the Bible asserts that there is no necessary incompatibility between it and the very nature of God himself. . . . Even if the Old Testament accounts of God's walking on the earth are not historically true, the point remains that he is the *kind* of God who *could* do so, if he chose. And in the New Testament, he did so choose.

What Cherbonnier never satisfactorily explains is why, if "there is no necessary incompatibility between [this present world] and the very nature of God himself," God's walking upon the earth, as described in the New Testament, should culminate in the long walk to Golgotha under the weight of a heavy cross. Cherbonnier asserts that tragedy attempts "to reconcile the spectator to [evil and suffering] by persuading him that they are necessary," and concludes that "all such attempts to explain evil only end by explaining it away." And again, "In holding that human disaster *need* not happen, the Bible takes a far more serious view of it than tragedy, which either capitulates in resignation or exhausts itself in futile protest." Jaspers is helpful at this point because he makes it perfectly clear that a view which regards evil as "unnecessary" is definitely untragic—his term for this view is "pre-tragic." He describes tragic knowledge, and goes on to say: "No such tragic outlook develops wherever man succeeds both in achieving a harmonious interpretation of the universe and in actually living in accord with it. That is to a great extent what happened in ancient, especially in pre-Buddhist, China. In such a civilization, all misery, unhappiness, and evil are merely temporary disturbances which never need occur."

The weakness in Cherbonnier's argument is not difficult to locate. He uses the terms "this present world" and "the world which the Bible describes" interchangeably, and he seems to assume that "the world which the Bible describes" is fully represented in the first chapter of Genesis. That is, he makes no distinction between the *created order* and the *fallen order*. According to Genesis 1, God created the world, and he "saw that it was good." Then, according to Genesis 3, Adam sinned; and from then on a different order of human existence obtained in the world. This distinction is perfectly clear in the first chapter of the fourth gospel: "The true light that enlightens every man was coming into the world; he was in the world, and the world was made through him, yet the world knew him not; he came to his own home, and his own people received him not" (John 1:9–11). As the created order, the world was Christ's "own home"; but as the fallen order, the world into which he came "knew him not." If a person is forcibly ejected from his own home and disowned by his own family, there is a real sense in which the home and family are no longer his, though he may have built the house with his own hands and populated it with his own flesh. It is for this reason that Jesus, according to more than one of the gospel writers, says "Foxes have holes, and the birds of the air have nests; but the Son of man has nowhere to lay his head" (Matt. 8:20, Luke 9:58). Genesis 3 is, after all, no less important to understanding "the kind of world the Bible describes" than Genesis 1 is.

Cherbonnier's argument culminates in this statement: "Where tragedy tends to call one and the same event both good, from one perspective, and evil, from the other, there is no trace of such ambivalence in the Bible." In the light of the New Testament, this assertion is simply amazing. What does the crucifixion mean to the Christian if not that it is at one and the same time a disaster and a miracle, the worst failure and the greatest success in world history? Those who crucified Christ simultaneously performed the greatest of sins and brought about the world's deliverance from sin. At one stroke, God abandoned his own son and redeemed the world. Yet, this attitude is possible only for the believer, who sees the crucifixion as both the epitome of the problem of evil and as the source of the world's salvation. To the unbeliever, who refuses to engage in what Cherbonnier scornfully calls "a constant flirtation with two perspectives at once," it is neither of these. St. Paul understood the matter clearly: "For the word of the cross is folly to those who are perishing, but to us who are being saved it is the power of God" (I Cor. 1:18).

Behind this double meaning of the crucifixion stands, of course, the double nature of Christ himself—from one perspective he is man, from the other he is God. Historically, Christianity has erred in proportion as it has lost sight of this twofold nature of Christ. At times the church has stressed the divine aspect to such an extent that it seemed to many Christians almost presumptuous to seek to emulate him—he is God, and we are clay. At other times it has emphasized the human element so strongly that to many he became a sentimentalized conception of "the good man." Either view robs the gospel narrative of its power, since that power depends finally upon the double perspective which, we are told, is characteristic of tragedy but utterly foreign to the Bible. We identify with Christ in his suffering because, like us, he is a man; and we are able to bear those sufferings only because he, unlike us, is God.

The double perspective from which the Christian views Christ as both man and God thus requires the cooperation of the believer no less than the double perspective of literary tragedy requires it of the sympathetic observer. The believer "must be willing to hold both perspectives before him in a kind of tension," and maintain "a conscious ambivalence. The moment he relaxes the tension between the two perspectives, the tragic effect [and, we argue, the power of the gospel] dissolves." If he sees Jesus merely as a man, he must reject the resurrection, and the gospel narrative becomes "a picture of unrelieved frustration." If he sees Jesus purely as God, then surely his "sufferings" were not in any sense unbearable to him—they seem in fact to be "much ado about nothing." Were we to take the same uncharitable view of the believer which Cherbonnier takes of the person who enters into the experience of literary tragedy, we could say that as long as one wears these "bifocal lenses" of belief, he is able to identify with Christ "sufficiently to derive a vicarious sense of dangerous living," and at the same time remain "secure in the knowledge" that Christ's sacrifice guarantees his [the believer's] salvation.

According to Cherbonnier, "Perhaps the furthest penetration by the tragic view of life into Christian usage . . . is the famous liturgical phrase, *felix culpa*." Following A. O. Lovejoy's commentary on Milton's *Paradise Lost*, he indicates that "whereas in the early part of the poem the fall of Adam is deplored as a 'ruinous enormity,' by the time the reader arrives at the Twelfth Book, Adam begins to describe his transgression as a ground for self-congratulation!" Cherbonnier does not, however, explain how this change of attitude is any different from the one which Peter undergoes between the occasion when he denies Christ not once but three times and the occasion when he preaches the sermon urging his listeners to be baptized in the name of Jesus, who had been "delivered up according to the definite plan and foreknowledge of God." Apparently, Peter regarded his connection with the final events of Jesus' life as a "ruinous enormity" at the time those events occurred, but as "a ground for self-congratulation" at some later point.

Such arguments as the ones we have just examined appear to have been devised as rationalizations for a conclusion that was formed on some other basis. One suspects that this other basis consists of two self-evident facts: (1) in retrospect, Christ upon the cross seems to the Christian triumphant rather than defeated, and (2) because the writers who devised and first exploited the tragic mode in literature lived before the time of Christ, they used that mode to convey insights which are pre-Christian. The first of these two facts is accounted for by the believer's acceptance of the double perspective which characterizes the observer's relation to tragedy in any form, and the second fact is obvious but irrelevant. If we conclude that there can be no Christian tragedy because tragedy is older than Christianity, we might almost as reasonably conclude that because the Greek language was devised before the Christian era to convey pre-Christian ideas, Greek could not be used (as it is in the New Testament) to communicate "what is essential to the Christian."

The relationship between Christianity and tragedy must be stated as a paradox. The same Jaspers who asserts that "no genuinely Christian tragedy can exist" provides the key to this relationship, though he apparently does so unconsciously. He ends one chapter by saying that "Christ is the deepest symbol of failure in this world, yet he is in no sense tragic. In his very failure he knows, fulfills, and consummates." The first paragraph of the next chapter contains this sentence: "Paradoxically, however, when man faces the tragic, he liberates himself from it." Even from these two statements we can see that Christ submits himself so totally to tragic experience that in the end he totally liberates himself from it. Though it may seem that "what is essential to the Christian cannot even emerge in tragedy," the fact is that *everything* which is essential to the Christian actually *does* emerge in the tragic narrative which we have in the four gospels. If some Christians believe that literary tragedy is incapable of communicating what is essentially Christian, it is only because the tragedy recorded in the New Testament seems to them so powerful that all other tragedies are trifling and pale in comparison.

We can say, then, with Niebuhr that Christianity stands beyond tragedy—but not because Christianity is untragic. On the contrary, it does so only because Christianity is so profoundly and uncompromisingly tragic that it ends by seeming to lose its tragic character, by coming out on the other side. That is to say, its catharsis is almost total. But in order to be a Christian, the individual must in turn submit himself to the tragic just as Jesus did. How else may we understand the words, "Whoever does not bear his own cross and come after me, cannot be my disciple" (Luke 14:27)? Christian tragedy *can* exist then, because even if "Christianity stands beyond tragedy," the raw material of literature is experience, and for anyone who accepts Christ's life as the model, experience is fundamentally tragic. Jesus himself framed the paradox with which we are confronted: "He who finds his life will lose it, and he who loses his life for my sake will find it" (Matt. 10:39). Losing one's life out of loyalty requires total submission to the tragic—no one can surrender his life in this way and remain serenely confident that all is well. If we are ever tempted to think otherwise, we should remember the words of Jesus upon the cross, "My God, my God, why hast thou forsaken me?"

This analysis does not pretend, of course, to demonstrate that literary Christian tragedy does exist, or, if it does, what form such tragedy takes. It merely shows that the arguments advanced to support the contention that "no genuinely Christian tragedy can exist" are basically unsound. It reopens a question which many people, both believers and skeptics, would have us regard as closed. If as Jaspers indicates, "A Christian is bound to misunderstand, say, Shakespeare," then we would be foolish to interpret *Hamlet* and *King Lear* as if they had any direct connection with historical Christianity. But we suspect that this assertion makes no better sense than saying that an ancient Greek was bound to misunderstand, say, Sophocles. No one claims that it is grossly misleading to interpret Sophocles in the light of Greek religion, and no really good reasons have been adduced for believing that we will surely be misled if we try to understand Shakespearean tragedy in the light of Christianity. On the contrary, it seems more likely that we will be led astray by denying categorically that Christianity is relevant to understanding Shakespearean drama, than by admitting the possibility that the New Testament may illuminate, for instance, Hamlet's dilemma.

William Whallon

Biblical Poetry
and Homeric Epic

_The characteristics of Hebrew poetry can be seen in rela-
tion to another tradition, Greek epic poetry. Although both
are traditional—they both use formulas or parallelism that
indicate oral composition—Old Testament writing is strikingly different from the Homeric epics. Hebrew poetry
shares with Homeric poetry its "horizontal" structure
(everyone is the same at the end as at the beginning), a
disregard for suspense (action occurs in the "foreground"),
and elevated poetic speech. In general, Old Testament prose
differs from Homeric and Hebraic poetry in characterization and style. The prose implies a background and develops action with suspense, and only the sparest detail is
given. Old Testament prose is seen as reportorial,
naturalistic, and non-formulaic. A study of what Hebrew
and Greek poetry share in common provides insight into
how a composition was transformed into writing._

_On the significance of poetry, particularly in connec-
tion with prophecy, see Freedman, above, pp. 77–100._

I N the first chapter of *Mimesis*—hereafter cited from the English translation by Willard R. Trask (Princeton, 1953), but with the page numbers from the German edition (Bern, 1946) in brackets—Erich Auerbach
contrasted the narrative about Odysseus' scar (from the nineteenth book
of the *Odyssey*) with the narrative about Abraham's offering of Isaac
(from the twenty-second chapter of Genesis). The analysis is brilliant;
and yet the two texts do not seem wholly comparable. For Homeric epic is
no more analogous to Old Testament prose than to the poetry; it is
episodic like the one, but formulaic like the other—the argument from
style that Homeric epic derived ultimately from an oral culture cannot be
extended to Old Testament prose but can in large measure be extended to
the poetry. So the passage about Odysseus' scar answers, in one way, to
the passage about the offering of Isaac, but in another way, equally good,

From William Whallon, *Formula, Character, and Context* (1969), pp. 214–20.

to a chapter from Habakkuk. In considering how Old Testament prose may be unlike the poetry, we shall keep Homeric epic as a touchstone, and bring Auerbach, quoting him as extensively as need be, under judgment.

A. OLD TESTAMENT POETRY LACKS DISTINCTIVE CHARACTERIZATION

Herein lies the reason why the great figures of the Old Testament are so much more fully developed, so much more fraught with their own biographical past, so much more distinct as individuals, than are the Homeric heroes. Achilles and Odysseus are splendidly described in many well-ordered words, epithets cling to them, their emotions are constantly displayed in their words and deeds—but they have no development, and their life-histories are clearly set forth once and for all. So little are the Homeric heroes presented as developing or having developed, that most of them—Nestor, Agamemnon, Achilles—appear to be of an age fixed from the very first. Even Odysseus, in whose case the long lapse of time and the many events which occurred offer so much opportunity for biographical development, shows almost nothing of it. Odysseus on his return is exactly the same as he was when he left Ithaca two decades earlier. But what a road, what a fate, lie between the Jacob who cheated his father out of his blessing and the old man whose favorite son has been torn to pieces by a wild beast!—between David the harp player, persecuted by his lord's jealousy, and the old king, surrounded by violent intrigues, whom Abishag the Shunnamite warmed in his bed, and he knew her not. The old man of whom we know how he has become what he is, is more of an individual than the young man; for it is only during the course of an eventful life that men are differentiated into full individuality; and it is this history of a personality which the Old Testament presents to us as the formation undergone by those whom God has chosen to be examples. Fraught with their development, sometimes even aged to the verge of dissolution, they show a distinct stamp of individuality entirely foreign to the Homeric heroes. (*Mimesis* 17–18 [22–23])

It will be convenient to borrow from Auerbach, for the sake of showing how far we agree with him, two spatial metaphors. The one concerns depth: it contrasts a background (of matters in obscurity) with a foreground (where all is made clear). The other contrasts verticality (or succession in time) with horizontality (or contemporaneity). Let us apply both metaphors to Old Testament prose and Homeric epic (after the manner of *Mimesis*), and then to Old Testament poetry as well.

Content. Old Testament prose implies a background and develops with suspense. The prosateur sets down only whatever matters are crucial; no ancillary material is allowed to claim attention for itself. Many things that might be expressed are left to be inferred. Nor can we accurately predict much of what is about to happen.

And Rebekah took goodly raiment of her eldest son Esau, which were with her in the house, and put them upon Jacob her younger son: And she put the skins of the kids of the goats upon his hands, and upon the smooth of his neck: And she gave the savoury meat and the bread, which she had prepared, into the hand of her son Jacob. And he came unto his father, and said, My father: and he said, Here am I; who art thou, my son? And Jacob said unto his father, I am Esau thy firstborn; I have done according as thou badest me: arise, I pray thee, sit and eat of my venison, that thy soul may bless me. And Isaac said unto his son, How is it that thou hast found it so quickly, my son? And he said, Because the Lord thy God brought it to me. And Isaac said unto Jacob, Come near, I pray thee, that I may feel thee, my son, whether thou be my very son Esau or not. And Jacob went near unto Isaac his father; and he felt him, and said, The voice is Jacob's voice, but the hands are the hands of Esau. (Gen. 27:15–22)

Homeric epic occurs in the foreground and has less suspense. The poet works into the narrative by one device or another whatever seems likely to hold the interest of his audience. He understands everything fully and leaves nothing obscure. We can predict some events because they are explicitly foretold.

And warm tears were flowing from their brows to the ground as they grieved in longing for their charioteer, and their rich manes were stained as they streamed from the yoke-pads by the yoke on both sides. Seeing the two of them in grief, the son of Cronus pitied them, and shaking his head he said to himself: Ah, wretched ones, why did we give you to lord Peleus, a mortal, when you yourselves are ageless and immortal? Was it that among unhappy men you should have your own sorrows? For I suppose that of all the things that breathe and creep on the earth there is nothing more miserable than man. But Hector Priamides is certainly not going to mount on you and the resplendent chariot; I will not allow it. Isn't it enough that as things are he has the arms and prides himself on them? But I shall send courage into your knees and your heart, so that you may save Automedon from the war and bring him to the hollow ships. For I shall still stretch out glory to the Trojans to slay, until they come to the well-benched ships, and the sun sets and the sacred darkness comes on. (*Il.* XVII. 437–55)

Old Testament poetry occurs in the foreground and has no suspense. Not details about political intrigues but truths known to every generation, not new facts but new insights, engage the poet's special eloquence. We lack any incentive to predict; nothing will take place that is memorable as history.

(Having been long barren, Hannah conceived a son; when he was weaned she prayed as follows:)

My heart rejoiceth in the Lord,
mine horn is exalted in the Lord:
my mouth is enlarged over mine enemies;
because I rejoice in thy salvation.
There is none holy as the Lord:
for there is none beside thee:
neither is there any rock like our God.
Talk no more so exceeding proudly;
let not arrogancy come out of your mouth:

for the Lord is a God of knowledge,
and by him actions are weighed.
The bows of the mighty men are broken,
and they that stumbled are girded with strength.
They that were full have hired out themselves for bread;
and they that were hungry ceased:
so that the barren hath born seven;
and she that hath many children is waxed feeble.
The Lord killeth, and maketh alive:
he bringeth down to the grave, and bringeth up.
The Lord maketh poor, and maketh rich:
he bringeth low, and lifteth up.
He raiseth up the poor of the dust,
and lifteth up the beggar from the dunghill,
to set them among princes,
and to make them inherit the throne of glory:
for the pillars of the earth are the Lord's,
and he hath set the world upon them.
He will keep the feet of his saints,
and the wicked shall be silent in darkness;
for by strength shall no man prevail.
The adversaries of the Lord shall be broken to pieces;
out of heaven shall he thunder upon them:
the Lord shall judge the ends of the earth;
and he shall give strength unto his king,
and exalt the horn of his anointed. (I Sam. 2:1–10)

Old Testament prose is vertical in showing a procession of figures after the usual fashion of a chronicle, and in showing that a long passage of time has affected certain figures in the usual way. But Homeric epic is horizontal since the casts of the *Iliad* and *Odyssey* are somewhat identical, and since the passage of time—each poem taking place in a few days, and only ten years lying between them—is too brief for much aging. And Old Testament poetry is horizontal in rather like manner: no great while is needed for the dialogue in Job, and everyone is the same at the end as at the beginning.

Style. Old Testament prose suggests a background by using only such descriptive elements as cannot be spared, and stands vertical because these elements always give point to the moment at hand; character is drawn without the use of clichés. But Homeric epic evenly illuminates its foreground with descriptive elements that are interesting for their own sake, and lies horizontal because these elements are timeless. Being loaded now with treasure to ransom the body of Hector (*Il.* XXIV. 189), and now with clothing that Nausicaa and her handmaids will wash at the shore (*Od.* VI. 72), a wagon is a "wagon well-wheeled, mule-drawn" (ἄμαξαν εὔτροχον ἡμιονείην). Character is sketched by assigning to everyone certain traits and titles that may be repeatedly mentioned without regard for their appropriateness in any particular passage. Not that all are alike: Achilles and Odysseus, since their names are identical in meter, could have shared their epithets between them, and the same is true for Hector and Ajax, or Athene and Apollo. But there is no change: there is never a time when we are sure that Achilles will not be called "swift-footed," and those who are prominent in both poems—Odysseus, Nestor, Menelaus, and Helen—are described in the same way early and late. Old Testament poetry creates a foreground of Homeric leisure and serenity by restating every concept, and lies horizontal because its idiom has a Homeric timelessness and inevitability. A mountain of any kind brings mention of a hill: "I will get me to the mountain of myrrh, and to the hill of frankincense" (S. of Sol. 4:6); "contend thou before the mountains, and let the hills hear thy voice" (Mic. 6:1). Character is not here an important subject, yet "Jacob" and "Israel," synonymous names, are balanced in forty verses; there is no development, no contrast.

It may be helpful to extend what Tolstoi, *What is Art? and Essays on Art,* (tr. by Aylmer Maude [London, n.d.], p. 208), remarked about Wagnerian opera: "There is one fixed combination of sounds, or *leit-motiv,* for each character, and this *leit-motiv* is repeated every time the person whom it represents appears; and when anyone is mentioned the *motiv* is heard which relates to that person. Moreover each article also has its own *leit-motiv* or chord. There is a *motiv* of the ring, a *motiv* of the helmet, a *motiv* of the apple, a *motiv* of fire, spear, sword, water, etc., and as soon as the ring, helmet, or apple is mentioned, the *motiv* or chord of the ring, helmet, or apple, is heard." None of this pertains to Old Testament prose, but if we change *leitmotiv* to *epithet* there are resemblances to Homeric epic, and if we change it to the *synonym,* or antonym, completing a word pair—there are resemblances to Old Testament poetry. With regard to background versus foreground, and verticality versus horizontality, both metaphors being applied in particular to characterization, Old Testament prose belongs on the left, Homeric epic and Old Testament poetry belong together on the right. Without debating whether, if all the factors were weighed, the figures of the Old Testament really would seem to have, as Auerbach claimed for them, an individuality foreign to the Homeric heroes, we observe that even the analysis behind this conclusion is valid only for the prose and not in the least for the poetry.

In contrasting Old Testament prose, on the one hand, with Homeric epic and Old Testament poetry, on the other, we say nothing about which is the nobler or has the more forcible effect on the mind. We say only that certain differences can be noted: the reportorial against the creative, the naturalistic against the nonnaturalistic, the suggestiveness of what is withheld as internal against the handsomeness of what is revealed as external, the nonformulaic against the formulaic, low against high style. To give these qualities in a slightly different order we may notice that, in contrasting Old Testament prose with Homeric epic, Auerbach defined the latter by its "fully externalized description, uniform illumination, uninterpreted connection, free expression, all events in the foreground, displaying unmistakable meanings, few elements of historical development and of psychological perspective" (*Mimesis* 23 [18]). Every term in the list applies also to Old Testament poetry.

B. OLD TESTAMENT POETRY CONSISTS OF NONNATURALISTIC SPEECH

With the utmost fullness, with an orderliness which even passion does not disturb, Homer's personages vent their inmost hearts in speech; what they do not say to others, they speak in their own minds, so that the reader is informed of it. Much that is terrible takes place in the Homeric poems, but it seldom takes place wordlessly: Polyphemus talks to Odysseus; Odysseus talks to the suitors when he begins to kill them; Hector and Achilles talk at length, before battle and after; and no speech is so filled with anger or scorn that the particles which express logical and grammatical connections are lacking or out of place. (*Mimesis* 6 [10])

One fact Auerbach failed to discuss is that, unlike Old Testament prose, Homeric epic and Old Testament poetry had special requirements, and became circumlocutory, and formulaic, as a consequence. A concept had to be expressed under exacting conditions (of meter in the one, parallelism in the other), and these conditions were fulfilled in perhaps the easiest way possible (by such means as the use of epithets to create phrases of the desired meter in the one, by the use of synonyms and antonyms to create word pairs of the desired parallelism in the other). And whenever the same problem recurred the poet ordinarily supplied the same answer because it came most quickly to mind. For this reason, Thetis, Diomedes, Andromache, and Eumaeus all speak with like epithets to accompany like nouns; Hannah, Job, Lemuel, and Isaiah all speak with the same word pairs. It was not from any wish for decorum, but primarily for the sake of convenience, that the poet never allowed his figures, no matter how strong the passions that might govern them, to mar their eloquence with solecisms, stammerings, and anacolutha. No one in Homeric epic used "swift-footed" because he intended to emphasize that term in particular, but solely because the poet needed to stretch out the name "Achilles"; no one in Old Testament poetry used "hills" because he was interested in them, but solely because the poet needed to complement the noun "mountains." Whether "swift-footed" or "hills" occurs in a line is accordingly somewhat fortuitous, the deciding factors being "Achilles" and meter, or "mountains" and parallelism. Here is a further aspect, not in Old Testament prose but in Homeric epic and Old Testament poetry, of an analogy with the *leitmotiv:* W. H. Auden, "Mimesis and Allegory," in *English Institute Annual, 1940* ([New York, 1941], pp. 5–6), remarks that it "was Wagner who showed the surrealists that the primitive, the illogical, the chance-determined was the true revolutionary art and who preceded Sibelius and Gertrude Stein in the discovery that if you repeat the same thing four times it has little effect, but that a remarkable effect can be gained by repeating it four hundred times."

Some speech in the Old Testament is prose, some poetry; but all the poetry—a fact noticed by few besides Paul Dhorme, O.P., *Le Livre de Job* (2d. ed. [Paris, 1926], p. li)—is speech. In the historical books the main narrative, in prose, is broken only for the quotation of a blessing (Gen. 49:1-27), a song of victory (Judg. 5), a prayer of thanksgiving (1 Sam. 2:1-10), or one of the other subjects of poetry. In Job the prologue and epilogue are in prose (except that Satan speaks in poetry: "From going to and fro in the earth, and from walking up and down in it"), and the assignment of the speeches and the introduction of Elihu are in prose; but Job and his friends converse in poetry, Elihu gives his monologue in poetry, and the Lord speaks in poetry from the whirlwind. In the Books of Psalms and Proverbs prose is used for attributing, now and then, a passage of poetry to an author, or for naming the circumstances behind its creation: and in the books of prophecy prose introduces, comments upon, and otherwise gives continuity to the words of the prophets, which are characteristically in poetry. The distinction between the forms, low against high style, is exact and uniform. In Homeric epic there is nothing comparable: the narrator speaks in the idiom of his heroes; the words of Priam resemble those of Telemachus, and both are like what the poet says as spectator; the high style is never interrupted. In this respect there is a distinction between the Old Testament and Homer, and it is precisely the opposite of what was asserted by Auerbach—who so far has been censurable only for having possibly misled us by giving all his attention to Old Testament prose and none to the poetry, but here for once is certainly mistaken:

> From the rule of the separation of styles which was later almost universally accepted and which specified that the realistic depiction of daily life was incompatible with the sublime and had a place only in comedy or, carefully stylized, in idyl—from any such rule Homer is still far removed. And yet he is closer to it than is the Old Testament. (*Mimesis* 22 [28])

This assertion, which stands near the close of the first chapter, is not peripheral or incidental to the arguments Auerbach developed throughout his book, for it reappears near the middle of the third chapter: "In the Judaeo-Christian tradition, as we have previously pointed out, there was no separating the elevated style from realism" (*Mimesis* 63 [68]). The assertion is not peripheral but central, and it is wrong. For the separation of styles is not further to seek in the Old Testament than in Homeric epic; it is immeasurably closer at hand; indeed it is obvious. Prose is used for the naturalistic description of events, poetry for all speech that is elevated or sustained.

V: APPROACHES TO A LITERARY CRITICISM OF THE BIBLE

Introduction

T HE six essays in this section are not meant to suggest that there are only six current approaches to biblical literary criticism. Nonetheless, they do represent important movements in this criticism, and coincidentally shed light on the question the literary critic poses of any work: What is literature? Taken together, they describe a large curve of scholarly interest that begins with the analytical task of recovering the "original" meaning of a text (its earliest "forms" and its original function in the living community). The essays move through an interest in the work itself; the work in its complex "unity." The final turn is taken in confronting the question of meaning itself, taking up the hermeneutic task of appropriating meaning that has been lost to us, and uncovering the structures that lie below the surface or "manifest" meaning of the text. The six approaches are form-critical, redaction-critical, rhetorical, logological, phenomenological, and structural:

Form criticism analyzes the text into "forms" which compose it and relates the "forms" to their original function in the community.

Redaction criticism studies the history of the text, its development from the point of view of the "redactor," or final editor, who has brought the material together.

Rhetorical criticism studies literary wholes in the text to show the shape or configuration of a piece, its unity and texture.

Logological criticism is a type of narrative analysis which relates story and symbol (or *mythos*) to the forms of logical propositions (or *logos*).

Phenomenological criticism describes, not the origin of the work of art, but how it is understood. It pursues the hermeneutical problem of the symbol by *de*symbolizing the once powerful but now diminished symbol and reinvesting it with meaning for us.

Structuralism exposes the latent content of narratives in the light of modern communication theory and linguistics.

With the possible exception of the form-critical method, the approaches discussed in the essays could be used to shed light on works by Shakespeare, Chaucer, or the *Beowulf*-poet. And form criticism might be

329

seen as a useful analytical tool in works rooted in traditional song or oral composition.

Faced with a text (which may be a biblical "book," but is usually smaller) that comes from a remote place or time, the reader is challenged to explain its meaning and, one hopes, to enter into it, in some way to participate in it. Some questions have already been asked in earlier sections about ways in which we should approach the Bible. But other questions remain. Is the text sure and certain? Is it a combination of several works put together? If in a foreign language—or in an earlier stage of the reader's native speech—can the translator of the words and concepts be trusted? What historical information is needed to gather a basic, literal understanding? Are influences from other societies and other traditions evident in the work? These are the kinds of questions that textual critics, "literary" critics (in the older sense used by biblical scholars), philologists, and literary historians seek to answer.

Furthermore, although literary critics and biblical scholars use different methods, they both ordinarily ask the same kinds of questions. It is useful to recall that for both the literary critic and the biblical scholar, the modern (and postmodern) twentieth-century approaches to the text developed as a reaction to the nineteenth-century preoccupation with scientific studies of texts, philology, influence-study, and developmental schema—in short, with the studies thought to be most objective, factual, and verifiable. The very remoteness in time and place was taken as a plus, since it allowed perspective and disinterested work on the text. (See the General Introduction, pp. 1–15.)

For biblical criticism, the most productive reaction (as Muilenburg points out, pp. 362–380) seemed to be form criticism. For the literary critic certain "formalist" schools, particularly new criticism, seemed to be most productive. Since "form" and "formalist" might appear to establish a similarity where none exists, a word of caution is offered. Ironically, James Muilenburg's call for something beyond form criticism is in many ways a call for a new criticism of biblical literature. Whereas the new critic is concerned precisely with those aspects of a literary work that give it its most intense, organic unity, the form critic is searching for types—forms—that can be lifted out of context in order to lay bare their origins in the traditions of the community. For example, a given psalm may include more than one form. Psalm 130, a "Song of Ascents," is part of a collection of Songs of Pilgrimage (Psalms 120–34), but it includes a "Watchman's Song" within it. One form may be rooted, for example, in the liturgy of the king's accession to the throne, and another in an agricultural festival. The *Sitz im Leben* concept—the place in the living community in which a form takes its original meaning—has come under attack, but it is still the mainstay of the form critic's attempt to find the types of songs, stories, and formulae found in the text.

In sharp contrast to this, the new critics' "formalist" approach has been to get back to the "poem itself" in its "own skin." The new critic examines patterns of imagery and the language most appropriate to the "autotelic" character of the literary work: ambiguity, paradox, and irony—the "concrete universals" that give immediacy to the work. The "texture" of the work, its intense unity, is what the new critic wants to exhibit.

The advantage of the new critical approach was to rid literary studies of various "fallacies" that seemed to burden them terribly. One was the delight in "isolated beauties," judging an author's work on the basis of a striking line or an impressive ("purple") passage and not attending to the work as a whole. A second critical shortcoming was called the "intentional fallacy." The main concern was the habit of ascribing a privileged position to what a writer says of his own work; what he "felt" in some way he was trying to do. Instead, one should attend to what was said in the work, not the biographical information surrounding it.

In its task of explicating or intensely studying the internal details of a literary work, new criticism hoped to find the "work itself" in its centripetal intensity and absolute uniqueness.

The productivity of new critical analysis of literary works is beginning to enter biblical scholarship. Although redaction criticism claims only to look at the diachronic, historically developed text, the redaction (actually redaction-historical) critic does study the nuances, ambiguous language, and image clusters of the text in order to point up the work of a given redactor, who has worked older, often traditional, forms into his own purpose. For example, Norman Perrin points out the way Matthew uses material found in Mark for Matthew's purpose. Since the redaction critic wants to take the historical development of the text to its final form, the unity of the final version is increasingly important to him. (See also Walker, pp. 156–165, and Mowinckel, pp. 173–190).

The resemblance of new criticism to James Muilenburg's rhetorical criticism is even more pronounced. Although the task of biblical criticism is much greater than the new critic usually faces, it is not fundamentally different. Not surprisingly, Muilenburg cited T. S. Eliot, whose criticism (particularly of the seventeenth-century metaphysical poets) was a model of the dry, dispassionate attention to the "work itself"—the hallmark of new criticism.

Whether Muilenburg's rhetorical criticism will look in practice like new critical studies, rhetorical criticism is certainly another reaction to form criticism, and an attempt to see the literary unity in biblical texts. The first task, according to Muilenburg, is "to define the limits or scope of the literary unity, to recognize precisely where and how it begins and where and how it ends." The rhetorical critic observes formal rhetorical devices, major motifs, the structure of a composition, and "the configuration of its component parts." Behind this task is the conviction, basic to any literary critical task, that the literary unity is "an indissoluble whole, an artistic and creative unity, a unique formulation."

It is not as easy to categorize Kenneth Burke's approach to biblical literature. His, too, is a kind of rhetorical criticism, but it is one which attends closely to the nature of symbolic language. For Burke, man, as symbol-using animal, speaks four kinds of words: words for the natural (like "tree" and "growth"); words for the socio-political realm (like "justice" and "monarchy"); words about words (the realm of dictionaries, grammar, poetics, and philology); and finally, words for the "supernatural." In Burke's analysis, the magnificent opening chapters of Genesis are dominated by imagery from nature and the social order. Burke is useful in his narrative theory: How—by what transformations— are the "principles" or the great themes yoked to a story form? Burke's solution, which should be contrasted with Edmund Leach's structural study of the same passages, lies in his analysis of the symbol. To this extent Burke is involved in a hermeneutic (the art of interpretation) such as John Macquarrie's. The problem of symbolic language is taken up again in the phenomenological analysis offered by Macquarrie. The varieties of symbolic expression, particularly in religious symbolism, have a dimension beyond "likeness." The religious symbol does not merely point to what in the real world is "like" light. The religious symbol calls forth an existential "response of commitment," which is at the very heart of religious symbolism. What, then, is to be done with ancient symbols used in the Bible that have been drained of the power to evoke the response of commitment? The case Macquarrie offers is the symbol of "light." His suggestion is that just as "estrangement" has enabled us today to recapture something lost in the old language of "sin," so "light" as an existential-ontological symbol reveals itself for us as "openness." Macquarrie terms this process "*de*symbolization."

The final three essays in this section—the essays by Burke, Macquarrie and Leach—do not focus on the text in the same historical, diachronic way as do the first three essays by Van Tilborg, Perrin, and Muilenburg. They differ in that the latter reflect the crisis in contemporary literary criticism that has been called the new literary history and postmodernism. The crisis pushes out in two directions. One emphasizes *a*temporal and *an*historical, synchronic features that "generate" texts. The task should be to reveal structural principles in the text, "latent" patterns underlying surface elements. The other push (phenomenological), on the other hand, is radically historical. The hermeneutical task is to break through a text whose symbols have become dead to us, revivifying it so that we can stand in its meaning.

Edmund Leach's structuralist study of the first four chapters of Genesis draws upon communication theory (cybernetics), the structural linguistics of Roman Jakobson, and the structural anthropology of Claude Lévi-Strauss. Why is a story retold in different variations? How do "mediating" figures work in a story? The *logic of myth* presents the problems of the society (in the myths Leach deals with, the problem is the opposition of incest and kin endogamy) in a way that the story resolves the problem. Binary opposites like life and death, light and dark, are resolved in redundancy and mediation.

From a search for the original situation of the forms of expression through a quest for the unity of the text to the recovery and restoration of its meaning for us: such is the arc described in the six essays of this section. Biblical texts provide examples of significant trends in twentieth-century literary criticism. But there is more. The "raid on the ultimate" Muilenburg writes about and the "response of commitment" Macquarrie explores remind us that for us the Bible is finally not just another example, not just an illustration among many. The Bible is "book," literature; in its numinosity and "ultimate concern," it does not become less book, but more. The essays suggest what the literary critic can open in the search for its meaning.

S. Van Tilborg

A Form-Criticism
of the Lord's Prayer

Form criticism attempts to analyze the biblical text into forms such as speeches, sermons, prayers, narratives, and songs. The importance of this method is that it allows us to recover the form in its original situation in the living community (its Sitz im Leben*)—to discover how a form functioned in society. (For the origins of the form-critical approach, see Muilenburg, pp. 362–380).*

In this example of the form-critical method, S. Van Tilborg examines the origin of the Lord's Prayer in a liturgical use of the Gethsemane story. From that situation Van Tilborg explains the "whole history of the development of the Lord's Prayer." The transformations of the form in the gospels (redactions) show the different authors' subtle modifications in view of their own theologies. (On redaction, see Perrin, pp. 344–361.)

I N the modern research of the form-criticism of the Lord's Prayer the article of M. D. Goulder[1] plays a role of importance. It is fascinating to become acquainted with an interpretation which has tried to take into account the long history that the text of the Lord's Prayer has undergone before it was inserted in the gospels of Matt. and Luke. The failure of the eschatological exegesis of the Lord's Prayer, as proposed by E. Lohmeyer,[2] J. Jeremias,[3] and R. E. Brown,[4] became evident not merely from the fact that these interpreters had to make use of extremely intricate reasoning and research to uphold this explanation. Several authors[5] had remained unconvinced by their arguments and rejected an eschatological interpretation for one or the other verse, or for several invocations.[6] The problem was dealt with in an even more fundamental way by E. Grässer,[7] who showed that the text of the Lord's Prayer, as we find it presently in the gospels, appears to have been developed at a time in which the delay of the Parousia was no longer a problem. If this is accepted the obstacles are removed for a form-criticism of the Lord's Prayer

From S. Van Tilborg, *Novum Testamentum*, 14 (1972), 94–105.

which tries to take into account all the data of the text. Every stage of the history of the text of the Lord's Prayer contributed to the meaning of the text and these meanings have exerted their influence upon the final text. Therefore, the only permissible approach to the interpretation of the text is to integrate these historical influences in the text-interpretations. The article of M. D. Goulder must be understood along these lines. However, since redaction-criticism has made such progress since the publication of Goulder's article, it is necessary to re-examine his conclusion that 'Jesus gave certain teaching on prayer by precept and example, which was recorded for the most part by St. Mark. This was written up into a formal prayer by St. Matthew, including certain explanations and additions in Matthean language and manner.... St. Matthew's Prayer was abbreviated and amended by St. Luke'.[8]

Whether or not the origin of the Lord's Prayer must be sought in a liturgical development of the Gethsemane story is decisive for every form-critical analysis of Matt. vi 9–13. Because the invocation γενηθήτω τὸ θέλημά σου is lacking in Luke xi 2, and corresponds with Matt. xxvi 42 (contrasting thereby with Matt. xxvi 39 and Mark xiv 36), it is assumed either that Matt. added vi 10b to the Lord's Prayer[9] or that the current rendition of Matt. xxvi 42 was influenced by Matt. vi 10b.[10] Although these arguments evince that Matt. vi 10b cannot have been borrowed directly from Mark xiv 36, they do not prove that Mark xiv 32–42 could not have played an active role in the development of the Lord's Prayer. Although with reference to the redactional character of γενηθήτω τὸ θέλημά σου we can indicate the typically Matthean formulae: ὡς ἐπίστευσας γενηθήτω σοι (viii 13), κατὰ τὴν πίστιν ὑμῶν γενηθήτω ὑμῖν (ix 29), and γενηθήτω σοι ὡς θέλεις (xv 28),[11] the combination of γενηθήτω τὸ τέλημά is found only in Matt. vi 10 and in Matt. xxvi 42. Elsewhere in Matt. there is mention of ποιέω τὸ θέλημα τοῦ πατρός μου (vii 21; xii 50 and xxi 31) and of εἶναι τὸ θέλημα ἔμπροσθεν τοῦ πατρὸς ὑμῶν (xviii 14). Because no further arguments are given to prove that Matt. vi 10b is redactional, it is acceptable that Matt. vi 10b was already part of the text of the Lord's Prayer before Matt. was written. Moreover, the supposition that Matt. xxvi 42 was changed under the influence of Matt. vi 10b does not prove in any way that Matt. vi 10b is redactional.

Every exegesis of the Lord's Prayer must take account of the striking fact that three formulae in Mark xiv 32–42 correspond to the text of the Lord's Prayer: ἀββα ὁ πατήρ (Mark xiv 36), οὐ τί ἐγὼ θέλω ἀλλὰ τί σύ (xiv 36) and προσεύχεσθε ἵνα μὴ ἔλθητε εἰς πειρασμόν (xiv 38). Even though none of these formulae occurs literally in the Lord's Prayer, the correspondence of their contents remains to be explained. Mark (or the tradition preceding him) has Jesus pray three times: at the end of the first day of Jesus' ministry (i 35), after the story of the feeding of the people (vi 46), and at the end of the life of Jesus (xiv 35). But only in the last text, which portrays a certain relationship with the Lord's Prayer, are we confronted with the contents of the prayer of Jesus. The conclusion, then, that in Mark's congregation the Lord's Prayer was unknown, but that it originated in a liturgical reflection upon the Gethsemane story is persuasive. The clearest proof of this, it seems to me, must be sought in the observation that in Matt. xxvi 36–46 as well as in Luke xxii 39–46, that is, in both parallels of Mark xiv 32–42, the influence of the Lord's Prayer is demonstrable. This could mean that the Lord's Prayer (at least in the three above-mentioned formulae) is older than the reconstruction of Mark xiv 32–42 in Matt. xxvi 36–46 and Luke xxii 39–46.

The numerous modifications of Matt. xxvi 36–46,[12] due to this reconstruction, are, however, closely related. In the first place it is striking that the three times Jesus goes to his disciples are given a clear historical character. In Mark only xiv 41 (καὶ ἔρχεται τὸ τρίτον) could lead one to conclude that the author has interpreted the previously mentioned walking up and down of Jesus as a leaving and returning. In Matt. this is developed more explicitly: xxvi 36: ἕως ἂν ἀπελθὼν ἐκεῖ; xxvi 42: πάλιν ἐκ δευτέρου ἀπελθὼν προσηύξατο; xxvi 43: καὶ ἐλθὼν πάλιν εὗρεν; xxvi 44: καὶ ἀφεὶς αὐτοὺς πάλιν ἀπελθὼν προσηύξατο ἐκ τρίτου τὸν αὐτὸν λόγον εἰπὼν πάλιν. Because of this it has become possible to accord a proper place to the prayer of Jesus, which in Mark xiv 35 and 36 is recorded partly in indirect and partly in direct speech. Twice Jesus is presented at prayer. However, the psychological acceptance of Jesus is given more prominence in his second prayer: εἰ δυνατόν ἐστιν (xxvi 39) and εἰ οὐ δύναται (xxvi 42).[13] Finally Matt. places greater emphasis upon the fact that it is an authentic prayer of Jesus himself. Jesus was the only one who remained watching and praying (cf. the addition μετ' αὐτῶν in xxvi 36, μετ' ἐμοῦ in xxvi 38, 40, πρὸς τοὺς μαθητὰς in xxvi 40, 45). These modifications are influenced by the paranetic motive to be unlike the disciples who left Jesus to pray alone. Matt. xxvi 36–46 is transformed into a story, uniquely concerned with the prayer of Jesus in Gethsemane. When we look at the texts of the prayers we see that, in contrast to Mark xiv 36, 38, their conformity with the text of the Lord's Prayer is much stronger: the ὥρα tradition is dropped, there is a reference to πάτερ μου (xxvi 39, 42), γενηθήτω τὸ θέλημά σου (xxvi 42), and Mt xxvi 41 states: ἵνα μὴ εἰσέλθητε εἰς πειρασμόν (compared with Mark xiv 38: ἵνα μὴ ἔλθητε εἰς πειρασμόν).

Also in Luke xxii 39–46 precisely the element of prayer is developed. By shortening the story the word προσεύχομαι (προσευχή) is accentuated (xxii 40, 41, 45, 46: i.e. there is a mention of prayer in every verse except in xxii 42, where the content of the prayer is presented). In this connection it is important to remember that in Luke xxii 39 the indication of the locality in which the prayer takes place has also been altered. Instead of Γεθσημανί Luke has the prayer take place in the ὄρος τῶν ἐλαιῶν, the typical place of Jesus' prayer (cf. Luke vi 12; ix 28).[14] Furthermore, the phrase προσεύχεσθε μὴ εἰσελθεῖν εἰς πειρασμόν is repeated in xxii 40 and in xxii 46, whereby some kind of inclusion takes place.[15] Luke conceives Jesus' prayer as a paranesis for the persecuted congregation. All in all it is apparent that Luke xxii 39–46, even more so than Matt xxvi 36–46, has been influenced by a text, which corresponds to the text which is assumed hypothetically to be the source of the Lord's Prayer: πάτερ (xxii 42), πλὴν μὴ τὸ θέλημά μου ἀλλὰ τὸ σὸν γινέσθω (xxii 42) (it is not only in Matt. that θέλημα and γίγνομαι are combined!) and ἵνα μὴ εἰσέλθητε εἰς πειρασμόν (xxii 46 and 40). (Here again an agreement between Matt. and Luke in contrast with Mark).

Evidently we may not conclude that at one time there existed a form of prayer which consisted only of the formulae: 'Father, your will be done, lead us not into temptation'. The texts of the different gospels differ too much to come to such a conclusion. Undeniably, however, the first form of the Lord's Prayer must have contained these three invocations. Otherwise the similar modifications of Matt. and Luke of the same text of Mark cannot be explained. However, there are other elements to be considered. Since Harnack,[16] Dalman,[17] and Fiebig[18] the conviction has grown that the Jewish prayer 'Qaddish yatom' has influenced the formation of the text of the Lord's Prayer. This thesis is not surprising since the beginning of the Qaddish prayer has a close similarity to the beginning of the Lord's Prayer. In the translation of B. Martin it reads: 'Magnified and sanctified be God's great name in the world he has created according to his will. May he establish his kingdom during your lifetime and days and during the lifetime of the whole house of Israel speedily and soon. And say: Amen'.[19] ἁγιασθήτω τὸ ὄνομά σου ἐλθέτω ἡ βασιλεία σου could have been borrowed directly from this prayer. Form-criticism is forced frequently to work with conjectures and suppositions, but the argument is appreciably strengthened if, as is the case here, it is possible to go beyond the level of mere possibility. Assuming that the Lord's Prayer has resulted from a reflection upon Mark's Gethsemane story, 'the will of God' text is common to both the hypothetical text of the Lord's Prayer and to the Qaddish text. In this way the two traditions are linked with one another. This is a thesis which is accepted implicitly by those who translate γενηθήτω τὸ θέλημα in their Hebrew-Aramaic reconstructed translation with יִתְעֲבֵיר רְעוּתָךְ.[20]

In any case alongside ἁγιασθήτω τὸ ὄνομά σου ἐλθέτω ἡ βασιλεία σου, the Q text of the Lord's Prayer contains also invocations for bread and for the remission of sins. Lohmeyer[21] has pointed out that this latter invocation is related to Mark xi 25. But also here there is no unequivocal tradition: the παραπτώματα of Mark xi 25 are ὀφειλήματα in Matt. vi 12 and ἁμαρτίας in Luke xi 4. However, an insight into this interrelationship is important because if the invocation for bread can be shown to be also a traditional prayer-logion of Jesus, the whole history of the development of the Lord's Prayer is explained. An original core of the prayer from the Gethsemane story would accordingly have been expanded into two directions. The mention of the will of God attracted the influence of the Qaddish prayer and the logion of Jesus concerning the πειρασμός attracted other logia of Jesus about prayer.[22] Is it possible to designate the 'beggar's culture',[23] in which Jesus lived with his disciples, as the original 'Sitz im Leben' of Matt. vi 11 (Luke xi 3)? If that would be the case, a traditional Jesus logion would be handed down in which it is said that one must give oneself up entirely to the care of the Father: a logion which is related directly to Mark vi 8, Matt. vi 25, 31 and par., and at the same time to Mekh 55b, in which R. Eleazar from Modiim comments upon Ex. xvi 4, with the words: 'He who has sufficiently to eat today and says: what will I eat tomorrow?, is of little faith'.[24]

This Jewish-Christian prayer, which must have existed in one form or another (and which is usually confused with the 'original' text of the Lord's Prayer, which at the same time would have to be also an authentic prayer of Jesus), was known in the congregations of Matt. and Luke, where it underwent its final redaction. Because a few recent studies exist about the modifications of Luke xi 2–4,[25] which along the lines of the above hypothesis are restricted to the changing of the aorist into the present (δίδου instead of δός, ἀφίομεν instead of ἀφήκαμεν), and to the changing of σήμερον into καθ' ἡμέραν and to the probable replacement of ἐλθέτω ἡ βασιλεία σου γενηθήτω τὸ θέλημά σου with ἐλθέτω τὸ πνεῦμαι σου, I will restrict myself to Matt. vi 9–13. Matt. makes use of the available material to make it correspond with his own theology, or rather, he reveals his own ideas in the subtle modifications of the existing text. Particularly the expression (πάτερ ἡμῶν) ὁ ἐν τοῖς οὐρανοῖς, which is only used in Matt.'s gospel (v 16, 45; vi 1, 9; vii 11, 21; x 32, 33; xii 50; xvi 17; xviii 10, 14, 19; and its parallel formula ὁ πατὴρ ὁ οὐράνιος in v 48; vi 14, 26, 32; xv 13; xviii 35 and xxiii 9) seems determined by the specific terminology of Matt.'s congregation.[26]

Whether the addition in Matt. vi 10c—ὡς ἐν οὐρανῷ καὶ ἐπὶ γῆς—is also redactional seems more difficult to determine. In the redactional Matt. xxviii 18 the same expression returns. Moreover, relatively speaking, the expression ἐπὶ τῆς γῆς (meaning 'on earth'—as opposed to 'not on earth', 'somewhere else', 'in heaven'—and not 'on the ground') is used more frequently by Matt. than by Mark and Luke (8/3/5): Matt. vi 10, 19; ix 6; xvi 19; xviii 18, 19; xxiii 9; xxviii 18; Mark ii 10; iv 31; ix 3; Luke ii 14; v 24; xviii 8; xxi 23, 25.

To pass judgment upon the redactional character of Matt. vi 12 is even more difficult than for Matt. vi 10c. Must the comparison ὡς καί, which is present in the text of Matt. but not in Luke, be called redactional? On the statistical level Matt. is the only one to use the expression ὡς καί (vi 12; xviii 33 and xx 14), but these are too few number to decide.

The invocation ἀλλὰ ῥῦσαι ἡμᾶς ἀπὸ τοῦ πονηροῦ allows us to move to less disputed grounds. Matt. has a strongly marked preference for the word πονηρός (26/2/13). Moreover, when he borrows this word from his *Vorlagen*, it is used mainly as an adjective, but in the material proper to Matt. the word received a typical meaning. Matt. is the only one who uses the word as a qualification for the Jewish leaders (cf. Matt. ix 4; xii 34, 39, 45; xvi 4; xxii 18). Besides, he expands the usage of the word considerably: as a plural pronoun οἱ πονηροὶ it is found in Matt. v 45; vii 11; xii 34; xiii 49; xxii 10 (of which Matt. vii 11 is borrowed from Q) and as a singular noun ὁ πονηρός (respectively τὸ πονηρόν) it is found in Matt. v 37, 39; vi 13; xiii 19, 38. Matt. vi 13b must be placed in this context. And if it seems unacceptable that Matt. himself added the final part of the Lord's Prayer, it is at least probable to suppose that the congregation in which he lived was influenced by these ideas in such a way that this invocation was added almost automatically.

But how do these modifications fit in the whole of the gospel of Matt.? Because it is possible to point out similar nuances in other texts, the conclusions of the statistical material are consolidated and at the same time clarify the meaning of the Matthean interpretation of the Lord's Prayer. Because the word heaven is mentioned twice (πάτερ ἡμῶν ὁ ἐν τοῖς οὐρανοῖς and ὡς ἐν οὐρανῷ καὶ ἐπὶ γῆς) and a comparison is made between heaven and earth, there is a suggestion of an opposition between the Father, who dwells in heaven, and the earth, which is man's dwelling place. We have cited the texts in which this opposition occurs elsewhere in Matt.'s gospel, namely vi 19; ix 6; xvi 19; xviii 18, 19; xxiii 9; xxviii 18. For our purposes the most important parallel is Matt. xxiii 9, because also here there is a reference to a Father in heaven. Attempts have been made to discover a Jewish background for this verse but this has led to several difficulties. Townsend[27] has pointed out that in Judaism the title 'abba' was never granted to living persons. This leaves us with only two possible explanations of Matt. xxiii 9. Either one follows a Jewish tradition, which granted the title 'father' to the renowned scribes of the past, so that Matt. xxiii 9 reads: 'Do not call any of your great spiritual leaders from the past "father", because only God is your father'. Or one follows the tradition from the Talmud, which calls no one except the patriarchs 'father' (Ber 26b) so that to understand Matt. xxiii 9 one must consult Matt. iii 9 and Luke iii 8: 'In Christianity not even the fatherhood of Abraham counts'. But to me neither of these explanations is very satisfactory. How is the opposition ἐπὶ τῆς γῆς–οὐράνιος to be understood? It would go too far to call the deceased rabbis or Abraham ἐπὶ τῆς γῆς. In my opinion it is not excluded that for the explanation of Matt. xxiii 9 we should turn to the Greek background of stoicism, which teaches the union of the human race with God as the only father. In any case this would offer also an explanation for Matt. xxiii 8c: πάντες δὲ ὑμεῖς ἀδελφοί ἐστε (ἐστε is to be translated as an imperative). Matt. xxiii 9 wants to say that all men must be brothers to one another, because the only father they have dwells in heaven. Now it is precisely with this sense in mind that Matt. xxiii 8c, 9 can function as a norm for the interpretation of Matt. vi 9–13. With his redactional transformation Matt. wants to impress upon his congregation that the mention of the name of God implies a task to men on earth. Since our Father dwells in heaven and we for that reason should be brothers, this will of the Father is to be realized on earth.

The relationship of Matt. vi 12 to Matt. vi 14–15 and xviii 35 has been recognized for some time and therefore it does not require extensive comment. It ought to be stressed, however, that Matt. himself (if he can indeed be called the author of the strict comparison ὡς καὶ, since the evidence of the statistical material is inconclusive) cannot be blamed for making the human attitude of forgiveness a model for God's attitude.[28] From the decidedly redactional character of Matt. vi 14–15 and xviii 35[29] it appears that the author of the gospel of Matt. did not see the mutual remission of sins as a human achievement, but more as a duty. For Matt. the emphasis is placed on the negative demand: if one does not do it, the Father will punish. Whatever the original meaning of the ὡς καὶ may have been, according to Matt. the comparison must be understood in this way.

Above I have given the related text material of Matt. vi 13b. According to Matt. humanity can be divided into the good and the evil (Matt. v 45), who will be separated only at the final judgment (xiii 49).[30] Matt.'s terms of reference are not the institutional church. The good and the evil are found in equal numbers on the roads (xxii 10). It is only because the servants invite everyone that the evil are also present at the wedding. Being good or evil is antecedent to whether or not one is a disciple of Jesus. According to Matt. it is not possible to outline concretely the evil in men as long as Jesus is accepted. Matt. makes only one exception. It becomes apparent from his redactional additions that the Jewish leaders are to be considered evil because they refused to accept Jesus as a healer (ix 4; xii 22–24), as an exorcist (xii 34, 43–45), or as a teacher (xxii 15–22); and because they asked for a sign (xii 38–42) and tried to put him to the test (xvi 1–4; xxii 18). Rejection of Jesus is the most certain proof of a person's wickedness, but this proof is not always given. In the interpretation of the parable of the seed and of the darnel among the wheat (xiii 18–23, 36–43) Matt. gives the reason for this. In the cosmos the sons of the kingdom live side by side with the sons of the wicked one (xiii 37, 38). At the source of this evil, however, we must look for the wicked one (xiii 19) who makes use of the present lack of discernment and removes the good seed.[31] A struggle ensues between the Son of man, the sower of the good seed, and the devil, the sower of the bad seed. The ultimate outcome may be known but the man must be watchful, for the wicked one works while everyone is asleep. Along these lines the addition of Matt. vi 13b ought to be understood. Matt. added the invocation because he wanted the faithful to be aware of evil. Indirectly the verse is determined christologically: it admonishes us not to give in to the evil one, but to follow Jesus also when tempted.

In the preceding study I have attempted to present a form-criticism of the Lord's Prayer. What are the results of this research? My point of departure has been that Mark's gospel does not contain the Lord's Prayer, but nevertheless discloses three texts reminiscent of the text of the Our Father: ἀββα ὁ πατήρ (xiv 36), οὐ τί ἐγὼ θέλω ἀλλὰ τί σύ (xiv 36), and προσεύχεσθε ἵνα μὴ ἔλθητε εἰς πειρασμόν (xiv 38). From there it is easy to conclude that in the congregation of Mark the Lord's Prayer was not known but that it originated in a liturgical reflection upon the Gethsemane story. This conclusion is strengthened by the observation that both in Matt. xxvi 36–46 and in Luke xxii 39–46 the influence of the Lord's Prayer can be demonstrated.

On the sole basis of the constellation of texts it is impossible, of course, to conclude that at any time a prayer form existed which consisted of the formulae 'Father, your will be done, lead us not into temptation'. But most probably the oldest text of the Lord's Prayer contained these invocations. In fact we observe that the Q-text of the Lord's Prayer has expanded this hypothetical core in two directions. The reference to the 'will of God' caused the influence of the Qaddish-prayer. The text then read, 'Father, hallowed be your name, your kingdom come, your will be done'. And the Jesus-logion concerning the πειρασμός attracted other prayer-logia of Jesus: the invocation of the bread and of the remission of sins so that the text developed into: 'give us today our daily bread, forgive us our guilt just as we forgive to others their guilt, lead us not into temptation'.

This Jewish-Christian prayer underwent its final transformation when it was assumed in the gospels of Matt. (and Luke). With reference to Matt. it may be assumed that the final redactor of the gospel of Matt. is responsible for the formulae (πάτερ ἡμῶν) ὁ ἐν τοῖς οὐρανοῖς (vi 9b) and ἀλλὰ ῥῦσαι ἡμᾶς ἀπὸ τοῦ πονηροῦ (vi 13b). Presumably he is also responsible for the addition ὡς ἐν οὐρανῷ καὶ επὶ γῆς (vi 10c) and possibly also for the comparison ὡς καὶ in vi 12. However, to indicate this redactional activity is of no·value unless at the same time it is interpreted against the background of the whole gospel. Through the redactional additions ὁ ἐν τοῖς ουρανοῖς and ὡς ἐν οὐρανῷ καὶ ἐπὶ γῆς an opposition is suggested between the Father, dwelling in heaven, and earth, the dwelling place of man. Matt. intended to refer to the redactional verse Matt. xxiii 8c–9: Since our Father dwells in heaven, we on earth must all be brothers. The redactional change in vi 12 (if it is indeed redactional) is meant to clarify that the mutual remission of sins must not be conceived as a human achievement, but as a duty. The redactional addition ἀλλὰ ῥῦσαι ἡμᾶς ἀπὸ τοῦ πονηροῦ in vi 13b is meant to remind the congregation that it must make a choice between Jesus and the evil one. Do not give in to the evil one but choose to follow Jesus also when tempted.

NOTES

1. M. D. Goulder, "The Composition of the Lord's Prayer", *JTS* 14 (1963), 32–45.
2. E. Lohmeyer, *Das Vaterunser*, Göttingen, 1962.
3. J. Jeremias, "The Lord's Prayer in Modern Research", *ET* 71 (1959/60), 141–146. (I used the French version: "Paroles de Jésus, Le sermon sur la Montagne, Le Notre Père", Paris, 1965.)
4. R. E. Brown, "The 'Pater noster' as an Eschatological Prayer", in *New Testament Studies*, Milwaukee, 1965, 217–253.
5. H. Schürmann, *Das Gebet des Herrn aus der Verkündigung Jesu erläutert*, Freiburg, 1965; H. van den Bussche, *Het Onze Vader*, Tielt/Den Haag, 1963; J. Carmignac, *Recherches sur le 'Notre Père'*, Paris, 1969; B. van Iersel, *H. Land* 13 (1960), 57–59, 65–69, 122–124, 137–139, 154–156, 165–167, 177–180.
6. The eschatological interpretation of the invocation of the remission of sins presents the greatest difficulties, but according to these authors also the invocation of the bread and the πειρασμός need not be interpreted in an eschatological fashion.
7. *Das Problem der Parusieverzögerung in den synoptischen Evangelien und in der Apostelgeschichte*, Berlin, 1960, 95–113.
8. M. D. Goulder, "The Composition of the Lord's Prayer", *JTS* 14 (1963), 35.
9. J. Jeremias, *Paroles de Jésus*, 75–80; M. Schürmann, "Die Bergpredigt", in 'Botschaft und Geschichte', Gesammelte Aufsätze, I, *Zur Evangelienforschung*, Tübingen, 1953, 127. They are particularly sensitive to the liturgical arguments. Jeremias points out that the three Matthean additions ('Father, who art in heaven'; 'your will be done,' and 'deliver us from evil') are found exactly at the end of the invocation or verse. Dibelius, referring to Ps. cxix 164, thinks that the congregation wanted to pray a sevenfold prayer to fulfil the psalm which mentions giving thanks to God seven times daily.
10. H. Schürmann, *Das Gebet des Herrn*, 66, note 101; W. Grundmann, *Das Evangelium nach Matthäus*.
11. W. Trilling, *Das wahre Israel*, 190, note 24. Moreover, H. Held has made it clear in "Matthäus als Interpret der Wundergeschichte", in Bornkamm-Barth, *Überlieferung und Auslegung im Matthäus-Evangelium*, Neukirchen, 1965, 227 and 263–284, that these formulae are used only in miracle stories. Therefore, the contrast between these formulae and the one that is used in the Lord's Prayer is greater than appears from the work of Trilling.
12. K. G. Kuhn says in "Jesus in Gethsemane", *EvTh* 12 (1952/53), 266–268, that Matt. elaborated further the double tradition of Mark xiv 32–42. But it may be asked whether Kuhn's distinction between the A tradition and the B tradition of Mark xiv 32–42 has been worked out adequately. According to Kuhn the A tradition consists of Mark xiv 32, 35, 40, 41 and the B tradition of Mark xiv 33, 34, 36, 37, 38, but the difference between the second person singular in xiv 37 (ἴσχυσας) and the second person plural in xiv 38 (γρηγορεῖτε κτλ) makes it improbable that Mark xiv 38 ought to belong to the B tradition. Also it is not clear why Mark xiv 36 must be connected with xiv 34. Could not καὶ ἔλεγεν point to an influence of Mark? For further criticism of Kuhn's article, cf. P. Benoit, "Les outrages à Jésus Prophète (Mc. xiv 65 par)", in *Neotestamentica et Patristica, Freundesgabe für O. Cullmann*, Leiden, 1962, 103 and recently in E. Linnemann, *Studien zur Passionsgeschichte*, Göttingen, 1970, 11–40.
13. See G. Strecker, *Der Weg der Gerechtigkeit*, 183.
14. H. Conzelmann, *Die Mitte der Zeit*, Tübingen, 1964, 38.

15. W. Ott, *Gebet und Heil. Der Bedeutung der Gebetsparanäse in der lukanischen Theologie*, München, 1965, 82–85.

16. A. von Harnack, "Die ursprungliche Gestalt des Vaterunsers", in *Sitzungsberichte der königlichen preussischen Akademie der Wissenschaften*, Berlin, 1904, 195–208 argues for the reconstruction of the original Lord's Prayer particularly by means of text-criticism.

17. G. Dalman, *Die Worte Jesu*, Darmstadt, 1965, 304–321.

18. P. Fiebig, *Das Vaterunser: Ursprung, Sinn und Bedeutung des christlichen Hauptgebets*, Gütersloh, 1927; cf. also J. Jeremias, *Paroles de Jésus*, 87–88 and R. Aron, *Les origines juives du Pater*, Maison-Dieu 85 (1966), 35–40.

19. B. Martin, *Prayer in Judaism*, New York, 1968, 147.

20. Because only then does it become clear that the two prayers are related terminologically; cf. G. Dalman, *Die Worte Jesu*, 314; E. Lohmeyer, *Das Vaterunser*, 15; K. G. Kuhn, *Achtzehngebet und Vaterunser und der Reim*, Tübingen, 1950, 32.

21. E. Lohmeyer, *Das Vaterunser*, 117–126; cf. also M. D. Goulder, "The Composition of the Lord's Prayer", *JTS* 14 (1963), 36–38.

22. Perhaps it is possible to say: 'attracted the content of all prayer logia of Jesus'. For if Mark xiii 18 is left out, because it is bound too much to the concrete situation of the text, then the Lord's Prayer has attracted all the logia about prayer.

23. In this connection the article of K. H. Rengstorf is very interesting ("Geben ist seliger denn Nehmen. Bemerkungen zu dem ausserevangelischen Herrenwort Apg 20, 35", in '*Die Leibhaftigkeit des Wortes*', *Festgabe für A. Köberle*, Hamburg, 1958, 23–33.) Cf. also J. Jeremias, *Die Gleichnisse Jesu*, Göttingen, 1965, 159; H. Schürmann, *Das Gebet des Herrn*, Freiburg, 1965, 85.

24. Strack-Billerbeck, I, 412; cf. also J. Dupont-P. Bonnard, *Le Notre Père, Notes Exégétiques*, Maison-Dieu 85 (1966), 22.

25. E. Grässer, *Das Problem der Parusieverzögerung*, 107–111; R. Leaney, "The Lucan Text of the Lord's Prayer (Lk. XI. 2-4)", *NT* 1 (1956), 103–111; W. Ott, *Gebet und Heil*, 112–122.

26. G. Strecker, *Der Weg der Gerechtigkeit*, 17.

27. J. T. Townsend, "Matthew 23, 9", *JTS* 12 (1961), 56–59; cf. also C. H. Dodd, *Historical Tradition in the Fourth Gospel*, Cambridge, 1963, 331–332.

28. See especially the work of J. Jeremias, *Paroles de Jésus*, 78.

29. The judgment about the redactional character of Matt. vi 14 must be seen in connection with the judgment about the integration of Mark xi 25 in Matthew's gospel. It appears that Mark xi 25 was incorporated in the text of the Lord's Prayer. This text existed before Matt. and since he was aware of the existence of Mark xi 25, he inserted it once more in his gospel. The redactional character of Matt. vi 15 is apparent from its connection with Matt. xviii 35. Matt. wanted to put the emphasis upon the negative character of punishment in the remission of sins. For Matt. xviii 35 cf. G. Strecker, *Der Weg der Gerechtigkeit*, 215; E. Linnemann, *Die Gleichnisse Jesu*, Göttingen, 1966, 111–119; J. Jeremias, *Die Gleichnisse Jesu*, 207–211; F. H. Breukelmann, "Eine Erklärung des Gleichnisses vom Schalksknecht, Matth. 18, 23–35", in '*PARRHESIA*', *K. Barth zum 80. Geburtstag*, Zürich, 1966, 216–287.

30. It remains an exegetical question whether through his conception of the final judgment, Matt. wanted to exert pressure upon his Christian congregations to eradicate the existing evils or whether in more general terms Matt. considered the factual living side by side of the good and the evil in the world-cosmos. It is not my intention to delve into this problem, but in my opinion Matt. xxv 32 and xxii 10 seem to indicate that Matt. thinks in terms of the whole world.

31. Here the same exegetical question of note 30 arises. A defense of the thesis that the congregation is a corpus mixtum can be found also in E. Klostermann, *Das Matthäusevangelium*, Tübingen, 1927, 123; H. J. Holtzmann, *Hand-Commentar zum NT*, Tübingen-Leipzig, 1901, 250; J. Schmid, *Das Evangelium nach Matthäus*, Regensburg, 1956, 225; W. Trilling, *Das wahre Israel*, 126; G. Bornkamm, *Enderwartung und Kirche im Matthäus-Evangelium*, Neukirchen, 1965, 40.

A defense that Matt. thinks of the whole cosmos, which does not coincide with the congregation, can be found in A. Vögtle, "Das christologische und ekklesiologische Anliegen von Mt. 28, 18-20", in *Studia Evangelica*, II, Berlin, 1964, 287–292; R. Walker, *Die Heilsgeschichte im ersten Evangelium*, Göttingen, 1967, 99–101.

Redaction Criticism at Work: A Sample

*Related to form criticism but moving in a different direc-
tion with the results of form-critical analysis is redaction
criticism. Redaction criticism attempts to put the forms
together, in the sense that it shows how an author or editor
(the redactor) has given final shape to the materials. Important here is the redactor's purpose in synthesizing the
materials.*

*The two directions of form criticism, leading back to
the original form and its function in the community, and
redaction criticism, leading back to the unity of the text as
we have received it, can also be seen in Van Tilborg, pp.
333–343.*

*By looking at three accounts of the same incident
(Jesus at Caesarea Philippi), Norman Perrin shows the significance of differences and the unity in each redaction.
The form is a story of the historical Jesus, but the purpose
relates to the Lord and his church. Further, each telling of
the story reveals the author's purpose.*

T HIS essay presents an example of the kind of thing redaction criticism does, and in this way we hope to help the discipline come alive
for the reader. We have chosen the account of the incident at Caesarea
Philippi, the story concerning the confession of Peter and the subsequent
teaching of Jesus on discipleship (Mark 8:27—9:1 with its parallels, Matt.
16:13-28 and Luke 9:18-27), because this story has always played a
large part in any attempt to reconstruct a life of Jesus. In this example,
therefore, the differences between a redaction-critical approach and the
older way of regarding it as essentially a historical narrative will be most
evident.

At this point we pause to make it clear that we are not concerned
here with arguing the case for redaction criticism as an approach to the

From Norman Perrin, *What is Redaction Criticism?* (1969), pp. 40–63.

Gospels in general or to this narrative in particular. The evidence and arguments which led the present writer to adopt form criticism and redaction criticism as the only legitimate approach to the Gospel narratives were set out in my *Rediscovering the Teaching of Jesus,* pp. 15–32, and there is no point in repeating them here. So far as this particular narrative is concerned, the way that redaction criticism is able to make sense of the phenomena demonstrably present in the texts is itself a validation of the methodology.

THE MARCAN NARRATIVE: MARK 8:27—9:1

The Marcan narrative has a remarkably clear structure and it should first be read in its entirety, with the reader resolutely leaving to one side any reminiscences of the Matthean or Lucan parallels and even more resolutely banishing from his mind reminiscences of lives of Jesus that he may have read. When we do this we arrive at the following general picture. Jesus and his disciples are on a journey from Bethsaida to some villages in the region of Caesarea Philippi and he asks them the double question: Who do men say . . . Who do you say that I am? They reply with a statement that represents the general opinion (such as Mark had already used in 6:14 f.), and then, through the mouth of Peter, with the fundamental confession of early Christianity: "You are the Christ." Jesus accepts this and charges them to keep it from anyone else, and he then goes on to teach them concerning the coming suffering of the Son of man (note: "Son of man," not "Christ"). Peter vehemently rejects this teaching, and Jesus, with an eye to the disciples as a group, in turn reprimands Peter in the strongest possible terms, identifying him in this moment as Satan. This dispute with Peter leads to a second block of teaching by Jesus, this time directed to the crowd as well as to the disciples, indicating that the disciple must be prepared to accept the possibility of martyrdom as the price of his discipleship. The narrative then reaches its climax in two sayings: the first issues a stern warning that those who fail the Son of man in the hour of trial will rue it at the Last Judgment; and the second offers a reassuring promise that those who stand firm will be delivered by the coming of the kingdom "in power."

Reading the narrative by itself in this way, one cannot help but be struck by a number of distinctive features. In particular there is the remarkable way in which the action moves backwards and forwards between the historical situation of the ministry of Jesus and the historical situation of the church for which Mark is writing. The reply to the first question refers to opinions available in the Palestinian situation of the ministry of Jesus, but the second block of teaching, in its present form, uses language derived from the situation of the early church ("take up his cross," ". . . and the gospel's"). The questions, answers, and teaching are on the lips of Jesus and Peter, but the titles involved are from the christological vocabulary of the early church. Further in this direction, we must note that, although the characters in the pericope bear names or designations derived from the circumstances of the ministry (i.e., "Jesus," "Peter," "the multitude"), they also equally represent the circumstances of the early church: "Jesus" is the Lord addressing his church, "Peter" represents fallible believers who confess correctly yet go on to interpret their confession incorrectly, and "the multitude" is the whole church membership for whom the general teaching which follows is designed. So we come to the all-important point so far as a redaction-critical view of the narrative is concerned: it has the form of a story about the historical Jesus and his disciples but a purpose in terms of the risen Lord and his church. Moreover, this purpose is a specifically Marcan purpose; it represents Mark's understanding of what the risen Lord has to say to the church of his day.

The fundamental premise of redaction criticism, then, is that the pericope can be analyzed from the perspective of a Marcan purpose. The goal of such an analysis is to understand the purpose and the theology that is revealed in the purpose. To this end we concern ourselves both with the individual parts of the narrative and with the story as a whole. In other words, we analyze the constituent parts of the narrative, such as the sayings, to see what they tell us of Mark as one who gathers, modifies, or creates tradition, and we analyze the total narrative in terms of its overall purposes, such as its setting in the framework of the Gospel as a whole, to see what this will tell us about Mark as an evangelist.

We shall begin with a discussion of four constituent parts of this narrative: the prediction of the passion (8:31); the teaching about discipleship (8:34–37); the climactic warning (8:38); and the climactic promise (9:1). In each case we shall raise the question of the previous history of the material in the tradition in order to set the stage for a consideration of the Marcan redactional work upon that material, and then we shall discuss both the redaction of the material by Mark and also the particular use which he has made of it.

THE PREDICTION OF THE PASSION: MARK 8:31

> And he began to teach them that the Son of man must suffer many things, and be rejected by the elders and the chief priests and the scribes, and be killed, and after three days rise again.

This is one of three passion predictions in Mark (8:31; 9:31; 10:33 f.). These sayings have such a complex history in the tradition that it is beyond our present capacity to unravel it in its details. This complexity is really what we should expect, for the problem of the crucified Messiah was the major problem for the early church, both in terms of the development of her own theology and of the development of an apologetic to Judaism, and she brought her every theological resource to bear upon it. The result of the church's wrestling with this problem is that the traditions that crystallized out of her struggle bear the marks of many different factors (use of various Old Testament passages in exegesis and "passion apologetic" [B. Lindars], a speculative Son of man theology, a development of a doctrine of divine necessity, emphasis upon the cross as redemptive and/or the resurrection as decisive victory, etc.). It is a task beyond our current resources to analyze these factors in their entirety, although we are increasingly developing insights into various parts of the tradition they represent.[1]

In this particular instance, therefore, we cannot learn anything about Mark and his theology from his redaction of tradition, but the matter is far different with regard to his use of it. Following in part Tödt's excellent analysis of this aspect of the Marcan theological purpose,[2] we note that the section of the Gospel 8:27—10:52 serves to introduce the passion narrative and to prepare the reader to understand it correctly. It presents to the reader the Marcan theological understanding of the cross; to use our own words, it offers a theological treatise on the meaning of the cross in narrative form. The section is a carefully composed unit held together by three geographical references: 8:27, ". . . to the villages of Caesarea Philippi" (north of Galilee); 9:30, ". . . from there and passed through Galilee"; 10:1, ". . . he left there and went to the region of Judea and beyond the Jordan" (i.e., he moves toward Jerusalem). Each of these three divisions of the unit has its own passion prediction (8:31; 9:31; 10:33 f.), and the dramatic tension is heightened by the fact that the last one includes a specific reference to the Jerusalem toward which the group is moving as the locale of the passion (Mark himself must be responsible for this aspect of the saying). So we learn from the sayings themselves, and from their function in the composition of the Gospel, something of the Marcan theology of the cross. Since we cannot isolate the Marcan redactional elements in the sayings themselves, we cannot determine how much of this theology is specifically Marcan and how much general early Christian, but the boldness of conception and the effectiveness of execution in presenting it in this narrative form is remarkable.

THE TEACHING ABOUT DISCIPLESHIP: MARK 8:34-37

And he called to him the multitude with his disciples, and said to them, "If any man would come after me, let him deny himself and take up his cross and follow me. For whoever would save his life will lose it; and whoever loses his life for my sake and the gospel's will save it. For what does it profit a man, to gain the whole world and forfeit his life? For what can a man give in return for his life?"

This section is made up of four sayings which very likely originally circulated separately in the tradition and then were gradually brought together because of their similarity of content and because of the common catchword "life." In the parallel passage in Matthew (16:24–26) all four sayings appear; in Luke (9:23–25) only the first three; in addition Matthew has versions of the first two joined together at his 10:38 f. and Luke has versions of them separately at his 14:27 and 17:33, Mark's verses 36 and 37 are found in Matthew and Luke only where they are following Mark (Luke omits verse 37), but they must have originally been separate sayings because they make quite different points: verse 36 that riches are of no avail at death and verse 37 that life is the highest good (Bultmann). So Mark has brought together a group of sayings which originally circulated separately, but in doing this he is only completing a process that was already going on in the tradition. In itself this is common editorial activity in the tradition and of no more theological significance for Mark than for the anonymous editors of the tradition who preceded him. However, the Marcan activity in introducing a group of sayings on the cost of discipleship at this particular point in the narrative does serve a definite theological purpose: it reflects the Marcan conviction that, as went the master, so must go the disciple, with all that this implies theologically. That this is definitely the result of deliberate editorial activity can be seen from the fact that it happens in each instance of a passion prediction and, moreover, there is a constant editorial pattern of prediction—misunderstanding—teaching: so in 8:31, passion prediction; 8:32 f., dispute between Jesus and Peter; 8:34–37, teaching about discipleship; and again, in 9:31, passion prediction; 9:33 f., report of a dispute about greatness; 9:35–37, teaching, and finally, 10:33 f., passion prediction; 10:35–41, request of James and John arising out of their misunderstanding of the nature of glory; 10:42–45, teaching. Furthermore, the three sets of teaching are carefully related to one another in content so as to make a total impact and to develop a total theological point. In the first one the disciple must be prepared to take up his cross, as did the master; in the second he must imitate the master in servanthood; in the third that servanthood is defined in a saying which both takes up the previous themes of cross and servanthood and presents these aspects of the Marcan theology in all their fullness: "For the Son of man also came not to be served but to serve, and to give his life as a ransom for many." The boldness and effectiveness of this method of stating a theme and developing an exhortation based upon it must again be described as remarkable.

THE CLIMACTIC WARNING: MARK 8:38

> For whoever is ashamed of me and of my words in this adulterous and sinful generation, of him will the Son of man also be ashamed, when he comes in the glory of his Father with the holy angels.

This saying has a history in the tradition prior to Mark which can be traced with comparative certainty.[3] In its very earliest form it probably ran (in Aramaic): "Everyone who acknowledges me before man, he will be acknowledged before the angels of God." It was taken up into that tradition of the early church which was concerned with the pronouncement of judgment upon offenders, which judgment however would be carried out by God at the *eschaton* (end time).[4] It was then translated into Greek and came to be known in the variety of versions which can be detected in Matthew 10:32 f. and parallel passage, Luke 12:8 f.:

> So every one who acknowledges me before men, I [Luke: the Son of man] also will acknowledge before my Father who is in heaven [Luke: the angels of God]; but whoever denies me before men, I also will deny before my Father who is in heaven [Luke: will be denied before the angels of God].

Here the important points to note are that the saying has become a double saying using the verbs "acknowledge" and "deny," and that the subject of the action in the second clause can now either be "I" or "the Son of man" or God (when the verb is in the passive). It must have been in some such version that Mark knew the saying, and the changes from this earlier version to the version in Mark 8:38 are due to Marcan redaction.

In the tradition from which the saying comes, the emphasis was upon the future judgment of God, and a specific form was created to express this judgment, namely, the form of a two-part sentence with the same verb in each part, expressing in the first part the activity being judged and in the second the nature of the judgment. This act of pronouncing judgment was carried out at the Eucharist and the form used for it came to be widely used in early Christian exhortation, no doubt because it carried with it something of the aura of that moment of solemn judgment at the Eucharist. It must have been for this reason that Mark chooses to use the form here. Intending this as the climactic warning of the pericope, he deliberately chooses a form which for his readers will strike the chord of the solemn judgment pronouncement of the church.

The changes in the actual saying from the version(s) detectable in Matthew 10:32 f. and parallel passages are similarly reflective of the Marcan purpose. The two most important of these changes are the generalizing of the specific double emphasis "acknowledge-deny" into the single "be ashamed,"[5] and the choice of "Son of man" to express the subject of the second clause rather than either of the other possibilities presented by the tradition, i.e., the first personal pronoun or the passive voice (the latter as a circumlocution for "God"). The first of these changes is due to the fact that the saying is now the warning part of a double climax of warning and promise (the promise being found in Mark 9:1) and so needs to become a single warning saying to balance the second saying, the promise. A double saying including both promise and warning would clearly be unbalanced when linked with a single saying expressing promise. The choice of "Son of man" has a double ground. On the one hand it makes a very effective combination to balance "Son of man" in the warning against "kingdom of God" in the promise, and on the other hand the use of "Son of man" here naturally recalls the "Son of man" in 8:31 (where, it should be noted, "Son of man" is introduced rather abruptly since "Christ" is actually the title upon which the contextual discussion turns). By means of this juxtaposition Mark is able to make the christ-ological point that the one whose cross is the example to be followed is also the one whose coming in judgment is to be anticipated. In this context we may note that the use of the verb "ashamed" becomes very effective indeed, a point which provides another reason for regarding this version of the saying as a Marcan product.

THE CLIMACTIC PROMISE: MARK 9:1

> And he said to them, "Truly, I say to you, there are some standing here who will not taste death before they see the kingdom of God come with power."

The present writer has wrestled with this saying throughout his academic career, and during the course of some ten years of work his opinion has moved from holding it to be a genuine saying of Jesus to accepting that it is a Marcan product.[6] To summarize what we have argued in more detail elsewhere, there are a number of features about the saying which call for an explanation: it has distinctively Marcan charac-teristics, and it is related in form to Mark 13:30 as it is in content to Mark 8:38. We shall discuss these matters in turn.

The Marcan characteristics are the reference to "seeing" the parousia and the use of the words "power" and "glory" in this kind of context. Mark speaks of seeing the parousia here in 9:1, again in 13:26, and for a third time in 14:62. Matthew follows Mark on each occasion (Matt. 16:28; 24:30; 26:64), but he never uses the verb "to see" in con-nection with the parousia elsewhere in his Gospel. Luke transforms Mark 9:1 into a non-parousia reference, as we shall argue below, and he follows Mark 13:26 (Luke 21:27), but he omits the reference to seeing in his version of Mark 14:62 (Luke 22:69). Luke, like Matthew, also has no such usage except in dependence on Mark. Mark uses "power" and "glory" in a parousia context in 8:38 ("glory") and 9:1 ("power"). Both Matthew (16:27 f.) and Luke (9:26 f.) follow him with regard to the use of "glory" but omit the reference to "power." Mark 10:37 has "in your glory" with reference to the parousia, Matthew (20:21) changes this to "in your kingdom"; Luke has no parallel. Mark 13:26 speaks of the Son of man "coming with great power and glory"; Matthew (24:30) and Luke (21:27) both follow this. Luke has no such usage elsewhere and Matthew only one, Matthew 25:31, which is the beginning of the parable of the sheep and the goats: "When the Son of man comes in his glory, and all the angels with him, then he will sit on his glorious throne." In view of Matthew 19:28, ". . . in the new world, when the Son of man shall sit on his glorious throne" (no parallels), this looks like a combination of Marcan and Matthean characteristics.

The relationship between Mark 9:1 and 13:30 in form and content is as follows: (1) Both begin with the identical solemn asseveration, "Truly, I say to you." (2) Both continue with a promise that is similar in content (9:1, ". . . there are some standing here who will not taste death before they see the kingdom of God come with power"; 13:30, ". . . this generation will not pass away before all these things take place") and exactly parallel in form. Both use in the Greek a clause introduced by *hoti* and both express the negation by the use of double negative with the subjunctive. (3) Both relate the promise to the coming of the eschaton.

The best explanation for this combination of data is the supposition that Mark himself has composed his 9:1 using the saying he has in his 13:30 as a model. Verse 13:30 itself is almost certainly non-Marcan. It is a general piece of Jewish Christian apocalyptic which has non-Marcan linguistic characteristics, and it fits its present context so very closely (it finally answers the question which introduces the apocalyptic discourse, 13:5–27, and the "these things" clearly are the things referred to in that discourse) that there can be little doubt but that the apocalyptic seer (neither Jesus nor Mark!) who is responsible for this discourse composed 13:30 in order to bring his discourse to an end.[7] With this as a model Mark has varied the content of the affirmation but not the form, adopting for his purpose some stock phraseology from Jewish apocalyptic. (Compare IV Ezra 6:25 f.: "And it shall be whosoever shall have survived all these things that I have foretold unto thee, he shall be saved and shall see my salvation. . . . And the men who have been taken up, who have not tasted death from their birth, shall appear.") The promise itself varies in content from 13:30 in that it is expressed in terms of the kingdom's coming in power. The use of "kingdom of God" in this context is undoubtedly due to the fact that such a usage is a feature of the Jesus tradition itself. As Mark had gone to Jewish apocalyptic for the raw materials of the first part of this saying, so he has gone to the tradition of the sayings of Jesus for those of the second part. He will have been motivated in part by the fact that in the Jesus tradition "the kingdom of God" is most often used in a context of promise or blessing. So it will have been natural for him to construct a kingdom saying in the form of a promise to balance the use of "Son of man" in the preceding warning. But although this kind of use of "kingdom of God," and of the verb "to come," were characteristic of the Jesus tradition, and, for that matter, of Jesus himself, both the tense of the verb (the perfect) and the phrase "in power" are Marcan. To put the verb in the perfect and to add "in power" is to stress the promise as a promise for an experience of complete fulfillment, all of which comes naturally in a saying intended as the climactic promise of a whole pericope.

We have spent some time on the arguments for the Marcan authorship of this particular saying because this is an important example of one kind of redactional possibility, namely, free composition by the redactor on the basis of traditional materials of various kinds. Indeed, one reason for choosing this narrative as an example is that within its comparatively brief compass we have instances of three distinct redactional possibilities: (1) the bringing together of previously existing independent sayings or shorter combinations of sayings (8:36–37); (2) the modification of a saying in an existing tradition of the church (8:38); (3) the creation of a new saying using materials already present in the traditions of the church and of Jewish apocalyptic.

So Mark 9:1 is a climactic promise constructed by Mark himself to bring to an end this dramatic incident. It balances the warning of the preceding saying and ends the whole on a note of assurance, an assurance expressed in the strongest terms which the traditions inherited by Mark could offer or which Mark could conceive.[8] A discussion of the exact meaning indicated by Mark in this assurance must wait until we have viewed the narrative as a whole from the perspective of Mark's intention, to which we now turn.

THE NARRATIVE AS A WHOLE

Having discussed in some detail four individual parts of the Caesarea Philippi narrative in Mark, we now must consider the narrative again in its entirety. When we do this, one thing noticeable is the very strong emphasis upon persecution and suffering. The Son of man "must suffer many things," the disciple must "deny himself and take up his cross"; there is the ever-present possibility of saving one's life only to lose it, of losing it only to save it, and so on. Moreover, as we noted earlier, the whole moves in a most remarkable manner between the historical situation of the ministry of Jesus and that of the early church, and it is quite evident that the pericope is concerned both with the sufferings of Jesus as Son of man on the one hand and with the potential sufferings of Christians "for my sake and the gospel's" on the other. The narrative presupposes a context of formal persecution for the readers. Recognizing this to be the case, a major purpose of the narrative then becomes apparent: the author is concerned with preparing the readers for that persecution by linking it backwards with the sufferings of Jesus and forwards with their own ultimate destiny. On the one hand, as went the Master, so must go the disciple; on the other, as goes the disciple now, so will go the Master with him at the End.

In a very real sense, therefore, this pericope is a tract for the times, and the times are those of formal persecution of Christians as Christians. We cannot now reconstruct the historical situation of the church to which Mark is addressing himself in the sense that we can name the Roman city or emperor concerned, but we can say that it is a situation in which persecution is a very real possibility and that preparation of his readers for this possibility is a very real part of the Marcan purpose.

If we turn next to a consideration of the narrative in its setting in the Gospel as a whole, then the first and most obvious thing to be noted is the fact that has been so often noted: this narrative is the watershed of the Gospel. Lives of Jesus without number have been built upon the supposition that there was a "Galilean springtime" in the ministry of Jesus, that this was followed by a darkening "via dolorosa" which led to Calvary, and that the transition from the one to the other came at Caesarea Philippi. That this supposition has so long endured is mute testimony to the skill of Mark as an author for, as we pointed out earlier, this narrative is certainly designed by him to introduce his particular theology of the cross. That he chose to do this in the form of narrative rather than theological treatise is his business; that his work has had such a tremendous impact upon subsequent generations is testimony to the effectiveness of his choice. A Marcan treatise on the cross might even have earned an honored place in the library of Christian theological literature, but the Marcan schematization of the ministry of Jesus has become part of the lifeblood of Christian devotional thinking. It is perhaps not out of place to add that the validity of the Marcan presentation is not dependent upon whether Caesarea Philippi "actually happened" but upon the meaningfulness of the cross as presented to Christian devotion in this way.

It is not our present purpose to summarize the Marcan theology of the cross presented in this pericope and subsequently through his Gospel. In our view Mark is a significant and creative literary figure and deserves to be read in the form in which he chose to write rather than in summary. Mark has the right to be read on his own terms, and after several generations of being read mistakenly, as a historian, he has earned the right to be read as a theologian. The reader is therefore invited to consider for himself the text of Mark and the theology of the cross which it presents. Our purpose is simply to point out that, from the viewpoint of redaction criticism, this is one way in which the text should be read.

A further emphasis in this narrative is that of Christology, and in this connection the narrative has a number of notable features. In the first place, we should notice that it uses the title "Christ": "Peter answered him, 'You are the Christ'" (8:29). At first sight this is by no means remarkable, for Peter is here formally representing the early church and therefore appropriately using the confessional title used by that church. But if we look at the Gospel as a whole, then we can see that, in general, the way Mark uses "Christ" focuses attention very sharply upon its use in this particular incident. The title occurs only seven times in Mark: 1:1; 8:29; 9:41; 12:35; 13:21; 14:61; 15:32. Of these seven instances one (9:41) is simply a way of saying "Christian," four (12:35; 13:21; 14:61; 15:32) are references to "the anointed one" of Jewish messianic expectation, and one (1:1) is clearly a part of the formal superscription to the Gospel as a whole. This throws the last one (8:29) into very strong relief and demands of us that we pay due attention to the fact that only here in the Gospel of Mark is Jesus formally acknowledged as the Messiah of Jewish expectation and the Christ of Christian worship. Clearly this narrative is concerned with Christology in a very special way. We must add to this observation the fact that verse 8:29 marks a very definite stage of development in the Marcan presentation of the disciples' understanding of Jesus.[9] In the first half of the Gospel (1:16—8:21) the disciples are imperceptive in the sense that they appear incapable of perceiving who Jesus is. "Despite the continuous manifestation of Jesus' messiahship before the disciples in countless healings, exorcisms, and nature miracles, they remain amazingly obtuse in the face of their involvement in the messianic drama" (Weeden). The fact is that a careful perusal of the first half of Mark's Gospel creates the impression that the disciples, although granted special privileges in their relationship with Jesus, are far less perceptive concerning him than are other people who meet him in the course of his ministry.[10] With the Caesarea Philippi narrative, however, all this changes. True, the disciples are as dim-witted about Jesus as they had always been—note, for example, that Peter is presented as one who cannot accept the idea of a suffering Messiah even when that suffering culminates in resurrection (8:31 f.)—but now there is a change from imperceptivity to misconception. Whereas before they had not been able to recognize Jesus as the Messiah, now they recognize him as Messiah but misunderstand the nature of that messiahship. Even this, however, is not the end. From Mark 14:10 onwards there is a further change in the disciples' understanding of Jesus. From this point on, they no longer simply misunderstand Jesus; now they totally reject him:[11] Judas betrays him; the inner group, Peter, James, and John, fails him in Gethsemane;

Peter, the disciple par excellence, denies him adamantly in the High Priest's courtyard.

This presentation of the disciples' relationship to, and understanding of, Jesus bears all the hallmarks of a careful schematization and this fact focuses attention upon the Caesarea Philippi narrative as a part of a Marcan christological argument. There is every reason to believe that one of the problems faced by the early church was that of understanding the true nature of her Christology. In the Greek world it was natural to think of "divine men"—"sons of God," who by their miraculous powers demonstrated the divine reality that was present in them as substance or power and that enabled them to enjoy ecstatic appearances and to do miracles[12]—and therefore to think of Jesus in these terms. Not the least of the purposes of Mark's Gospel seems to have been specifically to combat a "divine man" understanding of Christology. In the first part of his Gospel, Mark goes to considerable pains to present Jesus in such a light; he saturates the first half of his Gospel with wonder-working activities of Jesus and intersperses summaries of this activity which can only be read in these terms (1:32 ff.; 3:7 ff.; 6:53 ff.) so that the reader of his Gospel is left with only one possible conclusion: Peter confesses Jesus as a "divine man." In fact, if 1:1—8:29 were the only extant section of the Gospel, one would be forced to believe that from the Marcan perspective the only authentic understanding of Jesus was as a "divine man-Messiah." But it is precisely here that the Caesarea Philippi narrative plays its part. Here Peter confesses Jesus as the Messiah and goes on to interpret this messiahship in terms of a "divine man" Christology. Here, therefore, the Lord rejects this understanding of Christology in the most explicit terms possible: "Get behind me, Satan! For you are not on the side of God, but of man (8:33). The conclusion is inevitable: Mark presents the false understanding of Christology on the lips of Peter, a true understanding on the lips of Jesus. But in recognizing this, we are recognizing that the narrative is not concerned with the historical Peter's misunderstanding of the nature of Jesus' messiahship but with a false understanding of Christology prevalent in the church for which Mark is writing, i.e., with "the heresy that necessitated Mark's gospel" (Weeden). The purpose of the schematization of the disciples' misunderstanding of Jesus in Mark's Gospel is to press for an acceptance of a suffering servant Christology in the church for which Mark is writing.

One last aspect of this narrative which must concern us is that of the Messianic Secret (8:30). At several places in our work we have had occasion to call attention to this feature of Mark's Gospel because the recognition of it as a feature of the Gospel rather than of the historical ministry of Jesus has been a key factor in the development of redaction criticism. Anyone who would understand the theology of Mark has to wrestle with the meaning of the Messianic Secret in Mark. To review the various attempts to do this among contemporary scholars, or to make such an attempt ourselves, would be to go beyond the bounds of our present work; here we content ourselves with saying that this is one of the things redaction criticism has taught us to do.

We have concluded our discussion of the Caesarea Philippi narrative in Mark and we now turn to a discussion of the parallels in Matthew and Luke: Matthew 16:13–28 and Luke 9:18–27. As we do, the situation changes because now we have the source which both Matthew and Luke have used. On literary-critical grounds[13] we can show that both Matthew and Luke have used Mark as a source for their own Gospels, and they are certainly following Mark in their account of this particular incident. This means that we can now move with certainty in regard to redaction criticism because a simple comparison of Matthew and Luke with Mark will immediately throw into relief the redactional activity of Matthew and Luke respectively. Whereas with Mark we have to spend a lot of time and energy attempting to reconstruct the tradition he has used if we are to detect his redactional activity on that tradition, with Matthew and Luke, in a narrative such as this one, we have the tradition they have used before us in the form in which it came to them from Mark. Our knowledge of the redactional activity of Matthew and Luke is therefore both firm and extensive; we not only have one of their major sources, Mark, but we can also reconstruct another, the sayings source, Q. It is no accident that redaction criticism is able to do spectacularly successful work on the theology of Matthew and the theology of Luke.

THE MATTHEAN NARRATIVE: MATTHEW 16:13–28

If we repeat our previous practice with Mark and begin by reading this narrative straight through, we notice at once that there is here not one incident but two. Matthew 16:13–23 is a story complete in itself which should be given some such heading as "The Revelation to Peter." Peter's confession is now greeted by the paean of praise: "Blessed are you, Simon Bar-Jona! For flesh and blood has not revealed this to you, but my Father who is in heaven," which throws it into stark relief both as a confession and as an insight made possible only by divine revelation. This "Revelation to Peter" is followed by the commissioning of Peter as formal head of the church: "And I tell you, you are Peter, and on this rock I will build my church, and the powers of death shall not prevail against it. I will give you the keys of the kingdom of heaven, and whatever you bind on earth shall be bound in heaven, and whatever you loose on earth shall be loosed in heaven." This commissioning is clearly possible now because of the previous revelation; as the recipient of this revelation Peter fittingly becomes head of the Christian community. Then, in verse 21, there is a break in the narrative ("From that time Jesus began to show his disciples...."), and we get the transition to a second story, "The Misunderstanding of the Passion," an incident in which Matthew follows Mark in general content but with verbal changes that will concern us later.

The Matthean version is, then, a complete reworking of the narrative. Instead of a confession at Caesarea Philippi, we have both a revelation and a commissioning there, and the close connection between the confession and the subsequent misunderstanding characteristic of Mark, whose concerns are christological, is deliberately broken by Matthew, whose concerns are predominantly ecclesiological. This reworking is in part effected by verbal changes Matthew makes in the Marcan source, for example, Matthew's "From that time Jesus began" for Mark's "And he began" (Matt. 16:21; Mark 8:31), but for the most part they are due to the insertion of Matthew 16:17–19, a piece of tradition which has no parallel in Mark or Luke. Whence comes this formal blessing of Peter, this ceremonial appointment of him to hegemony in the early Christian church? The most probable answer is that it is from a story which originally concerned Christ's resurrection appearance to Peter, a story used by Matthew here and which has also left its traces on other parts of the New Testament, but which is otherwise lost to us.[14] The effect of the use of this piece of tradition by Matthew is unmistakable; it transforms the first part of the Marcan narrative into a new, self-contained incident in which Peter is granted a heavenly revelation of Jesus' true nature as Messiah and in which, on the basis of this revelation, he assumes full authority as founder and leader of the early church with the power to determine not only membership of that church but also of the ultimate kingdom of God. Here we have not only "outside the church there is no salvation" but also "within the church salvation is certain."

At this point it is interesting to note that there is a certain conflict between Matthew himself and the tradition he is using. It is true enough that Matthew has a marked ecclesiological interest; every "Introduction to the New Testament" points out that the Gospel of Matthew is a "church book," designed to meet the ecclesiastical needs of a Christian congregation toward the end of the first century, and in this sense the changes in the first part of the Marcan narrative are absolutely typical of Matthew's total procedure. Matthew himself certainly believes that "outside the church there is no salvation," but he also believes that there are many in the church who are by no means saved and that good and bad will continue side by side in the church until the sorting out process of the final judgment.[15] In the tradition used by him in verses 17–19 of this narrative, however, there is no hint of any reservation in this matter; as we have already said, "within the church salvation is certain" is the viewpoint here! Very likely this tradition was the product of circles concerned with honoring Peter as founder and leader of the church as against possible rivals, and, as one might expect, a partisan viewpoint is accompanied by a somewhat unsophisticated view of the church. Be that as it may, Matthew uses the tradition here because he too honors Peter and because he is concerned with the moment of revelation as a consequence of which the church is founded.

It should be noted in passing that, if the supposition is correct that the tradition originally concerned a resurrection appearance to Peter, then we have here another most important insight into the nature of Gospel narratives as conceived by the evangelists themselves. Not only is Matthew following Mark in moving readily between the ministry of Jesus, which is past, and the ministry of the church, which is present, but he is also adding a third element in that he moves equally readily from the more distant past of the ministry of Jesus to the more immediate past of a resurrection appearance to Peter, to the present of the church. It is clear that in Gospel narratives past—both more distant and more immediate— and present flow into one another in a way that we must regard as remarkable.

If we consider the wording of that part of Matthew 16:13-23 in which Matthew is following Mark, then two changes become immediately apparent: Jesus' first question, "Who do men say that I am?" has become in Matthew, "Who do men say that the Son of man is?" and Peter's confession, "You are the Christ," has become, "You are the Christ, the Son of the living God" (Matt. 16:13, 14). Both of these are significant. The first is part of a double change in that Matthew not only adds "Son of man" here but also rewrites the passion prediction (16:21, compare Mark 8:31) in order to avoid such a reference there; in effect he moves the "Son of man" reference from 16:21 to 16:13. Now the immediate effect of this is to make the question in 16:13 a nonsensical question, for the answer is now given in the question! It might be possible to suggest, as some commentators do, that "Son of man" here is a colorless self-designation, but this cannot be so because the fact that Matthew has moved the reference shows that it is for him a most meaningful one, and in any case in so heavily confessional a context as this the term must be regarded as being used confessionally. No, the truth of the matter is that Matthew is not here interested in a realistic question which will initiate a christological discussion, as is Mark; he is interested in the formal proclamation by Jesus of the existence of the Christian church and so "the sovereignty of the one who announces the period of his Church is solemnly enunciated at the beginning of the section" by using the name "Son of man" "as an emphatic heading."[16] So he moves the term to the beginning of the section in order to make the Jesus who is to proclaim the existence and authority of the church, with Peter as its leader, also proclaim himself as

Son of man. We shall have occasion to note below that for Matthew "Son of man" is a term of supreme authority.

The second change, the addition of "the Son of the living God" to the confession, is simpler. Recognizing the confession for what it is, the regular confession of the early Christian church, Matthew has cast it in the form used in the circles in which he moved. "Son of God" was not a messianic title in pre-Christian Judaism and so the confession would be impossible in the historical circumstances of the ministry of Jesus—not that that is of any concern to Matthew. The confession developed in early Christianity and it is particularly meaningful to Matthew himself, no doubt having been mediated to him by the church for which he wrote. He has a strong interest in this particular christological title and in theological and devotional thinking based upon its use: Matthew 2:15; 8:29; 14:33; 11:25–27.

The second of the two incidents into which Matthew divides the Marcan Caesarea Philippi narrative is much closer to the original than is the first. The major change comes at the end where the climactic warning and promise in Mark have been reworked in the interest of a particular Matthean doctrine of the Son of man (Matt. 16:27, 28; cf. Mark 8:38; 9:1). The Marcan reference to the coming of the Son of man has been made much more emphatic: "For the Son of man is to come . . ."; and in place of the Son of man being "ashamed" we have a developed doctrine of the judgment of the Son of man: "And then he will repay every man for what he has done." This last is a development in the direction of Jewish apocalyptic (cf. I Enoch 45:3 and chapter 46), and it is a doctrine in which Matthew has a particular interest (Matt. 13:41; 25:31). More than this, the final "kingdom" of Christian expectation can be for Matthew specifically the kingdom of the Son of man (see Matt. 13:41) and so the "before they see the kingdom of God come with power" of Mark 9:1 becomes, in Matthew 16:28, "before they see the Son of man coming in his kingdom." For Matthew "Son of man" is a title of supreme authority and that "Son of man" readily comes to assume functions which elsewhere in the Christian traditions are ascribed to God himself. Incidentally, the "Son of man" figure similarly assumes functions more normally attributed directly to God also in the Jewish apocalyptic traditions now represented by the so-called Similitudes of Enoch (I Enoch 37–71), traditions apparently known to Matthew.

THE LUCAN NARRATIVE: LUKE 9:18–27

This narrative begins with a verse that has long been the subject of discussion: "Now it happened that as he was praying alone the disciples were with him." This is nonsense, both in the English translation and in the original Greek, and the best explanation seems to be that Luke is deliberately combining the situation of Mark 6:46, "And after he had taken leave of them, he went into the hills to pray," with that of Mark 8:27, "And Jesus went on with his disciples. . . ." When we add to this the oft-noted fact that Luke has no parallels to Mark 6:44—8:26, then it seems most probable that his copy of Mark's Gospel was defective at this point. Newly discovered papyrus codices of the Gospels offer us exact parallels to this: John 6:11-35 is missing from the codex designated P⁶⁶ and Luke 18:18—22:4 from that designated P⁷⁵.

As regards more theologically motivated redaction, there are two major changes in the Lucan pericope as over against the Marcan. The first of these is the omission of the dispute between Jesus and Peter (Mark 8:32 f.). We argued above that this was part of a literary device by means of which Mark makes an essential christological point. Luke is not interested in the christological point (note in Luke 22:24-30 his spectacular choice of a version of the dispute about greatness which enables him to omit Mark 10:45), and he therefore omits this part of the narrative. It may even be that he found it offensive, although this we cannot know.[17]

The second change is that by a series of subtle touches—for example, the insertion of "daily" in verse 23, and the omission of "in this adulterous and sinful generation" in verse 26 and of "come with power" in verse 27—Luke has completely changed the tenor of the whole passage. The Marcan note of urgency in the face of a specific persecution preceding an imminent eschaton has become a challenge for a continual witnessing over an indefinite period of time. This is part of the Lucan rethinking of early Christian eschatology to which Hans Conzelmann has so convincingly called our attention, and since his work is so readily available we need do no more than mention this fact here.

NOTES

1. The two most important recent discussions are H. E. Tödt, *The Son of Man in the Synoptic Tradition*, trans. Dorothea M. Barton (Philadelphia: Westminster Press, 1965), pp. 141-221; and B. Lindars, *New Testament Apologetic* (Philadelphia: Westminster Press, 1962), pp. 75-137. I propose to approach the problem of the suffering Son of man sayings at a later date in light of the insights and arguments of my *Rediscovering the Teaching of Jesus*, (New York: Harper & Row, 1967), pp. 164-99.
2. Tödt, *Son of Man*, pp. 144-49.
3. We are now summarizing what we argued in detail in Perrin, *Rediscovering*, pp. 185-91, with the difference that we are not here concerned, as we were there, with the question as to whether any form of the saying can be held to go back to Jesus himself.
4. On this tradition, brilliantly isolated by Käsemann on form-critical grounds, see Perrin, *Rediscovering*, pp. 22 f.

5. On the details of the development of this tradition and for the arguments supporting the assertion made here, see Perrin, *Rediscovering*, pp. 185-99.

6. The changes and developments in the writer's opinion can be traced through the successive works, N. Perrin, *The Kingdom of God in the Teaching of Jesus* (Philadelphia: Westminster Press, 1963), and *Rediscovering*, pp. 16-20, 199-201.

7. We would reject the suggestion made, for example, by V. Taylor, *The Gospel According to St. Mark* (New York: St. Martin's Press, 1952), p. 521, that this saying was originally a genuine saying of Jesus referring to the destruction of Jerusalem which "has been adapted in the interests of contemporary apocalyptic." This is an ingenious attempt to salvage the saying as a genuine word of Jesus, but there is not one shred of evidence that the saying ever existed in a form other than that which it now has. See Perrin, *Rediscovering*, p. 200.

8. We have spoken of Mark throughout as a self-conscious—one might even say cold-blooded!—editor, redactor, and author. We should perhaps make the obvious fact that this is simply a scholarly convenience as we discuss what he did, and it is not meant to prejudge any questions with regard to inspiration, sense of having "the mind of the Lord," view of the tradition and its relationship to Jesus, etc. But before any such questions can be discussed, it is essential to be clear as to what Mark in fact did, and to determine this is, in part, the purpose of redaction criticism.

9. In this and what follows, we are indebted to Theodore J. Weeden.

10. Weeden, whom we are following at this point, refers to 5:28-31 where the disciples are oblivious to the healing power of Jesus' garments which was known to the hemorrhaging woman, to 8:4 where they have apparently gained no insight from the first feeding (6:30 ff.), and to 8:14-21 where they have failed to comprehend the supernatural capacity exhibited in the two feedings (6:30-44; 8:1-10).

11. The recognition of this fact is Weeden's special contribution to the discussion. Up to here he had been following, A. Kuby, "Zur Konzeption des Markus-Evangeliums," *Zeitschrift für die neutestamentliche Wissenschaft*, 49 (1958), 52-64, but the insights we follow from here on are his.

12. Cf. R. H. Fuller, *The Foundations of New Testament Christology*, (New York: Scribner's, 1965), p. 98.

13. See W. A. Beardslee, *Literary Criticism of the New Testament*, (Philadelphia: Fortress, 1970), and Perrin, *Rediscovering*, pp. 34 f.

14. R. H. Fuller, "The 'Thou Art Peter' Pericope and the Easter Appearances," *McCQ*, 20 (1966-67), 309-15.

15. Matt. 13:26-30; 13:47-50. Cf. G. Bornkamm, G. Barth, H. J. Held, *Tradition and Interpretation in Matthew*, (Philadelphia: Westminster, 1963), pp. 19 ff.

16. Tödt, *Son of Man*, p. 150. Tödt's discussion of the use of "Son of man" by Matthew here and elsewhere is most illuminating.

17. If we are to think in these terms, then we could say that Matthew will have been able to maintain it because it is mitigated by the preceding approval of Peter in the Matthean version of the narrative. It is interesting to note that all three evangelists have the account of the denial by Peter in their passion narratives (Mark 14:66-72; Matt. 26:69-75; Luke 22:56-61). The passion narrative in its essentials is certainly pre-Marcan and it may well have been this incident which led Mark to the literary device of the Petrine christological misunderstanding.

Form Criticism
and Beyond

James Muilenburg sketches the history and development of
form criticism (see Freedman, pp. 77–100, Van Tilborg,
pp. 333–343, Mowinckel, pp. 173–190, and Perrin, pp.
344–361). He suggests a new direction for biblical criticism
"beyond" form criticism to what he calls rhetorical criti-
cism. Just as form criticism was a response to the domina-
tion of literary criticism, which analyzes the biblical texts
into their "sources" (see, e.g., Perrin's comments, pp. 344–
361), so rhetorical criticism supplies elements not covered
in the analytical methods of form criticism.

The individual, personal, and unique features of a text
need to be considered as well as its typical features, the
forms and situation in the community (Sitz im Leben).
Stylistic and rhetorical differences must be studied as well
as the form in its original situation. Rhetorical criticism
studies the nature of literary composition, the structural
patterns employed in the literary unity, and devices used to
produce a "unified whole."

(On other ancient Near Eastern literature, see Kramer,
pp. 274–282, and Lambert, pp. 285–297.)

T HE impact of form criticism upon biblical studies has been profound,
comparable only to the subsequent influence of historical criticism
as it was classically formulated by Julius Wellhausen about a century ago.
Its pioneer and spiritual progenitor was Hermann Gunkel, for many years
professor of Old Testament at the University of Halle. The magnitude of
his contribution to biblical scholarship is to be explained in part by the
fact that historical criticism had come to an impasse, chiefly because of
the excesses of source analysis; in part, too, by Gunkel's extraordinary
literary insight and sensitivity, and, not least of all, by the influence
which diverse academic disciplines exerted upon him.[1] At an early age he
had read Johann Gottfried Herder's work *Vom Geist der Ebräischen*

From James Muilenburg, *Journal of Biblical Literature*, 88 (1969), 1–18.

Poesie (1782–83), with ever-growing excitement, and it kindled within him an appreciation not only of the quality of the ancient Oriental mentality, so characteristic of Herder's work, but also and more particularly of the manifold and varying ways in which it came to expression throughout the sacred records of the Old and New Testaments. Then there were his great contemporaries: Eduard Meyer and Leopold von Ranke, the historians; Heinrich Zimmern, the Assyriologist; Adolf Erman, the Egyptologist; and perhaps most important of all Eduard Norden, whose *Antike Kunstprosa* (1898) and *Agnostos Theos* (1913) anticipated Gunkel's own work in its recognition of the categories of style and their application to the NT records. Mention must also be made of his intimate friend and associate, Hugo Gressmann, who in his detailed studies of the Mosaic traditions pursued much the same methods as Gunkel,[2] and, more significantly, produced two monumental volumes on *Altorientalische Texte und Bilder* (1909[1]; 1927[2]), surpassed today only by the companion volumes, ANET, of James B. Pritchard (1950; 1954). Gunkel possessed for his time an extraordinary knowledge of the other literatures of the ancient Near East, and availed himself of their forms and types, their modes of discourse, and their rhetorical features in his delineation and elucidation of the biblical texts. What is more—and this is a matter of some consequence—he had profound psychological insight, influenced to a considerable degree by W. Wundt's *Völkerpsychologie,* which stood him in good stead as he sought to portray the cast and temper of the minds of the biblical narrators and poets, but also of the ordinary Israelite to whom their words were addressed. It is not too much to say that Gunkel has never been excelled in his ability to portray the spirit which animated the biblical writers, and he did not hesitate either in his lectures or in his seminars to draw upon the events of contemporary history or the experiences of the common man to explicate the interior meaning of a pericope.

One need not labor the benefits and merits of form-critical methodology. It is well to be reminded, however, not only of its distinctive features, but also of the many important contributions in monograph, commentary, and theology, in order that we may the better assess its rôle in contemporary biblical research. Professor Albright, writing in 1940, remarked that "the student of the ancient Near East finds that the methods of Norden and Gunkel are not only applicable, but are the only ones that can be applied,"[3] The first and most obvious achievement of *Gattungsforschung* is that it supplied a much-needed corrective to literary and historical criticism. In the light of recent developments, it is important to recall that Gunkel never repudiated this method, as his commentary on the Book of Genesis demonstrates, but rather averred that it was insufficient for answering the most pressing and natural queries of the reader. It was unable, for one thing, to compose a literary history of Israel because the data requisite for such a task were either wanting or, at best, meager. Again, it isolated Israel too sharply from its ethnic and cultural environment as it was reflected in the literary monuments of the peoples of the Near East. Further, the delineation of Israel's faith which emerged from the regnant historico-critical methodology was too simply construed and too unilinearly conceived. Not least of all, its exegesis and hermeneutics failed to penetrate deeply into the relevant texts. The second advantage of the form-critical methodology was that it addressed itself to the question of the literary genre represented by a pericope. In his programmatic essay on the literature of Israel in the second volume of Paul Hinneberg's *Die Kultur der Gegenwart,* Gunkel provided an admirable sketch of the numerous literary types represented in the OT, and many of the contributions to the first and second editions of *Die Religion in die Geschichte und Gegenwart* bore the stamp and impress of his critical methodology. It is here where his influence has been greatest and most salutary because the student must know what kind of literature it is that he is reading, to what literary category it belongs, and what its characteristic features are. The third merit of the method is its concern to discover the function that the literary genre was designed to serve in the life of the community or of the individual, to learn how it was employed and on what occasions, and to implement it, so far as possible, into its precise social or cultural milieu. Of special importance, especially in the light of later developments in OT scholarship, was its stress upon the oral provenance of the original genres in Israel, and beyond Israel, among the other peoples of the Near East. Finally, related to our foregoing discussion, is the comparison of the literary types with other exemplars within the OT and then, significantly, with representatives of the same type in the cognate literatures. Such an enterprise in comparison releases the Scriptures from bondage to parochialism.

The reflections of form-critical methodology are to be discerned all along the horizons of OT studies since the turn of the century, although it must be added that it has also been consistently ignored by substantial segments of OT scholarship. Thus R. H. Pfeiffer in his *magnum opus* on the *Introduction to the Old Testament* (1941) scarcely gives it a passing nod, in sharp contrast to the introductions of Otto Eissfeldt (1934[1]; Eng. trans. 1965), George Fohrer (1965; Eng. trans. 1968), Aage Bentzen (1948), and Artur Weiser (1948; Eng. trans. 1961), all of whom devote a large part of their works to the subject. In many commentaries, too, the literary types and forms are seldom mentioned. On the other hand, there have been many commentaries, such as those in the *Biblischer Kommentar* series, where they are discussed at some length. Equally significant is the important rôle that form criticism has played in hermeneutics. In theology, too, it has influenced not only the form and structure of the exposition, but also the understanding of the nature of biblical theology, as in the work of Gerhard von Rad, which is based upon form-critical presuppositions. Many words have been devoted to detailed studies of the particular literary genres, such as Israelite law,[4] the lament and dirge,[5] historical narrative,[6] the various types of Hebrew prophecy,[7] and wisdom.[8] In quite a different fashion, the method is reflected in recent studies of the covenant formulations,[9] the covenantal lawsuits,[10] and the covenant curses.[11]

Now, having attempted to do justice to the substantial gains made by the study of literary types, I should like to point to what seem to me to be some of its inadequacies, its occasional exaggerations, and especially its tendency to be too exclusive in its application of the method. In these reservations I do not stand alone, for signs are not wanting, both here and abroad, of discontent with the prevailing state of affairs, of a sense that the method has outrun its course. Thus its most thoroughgoing exponent, H. G. Reventlow, in a recent study of Psalm 8, comments: "One gets the impression that a definite method, precisely because it has demonstrated itself to be so uncommonly fruitful, has arrived at its limits."[12] It would be unfortunate if this were taken to mean that we have done with form criticism or that we should forfeit its manifest contributions to an understanding of the Scriptures. To be sure there are clamant voices being raised today against the methodology, and we are told that it is founded on an illusion, that it is too much influenced by classical and Germanic philology and therefore alien to the Semitic literary consciousness, and that it must be regarded as an aberration in the history of biblical scholarship.[13] If we are faced with such a stark either-or, my allegiance is completely on the side of the form critics, among whom, in any case, I should wish to be counted. Such criticisms as I now propose to make do not imply a rejection so much as an appeal to venture beyond the confines of form criticism into an inquiry into other literary features which are all too frequently ignored today. The first of these is the one that is most frequently launched against the method. The basic contention of Gunkel is that the ancient men of Israel, like their Near Eastern neighbors, were influenced in their speech and their literary compositions by convention and custom. We therefore encounter in a particular genre or *Gattung* the same structural forms, the same terminology and style, and the same *Sitz im Leben*. Surely this cannot be gainsaid. But there has been a proclivity among scholars in recent years to lay such stress upon the typical and representative that the individual, personal, and unique features of the particular pericope are all but lost to view. It is true, as Klaus Koch says in his book, *Was ist Formgeschichte?* (1964), that the criticism has force more for the prophetic books than for the laws and wisdom utterances; and I should add for the hymns and laments of the Psalter too, as a study of *Die Einleitung in die Psalmen* by Gunkel-Begrich will plainly show, although the formulations exhibit diversity and versatility here too. Let me attempt to illustrate my point. In the first major section of the Book of Jeremiah (2:1—4:4*) we have an impressive sequence of literary units of essentially the same *Gattung*, i.e., the *rib* or lawsuit or legal proceeding, and the *Sitz im Leben* is the court of law. Yet the literary formulation of these pericopes shows great variety, and very few of them are in any way a complete reproduction of the lawsuit as it was actually carried on at the gate of the city.[14] What we have here, for the most part, are excerpts or extracts, each complete in itself, to be sure, but refashioned into the conventional structures of metrical verse and animated by profuse images. Only the first (2:1-13) and the final pericopes (3:1—4:4*) are preserved with any degree of completeness. But what is more, precisely because the forms and styles are so diverse and are composed with such consummate skill, it is clear that we are dealing with limitations of a *Gattung*. Even when we compare such well-known exemplars of the type as Deut 32 and Mic 6:1-8, the stylistic and rhetorical differences outweigh the similarities. The conventional elements of the lawsuit genre are certainly present, and their recognition is basic to an understanding of the passage; but this is only the beginning of the story. To state our criticism in another way, form criticism by its very nature is bound to generalize because it is concerned with what is common to all the representatives of a genre, and therefore applies an external measure to the individual pericopes.[15] It does not focus sufficient attention upon what is unique and unrepeatable, upon the particularity of the formulation. Moreover, form and content are inextricably related. They form an integral whole. The two are one. Exclusive attention to the *Gattung* may actually obscure the thought and intention of the writer or speaker. The passage must be read and heard precisely as it is spoken. It is the creative synthesis of the particular formulation of the pericope with the content that makes it the distinctive composition that it is.

Another objection that has often been made of the criticism of literary types is its aversion to biographical or psychological interpretations and its resistance to historical commentary. This is to be explained only in part as a natural, even inevitable, consequence of its disregard of literary criticism. One has only to recall the rather extreme stress upon the nature of the prophetic experience of former times. The question is whether the specific text or passage gives any warrant for such ventures. There are cases, to be sure, as with Jeremiah and Ezekiel, where it is difficult to see how one can cavalierly omit psychological commentary of some kind. The call of Jeremiah, for example, is something more than the recitation of a conventional and inherited liturgy within the precincts of the temple,[16] and the so-called confessions of the prophet are more than the repetition and reproduction of fixed stereotypes, despite all the parallels that one may adduce from the OT and the Near Eastern texts for such a position. Perhaps more serious is the skepticism of all attempts to read a pericope in its historical context. The truth is that in a vast number of instances we are indeed left completely in the dark as to the occasion on which the words were spoken, and it is reasonable to assume that it was not of primary interest to the compilers of the traditions. This is notably the case with numerous passages in the prophetic writings. In Jeremiah, for example, more often than not, we are simply left to conjecture. Nevertheless, we have every reason to assume that there were situations which elicited particular utterances, and we are sufficiently informed about the history of the times to make conjecture perfectly legitimate. The prophets do not speak *in abstracto*, but concretely. Their formulations may reflect a cultic provenance as on the occasion of celebration of a national festival, although one must be on his guard against exaggeration here, especially against subsuming too many texts under the rubric of the covenant renewal festival, as in the case of Artur Weiser in his commentaries on Jeremiah and the Book of Psalms, or of the festival of the New Year, as in the case of Sigmund Mowinckel in his *Psalmenstudien.*

The foregoing observations have been designed to call attention to the perils involved in a too exclusive employment of form-critical methods, to warn against extremes in their application, and particularly to stress that there are other features in the literary compositions which lie beyond the province of the *Gattungsforscher*. It is important to emphasize that many scholars have used the method with great skill, sound judgment, and proper restraint, and, what is more, have taken account of literary features other than those revealed by the *Gattung*, such as H. W. Wolff's commentary on Hosea in the *Biblischer Kommentar* series. Further, we should recognize that there are numerous texts where the literary genre appears in pure form, and here the exclusive application of form-critical techniques has its justification, although one must be quick to add that even here there are differences in formulation. But there are many other passages where the literary genres are being imitated, not only among the prophets, but among the historians and lawgivers. Witness, for example, the radical transformation of the early Elohistic laws by the deuteronomists, or, perhaps equally impressively, the appropriation by the prophets of the curse formulae, not only within the OT, but also in the vassal treaties of the Near Eastern peoples.[17] Let me repeat: in numerous contexts old literary types and forms are imitated, and, precisely because they are imitated, they are employed with considerable fluidity, versatility, and, if one may venture the term, artistry. The upshot of this circumstance is that the circumspect scholar will not fail to supplement his form-critical analysis with a careful inspection of the literary unit in its precise and unique formulation. He will not be completely bound by the traditional elements and motifs of the literary genre; his task will not be completed until he has taken full account of the features which lie beyond the spectrum of the genre. If the exemplars of the *Gattung* were all identical in their formulations, the OT would be quite a different corpus from what it actually is.

It is often said that the Hebrew writers were not motivated by distinctively literary considerations, that aesthetics lay beyond the domain of their interests, and that a preoccupation with what has come to be described as stylistics only turns the exegete along bypaths unrelated to his central task. It may well be true that aesthetic concerns were never primary with them and that the conception of *belles lettres,* current in ancient Hellas, was alien to the men of Israel. But surely this must not be taken to mean that the OT does not offer us literature of a very high quality. For the more deeply one penetrates the formulations as they have been transmitted to us, the more sensitive he is to the rôles which words and motifs play in a composition; the more he concentrates on the ways in which thought has been woven into linguistic patterns, the better able he is to think the thoughts of the biblical writer after him. And this leads me to formulate a canon which should be obvious to us all: a responsible and proper articulation of the words in their linguistic patterns and in their precise formulations will reveal to us the texture and fabric of the writer's thought, not only what he thinks, but as he thinks it.

The field of stylistics or aesthetic criticism is flourishing today, and the literature that has gathered about it is impressive. Perhaps its foremost representative is Alonso Schökel, whose work, *Estudios de Poetica Hebraea* (1963), offers us not only an ample bibliography of the important works in the field, but also a detailed discussion of the stylistic phenomenology of the literature of the OT. In this respect it is a better work than Ed. König's *Stilistik, Rhetorik, und Poetik* (1900), an encyclopedic compendium of linguistic and rhetorical phenomena, which nevertheless has the merit of providing many illuminating parallels drawn from classical literature and of availing itself of the many stylistic studies from the earliest times and throughout the nineteenth century. It would be an error, therefore, to regard the modern school in isolation from the history of the OT scholarship, because from the time of Jerome and before and continuing on with the rabbis and until modern times there have been those who have occupied themselves with matters of style. One thinks of Bishop Lowth's influential work, *De sacra poesi Hebraeorum praelectiones academicae* (1753), and of Herder's work on Hebrew poetry (1772-83), but also of the many metrical studies, most notably Ed. Sievers' *Metrische Studien* (I, 1901; II, 1904-05; III, 1907).[18] Noteworthy, too, are the contributions of Heinrich Ewald, Karl Budde, and Bernhard Duhm, and more recently and above all of Umberto Cassuto. W. F. Albright has devoted himself to subjects which are to all intents and purposes stylistic, as *inter alia* his studies on the Song of Deborah and his most recent work on *Yahweh and the Gods of Canaan*

(1968). His students too have occupied themselves with stylistic matters, notably Frank M. Cross and D. N. Freedman in their doctoral dissertation on *Studies in Yahwistic Poetry* (1950) and in their studies of biblical poems.[19] Among the many others who have applied stylistic criteria to their examination of OT passages are Gerlis Gerleman in his study on the Song of Deborah,[20] L. Krinetski in his work on the Song of Songs,[21] Edwin Good in his analysis of the composition of the Book of Hosea,[22] R. A. Carlson in his scrutiny of the historical narratives of II Samuel in *David, the Chosen King* (1964), and William L. Holladay in his studies on Jeremiah.[23] The aspect of all these works which seems to me most fruitful and rewarding I should prefer to designate by a term other than stylistics. What I am interested in, above all, is understanding the nature of Hebrew literary composition, exhibiting the structural patterns that are employed for the fashioning of a literary unit, whether in poetry or in prose, and discerning the many and various devices by which the predications are formulated and ordered into a unified whole. Such an enterprise I should describe as rhetoric and the methodology as rhetorical criticism.

The first concern of the rhetorical critic, it goes without saying, is to define the limits or scope of the literary unit, to recognize precisely where and how it begins and where and how it ends. He will be quick to observe the formal rhetorical devices that are employed, but more important, the substance or content of these most strategic loci. An examination of the commentaries will reveal that there is great disagreement on this matter, and, what is more, more often than not, no defence is offered for the isolation of the pericope. It has even been averred that it does not really matter. On the contrary, it seems to me to be of considerable consequence, not only for an understanding of how the *Gattung* is being fashioned and designed, but also and more especially a grasp of the writer's intent and meaning. The literary unit is in any event an indissoluble whole, an artistic and creative unity, a unique formulation. The delimitation of the passage is essential if we are to learn how its major motif, usually stated at the beginning, is resolved. The latter point is of special importance because no rhetorical feature is more conspicuous and frequent among the poets and narrators of ancient Israel than the proclivity to bring the successive predications to their culmination. One must admit that the problem is not always simple because within a single literary unit we may have and often do have several points of climax. But to construe each of these as a conclusion to the poem is to disregard its structure, to resolve it into fragments, and to obscure the relation of the successive strophes to each other. This mistaken procedure has been followed by many scholars, and with unfortunate consequences.

Now the objection that has been most frequently raised to our contention is that too much subjectivity is involved in determining where the accents of the composition really lie. The objection has some force, to be sure, but in matters of this sort there is no substitute for literary sensitivity. Moreover, we need constantly to be reminded that we are dealing with an ancient Semitic literature and that we have at our disposal today abundant parallel materials from the peoples of the ancient Near East for comparison. But we need not dispose of our problem so, for there are many marks of composition which indicate where the finale has been reached. To the first of these I have already alluded, the presence of climactic or ballast lines, which may indeed appear at several junctures within a pericope, but at the close have an emphasis which bears the burden of the entire unit. A second clue for determining the scope of a pericope is to discern the relation of beginning and end, where the opening words are repeated or paraphrased at the close, what is known as ring composition, or, to employ the term already used by Ed. König many years ago and frequently employed by Dahood in his commentary on the Psalter, the *inclusio*. There are scores of illustrations of this phenomenon in all parts of the OT, beginning with the opening literary unit of the Book of Genesis. An impressive illustration is the literary complex of Jer 3:1—4:4, with deletion of the generally recognized prose insertions. While most scholars see more than one unit here, what we actually have before us is a superbly composed and beautifully ordered poem of three series of strophes of three strophes each. The major motif of turning or repentance is sounded in the opening casuistic legal formulation and is followed at once by the indictment:

> If a man sends his wife away,
> and she goes from him,
> and becomes another man's wife,
> will she return to him [with the corrected text]?
> Would not that land
> be utterly polluted?
> But you have played the harlot with many lovers,
> and would you return to me? (Jer 3:1).

The word שׁוּב appears in diverse syntactical constructions and in diverse stylistic contexts, and always in strategic collocations.[24] The poem has of course been influenced by the lawsuit, but it also contains a confessional lament and comes to a dramatic climax in the final strophe and in the form of the covenant conditional:

> If you do return, O Israel, Yahweh's Word!
> to me you should return (Jer 4:1a).

The whole poem is an Exhibit A of ancient Hebrew rhetoric, but it could easily be paralleled by numerous other exemplars quite as impressive.

The second major concern of the rhetorical critic is to recognize the structure of a composition and to discern the configuration of its component parts, to delineate the warp and woof out of which the literary fabric is woven, and to note the various rhetorical devices that are employed for marking, on the one hand, the sequence and movement of the pericope, and on the other, the shifts or breaks in the development of the writer's thought. It is our contention that the narrators and poets of ancient Israel and her Near Eastern neighbors were dominated not only by the formal and traditional modes of speech of the literary genres or types, but also by the techniques of narrative and poetic composition. Now the basic and most elemental of the structural features of the poetry of Israel, as of that of the other peoples of the ancient Near East, is the parallelism of its successive cola or stichoi. Our concern here is not with the different types of parallelism—synonymous, complementary, antithetic, or stairlike—but rather with the diversities of sequence of the several units within the successive cola, or within the successive and related bicola or tricola. It is precisely these diversities which give the poetry its distinctive and artistic character. It is always tantalizing to the translator that so often they cannot be reproduced into English or, for that matter, into the other Western tongues. In recent years much attention has been given to the repetitive tricola, which is amply illustrated in Ugaritic poetry.[25] But this repetitive style appears in numerous other types of formulation, and, what is more, is profusely illustrated in our earliest poetic precipitates:

> The kings came, they fought;
> > then fought the kings of Canaan,
> at Taanach, by the waters of Megiddo;
> > they got no spoils of silver.
> From heaven fought the stars,
> > from their courses they fought against Sisera.
> The torrent Kishon swept them away,
> > the onrushing torrent, the torrent Kishon.
> March on, my soul, with might (Judg 5:19-21).

Within so small a compass we have two instances of chiasmus, the four-fold repetition of the verb נִלְחָמוּ, the threefold repetition of נַחַל, and a concluding climactic shout. There are numerous cases of anaphora, the repetition of key words or lines at the beginning of successive predications, as in the series of curses in Deut 27:15-26 or of blessings in the following chapter (Deut 28:3-6), or the prophetic oracles of woe (Isa 5:8-22), or the repeated summons to praise (Ps 150), or the lamenting "How long" of Psalm 3. Jeremiah's vision of the return to primeval chaos is a classic instance of anaphora (Jer 4:23-26). In the oracle on the sword against Babylon as Yahweh's hammer and weapon, the line "with you I shatter in pieces" is repeated nine times (Jer 50:35-38). Examples of a different kind are Job's oaths of clearance (Job 31) and Wisdom's autobiography (Prov 8:22-31). These iterative features are much more profuse and elaborate in the ancient Near Eastern texts, but also more stereotyped.[26]

The second structural feature of Israel's poetic compositions is closely related to our foregoing observations concerning parallel structures and is particularly germane to responsible hermeneutical inquiry and exegetical exposition. The bicola or tricola appear in well-defined clusters or groups, which possess their own identity, integrity, and structure. They are most easily recognized in those instances where they close with a refrain, as in the prophetic castigations of Amos 4:6-11 or in Isaiah's stirring poem on the divine fury (9:7-20; 5:25-30) or the personal lament of Pss 42—43 or the song of trust of Psalm 46 in its original form or, most impressively, in the liturgy of thanksgiving of Psalm 107. They are readily identified, too, in the alphabetic acrostics of Psalms 9—10, 25, and 119 and in the first three chapters of Lamentations. But, as we shall have occasion to observe, there are many other ways to define their limits. In the literatures of the other peoples of the ancient Near East the same structural phenomena are present.[27] But how shall we name such clusters? The most common designation is the *strophe*, but some scholars have raised objections to it because they aver that it is drawn from the models of Greek lyrical verse and they cannot apply it to Semitic poetic forms. It is true that in an earlier period of rhetorical study scholars were too much dominated by Greek prototypes and sought to relate the strophes to each other in a fashion for which there was little warrant in the biblical text. If we must confine our understanding to the Greek conception of a strophe, then it is better not to employ it, and to use the word *stanza* instead. The second objection to the term is that a strophe is to be understood as a metrical unit, i.e., by a consistent metrical scheme. There is also some force in this objection. Many poems do indeed have metrical uniformity, but often this is not the case. Indeed, I should contend that the Hebrew poet frequently avoids metrical consistency. It is precisely the break in the meter that gives the colon or bicolon its designed stress and importance. But we can say with some confidence that strophes have prevailingly consistent meters. My chief defense for employing the word *strophe* is that it has become acclimated to current terminology, not only by biblical scholars, but also by those whose province is Near Eastern literature. By a strophe we mean a series of bicola or tricola with a beginning and ending, possessing unity of thought and structure. The prosody group must coincide with the sense. But there is still another observation to be made which is of the first importance for our understanding of Hebrew poetry. While very many poems have the same number of lines in each strophe, it is by no means necessary that they be of the same length, although in the majority of cases they are indeed so. Where we have variety in the number of lines in successive strophes, a pattern is usually discernible. In any event, the time has not yet passed when scholars resort to the precarious practice of emendation in order to produce regularity. Just as we have outlived the practice of deleting words *metri causa* for the sake of consistency, so it is to be hoped that we refuse to produce strophic uniformity by excision of lines unless there is textual support for the alteration.

Perhaps there is no enterprise more revealing for our understanding of the nature of biblical rhetoric than an intensive scrutiny of the composition of the strophes, the manifold technical devices employed for their construction, and the stylistic phenomena which give them their unity. Such a study is obviously beyond the province of our present investigation. We may call attention, however, to a number of features which occur with such frequency and in such widely diverse contexts that they may be said to characterize Hebrew and to a considerable extent ancient Near Eastern modes of literary composition. We have already mentioned the refrains which appear at the close of the strophes. There are not a few examples of where they open in the same fashion. Thus the succession of oracles against the nations in Amos 1:3—2:16 are all wrought in essentially the same mold, and the stylistically related sequence of oracles in Ezek 25:3–17 follows precisely the same pattern. Psalm 29 is, of course, a familiar example with its iteration of קוֹל יהוה in five of the seven strophes. In the opening poem of Second Isaiah (40:1–11) the proem comes to a climax in the cry, קְרָאוּ אֵלֶיהָ. This now serves as a key to the structure of the lines that follow: קוֹל קוֹרֵא (1a), קוֹל אֹמֵר קְרָא (6a), and הָרִימִי בַכֹּחַ קוֹלֵךְ (9b). The poem which follows is a superb specimen of Hebrew literary craft and exhibits the same sense of form by the repetition of key words at the beginning of each strophe, and the succession of interrogatives couched in almost identical fashion reach their climax in the awesome וּרְאוּ מִי־בָרָא אֵלֶּה, which is answered in the final strophe by the words to which all the lines have been pointing:

> Yahweh is an everlasting God,
>> Creator of the ends of the earth (40:28b).

Perhaps the most convincing argument for the existence of strophes in Hebrew poetry as in the poetry of other ancient Near Eastern peoples is the presence within a composition of turning points or breaks or shifts, whether of the speaker or the one addressed or of motif and theme. While this feature is common to a number of literary genres, it is especially striking in the personal and communal laments. Psalm 22, which fairly teems with illuminating rhetorical features, will illustrate. We cite the opening lines of each strophe:

> My God, my God, why hast thou abandoned me? (1–2)
> But Thou art holy (3–5)

> But I am a worm and no man (6-8)
> Yet thou art he who took me from my mother's womb (9-11)
> I am poured out like water (14-15)
> Yea, dogs are round about me (16-18)
> But thou, O Yahweh, be not far off (19-21)
> I will tell of thy name to my brethren (22-24)
> From thee comes my praise in the great congregation (25-28)
> Yea to him shall all the proud of the earth bow down (29-31)
>   (emended text. See B. H.).

Particles play a major rôle in all Hebrew poetry and reveal the rhetorical cast of Semitic literary mentality in a striking way. Chief among them is the deictic and emphatic particle כִּי, which performs a vast variety of functions and is susceptible of many different renderings, above all, perhaps, the function of motivation where it is understood causally.[28] It is not surprising, therefore, that it should appear in strategic collocations, such as the beginnings and endings of the strophes. For the former we may cite Isaiah 34:

> For Yahweh is enraged against all the nations (32:2a)
> For my sword has drunk its fill in the heavens (34:5a)
> For Yahweh has a sacrifice in Bozrah (34:6c)
> For Yahweh has a day of vengeance (34:8a).

The particle appears frequently in the hymns of the Psalter immediately following the invocation to praise, as in Psalm 95:

> For Yahweh is a great God,
>   and a great King above all gods (95:3),

or later in the same hymn:

> For he is our God,
>   and we are the people of his pasture (95:7).

The motivations also conclude a strophe or poem:

> For Yahweh knows the way of the righteous,
>   but the way of the wicked shall perish (Ps 1:6);

or, as frequently in Jeremiah:

> For I bring evil from the north
>   and great destruction (Jer 4:6b);
>
> For the fierce anger of Yahweh
>   has not turned away from us (Jer 4:8b);
>
> For their transgressions are many,
>   their apostasies great (Jer 5:6c).

Significantly, in the closing poem of Second Isaiah's eschatological "drama" (Isa 55) the particle is employed with extraordinary force, both at the opening and closing bicola of the strophes, and goes far to explain the impact that the poem has upon the reader. As the poems open with the threefold use of the particle in the opening strophe, so they close with a fivefold repetition of the word.

A second particle, frequently associated with כִּי, is הִנֵּה or הֵן, the word which calls for our attention. Characteristically it appears in striking contexts, either by introducing a poem or strophe or by bringing it to its culmination. Thus the third and climactic strophe of the long and well-structured poem of Isa 40:12–31 begins dramatically after the long series of interrogatives:

> Behold (הֵן), the nations are like a drop from a bucket,
>   and are accounted as dust on the scales;
> Behold, he takes up the isles like fine dust (40:15).

The poem which follows is composed of three series of three strophes each, and the climax falls in each case upon the third strophe. The "behold" always appears in crucial or climactic contexts. The judgment of the nations appears at the close of two strophes:

> Behold, you are nothing,
>   and your work is nought;
>   an abomination is he who chooses you (Isa 41:24);
> Behold, they are all a delusion;
>   their works are nothing;
>   their molten images are empty wind (Isa 41:29).

It is at this point that the Servant of Yahweh is introduced:

> Behold my servant, whom I uphold,
>   my chosen, in whom I delight;
> I have put my spirit upon him,
>   he will bring forth justice to the nations (42:1).

The last of the so-called Servant poems begins in the same way:

> Behold, my servant yet shall prosper,
>   he shall be exalted and lifted up,
>   and shall be very high (Isa 52:13).

The particle may appear in series, as in Isa 65:13–14:

> Therefore thus says Yahweh God:
> "Behold, my servants shall eat,
>   but you shall be hungry;
> behold, my servants shall drink,
>   but you shall be thirsty;
> behold, my servants shall rejoice,
>   but you shall be put to shame;
> behold, my servants shall sing for gladness of heart,
>   but you shall cry out for pain of heart,
>   and shall wail for anguish of spirit.

Frequently it brings the strophe or poem to a climax:

Behold your God!
Behold, the Lord Yahweh comes with might,
and his arm rules for him;
behold, his reward is with him,
and his recompense before him (Isa 40:9–10).

The particle appears in many other modes and guises in the OT, as, for example, in introducing oracles of judgment where הִנְנִי is followed by the active participle.[29]

There are other particles which would reward our study, among which we may mention לָכֵן, which characteristically introduces the threat or verdict in the oracles of judgment, or לָמָּה, with which the laments so frequently open, or וְעַתָּה, so central to the covenant formulations, but perpetuated in the prophets and singers of Israel.

Numerous other stylistic features delineate the form and structure of the strophes. Most frequent are the vocatives addressed to God in the invocations. Take the opening cola of the successive strophes in Psalm 7:

O Yahweh, my God, in thee do I take refuge (7:1a [Heb. 2a]);
O Yahweh, my God, if I have done this (7:3a [Heb. 4a]);
Arise, O Yahweh, in thy anger (7:6a [Heb. 7a]).

Or the *inclusio* of Psalm 8:

O Yahweh, my Lord,
how spacious is thy name in all the earth (8:1, 9 [Heb. 2, 10]);

or the entrance liturgy:

O Yahweh, who shall sojourn in thy tent?
Who shall dwell on thy holy hill? (15:1).[30]

Rhetorical questions of different kinds and in different literary types appear in strategic collocations. As we should expect, they are quite characteristic in the legal encounters:

What wrong was it then that your fathers found in me
that they went far from me? (Jer 2:5);
Why do you bring a suit against me? (Jer 2:29).[31]

The questions often provide the climactic line of the strophe:

How long must I see the standard,
and hear the sound of the trumpet? (Jer 4:21),

or in the moving outcry of the prophet:

Is there no balm in Gilead?
Is there no physician there?
Why then has the health of the daughter, my people, not been restored?
(Jer 8:22).

Especially striking is the threefold repetition of a keyword within a single strophe. This phenomenon is so frequent and the words are so strategically placed that it cannot be said to be fortuitous. We have observed it in connection with our study of the particles. We select an example almost at random, though it is lost in translation:

קוּמִי אוֹרִי כִּי בָא אוֹרֵךְ וּכְבוֹד יְהֹוָה עָלַיִךְ זָרָח:
כִּי־הִנֵּה הַחֹשֶׁךְ יְכַסֶּה־אֶרֶץ וַעֲרָפֶל לְאֻמִּים
וְעָלַיִךְ יִזְרַח יְהֹוָה וּכְבוֹדוֹ עָלַיִךְ יֵרָאֶה:
וְהָלְכוּ גוֹיִם לְאוֹרֵךְ וּמְלָכִים לְנֹגַהּ זַרְחֵךְ:   (Isa 60:1–3).

Amos' oracle on the Day of Yahweh is another good example (Amos 5:16–20). If we may accept the present masoretic text of Isa 55:1, it is not without significance that the prophet's final poem opens with the urgent invitations, which are all the more impressive because of their assonance:

> Ho, every one who thirsts,
>   come (לְכוּ) to the waters;
> and he who has no money,
>   come (לְכוּ), buy and eat!
> Come (לְכוּ), buy wine and milk
>   without money and without price (Isa 55:1).[32]

Repetition serves many and diverse functions in the literary compositions of ancient Israel, whether in the construction of parallel cola or parallel bicola, or in the structure of the strophes, or in the fashioning and ordering of the complete literary units. The repeated words or lines do not appear haphazardly or fortuitously, but rather in rhetorically significant collocations. This phenomenon is to be explained perhaps in many instances by the originally spoken provenance of the passage, or by its employment in cultic celebrations, or, indeed, by the speaking mentality of the ancient Israelite. It served as an effective mnemonic device. It is the key word which may often guide us in our isolation of a literary unit, which gives to it its unity and focus, which helps us to articulate the structure of the composition and to discern the pattern or texture into which the words are woven. It is noteworthy that repetitions are most abundant in crucial contexts. Perhaps the most familiar of these is the call of Abram (Gen 12:1–3) which opens the Yahwist patriarchal narratives. As Ephraim Speiser has seen, it is a well-constructed poem of three diminutive strophes of three lines each. But what is notable here is the fivefold repetition of the world *bless* in differing syntactical forms, which underscores the power of the blessing that is to attend not only Abram, but all the nations of the earth. It is not surprising, therefore, that the motif should recur again and again and always in decisive places. An example of another kind is the much controverted verse at the beginning of the book of Hosea:

לֵךְ קַח־לְךָ אֵשֶׁת זְנוּנִים וְיַלְדֵי זְנוּנִים
כִּי־זָנֹה תִזְנֶה הָאָרֶץ מֵאַחֲרֵי יְהֹוָה   (1:2).

In the following chapter the motif of the new covenant reaches its climax in another repetitive text:

And I will betroth you to me for ever; I will betroth you to me in righteousness and in justice, in steadfast love, and in compassion. I will betroth you to
me in faithfulness; and you shall know that I am Yahweh (Hos 2:19-20
[Heb. 21-22]).

The structure of the first chapter of Ezekiel is determined by the recurring motif of the *demuth* at the beginning of each of its major divisions,
and in the finale reaches its climax by the dramatic threefold repetition:

And above the firmament over their heads was the likeness of a throne, in
appearance like sapphire; and seated above the likeness of a throne was a
likeness as it were in human form (Ezek 1:26).

Persistent and painstaking attention to the modes of Hebrew literary
composition will reveal that the pericopes exhibit linguistic patterns,
word formations ordered or arranged in particular ways, verbal sequences
which move in fixed structures from beginning to end. It is clear that
they have been skillfully wrought in many different ways, often with
consummate skill and artistry. It is also apparent that they have been
influenced by conventional rhetorical practices. This inevitably poses a
question for which I have no answer. From whom did the poets and
prophets of Israel acquire their styles and literary habits? Surely they
cannot be explained by spontaneity. They must have been learned and
mastered from some source, but what this source was is a perplexing
problem. Are we to look to the schools of wisdom for an explanation? It is
difficult to say. But there is another question into which we have not
gone. How are we to explain the numerous and extraordinary literary
affinities of the *Gattungen* or genres and other stylistic formulations of
Israel's literature with the literatures of the other peoples of the Near
East? Were the prophets and poets familiar with these records? If not,
how are we to explain them? If so, in what ways?

But there are other latitudes which we have not undertaken to explore. T. S. Eliot once described a poem as a "raid on the inarticulate." In
the Scriptures we have a literary deposit of those who were confronted by
the ultimate questions of life and human destiny, of God and man, of the
past out of which the historical people has come and of the future into
which it is moving, a speech which seeks to be commensurate with man's
ultimate concerns, "a raid on the ultimate," if you will.

Finally, it has not been our intent to offer an alternative to form
criticism or a substitute for it, but rather to call attention to an approach of
eminent lineage which may supplement our form-critical studies. For
after all has been said and done about the forms and types of biblical
speech, there still remains the task of discerning the actuality of the
particular text, and it is with this, we aver, that we must reckon, as best
we can, for it is this concreteness which marks the material with which
we are dealing. In a word, then, we affirm the necessity of form criticism,

but we also lay claim to the legitimacy of what we have called rhetorical criticism. Form criticism and beyond.

NOTES

1. W. Baumgartner, "Zum 100 Geburtstag von Hermann Gunkel," *VTSup* (1962), pp. 1–18.

2. H. Gunkel, *Mose und seine Zeit* (1913).

3. W. Albright, *From the Stone Age to Christianity*, p. 44.

4. G. von Rad, *Deuteronomium-Studien* (1948; Eng. trans. 1953); A. Alt, *Die Ursprünge des israelitischen Rechts* in *Kleine Schriften zur Geschichte des Volkes Israel*, I (1959), pp. 278–332; Eng. trans. in *Essays on Old Testament History and Religion* (1966), pp. 79–132; Karlheinz Rabast, *Das apodiktische Recht im Deuteronomium und im Heiligkeitsgesetz* (1949).

5. Hedwig Jahnow, *Das hebräische Leichenlied im Rahmen der Völkerdichtung*, *BZAW*, 36 (1923).

6. R. A. Carlson, *David, the Chosen King* (1964).

7. J. Lindblom, *Die literarische Gattung der prophetischen Literatur* (1924); and *Prophecy in Ancient Israel* (1962); C. Westermann, *Grundformen prophetischer Rede* (1960), Eng. trans., *Basic Forms of Prophetic Speech* (1967).

8. W. Baumgartner, *Israelitische und altorientalische Weisheit* (1933); J. Fichtner, "Die altorientalische Weisheit in ihrer israelitisch-jüdischen Ausprägung," *BZAW*, 62 (1933); J. Hempel, *Die althebräische Literatur und ihr hellenistisch-jüdisches Nachleben* (1930).

9. V. Korošec, *Hethitische Staatsverträge* in *Leipziger rechtswissenschaftliche Studien* (1931); G. E. Mendenhall, *Law and Covenant in Israel and the Ancient Near East* (1955); K. Baltzer, *Das Bundesformular. Wissenschaftliche Monographien zum alten Testament* (1960); Dennis J. McCarthy, *Treaty and Covenant, Analecta Biblica*, 21 (1963).

10. H. B. Huffmon, "The Covenant Lawsuit in the Prophets," *JBL*, 78 (1959), pp. 285–95; G. E. Wright, "The Lawsuit of God: a Form-Critical Study of Deuteronomy 32," in *Israel's Prophetic Heritage* (1962), pp. 26–67; Julien Harvey, S.J., "Le 'Ribpattern,' requisitoire prophétique sur la rupture de l'alliance," *Biblica*, 45 (1962), pp. 172–96.

11. Delbert R. Hillers, "Treaty Curses and the Old Testament Prophets," in *Biblica et Orientalia*, 16 (1964); H. J. Franken, "The Vassal-Treaties of Esarhaddon and the Dating of Deuteronomy," *Oudtestamentische Studiën*, 14 (1965), pp. 122–54.

12. H. G. Reventlow, "Der Psalm 8" in *Poetica: Zeitschrift für Sprach- und Literatur-Wissenschaft*, I, (1967), pp. 304–32.

13. Meir Weiss, "Wege der neuen Dichtungswissenschaft in ihrer Anwendung auf die Psalmenforschung," *Biblica*, 42 (1961), pp. 255–302.

14. Ludwig Köhler, "Justice in the Gate," in *Hebrew Man* (1956), pp. 148–75.

15. H. G. Reventlow, "Der Psalm 8" in *Poetica*, p. 304.

16. H. G. Reventlow, *Liturgie und prophetisches Ich bei Jeremia* (1963), pp. 24–77.

17. See n. 11.

18. For literature on the subject see Otto Eissfeldt, *The Old Testament: An Introduction* (1967), p. 57.

19. "A Royal Song of Thanksgiving—II Samuel 22 = Psalm 18," *JBL*, 62 (1953), pp. 15–34; "The Song of Miriam," *JNES*, 14 (1955), pp. 237–50; "The Blessing of Moses," *JBL*, 67 (1948), pp. 191–210. See also Freedman's "Archaic Forms in Early Hebrew Poetry," *ZAW*, 72 (1960), pp. 101–07.

20. "The Song of Deborah in the Light of Stylistics," *VT*, I (1951), pp. 168–80.

21. G. Gerleman, *Das Hohelied* (1964).

22. "The Composition of Hosea," *Svensk Exegetisk Årsbok*, 31 (1966), pp. 211–63.

23. "Prototype and Copies, A New Approach to the Poetry-Prose Problem in the Book of Jeremiah," *JBL*, 79 (1960), 351–67; "The Recovery of Poetic Passages of Jeremiah," *JBL*, 85 (1966), pp. 401–35.

24. William L. Holladay, *The Root SÛBH in the Old Testament* (1958).

25. H. L. Ginsberg, "The Rebellion and Death of Ba'lu," *Orientalia*, 5 (1936), pp. 161-98; W. F. Albright, "The Psalm of Habakkuk," *Studies in Old Testament Prophecy*, ed. by H. H. Rowley (1950), pp. 1-18; *idem, Yahweh and the Gods of Canaan* (1968), pp. 4-27; J. H. Patton, *Canaanite Parallels in the Book of Psalms* (1944), pp. 5-11.

26. S. N. Kramer, *The Sumerians* (1963), pp. 174 ff., 254, 256, 263; A. Falkenstein and W. von Soden, *Sumerische und Akkadische Hymnen und Gebete*, pp. 59 f., 67 f.; J. B. Pritchard, *ANET*, pp. 385b-86a, 390, 391b-92.

27. See A. Falkenstein and W. von Soden, *Sumerische und Akkadische Hymmen*, pp. 37 ff.

28. James Muilenburg, "The Linguistic and Rhetorical Usages of the Particle in the Old Testament," *HUCA*, 32 (1961), pp. 135-60.

29. Paul Humbert, *Opuscules d'un Hebräisant* (1958), pp. 54-59.

30. Cf. also Pss 3:1 (Heb. 2), 6:1 (Heb. 2), 22:1 (Heb. 2), 25:1, 26:1, 28:1, 31:1 (Heb. 2), 43:1, 51:1 (Heb.2).

31. Cf. also Pss 2:1, 10:1, 15:1, 35:17, 49:5 (Heb. 6), 52:1 (Heb. 2), 58:1 (Heb. 2), 60:9 (Heb. 11), 62:3 (Heb. 4); Jer 5:7a; also Isa 10:11, 14:32, 42:1-4; Jer 5:21d, 9:9.

32. Cf. Judg 5:19-21; Pss 25:1-3, 34:1-3 (Heb. 2-4), 7-10 (Heb. 8-11), 121:7-8, 139:11-12 (Heb. 12-13), 145:1-3; Isa 55:6-9; Jer 5:15c-17.

The First Three Chapters of Genesis

*The study of imagery and narrative has occupied literary
critics for some time. Another "rhetorical" approach, offered by Kenneth Burke, is logology. Logology is Burke's
term for transformations of imagery and story into logical propositions. (Logology literally means "words about
words.") Story involves temporal sequence (plot) and personality (character). How story involves "principles" is explored in the study Burke offers of the first three chapters of
Genesis.*

*Nature and the social order provide symbols that are at
the very center of human existence. Burke's method in dealing with the great concerns in Genesis—order, the Fall,
mortification, death, dominion, guilt, and sacrifice—
should be contrasted with Edmund Leach's structuralist
reading of the same material, pp. 411–422.*

*Burke's study, which moves back and forth between the
modern and ancient world, does not rest simply in the original meaning of the text, but moves away to universal and
open-ended symbolic analysis.*

Burke believes that man is:

1) the symbol-using animal;

2) the inventor of the negative;

*3) separated from his "natural condition" by instru-
ments of his own making; and*

4) goaded by the spirit of hierarchy.

*Such beliefs stand behind his logological study of
Genesis.*

PRINCIPLES OF GOVERNANCE STATED NARRATIVELY

I MAGINE that you wanted to say, "The world can be divided into six
major classifications." That is, you wanted to deal with "the principles

From Kenneth Burke, *The Rhetoric of Religion* (1961), pp. 201–22.

of Order," beginning with the natural order, and placing man's socio-political order with reference to it. But you wanted to treat of these matters in *narrative* terms, which necessarily involve *temporal* sequence (in contrast with the cycle of terms for "Order," that merely cluster about one another, variously implying one another, but in no one fixed sequence).

Stated narratively (in the style of Genesis, *Bereshith*, Beginning), such an idea of principles, or "firsts," would not be stated simply in terms of classification, as were we to say, "The first of six primary classes would be such-and-such, the second such-and-such" and so on. Rather, a completely narrative style would properly translate the idea of six classes or categories into terms of time, as were we to assign each of the classes to a separate "day." Thus, instead of saying, "And that completes the first broad division, or classification, of our subject-matter," we'd say, "And the evening and the morning were the first day" (or, more accurately, the "One" Day). And so on, through the six broad classes, ending, "last but not least," on the category of man and his dominion.

Further, a completely narrative style would *personalize* the principle of classification. This role is performed by the references to God's creative fiat, which from the very start infuses the sheerly natural order with the verbal principle (the makings of that "reason" which we take to be so essential an aspect of human personality).

Logologically, the statement that God made man in his image would be translated as: The principle of personality implicit in the idea of the first creative fiats, whereby all things are approached in terms of the word, applies also to the feeling for symbol-systems on the part of the human animal, who would come to read nature as if it were a book. Insofar as God's words infused the natural order with their genius, and insofar as God is represented as speaking words to the first man and woman, the principle of human personality (which is at the very start identified with *dominion*) has its analogue in the notion of God as a super-person, and of nature as the act of such a super-agent. (That is, we take symbol-using to be a distinctive ingredient of "personality.")

Though technically there is a kind of "proto-fall" implicit in the principle of divisiveness that characterizes the Bible's view of the Creation, and though the principle of subjection is already present (in the general outlines of a government with God at its head, and mankind as subject to His authority while in turn having dominion over all else in the natural realm), the Covenant (as first announced in the first chapter) is necessarily Edenic, in a state of "innocence," since no negative command has yet been pronounced. From the dialectical point of view (in line with the Order-Disorder pair) we may note that there is a possibility of "evil" implicit in the reference to all six primary classifications as "good." But in all three points (the divisiveness, the order of dominion, and the universal goodness) the explicit negative is lacking. In fact, the nearest approach to an outright negative (and that not of a moralistic, hortatory sort) is in the reference to the "void" (*bohu*) which preceded God's classificatory acts. Rashi says that the word translated as "formless" (*tohu*) "has the meaning of astonishment and amazement." Incidentally, in connection with Genesis 1:29, *The Interpreter's Bible* suggests another implicit negative, in that the explicit permitting of a vegetarian diet implies that Adam may *not* eat flesh.

In the first chapter of Genesis, the stress is upon the creative fiat as a means of classification. It says in effect, "What hath God wrought (by his Word)?" The second chapter's revised account of the Creation shifts the emphasis to matters of dominion, saying in effect, "What hath God ordained (by his words)?" The seventh "day" (or category), which is placed at the beginning of the second chapter, has a special dialectical interest in its role as a transition between the two emphases.

In one sense, the idea of the Sabbath is implicitly a negative, being conceived as antithetical to all the six foregoing categories, which are classifiable together under the single head of "work," in contrast with this seventh category, of "rest." That is, work and rest are "polar" terms, dialectical opposites. (In his *Politics*, Aristotle's terms bring out this negative relation explicitly, since his word for business activity is *ascholein*, that is, "*not* to be at leisure," though we should tend rather to use the negative the other way round, defining "rest" as "not to be at work.")

This seventh category (of rest after toil) obviously serves well as transition between Order (of God as principle of origination) and Order (of God as principle of sovereignty). *Leisure* arises as an "institution" only when conditions of dominion have regularized the patterns of *work*. And fittingly, just after this transitional passage, the very name of God undergoes a change (the quality of which is well indicated in our translations by a shift from "God" to "Lord God").[1] Whereas in 1:29 *God* tells the man and woman that the fruit of "every tree" is permitted them, here the *Lord God* (2:17) notably revises thus: "But of the tree of the knowledge of good and evil, thou shalt not eat of it: for in the day that thou eatest thereof thou shalt surely die." Here, with the stress upon governance, enters the negative of command.

When, later, the serpent tempts "the woman" (3:4), saying that "Ye shall not surely die," his statement is proved partially correct, to the extent that they did not die on the day on which they ate of the forbidden fruit. In any case, 3:19 pronounces the formula that has been theologically interpreted as deriving mankind's physical death from our first parents' first disobedience: "In the sweat of thy face shalt thou eat bread, till thou return unto the ground; for out of it wast thou taken: for dust thou art, and unto dust shalt thou return."

The Interpreter's Bible (p. 512) denies there is any suggestion that man would have lived forever had he not eaten of the forbidden fruit.

Chapter 3, verse 20 is taken to imply simply that man would have regarded death as his natural end, rather than as "the last fearful frustration." Thus, the fear of death is said to be "the consequence of the disorder in man's relationships," when they are characterized "by domination" (along with the fear that the subject will break free of their subjection). This seems to be at odds with the position taken by the Scofield Bible which, in the light of Paul's statements in Romans 5:12–21 ("by one man sin entered the world, and death by sin"—and "by one man's offence death reigned by one") interprets the passage as meaning that "physical death" is due to a "universal sinful *state,* or nature" which is "our heritance from Adam."

It is within neither our present purpose nor our competency to interpret this verse theologically. But here is how it would look logologically.

First, we would note that in referring to "disorder" and "domination," *The Interpreter's Bible* is but referring to "Order" and "Dominion," as seen from another angle. For a mode of domination is a mode of dominion; and a socio-political order is by nature a ziggurat-like structure which, as the story of the Tower makes obvious, can stand for the principle of Disorder.

If we are right in our notion that the idea of Mortification is integral to the idea of Dominion (as the scrupulous subject must seek to "slay" within himself whatever impulses run counter to the authoritative demands of sovereignty), then all about a story of the "first" dominion and the "first" disobedience there should hover the theme of the "first" mortification.

But "mortification" is a weak term, as compared with "death." And thus, in the essentializing ways proper to the narrative style, this stronger, more dramatic term replaces the weaker, more "philosophic" one. "Death" would be the proper narrative-dramatic way of saying "Mortification." By this arrangement, the natural order is once again seen through the eyes of the socio-political order, as the idea of mortification in the toil and subjection of Governance is replaced by the image of death in nature.

From the standpoint sheerly of imagery (once the idea of mortification has been reduced to the idea of death, and the idea of death has been reduced to the image of a dead body rotting back into the ground), we now note a kind of "imagistic proto-fall," in the pun of 2:7, where the Lord God is shown creating man (*adham*) out of the ground (*adhamah*). Here would be an imagistic way of saying that man in his physical nature is essentially but earth, the sort of thing a body becomes when it decays; or that man is *first of all* but earth, as regards his place in the sheerly natural order. You'd define in narrative or temporal terms by showing what he came from. But insofar as he is what he came from, then such a definition would be completed in narrative terms by the image of his return to his origins. In this sense, the account of man's forming (in 2:7) ambiguously lays the conditions for his "return" to such origins, as the Lord God makes explicit in 3:19, when again the subject is the relation between *adham* and the *adhamah:* "For dust thou art, and unto dust shalt thou return." Here would be a matter of sheer imagistic consistency, for making the stages of a narrative be all of one piece.

But the death motif here is explicitly related to another aspect of Order or Dominion: the sweat of toil. And looking back a bit further, we find that this severe second Covenant (the "Adamic") also subjected woman to the rule of the husband—another aspect of Dominion. And there is to be an eternal enmity between man and the serpent (the image, or narrative personification, of the principle of Temptation, which we have also found to be intrinsic to the motives clustering about the idea of Order).

Logologically, then, the narrative would seem to be saying something like this: Even if you begin by thinking of death as a merely natural phenomenon, once you come to approach it in terms of conscience-laden *mortification* you get a new slant on it. For death then becomes seen, in terms of the socio-political order, as a kind of *capital punishment.* But something of so eschatological a nature is essentially a "first" (since "ends," too, are principles—and here is a place at which firsts and lasts meet, so far as narrative terms for the defining of essences are concerned). Accordingly death in the natural order becomes conceived as the fulfillment or completion of mortification in the socio-political order, but with the difference that, as with capital punishment in the sentencing of transgressions against sovereignty, it is not in itself deemed wholly "redemptive," since it needs further modifications, along the lines of placement in an undying Heavenly Kingdom after death. And this completes the pattern of Order: the symmetry of the socio-political (*cum* verbal), the natural, and the supernatural.

RESTATEMENT ON DEATH AND MORTIFICATION

If the point about the relation between Death and Mortification is already clear, the reader should skip this section. But in case the point is not yet clear, we should make one more try, in the effort to show how the step from conscience-laden guiltiness to a regimen of mortification can be narratively translated into terms of the step from "sin" to "death." It is important, because the principle of mortification is integral to the idea of redemptive sacrifice which we have associated with the idea of Order. The secular variants of mortification, we might say, lie on the "suicidal" slope of human motiviation, while the secular variants of redemption by sacrifice of a chosen victim are on the slope of homicide.

Conscience-laden repression is the symbol-using animal's response to conditions in the socio-political order. The *physical* symptoms that go with it seem like a kind of death. Thus, though the *word* for the attitude called "mortification" is borrowed from the *natural* order, the *feeling* itself is a response to various situations of dominion in the socio-political order. This terministic bridge leading from the natural order to the socio-political order thus can serve in reverse as a route from the socio-political order to the natural order. Then, instead of saying that "conscience-laden repression is *like* death," we turn the equation into a quasi-temporal sequence, saying that death "comes from" sin. We shall revert to the matter later, when considering formally how terms that are logically synonymous or that tautologically imply one another can be treated narratively as proceeding from one to the other, like cause to effect.

Logologically, one would identify the principle of personality with the ability to master symbol-systems. Intrinsic to such a personality is the "moral sense," that is, the sense of "yes and no" that goes with the thou-shalt-not's of Order. Grounded in language (as the makings of "reason") such conscience gets its high development from the commands and ordinances of governance. A corresponding logological analogue of personal immortality could be derived from the nature of a *personal name*, which can be said to survive the physical death of the particular person who bore it, as the idea of Napoleon's essence (the character summed up in his name) can be verbally distinguished from the idea of his "existence." So long as we can "recall" a departed ancestor by name in recalling the quality of the personality associated with his name, he can be said to "still be with us in spirit." And from the strictly logological point of view, the proposition that man necessarily conceives of God in accordance with the personal principle of the verbal would be statable in narrative style as the statement that God is an order-giving super-person who created man in His image. This is how the proposition should be put narratively, regardless of whether or not it is believed theologically.

Similarly, like St. Paul, we may choose to interpret the Biblical account of the Creation and Fall as saying literally that, whereas other animals die naturally (even without being subject to the kind of covenant that, by verbally defining sin, makes "sin" possible), all members of the human species die not as the result of a natural process but because the first member of the species "sinned." That is, death in man's case is primarily associated with the principle of personality (or "conscience"), such as the Bible explicitly relates to a verbal Covenant made by the first and foremost exponent of the creative verbal principle, in its relation to the idea of Order. Otherwise put: When death is viewed "personally," in moralistic terms colored by conditions of governance (the moral order), it is conceived not just as a natural process, but as a kind of "capital punishment."

But a strictly logological analysis of the mythic idiom (of the style natural to narrative) suggests a possibility of this sort: Even if one did not believe in Paul's theological interpretation of the story, even if one did not literally believe that all men's physical death is the result of the first man's disobedience, the Biblical narrative's way of associating "sin" with "death" would be the correct way of telling this story.

Suppose you wanted to say merely: "Order gives rise to a sense of guilt, and insofar as one conscientiously seeks to obey the law by policing his impulses from within, he has the feel of killing these impulses." Then, within the resources proper to narrative, your proper course would be to look for the strongest possible way of saying, "It is as though even physical death were a kind of capital punishment laid upon the human conscience." And that's what the story does, as starkly as can be. And that's how it should be stated narratively in either case, whether you give it the literal theological interpretation that Paul did, or interpret it metaphorically.

Theology is under the sign of what Coleridge would call the "Greek philosopheme." The narrative style of Genesis is under the sign of what Coleridge would call "Hebrew archaeology." Each style is concerned with "principles," after its fashion, Genesis appropriately using the "mythic" language of *temporal* firsts. (Coleridge's special use of the word "archaeology" is particularly apt here, inasmuch as *archai* are either philosophic first principles or beginnings in time.)

I discussed this ambiguity in the section "The Temporizing of Motives" in my *A Grammar of Motives*. But now we are attempting to bring out a slightly different aspect of the question. We are suggesting that, as regards the logological approach to the relation between Order and Guilt, the Biblical narrative as it now is would be "correctly" couched, whether you agree with Paul's theological interpretation of "original sin," or whether you view the narrative simply as a mythic way of describing a purely secular experience: the sense of "mortification" that goes with any scrupulous ("essential") attempt at the voluntary suppression of unruly appetites.

Such a speculation would suggest that the "archaeological" mode of expression allows naturally for a wider range of interpretation than does the "philosopheme" and its equivalents in formal theology. The narrative is naturally more "liberal." Yet this very liberality may in the end goad to theological controversy, insofar as theological attempts are made to force upon the narrative utterance a stricter frame of interpretation than the style is naturally adapted to. (A further step here is the possibility whereby the theologian may be said to be inspired in his own way; and thus, whereas he cites the original narrative as authority from God, his narrowing of the possible interpretation may later be viewed as itself done on authority from God.)

If you wanted to say, "It's essentially as though this were killing us," your narrative way of stating such an essence or principle would be the same, whether you meant it literally or figuratively. In either case, you wouldn't just say, "The sense of *mortification* is profoundly interwoven with the sense of guilt." Rather, you'd say, "The *very meaning of death itself* derives from such guilt." Or, more accurately still, you'd simply show man sinning, then you'd show the outraged sovereign telling him that he's going to die. And if he was the "first" man, then the tie-up between the idea of guilt and the imagery of death in his case would *stand for* such a "primal" tie-up in general.

However, note how this ambiguous quality of narrative firsts can tend to get things turned around, when theologically translated into the abstract principles of "philosophemes." For whereas narratively you would use a natural image (death—return to dust) to suggest a spiritual idea (guilt as regards the temptations implicit in a Covenant), now in effect the idea permeates the condition of nature, and in this reversal the idea of natural *death* becomes infused with the idea of moral *mortification,* whereas you had begun by borrowing the idea of physical death as a term for naming the mental condition which seemed analogous to it.

THE NARRATIVE PRINCIPLE IN IMAGERY

Besides discussing the way in which the narrative style translates principles into terms of temporal priority and personality, we should consider the peculiar role of imagery in such "archaeology."

One problem here is in trying to decide just how the concept of imagery should be limited. There is a sense in which all the things listed in the account of the Creation could be considered as images (lists of positive natural things deemed permeated by the principle or idea of divine authorship and authority). Here would be waters, sun, land, moon, stars, the various living things, etc., as defined by the "Spirit of God."

The formula, "Let there be light," could be said to introduce (in terms of an act and an image) the "principle of elucidation" at the very start, and in terms of a darkness-light pair that, though both are in their way "positive" so far as their sheer physical character is concerned, are related dialectically as the flat negation of each other. Incidentally, also, the relation between the pre-Creative darkness and the Creative light also at the very start introduces, in actual imagery, the idea of the Order-Disorder pair—and it sets the conditions for expressing the imagistic treatment of the Counter-Order as a "Kingdom of Darkness."

The explicit statement that man is made in God's image would be logologically translated: "God and man are characterized by a common motivational principle," which we would take to be the principle of personality that goes with skill at symbol-using. This kinship is reaffirmed in the account of Adam's naming the various animals, though also there is a notable difference in the degree of authority and authorship, as befits this hierarchal view of Order.

The reference to the mist in chapter 2, we are told in *The Interpreter's Bible,* once followed verse 8, on the Lord God's planting of the garden, and originally read: ". . . and a mist used to go up from the earth and water the garden." The same comment adds: "This is a statement to the effect that the garden was irrigated supernaturally—the word rendered *mist* has probably a mythological connotation[2]—not by human labor." Whatever such a mist may be mythologically or theologically (where it has sometimes been interpreted as standing for "error") there is a possible logological explanation for it, in keeping with the fact that an account of "firsts" naturally favors imagery associated with childhood. Such an image could well stand narratively, or "mythically," for the word-using animal's vague memory of that early period in his life when he was emerging into speech out of infancy. For at that time, the very growth of his feeling for words would be felt as a kind of confusion, or indistinctness, while a bit of linguistic cosmos (or verbal light) was gradually being separated from a comparative chaos (or inarticulate darkness) of one's infantile beginnings. That is, whereas speechlessness probably has not the slightest suggestion of confusion or deprivation to an animal that is not born with the aptitude for speaking, the speechless state should be quite different with the human being's period of emergence from infancy into articulacy. Yet, at the same time, it could be endowed with "promissory" or "fertile" connotations, insofar as the mist-wanderer was moving towards clarity.

At least, there is a notable example of such a mist in Flaubert's *Temptation of Saint Anthony.* For as the work proceeds, it develops after the fashion of a swiftly accelerating *regression,* going back finally to the imagining of an initial source in "pure" matter (as maternal principle). Flaubert's book traces plenitude back to its beginnings in a principle of heretic, unitary matter. In this reverse development, the fog of a monster's breath marks the line of division between the realm of the verbal and the realm of infantile formlessness (where all things are patchy combinations wholly alien to the realm of Order as we know it). Similarly the fog-people of Wagner's *Niebelungen* cycle seem to have such a quality (particularly in the *Nebelheim* of *Das Rheingold,* surely the most "infantile" of the plays, though all are somewhat like fairy stories).

The complicating element to do with images, when used as the narrative embodying of principles, or ideas, is that the images bring up possibilities of development in their own right. Thus, there is a kind of "deathiness" implicit in the very term, "tree of life." One might think of it as being cut down, for instance. The Biblical story relates it contrastingly to the forbidden fruit (which turns out to be a tree of death). But there is still the business of denying access to the tree *as a tree;* hence the arrangement whereby, after the expulsion, a flaming sword is set up, "which turned every way, to keep the way of the tree of life." The sword would seem most directly related to the idea of keeping people away from a tree; yet it also would fit with the idea of "protecting" life (though here, ironically, its kind of "protection" involves a *denial,* and thus another aspect of the negatives of dominion, with its principle of "capital punishment," or in general, "mortification").

Later we shall discuss the implications of the imagery to do with the unnatural obstetrics of Genesis, the possible logological interpretation of nakedness, the imagery of eating, and the role of the serpent as simultaneously the image and personal representative of the principle of temptation.

Perhaps the only other major imaginal deployment in the first three chapters concerns the Lord God's irate words to Adam (3:17): "Cursed is the ground for thy sake." On this point, our Scofield Bible says the earth is cursed because "It is better for fallen man to battle with a reluctant earth than to live without toil." But from the strictly logological point of view, Rashi's commentary seems more in keeping with the principle of firstness that infuses these chapters: "This is similar to one who goes forth to do evil; and people curse the breasts from which he suckled." Rashi here treats of a symmetry involving scene, agent, and act. The Lord God, to curse this agent thoroughly, curses the very ground he walks on. We might also remember, as regards the *adham-adhamah* pun, that this is the deathly, dominion-spirited ground from which he came.

To be sure, images also hover about ideas, as stated in the style of philosophemes. Also, ideas always contain an element of personality, as Plato's dialogues make apparent. And the Hobbesian notion of a quasi-original Covenant indicates how the pressure of narrative thinking affects our ideas of laws, principles, summations. But though the "archaeological" style cannot be distinguished categorically from the "philosopheme," one can at least distinguish their different slopes, or trends, and can in time spot the kinds of development that are specific to death.

DOMINION, GUILT, SACRIFICE

In sum, when we turn from the consideration of a terministic cycle in which the various terms mutually imply one another, to the consideration of the narrative terminology in these opening chapters of Genesis, we note that the narrative terms allow the idea of Order to be "processed." Here one can start with the creation of a natural order (though conceiving it as infused with a verbal principle); one can next proceed to an idea of innocence untroubled by thou-shalt-not's; one can next introduce a thou-shalt-not; one can next depict the thou-shalt-not as violated; one can next depict a new Covenant propounded on the basis of this violation, and with capital punishment; one can later introduce the principle of sacrifice, as would become wholly clear when we came to the Noachian Covenant where, after the great cleansing by water, God gave Noah the rainbow sign: "And Noah builded an altar unto the Lord; and took of every clean beast, and of every clean fowl, and offered burnt-offerings on the altar" (8:20). Then gradually thereafter, more and more clearly, comes the emergence of the turn from mere sacrifice to the idea of outright redemption by victimage.

The Scofield editor says of the Noachian Covenant: "It's distinctive feature is the institution, for the first time, of human government—the government of man by man. The highest function of government is the judicial taking of life. All other governmental powers are implied in that. It follows that the third dispensation is distinctively that of human government."

Still, there is a notable difference between the idea of the kill in the sacrifice of an animal and the idea of the kill as per 9:6: "Whoso sheddeth man's blood, by man shall his blood be shed." This is the *lex talionis,* the principle of human justice, conceived after the nature of the scales, and grounded in the idea of an ultimate authority. It is not the idea of vicarious sacrifice. That is found implicitly in Noah's sacrifice of the clean animals as burnt-offerings.

But ultimately the idea of cleanliness attains its full modicum of *personality,* in the idea of a fitting personal sacrifice. The principle of personal victimage was introduced incipiently, so far as theology goes, in connection with the next Covenant, involving Abraham's willingness to sacrifice his beloved son, Isaac, on the Altar of God's Governance—while the principle of personal victimage was also clearly there, in the idea of Israel itself as victim. It was completed in Paul's view of Christ, and the New Kingdom.

We should also note that, in proportion as the idea of a *personal* victim developed, there arose the incentives to provide a judicial rationale for the sacrifice more in line with the kind of thinking represented by the *lex talionis.* Thus the idea of a personally fit victim could lead to many different notions, such as: (1) the ideal of a perfect victim (Christ); (2) the Greeks' "enlightened" use of criminals who had been condemned to death, but were kept on reserve for state occasions when some ritual sacrifice was deemed necessary; (3) Hitler's "idealizing" of the Jew as "perfect" enemy.

Whereas the terms of Order, considered tautologically, go round and round like the wheel seen by Ezekiel, endlessly implicating one another, when their functions are embodied in narrative style the cycle can be translated into terms of an irreversible linear progression. But with the principle of authority personalized as God, the principle of disobedience as Adam (the "old Adam in all of us"), the principle of temptation as an Aesopian serpent, Eve as mediator in the bad sense of the word, and the idea of temptation reduced imagistically to terms of eating (the perfect image of a "first" appetite, or essential temptation, beginning as it does with the infantile, yet surviving in the adult), such reduction of the tautological cycle to a narrative linear progression makes possible the notion of an *outcome*.

Thus when we read of one broken covenant after another, and see the sacrificial principle forever reaffirmed anew, narratively this succession may be interpreted as movement towards a fulfillment, though from the standpoint of the tautological cycle they "go on endlessly" implicating one another. Logologically, many forms of victimage are seen as variants of the sacrificial motive. Burnt offerings, Azazel, Isaac, Israel in exile and the various "remnants" who undergo tribulations in behalf of righteousness can all be listed, along with Christ, as "reindividuations of the sacrificial principle." But a theological view of the narrative can lead to a more "promissory" kind of classification, whereby all sacrifices and sufferings preceding the Crucifixion can be classed as "types of Christ." When the devout admonish that "Christ's Crucifixion is repeated endlessly each time we sin," they are stating a theological equivalent of our logological point about the relation between the linear-temporal and the cyclical-tautological.

Logologically, the "fall" and the "redemption" are but parts of the same cycle, with each implying the other. The order can be reversed, for the terms in which we conceive of redemption can help shape the terms in which we conceive of the guilt that is to be redeemed. In this sense, it is "prior" to the guilt which it is thought to follow (quite as the quality of a "cure" can qualify our idea of the "disease" for which it is thought to be the cure—or as a mode of "wish-fulfillment" can paradoxically serve to reinforce the intensity of the wishes). But narratively, they stand at opposite ends of a long development, that makes one "Book" of the two Testaments taken together.

Thus, whereas narratively the Lord God's thou-shalt-not preceded the serpent's tempting of Eve, by appealing to the imagination, in mixing imagery of food with imagery of rule ("and ye shall be as *Elohim*"), and whereas the tempting preceded the fall, logologically the thou-shalt-not is itself implicitly a condition of temptation, since the negative contains the principle of its own annihilation. For insofar as a thou-shalt-not, which is intrinsic to Order verbally guided, introduces the principle of negativity, here technically is the inducement to round out the symmetry by carrying the same principle of negativity one step farther, and negating the negation. That is the only kind of "self-corrective" the negative as such has.

This principle of yes and no, so essential to the personal, verbal, "doctrinal" "sense of right and wrong," is potentially a problem from the very start. And when you add to it the "No trespassing" signs of empire, which both stimulate desires and demand their repression, you see why we hold that guilt is intrinsic to the idea of a Covenant. The question then becomes: Is victimage (redemption by vicarious atonement) equally intrinsic to the idea of guilt? The Bible, viewed either logologically or theologically, seems to be saying that it is.

One notable misfortune of the narrative is its ambiguities with regard to the relations between the sexes, unless logologically discounted. If man, as seen from the standpoint of a patriarchal society, is deemed "essentially superior" to woman, of whom he is "lord and master," it follows that, so far as the narrative way of stating such social superiority is concerned, man must be shown to "come first." Accordingly, as regards the *first* parturition, in contrast with ordinary childbirth, woman must be depicted as being born of man. This is the only way to make him absolutely first in narrative terms. Thus the punishment pronounced on Eve (3:16): "Thy desire shall be to thy husband, and he shall rule over thee" was ambiguously foretold (2:21, 22) where Eve is derived from Adam's rib.

A similar narrative mode of proclaiming man's essential social superiority appears in Aeschylus' *Eumenides*. Here, Athena, in her role as Goddess of Justice, gives her deciding vote at the "first" trial in the "first" law court—and appropriately she remarks that, though she is a woman, she was born not of woman but from the head of Zeus. (Her decision, incidentally, involves in another way the socio-political modifying of natural childbirth, since she frees Orestes of the charge of matricide by holding that he could not really have a mother, descent being through the male line, with the woman acting but as a kind of incubator for the male seed.)

The consciousness of nakedness as the result of the fall likewise seems to have been interpreted too simply, without reference to the major stress upon the matter of a *Covenant*. The approach from the standpoint of "Order" would be somewhat roundabout, along these lines: Social order leads to differentiations of status, which are indicated by differences in *clothing*. Thus, the same socio-political conditions that go with a Covenant would also go with clothing, thereby making one conscious of nakedness. The Biblical narrative itself makes clear that, under the conditions of Governance, sexual differentiation was primarily a matter of relative status. In a situation where man is to woman as master is to servant, and where the differences between the sexes were attested by clothes, nakedness would be too equalitarian.

But after sexual differentiation by clothing had been continued for a sufficient length of time, people began to assume a far greater difference between "social" and "sexual" motives than actually exists, and this is true also of modern psychoanalysis—until now we'd need a kind of ironic dissociation such as Marx proposed in connection with the "fetishism of commodities," before we could come even remotely near to realizing the extent of the social motives hidden in our ideas of sheerly "physical" sexuality. However, this marvelously accurate image of nakedness, interpreted from the standpoint of the estrangements resulting from Order in the sense of divergent rank, has been interpreted so greatly in purely sexual terms that often people seem even to think of Adam's original transgression as essentially sexual. Insofar as clothes imply social astrangement or differentiation by status, they are by the same token a kind of "fall." In themselves they are at odds with the natural order; yet nakedness is at odds with the order of our "second nature."

One final point, and our discussion of the specifically narrative resources here is finished. The opening sentence of Aristotle's *Nichomachaean Ethics* can serve best as our text: "Every art and every inquiry, and likewise every action and practical pursuit, is thought to aim at some good: hence it has rightly been said that the Good is that at which all things aim." Thus, whenever the Biblical account says, "And God saw that it was good," we might take the formula as having for its purely technical equivalent some such statement as, "And it was endowed with the principle of purpose." Since words like "aim," "end," "purpose" are our most generalized terms for such an idea, it follows that the equating of "to be" with "to be good" (as in the first chapter of Genesis) is a way of stating ethically, dramatically, narratively that a thing's "purpose" is technically one with its *esse*. Natural things, by their nature as creatures, are to be viewed as the *actualities* of God, hence as embodying a "design" (and they fit perfectly with Aristotle's stress, which is concerned with the varieties of "action," rather than with objects or things or processes in the sheerly neutral sense in which wholly impersonal, pragmatic science might view them).

All told, the idea of *purpose*, so essential to the narrative principle of *personality*, is here ingrained in the idea of Order, by being identified with the "good," whereby all things, by their mere act of being, contained in themselves the aim of their being.

No, that isn't quite the case. For their nature as "actualities" depends upon their nature as God's acts. Accordingly, in the last analysis, their aim involves their relation to the aims of their author (as the words in a well-formed book derive their aim from the purpose of the book as a whole—the Bible being a quite "bookish" view of the creative process).

Two further observations: (1) Recall, once more, that by the sheer dialectics of the case, this pronouncing of things as "good" brought up the possibilities of "evil"; (2) Think how Spinoza's *Ethics* in effect restated the Biblical narrative (though translating it from terms of "archaeology" into the circular terms of the "philosopheme," treating of Creation "in principle"). Think of his word for purpose, *conatus*, the endeavor of each thing to go on being itself, unless or until prevented by the determinations imposed upon it by other things likewise endeavoring to go on being themselves. And he also had his technical equivalent of the particular thing's relation to an over-all principle at once outside itself and permeating its very essence. The sacrificial principle in Spinoza would seem to take the form of a benign mortification, a peaceful, systematic distrust of the goads of the gods of empire.

NOTES

1. Grammatically, the word for God in the first chapter, "Elohim," is a plural. Philologists may interpret this as indicating a usage that survives from an earlier polytheistic period in the development of Jewish monotheism. Or Christian theologians can interpret it as the first emergence of a Trinitarian position; thus early in the text, with the Creator as first person of the Trinity, the Spirit that hovered over the waters as third person, and the creative Word as second person. (Incidentally, the words translated as "Lord God" in chapter II are *Jehovah-Elohim*. Later, in connection with the Abrahamic Covenant, the words translated as "Lord God" are *Adonai Jehovah*. *Adonai*, which means "master," applies to both God and man—and when applied to man it also includes the idea of husband as master.) The distinction between authority and authorship is approached from another angle in Augustine's *Confessions* I, where God is called the *ordinator* and *creator* of all natural things; but of sin he is said to be only the *ordinator*.

2. "The Book of Genesis. Exegesis," by Cuthbert A. Simpson, in *The Interpreter's Bible* (Nashville: Abingdon Press, 1960), I, 493.

_____John Macquarrie_____

Symbolism Case Study:
Light as a Religious Symbol

The problem of symbolic language is a problem in her-
meneutics, or the principles of interpretation. John Mac-
quarrie begins his phenomenological study of the symbol by
distinguishing it from myth. (On myth, see essays by
Kramer, pp. 272–284, Lambert, pp. 285–297, and Leach, pp.
411–422.) Macquarrie then attempts to distinguish between
the religious and the aesthetic symbol. Basically, the distinc-
tion is that the religious symbol calls forth an existential
response—a "response of commitment." "Father," the Cross,
water, and particularly the symbol of light are examined by
Macquarrie. Of special importance is the need to interpret
and reinterpret symbols. The reinterpretation is desymbol-
izing the symbol. (For a different view of the symbol, see
Alonso Schökel, pp. 24–56, Muilenburg, pp. 362–380, and
Burke, pp. 381–395, who distinguish the religious and
aesthetic dimenions in other ways.)

After a brief survey of the way light imagery is used in
pre-biblical and biblical writings, Macquarrie confronts his
central question: If for us the power of the light symbol
would seem to be lost, how may we reinterpret light in a
way that restores something of the force it once had? To
restore its original numinous power, Macquarrie redefines
light as "openness," to which he provides an "existential-
ontological" approach.

B ULTMANN'S 'demythologizing', in spite of its negative-sounding
name, does not aim at the elimination of myth but at its interpretation, and more specifically, its existential interpretation. Mythological
language cannot be entirely translated into existential language, in spite
of the proven affinities between the two. One reason is that, as in all
interpretation, there is a kind of reciprocity between the two languages,

From John Macquarrie, *God-Talk: An Examination of the Language and Logic of Theology*
(1967), pp. 192–211.

so that one is not absorbed into the other but rather each helps to throw light on the other. In this specific case, the language of existence helps to light up the obscure expressions of myth, but then in turn the concrete drama of the myth throws light in a new way on the structures of existence. The other reason is that myth is more than just an anthropological language; it has a further dimension, which we might call ontological or theological or cosmological. This cannot be translated into existential language, and we find it appearing in Bultmann as what he calls 'analogical' language. In any case, here again the language of myth is resistant to attempts to get rid of its concrete, pictorial character, for it wants to speak of a level of reality transcending the human level, and if we are to speak at all of the ultimate mysteries of God and Being, we cannot avoid using an indirect language of images.

So we are brought before the problem of symbolic language. 'Symbolic' language, in the widest sense, is different from myth. The point is that myth has an immediacy in which symbols and what they symbolize have not been sorted out. But a consciously symbolic language is much more sophisticated, and has some understanding of the complexity of its own logic. In such a language, the symbol and the symbolizandum are consciously distinguished. Perhaps the most familiar and the most profound symbols have their home, so to speak, in myth and in the unconscious, but they can become detached from this 'dreaming' background, as it were, and may continue to be used in very fruitful ways by men who have become 'awake' to their symbolic character.

Apart from making this rough distinction of symbol from myth, and thereby showing how symbols may continue to be useful and even indispensable in a post-mythical world, we have not tried to pin down too precisely what we mean by a 'symbol'. The word has an extremely wide range, and there is a sense in which all language is symbolic—every word is a symbol, and even the letters, out of which written words are made, are symbols. On the other hand, there are a great many symbols that are not words. Since we ourselves are concerned in this study with language, we are more interested in verbal symbols than in, let us say, flags, emblems and the like; yet it is not possible or desirable to discuss a word without also discussing the thing or the phenomenon for which the word stands, and whose properties or characteristics have made possible the particular symbolic use of the language. On the other hand, although we are concerned with verbal symbols primarily, we are obviously not interested in *all* words, though all words can be called 'symbols'. Our interest lies in those words which are 'symbolic' in a narrower sense, namely, words which stand for a thing or phenomenon which is itself a symbol, insofar as it stands for something else; so that the word, in such a case, refers indirectly through its immediate referend to whatever this may symbolize. If I may anticipate the study of a special case to which we shall come later, I may give an illustration at this point. In the Nicene Creed, it is asserted that Jesus Christ is 'Light of Light'. Now this expression is symbolic, that is to say, the words are symbolic. More than this, however, the actual phenomenon of light is considered a symbol of the divine. Thus the words immediately refer to light, but in the universe of discourse in which they are used, they bounce off their immediate referend, if I may use such an expression, and point to the mystery of Christ's deity.

Yet even if we pin down the notion of symbolism in this way, our usage is still very imprecise. What has been described is indirect or oblique language in general. Is all such indirect language to be called 'symbolic'? Or are we to make further distinctions between 'symbols', 'analogues', 'images', 'metaphors' or whatever other expressions may be used? Bultmann, for instance, does distinguish between 'symbol', 'analogue' and 'metaphor', though his distinctions are never made very clear and he is not consistent in maintaining them.

If we try to move toward a more exact differentiation among the various terms that we have noted, a first useful step would be to separate metaphor from symbols, analogues and images. The expression 'metaphor' is used mostly in literary contexts; and although 'symbols', 'analogues' and 'images' are all expressions that can be used in a variety of contexts, we are thinking of them here primarily in their religious and theological use. Now, it seems to me that we can separate metaphors from the other three chiefly in terms of our existential response. As far as the metaphor is concerned, our response to it is an aesthetic one. A well-chosen metaphor sharpens our perception so that we notice features of the situation that we would not have noticed otherwise. We share in the way the poet has seen whatever he is describing to us. Now surely the symbols, analogues and images of religious discourse likewise sharpen our perception, and the manner in which they do this has obvious affinities with the way in which literary metaphors function. But the response, in the case of the religious expression, is not an aesthetic one. It does indeed involve feeling, though it would be the feeling associated with the sense of the numinous rather than with the sense of the beautiful. It also involves insight, and our major problem is to elucidate the kind of insight that such religious symbols and the like may bring, that is to say, to elucidate their cognitive dimension. But perhaps the chief difference is that the religious symbol, analogue or image calls from us a response of commitment. When Matthew Arnold writes, 'And still the men were plunged in sleep', this is a vivid metaphor that presents a situation to us in a sensitive and dramatic way, and perhaps even involves us in this situation; but it involves us aesthetically rather than personally or morally. On the other hand, when we think of some of the images that were applied by the first Christians to Christ, these involved a faith-commitment to him. To call him 'Lord' or 'Son of God' or 'eternal Word' or even 'good Shepherd' or 'true Vine' is not so much to light up his being (though this is included) as to respond to him by accepting him and declaring one's allegiance to him or obedience to him. Generally speaking, then, it seems to me that in the way they affect us and in the existential response that they call forth, religious symbols and allied expressions have to be distinguished from the metaphors and other figurative expressions used in literature. That there are resemblances, we need not deny; and that the poet too can evoke commitment, we need not deny, though then he is probably writing as a prophet, rather than a poet pure and simple. But even when we allow these things, we can still see that the oblique language of religion has its own distinctive characteristics.

Can we now make some further distinctions as among 'symbols', 'analogues' and 'images', the three expressions which we have been using up till now? In common usage, I believe that these expressions frequently overlap, so that such distinctions as we make will have a somewhat arbitrary character. Perhaps we could agree to use the word 'image' as a broad generic term that would cover any kind of pictorial language. The question would then arise about how we distinguish between symbols and analogues within the general field of images. It is obvious that many theologians have in fact made such a distinction, although one would have to add that the dividing line is not always a very clear one. But there is a rather obvious difference, which although it may seem a trivial matter in itself, suggests a point of departure. The difference is that the best analogues are almost self-interpreting, whereas symbols frequently require much explanation of background before we begin to see where they are pointing. This difference may sometimes be a relative one, and depends simply on the fact that the best analogues assume a background of ideas and relationships that is universally known, while even quite well-known symbols imply a narrower background of ideas, perhaps deriving from the history of a specific community. But I think there is more to the difference than this.

Analogy would seem to depend on some intrinsic likeness between the analogue and that for which it stands. We do not, for the moment, pause to ask the difficult question about what is meant precisely by 'likeness' or 'similarity'. In the case of religious analogues, the likeness would usually be found in some personal characteristic or relationship. For instance, when we speak of God as our Father, we are employing an analogue which depends on an intrinsic likeness, in some respects at least, between the parent-child relation and the relation of God to his creatures. I say that an analogy of this kind is almost self-interpreting (whatever its ultimate difficulties may be) because it seems to imply some straightforward likeness and because also the parent-child relation is universally known in human experience. Such an analogy gains the widest currency and perhaps we could scarcely imagine the possibility of ever dispensing with it. It is true that in some cases the analogue might be less than self-interpreting. There is the case of the child who has never known parental love, and for whom the analogue of God's fatherhood needs to be unfolded through the experience of love in a Christian community; again, human fatherhood is frequently so cheapened and debased that it may afford only a very distant glimpse of what is meant by divine fatherhood, and needs to be itself judged in the light of the God-creature relation, to which it has afforded a clue; or again, one would need to take account of Freud's theories about the projection of the father-image, and ensure that this particular analogue is not allowed to degenerate into something infantile and neurotic. Nevertheless, this kind of analogue seems to have an extraordinary stability and universality, as well as a direct and readily intelligible power of address.

To say that it is 'likeness' that makes possible analogy is not to imply that symbolism is something purely subjective, and that there is no kind of intrinsic relation between the symbol and that which it symbolizes. It may well be the case that there are relations other than likeness that make possible a symbolism that has some ontological validity and is not exhaustively accounted for in terms of existential response. Tillich, for instance, speaks of 'participation', and as an illustration he mentions a national flag, which is said to 'participate' in the being of the nation to which it belongs.[1] Admittedly, this notion of 'participation' is not made very clear, though it seems obvious that it is something much more concrete than the participation of a particular in a universal, the way in which the notion of 'participation' (*methexis*) has usually been understood from Plato onward. But it is also clear that this participation is something very different from 'likeness'. We would never dream of calling a flag an 'analogue' of the country to which it belongs, and even if we thought of it as more than a merely extrinsic or conventional symbol, we would not suppose that the intrinsic relation, whatever it might be, is one of likeness.

Perhaps we may get some help at this point if we recall the so-called 'picture' theory of language. According to this theory, our language somehow reproduces the structure of the facts about which we are talking and so, presumably, has some kind of formal 'likeness' to the facts. But while the proponents of this theory, such as Earl Russell, believed themselves to be championing the cause of science and empiricism, they get no support from contemporary physics, in which the relation between language and facts is much more complex than a relation of simple likeness.

The point has been developed in relation to religious language by Ian Ramsey, who bases himself in turn on some views about scientific models put forward by Max Black.[2] Here we are introducing a new word into the discussion—the word 'model'. I do not think, however, that this need be taken as an additional complication. As the word is used by Ramsey, it has a fairly broad generic range (like the word 'image') and seems to cover both analogues and symbols. Ramsey's point is that there is a big difference between the way scientific models were understood in the nineteenth century and the way they are understood today. In the nineteenth century, these models were supposed to be 'picture' models, reproducing or copying on a different scale selected features of the reality which they were supposed to represent. I suppose that the model of the atom as a miniature solar system, if taken more or less literally, would be an example of a 'picture' model. But the kind of models used in contemporary science are different. It is accepted that the atom cannot be pictured at all, and although we may talk of 'particles', 'waves' and the like, this language is not to be taken literally. We cannot understand the atom in the way the nineteenth century physicist wanted to understand it, that is to say, by constructing a mental model that would reproduce the essential features of the atom. Yet, on the other hand, it is clear that people today do in fact understand the atom better than people did in the nineteenth century. The models that are used today—Ramsey calls them 'disclosure' models—are not pictures based on one-to-one likeness between features of the picture and corresponding features in the original, yet the fact that they enable us to operate with the atom and to harness atomic power shows that somehow they stand in real relatedness to the nature of the atom. These contemporary scientific models are symbols, rather than pictures. One might almost call them 'ciphers', in Jaspers' use of this term,[3] that is to say, words that stand for something that is in itself quite incomprehensible, and yet words that somehow give us some way of coming to terms with the mystery. But I doubt if Jaspers himself would use the term 'ciphers' in this way.

John McIntyre has made an interesting comparison between the non-picturing models about which we have been talking and the so-called 'secondary' qualities given in sense-perception.[4] These secondary qualities, we suppose, do not belong to things apart from our perceiving them—the rose is not 'really' red, or the sky blue. Yet on the other hand these secondary qualities are not just subjective ideas in our minds, unrelated to the external world. This comparison is, of course, itself an analogy, and it must not be pressed too far, but it does at least give us an example of how we may know something through properties or characteristics different from but not unrelated to the properties or characteristics of the thing itself.

Actually, we use the word 'symbol' to cover a whole range of possible relations between the symbol and the symbolizandum, extending from something very close to a purely conventional and extrinsic relation at one extreme to something near to the 'likeness' of analogy at the other. A mathematical symbol would seem to be a matter of convention, and to have no intrinsic connection with what it symbolizes. A letter of the alphabet might seem to be just as conventional, though it must be remembered that letters which now represent sounds to which they have no intrinsic relation have been derived from ideograms which originally pictured objects or ideas. A national flag would seem to acquire its relation to or 'participation' in the life of a nation through its association with the history of that nation; but it is hard to know whether this ever becomes an intrinsic relation, or whether Tillich is justified in putting the flag so definitely among symbols rather than among what he calls 'signs'. Such a symbol as the cross might seem to be in similar condition. It is a symbol of God's love within the Christian community because of the associations which it has there with the death of Jesus Christ; but in pre-Christian times, or in a country that knew nothing of the Christian religion, the cross would not be such a symbol. Yet just because of its distinctive shape, the cross has served as a symbol of other qualities in non-Christian and pre-Christian cultures—of immortality in ancient Egypt and of fertility in Central America, to mention only two widely divergent cases. Thus, apart from its historical associations in the Christian religion, one would have to say that the cross has a kind of intrinsic symbolic power, though this has been differently understood in different cultures. Water, on the other hand, seems to be in still another class. Apart altogether from the history of its use in different cults, its everyday use in washing gives to it an almost universal and intrinsic symbolic power as representing cleansing. When we come to such a symbol as light, of which I shall have more to say shortly, the dividing line between symbols and analogues has become very ill-defined, for one could argue that there is a measure of 'likeness' between some features of light and some features of God as he is known in religious experience.

While there is a wide range of religious symbols and while the degree of affinity between the symbol and what is symbolized varies, it would seem that there is always some affinity, and that religious symbols are never just extrinsic or accidental. By its very participation in the history of a community or in the experience of mankind, a symbol establishes itself, exerts its own power and claims its own right. Such a symbol is much more than a mere conventional sign like, say, the plus sign in arithmetic or algebra. The operation of addition could get along just as well with some other sign, though it may be worth noting that even the addition sign does not seem to be entirely arbitrary, for it consists of one stroke added to another, and to this extent is intrinsically related to what it signifies. Still, it could be changed by agreement. But it would be unthinkable for Christianity to dispense with the cross or change it for some other symbol, just as presumably it would also be impossible to discard such fundamental analogies as that of the fatherhood of God.

But if symbols, or at any rate some symbols, are just as much built into the Christian faith as some of its central analogues, why is it the case—as we have asserted earlier—that the analogues have a kind of self-interpreting quality, whereas the symbols may have a kind of obscurity that calls for their reinterpretation and refurbishing in an enterprise rather similar to the interpretation of myth?[5] To this it may be replied that symbols only remain symbols for as long as they successfully point to the reality which they symbolize, and relate that reality to our human existence. This, in turn, depends like all successful communication on a background of shared ideas within which the symbols can operate.

Even the cross could become an empty symbol, and for this reason we not only exhibit the cross in our churches or make the sign of the cross in our worship, but also preach the cross and continually call to mind its meaning in the Christian story and the theology based on this story. There is a double activity here, typifying again the hermeneutic circle whereby we move back and forth from one medium to another, and find that each interprets the other. The symbol lights up for us levels of meaning and of reality in ways that perhaps conceptual language could not do, above all, if it is an abstract language; yet without conceptual elucidation of the symbol's meaning, it would lapse into utter obscurity and could not perform its function.

I propose now to illustrate and clarify these general remarks about symbols and symbolism by taking a concrete example of a religious symbol and subjecting it to closer study. We shall try to see what are the dimensions of meaning in this symbol, and we shall consider also how far it typifies the tendency of symbols to lapse back into obscurity, and what kind of interpretation or reinterpretation it demands—in other words, what kind of 'desymbolizing' is called for, if we remember that this expression implies just as positive a hermeneutic as does 'demythologizing'. The example chosen for this case study, if I may call it such, is not so central as the cross in the Christian faith. It is nevertheless a very important symbol, and one that is found not only in Christianity but in many other religions besides. It is the symbol of light.

An examination of a symbol like light is an interesting pointer to those unifying factors which, in spite of all differences, run through the religious faiths of mankind. A study of the shared imagery might turn out to be one useful way of promoting communication and co-operation among faiths. But however that may be, the symbol of light is one that has been known far beyond the borders of Christendom, and it has had a very long history among the religions of the world. The very name of one of these religions, Buddhism, implies that 'enlightenment' is of the essence of religion, for a Buddha is simply one who has become enlightened. Edwyn Bevan, in an admirable discussion of this symbol, [6] has briefly traced something of the history of this image in the religious vision of ancient peoples. He begins from the sun-gods of Egypt and other countries of the Near East, continues through the dualistic world-view of Zoroastrianism, with its depiction of the cosmic struggle between light and darkness, and comes on to the use of the symbol in Hellenistic times, when, as Bevan believed, it acquired a special importance. In this period, light figured prominently in Gnosticism, neo-Platonism, the writings of Philo, and generally in the religion and philosophy of the Graeco-Roman world. To the examples adduced by Bevan, one could now add a mention of the light symbol in the Qumran community, one of whose documents dealt with 'The War of the Sons of Light with the Sons of Darkness'.[7]

But what is important in Bevan's treatment is not so much his bringing together of historical examples as rather his masterly exploration of the symbol itself and its power to direct us into many dimensions of experience. Prominent in Bevan's account is what we have called the element of 'existential response', that is to say, the feelings and commitments which this symbol awakens in us, and which we may suppose are likewise feelings and commitments appropriate to the religious realities which light is taken to symbolize. But there are hints also of the ontological dimensions of the symbol, as lighting up something of the mystery of these religious realities themselves. The problem of desymbolizing begins to show itself as remarkably parallel to the problem of demythologizing. In both cases, existential interpretation is an important step toward elucidating the meaning, but in neither case is such interpretation exhaustive.

Perhaps it is only when one begins to look for it that one realizes how pervasive the light symbol is in Christian thought and worship. Its place in the Bible itself has been well shown by A. G. Hebert. He uses a typological method of exegesis and believes that we can discern certain great images or symbols that recur throughout the Bible; if we follow these up, it is claimed, we find them building themselves together in revelatory patterns. Applying this method to the symbol of light, he notes that there was light in the beginning of the creation, when God said, 'Let there be light'. There was light at the theophany to Moses in the desert, and in the exodus, in the pillar of fire. The light symbol recurs in the New Testament, for it is present at the beginning of the incarnation, at the birth of Christ, just as it had been at the beginning of the creation. There is light too at the transfiguration. In St John's Gospel, Christ declares himself to be the light of the world, while in the First Epistle of St John, it is asserted that God *is* light. This identification of God with light may, incidentally, be cited as illustrating a kind of transition point between myth and conscious symbolism. For many persons in the first century, especially in the dualistic Gnostic cults, God and light were literally one and the same. Presumably in St John's Epistle, the literal identification of light with God has given way to a conscious use of the light symbol to stand for God. Yet it may well have been the case that the distinction between symbol and symbolizandum was still blurred. This seems even probable when we remember that the contrast between light and darkness is one element in the so-called 'Johannine dualism', and that Bultmann and others have seen in this dualism (as well as in other things) evidence of a Gnostic influence in the Johannine literature.[8]

But let us come back to Father Hebert's remarks on the light symbol in the Bible. In this poetic kind of language, one does not look for complete consistency. Sometimes God is represented as the author of light, sometimes he is associated with light, sometimes light marks his presence, sometimes he is identified with light. According to Hebert, the symbol of light 'is used to describe the work of God in the whole order of creation and redemption, and it dwells in the imagination as exact theological definitions cannot do'.[9] Even if we have reservations about aspects of Hebert's typological style of exegesis, we can acknowledge the claim that he makes for the poetic, evocative force of symbolic language, as a kind of language that can somehow work upon men and lead them to insight and even action, where a more exact conceptual language might fail.

The importance of the symbol of light in Christianity may be seen further if we consider its place in liturgy and devotion. Right through the Christian year, the symbol of light figures very prominently. In the Anglican Book of Common Prayer, the collect said throughout the season of Advent begins with the petition that God may 'give us grace that we may cast away the works of darkness, and put upon us the armour of light'. Christmastide tells how the 'glory of the Lord' shone round about the shepherds, and also of the 'true light' that came into the world.[10] Epiphany is perhaps *par excellence* the season of the light symbol. In the Gospel, we read the story of how the wise men were guided by the star to Jesus.[11] In the Epistle, St Paul asserts that the God who had said in the beginning, 'Let there be light!' has shone in our hearts to give 'the light of the knowledge of his glory in the face of Christ.[12] From the Old Testament, we hear the voice of the prophet: 'Arise, shine, for thy light is come, and the glory of the Lord has risen upon you'.[13] Of course, the very word 'Epiphany' is derived from the same root as the Greek word *phōs,* 'light'. Epiphany simply means a 'coming to the light', a manifestation or shining forth in which something that has hitherto been veiled or hidden is now brought into the open. It is not necessary for us to pursue the theme of light through the remainder of the Church's year, but it keeps recurring. We may remember too that on various Saints' Days, the theme of light occurs. Soon after the Epiphany we commemorate St Paul's conversion and recall how 'there shone round about him a light from heaven'.[14]

It is not my intention to try to explore the evocative connotations that the symbol of light carries with it, either in the general religious experience of mankind or in the context of the Bible or of Christian worship. It would in any case be difficult to add anything worthwhile to the perceptive comments of Bevan, Hebert and others. Rather, we shall consider this symbol in a more general way, hoping that this may help us toward a better understanding of religious symbols as such. The power of a symbol to awaken an existential response must be related to its power to yield insight into some ontological reality. When this fails to happen, the symbol becomes obscure, its power is weakened and it may eventually fall out of use. So we may begin by asking about the power and effectiveness of the symbol for our times, and this will lead us into the question of its meaning and the possibilities for reinterpretation. Even the most powerful symbols eventually grow old and die, so that they can no longer speak to men with their former persuasiveness. There are two reasons for suspecting that the symbol of light, whatever its past power may have been, is no longer one that can easily speak to men in modern times.

The first reason is simply that our prosaic, matter-of-fact attitude to the world gives us quite a different feeling for light from that which men presumably had for it in ancient times. For them, light was a mysterious effluence, already possessed of something like a numinous character. For us, light has become just another physical phenomenon; and more than that, it is something that we have at our disposal, for we now make our own light and use it when we will, and are not dependent on the 'great lights' of the sky that once 'ruled' the day and the night.[15] Like all other physical phenomena, light is for us profane, secular, matter-of-fact. Even if it is ultimately a mystery, we can nevertheless place it in our scheme of the physical universe. We can think of it as waves, whose frequency and intensity we can measure; or as packets of energy, whose very mass we can likewise measure. Even by the most strenuous effort of imagination, we could hardly feel for light as people once did. But without its ancient connotations, light can hardly function for us with the power of a symbol, that is to say, with power to shape our lives; at best, it might remain as a metaphor, operating on the literary and aesthetic level.

The second reason suggesting that the power of the light symbol has declined is that, as a symbol drawn from nature, it lacks a personal or existential dimension, even if it has possibilities for eliciting an existential response. When we remember how thoroughly personalized is the Bible's talk of God, it is perhaps rather surprising to find a naturalistic symbol figuring so prominently as does the symbol of light. Even if we agree with those scholars who maintain that the talk of light and darkness in the Johannine literature comes out of a Gnostic background, there are still plenty of other areas of the Bible that speak of light. The light symbol is indeed so firmly established in the Old Testament that one could argue that it is unnecessary to look to Near Eastern dualism for the role assigned to this symbol in the Fourth Gospel. But we need not concern ourselves with this question about origins. However, let us notice that the very Epistle which makes central the naturalistic symbol of light in asserting 'God is light', also contains the assertion 'God is love', and in this passage makes central a personal image.[16] Most Christians would probably think that this second and personal way of talking about God is much more adequate than the first, because it points to him by employing a symbol—or, to speak more precisely, an analogue—drawn from human existence, not from inanimate nature. We are participants in human existence and know it from the inside, whereas we know nature only from without. But admittedly, the passages about light in the New Testament are given an existential application: for instance, both our Lord's declaration that he is the light of the world and the assertion that God is light are followed by statements about walking in the light. Nevertheless, the symbol is itself an impersonal one.

The question then arises whether we can find some way of reinterpreting this ancient symbol of light, so as to restore something of the force which it presumably once had, and keep it from degenerating into a mere metaphor. Is there some expression that might help to bring to life something of the meaning of the symbol of light that belonged to it when light was still a mysterious and even numinous effluence? Perhaps this means finding an expression that will introduce an existential dimension into the naturalistic symbol—a symbol which has been progressively depersonalized as nature has been stripped of any animistic interpretation. We must look for some interpretative idea that will allow us to grasp the language of the biblical writers—and/or allow it to grasp us—as not just a figurative flight of poetic imagery, but as having to do with the 'light of life',[17] our life here and now.

Let me now suggest that an expression which can perhaps help to revivify the biblical symbol of light is 'openness'. We cannot think of 'openness' as simply a word that can be substituted for mentions of 'light', but it is a word that can help us to understand an important dimension of the light symbol, a dimension that has been obscured in the general decay of the symbol that has gone on concomitantly with the secularization of nature. Roughly speaking, one might say that the word 'openness' can do for the symbol of light what the word 'estrangement' has done in much contemporary theology for the moribund word 'sin'. 'Estrangement' is certainly not a substitute for 'sin', but it does refurbish the old word by pointing to a basic structure to which 'sin' refers. In similar fashion, the word 'openness' draws our attention to a basic structure intended by the light symbol, for only where conditions of openness obtain can there be light. In the depth of a forest, for instance, it is where the wood has been opening up that the light comes in, and we call such an open place a 'clearing' or a 'glade', a place that is bright.[18]

The interpretation of the symbol of light in terms of openness is an existential-ontological one, related to the basic logic of all theological discourse. The interpretation begins from the existential side, for we find the first clues to what is meant by 'openness' simply by considering ourselves. What makes us, as human beings, different from rocks and stars and even animals is just the astonishing multiplicity of ways in which we stand open. We are open to the past through memory and open to the future through anticipation, and so we are open to the possibility of becoming responsible selves. Again, we are open to our world, so that we can understand it and, within limits, transform it and become creative within it. We are open to other human beings (themselves having this kind of openness) so that we can enter into personal relations with them and push outward the horizons of genuine community. Surely we are open also to God, the Being within which we and all that is have our limited beings.

And yet, as soon as we say these things, we see that all of them have to be contradicted. This openness of ours is ambiguous and variable in its character. We have it as a potentiality of our being, but in fact we oscillate between being open and being shut up. We shut out our past by 'forgetting' what is unpleasant to us, and we withdraw from the disturbing responsibilities of the future. We mark out for ourselves a corner of the world that we want to possess. We throw up barriers against the neighbour. Likewise we can go far toward shutting out any ultimate concern by immersing ourselves in what is immediate or even petty.

It is in this ambivalent and even contradictory situation that there is addressed 'the message that we have heard from the beginning', the message that God is light. The statement 'God is light' could be translated into the language of openness by saying: 'Openness is constitutive for being'. The more openness, the fuller being and the more expansion in being; but where openness is obstructed, being is narrowed down and thinned away. Openness is the very law of being, so to speak, because Being itself or God is constituted by openness.

It is not difficult to relate this ontological interpretation of the symbol of light to some of the central Christian doctrines. God is not closed in himself, like, perhaps, the 'uncarved block' of Chinese mysticism. He does not preserve himself intact, if one may so speak, but goes into the openness of the creation, conferring being, and even, in the case of the creation of man, conferring responsibility for being and a measure of his own creativity. God takes the risk that is inseparable from all openness, for to come into the open is to be exposed. Yet this very coming forth is what makes him God, what allows us to call by this holy name the ultimate Being of the world; for we could not call a self-enclosed Being 'God'. It is true that the depths of God remain veiled, yet there is an openness in God so that he is not merely opaque to us. This openness, which can be called both 'light' and 'love', belongs to his very essence.

But in saying this, we seem also to be asserting an analogy or likeness between God and man, insofar as we have spoken of both of them in terms of openness. The openness of God (Being) is of course prior to the openness of man, and determinative for it. Since this openness is the very law of Being, as it were, then in the case of human existence too, it is the man who would save himself by gathering up his being that actually becomes less in his being and eventually loses it; while the man who loses his being by going out into the risk of openness in its many dimensions is the man who really *ex-sists,* who really *is.*

Christ is the 'light of the world'[19] because in him the full openness of God and the potential openness of man have converged. In the Eastern churches, the Epiphany is specially associated with Christ's baptism and so with its imagery of the divine Spirit descending upon Jesus and dwelling with him. Jesus, we may say, was the man fundamentally open to the Father, and this is the basic openness on which all other kinds of human openness depend. We can think of Christ as the God-man because he moves out to fulfil the openness that is potential in all human existence. What is ambiguous and obscured in everyday human existing is revealed and manifested in the Christ. Here is openness to the world, openness to the neighbour, the manifestation of God's openness in the flesh. This thought of Christ's openness, moreover, gives us a clue to the mystery of what we mean by "incarnation'. A human life that has gone out in complete openness is the manifestation in the flesh of the openness of God. This is possible because human 'nature', as an existence, is not a closed nature but an open and dynamic one.

The symbol of light serves to point to these fundamental structures of openness—in human existence, in Christ, in God.

NOTES

1. *Dynamics of Faith* (New York: Harper & Row, 1957), p. 42.
2. *Models and Mystery* (London: Oxford University Press, 1964), pp. 2ff.
3. Rudolf Bultmann, *Kerygma and Myth* (New York: Harper, 1961), II, 169.
4. *The Shape of Christology* (London: SCM Press, 1966), p. 67.
5. Bultmann does in fact speak of a 'desymbolizing' as well as a 'demythologizing'.
6. *Symbolism and Belief* (London: Allen & Unwin, 1938), pp. 125ff.
7. Millar Burrows, *The Dead Sea Scrolls* (London: Secker & Warburg, 1956), pp. 390ff.
8. Rudolf Bultmann, *Theology of the New Testament,* (New York: Scribner's, 1955), II, 21.
9. *The Bible from Within* (London: Oxford University Press, 1950), p. 176.
10. Luke 2.9; John 1.9.
11. Matt. 2.9.
12. II Cor. 4.6.
13. Isa. 60.1.
14. Acts 9.3.

15. Gen. 1.16.

16. I John 1.5; 4.8.

17. John 8.12.

18. The German word for a clearing, *Lichtung,* makes even more obvious the connection with light (*Licht*), Cf. Heidegger, *Being and Time,* trans. John Macquarrie and Edward Robinson (New York: Harper & Row, 1962), p. 171.

19. John 8.12.

Genesis as Myth

In sharp contrast to the phenomenological method of John Macquarrie, Edmund Leach's essay is an example of structuralism. The structural study of myth involves its "non-rationality," that is, the myth does not mean what it appears to mean. The binary and redundant character of myth leads Edmund Leach to modern communications theory. Drawing on the work of linguists such as Roman Jakobson and anthropologists such as Claude Lévi-Strauss for his method, Leach analyzes the first four chapters of Genesis.

Mediating figures—anomalous and abnormal figures which stand between binary opposites—allow for the resolution of problems through myths. (An example is the problem of death.) Creation stories in Genesis are shown to be variants of the Oedipus myth, concerned with the theme of incest and kin endogamy (marrying within one's tribe or kin group). Myths cannot be examined apart from one another. The variations as the story is retold (repeating structural elements) reveal the message of the story.

On myth, see also Kramer, pp. 272–284, and Lambert, pp. 285–297.

A DISTINGUISHED German theologian has defined myth as 'the expression of unobservable realities in terms of observable phenomena'.[1] All stories which occur in the Bible are myths for the devout Christian, whether they correspond to historical fact or not. All human societies have myths in this sense, and normally the myths to which the greatest importance is attached are those which are the least probable. The nonrationality of myth is its very essence, for religion requires a demonstration of faith by the suspension of critical doubt.

But if myths do not mean what they appear to mean, how do they come to mean anything at all? What is the nature of the esoteric mode of

From Edmund Leach, *Genesis as Myth and Other Essays* (1969), pp. 7–23.

communication by which myth is felt to give 'expression to unobservable realities'?

This is an old problem which has lately taken on a new shape because, if myth be a mode of communication, then a part of the theory which is embodied in digital computer systems ought to be relevant. The merit of this approach is that it draws special attention to precisely those features of myth which have formerly been regarded as accidental defects. It is common to all mythological systems that all important stories recur in several different versions. Man is created in Genesis (i. 27) and then he is created all over again (ii. 7). And, as if two first men were not enough, we also have Noah in chapter viii. Likewise in the New Testament, why must there be four gospels each telling the 'same' story yet sometimes flatly contradictory on details of fact? Another noticeable characteristic of mythical stories is their markedly binary aspect; myth is constantly setting up opposing categories: 'In the beginning God created the heaven and the earth'; 'They crucified him and two others with him, on either side one, and Jesus in the midst'; 'I am the Alpha and the Omega, the beginning and the end, saith the Lord.' So always it is in myth—God against the world and the world itself for ever dividing into opposites on either side: male and female, living and dead, good and evil, first and last.

Now, in the language of communication engineers, the first of these common characteristics of myth is called *redundancy,* while the second is strongly reminiscent of the unit of information—the *bit.* 'Information' in this technical sense is a measure of the freedom of choice in selecting a message. If there are only two messages and it is arbitrary which you choose, then 'information is unity', that is = 1 bit.[2] (Bit stands for binary digit.)

Communication engineers employ these concepts for the analysis of problems which arise when a particular individual (the sender) wishes to transmit a coded message correctly to another individual (the receiver) against a background of interference (noise). 'Information' refers on the one hand to the degrees of choice open to the sender in encoding his transmission, and on the other to the degrees of choice open to the receiver in interpreting what he receives (which will include noise in addition to the original transmitted signal). In this situation a high level of redundancy makes it easy to correct errors introduced by noise.

Now in the mind of the believer, myth does indeed convey messages which are the Word of God. To such a man the redundancy of myth is a very reassuring fact. Any particular myth in isolation is like a coded message badly snarled up with noisy interference. Even the most confident devotee might feel a little uncertain as to what precisely is being said. But, as a result of redundancy, the believer can feel that, even when the details vary, each alternative version of a myth confirms his understanding and reinforces the essential meaning of all the others.

The anthropologist's viewpoint is different. He rejects the idea of a supernatural sender. He observes only a variety of possible receivers. Here redundancy increases information—that is the uncertainty of the possible means of decoding the message. This explains what is surely the most striking of all religious phenomena—the passionate adherence to sectarian belief. The whole of Christendom shares a single corpus of mythology, so it is surely very remarkable that the members of each particular Christian sect are able to convince themselves that they alone possess the secret of revealed truth. The abstract propositions of communication theory help us to understand this paradox.

But if the true believer can interpret his own mythology in almost any way he chooses, what principle governs the formation of the original myth? Is it random chance that a myth assumes one pattern rather than another? The binary structure of myth suggests otherwise.

Binary oppositions are intrinsic to the process of human thought. Any description of the world must discriminate categories in the form 'p is what not-p is not'. An object is alive or not alive and one could not formulate the concept 'alive' except as the converse of its partner 'dead'. So also human beings are male or not male, and persons of the opposite sex are either available as sexual partners or not available. Universally these are the most fundamentally important oppositions in all human experience.

Religion everywhere is preoccupied with the first, the antinomy of life and death. Religion seeks to deny the binary link between the two words; it does this by creating the mystical idea of 'another world', a land of the dead where life is perpetual. The attributes of this other world are necessarily those which are not of this world; imperfection here is balanced by perfection there. But this logical ordering of ideas has a disconcerting consequence—God comes to belong to the other world. The central 'problem' of religion is then to re-establish some kind of bridge between Man and God.

This pattern is built into the structure of every mythical system; the myth first discriminates between gods and men and then becomes preoccupied with the relations and intermediaries which link men and gods together. This much is already implicit in our initial definition.

So too with sex relations. Every human society has rules of incest and exogamy. Though the rules vary, they always have the implication that for any particular male individual all women are divided by at least one binary distinction, there are women of *our kind* with whom sex relations would be incestuous and there are women of the *other kind* with whom sex relations are allowed. But here again we are immediately led into paradox. How was it in the beginning? If our first parents were persons of two kinds, what was the other kind? But if they were both of our kind, then their relations must have been incestuous and we are all born in sin. The myths of the world offer many different solutions to this childish intellectual puzzle, but the prominence which it receives shows that it entails the most profound moral issues. The crux is as before. If the logic of our thought leads us to distinguish *we* from *they*, how can we bridge the gap and establish social and sexual relations with 'the others' without throwing our categories into confusion?

So, despite all variations of theology, this aspect of myth is a constant. In every myth system we will find a persistent sequence of binary discriminations as between human/superhuman, mortal/immortal, male/female, legitimate/illegitimate, good/bad—followed by a 'mediation' of the paired categories thus distinguished.

'Mediation' (in this sense) is always achieved by introducing a third category which is 'abnormal' or 'anomalous' in terms of ordinary 'rational' categories. Thus myths are full of fabulous monsters, incarnate gods, virgin mothers. This middle ground is abnormal, non-natural, holy. It is typically the focus of all taboo and ritual observance.

This approach to myth analysis derives originally from the techniques of structural linguistics associated with the name of Roman Jakobson[3] but is more immediately due to Claude Lévi-Strauss, one of whose examples may serve to illustrate the general principle.

Certain Pueblo Indian myths focus on the opposition between life and death. In these myths we find a threefold category distinction: agriculture (means to life), war (means to death), and hunting (a mediating category since it is means to life for men but means to death for animals). Other myths of the same cluster deploy a different triad: grass-eating animals (which live without killing), predators (which live by killing), and carrion-eating creatures (mediators, since they eat meat but do not kill in order to eat). In accumulation this total set of associated symbols serves to imply that life and death are *not* just the back and the front of the same penny, that death is *not* the necessary consequence of life.[4]

My Figure 1 (see pp. 416–417) has been designed to display an analogous structure for the case of the first four chapters of Genesis. The three horizontal bands of the diagram correspond to (A) the story of the seven-day creation, (B) the story of the Garden of Eden, and (C) the story of Cain and Abel. The diagram can also be read vertically: column 1 in band (B) corresponds to column 1 in band (A) and so on. The detailed analysis is as follows.

UPPER BAND: A

First Day. (i. 1–5; not on diagram). Heaven distinguished from Earth; Light from Darkness; Day from Night; Evening from Morning.

Second Day. (i. 6-8; col. 1 of diagram). (Fertile) water (rain) above; (infertile) water (sea) below. Mediated by firmament (sky).

Third Day. (i. 9-10; col. 2 and i. 11-12; col. 3). Sea opposed to dry land.

Mediated by 'grass, herb-yielding seed (cereals), fruit trees'. These grow on dry land but need water. They are classed as things 'whose seed is in itself' and thereby contrasted with bisexual animals, birds, etc.

The creation of the world as a static (that is, dead) entity is now complete and this whole phase of the creation is opposed to the creation of moving (that is, living) things.

Fourth Day. (i. 13-18; col. 4). Mobile sun and moon are placed in the fixed firmament of col. 1. Light and darkness become alternations (life and death become alternates).

Fifth Day. (i. 20-23; col. 5). Fish and birds are living things corresponding to the sea/land opposition of col. 2 but they also mediate the col. 1 oppositions between sky and earth and between salt water and fresh water.

Sixth Day. (i. 24-25; col. 6). Cattle (domestic animals), beasts (wild animals), creeping things. These correspond to the static triad of col. 3. But only the grass is allocated to the animals. Everything else, including the meat of the animals, is for Man's use (i. 29-30). Later at Leviticus xi creatures which do not fit this exact ordering of the world—for instance water creatures with no fins, animals and birds which eat meat or fish—are classed as 'abominations'. Creeping Things are anomalous with respect to the major categories, Fowl, Fish, Cattle, Beast, and are thus abominations *ab initio* (Leviticus xi. 41-42). This classification in turn leads to an anomalous contradiction. In order to allow the Israelites to eat locusts the author of Leviticus xi had to introduce a special qualification to the prohibition against eating creeping things: 'Yet these ye *may* eat: of every flying creeping thing that goeth on all four which have legs above their feet, to leap withal upon the earth' (v. 21). The procedures of binary discrimination could scarcely be carried further!

(i. 26-27; col. 7). Man and Woman are created simultaneously.

The whole system of living creatures is instructed to 'be fruitful and multiply', but the problems of Life versus Death and Incest versus Procreation are not faced at all.

CENTRE BAND: B

The Garden of Eden story which now follows tackles from the start these very problems which have been evaded in the first version. We start again

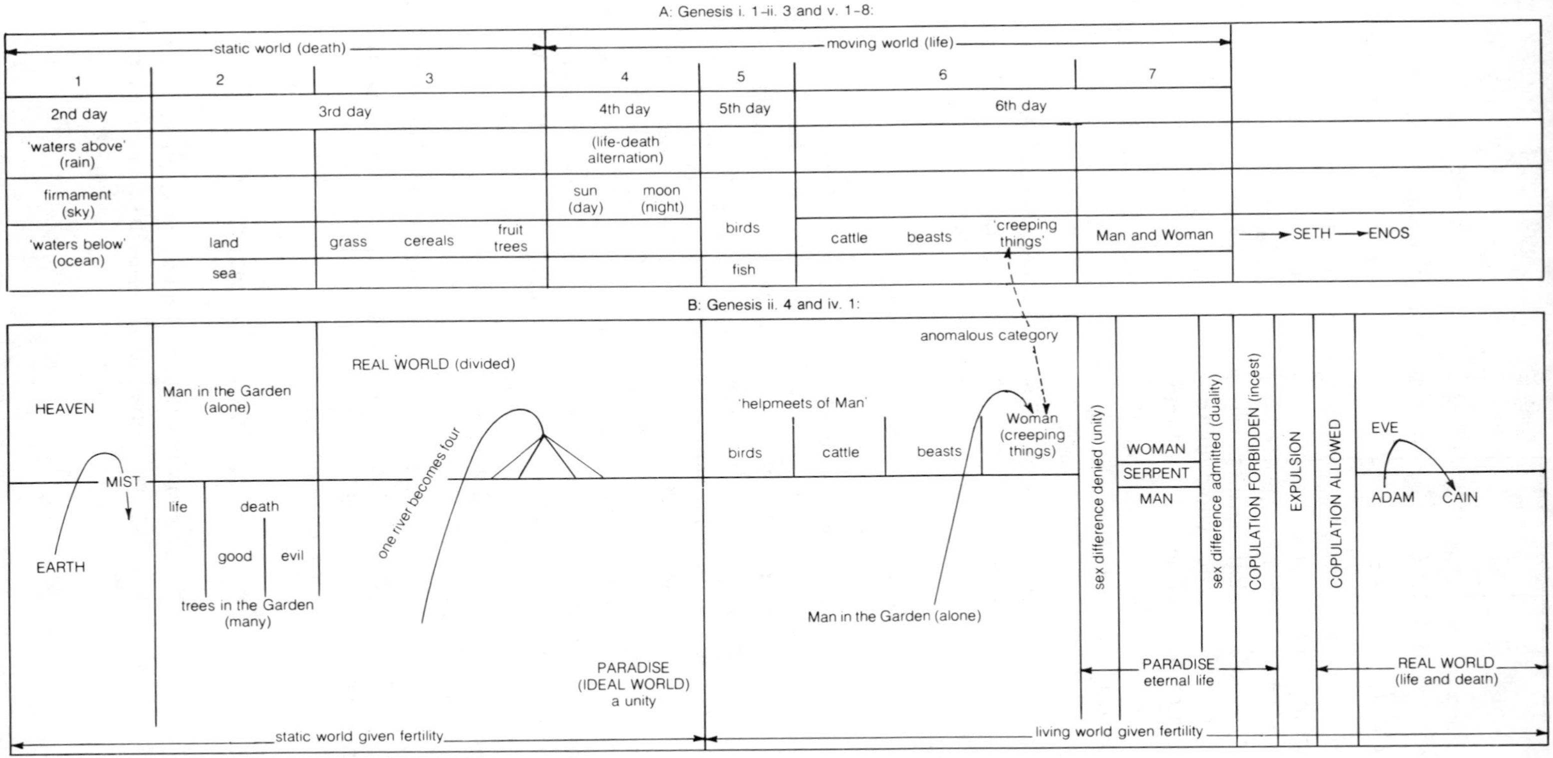
A: Genesis i. 1–ii. 3 and v. 1–8:
static world (death)
moving world (life)
1
2
3
4
5
6
7
2nd day
3rd day
4th day
5th day
6th day
'waters above' (rain)
(life-death alternation)
firmament (sky)
sun (day)
moon (night)
'waters below' (ocean)
land
sea
grass
cereals
fruit trees
birds
fish
cattle
beasts
'creeping things'
Man and Woman
SETH
ENOS
B: Genesis ii. 4 and iv. 1:
HEAVEN
MIST
EARTH
Man in the Garden (alone)
life
death
good
evil
trees in the Garden (many)
REAL WORLD (divided)
one river becomes four
PARADISE (IDEAL WORLD) a unity
'helpmeets of Man'
birds
cattle
beasts
anomalous category
Woman (creeping things)
Man in the Garden (alone)
sex difference denied (unity)
WOMAN
SERPENT
MAN
sex difference admitted (duality)
PARADISE eternal life
COPULATION FORBIDDEN (incest)
EXPULSION
COPULATION ALLOWED
EVE
ADAM
CAIN
REAL WORLD (life and death)
static world given fertility
living world given fertility

C: Genesis iv. 2-16:

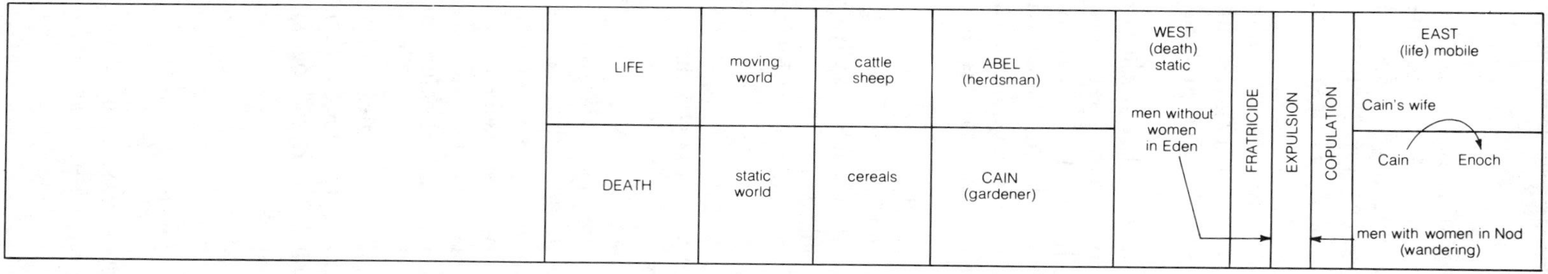

Fig. 1 The four chapters of Genesis contain three separate creation stories. Horizontal bands correspond to (a) seven-day creation; (b) Garden of Eden; and (c) Cain and Abel. Each story sets up the opposition Death versus Life, God versus Man. World is 'made alive' by using categories of 'woman' and 'creeping thing' to mediate this opposition.

with the opposition Heaven versus Earth, but this is mediated by a fertilizing mist drawn from the dry, infertile earth (ii. 4–6). This theme, which blurs the distinction life/death, is repeated. Living Adam is formed from the dead dust of the ground (ii. 7); so are the animals (ii. 19); the garden is fertilized by a river which 'went out of Eden' (ii. 10); finally fertile Eve is formed from a rib of infertile Adam (ii. 22–23).

The opposition Heaven/Earth is followed by further oppositions— Man/Garden (ii. 15); Tree of Life/Tree of Death (ii. 9, 17); the latter is called the tree of the 'knowledge of good and evil,' which means the knowledge of sexual difference.

Recurrent also is the theme that unity in the other world (Eden, Paradise) becomes duality in this world. Outside Eden the river splits into four and divides the world into separate lands (ii. 10–14). In Eden, Adam can exist by himself, Life can exist by itself; in this world, there are men and women, life and death. This repeats the contrast between monosexual plants and bisexual animals which is stressed in the first story.

The other living creatures are now created specifically because of the loneliness of Man in Eden (ii. 18). The categories are Cattle, Birds, Beasts. None of these is adequate as a helpmeet for Man. So finally Eve is drawn from Adam's rib . . . 'they are of one flesh' (ii. 18–24).

Comparison of Band A and Band B at this stage shows that Eve in the second story replaces the 'Creeping Things' of the first story. Just as Creeping Things were anomalous with respect to Fish, Fowl, Cattle and Beast, so Eve is anomalous to the opposition of Man versus Animal. And, as a final mediation (chapter iii), the Serpent, a creeping thing, is anomalous to the opposition Man versus Woman.

Christian artists have always been sensitive to this fact; they manage to give the monster a somewhat hermaphrodite appearance while still indicating some kind of identification between the Serpent and Eve herself. Hugo Van der Goes, in 'The Fall' at the Kunst-historisches Museum, Vienna, puts Eve and the Serpent in the same posture. Michelangelo makes Adam and Eve both gaze with loving adoration on the Serpent, but the Serpent has Eve's face.[5]

Adam and Eve eat the forbidden fruit and become aware of sexual difference; death becomes inevitable (iii. 3–8). But now for the first time pregnancy and reproduction become possible. Eve does not become pregnant until after she has been expelled from Paradise (iv. 1).

LOWER BAND

Cain the Gardener and Abel the Herdsman repeat the antithesis between the first three days of the Creation and the last three days in the first

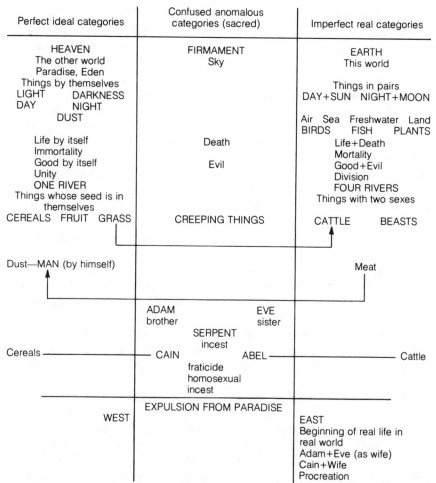

Perfect ideal categories	Confused anomalous categories (sacred)	Imperfect real categories
HEAVEN The other world Paradise, Eden	FIRMAMENT Sky	EARTH This world
Things by themselves LIGHT DARKNESS DAY NIGHT DUST		Things in pairs DAY+SUN NIGHT+MOON
		Air Sea Freshwater Land BIRDS FISH PLANTS
Life by itself Immortality Good by itself Unity ONE RIVER Things whose seed is in themselves	Death Evil	Life+Death Mortality Good+Evil Division FOUR RIVERS Things with two sexes
CEREALS FRUIT GRASS	CREEPING THINGS	CATTLE BEASTS
Dust—MAN (by himself)		Meat
	ADAM EVE brother sister SERPENT incest	
Cereals ————————	— CAIN ABEL — fraticide homosexual incest	———————— Cattle
WEST	EXPULSION FROM PARADISE	EAST Beginning of real life in real world Adam+Eve (as wife) Cain+Wife Procreation

Fig. 2   Incest categories have a logical basis in all myths. Similarity between myths is seen most clearly if they are analyzed in a binary form as shown in this table.

story. Abel's living world is more pleasing to God (iv. 4–5). Cain's fratricide compares with Adam's incest, and so God's questioning and cursing of Cain (iv. 9–12) has the same form and sequence as God's questioning and cursing of Adam, Eve and the Serpent (ii. 9–19). The latter part of iii. 16 is later repeated exactly (iv. 7), so Cain's sin was not only fratricide but also incestuous homosexually. In order that immortal monosexual existence in Paradise may be exchanged for fertile heterosexual existence in reality, Cain, like Adam, must acquire a wife (iv. 17). To this end Adam must eliminate a sister; Cain a brother. The symmetry is complete.

The issue here is the logical basis of incest categories, and closely analogous patterns must occur in all mythologies regardless of their superficial content. Cross-cultural comparison becomes easier if we represent the analysis as a systematic pattern of binary discrimination as in Figure 2.

Adam/Eve and Cain/Abel are then seen to be variants of a theme which can also occur in other forms, as in the well-known myth of Oedipus. The actual symbolism in these two cases is nearly identical. Oedipus, like Adam and Cain, is initially earthbound and immobile. The conclusion of the Athenian version of the Oedipus story is that he is an exiled wanderer, protected by the gods. So also is Cain (iv. 14–15). The Bible also includes the converse of this pattern. In Genesis xxviii Jacob is a lonely exile and wanderer under God's protection, but (xxxii. 24–32) he is renamed Israel and thus given the status of a first ancestor with a territorial autochthonous base, and he is tamed by God. Although Jacob dies abroad in Egypt, he is buried on his own ancestral soil in Israel (xl. 29–32; l. 5–7).

In the Oedipus story, in place of Eve's Serpent we have Jocasta's Sphinx. Like Jocasta the Sphinx is female, like Jocasta the Sphinx commits suicide, like the Serpent the Sphinx leads men to their doom by verbal cunning, like the Serpent the Sphinx is an anomalous monster. Eve listens to the Serpent's words and betrays Adam into incest; Oedipus solves the Sphinx riddle and is led into incest. Again, Oedipus's patricide replaces Cain's fratricide—Oedipus, incidentally, meets Laius 'at a cross roads'.

Parallels of this kind seem too close to be accidental, but this kind of algebra is unfamiliar, and more evidence will be needed to convince the sceptical. Genesis contains several further examples of first ancestors.

Firstly, Noah survived the destruction of the world by flood together with three sons and their wives. Prior to this the population of the world had included three kinds of being—'sons of God', 'daughters of men' and 'giants' who were the offspring of the union of the other two (vi. 1–4). Since the forbears of Noah's daughters-in-law have all been destroyed by the Flood, Noah becomes a unique ancestor of all mankind without the implication of incest. Chapter ix. 1–7, addressed to Noah, is almost the duplicate of i. 27–30, addressed to Adam.

Though heterosexual incest is evaded, the theme of homosexual incest in the Cain and Abel story recurs in the Noah saga when drunken Noah is seduced by his own son Ham (ix. 21–25). The Canaanites, descendants of Ham, are for this reason accursed. (That a homosexual act is intended is evident from the language 'Ham saw the nakedness of his father'. Compare Leviticus xviii. 6–19, where 'to uncover the nakedness of' consistently means to have sexual relations with.)

In the second place, Lot survives the destruction of the world by fire, together with two nubile daughters. Drunken Lot is seduced by his own daughters (xix. 30–38). The Moabites and the Ammonites, descendants of these daughters, are for this reason accursed. In chapter xix the men of Sodom endeavour to have homosexual relations with two angels who are visiting Lot. Lot offers his nubile daughters instead, but they escape unscathed. The implication is that Lot's incest is less grave than heterosexual relations with a foreigner, and still less grave than homosexual relations.

Thirdly, the affair of the Sodomites and the Angels contains echoes of 'the sons of God' and 'the daughters of men' but links superficially with chapter xviii where Abraham receives a visit from God and two angels who promise that his aging and barren wife Sarah shall bear a son. Sarah is Abraham's half-sister by the same father (xx. 12) and his relations with her are unambiguously incestuous (Leviticus xviii. 9). Abraham loans Sarah to Pharaoh saying that she is his sister (xii. 19). He does the same with King Abimelech (xx. 2). Isaac repeats the game with Abimelech (xxvi. 9–11) but with a difference. Isaac's wife Rebekah is his father's brother's son's daughter (second cousin) and the relation is *not* in fact incestuous. The barrenness of Sarah is an aspect of her incest. The supernatural intervention which ultimately ensures that she shall bear a child is evidence that the incest is condoned. Pharaoh and Abimelech both suffer supernatural penalties for the lesser offence of adultery, but Abraham, the incestuous husband, survives unscathed.

There are other stories in the same set. Hagar, Sarah's Egyptian slave, bears a son Ishmael to Abraham whose descendants are wanderers of low status. Sarah's son Isaac is marked out as of higher status than the sons of Abraham's concubines, who are sent away to 'the east country' (cf. wandering Cain who made his home in Nod 'eastward of Eden'). Isaac marries a kinswoman in preference to a Canaanite woman. Esau's marriage to a Hittite woman is marked as a sin. In contrast his younger and favoured twin brother Jacob marries two daughters of his mother's brother who is, in turn, Jacob's father's father's brother's son's son.

All in all, this long series of repetitive and inverted tales asserts:

(a) the overriding virtue of close kin endogamy;
(b) that the sacred hero-ancestor Abraham can carry this so far that he marries his paternal half-sister (an incestuous relationship). Abraham is thus likened to Pharaoh, for the Pharaohs of Egypt regularly married their paternal half-sisters; and
(c) that a rank order is established which places the tribal neighbours of the Israelites in varying degrees of inferior status depending upon the nature of the defect in their original ancestry as compared with the pure descent of Jacob (Israel).

The myth requires that the Israelites be descended unambiguously from Terah, the father of Abraham. This is achieved only at the cost of a breach of the incest rule; but by reciting a large number of similar stories which entail even greater breaches of sexual morality, the relations of Abraham and Sarah finally stand out as uniquely virtuous. Just as Adam and Eve are virtuous as compared to Cain and Abel, so Abraham's incest can pass unnoticed in the context of such outrageous characters as Ham, Lot's daughters, and the men of Sodom.

I have concentrated here upon the issue of sexual rules and transgressions so as to show how a multiplicity of repetitions, inversions, and variations can add up to a consistent 'message'. I do not wish to imply that this is the only structural pattern which these myths contain.

The novelty of the analysis which I have presented does not lie in the facts but in the procedure. Instead of taking each myth as a thing in itself with a 'meaning' peculiar to itself, it is assumed, from the start, that every myth is one of a complex and that any pattern which occurs in one myth will recur, in the same or other variations, in other parts of the complex. The structure that is common to all variations becomes apparent when different versions are 'superimposed' one upon the other.

Whenever a corpus of mythology is recited in its religious setting such structural patterns are 'felt' to be present, and convey meaning much as poetry conveys meaning. Even though the ordinary listener is not fully conscious of what has been communicated, the 'message' is there in a quite objective sense. If the labour of programming could be performed, the actual analysis could be done by a computer far better than by any human. Furthermore, it seems evident that much the same patterns exist in the most diverse kinds of mythology. This seems to me to be a fact of great psychological, sociological, and scientific significance. Here truly are observable phenomena which are the expression of unobservable realities.

NOTES

1. J. Schniewind in H. W. Bartsch, *Kerygma and Myth: A Theological Debate* (London: S.P.C.K., 1953), p. 47.

2. C. Shannon and W. Weaver, *The Mathematical Theory of Communication* (Urbana: University of Illinois Press, 1949).

3. R. Jakobson and M. Halle, *Fundamentals of Language* (The Hague: Mouton, 1956).

4. C. Lévi-Strauss, 'The Structural Study of Myth', *Myth: A Symposium*, ed. T. A. Sebeok (Bloomington: University of Indiana Press, 1955).

5. G. Groddeck, *The World of Man* (London: C. W. Daniel, 1934); see also E. R. Leach, *Transactions of the New York Academy of Sciences*, No. 23 (New York, 1961), pp. 386–96.

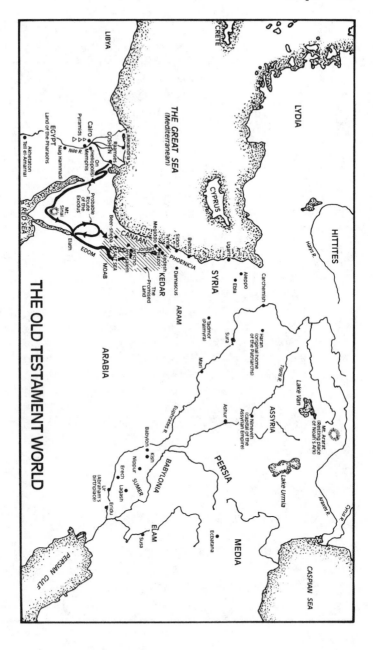

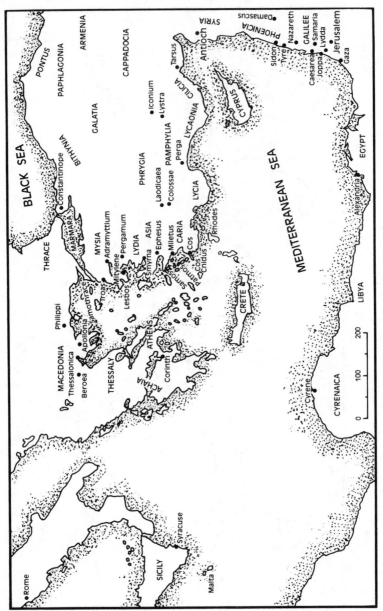

New Testament World

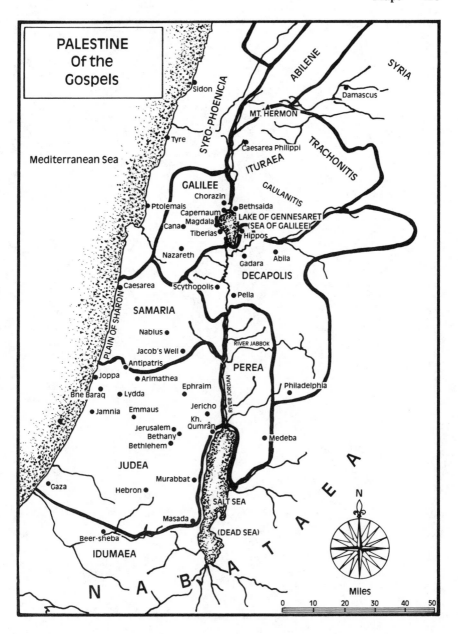

PALESTINE
Of the
Gospels

Mediterranean Sea

SYRO-PHOENICIA

ABILENE

SYRIA

Sidon

Damascus

MT. HERMON

Tyre

Caesarea Philippi

TRACHONITIS

ITURAEA

GALILEE

GAULANITIS

Chorazin

Ptolemais

Bethsaida

Capernaum

LAKE OF GENNESARET
(SEA OF GALILEE)

Magdala

Cana

Tiberias

Hippos

Nazareth

Abila

Gadara

DECAPOLIS

Caesarea

Scythopolis

Pella

PLAIN OF SHARON

SAMARIA

Nablus

RIVER JABBOK

Jacob's Well

Antipatris

PEREA

Joppa

Arimathea

Philadelphia

Bne Baraq

Lydda

Ephraim

RIVER JORDAN

Jamnia

Emmaus

Jericho

Jerusalem

Kh.
Qumrân

Bethany

Medeba

Bethlehem

JUDEA

NABATAEA

Gaza

Murabbat

Hebron

SALT SEA

Masada

(DEAD SEA)

Beer-sheba

IDUMAEA

N

Miles

0   10   20   30   40   50

General Index

98, 108, **245–47,** 248–49, 388
Homer (-ic) (includes *Iliad* and *Odyssey*) 7, 20, 59, 100 n.28, 128, 129, 171, 256, 264 n.4, 269, 290, **318–25**
homily 47
Hooke, S. H. 136, 145 n.13
Hooker, M. D. 162 n.3
Hopkins, Gerard Manley 2, 3, 21, 38
Horace 30
Horeb, *see* Sinai
Horne, T. H. 117 n.18
Horner, Thomas M. 173
Hort, F. J. A. 236, 240, 241, 243
Hosea 3, 21, 32, 33, 34, 94
Housman, A. E. 64, 244, 252 n.9
Huffmon, H. B. 133 n.35, 379 n.10
Hughes, Archibald 118 n.39
Humbert, Paul 380 n.29
humors 63
Hurrian(s) 276, 287, 295
Husserl, Edmund 52
Hyatt, J. P. 134
Hyland, C. F. 99 n.14
Hymn(s) 11, 41, 47, 72, 87, 93, 96, 219, 272, 273, 274, 365
Hytier, J. 54 n.7

Ignatius 208
illumine 221
illusions 70
Image and Symbol 3, 4, 7, 11, 14, 21, 22, 33, 48, **57–66,** 134, 157, 178, 181, 255–56, 316, 329, 331, 332, 366, **381–95, 396–41;** *see also* myth
animal 58, 144, 199, 390, 391, 415, 418
Apocalyptic 7, 21, 57–66
city 21, 58, 63, 65, 66
clothes, nakedness 1, 393, 394
Communion (food, eating) 60, 390, 392
cross 396, 402, 403
demonic 7, 21, 57–66, 153

divine 398
dragon 291, 293
father 396, 399, 400, 402
fertility 402, 414
fire 61, 62, 404
flag 397, 402
garden (Eden, Paradise) 21, 58, 62, 63, 200, 277, 382, 383, 389, 414, 415, 418
heaven 339, 340, 356, 358, 385, 412, 414, 418
immortality 402
light 14, 33, 38, 58, 62, 332, 388, 389, 390, **396–410,** 414, 415
nature 1
marriage 32
martial 197
Promised Land 32
rule 392
sea 200, 277, 278, 286, 288, 291, 292, 295, 414
serpent 383, 385, 389, 390, 392, 418
sheepfold (shepherd) 21, 58, 60
tree 21, 37, 38, 42, 61, 65, 69, 72, 116, 124, 195, 199, 200, 390, 407, 415, 418
water (includes baptism) 62, 63, 199, 396, 402, 414, 415
world (includes universe, world, firmament) 58–66, 125, 135, 275, 277, 278, 290, 406, 408, 413, 414, 415, 418
imagination 7, 8, 27
Inanna 20, 23 n.2, 274, 281
incantation 87
India 278
inerrancy, *see* erring
insight 24, 33, 38, 50
inspire (-ation) 2, 3, 6, 7, 19, 20, 21, 22, **24–56,** 67, 71
intention 3, 10, 28, 46, 84
Intertestamental **191–203**
intuition 7, 20, 24, 31, 33, 34, 37, 40, 41, 45, 46, 48, 49, 50

Iraq 269
Irenaeus 118 n.28, 203 n.23, 240
irony 7, 45, 331
Isaac 318, 391, 392, 421
Isaiah 7, 40, 44, 62, 65, 143, 161, 191, 192, 193, 323
Ishme-Dagan 275
Ishmael 232, 421
Israel 33

"J," *see* Yahwist
Jacob (includes "Testament of Jacob") 61, 90, 91, 93, 196, 200, 254, 319, 421
Jacobsen, Thorkild 283 n.2, 296 n.14, 296 n.18
Jahnow, Hedwig 379 n.5
Jakobson, Roman 333, 411, 414, 422 n.3
James, the disciple 348, 354
James I (of England) 256, 259
Jamnia 208, 215, 216
Jehoshaphat 154
Jeremiah 7, 21, 37, 41, 69, 85, 97, 105, 106, 107, 113, 128, 140, 143, 161, 199, 366
Jeremias, J. 96, 334, 342 n.9, 343 n.18, 343 n.23, 343 n.28, 343 n.29
Jericho 168
Jerome 208, 209, 228, 233, 249, 250, 368
Jerusalem 61, 72, 128, 137, 156, 160, 161, 180, 187, 194, 198, 200, 210, 213, 215, 225, 240, 255, 281, 347
Jerusalem Bible, *see* Bible
Jerusalem Christianity 207
Jewish Christianity 156
Job 59, 275, 281, 323
Jocz, Jakob 119 n.50
Johannine authorship 406
Johannine dualism 405
John the Baptist 95, 197, 308
John of St. Thomas 52
John, the disciple 250, 348, 354
John Rylands Papyrus 458, see papyri

Index of Biblical Passages

OLD TESTAMENT

443

NEW TESTAMENT